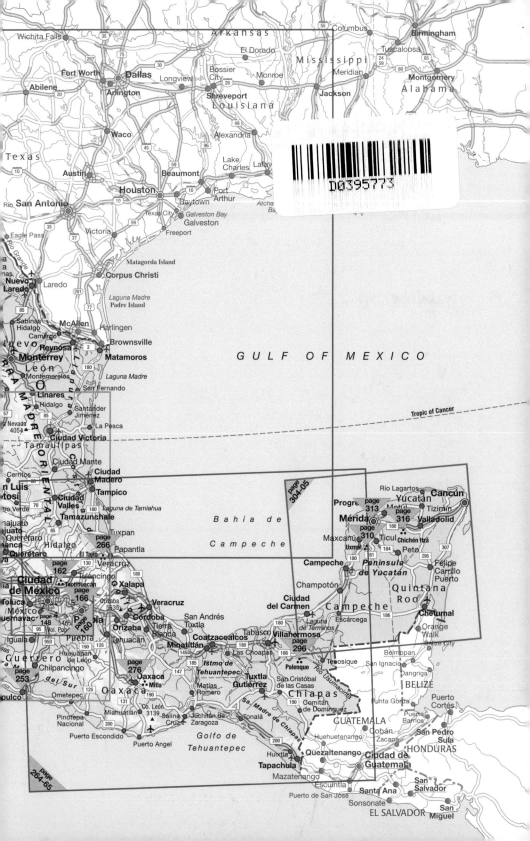

INSIGHT GUIDES
MEXICO

APA PUBLICATIONS L

Part of the Langenscheidt Publishing Group

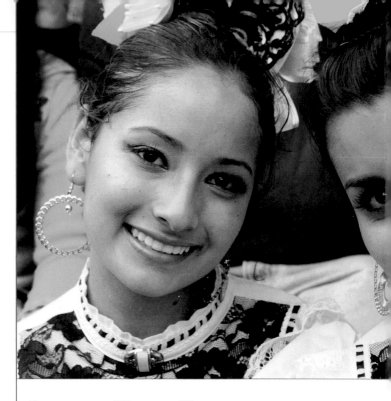

✴ INSIGHT GUIDE

MEXICO

Editorial
Project Editor
Alyse Dar
Art Director
Steven Lawrence
Picture Manager
Tom Smyth
Series Manager
Rachel Fox

Distribution

UK & Ireland
GeoCenter International Ltd
Meridian House, Churchill Way West
Basingstoke, Hampshire RG21 6YR
sales@geocenter.co.uk

United States
Langenscheidt Publishers, Inc.
36–36 33rd Street 4th Floor
Long Island City, NY 11106
orders@langenscheidt.com

Australia
Universal Publishers
1 Waterloo Road
Macquarie Park, NSW 2113
sales@universalpublishers.com.au

New Zealand
Hema Maps New Zealand Ltd (HNZ)
Unit 2, 10 Cryers Road
East Tamaki, Auckland 2013
sales.hema@clear.net.nz

Worldwide
Apa Publications GmbH & Co.
Verlag KG (Singapore branch)
38 Joo Koon Road, Singapore 628990
apasin@signet.com.sg

Printing

CTPS-China

©2010 Apa Publications GmbH & Co.
Verlag KG (Singapore branch)
All Rights Reserved

First Edition 1983
Eighth Edition 2010

CONTACTING THE EDITORS
We would appreciate it if readers
would alert us to errors or outdated information by writing to:
Insight Guides, P.O. Box 7910,
London SE1 1WE, England.
insight@apaguide.co.uk
NO part of this book may be reproduced,
stored in a retrieval system or transmitted
in any form or means electronic, mechanical, photocopying, recording or otherwise, without prior written permission of
Apa Publications. Brief text quotations
with use of photographs are exempted
for book review purposes only. Information has been obtained from sources
believed to be reliable, but its accuracy
and completeness, and the opinions
based thereon, are not guaranteed.

www.insightguides.com

ABOUT THIS BOOK

The first Insight Guide pioneered the use of creative full-color photography in travel guides in 1970. Since then, we have expanded our range to cater for our readers' need not only for reliable information about their chosen destination but also for a real understanding of the culture and workings of that destination. Now, when the internet can supply inexhaustible (but not always reliable) facts, our books marry text and pictures to provide those much more elusive qualities: knowledge and discernment. To achieve this, they rely heavily on the authority of locally based writers and photographers.

Insight Guide: Mexico is structured to convey an understanding of the country and its people as well as to guide readers through its attractions.

◆ The **Features** section, indicated by a pink bar at the top of each page, covers the political, cultural, and social history of the country and includes illuminating essays on fiestas, music, food, and crafts in a series of lively, informative essays.
◆ The main **Places** section, indicated by a blue bar, is a complete guide to all the sights and areas worth visiting. Places of special interest are coordinated by number with the maps.
◆ The **Travel Tips** listings section, with a yellow bar, provides full information on transportation, hotels, and activities from culture to shopping to sports, an A–Z section of essential practical information, and a handy phrasebook with Spanish words and expressions. An easy-to-find contents list for Travel Tips is printed on the back flap, which also serves as a bookmark.

LEFT: Guadalajara folkloric dancers.

Jalisco and Michoacán, Acapulco and Pacific Beaches. He also wrote the new Adventure Tourism feature and contributed practical information for the Travel Tips. Bartlett has written for a wide variety of travel publications including newspapers, magazines, radio, video and travel guides. He is an expert on Japan, Korea, and Mexico, all of which he visits frequently, and often travels within the United States. When not on the road he divides his time between Cape Cod and Baja California where he surfs, takes photographs, and writes fiction.

This version builds on earlier editions produced by **Felicity Laughton** and **Kal Müller**, and edited by **Martha Ellen Zenfell**, with subsequent contributions from writers **John Wilcock**, **Margaret King**, **Mike Nelson**, **Barbara Ann Rosenberg**, **José-Antonio Guzmán**, **Patricia Díaz**, **Guillermo García-Oropeza**, **Wendy Luft**, **Donna Dailey**, **Mike Gerrard**, **Andrea Dubrowski**, **Chloe Sayers**, **Barbara McKinnon**, and **Ron Mader**.

Most of the stunning photographs in this edition were taken by experienced travel photographers **Anna Mockford** and **Nick Bonetti**. **Alex Havret** contributed the images for the Yucatán Peninsula chapter. The book was proofread by **Pam Barrett**. **Helen Peters** compiled the index and **Catherine Dreghorn** provided editorial assistance.

The contributors

This new edition was commissioned and edited by **Alyse Dar** at Insight Guides' London office.

The chapters on Mexico's people, its history and the land, Mexico City, the Gulf Coast, Tabasco and Chiapas, the Yucatán Peninsula, and the general practical information for the redesigned Travel Tips were rewritten and revised by **Nick Rider**, who has a Ph.D in history and has written books on France, Spain, and Mexico, including the *Insight Smart Guide: Cancún and Yucatán*. Rider also compiled the Best of Mexico and wrote new features on pre-Hispanic sites, Los Charros, and Zapatistas.

Ray Bartlett comprehensively updated the features on crafts, muralists, fiestas, food, and music as well as the Places chapters covering Baja California, the Sierras, the El Bajío and Colonial Heartland,

Map Legend

⎯ ⸱ ⎯	International Boundary
⎯ ⎯	State Boundary
⊖	Border Crossing
⎯ ⎯	National Park/Reserve
⎯ ⎯	Ferry Route
🚇	Metro
✈	Airport: International/Regional
🚌	Bus Station
❶	Tourist Information
✉	Post Office
†	Church/Ruins
†	Monastery
☾	Mosque
✡	Synagogue
🏰	Castle/Ruins
∴	Archeological Site
∩	Cave
👤	Statue/Monument
★	Place of Interest

The main places of interest in the Places section are coordinated by number with a full-color map (eg ❶), and a symbol at the top of every right-hand page tells you where to find the map.

Contents

LEFT: Pirámide de la Luna, Teotihuacán.

Maps

THE BEST OF MEXICO: TOP ATTRACTIONS

With dramatic ancient relics, exuberant cities, placid colonial towns, and stunning landscapes, Mexico offers an immense variety. Here are some of its foremost highlights

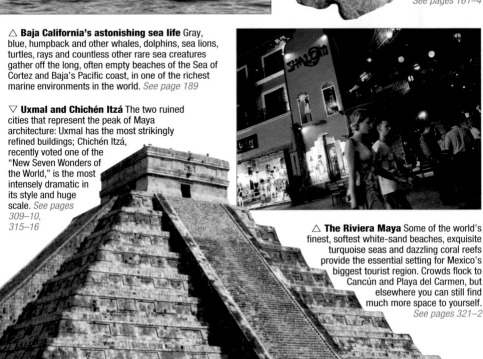

◁ **Teotihuacán** The immense pyramids and majestic, silent geography of this giant city, abandoned since around AD 650, encapsulate the mystery and dramatic grandeur of Mexico's ancient cultures. *See pages 161–4*

△ **Baja California's astonishing sea life** Gray, blue, humpback and other whales, dolphins, sea lions, turtles, rays and countless other rare sea creatures gather off the long, often empty beaches of the Sea of Cortez and Baja's Pacific coast, in one of the richest marine environments in the world. *See page 189*

▽ **Uxmal and Chichén Itzá** The two ruined cities that represent the peak of Maya architecture: Uxmal has the most strikingly refined buildings; Chichén Itzá, recently voted one of the "New Seven Wonders of the World," is the most intensely dramatic in its style and huge scale. *See pages 309–10, 315–16*

△ **The Riviera Maya** Some of the world's finest, softest white-sand beaches, exquisite turquoise seas and dazzling coral reefs provide the essential setting for Mexico's biggest tourist region. Crowds flock to Cancún and Playa del Carmen, but elsewhere you can still find much more space to yourself. *See pages 321–2*

▷ **Colonial Oaxaca** With its colonnaded main square, extravagant churches, distinctive cuisine, rich craft traditions, and constant calendar of highly colored, intricate fiestas, and its utterly delightful hotels with plant-shaded old patios, Oaxaca epitomizes the rare charm of Mexico's colonial cities. *See pages 275–9*

△ **Mexico City** Vast, sprawling, sometimes overwhelming, the capital is almost a continent by itself, within which there are fabulous museums, exquisite restaurants, imposing plazas, placid districts full of old-village charm, and an enormously varied, vibrant, constantly surprising humanity. *See pages 131–55*

◁ **Mexican Folk Art** Made with enormous skill and an ever-exuberant love of color, using materials from fine silks to recycled cans, Mexico's endlessly varied ceramics, textiles, woodcarvings and other folk arts are an irresistible demonstration of the country's imagination and creativity. *See pages 107–11*

△ **Palenque** Rising out of the Chiapas rain forest, Palenque is the most atmospheric of all the Maya cities, and its temples, multi-roomed palace and their refined carvings and inscriptions have yielded up the most complete history of the dynasty of its kings. *See pages 295–6*

▷ **Copper Canyon** Deeper and four times wider than the Grand Canyon, crossed by a spectacular railroad, the *Barranca del Cobre* is an awesome rift in the world's surface, an intricate maze of gorges, waterfalls and giant rock walls, home to the Tarahumara people, and with unforgettable hiking and biking routes. *See pages 202–3*

△ **Pacific Beaches** Mexico's long, long Pacific coast is lined by fabulous, palm-ringed beaches, many with crashing waves that provide some of the world's best surfing spots. Behind some beaches there are gleaming resorts like Ixtapa-Zihuatanejo, Acapulco and Huatulco, but elsewhere there are laid-back villages, and miles of idyllic bays you can have just to yourself. *See pages 256–7 and 282–3*

THE BEST OF MEXICO: EDITOR'S CHOICE

Mexico's special options include mingling with the crowds at fabulously colorful fiestas or teeming markets, climbing awe-inspiring pyramids, lying back on exquisite beaches... this is our selection of its most memorable experiences

BEST CITIES

● **Mexico City**
The city that has everything, from ancient ruins and teeming markets to all-night clubs and ultra-chic hotels. See pages 131–55.

● **Puebla**
A busy modern university city, but still a multi-colored jewel of colonial architecture, with many of its old buildings clad in bright Talavera tiles. See pages 165–70.

● **Cuernavaca**
Famed for its exquisite year-round climate, with magnificent gardens spread around its steep hills, the old town of Cuernavaca has an ideal mix of a lush natural setting and gracious colonial architecture. See pages 171–3.

● **Guanajuato**
The most attractive of the colonial "silver towns," with narrow streets of churches and 18th-century mansions winding up and down the flanks of a dramatic ravine. See pages 222–5.

● **Oaxaca**
One of the cities with the most special atmosphere, the most special cuisine, the most intriguing culture and traditions. See pages 275–9.

● **San Cristóbal de las Casas**
Maya and Spanish traditions are inextricably intertwined in the fascinating capital of the Chiapas highlands, together with a touch of modern style. See pages 292–4.

BEST ANCIENT SITES

● **Templo Mayor**
Mexico City. The core of Aztec Tenochtitlán, discovered only in the 1970s right next to the city's modern heart, the Zócalo. See pages 136–7.

● **Teotihuacán**
From the massive Pyramid of the Sun to the Avenue of the Dead, "the place where men became gods" cannot fail to be awe-inspiring. See pages 161–2.

● **Monte Albán**
A spectacular feat of ancient engineering, built by levelling off an entire mountain top high above Oaxaca. See page 279.

● **Palenque**
A ruined city where it's still easy to imagine King Pakal and his

descendants stalking the patios of their palace. See pages 295–6.

● **Bonampak**
Deep in the Chiapas jungle, one small temple in this remote Maya site contains the finest of all surviving pre-Hispanic wall paintings. See page 297.

● **Uxmal**
The most sophisticated architecture of any Maya city and startlingly modern in its rhythmic geometry. See pages 309–11.

● **Chichén Itzá**
The giant temples, ball court and Castillo Pyramid of Chichén can seem like a set for a science-fiction movie, rising up out of the flat Yucatán. See pages 315–6.

ABOVE: Templo Mayor. **LEFT:** colors of Guanajuato.

BEST BEACHES

● **Bahía Concepción** South of Mulegé are miles of wild, often empty, beaches with water of ever-changing colors. *See page 191.*

● **Puerto Vallarta and the Costa Alegre** The most beautiful of the big Pacific resorts; seekers after solitude can find plenty of empty coves ringed by fabulously lush forest down the Costa Alegre to the south. *See pages 247–9.*

● **Playa Troncones** North of Ixtapa-Zihuatanejo, with an idyllic laid-back feel, remote Troncones beach is a surfers' mecca, but

also great for kayaking and turtle-watching. *See page 252.*

● **Zicatela and Zipolite** Puerto Escondido's Zicatela beach has the the country's most spectacular surf; Zipolite, further east, is perhaps the ultimate tropical hang-out. *See page 282.*

● **Cancún** Every kind of entertainment to hand, and a giant 23km (14-mile) strip of white, white sand. *See page 318.*

● **Tulum,** Quintana Roo. One of the most beautiful 14km (9 miles) of white sand imaginable, and with a ruined Maya city above it. *See page 322.*

ABOVE: powerful breakers pound the Zicatela shore.

BEST ADVENTURES

● **Hiking Copper Canyon** Tarahumara guides can lead you through the forests, gorges and great vistas of one of the world's most extraordinary landscapes. *See pages 198, 202–3.*

● **Surfing the Pacific Coast** Baja, Troncones and Puerto Escondido offer some of the ocean's most challenging breaks. *See pages 193, 247, 252, 282.*

● **Find the Monarchs** Michoacán and Mexico State. Hike or ride horseback into the remote high-mountain valleys that are the winter home of millions of Monarch butterflies. *See page 239.*

● **Rafting the rivers of Veracruz** Speed through tree-shrouded canyons on the flashing whitewater Río Filobobos, and hike far away from any road. *See page 267.*

● **Cavern and Cave Diving and Snorkeling** The Yucatán's hundreds of kilometers of under-water caves are a magnet for divers, and even the less-experienced can see a lot just with a snorkel. *See pages 84–5, 300–1.*

● **Dive the Great Maya Reefs** Cozumel and the Riviera Maya. Colorful coral and fish, and a huge range of dives from inshore reefs to vast undersea walls, caverns and wrecks. *See pages 320–2.*

BEST FIESTAS

● **Carnaval** Late Jan–Feb. Celebrations take many forms, from Rio-style extravagance to intense Catholic-Maya rituals. *See pages 90–1.*

● **La Guelaguetza** July. The most brilliantly colorful demonstration of Mexico's music and folklore. *See page 365.*

● **Feria de Huamantla** Aug. With flower-carpets created across the town in one night, to be destroyed by crazy bull-running the next day, this

is a classic Mexican mix of piety, craftsmanship, color, and wild partying. *See page 90.*

● **Day of the Dead** Oct 31–Nov 2. Among the best places to experience this most Mexican of fiestas are Lake Pátzcuaro, Michoacán, and Oaxaca. *See pages 92–3.*

● **La Vírgen de Guadalupe** Dec 12. The entire country gets involved in this homage to its foremost patron, with intense pilgrimages and religious processions. *See page 29.*

ABOVE: Day of the Dead figurine.
RIGHT: divers exploring the Dos Ojos waterhole, Tulum.

¡QUE VIVA MÉXICO!

Fabulous beaches, spectacular
festivals, ancient cultures, and dynamic cities –
Mexico is a tropical treasure trove

Mexico, as we know it today, has only existed for a little over 160 years. Before, its borders stretched north through Texas, New Mexico, Arizona, and California. Now, although it is only one quarter the size of its northern neighbor, it is still a vast country full of surprises and startling contrasts, geographical and social.

In Monterrey, glass-and-steel office towers and factories rise out of the desert; in northern Veracruz and along the Tabasco coast, oil rigs loom up like exclamation points, while in the capital, Mexico City, the sheer density of snorting traffic overwhelms any first-time visitor. On Mexico's Pacific and Caribbean beaches some 20 million visitors each year bask under the tropical sun and party through the balmy nights. And yet, not far away, you can find the pyramids left by ancient Mesoamerican civilizations, and forests and lagoons full of rare wildlife. In villages and mountain valleys, indigenous Mexicans continue to perform age-old rituals.

Fiery murals blanket many of Mexico City's public walls, but thick smog blankets the sky, all too often obscuring the snow-capped volcanoes – Popocatépetl and Iztaccíhuatl – only 60km (37 miles) to the southeast. With a population over 22 million, Mexico City is one of the biggest megalopolises on earth.

Yet beyond the sprawl of the ever-expanding Distrito Federal, the air is often still wonderfully clear, and, although Mexico has 332,000km (207,000 miles) of roads there are still many spectacular parts of the country that are remote and inaccessible. And even apparently plain-looking towns on main highways can surprise you with a raucous fiesta that seems utterly bizarre.

Two-thirds of Mexico's 110 million people are under the age of 30. Most Mexicans are Spanish-speaking, mixed-race mestizos, but some 60 native languages are still spoken, by more than 50 indigenous groups.

So, how do you explain it all – this fantastic, frenetic country? "One does not explain Mexico," says the philosopher Manuel Zamacona in *Where the Air is Clear*. "One believes in Mexico, with fury, with passion..." ❏

PRECEDING PAGES: raising the flag on the Zócalo; VW Beetle on a colorful San Miguel de Allende street; rodeo event in Zacatecas; Lake Pátzcuaro; **FAR LEFT:** Dance of the Concheros, Chichimecas statue, Querétaro **FROM TOP:** spectators at a bullfight in the Yucatán. **ABOVE LEFT:** a shining example of quaffable Mexican beer.

THE MEXICAN MOSAIC

The product of many, very disparate influences, Mexico's people and their cultural tapestry have a constant ability to surprise

Mexicans are peculiarly concerned with their identity. To most outsiders, theirs is one of the most recognizable countries in the world, with its own distinctive music, food and colorful visual style, and a set of unmistakable symbols, from *mariachis* to *charro* cowboys and traditional blouses. Many Mexican writers, on the other hand, have spent a great deal of time considering the nature of *Mexicanidad*, "Mexican-ness," and Mexicans' place in the world.

In good part this is because Mexico is genuinely very difficult to sum up. Mexican men especially can be loud and boisterous at times, lovers of the fiestas that are a national trademark, but oddly reserved at others. Extravagant displays of sentimental patriotism are another feature of Mexican life, from the nightly flag-lowering ceremony in Mexico City's Zócalo and the major national holidays, to the drunken singing of patriotic songs, but Mexicans can also be unremittingly negative about their own country. One could also say that Mexicans are very religious, and reverential towards religious symbols, but amid the piety you can also easily find plenty of raucous, earthy, often off-the-wall humor. It is true to say that most Mexicans, above all in the south, place great value on courtesy; it's also true that some can catch you out by being extremely brusque. A nation often associated with machismo can be amazingly accepting of homosexuality, and contains communities that are declaredly matriarchal. Lately, through the drug wars, parts of Mexico have been heavily associated with violence, and their crime statistics are frightening; but, arrive in country areas elsewhere, or even small towns, and all you will feel is a pervasive courtesy and gentleness.

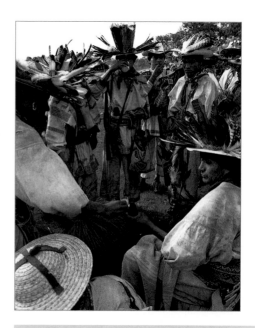

Under Spanish rule, an attempt was made to keep racial mixing at bay by means of a complex scale of legal castes, arranged according to the amount of a person's European ancestry.

The degree of disconnect between these last two images, especially, is something foreigners find baffling. In their folk arts and fiestas, Mexicans also show immense inventiveness and creativity, and yet economically the country has often seemed dogged by inertia. Paradoxes, and the unexpected, are actually part of the essence of Mexico, and even more so now that the country's middle classes are determinedly embracing a modern, consumerist way of life.

This is a country that, more than most, defies generalizations, so that the best one can hope for is to capture just some parts of a changing mosaic. Negotiating, and appreciating, all these contrasts is central to enjoying the country. Mexico is a continent in itself: neither a very old country, nor a very new one. It is both at the same time. It has the most leading-edge modern technology, while nearby people are living according to 2,000-year-old traditions.

Mestizaje

Many of these paradoxes can be traced back to modern Mexico's very origins in colonial society. When Europeans settled North America or Australia, they generally pushed the native inhabitants aside, or exterminated them. In Mexico and Latin America, the Spaniards dominated the local population, eliminated their rulers, exploited and blatantly mistreated them, but they also lived with them and mixed with them. The Catholic Church, instead of keeping "Indians" at bay Puritan-style, insisted that they be baptized and converted, even if this only produced a "syncretic religion," the often-bizarre mixes of Catholic and pre-Conquest beliefs that are characteristic of many indigenous communities today.

The great majority of Mexico's 110 million people today are mestizos, or "mixed race," of both European and indigenous American descent. This process of *mestizaje* or "racial mixing" that has taken place since the Conquest is the central element in Mexican identity. Rather than the one Spanish Catholic tradition overwhelming the older native American one, the two became subtly entangled, to the extent where no one can quite tell where one begins and the other ends, and indigenous American traditions are still visible in every part of Mexico, not just museum exhibits of national folklore. The complex intertwining of the two is expressed in countless aspects of Mexican life, from the ever-present cult of the Virgin of Guadalupe (*see page 29*) and the celebrations of the Day of the Dead to the delicious, rich variety of Mexico's regional cuisines. Other communities have arrived in Mexico since the first

Spanish colonists – Africans brought by the Spaniards as slaves to Veracruz and Guerrero, 20th-century Spanish refugees, Jews, Poles and other eastern Europeans, and Lebanese – but they have found their place alongside the dominant mestizo culture.

Today "multiculturalism" is often seen as a positive, and Mexico City's Plaza de las Tres Culturas is one of many monuments around Mexico that celebrate the country's "Three Cultures" – pre-Hispanic, Spanish, and the modern Mexican synthesis. For many Mexicans, however, having mixed origins has often been a source of neurotic insecurity, as if it would be simpler

just to be one or the other. The Conquest, after all, was not some peaceful meeting of cultures but a bloody drama, and has often been compared to a mass rape. One of the best-known, most emblematic figures in the Conquest is *La Malinche*, the indigenous princess who became Hernán Cortés' interpreter and mistress, and so mother to one of the first mestizos, before being cast aside when Cortés married a Spanish aristocrat. The powerful, sombre mural by José Clemente Orozco showing *Cortés and Malinche* as a kind of Adam-and-Eve to the new Mexican people, in the Colegio de San Ildefonso in the capital, sums up all the many, frequently contradictory feelings Mexicans can have towards their dual origins.

LEFT: ancient traditions at a Huichol gathering.
RIGHT: young Monterrey boys playing with a wrestling toy in a local park.

A national culture

At one time Mexicans were pretty much offi-cially encouraged to indulge in self-hatred, and to see the presence of so much indigenous blood in the country as a failing, above all dur-ing the dictatorship of Porfirio Díaz at the end of the 19th century. European models were seen as superior in all things, and although General Díaz was himself very much a mestizo from Oaxaca – as is evident in any photograph – he and his followers made it virtually an article of state policy that one of Mexico's major prob-lems was its own people, and especially the indigenous communities, who were lazy, apa-

thetic and lacking any initiative. Hence they looked around determinedly for new migrants – Germans, Japanese, Lebanese – to improve the stock and boost the economy.

This produced an intense reaction in the vast upheaval of the 1910 Revolution. The cultural revolution that followed was one of its most lasting consequences, and laid down the basis of the new, inclusive national culture that sur-vives today. In his great murals in the Palacio Nacional in Mexico City Diego Rivera idealized the pre-Conquest world, while his bohemian partner Frida Kahlo began dressing in the bril-liantly colored blouses of the Zapotec women of Tehuantepec. "Aztec" and other pre-Hispanic motifs became a feature – often a cliché – of new Mexican architecture, and the state took its first steps towards taking charge of Mexico's immense archeological heritage, which had previously only been of interest to foreigners. In a complete break with previous centuries, instead of Mexico's pre-Hispanic past and tradi-tions being ignored and treated with contempt, they were comprehensively re-evaluated, cele-brated, even venerated, as an essential part of the national identity.

And yet, as usual in Mexico, there is still plenty of room for paradox and ambiguity. The many indigenous communities, especially, may have been enshrined as symbols of the nation, but everyday attitudes towards them can be very variable. Many indigenous communities complain that they are still treated as primitive, and discriminated against, one of the sources of the Zapatista conflict in Chiapas. The inte-gration of the indigenous way of life – based

HISTORIC TITLES

One practice that came in flamboyantly with the Mexican Revolution, and which has survived, is the revival of per-sonal names of Mexica or Aztec, and sometimes Maya, origin. The radical artist Gerardo Murillo was a forerunner in the trend, by taking the name "Doctor Atl" (from the Náhuatl for water). Others followed, and for a while it was very fashionable for officials of the new revolutionary political regime to take on names reminiscent of the Aztec warrior aristocracy, or to give them to their children. Most popular of all was Cuauhtémoc, name of the heroic last Aztec emperor who led the final defense of Tenochtitlán; the most prominent examples are Cuauhtémoc Cárdenas, former mayor of Mexico City and son of the great 1930s

president Lázaro Cárdenas, and Cuauhtémoc Blanco, Mex-ico's best-loved soccer player. Other names that have stayed common are Tenoch, short for Tenochtitlán, for boys, and Xóchitl, from the nahuatl for flower, for girls.

Before the Revolution no Mexican with any wealth or social position would have given their children an indig-enous name. Even today, it can still seem strange to come upon a well-groomed, suited gentleman introduced with the name of a Mexica warrior (plus, foreigners, including other Spanish-speakers, commonly have no idea how to pronounce these names and words ending in –tl). But, they remain another sign of Mexico's much-treasured sense of identity.

on community, tradition, and a sense of maintaining a balance in the universe rather than change – with a more individualistic Western outlook is a still-continuing process that goes on in people's heads and hearts, rather than any settled matter.

Indigenous peoples

Around 10–11 percent of Mexico's population, or about 11 million people, is still made up of indigenous communities (pueblos indígenas), in one of over 60 different groups who have all maintained their identities and resisted full integration into Hispanic-mestizo culture ever since the Conquest. After centuries of mestizaje, however, the limits of these peoples are often a little vague, and rather than just genetics a truer test of belonging is whether someone lives in a community, maintains its traditions and speaks one of the many indigenous languages. As said, the attitudes of other Mexicans to them are very mixed. Cultured middle-class opinion acknowledges them and their traditions and crafts as special national symbols, but in economic life they are commonly at a constant disadvantage. Poor mestizos frequently admire the "Indians'" pugnacious exercise of community solidarity, but, since they themselves are excluded from it, also often find it threatening and an irritation.

With their colorful, intricate crafts, complex, strange beliefs and sense of contact with an ancestral past the indigenous peoples are often the Mexicans that are most fascinating to foreigners, especially those communities, several in the north, that have maintained their traditions in the purest form. The Tarahumara of Copper Canyon are one such group, known for their extreme endurance, as seen in their ritual sport of rarajipari, a kind of soccer game played for several days over mountain tops. The Seri are another group, a tiny community of under 1,000 who live by fishing on the shores of the Sea of Cortés in Sonora, and are known for their striking basketware. Northern Jalisco is the home of one of the most famous communities, the Huicholes, known for their stunningly colorful woven images, their beautiful embroidered shirts and their use of the cactus-drug peyote in shamanic rituals. Each community has its own, particular set of beliefs, often

incorporating a few Catholic elements beside ancient, entirely pre-Hispanic gods and earth spirits, which have been study material for legions of anthropologists. Equally, each group has a powerful sense of community life, over and above each individual within it, and in most cases there is a similarly ancient system of authority based on councils of elders, with, in many, a complex rotation of responsibilities between the men of the community.

These communities in northern and central Mexico, however, have typically maintained their traditions in such pure form because they have retreated to remote places, as far as

possible from mainstream Mexican society, and often keep all contacts with the mestizo world to an absolute minimum. In cities in the same regions, however, such as Chihuahua or Guadalajara, there is often scarcely any sign of an indigenous presence at all. It is in contrast to the south of Mexico, in Oaxaca, Chiapas and the Yucatán Peninsula, where the Mixtecs, Zapotecs, Maya and others still make up half or even more of the population, where the multi-faceted indigenous heritage is all pervasive, visible in every market and on every street, an inescapable part of everyday life.

In Oaxaca, it is reflected in the explosive variety of local craft work, or the completely unexpected ways of towns such as Zapotec Juchitán,

LEFT: some Tarahumaras still live in caves.
RIGHT: a woman from the long-suffering Seri tribe.

which is traditionally matriarchal, and where women like to have gay sons since they are more helpful than straight ones. In Chiapas, though the Highland Maya communities have long kept themselves apart like the smaller groups of the north, in recent years they have flooded in to towns like San Cristóbal de Las Casas. In

In the work of one of Mexico's greatest living artists, the Oaxaca painter and engraver Francisco Toledo, indigenous imagery has been brought directly into contemporary art.

the Yucatán, the influence of the Maya, gentle and reticent, is everywhere, and gives local life its distinctive tone and charm. Another aspect of the south is that the macho brashness often found in northern Mexican cities is far less evident, giving way to a much softer, courteous, tropical grace.

Tradition and its novelties

Whether in loud, industrial Monterrey or the placid, heavily indigenous colonial cities of the south, the interaction between pre-Hispanic, Spanish and other influences equally plays itself out in many aspects of the life of the 89 percent of the population who are not part of strictly indigenous communities. This is

perhaps most marked in fields where the two main influences actually agree, and so reinforce rather than oppose each other. One of the most striking is the importance given to tradition in itself, a characteristic of the ancient Mexican peoples but also highly regarded in the past by the Spaniards. Compared especially to English-speakers, for whom, some say, "life is what you make it" and can theoretically be invented new every day, Mexicans historically have a strong sense of tradition as setting down the basic markers of behavior, in food, music, the pattern of daily life, and traditions have often been seen as a refuge, an important source of stability in a shifting world.

The sense of time is one particular area where pre-Hispanic and Spanish elements coincide. All the pre-Conquest cultures, but above all the Maya, were obsessed with marking the passage of time and the movements of the heavens, as indications of the cycles of the universe. The Spanish Catholic Church, equally, brought with it an intricate calendar of saints' days and other festivals. These two sides of a coin combined together perfectly, and the result was a devotion to fiestas even stronger than anything in Spain itself. The great Nobel Prize-winning poet Octavio Paz wrote in his remarkable dissection of his country's psychology *The Labyrinth of Solitude* that "we are a ritualistic people," and the fiesta remains one of the foremost Mexican institutions. Not only does each town and village have one to honor its principal patron saint, but there are also special fiestas for individual districts, churches, trades, and of course the big national ones like the Virgin of Guadalupe. Fiestas are occasions for collective enjoyment with all one's neighbors, when the everyday look of things is transformed by color, music, fireworks. Many incorporate strange, part pre-Hispanic traditions, and/or are occasions for wonderful demonstrations of popular skills and creativity, so that fiestas can themselves be reinvented within a tradition. Utilitarian minds can be horrified when they discover what proportion of its resources a poor village will spend on fiestas, but just to treat every day as the same, Protestant-style, would seem to most Mexicans ridiculously dull.

The love of color and decoration is another Mexican characteristic of pre-Conquest origin that seems to run in tandem with the love of fiestas, and is seen at its best in curious details like the painted papier-mâché butterflies made in many regions, or the endless range of textile designs. In the 1540s the Spanish Friar Diego de Landa wrote with great admiration of the way the Maya decorated their homes with flowers, and the association of flowers and color with the sacred can be seen in the story of the Virgin of Guadalupe *(see page 29)*. In this case, the modern Mexican enjoyment of color is a tradition that has also been deliberately revived, as it was artists such as Frida Kahlo who made an appreciation of Mexico's brilliant indigenous colors newly fashionable after the Revolution.

The importance of family is another inescapable feature of Mexican life. This could perhaps be not so much a matter of time-honored tradition as a reflection of people's lack of confidence in any other institution (except perhaps the Virgin of Guadalupe), particularly politics and government. Children are naturally the focus of the family, and are liberally smothered with affection; the American traveler Charles Macomb Flandreau was so impressed by what he saw here in the 1900s that he wrote that *all* children should be born Mexican, to give them a good start in life. Equally, many indigenous people in particular do not really understand how anyone can *not* have several children. Among country people, particularly, this emphasis on caring for family contributes to the atmosphere of warmth and kindliness, the attitude of quiet, live-and-let-live tolerance, that is palpable in many small towns and villages.

Solitude and sentiment

Alongside this color and friendly warmth there are, as always in Mexico, other more complex and contradictory characteristics, such as the much-remarked reserve of Mexican men in particular. Quiet courtesy and apparent affability can sometimes fade into an almost oriental distance and formality. Equally, the counterpoint to this traditional Mexican liking for courtesy is the brash, sharp street-talk of many youth in Mexico City and other big cities, which goes to another extreme with chippy attitude and torrents of obscenities. Octavio Paz wrote that the central condition of the Mexican man was solitude, and that much of his behavior – from

elaborate formality to the exaggerated sociability of the fiesta – represented only different means of defense, to keep people at bay and protect his isolation. Some say that the reliance on family is itself part of this, in that many Mexicans do not, ultimately, trust anyone outside their immediate family or circle of *compadres* (lifelong friends), an attitude that has naturally contributed to recurrent political corruption. Paz argued too that as a result of his own chronic insecurities the Mexican really saw no point in trusting others, and felt that there were only two attitudes to take when dealing with others: take advantage of them, or have them

take advantage of you; "screw or be screwed," in the language of the street.

The views of Paz have often been criticized since they first appeared in the 1990s, and the image of the Mexican male ready to challenge all he meets has become an often-ridiculed cliché, but this all-or-nothing approach is certainly enshrined in popular culture, particularly the classic Mexican popular culture of *mariachis*, *ranchera* songs and the great Mexican movies of the 1940s that are still favorites on TV. These have in common that they are melodramatic, romantic, and unreservedly sentimental, but in a peculiarly negative, even vaguely masochistic, way. The great leading men of Mexican cinema – Jorge Negrete, Pedro Infante – perfected a kind

LEFT: an Independence Day performance by Ballet Folklórico in San Miguel de Allende's El Jardín.
RIGHT: the actor and singer Jorge Negrete, on the right.

of haughty male smoulder; their heroines, like the superstar María Félix, smouldered haughtily back. Passion was at the center of the story, but nearly always with the idea that their love was ultimately doomed. The most popular *rancheras* always deal in tragedy, in betrayal, the futility of love. According to Mexican journalist Alma Guillermoprieto, a Mexican's idea of a good party is not one where everybody ends up laughing, but one where at least some of the guests, helped by a few tequilas, end up crying their eyes out on each others' shoulders after singing some sentimental old traditional songs, releasing pent-up emotion and so perhaps breaking

out of their proverbial solitude. In film and in song, love is always worth embarking upon, but with the implication that it's more likely to lead to disappointment than the naïve and drama-free world of happy-ever-after. In the south, the macho bravado of the northern *rancheras* and *corridos* is absent in traditional music such as the *boleros* of the guitar trios of Yucatán, but is replaced by a much more languid, tropical, but still hugely sentimental romanticism.

Most recently, the stereotypical image of the northern Mexican male as in a doomed struggle with the world has also been taken up keenly by those most macho of modern Mexicans the

PICK YOUR TELENOVELA

Mexico has a modern institution that easily rivals fiestas in popularity, in part because it's available every day: *telenovelas*, the soap operas that dominate the TV schedules, with at least 10 ongoing on one or other channel at any one time. They differ from most English-speaking TV soaps in that they are not never-ending, but each is a mini-series, with about 100 episodes leading up to a very clear, dramatic end. They are among Mexico's most successful exports, as they gather huge audiences not only throughout the Hispanic world but also in Russia, China and many Arab countries.

Telenovelas nearly always stick to a few well-tried formulas; melodrama, as in so much of Mexican popular culture, is the key, and family tensions are at least somewhere in each

tale. One favorite storyline is the poor girl who falls in love with a rich man and has to overcome the opposition of her family and rivals to reach the happy ending. Historical romances give an opportunity for different costumes and more variety. One traditional constant has been that most of the actors are unusually white-skinned for Mexico, and in modern settings even the "poor" characters seem unusually comfortable, considering that these series are gobbled up by mestizo and indigenous people living in very different conditions throughout the country. Aware of this criticism, some producers have tried to introduce social issues, and give their *telenovelas* a more realistic look. But it's hard to change a formula when the fantasy has been so successful.

narcos or drug traffickers, many of whom, like all the Mafia mobsters who modeled themselves on characters from *The Godfather*, exult in their self-cultivated image as lonely heroes ready to take on the FBI, the Mexican army and anyone else who crosses their path. And there is perhaps no better evidence for Paz's thesis on the solitude and distrust of a certain kind of Mexican male than the *narcos'* terrifying readiness to turn on and murder each other.

The modern world

Naturally, though, even such a multi-faceted weight of traditions can still not explain Mexico completely, for no country stands still. Mexico especially has undergone vast changes in the last century, and is still feeling them everyday, in its skin. First of all has been massive urbanization, beginning in the 1930s but reaching galloping pace from the 1960s onwards. Curiously, one of the first effects of urbanization was perhaps to increase the prominence of tradition, since it was in the 1940s that *mariachi* music – via radio – and other classic images of "Mexicanness" such as the movie heroes with their moustaches and big sombreros first became popular throughout the country, as reassuringly familiar images of rural life for new city dwellers. In the last few decades, though, urban growth has gone beyond all expectations, above all in the immense, sprawling mass – sometimes just called *el monstruo*, "the monster" – of Mexico City, creating huge challenges to traditional ways of life and generating entirely new ones.

With its size, pollution, traffic chaos, and dire warnings from locals on how not to take a taxi and which areas not to stray into, its catalog of environmental and other problems, Mexico's capital can appear out of control. In its worst problem areas – easily avoided by most visitors – the tension created by crime and insecurity is unavoidable. However, it can also be seen as an example of the resilience of ordinary Mexican people, with very few resources. Even in the most ragged districts, with the greatest deficiencies in housing, water supply, power and other basics of modern urban life, people establish local organizations, build up local networks, place religious shrines and flowers on street

corners, and generally try to take care of their neighborhood. New urban Mexicans enthusiastically keep up district fiestas – or observe some they have brought with them from the countryside – and also invent new traditions, such as their crazy love of masked wrestlers.

Mexico's biggest problem, as it has long been, is its difficulty in providing a decent standard of life for a great proportion of its population, in the great city and especially across vast areas of the countryside. This has greater impact than the corrosive impact of drug violence – to which it also contributes, since, the fewer the economic opportunities, the fewer the alternatives there

are to accepting the pressures and blandishments of the drug lords. The scale of migration and dependency on it has placed immense strain on traditional family life, as whole villages are left made up of old people, sometimes nearly all women, caring for small children after their parents have left for Mexico City or *El Norte*, the US border, and the first question hanging in the air when anyone reaches teenage years is when they might leave. It is another indication of Mexican resilience, and ability to improvise, that so much of social life has survived in such circumstances. Outside Mexico, Mexican migration is often presented as a problem above all for the US, as to whether or not people should be let in, but it is interesting to note that in Mexico's last

LEFT: musicians performing "Danza de los Viejitos" in Plaza Vasco de Quiroga, Pátzcuaro. **RIGHT:** rural and urban poverty is still a major concern in modern Mexico.

presidential election year of 2006 both the mainstream left candidate Andrés Manuel López Obrador and the radical "Other Campaign" promoted by the Zapatista spokesman Marcos focused instead on the huge pain migration creates within the country, and the need for Mexico itself to offer its poorest people valid alternatives.

Beyond the overriding problem of rural poverty, the modern world has also exerted particular pressures on indigenous communities, despite their apparent protective ring of tradition. In Chiapas, many Maya have joined in a frontal challenge to their place in

Middle Mexico

Yet again, of course, these tensions represent only parts of the Mexican reality. Another – often passed over by foreigners, but hugely important – is the urban middle class, that substantial section of the population able to be fully in touch with the modern world. Some of the richest, in a tradition of wealthy Mexicans that goes back centuries, go whole-hog to embrace foreign, and especially American, culture. An acrid debate has flowed in Mexico recently over the accusation that many well-heeled teenagers are more familiar with Halloween parties copied from movies than they are with the Day of the

society through the Zapatista movement, but this has also led to clashes with other, more traditional Maya groups. More challenging to indigenous life across Mexico as a whole has been the arrival of evangelical Protestantism. Most indigenous communities had long got used largely to ignoring the official Catholic Church, but since the 1940s many have been emphatically targeted by a variety of mostly US-based evangelical sects, who have won many converts. Since so much of indigenous life has traditionally revolved around shared rituals, any division in religion is profoundly disruptive of community life. And without the community, indigenous people are all the more vulnerable in the outside world.

Dead. Others, however, have a far more creative approach to their own background, as seen in the wonderful, but wholly Mexican, inventiveness of the country's pop music and arts scene.

Mexico has always struggled to combine its great weight of tradition with modernity. Its political system is another example; while extensively democratized since the 1990s, it retains huge elements of long-established cronyism and inertia, and yet now faces its greatest test in the confrontation with the drug cartels. Nevertheless, Mexicans have a long record of imaginatively recreating and adapting their own culture. ❏

ABOVE: staying connected through Wi-fi in a Querétaro park.

Guadalupe: the Ever-present Virgin

The Virgin of Guadalupe is found everywhere in Mexico, and ensures that Catholicism here, like so many things, has a very special national tone and color.

A mind-boggling 6 million pilgrims arrive at the vast Basílica de Nuestra Señora de Guadalupe in Mexico City every year to pay tribute to Mexico's patron, making this the most-visited single Catholic site in the world. Some arrive on foot, from the remotest parts of Mexico. Individuals come to ask for help or to make a pledge to the Virgin; business groups often send representatives, and sometimes a whole village will arrive.

In the week before the day of the Virgin of Guadalupe, December 12, devotees run along roads throughout Mexico carrying flaming torches, on pilgrimages to local churches dedicated to her. The red, white and green image of the Virgin can be seen in airports, on T-shirts and picked out in flowers covering whole hillsides, and there is one in nearly every home. She is one of the most pervasive religious images in the world.

Octavio Paz wrote that the Virgin of Guadalupe is the real core of Mexican Catholicism, ahead of Christ or God the Father, and some writers say Mexicans are not really Catholics but *Guadalupanos*. She is entwined with Mexican life in innumerable ways, a symbol of the racial and cultural mix that is Mexico.

The shrine of Guadalupe is on the hill of Tepeyac, which was outside Mexico City in 1531, when, the traditional account goes, the Virgin Mary appeared there to a recently baptized Mexica peasant, Juan Diego, original name Cuauhtlatoatzin. Speaking in Náhuatl, she told him she wanted a temple built there, for all the people in Mexico who loved her. Diego took the message to the Spanish bishop, but was turned away and mistreated; he begged the Virgin to use someone important instead, but she insisted she had chosen him as her messenger. He tried again, until the bishop sneered that, if Diego's apparitions were true, he should show them a sign. The Virgin appeared again, and told Juan to go back to Tepeyac and gather everything he found there.

RIGHT: the Virgin of Guadalupe.

At the top of the hill, normally an arid, rocky place, he found a field of dazzling, exquisite flowers. Carrying as many as he could in his plain *tilma*, or poncho, he returned to the city. The Spaniards abused him again, but when his *tilma* fell open and the flowers spread across the floor, the image of the Virgin appeared through them, leaving the bishop stunned and ashamed. Juan Diego's *tilma* is now the centerpiece of the Basilica of Guadalupe, and he himself was made a saint in 2002.

This was the first manifestation of the Virgin Mary anywhere in the Americas recognized by the Catholic Church; it was also a remarkable coming together of the new beliefs and the old. Tepeyac hill had previously been a shrine to an Aztec fertility

goddess, Tonantzin. The emphasis on the downtrodden Indian as the Virgin's messenger, and the inclusion of such pre-Hispanic elements as the role of flowers and color as symbols of divine life, also had resonance.

The cult of Guadalupe gave Catholicism here a distinct, Mexican identity, separating it from its Spanish roots, which also made the Virgin a patriotic as well as a religious symbol. When Hidalgo called for revolt against Spain in 1810, he invoked the protection of the Virgin of Guadalupe for an independent Mexico, and military leaders from Porfirio Díaz to the revolutionary Emiliano Zapata have ridden under her banner. And today, no sensible politician would ever dare criticize the Virgin of Guadalupe. ❑

DECISIVE DATES

PRE-HISPANIC ERA

c.20,000 BC
First human migrations to the Americas from Asia across the Bering Straits.

c.18–10,000 BC
Settlements of hunter-gatherers established in the Valley of Mexico.

c.2000 BC
The beginning of agriculture, with the cultivation of corn, beans and chilies.

1600–300 BC
Preclassic period. The Olmec culture, the "mother culture" of Mesoamerica, develops near the Gulf Coast, with centers at San Lorenzo (Veracruz) and La Venta (Tabasco).

300 BC–AD 250
Late Preclassic period. The Pyramid of the Sun and other major structures are built at Teotihuacán. A distinctive Maya civilization takes shape in the south.

AD 250–800
The Classic era of Meso-america: many different cultures flourish, and create large, complex centers. Teoti-huacán dominates a huge area until its still-unexplained collapse around 650. In the south, Maya civilization reaches its peak in over 60 city states.

AD 800–1000
The Great Collapse: many cultures go into a rapid decline. The Collapse is most acute among the Maya, and most southern Maya cities are abandoned over the next two centuries.

AD 1000–1520
The Postclassic. Warlike Tula emerges as a new center in the Highlands from 900–1100. Mixtec civilization expands in Oaxaca. Around 1200, the Aztecs occupy the Valley of Mexico.

1325
Aztecs found their capital Ten-ochtitlán on an island in Lake Texcoco, site of present-day Mexico City.

SPANISH CONQUEST AND THE COLONIAL ERA

1517
Francisco Hernández de Cór-doba makes first Spanish landing in Mexico.

1519
Hernán Cortés and his con-quistadores land at Veracruz and march to Tenochtitlán, where they are initially greeted as honored guests by Moctezuma II.

1520–21
Cortés and his men take Tenochtitlán and overthrow the Aztec empire.

1526–42
Spaniards conquer Maya Yucatán in the face of fierce resistance.

INDEPENDENCE 1810–1910

1810–21
Miguel Hidalgo makes his famous *Grito de Dolores* – Cry for Independence – initiating Mexico's bloody 10-year war of independence.

1821–2
Agustín de Iturbide, Mexican-born commander of the Spanish army, changes sides and so allows Mexico to become independent, declaring himself its first emperor.

1823
Iturbide is overthrown and Mexico becomes a republic.

1836
Texas gains independence.

1846–8
The United States invades Mexico and takes Mexico City. In the concluding Treaty of Guadalupe Hidalgo, Mexico cedes Texas, New Mexico, Arizona and California – half its territory – to the USA.

1847–50
"Caste War," a massive Maya revolt, in Yucatán.

1855–9
Wars of La Reforma, as liberals led by Benito Juárez struggle against conservatives to give Mexico a modern state.

1862–7
French troops occupy Mexico City and attempt to impose the Austrian prince Maximilian as a new emperor of Mexico. Following another bitter war Juárez is restored as president and Maximilian is executed.

1876–1910
General Porfirio Díaz establishes a 34-year dictatorship,

PRECEDING PAGES: Maya architecture, Chichén Itzá. FAR LEFT: colossal basalt Olmec head, Museo de Antropología de Xalapa. MIDDLE LEFT: Aztec codex painting. TOP LEFT: engraving of Hernán Cortés by W. Holl. TOP RIGHT: Porfirio Díaz. RIGHT: President Felipe Calderón.

the Porfiriato. Foreign investment is encouraged and the economy expands enormously, but chronic poverty worsens in many parts of the country.

MEXICAN REVOLUTION AND ITS AFTERMATH, 1910–80

1911
Armed rebellions finally oust Díaz, and instal Francisco Madero as president.

1913
Reactionary generals assassinate Madero, but are resisted by revolutionary groups.

1917
New Constitution announced; Venustiano Carranza elected president.

1929
The official state political party, the Partido Nacional Revolucionario – later known as the Partido Revolucionario Institucional (PRI) – is founded to bring together all the different groups that were identified with the Revolution.

1938
President Cárdenas nationalizes Mexico's oil.

THE MODERN ERA

1994
Ejército Zapatista de Liberación Nacional (EZLN) seizes San Cristóbal and other towns in Chiapas.

1997
PRI loses the mayoralty of Mexico City to the left-wing PRD.

2000
Partido de Acción Nacional (PAN) candidate Vicente Fox is elected the first non-PRI president of Mexico in 71 years.

2006
Felipe Calderón (PAN) is declared winner of the presidential elections by the narrowest of margins over Andrés Manuel López Obrador of the PRD.

2007–9
President Calderón launches massive military and police campaign against drug cartels; violence intensifies, especially in cities on the US border.

2009
The US and global economic crisis has a severe impact on Mexico.

PRE-HISPANIC CIVILIZATIONS

The Maya and Aztecs are the best-known cultures, but ancient Mexico contained a remarkable array of diverse, complex peoples

According to archeological research, Mexico has been inhabited for around 20,000 years. It all began in Siberia, with ancient hunter-gatherer peoples crossing the Bering Straits in search of food during the Ice Ages. From Alaska they moved south down the coast, and eventually reached Mexico and Central and South America .

Some time around 9000–7000 BC, people in what is now Mexico first began to use a crude stone implement to grind wild corn into maize flour. This was the forerunner of the *metate*, the slab upon which rural Mexicans still grind corn today. By 5000 BC ancient Mexicans had begun to grow maize and beans, and around 2000 BC they began to mix lime powder with corn to create the much more nutritious *nixtamal* flour, the essential ingredient for making corn tortillas. These have been the staples of the Mexican diet ever since.

The Mesoamerican timeline

Mesoamerica is the term commonly used for the cultural region that in pre-Columbian times extended through Mexico, Guatemala and much of Central America. Within it there were two main "hubs," the Central Highlands and the southern Maya region from Guatemala up into Yucatán, with many "offshoots" such as the valleys of Oaxaca. Our knowledge of Mesoamerican civilizations is continually changing and expanding, and has been transformed by discoveries in the last 30 or 40 years

A common Mesoamerican historical division into "eras" has been developed. Very broadly,

the first complex cultures emerged in what is known as the "Preclassic" era, from about 1600 to 300 BC; this was followed by a transitional period usually called the "Late Preclassic," from about 300 BC to AD 250, when the growth of major cultures such as Teotihuacán or the southern Maya accelerated. The Classic era of Mesoamerica, from about AD 250 to 800, saw these civilizations reach their greatest wealth and extent, but was followed by a period often called the "Collapse," when some cultures, above all the southern Maya, went into rapid decline, for reasons that are still continually debated. In the "Postclassic," from about 1000 to the Spanish Conquest, the Maya revived on a more

LEFT: colossal Olmec head.
RIGHT: Coatlicue, the Aztec goddess of the Earth.

limited scale in Yucatán, while cultures proliferated in the Central Highlands, culminating in the empire of the Aztecs.

The mother culture

The first of Mexico's great ancient cultures was that of the Olmecs, who flourished, not in either of Mesoamerica's hubs, but in the apparently unfavorable setting of the low-lying jungles and delta swamps of southern Veracruz and Tabasco, between about 1200 and 400 BC.

Many things about the Olmecs, or "people from the land of rubber," remain an enigma. We know they were the first builders of large,

well-organized centers or "cities," and that they channeled water to grow their crops. But unlike the Maya, the Olmec did not have a writing system that can be deciphered, so we must rely entirely on the testimony of their art.

Their best-known legacies are the astounding, monolithic basalt heads – many of which are now in Parque La Venta in Villahermosa – measuring up to 3 meters (10ft) in height, and weighing between 6 and 50 tons. No one can be certain what they portray, but it is widely believed they are gigantic portraits of Olmec rulers. All 17 discovered have generally similar features – flat wide noses, thickened lips – but all are different from each other. Their slightly "African" appearance has given rise to suggestions the Olmecs had some kind of contacts with the other side of the Atlantic, but this idea has been thoroughly discredited, and it is believed the heads were given their apparently non-Native American features to increase their dramatic effect and evoke the jaguar that was such a theme in Olmec imagery.

One of the great mysteries about the Olmecs is how these heads and other monuments were ever made. The Olmecs had only simple tools, but these heads are carved out of hard basalt from the Tuxtla mountains, up to 100km (60 miles) from the centers where they were found. It can only be assumed they were hauled down from the hills or on rafts along rivers, but exactly how remains unknown. The enormous workforce required is proof in itself of an organized, hierarchical society.

Not all Olmec art is monumental; there are also exquisite jade miniatures, and delicate

THE BALL GAME

The ancient Mesoamerican ball game is one of the world's oldest sports, traced back 4,000 years. It seems it was played for sport and to keep warriors fit for war, but it also had huge ritual significance. In societies preoccupied by cosmic forces and cycles of time, it represented a chance to challenge destiny. In the Maya myths known as the *Popol-Vuh*, the "Hero-Twins" Hunahpú and Xbalanqué play the game with the Lords of Death for days and nights on end, and eventually defeat them. It also played a part in sacrifice, with losing players – often already captives – put to death.

It's impossible to know exactly how it was

played, but it seems that in the relatively small, earlier-style courts most common among the Classic Maya and in Veracruz, it was played between two or four players, and scoring was achieved just by getting the ball past the opponent and out the far end of the court. In later, larger courts – like the enormous one at Chichén Itzá – games were probably played between teams of around seven, and scoring required players to get the heavy, rubber ball through stone rings either side of the court. In both styles, players could not touch the ball with hands or feet, but only with their heads, shoulders and especially hips, protected by leather belts.

pottery and obsidian jewelry. The Olmecs created an extensive trading network to obtain materials such as jade, obsidian and serpentine, and Olmec relics have been found in Puebla, the Valley of Mexico, Oaxaca and Guatemala.

As in all pre-Hispanic cultures, Olmec art and religion were inseparable. A recurring motif in Olmec art is the jaguar, as the terrifying forest predator played a central role in Olmec religion. The Olmecs were the first people to set out the essential Mesoamerican cosmological vision of existence as divided into three, between the heavens, this world and a threatening underworld, all equally "alive" and with constant con-

400 BC, the first of several Mesoamerican "collapses" that give rise to constant discussion of their possible causes. However, as the "mother culture" of Mesoamerica the Olmecs had laid down patterns – in their cosmic vision, social organization, the role of monumental cities with symbolic temple-pyramids as the "core" of each community, even the ball game – that would influence all subsequent civilizations in the region.

The south: the Maya

Strongly influenced by the Olmecs, the Maya first emerged as a city-building culture in Chi-

tact between them. This vision allowed space for a complex variety of gods and mythical or semi-mythical creatures.

The first great Olmec center, San Lorenzo in Veracruz, grew up around 1300 BC. It was largely abandoned around 900 BC, but was succeeded by two more Olmec centers, at La Venta in Tabasco and Tres Zapotes to the northwest, which each thrived for another 400–500 years.

Olmec civilization finally came to an end with the disintegration of La Venta around

LEFT: "The Wrestler," an Olmec sculpture.
ABOVE: dating from pre-Hispanic times, the Maya backstrap loom is still in use today.

apas and central Guatemala around the beginning of the Late Preclassic (around 300 BC), and spread across the whole of modern Guatemala, Belize, part of Honduras, Tabasco, and the Yucatán Peninsula. In the Classic era the Maya were the most sophisticated of all the ancient Mesoamerican cultures, in art, astronomy, mathematics – using the concept of zero centuries before it was known in Europe – and many other fields. The Maya had the only really complete glyph writing system in pre-Hispanic America, used in bark books, on ceramics and in thousands of carved inscriptions. Maya glyphs have only been extensively deciphered since the 1960s, but this has made it possible for the Classic Maya to become the only ancient Mesoamerican people with an extensive history of known names, rulers and dates.

The Maya were also among the region's finest builders, and their harmoniously proportioned buildings are often beautifully decorated with fine carving or stucco. Like other Mesoamerican cultures they never discovered the true arch, but the Maya did invent what is known as the corbelled vault, or "Maya arch," an upturned V of flat slabs topped by a coping stone.

One of the most important discoveries in the Maya world came in 1952, when a rich burial chamber was found in the Temple of

of the stars with astonishing precision. The Maya needed such exact calendars because co-ordination of the heavenly bodies affected everything they did. Their vision of the world was cyclical: since the stars and the universe move in regular cycles, they expected events on earth to repeat themselves too, as the planting season does each year.

The ending of each 20-year *katun* period was marked with special ceremonies, and political events, such as battles and the accessions of kings, were also timed to coincide with the stars. This is also why so many monuments were rigorously inscribed with Long Count

Inscriptions at Palenque, the tomb of the city's greatest ruler, Pakal "the Great" (ruled AD 615–83). Since then many more tombs have been excavated beneath Maya pyramids, notably at Calakmul. Another major find was that of the extraordinary battle murals at Bonampak – the only full-size survivors of thousands of Maya wall paintings – which revolutionized our knowledge of Maya art and warfare, with intricate details of dress, musicians, and rituals.

Time keepers

The passage of time was all-important to the Maya, and no other culture was so obsessed with recording time, plotting the movements

dates, making it possible to "date" Maya history with such precision.

Gods of the Maya

The Maya pantheon was as complicated as their calendar. Though commonly translated as "gods," Maya and other Mesoamerican deities would be better described as spiritual or natural forces. For the Maya there were at least 166, each of which could express itself in several different ways. Since the Maya believed themselves to be descended from people of corn, the staff of life, the Maize God, sometimes called Yum Kaax, was of funda-

ABOVE: Maya mural painting in Bonampak, Chiapas.
RIGHT: Palenque's Temple of Inscriptions.

The memory of the giant city of Teotihuacán always remained in the minds and folklore of the peoples of central Mexico, as the place where civilized life began.

mental importance, and in the Yucatán Chac, the Rain God, Itzamná, the Sun God, and his wife Ixchel, Goddess of the Moon, and of weavers, and women, were all prominent. The Maya were also ready to "absorb" gods from other cultures, such as the Teotihuacán war god Tlaloc.

Sacrifice was a central feature of Maya religion, as it was in all Mesoamerican cultures. Humans and spiritual forces were conceived as interdependent: in the same way that humans were "fed" by the gods, with rain and corn, so too the gods needed to be "fed" to survive, above all with human blood. Royal blood was especially powerful, and in elaborate rituals Maya kings and queens let their own blood from ears, tongues or penises. Wars were also fought to secure prisoners to be killed as sacrifices.

Common ground

The Maya had a common culture, but were never politically united. They were divided, in the Classic era, into around 60 separate city-states, each with a hereditary *ahau* or "sacred king," who was simultaneously the community's ruler and its great shaman, its link to the heavens. They were often at war with each other, and the deciphering of Maya inscriptions has revealed a complex history of battles, rivalries, alliances and dynastic struggles.

In the early Classic era, many Maya cities had strong links with Teotihuacán. Some Maya centers were linked by stone roads, or *sacbeob*. Maya communities enjoyed a virtual "boom" in size and building from about 600 to 800, when the largest cities, such as Palenque or Calakmul, had populations of 60–70,000.

Then, remarkably quickly, Classic Maya civilization entered a fatal decline. The "Maya Collapse" is one of history's great enigmas, and there are many theories to explain it. It seems most likely the Maya were torn apart by a spiral of environmental and political disasters. The growth in population itself stretched their

MAYA CALCULATIONS

The Maya used a simple bar-and-dot number system, with three symbols: a shell (often more like an eye or a cacao bean) for zero, a dot for one and a bar for five. While our numbers go from right to left by factor 10 (ie 2,345), larger Maya numbers were written in vertical columns from bottom to top, increasing by 20 in each row, as in the example here:

34,448

- • • • • $4 \times 8,000 = 32,000$
- —•— $6 \times 400 = 2,400$
- • • $2 \times 20 = 40$
- ••• 8

An essential use of numbers was to mark time. Dates could be identified with three calendars. Two were used throughout Mesoamerica: the 260-day *tzolkin* cycle and the 365-day *haab* year, which were normally used together, interlocking like cog-wheels in a cycle that repeats every 52 years. More intricate was the "Long Count" perhaps first developed in Oaxaca but only used by the Classic Maya. Again it is mainly based on 20: 20 days make up one uinal month, 18 of which form a 360-day *tun* or year. Twenty *tuns* make a *katun*, and 20 *katuns* a *baktun* (around 400 years) of which 13 make up a Great Cycle (around 5,200 conventional years), the most important division in the movement of time, although even more vast multiples could be used too. The current Great Cycle began in August 3114 BC and will end in December 2012, when, some say, a whole new creation may begin.

agricultural techniques to the limit: soils were exhausted, ever more forest was cut down, productivity fell, and malnutrition spread. The main response of the *ahau* lords was more wars, which only made things worse. A crisis point seems to have been reached with a general

> For all the Mesoamerican cultures natural phenomena – caves, waterfalls, mountains, animals – could represent spiritual forces, and act as conduits between the three levels of existence.

collapse in faith in *ahau* rule: over a century, beginning around 800, virtually all the dynasties of the southern Maya cities fell, taking much of refined Maya culture with them, and the cities themselves were mostly abandoned over the next 200 years.

The "Collapse" arrived later, and was never as complete, in northern Yucatán, where cities such as Uxmal and Chichén Itzá were still reaching their peak around 900, but by the year 1000 they too had suffered a decline, often terminal. The southern Maya cities never revived, but from around 1200 Maya culture raised its head again on a smaller scale in Yucatán, reflected in the fierce resistance given to the Spaniards in the 1530s.

Central Highlands and Teotihuacán

In contrast to the Maya, the first great civilization on Mexico's highland plateau was highly centralized, around the vast city of Teotihuacán, just north of modern Mexico City. It first emerged some 200 years before the Christian era, and many of its main structures, including the 75-meter (246-ft) -high Pyramid of the Sun, had been built by AD 100. Everything about Teotihuacán was immense: at its peak it probably had more than 150,000 people. It was a ghost town when the Aztecs arrived in the 1300s, but its ruins were so awe-inspiring that they revered it as "The Place of the Gods," and believed the Sun and the Moon had been created there. However, the Teotihuacános did not develop a full writing system like the Maya, so their history has remained far more vague and anonymous.

The exact origins of Teotihuacán are another mystery, though it too was influenced by the Olmecs. It was a warrior city, conquering other peoples around it, but was also a great commercial hub, with trading links throughout Mesoamerica. It controlled large deposits of obsidian, treasured for making tools, weapons, and jewelry, and Teotihuacán craftsmen excelled in jewelry and ceramics. Pyramids and other structures were adorned with fine carvings and spectacular painted murals.

Influential gods

So pre-eminent was Teotihuacán that its influence was felt throughout Mesoamerica, in art, architecture, warfare and religion. One of its foremost deities was the goggle-eyed Tlaloc, god of rain and fertility: in the *Paradise of Tlaloc* mural people are shown frolicking, singing and dancing in a lush, fertile land. However, like most Mesoamerican gods he could have positive and negative aspects, for he was also associated with lightning and war, in which guise he was "adopted" by many Maya cities, along with Teotihuacano fighting techniques. The cult of Quetzalcóatl, the plumed-serpent god of wind and the dawn, also developed in Teotihuacán. He would be one of the gods most revered by the Aztecs, and in late Classic and Postclassic Yucatán, where he was given the Maya name Kukulcán.

Nevertheless, despite – or perhaps because of – its power and wealth, Teotihuacán also suffered a general collapse, around 600–650. As with the Maya 200 years later, there is still no definitive explanation why, but it seems likely it was due to a similar amalgam of overpopulation, agricultural crisis, drought, revolt and invasion.

The Toltecs

The centuries after the fall of Teotihuacán saw smaller-scale cultures rise and fall in the Central Highlands. Some time around 850 a group of Chichimecas, nomadic hunters from the northern deserts, settled down around a new city at Tula, now in Hidalgo state. The Aztecs later called them "Toltecs," but since this could also mean "craftsmen" it has never been clear whether this identified them as a distinct ethnic group or simply meant that they had become "civilized."

Tula society was highly militaristic, and at one time dominated much of central Mexico. While every culture practiced sacrifice, the Toltecs are thought to have been the first to carry out the mass human sacrifices so prominent among the Aztecs.

The Toltecs were also skilled masons, weavers and featherworkers. Apart from the serpent, predominant motifs in Toltec sculpture – overwhelmingly revolving around power, war and sacrifice – include the *chacmool* figures, reclining back to receive sacrificial hearts; the famous *Atlantes*, massive columns of warriors; eagles and jaguars devouring human hearts, and the *tzompantli*, or human skull rack. It was long thought that the presence of similar sculptures at the Maya city of Chichén Itzá indicated that there had been a Toltec invasion of Yucatán, but it is now believed that this was due to a more diffuse spread of central Mexican influences, and that no such "Toltec invasion" ever happened. Nevertheless, Toltec commercial ties were far-reaching, and artifacts from Tula have been found as far north as Paquimé in Chihuahua, and even in northern New Mexico. However, Toltec power was fairly short-lived, and Tula, like Teotihuacán before it, was partly destroyed by fire some time in the 1170s.

The Aztecs

Some time around 1200, another formerly nomadic people arrived in the Valley of Mexico. They called themselves the Mexica – the origin of the name Mexico – and like other migrant peoples in the same area spoke a variant of the Náhuatl language. The Aztecs later elaborated extensive "histories" of their origins, combining fact and myth in a way that makes the two very hard to disentangle. According to legend, the Mexica once lived on an island in a lake called Aztlán, somewhere in the north of Mexico. However, they were oppressed there by other tribes, and so their paramount god Huitzilopochtli instructed them to leave, summoning up a vision of an eagle perched on a cactus and devouring a serpent, and telling them to stop only when they saw a similar vision again.

Guided by Huitzilopochtli, they wandered for over a century, until, on an island in Lake Texcoco in the Valley of Mexico, they finally saw the prophesied eagle. About a year later, in 1325, the Mexica founded what was to be the great city of Tenochtitlán, named for their leader Tenoch, and which means "Place of the Cactus." Their cosmic symbol – the eagle representing the sky and the sun, the snake symbolizing the earth, and the cactus as sustenance of a wandering desert people – is today the national emblem of Mexico.

The Triple Alliance

At first they lived off snake meat, fish, and ducks. However, the shallow lake was ideal for

LEFT: a view of the smaller pyramids of Teotihuacán with the mighty Temple of the Sun in the distance.
RIGHT: Mixtec skull overlaid with turquoise mosaic.

the network of *chinampas* or drained-marsh gardens that was created around the central island, and which soon became extraordinarily productive. The lake also provided an easy, fast means of communication.

The Mexicas were originally only one of many Highland settlements, but in 1428 they formed an alliance with two smaller Náhuatl-speaking cities nearby, Tlacopán and Texcoco. Led by the Mexica king or *Tlatoani*, this "triple alliance" formed the core of what would later be called the Aztec Empire. Under Moctezuma I (1440–69), especially, Tenochtitlán became an imperial capital, as campaigns were launched

against Oaxaca and the Gulf Coast. Under later *Tlatoani*, Aztec power extended from coast to coast and even as far south as the Pacific coast of Guatemala, where they went in search of cacao.

The Aztecs demanded obedience from cities they defeated – so that they are one of the few great powers of pre-Hispanic America that can justifiably be called an empire – but were not interested in occupying the lands of the vanquished. They left the conquered peoples with their own leaders, but demanded hefty tributes of luxuries such as shells, quetzal feathers, jaguar skins, precious stones, and cacao.

Huge numbers of prisoners were also taken to Tenochtitlán to be sacrificed. The dedication of the temple-pyramid of Huitzilopochtli

in 1487 required the sacrifice of thousands of prisoners who, according to some accounts, were marshalled four abreast, then driven to the sanctuary on top of the pyramid for priests to tear out their hearts.

Five suns

More than 2,000 spiritual forces were worshipped in the complex Aztec pantheon, but the main temples at Tenochtitlán were dedicated to Huitzilopochtli – "Hummingbird," the Sun God and the city's chief protector – and to Tlaloc. Two other major temples stood nearby: one was dedicated to Tezcatlipoca ("Smoking-mirror"), and the other was the round temple of Quetzalcóatl. The Mexica believed the world had been through five time spans, or suns, each one lasting for several hundred years.

Each of the first four suns was presided over by a different god – the Earth god Tezcatlipoca, Quetzalcóatl the god of the Wind, Tlaloc the god of Rain and Fire, and Chalchiuhtlicue, a female water god – and were ended by titanic struggles between them. The fifth sun, the contemporary era, was said to have begun when Tezcatlipoca and Quetzalcóatl joined together at Teotihuacán to recreate the world

Aztec art

The Aztecs also developed powerful artistic styles. They were skilled sculptors, potters, jewelers and painters, and though they did not have a full writing system like the Maya, their illustrated books – the codices – are vivid and beautiful. As well as the highly stylized

> *At a time when most Europeans never washed at all, many Aztecs took daily baths, and hundreds of men were employed to clean the streets of Tenochtitlán every night.*

temple sculptures, there was a strong strain of naturalism in Aztec representation of grasshoppers, coyotes, frogs, rabbits, monkeys, and other animals.

Perhaps the greatest masterpiece of Aztec art, however, was the magnificent city of Tenochtitlán itself in the middle of the lake, with vibrant markets and surrounded by gardens fed by an intricate system of dikes.

Oaxaca: Zapotec and Mixtec

The ritual center of Monte Albán, in a remarkable location on a mountain top above the city of Oaxaca, was one of the oldest and most enduring settlements in ancient Mexico. Its first structures date from around 500 BC, and it was occupied, built and rebuilt for over a thousand years, until after AD 750. The greatest achievement of the Zapotec culture, in the early Classic it was the hub of a vigorous "state" that controlled much of modern Oaxaca.

The Zapotecs developed an extensive glyph writing system, and used the same bar and dot numbers as the Maya. Zapotec art was notably

tecs, but also built new centers of their own, the most striking of them Mitla, east of Oaxaca City, where the long, low "palaces" are decorated in finely cut stone mosaic, with a geometrical style slightly reminiscent of late Maya buildings such as Uxmal in the Yucatán.

The Mixtecs were famed as master craftsmen, goldsmiths and potters, and their superbly painted polychrome pottery was traded and imitated from central Mexico to Guatemala. They also left especially rich tombs: Tomb 7 at Mitla was found to contain more than 500 pieces of intricate jewelry and other precious artifacts, the greatest single treasure trove found in Mesoamer-

sophisticated, and among its greatest works are the extraordinary bas-reliefs at Monte Albán called *Los Danzantes* (The Dancers). Their ceramic funerary effigy urns, depicting seated deities wearing flamboyant costumes and jewelry, are unique. They were placed in elaborate stone tombs, where they were believed to guard the noble dead.

About AD 1000 the Mixtecs, originally from the Cholula-Puebla area farther north, moved down into Oaxaca and took over Monte Albán, already in decline. They mixed with the Zapo-

ica. The Mixtec *codices* or deer-skin manuscripts, up to 12 meters (39ft) in length, are a vital source of information on pre-Conquest America.

The Aztecs greatly prized Mixtec jewelry and mosaics, which in part was their downfall, for in the 1490s the *Tlatoani* Ahuitzotl invaded Oaxaca and conquered both Zapotecs and Mixtecs. They never disappeared, however, and there are still large numbers of Zapotec- and Mixtec-speaking people in Oaxaca today. Many have also emigrated to the US.

The Gulf Coast: the Veracruz culture and Huastecs

LEFT: detail of the large puma mural discovered at the ruined Maya city of Teotihuacán. **ABOVE:** Diego Rivera mural depicting the city of El Tajín.

The fertile, tropical Gulf Coast of Mexico was home not only to the Olmecs but also, later, to the Totonacs in central Veracruz and the Huastecs in the north.

Totonac was the name of the people who lived in Veracruz at the time the Spaniards arrived (and are still numerous today), and is also often used to refer to the culture that

The Veracruz and Huastec peoples made figurines to push about on wheels, but only as toys, perhaps because there was no point in making wheeled carts with no animals to pull them.

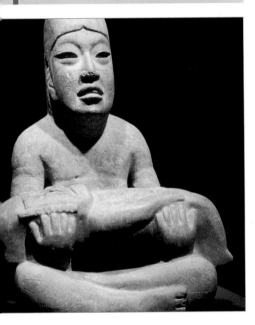

flourished through the Classic era in central Veracruz, although some experts dispute that these were the same people. The most prominent ancient Veracruz centers are at Remojadas, a relatively small site that is closed to visitors, and El Tajín. The Remojadas culture is not known for its monumental architecture, but was outstanding for its mastery of clay. The dead were buried with clay vessels and figurines, often painted with fine geometric designs, hundreds of which are now in the region's museums.

The *sonrientes* or "smiling face" figurines, often also in the form of whistles or rattles, are this culture's most distinctive creation. Compared with the often fearsome style of

Maya or Aztec sculpture, these jolly little figures of men and women, bring an instant change of tone. Their symbolism has been variously interpreted. Some think they portray the ritualistic use of hallucinogenic substances (hence the smile), while others see them simply as an expression of the generally festive character of the coastal people.

The great hub of the Veracruz culture was the huge city of El Tajín, with its famous Pyramid of the Niches. Veracruz culture seems to have been more obsessed than any other in Mesoamerica with the ritual ball game: some 17 courts have been found at El Tajín, and carvings depict many rituals and sacrifices related to the game. The many beautiful carved stone *hachas* (axes), *palmas* (palms) and *yugos* (yokes) at the site were also part of the ball game ceremony. Building continued at El Tajín until about 1200, but later it was attacked by primitive invaders, and by the time of the Conquest it had already been abandoned.

The Huastecs

The pre-Conquest Huastecs occupied an area extending from northern Veracruz into the surrounding states, and many of their descendants still live in this region, La Huasteca, today. Curiously, their language is of Maya origin, and there are many theories as to when and why they moved north, probably some time in the Preclassic era, about 1000 BC.

Considered primitive by their neighbors – in part because they usually went naked – the Huastecs only became prominent in the Postclassic era. Their buildings are relatively crude, and they are best known for their extraordinary art work, especially the highly stylized sandstone sculptures that depict almost abstract body shapes of women and men, many with conical headdresses, and bent-over figures of hunchbacks.

The Aztecs conquered the Huastecs some time around 1450. The Mexica were shocked by the Huastecs, who faced their enemy naked, their bodies painted with brilliant colors, their heads flattened and deformed.

Western and northern cultures

Much less is known about the cultures of western Mexico, although effigy pottery found in caves and tombs has revealed much about the beliefs of the people who inhabited this area 2,000 years ago. The settlements of Colima, Jalisco and Nayarit never merged into unified kingdoms, but remained under chieftains who controlled small areas, often warring with each other.

Life after death was, as usual, a central element in their beliefs, and so men were buried with ceramic replicas of their wives, servants and slaves to enhance their lives in the afterworld. Lacking the refinement of the Maya or the skill of the Mixtecs, the work of the western potters is distinctive, thanks to its simplicity of design, and joyfulness. They portrayed everyday life as well as spiritual themes: a

The Tarascans

Thanks to the Spaniards, we know a good deal more about the Tarascans of Michoacán, an independent kingdom, which by the time the Spaniards arrived, had been resisting invasions by the Aztecs for over a hundred years. Shortly after the Conquest a priest, Friar Jerónimo de Acalá, compiled his *Chronicles of Michoacán*, a history of the Purépecha, as the Tarascans called themselves, that gives an insight into their culture.

Michoacán means "Place of the Fishermen," a reference to Lake Pátzcuaro, the centre of Tarascan life. However, the religion of the Purépecha was based not on water but on volcanoes. The

ball game with spectators, lovers embracing, phallic dances, musicians, warriors and animals; one of their most common models was the *itzcuintli*, the plump and hairless native Mexican dog.

The peoples of the Central Highlands customarily dismissed those to the north of them as primitive, nomadic Chichimecas. However, in the Postclassic era, around 1200, yet another city developed in the far northwestern desert of Chihuahua at Paquimé, part of a culture that extended into Arizona.

chief deity, Curicáueri, the "Great Burner," represented the young Sun. In his honor, the Purépecha kept fires burning constantly on top of huge stone structures called *yácatas*, the largest of them at Tzintzuntzan, their lakeside capital.

As an enemy of the Aztecs, the last Tarascan king, Tangáxuan II, thought the Spaniards could perhaps become his allies. Spanish emissaries arrived in 1522, and rather than resist he agreed to accept the overlordship of Cortés while retaining his own autonomy. However, once the conquistadors discovered that he was passing on to them only a small part of the tribute he gathered from his people, retaliation was swift. Tangáxuan was burned alive, and the Tarascans were subjected to Spanish rule. ❑

LEFT: Olmec statue of a priest holding a supernatural infant. **ABOVE:** dramatic rock formations along Cañón de la Huasteca in the homeland of the Huastecs.

THE ANCIENT MEXICAN WORLD

Mexico's ruined cities are echoes of a 3,000-year-long history, and a complex, intricately interconnected world that can at times seem familiar, and at others feels very alien

Perhaps the most astonishing feature of the pre-Conquest civilizations of Mexico is their sheer variety, scale and extent. World-famous ruins such as Teotihuacán or Chichén Itzá are only a few among hundreds of sites, from Paquimé near the New Mexico border to the forest cities of the Yucatán and Chiapas in the south, part of a Maya region that extended still further into Guatemala and Honduras. A complex series of cultures developed and succeeded each other for nearly 3,000 years, from the emergence of the first Olmec communities in Veracruz and Tabasco around 1300 BC to the time of the Spanish Conquest. They adapted to every part of the region, from the northern deserts and highland valleys to the rain forests of the south. Look beyond the most obvious features, and exploring their differences, individualities and enigmas is endlessly fascinating.

Architecturally the pre-Hispanic cultures were commonly crude in some ways – their reliance on pyramid-mounds rather than load-bearing walls for height – and sophisticated in others – carving, water management. The central place of ritual was reflected in the theatricality of major buildings. While the great pyramids and plazas grab the eye first, just as interesting can be the details found in palaces and residential areas at sites such as El Tajín, Palenque or Kohunlich, which give a feel of daily life. Nor is ancient Mexico a closed book, for more sites are being excavated, and more learnt about them, all the time.

ABOVE: jade was one of the most precious materials in ancient Mesoamerica, used to create treasure like this Olmec face mask.

RIGHT: Olmec carvings often show mythological and supernatural creatures like this "human-jaguar."

LEFT AND BELOW: the only complete surviving Maya murals, at Bonampak in Chiapas, portray courtly ceremonies, rituals, and a bloody AD 792 battle.

BELOW: Maya astronomers tracked the movement of the stars at the Chichén Itzá observatory.

ABOVE: the adobe city of Paquimé flourished in the arid valleys of Chihuahua from around AD 1000–1400.

ABOVE: early representation of the Voladores de Papantla.
RIGHT: the Niches Pyramid at El Tajín, Veracruz, dates from around AD 700.

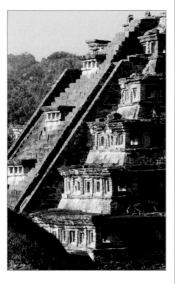

ANCIENT ARTS

The artistic creations of the ancient cultures were as inventive as their buildings. Many symbolized the power of their rulers or were associated with rituals and sacrifice, such as the fearful carved altars, or the elaborate Maya ceramic incense-burners representing supernatural beings. Others show a less forbidding side of each culture, such as the disarming "smiling head" sculptures of Veracruz. Among the Mixtecs and the Maya, scenes of everyday life, as well as legends, were painted on ceramic pots. And a Maya specialty were the tiny Jaina figurines, charming figures that give an image of a whole society.

All the cultures had a very vivid, imaginative visual sense, which has survived unbroken in Mexican folk arts today. The Maya had the most complete glyph writing system, followed by the Mixtecs, who left many books. Other cultures excelled in jewelry or more abstract designs. Many cultures had sophisticated painting traditions, but only a few examples have survived, such as the murals at Teotihuacán, Mitla and above all Bonampak, Chiapas.

The ideal first stop to get an idea of the range of pre-Hispanic art is the Museo de Antropología in Mexico City, but there are other fine collections in Xalapa, Palenque and Mérida.

RIGHT: gold was very scarce in ancient Mexico since it had to be imported from South America; but from around AD 1200, cultures such as the Mixtecs and the Aztecs produced gold figurines and other artifacts.

CONQUEST AND COLONIAL RULE

Spanish adventurers and Mexico's indigenous cultures locked together in an epic struggle, and the fissures in the society this created can still be seen 500 years later

The Spanish conquest of Mexico centered on the violent clash between two empires, both of which were cultured, cruel and well organized. But it was there the similarities stopped.

From an outsider's point of view, this is one of the world's most exciting adventure stories. Against tens of thousands of Aztec warriors, Hernán Cortés, the leader of the Spanish conquistadors, initially had fewer than 400 soldiers, 16 horses – "fearsome beasts," never before seen in the New World – 10 heavy guns and four lighter pieces of artillery. The success of Cortés' expedition would have been impossible without the help of other indigenous groups hostile to the Aztecs, and who were sick of paying tribute to Tenochtitlán: most of all the Tlaxcalans, who provided thousands of men to fight alongside the Spaniards.

When Cortés arrived in Mexico he was a mutineer on the run from a Spanish royal governor, and could only expect severe punishment if he returned empty-handed.

News of gold

The first Spanish expedition to set foot in Mexico was led by Francisco Hernández de Córdoba, who in February 1517 sailed west with three ships from Cuba, conquered by the Spaniards six years earlier. They landed first on Isla de Mujeres and sailed west around Yucatán, turning back after a skirmish with the Maya lord of Kin Pech (modern Campeche). Nevertheless, they had already seen buildings and goods of a sophistication far beyond anything the Spaniards had found on the Caribbean islands.

The following year another expedition, led by Juan de Grijalva, sailed south around the Yucatán coast and landed in what is now Veracruz state, where they first saw some of the wealth, fine textiles and above all gold of the Aztec empire. Once news of this reached Cuba, it could be said that Mexico's fate was sealed.

Hernán Cortés had been just 19 years old when he arrived on Hispaniola in 1504. Later he obtained land in Cuba, but, intelligent and ruthless, he craved more wealth and

ABOVE: schoolbook portrait of Hernán Cortés.
RIGHT: Cortés enters Tenochtitlán (detail of a painted screen from the colonial period).

adventure. In 1519 the governor of Cuba, Diego de Velázquez, proposed that he lead a third, larger expedition of 11 ships, men and horses to Mexico. However, like most conquistadors both men were intensely ambitious and suspicious of each other, and the rivalry between them would play its part in subsequent events. Distrusting Cortés, Velázquez tried to cancel the expedition, but Cortés ignored the order and set sail regardless.

Burning the boats

Like Grijalva, Cortés landed first on Cozumel, and then sailed west around the Yucatán. He won a victory against a local chieftain in western Campeche, after which, in Mesoamerican tradition, he was given tribute that included 20 women slaves, among them *La Malinche*, who would become Cortés' invaluable interpreter. On April 22, 1519 they landed again at a point further north, where Cortés decided to found the first Spanish settlement in Mexico, naming it "The Rich Town of the True Cross," or Veracruz.

The next thing he did was order the destruction of all but one of his ships. Cutting himself off from any line of retreat, he clearly intended to make his men as desperate to conquer or die as he was.

The journey to Tenochtitlán

The Spaniards were well received by the Totonacs of nearby Cempoala, and Cortés soon became aware of the advantages he could gain by exploiting the resentment of other communities at Aztec domination. In Tenochtitlán, reports of the Spanish landings were heard by

the Aztec emperor or *Tlatoani*, Moctezuma II. The reasons for his strangely passive response have been a great cause of speculation. Traditional accounts from Spaniards and Aztec chroniclers – who blamed him for their defeat – portray Moctezuma as refined but weak, indecisive and fearful.

It was said that there had been bad omens in the previous year, and that Moctezuma was acutely aware of the legend foretelling the return from the east of the god-king Quetzalcóatl. The description of the Spanish arriving in their "floating towers" coincided with the legend, as they, like Quetzalcóatl, were fair-skinned and

---

MALINCHE, MYTH AND REALITY

La Malinche, original name probably *Malintzin*, is a powerfully symbolic figure in the conquest of Mexico. She appears to have been the daughter of a lord from southern Veracruz, but was made a slave at Xicalango in Campeche, where she was given to Cortés after his first victory. She spoke Nahuatl and Maya languages, and began to serve Cortés as an interpreter. He already had with him Jerónimo de Aguilar, a priest who had learnt Yucatec Maya while shipwrecked in Yucatán, and between them they gave Cortés a doorway into Mexico. She soon learnt Spanish herself, so that she could translate directly, and is said to have given Cortés vital advice in outwitting the Aztec lords. She also bore Cortés's first son, Martín, one of the first of the mestizos who now make up most of Mexico's population. Malinche can thus be endlessly reinterpreted. The most traditional Mexican view of her is as a traitor, Cortés' whore, selling herself and then cast aside when he married a Spanish noblewoman. *Malinchista* is a word of contempt for any Mexican fascinated with all things foreign. Others see her as an intelligent survivor. And the same contempt is not heaped on men who played a part in Cortés' success, such as the largely forgotten king of Tlaxcala, Xicotencatl.

bearded. Recent accounts cast doubt on the strength of these legends, but, for whatever reason, Moctezuma did not send warriors to meet Cortés but messengers, who tried to persuade him not to venture further inland. Cortés, however, ignored them.

Leaving 150 men at Veracruz, Cortés took his time to make the 312km (194-mile) march to Tenochtitlán, stopping at Tlaxcala, where he gained his most vital allies. When the invaders – accompanied by several thousand Tlaxcalans – finally reached the outskirts of Tenochtitlán, on November 8, 1519, they beheld a marvelous city, then one of the largest in the world, set in a

him and his men to be quartered in the former palace of his own father, Axayacatal.

Guests of Moctezuma

There followed weeks of meandering discussions between Moctezuma and Cortés. The *Tlatoani* entertained the Spaniards in luxury, but would promise nothing. Cortés and his men were increasingly bold and restive; Aztec lords, meanwhile, resented their presence and urged Moctezuma to attack them, but he refused to comply. Eventually, in a daring stroke Cortés's men seized Moctezuma and insisted he move into their palace with them, effectively taking

lake, with broad main streets, temples, terraces, gardens, and distant snowcapped mountains.

An essential source on the Conquest is Bernal Díaz, a common soldier who served on all three expeditions to Mexico. In his journal he described the wonder he felt when he first saw the Aztec capital. "[The city] seemed like an enchanted vision from the tale of Amadis," he wrote. "Indeed some of our soldiers asked whether it was not all a dream." The Spaniards saw the people, the canals, the bridges and the boats gliding on the lake, carrying produce to the great market of Tlatelolco, patronized by some 20,000 people a day.

Moctezuma greeted Cortés with great ceremony, gave him many gifts and arranged for

him hostage. Even then, he still sought to keep his people from rebelling.

Then, news arrived that a much larger Spanish force had landed at Veracruz under Pánfilo de Narváez, sent by Governor Velázquez to arrest Cortés and take over the expedition. In yet another demonstration of his phenomenal willpower, Cortés left Pedro de Alvarado in command in Tenochtitlán with 80 men, and traveled remarkably quickly back to the coast, where he ambushed and imprisoned Narváez and persuaded his men – more than 1,000 Spanish troops – to join him. With this much larger army, he set off back into the highlands.

In Tenochtitlán, the situation had exploded. Alvarado was brutal but lacked Cortés's cunning. Things came to a head at a festival for the god Huitzilopochtli on May 10, 1520. Exactly what happened is unclear, but the Spaniards, perhaps fearing an attack, set upon the crowd at the Templo Mayor, killing hundreds of priests and nobles. The city rose against them, and the Spaniards were chased back into the palace, taking Moctezuma with them.

Despite this Cortés was still able to rejoin Alvarado with his reinforcements, but they were now besieged. Cortés looked to Moctezuma to cool the situation, but, according to Díaz, when he appealed to his people he was met with a hail of stones, and died soon afterwards. He was succeeded by his brother Cuitlahuac, who began to organize Aztec resistance.

The Sad Night

Cortés realized their only hope of survival was to escape from Tenochtitlán. On the night of June 30, the Spaniards attempted to break out in silence, padding their horses' hooves to escape detection. However, they were seen crossing one of the causeways linking the island city, and attacked by thousands of warriors, many in canoes on the lake. The Spaniards fought back, then ran for their lives while the Aztecs, no longer fearful of the invaders, harassed them along the bridges and paths.

Bernal Díaz wrote that during this *Noche Triste* (Sad Night), as it became known, the Spanish lost more than half their men, all their artillery and munitions, and many of their horses. Many died from greed, as, weighed down with Aztec gold, they could not fight or swim to safety or even move effectively.

The end of Tenochtitlán

However, the Aztecs failed to follow up their victory. In October 1520 Tenochtitlán was hit

by a devastating epidemic of smallpox, brought by the Spaniards, which killed thousands, including Cuitlahuac himself. Aztec society was still more in disarray, with many of its ruling and warrior elite dead, and Cuitlahuac's young nephew and successor Cuauhtémoc chose to stay in the city, perhaps believing it was now safe from attack.

Cortés and his few surviving men were thus

> Since the Mexican Revolution Cuauhtémoc, the 18-year-old last Tlatoani *who defended Tenochtitlán, has been enshrined as a national hero, and Cuauhtémoc is a popular name for a man.*

FAR LEFT: book illustration depicting human sacrifice. **LEFT:** Hernán Cortés. **ABOVE:** Moctezuma is captured. **RIGHT:** Cortés weeps on the night of his defeat.

able to reach Tlaxcala, after living on berries and ears of corn from the fields. Once there, undaunted, he launched into a whirlwind of activity. He set out on a round of diplomacy to win the support not just of the Tlaxcalans but many other Highland states, making all kinds of promises in return for their support, most of which were disowned by later Spanish governors. He also received fresh reinforcements from Cuba, intended for Narváez.

When he moved again on Tenochtitlán, in February 1521, Cortés had 86 horsemen, 818 Spanish foot soldiers and around 80,000 indigenous warriors, and had prepared a careful plan

for the assault on the city. His master-stroke was to have 13 small ships built on Lake Texcoco, some with cannon, to allow the Spaniards to enforce a complete siege.

They still did not have an easy victory. Cuauhtémoc proved an inventive commander, and the assault on Tenochtitlán lasted for months, between the siege, Aztec breakouts, and frontal attacks. The Spaniards conquered the causeways first, and then the city, street by street. Their numbers severely reduced by smallpox and famine, the Aztecs were less and less able to fight. Cuauhtémoc was captured, and the Aztecs surrendered on August 13, 1521.

Tenochtitlán had lost perhaps 100,000 people, and the Spaniards and their allies sacked

what was left. Cortés had the center completely razed to be rebuilt as a new, Spanish city, with the remaining indigenous communities confined to the outskirts. The dismantling of the Aztec empire was near-complete.

The spread of Spanish power

The overthrow of the greatest state in Mesoamerica gave the Spaniards an aura of immense power, and an essential base from which to extend their tentacles throughout the region. Beginning in 1522 Cortés' men took control of the Tarascan kingdom in Michoacán, and in 1524 Pedro de Alvarado led a bloody march southwards through Chiapas to conquer Guatemala and Honduras. The "Chichimeca" deserts north of Zacatecas, however, would be settled by the Spaniards only gradually, over the next 200 years.

Yucatán proved a particularly hard nut for the Spaniards to crack. In 1526 the commission to conquer it was granted by Charles V of Spain to Francisco de Montejo. However, it would take three attempts before Montejo, his son and his nephew (both also called Francisco de Montejo) were able to inflict a decisive defeat on the Maya lords and found their new capital of Mérida, in 1542. And even then, the last independent Maya kingdom, on Lake Petén-Itzá in Guatemala, continued to survive until 1697.

The conquistadors were driven by lust for gold, but also by a sense of divine mission. They believed God was on their side. Bernal Díaz said their triumph was achieved "not of our volition, but by the guidance of God. For what soldiers in the world, numbering only 400... would have

THE MANILA GALLEONS

New Spain was not only a source of wealth for Spain by itself, it also became its route to the riches of the Orient. From 1565 until 1815, one or two ships sailed each year from the Philippines to Acapulco, loaded with Asian spices and other treasures, and back again with Mexican silver to pay for them. From Acapulco the cargoes were carried overland to Mexico City and then Veracruz, to be shipped onwards to Spain.

The Spaniards used this route to avoid the pirates of the Indian Ocean and, later, hostile colonies around the coasts of Africa. This trans-Pacific trade left many influences in southwest Mexico, such as the lacquer-work of Michoacán, Guerrero and Chiapas.

dared to enter a city as strong as Mexico, which is larger than Venice and more than 4,500 miles away from our own Castile?"

Imperial system

Spain governed Mexico for three centuries. At the beginning of the 16th century Spain was one of the most dynamic countries in Europe, with a new burst of energy after the final expulsion of the Moors in 1492. Its different Christian kingdoms had recently been unified under one crown, although they still did not form one state, and the new American colonies were actually claimed for Castile. Castile was an absolute

was only the most prominent of the many who bitterly resented their treatment: initially confirmed as Governor of New Spain, he was later made subordinate to an *Audiencia* or high court of royal officials, and then passed over for the post of Viceroy in favour of a more aristocratic candidate.

The Spanish Crown aimed to bring order to its colonies with a set of rules. They were all to be governed in line with the *Leyes de Indias*, the "Laws of the Indies," which attempted to cover every possible field: the role of governors, the treatment of indigenous people, taxation and so on.

monarchy, and below the Crown the two most powerful elements in society were the aristocracy and the Catholic Church. A rigid hierarchy prevailed, and any deviations from Catholic orthodoxy were not permitted.

The same pattern of society would be extended to "New Spain," as Mexico was now called, as the Crown asserted its authority. Charles V and his ministers distrusted the freebooting conquistadors – many of whom were fighting each other for the spoils of conquest – and set out to bring them under control. Cortés

LEFT: San Rafael and Tobias by Miguel Cabrera (1695–1768), Mexico's most famous colonial artist.
ABOVE: Spanish missionary addressing an Indian group.

Encomenderos and friars

Spanish colonists were initially rewarded through the *encomienda* system, with which they were "entrusted" (*encomendado*) an area of land and all the indigenous people on it, with the right to their labor and the (often theoretical) obligation to teach them Christianity. This effectively gave *encomenderos* the power of life and death, and denunciations were rife of the abuses of the system, with many cases of indigenous people being literally worked to death.

The main challenge to *encomendero* power came from the Church and particularly the various orders of friars – Franciscans, Dominicans – who arrived on the heels of the military conquerors to begin the "Spiritual Conquest" of the Americas, the conversion of its people to Catholicism. This required a phenomenal effort by the Spanish Church, but was of fundamental importance to Church and Crown, as a God-given mission that could excuse, even sometimes justify, the cruelty of other aspects

> The Leyes de Indias *stipulated the grid layout of all Spanish colonial cities, around a central plaza with a cathedral or church on the east side, a governors' palace on the north and town hall on the west.*

Disappearing peoples

Encomenderos complained that friars and Crown officials only denounced mistreatment of indigenous people because they wanted power and local labor for themselves, but there were also priests who were dedicated defenders of indigenous people, such as Bishop Vasco de Quiroga in Michoacán, and the extraordinary Bartolomé de Las Casas in Chiapas, who in his *Brief History of the Destruction of the Indies* questioned the whole moral basis of the Conquest. In 1542 he even persuaded Charles V to revise the *Leyes de Indias*, giving indigenous people more protection from the Crown. The difficulty was

of the Conquest. Different missionary orders were given responsibility for entire parts of the country, such as the Dominicans in Oaxaca and Chiapas, the Franciscans in Yucatán.

The missionaries concentrated many of their efforts on teaching the children of the native aristocracy. In 1528, the Colegio de Santa Cruz in Tlatelolco was founded for this purpose. For a wider audience, open-air "Indian chapels" (*capillas de indias*) were built to hold services for as large a number of indigenous people as possible. One of the most important moments in the *conquista espiritual* came in 1531 with the beginning of the cult of the Virgin of Guadalupe, a vital step in giving Catholicism a distinctly Mexican – mestizo – tone (*see page 29*).

in getting laws to apply on the ground, and throughout the colonial era there were complaints that many settlers treated colonised people as slaves.

Las Casas was also perhaps mistaken in thinking that conquistador brutality was the immediate cause of something all the Spaniards could see around them: the catastrophic decline in the indigenous population. In 1520 Mesoamerica had a population of at least 12 million; a century later, almost 90 percent had disappeared. Indigenous people had no defenses against European diseases, above all smallpox; at the same time, the disruption of the traditional economy had a disastrous effect on the food supply. This population collapse was not at all uniform, and some areas – notably Oaxaca, Chiapas and Yucatán in the south – retained large indigenous populations, but in many areas of the Central Highlands an ever-greater proportion of the survivors was made up of mixed-race mestizos.

It did not take very long for the Spanish to discover silver in Zacatecas, Pachuca and Guanajuato, and by 1548 more than 50 silver mines were in operation. Indigenous people were forcibly recruited to work in them, and when their numbers fell African slaves were imported. By 1800 Mexico was producing 66 percent of the world's silver.

begun to build chapels and monasteries as soon as they arrived in Mexico in the 1520s, but the great age of colonial religious building was the 17th century, when magnificent Baroque churches spread across the country.

The great sources of wealth were mining, agriculture and trade. Cattle and horses the Spaniards had introduced into the country flourished, and huge areas were given over to ranching. Sugar cane was another Spanish introduction. The *encomienda* system largely gave way to one of hacienda estates, so that settlers swopped direct control over indigenous people for ownership of often vast extensions

Colonial life

In most of New Spain life settled into a fairly unchanging pattern as the Conquest receded into the past. It was based on the aristocratic Castilian model of society, and the sectors the Spanish Crown relied on to run its empire – the Spanish aristocracy, local landowners and the Church – were not ones to encourage innovation.

The Catholic Church was omnipresent and enormously wealthy, receiving a 10 percent tithe from agriculture, commerce, mining, and the native economy. The missionary orders had

of land. Even so, indigenous families were still commonly bound to the same hacienda for generations, by debt servitude or just the lack of enough land of their own.

The Spanish Crown, interested above all in ensuring that its empire added to its own wealth, banned Mexico and its other American colonies from trading with any European country except Spain. Inter-colonial trade was also prohibited, since it would compete with imports from the Iberian peninsula.

The castes of New Spain

Spanish Mexico had a rigid social hierarchy, based on race, wealth and place of birth. At the top were Spanish-born aristocrats, for only they

LEFT: at the beginning of the 18th century, Mexico City was still surrounded by a lake. **ABOVE:** Apache prisoners were forced to work in the silver mines.

could occupy the most important state offices. Below them were the criollos, Mexican-born but of entirely white blood, many very rich and increasingly frustrated at the Spaniards' monopoly on power. Below them was a medley of new peoples: mestizos of Spanish and Native American blood were the most prominent, but there were also many *castas* (castes), with varying quantities of Spanish, indigenous, African and Oriental genes. By the 18th century, criollos and mestizos formed around half the population. At the bottom were the indigenous peoples, who for most of the colonial era were not even allowed to set foot in the centers of the Spanish cities.

the Spanish throne. Suddenly, the center of government had ceased to exist. Criollo grandees demanded to be represented in the regency that took charge of New Spain, but the Spanish officials or *peninsulares* stubbornly resisted. Other criollos looked for more radical change, and secret meetings discussed rebellion. One such group, meeting in Querétaro, included the parish priest of the small town of Dolores, Miguel Hidalgo.

They planned an uprising for the end of 1810, but the government got word of the plot. Rather than be arrested, on September 16, 1810, Father Hidalgo gave an impassioned speech to

In 1759 an energetic monarch, Carlos III, became king of Spain and tried to shake up his decaying empire. Spanish governors were instructed to introduce economic reforms and even challenge the power of the Church, seen as obstructing that of the state. Among many criollos, however, this burst of activity only spurred the thought that they could do better by themselves.

The cry of independence

Discontent with Spanish rule was widespread – encouraged by the Enlightenment, the independence of the United States and the French Revolution – but gave rise to little action until Napoleon occupied Spain in 1808, imprisoned the royal family and put his own brother on

Miguel Hidalgo was a very free-thinking Catholic priest: he did not believe in the virgin birth, the supremacy of the pope or priestly celibacy, and fathered five children.

his congregation in Dolores. From the pulpit he called on them to join in a fight for freedom and to take back the land "stolen" from their forefathers, ending by shouting "Long live the Virgin of Guadalupe" and "death to bad government." This was the famous *Grito de Dolores*, the "shout" for independence.

It has never been clear how far Hidalgo intended to go, but a characteristic of Mexican revolutions is that small actions can have huge, unanticipated consequences. His *grito* started a peasant revolution.

Bitter battles

Armed with machetes, shovels and slings, poor mestizos and Indians flocked to join Hidalgo, and within a few weeks he had an army of 50,000 that captured Guanajuato, Zacatecas and Guadalajara. He issued decrees abolishing slavery, and the tributes paid by indigenous people to the Church and criollo landowners. However, his ragged army also massacred whites, Spaniards and criollos in Guanajuato and Guadala-

and convened a congress at Chilpancingo in 1813 that sketched out the basis of an independent state, with civil rights for all. However, he too was caught and executed, in 1815. He was succeeded by one of his lieutenants, Vicente Guerrero, and the struggle continued as a bitter guerrilla war.

Change to keep things the same

By 1819, the insurgents had largely been contained. Then, things turned upside down. In January 1820 a rising by liberal army officers took over the government in Spain. In Mexico, rumors spread that the mother country's new administration would bombard them with

jara. Many criollos, horrified at the prospect of social upheaval, rallied to support the Spanish viceroy. The result was years of bloody war.

At the beginning of 1811 the rebels were driven back, and Hidalgo was captured and executed in July. His role as leader of the fight for independence was taken by José María Morelos, another priest, and a mestizo from Valladolid in Michoacán, now named Morelia in his honor. A brilliant general, Morelos led successful campaigns across Michoacán, Guerrero and Oaxaca,

radical decrees challenging the powers of the Church and landowners, and wealthy criollos saw new attractions in independence.

A criollo general in the Spanish army, Agustín de Iturbide, made contact with Guerrero, and called on him as a patriot to join him in support of the so-called "Three Guarantees:" the independence of Mexico; Catholicism as the sole religion; and the "union" of all Mexicans, with the abolition of the Spanish legal distinctions between ethnic groups and classes. Guerrero agreed, and this left the Spaniards with few options. A newly arrived Viceroy, Juan O'Donojú, signed a treaty that finally converted New Spain into Mexico on August 24, 1821. ❏

FAR LEFT: painted tiles from colonial Casa Sandoval. **LEFT:** royal fiesta in Mexico City's Chapultepec Park (18th century). **ABOVE:** *Pima Indians convoying a Silver Train in Mexico* by Frederic Remington, 1887.

New Spain's Heritage in Stone

The ornate styles of Imperial Spain blended with Mexican sensibilities and love of decoration to create a unique architectural synthesis.

In Mexico, the legacy of the past is rarely far away. Pre-Hispanic pyramids, monasteries, Baroque churches and ruined haciendas lie off busy high-

ways. After the Spanish Conquest, the fusion of cultures gave rise to a multiplicity of architectural styles. The missionary friars were the most prolific builders of the 16th century. Far from Spain, in an alien climate and an alien land, they brought with them elements from Romanesque, Gothic, Renaissance and other Old World architectures. Even an unusual Spanish style such as Mudéjar – the Moorish-influenced architecture produced by Muslim craftsmen under Christian rule – left its mark in Mexico from 1562, notably in the great *Pila* or well in Chiapa de Corzo, Chiapas.

In villages such as Actopan, Huejotzingo and Yecapixtla, immense monasteries still dominate the landscape. These fortress-like structures were often built with stones from "pagan" pyramids and

temples. Work was carried out by native craftsmen, who were instructed in carpentry, masonry, metal-working and other European skills. The glory of the Church Militant found expression in immense altarpieces, gilded images, mural paintings, and carved decoration of wood and stone. Such creations were not mere copies of European models. With time they increasingly reflected an indigenous sensibility, as local craftsmen reinterpreted European imagery. This intermingling of European and indigenous art – sometimes producing bizarre anomalies – is called *tequitqui* by art historians.

Different missionary orders favored different styles. The austere Franciscans in the Yucatán disliked extravagance and built in a plain, late-medieval style that was already archaic in Europe, as seen in the massive monastery in Izamal or countless Yucatán village churches. The Augustinians in the Central Highlands and the Dominicans in Oaxaca and Chiapas had a much greater taste for artistic refinement and contemporary styles, whether Renaissance or the elegant Spanish style known as "plateresque," because it was said to reproduce the effects of silverware *(plata)* in stone. One of the finest examples of plateresque is the 1560s monastery of San Antonio Acolmán north of Mexico City, and the style can also be seen in non-monastic churches such as the first stages of Mexico City Cathedral, begun in the 1570s, and Mérida Cathedral, completed in 1598.

Baroque zenith

In the 17th century, Mexican architecture became increasingly ornate. High Baroque, the favourite style of Imperial Spain at its peak, encouraged exuberance and invention, and was enthusiastically taken up in Mexico. By 1750, Baroque had become ultra-Baroque, with the arrival of the Churrigueresque style. Originated by the architect-sculptor José Churriguera in Salamanca in Spain, this involved covering every last part of facades and altars with intricate decoration; in Mexico it matched perfectly with local tastes, and was taken to its limits. This was the greatest period of church-building in colonial Mexico, reflecting 18th-century prosperity, and churches and cathedrals were characterized by lavish complexity and richness of detail.

The Sagrario beside Mexico City Cathedral and Zacatecas Cathedral have two of the most astonishing Churrigueresque facades, but there are many more. Gold-clad altarpieces – replete with twisted columns, angels and medallions – dazzled the faithful of Tepotzotlán, Taxco or Querétaro.

In small towns and villages, local craftsmen drew inspiration from what they saw in cities. Their eclectic creations are described as *barroco popular*. Stucco, carved to imitate stone, embellished facades in the Sierra Gorda of Querétaro. A particular Mexican addition to Churriguesque was color: in Puebla, multi-colored glazed tiles covered church exteriors, and at San Francisco Acatepec, outside the city, they encased cornices, capitals and columns. Clusters of flowers, fruit, animals and cherubs cover the walls and ceiling at Santa María Tonantzintla.

Neoclassicism, imported at the end of the 18th century, condemned Baroque as showy and vulgar. It was used in the final stages of Mexico City Cathedral – the dome – and would be copied in many public buildings erected in the first years of independence, as a more "modern" style. Some church interiors were stripped of decoration. Yet many Baroque churches and cathedrals survived intact. Decked out today with flowers, candles and plaster saints – sometimes even neon crosses – they meet the aesthetic and spiritual needs of Mexican worshippers.

Cities and palaces

In the viceregal capital, the ruling class displayed an appetite for luxury. After the destruction of Tenochtitlán Aztec structures were replaced by grand residences and government buildings. Fray Alonso Ponce, visiting in 1585, praised its "very good houses and handsome streets." Today, little remains of 16th-century civil architecture. Buildings not demolished by later generations have been modified to suit changing tastes.

Aristocratic residences of the Baroque era had two or more stories. Lavish exteriors incorporated corner towers, statues in niches, balconies, and monumental entrances topped by coats of arms. Inside, an imposing stairway led from the main patio to the upper levels. Wealthy families built their city mansions with income from country estates. In the 1730s the Condesa del Valle de Orizaba had her 16th-century Mexico City house rebuilt and decorated with blue-and-white Puebla tiles. Popularly known as *La Casa de los Azulejos* (House of Tiles), it now contains Sanborn's restaurant. Outside the capital, fine houses were built in

cities such as Puebla, where Baroque facades were often encrusted with stucco. One such mansion, resplendent with icing-like ornamentation and now a museum, is aptly known as *La Casa del Alfeñique* (The Sugar-Frosted House).

Haciendas

Landowners with haciendas or country estates made fortunes from farming and mining. Haciendas, many established in the 16th century, were constantly remolded to meet prevailing needs, including after independence. Many surviving hacienda buildings have thus acquired a timeless quality, which makes them hard to date.

Haciendas are among the emblematic buildings of the Mexican countryside. Self-sufficient, haciendas operated along feudal lines. Thick, powerful walls protected the great house, with its lofty rooms, well-shaded verandahs and plant-filled patios. The walls also enclosed the chapel, laborers' dwellings, the cemetery, the stables, cattle yards and granaries. Today several haciendas have been transformed into very special luxury hotels with delightful gardens, such as Hacienda Temozón and other haciendas in Yucatán, or Hacienda de San Gabriel near Cuernavaca. The Hacienda El Lencero outside Xalapa in Veracruz, once home to the 19th-century dictator Santa Anna, is now a museum. Others are still left to decay, as they have been since the 1910 Revolution. ❑

LEFT: Baroque south entrance of Zacatecas Cathedral.
RIGHT: a shady hacienda patio in the Yucatán.

INDEPENDENCE AND REVOLUTION

Dreams of freedom, equality and independence were pursued by Mexicans in the face of cynical dictators, foreign invasions, and social upheaval

The new state was born with very mixed motives. The Ejército Trigarante or "Army of the Three Guarantees" that entered Mexico City amid great enthusiasm in 1821 included revolutionaries who had been fighting as guerrillas for 10 years, but its commander General Iturbide had taken up the cause of independence precisely to defend the privileges of colonial society. The immense tensions this situation created would be played out over the next century.

Many conservatives still considered a monarchy to be an essential guardian of social order. In 1822, in a lavish ceremony, Iturbide was crowned Emperor Agustín I. But his rejoicing was short-lived; less than a year later one of his cronies, General Antonio López de Santa Anna, rebelled and forced him to abdicate. When Iturbide tried to return in 1824, he was caught and executed.

Shaky republic

The Constitution of 1824 finally made Mexico a republic, and Guadalupe Victoria, a stalwart of the fight for independence alongside Hidalgo

Santa Anna said that Mexicans were "not fit" for liberty and needed "despotism" to keep them in line, and called himself the "Napoleon of the West" and the "Mexican Caesar."

and Morelos, became its first president. But it was Santa Anna who dominated the political scene for the next three decades. Born into a

criollo landowning family in Veracruz, like Iturbide he had fought for Spain throughout most of the independence wars.

Independent Mexico found itself to be a vast country with vast problems. Trade and mining had been paralyzed. Communications in the troubled land were almost impossible. The mestizo and indigenous majority lived in dire poverty, apathetic toward, and cut off from, politics.

Mexico's political conflicts coalesced into a divide ostensibly between conservative "centralists" in favor of an authoritarian state and a powerful role for the Catholic Church, and more liberal "federalists," but even Santa Anna, generally the standard-bearer of conservatism,

LEFT: Lázaro Cárdenas signs peasants' land deed.
RIGHT: General Antonio López de Santa Anna.

changed sides when his intrigues demanded. In many areas the only real power was held by local landowners and bosses called *caciques*.

From 1821 to 1855 Mexico was in constant turmoil. In 30 years there were 50 governments, almost all the result of military coups, and 11 of them presided over by Santa Anna, dubbed the "perpetual dictator." Mexico's weakness tempted foreign powers to intervene, spurred on by myths about its mineral riches.

Catastrophe

Santa Anna is remembered above all in Mexico as the man who lost half the nation's territory to the United States. In 1835 he tried to tear up Mexico's 1824 Constitution and create a centralized dictatorship. American settlers in Texas reacted by declaring independence. Santa Anna marched north, and famously massacred Texans at the Alamo before being beaten by Sam Houston at the battle of San Jacinto. Humiliated, Santa Anna was forced to accept Texan independence. A new government in Mexico City disowned this agreement, but was powerless to reverse it.

Santa Anna did not only antagonize Anglo settlers in Texas, for other states rebelled against him. Most successful was Yucatán (the entire peninsula, not just modern Yucatán state),

NATIONAL HEROES: JUÁREZ

If Santa Anna was an early archetype of tawdry corruption in Mexican politics, Benito Juárez was its foremost symbol of integrity, with a stature comparable only to Abraham Lincoln as his country's greatest statesman. Born in 1806 in a village north of Oaxaca, he was of pure Zapotec stock, and spoke only Zapotec as a child. His parents died when he was three, and he worked in the fields until, aged 12, he walked to Oaxaca City.

His intelligence was obvious, and a local priest arranged for his education. Instead of entering the priesthood, however, he decided to become a lawyer. His rigid belief that a fair application of law would provide a solution to Mexico's inequalities was the source of many of his strengths and weaknesses. His most-repeated quotation is "respect for the rights of others, is peace."

Above all, he was known as utterly incorruptible. His unbending determination was vital to the survival of the liberal cause and Mexican independence through the struggles of the 1850s and 1860s. And yet, some of the measures in his great Reform program, ending traditional restrictions on land sales, would themselves be used by landowners under the Díaz regime to grab even vaster estates.

which had had its own administration under Spanish rule. Yucatán too declared independence, and beat off an army sent by Santa Anna to Campeche in 1842.

In 1845 the US Congress voted to annex Texas. This sparked the Mexican–American War, described by future president and general Ulysses Grant as "one of the most unjust [wars] ever waged by a stronger against a weaker nation." US troops captured Monterrey and most of California, while an army under General Winfield Scott disembarked in Veracruz and occupied Mexico City.

In 1848, by the Treaty of Guadalupe Hidalgo, Mexico ceded Texas, California, Nevada, Utah and most of New Mexico and Arizona to the United States. In 1853, Santa Anna sold off one last portion of New Mexico and Arizona for $10 million, in the Gadsden Purchase.

In the meantime an entirely separate drama had taken place at the other end of the country. The Maya had risen in rebellion across then-independent Yucatán in 1847, in a savage struggle that became known as the "Caste War." The largest indigenous revolt in Mexico since the Conquest, it very nearly succeeded. In fear of their lives, Yucatán's criollo elite agreed to return to Mexico, in return for aid against the Maya.

Juárez and the Reform

In 1855 a liberal revolt drove Santa Anna from power for the last time, and set out at last to give Mexico the institutions of a modern, democratic state, with a sweeping program known as *La Reforma*, The Reform. The key figure in the new government, as justice minister and later president, was Benito Juárez. Reform laws attacked the privileges of the Catholic Church, which liberals saw as consigning the country to social and economic paralysis. Church and communal properties were broken up. In 1857, a new constitution guaranteed freedom of religion and other fundamental liberties.

Juárez's revolutionary venture met with fierce opposition from conservatives. For three years, from 1858–60, the two parties fought the bitter War of Reform. Juárez emerged triumphant, and on January 1, 1861, the liberal forces marched into Mexico City.

LEFT: 19th-century woodcut depicting Mexican troops on the march during the Mexican-American War.
RIGHT: Emperor Maximilian of Mexico.

French invasion

But this victory was short-lived. The new government was bankrupt, and Juárez had to suspend payment of Mexico's foreign debt. Spain, Britain and France protested, and sent a joint force to Veracruz to secure their money.

The French Emperor Napoleon III, however, had greater ambitions. Encouraged by Mexican conservatives, who refused to accept defeat, he ordered his troops to advance on Mexico City. After a brief though famous Mexican victory under Ignacio Zaragoza at Puebla on May 5, 1862 (the *Cinco de Mayo*, now a holiday), the French took over most of the country. Napo-

leon invited Maximilian of Habsburg, an Austrian archduke, to become emperor of Mexico under French protection.

Emperor Maximilian and his Belgian Empress María Carlota moved into Chapultepec Castle (*see page 145*), but their reign was brief. Ironically, Maximilian was too liberal for Mexican conservatives; a romantic idealist, he unsuccessfully invited Juárez to become his prime minister. Then, after the American Civil War ended in 1865, the US government put pressure on Napoleon to withdraw his troops. Without the French to support him, Maximilian was captured in Querétaro. The 35-year-old prince was shot at dawn on June 19, 1867.

The Republic was restored, and Juárez set about

putting the *Reforma* into practice. He died in office in 1872, of a heart attack. However, all the struggles of the previous years had not ensured stability, and in 1876 there was yet another military takeover, led by General Porfirio Díaz.

Don Porfirio

Díaz, also a son of Oaxaca, had been a hero of the fight against the French under Juárez. He was to dominate Mexico's political scene for 34 years, an era known as the *Porfiriato.*

Unlike previous military strongmen, he always claimed to be defending the Constitution. He stressed the need for effective government, and

the pacification of the country. Political liberty would come later, he promised; what Mexico needed first was strict administration and very little politicking. He used the army and the *rurales*, his much-feared rural police force, to enforce his program. Díaz acted as the great ringmaster of Mexican politics. He knew exactly how to handle truculent local bosses, doling out favors. Conservative former followers of Maximilian were enticed on board, and a rapprochement shrewdly sought with the Church. Open opposition was ruthlessly snuffed out.

Boomtime

Having established order, General Díaz set about modernizing the country. Business-minded ministers known as *científicos* (scientists) mapped out plans to bring Mexico into the industrial age. Foreign investment was welcomed, and capital poured in. An impressive 19,000km (12,000-mile) railroad network was laid, creating a whole new set of economic possibilities. Steel mills in Monterrey processed iron ore railed in from Durango, and cotton from the north was processed in central Mexico. Railroads also allowed the expansion of mining, not only of gold and silver but also coal, lead, antimony and copper.

Landowners could send cattle and cash crops such as wheat, sugar, and coffee to the cities and for export. In the Yucatán sisal rope, made from the *henequén* cactus – "green gold" – and in huge demand before the invention of artificial fibers, created vast fortunes, and *henequén* haciendas extended across the countryside.

The Díaz regime won great international praise for the order and progress it had brought to Mexico. Díaz favored European investors for some sectors – notably railroads – in order to reduce Mexican dependence on the United States. Nevertheless, American companies still made huge investments – and huge profits – in Mexico. By 1910, foreigners controlled three-quarters of the nation's mineral and oil rights.

The *Porfiriato* boom transformed many Mexican cities. Grandiose French- or Italian-influenced architecture was favored by the Europeanized elite. In Mexico City, buildings such as the Palacio de Bellas Artes and the central Post Office all date from this period. Mérida, home of the Yucatán *henequeneros*, acquired a "Parisian-style" boulevard, the Paseo de Montejo.

At the same time, millions were barely managing to survive. As export agriculture boomed,

> The great dictator Porfirio Díaz is appreciated for his most famous remark: "Poor Mexico!... So far from God, and so close to the United States."

production of food staples actually fell, and prices rose. Rural villages were particularly affected by the break up of communal lands – originated by Juárez's reform – which gave ample scope for big landowners to seize village lands. The ignorant mestizo and indigenous poor, it was said, could not be allowed to stand in the way of progress. Most productive land thus wound up in the hands of some 6,000 *hacendados*, whose holdings ranged from 1,000 hectares (2,500 acres) to areas the size of a small country.

End of an era

Elections under Porfirio Díaz were carefully managed. Then, in an interview with a US journalist in 1908, Díaz said Mexico was now ready for democracy, and that he would welcome real opposition. People took him at his word. For the 1910 elections, opposition coalesced around a wealthy liberal, Francisco Madero.

went hungry, were tortured and shot, and more than a million died.

Groups across Mexico rose up in support of Madero, and Porfirio Díaz was finally ousted in May 1911. Madero, however, declared he would only take up the presidency after fresh, clean elections in November. A cultivated, philanthropic hacienda owner from Coahuila, he was a democratic reformer who wanted an end to social injustice, but always insisted on carefully following established legal processes. He lacked any sense of urgency, and so did nothing to challenge the power of Díaz appointees in the army and the states. He even allowed a former

Díaz, aged 80, had him arrested and declared himself the winner for a seventh presidential term. But things did not end there. Madero escaped, and an armed rebellion began on November 20, 1910.

Revolution

The Mexican Revolution of 1910 – the one always written with a capital R – was no straightforward, united fight for freedom and democracy against the oppressive regime of the *Porfiriato*. It was an explosion of rage that led to a decade of violence and starvation. People

Díaz supporter, Francisco León de la Barra, to become interim president while he waited for the November election.

Tierra y Libertad

This could not satisfy the passions unleashed by the revolt against Díaz. Many of the movements that had won the first revolution for Madero expected determined, radical change, foremost among them the peasants in Morelos and the south led by Emiliano Zapata. Instead, under De la Barra troops were sent to Morelos to return to the haciendas land taken by the Zapatistas.

Zapata lost patience with Madero, and in November 1911 the Zapatistas proclaimed their

LEFT: a mural of Porfirio Díaz by David Siqueiros.
ABOVE: Madero enters Guernavaca in 1911.

radical program the *Plan de Ayala* and took up arms against the new government around the slogan *Tierra y Libertad* (Land and Freedom). To this day Zapata is to most Mexicans the Revolution's greatest hero, and has never lost the power to inspire, as seen in the Zapatistas of Chiapas.

Other revolts burst out around the country. Madero relied increasingly on the army to keep order, but its generals regarded him with contempt. Foreign investors called for a restoration of order. At the end of 1912, the old dictator's nephew Félix Díaz and US ambassador Henry Lane Wilson conspired with the army commander Victoriano Huerta for the latter to lead a counter-revolution. In the "10 tragic days" in February 1913, Madero was tricked by Huerta, arrested, and murdered.

Shifting alliances

Huerta assumed he could walk into the presidency, but the sheer brutality of Madero's elimination galvanized resistance. The Zapatistas fought back with renewed determination in the south, while a powerful movement formed in the north around the governor of Coahuila, Venustiano Carranza, in loose alliance with Pancho Villa and his ragged "Division of the North." After savage fighting, Huerta

NATIONAL HEROES: ZAPATA AND VILLA

Emiliano Zapata and Francisco (Pancho) Villa are two worldwide symbols of the Mexican Revolution. Zapata was a mostly indigenous peasant from Anenecuilco, a village in Morelos. In 1909, he was chosen to speak for the village in a dispute with a *hacendado* who was seizing its land to extend his sugar estates. Zapata's creed was a simple one to which he stayed forever loyal: that village communities should be given back their lands and guaranteed them in perpetuity. Peasants throughout southern Mexico could see themselves in him: he was taciturn, and in meetings with politicians often let others talk for him; he never felt comfortable outside his own patch. He also had, like Juárez, an image of unflinching, unbreakable integrity.

Pancho Villa was never short of a word, and so could be equally typical of the north. Born in Durango and orphaned when very young, he survived at different times as a miner, a bandit and a horse thief. In 1910 he joined a revolutionary band in Chihuahua, and gained a reputation with a string of exploits that have entered Mexican folklore.

His clashes with more conventional leaders such as Carranza – who despised him as a dangerous idiot – were part political, part very personal. His radicalism was instinctive, not systematic: in Chihuahua, he raised wages, lowered prices and built schools. Pancho Villa also married more than 70 women, without divorcing any of them.

was driven from Mexico City in mid-1914.

The victorious revolutionaries, however, were in no agreement on what should happen next. For all its apparent shapelessness, fought by different groups who often had little contact with each other, the Mexican Revolution is said to have been driven by four common impulses: it was expected to bring Mexico democracy; national independence, and an end to the subservience to foreign interests of the Díaz era; modernization, in a way that benefited the whole country; and agrarian reform, with justice for the rural poor. The importance given to these goals, though, varied a great deal. For the northern "Constitutionalists" around Carranza, an effective, inclusive government was their first priority.

A convention held in Aguascalientes failed to reach any consensus. Fighting soon broke out between supporters of Villa and Zapata, who called for rapid change, and those of Carranza. At the end of 1914 Villa and Zapata occupied Mexico City, and Zapata's peasant soldiers were famously photographed in Sanborn's restaurant. However, they failed to capitalize on their success.

The Constitutionalists gained ground, led by the Revolution's most able general, Alvaro Obregón, another northerner, from Sonora. At Celaya in April 1915 he destroyed Villa's forces by using barbed wire, machine guns and other techniques of modern warfare. Villa retreated northwards. Enraged by US support for Carranza, he raided Columbus, New Mexico, in 1916, which led the US Army to follow him in futile pursuit for 11 months. Zapata meanwhile retreated to Morelos, as he had always tended to do.

A new constitution

In 1917 Venustiano Carranza convened an assembly in Querétaro to agree a new Constitution. He wanted only a few amendments to the Constitution of 1857, but it was part of the Mexican Revolution's peculiar, diffuse nature that, since victory was never entirely clear-cut, no one leader could ever impose a single vision on it, and progress could only be made by giving out concessions to other sectors. To Carranza's disgust, the delegates agreed

LEFT: Pancho Villa sits in the presidential chair with Emiliano Zapata to his right. **RIGHT:** the governor of Coahuila, Venustiano Carranza.

many radical propositions, guaranteeing the right to strike and form unions, and an eight-hour working day. Even though Zapata was still fighting Carranza, to win the support of the rural poor some of the Zapatistas' central demands were included, in the famous Article 27. For a century, agrarian changes in Mexico had focused on creating large estates or dividing land into small, individual farms. Article 27 not only made it mandatory for great haciendas to be broken up, it allowed villages to work their lands individually or collectively, in line with indigenous tradition. How this could be put into practice would be a new source

of argument, but the 1917 Constitution had enshrined a whole range of social aspirations in law.

Within this colossal drama every state in Mexico had its own stories. And the Revolution continued to devour its own. In April 1919 one of Carranza's generals tricked Zapata into a meeting, and had him shot. A rift developed between Carranza and Obregón, and in 1920, when Carranza seemed set on extending his power beyond his presidential term, Obregón led a revolt. Carranza was killed while escaping, by an ex-Villista band. Villa himself ostensibly made peace with Obregón and retired to his hacienda, but was ambushed and assassinated in his car one afternoon in 1923.

Reconstruction

Obregón began the "consolidation" of the Revolution, in an exhausted country. Like his closest associate and fellow Sonoran Plutarco Elías Calles, he believed in "national capitalism," not socialism. However, he was far more aware than Carranza of the need to answer the urgent needs of Mexico's poor. During the Revolution he had already forged contacts with labor unions in the cities, and as president introduced pro-labor measures and encouraged the growth of friendly unions, as a power base. Land reform was begun in states where it was supported by strong local movements, like Morelos and Yucatán.

the *Porfiriato*, and many Revolutionary leaders saw it as a permanent threat to Mexico's progress. Conflict intensified after 1924 under Obregón's successor, Plutarco Elías Calles, for whom anti-clericalism was a virtual obsession. Anti-Catholic laws were rigidly enforced, and Catholic guerrillas, known as *Cristeros*, with the war cry ¡*Viva Cristo Rey!* (Long Live Christ the King) clashed with *federales* in Jalisco, Michoacán, Guanajuato and Colima. Tensions only abated after Calles lost his hold on power.

In 1928 Obregón planned a return to the presidency with Calles, causing deep disquiet among old revolutionaries who feared a repeat

The 1920s also saw the flowering of one of the most profound changes brought by the Revolution, its cultural transformation. In sharp reaction against the contempt poured on everything uniquely Mexican under Díaz, artists such as Rivera, Siqueiros and Orozco used pre-Hispanic motifs and images from folk art to create a dynamic style that ignored European models. Their foremost expression was in the world-famous murals on public buildings, many commissioned by Obregón's education minister José Vasconcelos, who built schools across the country.

The revolutionary government also became mired in a fierce battle with the Catholic Church. It had regained strength during

Before the Revolution Mexico had shunned its indigenous and folk heritage: in the 1920s and 1930s artists and writers reveled in them to create an entirely new set of national symbols.

of Díaz's multiple terms in office. Obregón won the election, but was shot dead a few weeks later, not by one of his former comrades but by a young Catholic.

The official party

With Obregón dead, the three presidents who followed were all puppets of Calles. The Revolution's greatest power broker, he had already decided to give it some institutional continuity. So far the Revolution had been dominated by particular leaders, their clashes and alliances. Most political parties were based in individual states. In 1929 Calles invited all the many parties, groups and local leaders around the country identified with the Revolution to join together in a single party, the Partido Nacional Revolucionario or PNR. It would also include all the pro-government labor and peasants' unions.

If the PNR was sufficiently inclusive, Calles reasoned, its success would be assured without too much electoral manipulation. The presi-

boss to become the most revered – indeed loved – Mexican president since Juárez. No one else did as much to put the social aspirations of the Revolution into practice.

Above all, Cárdenas took land reform seriously. Over 18 million hectares (45 million acres) of land was redistributed to the communally-owned villages or *ejidos*, against less than one million under Obregón. By the end of his presidential term, Cárdenas had distributed land to almost one-third of the population.

Cárdenas equally encouraged labor unions, giving them a permanent place in government. In so doing he also used them to reinforce the

dential succession could be argued out within the party, rather than with street fights. For still more stability, presidential terms would be extended to a *sexenio*, six years. The "official party" thus created would remain in power under different names for 71 years.

Cárdenas

The PNR candidate for president in 1934, Lázaro Cárdenas, had also been a Calles protégé, but once in office he broke with his old

LEFT: General Obregón and his wife.
ABOVE: women donating chickens during a countrywide campaign to raise funds to pay for the nationalization of the oil industry.

all-encompassing bureaucratic structures of the national party, subsequently renamed the PRM (Partido de la Revolución Mexicana) and later Partido de la Revolución Institucional (Party of the Institutional Revolution, or PRI).

Nevertheless, Cárdenas's presidency is often remembered as a golden, hopeful age, and his status as a national hero was cemented forever in March 1938 when he nationalized Mexico's oil, until then controlled by US and British companies. Mexicans cheered; the British were incensed, but in the troubled international climate of the 1930s neither Britain nor the US could afford a major confrontation in Latin America, and both, eventually, had to accept the decision. ❏

MODERN MEXICO

Mexicans have few illusions about politicians, but in 70 years the country has left behind one-party rule to become an imperfect and argumentative democracy

Between World War II and the early 21st century Mexico's population jumped from 20 million to 110 million. Few countries in the world underwent greater transformations in those years. Mexico has been through several economic booms, and become part of the modern world. But it still faces some of its old problems, as well as entirely new ones.

The reign of the PRI

For most of those years Mexico was governed uninterruptedly by the Partido de la Revolución Institucional, or PRI. The party structures created by Calles and Cárdenas grew into a vast, intricate bureaucracy, extending into every part of the country. The tangled web of affiliated labor unions such as the Confederación de Trabajadores Mexicanos (CTM, Confederation of Mexican Workers) or the Confederación Nacional Campesina (CNC, National Confederation of Farm Workers) played an essential

As the era of revolutionary jefes on horseback faded into memory it was replaced by another era of ribbon-cutting ceremonies, speeches, and official cars.

role in ensuring support. Millions of Mexicans knew they could only get a job through membership of the union, and in return were expected to show loyalty at election time.

LEFT: contemporary metallic sculpture in Mexico City.
RIGHT: violent outbreaks between rival revolutionary and independent party supporters during elections.

Unions and other PRI organizations were run in a rigidly top-down manner. As a reaction against dictators like Díaz or Santa Anna, it was a principle of the Revolution that elected officials, from town mayors to the president, could only serve one six-year term. This, however, only replaced personal rule with the collective domination of the party bureaucracy. Office-holders customarily played a part in nominating their successor, and the result was a pervasive atmosphere of cronyism and corruption.

The party that exercised such power was, however, flexible, its positions as diffuse and hard to define as the Revolution it "expressed." In the tradition of the Revolution, its habit was not to resolve – or override – contradictions but find a compromise, however odd the result. The PRI could display a style close to Soviet Communism in its labor unions, but at the same time gave all kinds of support – including keeping down wages – to "national capitalism," enabling friends of the regime to amass giant fortunes. Nationalist rhetoric provided a cover-all for many policies, and after a brief closeness during World War II, later PRI governments were often pointedly suspicious of the US.

The PRI's main purpose became keeping itself in power. For many years the party held every major elected office in Mexico.

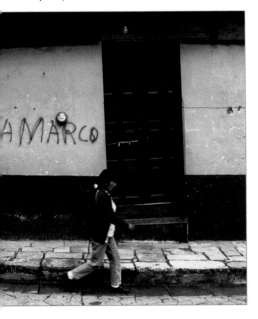

Better days

For years the regime also seemed remarkably successful. Of the four "goals" of the Mexican Revolution – democracy, national independence, modernization and land reform – nationalism and modernity were pre-eminent after 1940. Mexico benefited a great deal economically from World War II, joining the war on the Allied side in 1942 and supplying goods to the United States, and on this basis President Miguel Alemán (in office 1946–52) set out a program for industrialization. Major infrastructure projects were undertaken by giant state-run enterprises like Pemex (the national oil company), in collaboration with home-grown private business. Nationalist tariff policies kept out US and other

competition. Politicians and party officials were closely involved, handing out contracts, which gave still more room for corruption.

Implicit in Alemán's policies was the attitude that certain social consequences – uncontroled urbanization, inflation, more inequality – were acceptable so long as growth was achieved. Nevertheless, this did provide a basis for a rapid expansion of Mexican industry, which could sell into a growing market. Moreover, this was one period of expansion in Mexico that benefited large numbers of ordinary people. The middle class in the cities, especially, saw their living standards rise steadily during the 1940s and 1950s.

Agrarian reform never again received the same attention as under Lázaro Cárdenas. A "Banco Ejidal" and other organizations had been created to help *ejido* communal villages farm more effectively, but like so many PRI institutions these developed into a top-heavy, increasingly corrupt bureaucracy. The complaint was often made that *ejidatarios* (members of *ejidos*) had gone from being peons on haciendas to peons of the Banco Ejidal. At the same time, government policy shifted to encouraging more productive private agriculture, in the interests of rapid development. This made it still harder for *ejidos* to compete. Instead of a means for taking them out of poverty, the *ejido* came to be seen by Mexican country people only as a last defense against complete exposure to the market. Attitudes to the rural poor became one of post-Revolutionary Mexico's many paradoxes: despite the prime position of peasant revolt in revolutionary mythology – and the hundreds of villages called "Reforma Agraria" or "Tierra y Libertad" – in practice officials often showed little interest in rural poverty, and treated it as something no one could expect to do much about.

The system in decay

The PRI machine began to falter in the 1960s. The economy stagnated, running into the buffers of population growth and its own inflexibility. The growth of Mexico's cities – formerly seen as a symbol of progress – began to spiral out of control, above all in Mexico City itself, as millions of people flooded into the capital from the countryside, seeking jobs and needing services – light, water, transportation – that the system was scarcely able to provide, and creating a string of huge new environmental problems. Tensions became more evident in the countryside, and student demonstrations before Mexico City's Olympic Games in 1968 were brutally suppressed. Respite came thanks to the global oil price hike in the 1970s, which brought another spectacular boom. Tourist income began to flow too, especially into the Yucatán peninsula after the creation of Cancún. This, however, conformed to a common pattern for Mexican booms: it was possible for Mexico to have the highest growth rates in the world for a few years, for many people to feel better and for some to get extremely rich, while chronic poverty was untouched or even got worse.

The oil boom came to an equally sudden end in 1982, with a collapse of the peso. Opposition grew, and the PRI began to lose state governorships, especially to the Partido de Acción Nacional (PAN), a conservative, free-market party. The PRI's maneuvers to hold back opposition became more blatant. The PRI candidate for president in 1988, Carlos Salinas de Gortari, was only able to win through crude election-rigging against the leftist Cuauhtémoc Cárdenas, son of the revered 1930s president.

Salinas agreed with international observers who saw Mexico's neo-Soviet system of state enterprises as a block to growth. He set out to open Mexico up to the world – and especially the US – economy, with privatizations of banks, telephones and other sectors, and a new welcome to foreign investment. Another supercharged boom began. Food prices rose; the flow of the poor into the mushrooming megalopolis of Mexico City and toward the United States accelerated, but this was not given too much attention when other economic indicators seemed so positive.

The culmination of Salinas's program was to be the introduction of the NAFTA agreement on January 1, 1994, which required the amendment of the iconic Article 27 of the Constitution, to make it easier to break up *ejidos*. Then, on the same day, the Zapatista rebels emerged from the forests of Chiapas, making it evident the Salinas boom had only covered over the fissures created by chronic poverty. Their masked spokesman, Subcomandante Marcos, won huge sympathy throughout Mexico by describing the Salinas regime as a sham. Foreign investors fled

again, precipitating a massive downturn. No longer a guarantee of stability, the PRI was falling apart. For six years it stumbled on, as corruption scandals emerged so draw-dropping that even world-weary Mexicans could be shocked.

A new era

Faced with a barrage of opposition, the PRI had to allow cleaner elections. In 1997 it lost its majority in the Federal Congress, and the mayoralty of Mexico City was won by the left-wing Partido de la Revolución Democrática (PRD), founded by Cuauhtémoc Cárdenas. Then, in 2000 the presidency was won by Vicente Fox of

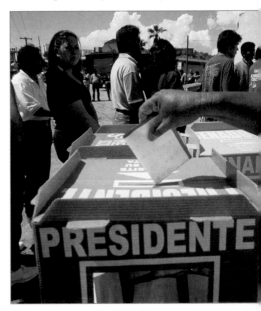

THE PERFECT DICTATORSHIP

Peruvian novelist Mario Vargas Llosa described the rule of the PRI as "the perfect dictatorship," because no one could ever quite say it was one. The party presented itself as Mexico's only viable option for government, and expected only minor opposition from its right and left. Dissent was not always silenced, and intellectual and cultural life was allowed a good deal of latitude. If open opposition arose, a common response was "co-option," calling in a movement's leaders and offering them a job in party organizations. If resistance continued, most elections could be controlled, and the PRI did not flinch from using outright repression as a final option.

LEFT: pro-Zapatista graffiti and bullet holes on a San Cristóbal de las Casas building recall the 1994 uprising.
RIGHT: casting a ballot in the 2000 presidential election.

the PAN. Many other PRI strongholds fell to the PAN or the PRD over the next few months.

Mexico, it was widely said, could at last be called a true democracy. After 71 years of one-party rule, Mexicans got used to their new democracy remarkably quickly, but without

The privatizations of banks and other major economic sectors since the 1990s have encouraged the entrenchment of a super-rich elite, such as Mexico's pre-eminent billionaire, Carlos Slim, the world's richest man.

many romantic illusions. Issues the old system kept hidden are now widely aired. There is vigorous political debate – many Mexicans would say too much, and too much about politicians' cat-fights rather than any real issues. The system of power is more fluid but still very opaque, with a great deal still done behind the scenes, and so there exists the usual space for corruption. Some commentators suggest Mexico has essentially exchanged a system of domination by a single elite for one of rotation between three, of the PAN, PRI and PRD. Federal, state and local authorities have taken more steps to deal with Mexico's long-accumulating environmental problems, especially in the capital, but a great deal remains to be done. Hopes of radi-

cal change have largely gone unsatisfied: during his campaign President Fox had said he could resolve the Chiapas conflict "in 15 minutes," but in 2001 a proposed solution was allowed to fall apart in the face of PAN and PRI opposition in Congress, and the Chiapas situation has again been allowed to stagnate, as a problem that can be isolated and ignored.

Mexico is now fully a part of the global economy – the eleventh-largest in the world – and especially interlinked with the US. Pemex is virtually the only survivor of once-vast nationalized industries, its privatization resisted by many Mexicans who see oil ownership as essential for national sovereignty. Tourism is now a major source of income. Meanwhile, collusion between vested interests and politicians remains a fact of economic life, contributing to the economy's inflexibility, and extremes of wealth, and so Mexico's longest-running problems, have widened.

As another presidential election approached in 2006, a new figurehead for the left appeared in Andrés Manuel López Obrador (AMLO, for short), former PRD mayor of Mexico City. An abrasive populist who polarizes opinion inside and outside his own party, AMLO saw his popularity rocket as he promised a "new beginning," with action at last to tackle Mexico's blatant inequalities, and called on everyone interested in genuine change in Mexico to support him. Appeals to the Zapatistas in Chiapas to back him were rebuffed, but nevertheless in the July 2006 election he came within a whisker of the presidency: Felipe Calderón of the PAN won by a margin of 0.58 percent, out of 42 million voters. López Obrador denounced the result as a fraud, and later staged his own separate inauguration as "the Legitimate President of Mexico." However, this only meant that the PRD has been frequently paralyzed ever since by infighting between AMLO supporters and others who saw his "inauguration" as futile grandstanding.

Following this controversy, Calderón chose to make his mark early, by incorporating some of López Obrador's social proposals into his program, and most controversially by launching an offensive against Mexico's drug cartels *(see page 75)*. The results have been a severe shock, but modern Mexico has demonstrated a remarkable ability to overcome crises. ❏

LEFT: PAN's Felipe Calderón was elected president in 2006, defeating Manuel López by a very narrow margin.

21st-Century Challenges

Mexico is now facing two major tests, both linked to its ever-complex relationship with the United States.

Two issues dominate headlines on Mexico. One has been around forever: the need to provide decent living standards for most Mexicans. The other is a recent explosion: the battle with the drug cartels. Both reflect the way Mexico is now intertwined with the United States.

For years Mexico sought to keep US domination at bay by building a self-sufficient economy behind tariff walls. Since this model stagnated, politicians took a bet on embracing the bear next door as the easiest means to economic progress. Millions of ordinary Mexicans, of course, have done so by themselves, migrating northwards. Since the 1994 NAFTA agreement, *maquiladoras* (assembly plants for export goods) oriented to the US market have proliferated across Mexico.

This has left Mexico acutely vulnerable to fluctuations in the USA – as the recession bit in 2008, Mexico's exports fell by 32 percent. One likely result is renewed emigration. Critics say a more stable economy can only be built by creating more stable demand within Mexico, through tackling its inequalities of wealth.

The other issue was created by American society's vast demand for narcotics, and the money it spends on them. Every country has criminals: the difference with the drugs trade is that it pumps criminal gangs, the "cartels," with resources greater than whole state budgets.

Determined to demonstrate his authority after his contested election, President Felipe Calderón attacked Mexico's cartels straight after his inauguration in 2007, using the army in place of infiltrated local police forces. Calderón has been criticized for doing so without sufficient preparation, and without realizing just what a hornets' nest he was stirring up.

The cartels made it clear that if the government wanted a fight, it would have one. Over 7,000 people died in drug-related violence in 2008–9. Law officials have been assassinated, soldiers and

policemen not bought off are brazenly threatened, and *narcos* (traffickers) have fought each other in savage turf wars.

Beyond the demand, the other way the US is involved is as a weapons supplier, as US officials increasingly recognize. Within Mexico, firearms are actually hard to obtain; however, there is an uncontrolled market in military-standard weapons in the United States. Of more than 12,000 weapons seized from the cartels in 2008, 90 percent were bought in the USA.

All this led a US military think-tank to ponder (within a 2008 report on global scenarios) whether the drug war could lead to Mexico becoming a

"failed state," sparking wildly exaggerated media reports that changed this speculation to a prediction. This gives a distorted picture. The Mexican government has given itself a huge test. Many Mexicans remain unconvinced this has been worth taking on. Nevertheless, the Calderón government can point to important successes: vast amounts of drugs impounded, weapons seized, drug lords locked up.

Talk of Mexico's impending collapse is over the top: however much chaos there is in border towns like Ciudad Juárez, they are only a small part of a huge country. Very few tourist travelers are ever caught up in drug violence. The cartels try to extend their tentacles, but in most of Mexico the drug war is a news story, not part of everyday life. ❑

RIGHT: a member of the La Familia drug cartel is presented to the media in Mexico City.

SMOKING MOUNTAINS AND FLOWERING DESERTS

A land of extremes, from deserts to rain forests, from soaring volcanoes to vast underwater caverns, Mexico is both barren and lush, rugged and pastoral

There are many Mexicos, it has often been said. Dramatic physical features make for striking divisions between different parts of the country. Two great mountain ranges, the Sierra Madre Occidental and Sierra Madre Oriental, run down from the US border, flanking the Pacific and Gulf coasts. They meet in the Central Highlands, Mexico's historic heart: covering an area of about 640km (400 miles) from east to west and less than 320km (200 miles) from north to south, this region represents just one-tenth of all Mexico, but contains almost half the country's population. The Central Highlands in turn have a very marked "core," where rivers run not down to the sea but into a giant bowl in the mountains known as the Valle de México, the Valley of Mexico, with Mexico City at its center.

Across the center of the Republic, a 160km (100-mile) belt of mountains stretches between Puerto Vallarta on the Pacific coast and Veracruz on the Gulf. South of this volcanic axis, lesser mountains form the Sierra Madre del Sur, narrowing down at the Isthmus of Tehuantepec – Mexico's so-called waist, with a width of only 160km (100 miles). East of the Isthmus the mountains surge up again into the Sierra Madre de Chiapas, which continue south into Guatemala; to the north, the terrain is very different, even unique, in the Yucatán Peninsula, a vast limestone sheet covered by thin soil, ironed flat by nature.

Rainfall and forests

Mountains and highlands characterize much of Mexico, but deserts dominate the north. The Great Arizona Desert continues south of the

border through Sonora, Chihuahua, Baja California and several other states, with vast, arid, empty landscapes where – apart from the desert flowers that form sudden flashes of color for a few weeks each year – crops can generally be grown only with the help of irrigation.

Nature in Mexico has always tended to extremes. Many of the northern desert areas get as little as 10cm (4ins) of rain a year. It seems almost perverse that on the Gulf coast, too much rain – as much as 6 meters (240ins) each year – obliges farmers to hack away unwanted growth. Rainfall is also erratic in the central highlands: sometimes a trickle, sometimes a flood .

The denuding of forests by the indiscriminate

PRECEDING PAGES: Popocatépetl. **LEFT:** vantage point for vultures. **RIGHT:** *bandilleros* and maguey cacti.

cutting of timber has long been a major cause of problems, accentuating those stemming from the variability and unpredictability of rainfall. This began in colonial times, when many areas were stripped of trees for planting crops, or for large-scale mining. The silver-mining region of Zacatecas is an example of woodland that was transformed to savannah by tree-cutters. In many regions the water table has fallen and climate change has ensued as a result. In the last 50 years, the extension of roads into once-remote rain forest areas of the south has led to large-scale deforestation there, especially in Tabasco and northern Chiapas.

to integrate effectively into their main territories all the great northern reaches that the conquistadors had claimed, and when the time came the United States was able to seize these lands without much of a struggle.

In the south, too, many regions had only fragile connections with the Valley of Mexico

> *In colonial times, it took over a year to make the 2,600km (1,600-mile) round trip from Zacatecas to New Mexico and back across the Chihuahua desert.*

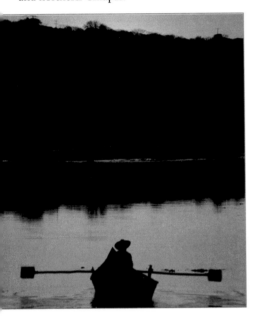

for decades. The Yucatán Peninsula, meanwhile, was virtually an island, with no usable land link with central Mexico through the swamps and forests of Tabasco until the 1940s. Instead, most contacts were carried on by boat, between Veracruz and Campeche or Progreso.

During the dictatorship of Porfirio Díaz (1876–1910), foreign capital poured into Mexico and helped finance the building of roads and railroads, especially between Mexico City and the north. This made it possible to exploit untapped natural resources, such as metals and oil. The governments that followed the 1910 Revolution made improving communications a priority, and in the 1940s the Mexican section of the Pan-American Highway was completed, the first road from one end of the country to the other. While Mexico's railroads have been allowed to fall into decay, road-building has gone on ever since, creating some of the world's most spectacular mountain highways.

Rivers and roads

Apart from a few in the south – notably the Grijalva and the Usumacinta, which flow into the Gulf in Tabasco – Mexico's rivers are mostly unnavigable, and communicating between one part of the country and another has always posed special problems. Throughout the colonial period, the road from Mexico City to Veracruz served as the umbilical cord between the New World and Spain; in the late 16th century land links were also opened to the agriculturally rich Bajío north of Mexico City, and on to the mining district of Zacatecas. However, attempts to extend significant Spanish colonization into New Mexico failed. Neither Spain nor freshly independent Mexico had the resources

Volcanoes, cascades and caverns

All the ancient cultures of Mexico saw the land around them as alive with spiritual forces, which could be both friendly and hostile. It's easy to see why, for many features of the Mexican landscape are spectacular, strange and volatile. Among the most prominent are its many volcanoes, of which the most famous are the two giants that loom up over the Valley of Mexico, Popocatépetl (5,465 meters/17,845ft high), the "Smoking Mountain" or *El Popo* that as recently as 2000 spewed out high-reaching fumaroles and dust towards Mexico City; and its extinct neighbor, Iztaccíhuatl, the "Sleeping Woman" (5,230 meters/17,155ft; *see also page 165*). Mexico's highest mountain the Pico de

Orizaba or Citlaltépetl ("Star Mountain" in Náhuatl), 5,636 meters (18,490ft) high and visible from the road between Mexico City and Veracruz, is also a volcano, currently dormant but not extinct (its last eruption was in 1687).

The youngest of Mexico's volcanoes, Paricutín in Michoacán, was born only in February 1943, when local farmer Dionisio Pulido saw a burst of gas and ashes emerging from a cornfield one afternoon. Awestruck, he returned with his *compadres* (friends) the next day to discover a cone already 6 meters (20ft) high. The eruption intensified soon after, hurling molten rock 100 meters (328ft) into the air and putting on a fiery display of orange lava. During its nine active years the fissure covered the village of San Juan Parangaricutiro in ash, and eventually created a cinder-cone mountain 424 meters (1,391ft) high. Since 1952, Paricutín has again been quiet.

In the far south, the massive Tacaná volcano (4,092 meters/13,425ft) that sits astride the border between Chiapas and Guatemala is also potentially still active. Its last significant belch of gas and ash occurred in 1986, but the mountain is still constantly monitored.

Mexico's rivers may not be much use as means of communications, but they are often stunning natural sights. The rivers that run down the eastern Sierra Madre to the Gulf descend several thousand meters in only some 100km (62 miles), along spectacular gorges, rapids and waterfalls, so that rivers like the Filobobos in Veracruz are ideal for rafting and other adventure sports. In the Central Highlands, mountain rivers such as the Amacuzac in Morelos are equally stunning. In the Lacandón forests of Chiapas, many rivers form "ladders" of cascades, torrents, rapids and exquisite rock pools, often extending over several kilometers.

The Yucatán Peninsula has perhaps the most mysterious landscape of all. There are no rivers of any kind. Instead, rainwater runs straight through the soft limestone, forming a vast labyrinth of caverns and underground watercourses. Investigations by cave divers have shown that most are connected, forming the longest underground river systems in the world. Openings through the rock called

cenotes – often large, beautiful pools, where a cave roof has fallen in – have been the main (or only) source of water for the Yucatán's people. Nutrients from these mineral-rich caves flow out to the sea, to feed the dazzling coral reefs along the Caribbean coast.

Wildlife

Urban areas in Mexico tend to be seriously polluted, and elsewhere deforestation, soil erosion, and the effects of uncontrolled building pose serious ecological threats. Nevertheless, there remain vast thinly-inhabited areas of the country that are still isolated and inaccessible, and in

The Ox Bel Ha cave system, entered near Tulum, is the longest underwater cave system yet discovered anywhere in the world, and has been explored – so far – to a length of 172km (106 miles).

which wild animals can roam relatively freely.

Mexico is a paradise for the nature-lover. It has 2,896 species of vertebrates, including 520 mammals, 1,424 species of birds, 685 kinds of reptiles, and 267 amphibians. Some are protected in national parks, and others in wildlife refuges. In all, there are more than 50 reserves of different kinds in Mexico.

LEFT: rowing at dusk near El Presa dam, San Miguel de Allende. **RIGHT:** beautiful *cenote* Samula in Dzitnup, near Valladolid in the Yucatán.

Tough hikers can sight great horned sheep in San Pedro Mártir National Park in the mountainous interior of Baja California, and in the Cumbres de Monterrey National Park there are black bears. Off the coast of the Baja Peninsula, the islands of San Benito and Guadalupe (the latter of which is a Biosphere Reserve) are a refuge for fur seals and other species, while the waters around them contain major concentrations of great white sharks. Sea lions bask on many of the small islands around Baja, some of which are also home to the endangered green turtle (Chelonia mydas).

The most spectacular of the mammals are

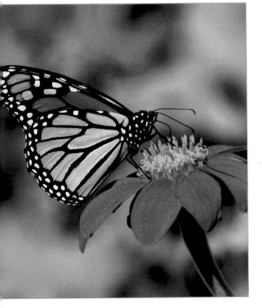

the gray and other varieties of whales, which migrate yearly from Alaska's Bering Sea to Baja California to mate and calve. For years whales were hunted to near extinction but, thanks to official protection – and despite problems caused by other commercial fisheries in the area – there has been a strong recovery in recent decades. Whales are now easy to spot in their breeding grounds around Laguna San Ignacio on the Pacific coast and in the Sea of Cortés, especially in the December–April breeding season.

From eagles and vultures to hummingbirds and pelicans, birds are never far from view in Mexico; in some parts, wild flocks of parrots are as common a sight (and sound) as the caged macaws in the patios of restaurants or hotels.

As well as having hundreds of native species, Mexico is the winter terminus for many more. Some favor the Pacific coast, and areas such as the San Juan Estuary near San Blas in Nayarit. In Yucatán, thousands of pink flamingos and other water birds flock to the mangrove wetlands around the coast, which can most easily be visited at Celestún, west of Mérida, and Río Lagartos on the north coast.

But perhaps the most spectacular sight of all is found inland, in Central Mexico. Each winter, millions of Monarch butterflies transform the Michoacán landscape when they arrive at their breeding grounds high up in mountain valleys after flying thousands of miles, all the way from Canada and the United States (see page 239). ❏

LEFT: millions of Monarch butterflies migrate to Mexico in winter. **RIGHT:** the village of Tapalpa, Jalisco, at dawn.

PROTECTING NATURAL MEXICO

Ecotourism has become ever more popular in Mexico, as it has across the world. Some of the resulting projects are themselves destructive of the natural attractions they aim to open up – through, for example, careless waste management – but there are many schemes that take care to keep their impact as low as possible. Parallel to this growth has been the expansion of reserve areas, generally with one of three grades of protection: *Reservas de la Biósfera* or Biosphere Reserves, *Parques Nacionales* or National Parks, and protected areas (AFPP).

In the north, Copper Canyon (Barranca del Cobre) – seven times the size of the Grand Canyon – and nearby Cascada de Basaseáchic, with the highest single-drop waterfall in

North America, are both now national parks. In the south, Montes Azules Biosphere Reserve near the Guatemalan border is one of the last wild homes of the red macaw.

One of the most ambitious projects is the vast Sian Ka'an Biosphere Reserve, just south of the Riviera Maya. Its range of habitats includes rain forest, coastal lagoons, mangroves and coral reefs, containing turtles, howler monkeys, crocodiles, pumas, jaguars, and hundreds of species of birds and fish. The largest of all Mexico's forest reserves, though, is the Calakmul Biosphere in southern Campeche, a giant expanse around the ruined Maya city of Calakmul.

ADVENTURE TOURISM

From north to south, in mountains and deserts, even underwater – Mexico offers thrills of a lifetime

Few countries in the world offer more for the thrill seeker than Mexico. Plop a finger on the map and you'll likely find countless opportunities to plunge, soar, zip, or even scream. Even otherwise placid tourist spots such as Los Cabos in Baja offer parasailing and ATV rides, but adrenalin junkies will find plenty to keep them occupied.

Baja's fame as a surfing mecca began in the sixties, when those searching for endless waves (if not Endless Summer) started trekking down the 1,600km (1,000-mile) long dirt roads to find beach breaks. This mystique has remained, and Baja offers some of the most spectacular surfing anywhere. Adventure seekers will find more than just waves however: ancient pilgrimage routes, lost treasure, breathtaking hikes through the astonishing "green desert" all beckon. Mainland destinations such as Sayulita and Puerto Escondido (famous as the "Mexican Pipeline") draw increasing numbers of surfers each year.

Mexico is as varied and spectacular under water as above it. The eerie stillness of freshwater cenotes in Yucatán, the dazzling jewels of the world's second longest barrier reef off Quintana Roo and Cozumél, and the sun-dappled azure of the Sea of Cortés all provide divers with a lifetime's worth of memories.

Jungles offer more than just mosquitoes and humidity: some of the planet's last surviving populations of jaguars still roam in the dense forests in Chiapas, Quintana Roo, and Yucatán. and fascinating birdlife teems in the estuaries in coastal flatlands and Acapulco.

Adventures lie around every corner... go out and explore!

LEFT: rent an all-terrain vehicle and cruise across the sand.

ABOVE: ziplining through the canopy near the mountain village of La Noria delivers exhilartion with scenic views.

ABOVE: swim with a whale shark in Baja's La Paz Bay.
BELOW: a woman tests her skill and strength on a free climb in the rugged desert terrain near La Paz.

ECO OR NOT? THAT IS THE QUESTION

ABOVE: a surfer rides a powerful wave at Puerto Escondido, also known as the "Mexican Pipeline."

Adventure tourism and "eco" tourism are often bandied about and the catch phrase seems to have caught on everywhere– but just because the word has "eco" in it doesn't mean your trip won't be harming the environment. Those going on buggy or horse rides should be sure to ask whether this will be on marked trails or through privately owned lands. Search on the internet to check that you're going with a well-known organization that has concern for the environment. National parks are fragile ecosystems and can be easily overwhelmed by large numbers of tourists. Help minimize your effect on the planet by being sure to place your trash in marked receptacles, or consider carrying it with you back to your hotel. Always make sure to close faucets and preserve water, especially in places like Baja or northern Mexico where rains are infrequent. When hiking, stay on the trails so as not to widen them. Divers, snorkelers, and surfers should always take care to avoid direct contact with the fragile coral reef, which takes decades to grow.

TOP RIGHT: coral colonies are beautiful but fragile, growing only a few inches each year.
ABOVE: get your heart racing in a parasail ride high above one of Mexico's beautiful bays.
LEFT: snorkeling is an easy and inexpensive way to see what lies beneath the sea.
RIGHT: a mountain biker races up a steep rock formation.

FIESTAS

Witness if you can the rituals, costumes, masks, fireworks, song and dance that make Mexico's fiestas an explosion of exuberance

There is always a fiesta taking place somewhere in Mexico. Apart from the national civic celebrations, every city, town, village, or *barrio* (neighborhood) has its own fiesta, often in honor of the local patron saint. Visitors have a good chance of happening upon one of Mexico's wonderful fiestas – particularly at certain, more traditionally festive times. The calendar lists more than 5,000 every year – that is an average of nearly 14 fiestas a day.

An exuberant blend

Fiestas are a vital part of community life in Mexico. Many can be traced back to pagan pre-Hispanic rituals which relate to ancient customs and aspects of nature such as fertility or the harvest. Others were brought over from Europe with Christianity and have a marked Spanish flavor. But most Mexican fiestas, like the people themselves, are a combination of both.

Fiestas vary greatly from region to region and no two are ever the same, although music, dance, street parades, fireworks and fire-crackers are almost always present. On religious occasions there are also processions, the reciting of rosaries and the chanting of *novenas* (prayers).

Mexican fireworks are quite breathtaking and unlike any display you are ever likely to witness again. As a general rule, the bigger or richer the town the more impressive the show. Specialized craftsmen are brought in for the occasion to make the *castillos* (castles) and *toritos* (little bulls). The *castillos* are enormous wicker structures, up to 20 meters (66ft) high, to which hundreds of fireworks are wired so as to create a

PIÑATAS

The most colorful stall in any Mexican market is the one selling *piñatas*, the terracotta pots decorated with papier-mâché and brightly colored shredded tissue paper. *Piñatas* shaped like a three-dimensional stars are a traditional part of Christmas festivities. They also come in the form of fruit, vegetables, animals, clowns, or even the Disney character of the month. The *piñata* is hung in the patio or street and, one by one, blindfolded children try to hit and break it with a stick. As soon as the pot breaks, candy, fruit, peanuts, and sticks of sugar cane cascade to the ground and the children dive in to grab all they can.

PRECEDING PAGES: a Day of the Dead costume. **LEFT:** San Miguel de Allende. **RIGHT:** Guadalajara carnival dancers.

show of spectacular effects. For the *toritos*, especially famous in Cholula, Puebla, the wicker framework, shaped like a bull, is worn by a man who twists, turns and charges at the crowds with the fireworks exploding all around.

Fiestas take place in the center of town, around the church and main plaza. A marketplace springs up, with stalls selling crafts, trinkets, mementoes and the hard-to-resist *antojitos*. A national favorite, *antojitos* include a whole range of Mexican food, from beautifully decorative peeled and cut fruits eaten with lime juice, salt and chili powder, to the ubiquitous tacos, tamales and quesadillas.

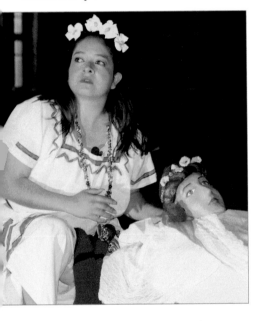

The *lotería*, a Mexican version of bingo, is usually present too, with its traditional figures of the devil, the moon, the soldier, the señorita, the drunkard, the dandy and, of course, Death. Also common to most parts of the country are bullfighting, horse racing (*see Charros photo feature, page 245*) and cock fighting. In some towns – like Huamantla in Tlaxcala or Tlacotalpán in Veracruz – they practice Pamplona-style bull-running through the streets. In Huamantla the bulls run through 12km (7 miles) of streets which, on *La Noche que Nadie Duerme* (The Night when Nobody Sleeps), have been beautifully decorated with colored sawdust and flowers for the feast of the Assumption (August 14).

Song and dance

The variety of traditional music and dance performed at fiestas is enormous. Apart from the obvious Jarabe Tapatío (Mexican Hat Dance), there are dozens more. Some, like the *concheros*, have survived the Conquest; others interpret it. The masked protagonists of the *Danza de la Conquista* (Dance of the Conquest), in Jalisco and Michoacán, are Moctezuma, Cortés and La Malinche, as well as armed Spanish soldiers and the jaguar and eagle warriors with their feather headdresses.

The best-known of the many dances formerly dedicated to Huehuetéotl, the "Old God," deity of fire and time, is the extraordinary *Danza de los Viejitos* (Dance of the Old Men) in Michoacán. In Puebla, the Quetzal dancers wear huge, brilliantly colored and feathered headdresses, whilst in Sonora, the Yaqui perform the *Danza del Venado* (Stag Dance), and in Veracruz the Voladores "fly" around a 32-meter (105ft) pole (*see page 265*) in a hypnotic re-enactment of a Totonac ritual.

> The Festival Cervantino in Guanajuato began in 1972 when a group of drama students performed works by Cervantes, the author of Don Quijote.

Other dances, introduced by the Spanish missionaries, pitch Moors against Christians and include such unlikely characters as Charlemagne and the Knights of the Round Table, as well as the more familiar Angel, Devil, Priest, Maiden and Death. Newer festivals, such as the Festival Cervantino, celebrate dramatic arts from all over the world.

Religious fiestas

Carnaval is celebrated the week before the beginning of Lent, in February or March. It is, traditionally, the last chance to let your hair down before the 40-day abstinence that precedes Easter. The famous carnivals of Veracruz and Mazatlán (the former claims to be the biggest outside Rio de Janeiro), as well as those of Campeche, Cozumél, Mérida and other parts of the Republic, are celebrated with colorful parades, extravagant costumes, fireworks, day-and-night dancing, eating and drinking. The fiesta in Veracruz starts with the ceremonial

Quema del Mal Humor (Burning of Bad Temper), and reaches its climax several sleepless days later, on Shrove Tuesday (Mardi Gras). The next day, Ash Wednesday, sees the burial of Juan Carnaval and the symbolic beginning of a new era.

Brightly colored papier-mâché devils, or Judases, are sold on street corners the week before Easter and are traditionally burned on the Saturday. Easter in Mexico is a time for candle-lit processions and impressive passion plays that can last for days. Many people flock to Taxco each year, and millions watch the "crucifixion" at Iztapalapa in Mexico City.

celebrated on the nine days leading up to Christmas, commemorate the journey of Mary and Joseph to Bethlehem and are traditionally accompanied by the breaking of the *piñata*. Christmas itself is celebrated on the night of December 24, with a big dinner and Mass the next morning. Some families still put up the traditional *nacimiento* – or nativity scene – although, influenced by the US, Christmas trees are now more widespread. Customs vary in different regions of the country: in some parts the children receive gifts from the "infant Jesus," while in others it is the Three Kings who bring the gifts on January 6.

The Feria de San Marcos, around April 25, is a lively affair in Aguascalientes, while Corpus Christi – when children go to church dressed as indigenous people and carrying tiny straw donkeys – is especially interesting in Papantla, Veracruz. The Day of the Dead is Mexico's answer to All Souls' Day, the ultimate combination of pre-Hispanic and Christian ritual *(see pages 92–3)*. Even the celebrations on December 12, when all Mexico commemorates the Virgen de Guadalupe *(see page 29)*, has Aztec as well as Catholic origins. The *posadas*,

Patriotic fiestas

Although religious celebrations are usually the most elaborate, there are lively fiestas in Mexico's political calendar too. National flags are for sale everywhere in September, *El Mes de la Patria* (Fatherland Month), which traditionally begins with the president's state of the nation address (September 1) and builds up to Independence Day celebrations on September 16.

On November 20 schoolchildren parade through the streets dressed as Zapata or Pancho Villa to celebrate the Day of the Revolution, while May 5 marks the Mexican defeat of the French army (albeit short-lived) at the Battle of Puebla. ❏

LEFT: a Festival Cervantino street theater performance.
ABOVE: Independence Day procession of military bands, San Miguel de Allende.

IN HONOR OF THEIR ANCESTORS

Every year on the first two days of November, the people of Mexico recall their dead relations in a meaningful but festive ceremony

Of the many religious festivals celebrated throughout the year in Mexico, the *Día de los Muertos* (Day of the Dead) is probably the most fascinating to any outsider and the one that is truest to the country's mestizo spirit. The original celebration can be traced to pre-Hispanic rituals dedicated to Mictlantecuhtli, the Mexican lord of the underworld, and Huitzilopochtli, the Aztec war deity to whom so many were sacrificed. After the Conquest, in an attempt to turn the fiesta into a Christian celebration, Spanish priests moved the date to coincide with that of All Souls' Day. Far from a macabre, grisly dwelling on darkness and death, Day of the Dead has become a fiesta that celebrates life as much as death, a fun-filled family affair where young and old pay colorful tribute to the spirits that surround them.

Nowadays the fiesta blends both pre-Hispanic and Christian rituals, and celebrations vary from state to state, a warm tradition that brings families together and is anything but somber. The most famous are the Purépecha traditions in Michoacán, where all-night vigils in the cemeteries and candlelit boat processions across the lake to the tiny island of Janitzio attract visitors from all over the world.

ABOVE: market stalls fill up with sugar and chocolate skulls – reminiscent of the Aztec *tzompantli* (skull racks). There are also lively and humorous skeletons and coffins made of clay and papier-mâché

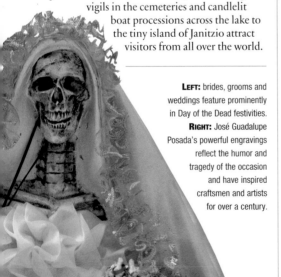

LEFT: brides, grooms and weddings feature prominently in Day of the Dead festivities.
RIGHT: José Guadalupe Posada's powerful engravings reflect the humor and tragedy of the occasion and have inspired craftsmen and artists for over a century.

LITTLE ANGELS RETURNING HOME

It is believed that the souls of the children who have died (called *angelitos* – "little angels") return to their earthly homes on November 1, while those of the adults arrive the following day. A candle is lit for each returning soul and beautiful *ofrendas*, or shrines, are made in homes all over the country.

Photos of the loved ones are placed around the table along with a variety of their favorite foods or *antojitos*, the traditional *pan de muerto* (bread of the dead) and a glass of tequila or mug of *atole* (cornmeal drink). The shrine is decorated with ornately cut tissue paper and orange *cempasúchil* flowers. Little chocolate or sugar skulls, and other decorations are placed around the *ofrenda*, and an incense called *copal* is burned. Sometimes a path of orange petals is strewn from the street to the shrine to help the souls find their way home, in this intimate tribute to lost loved ones.

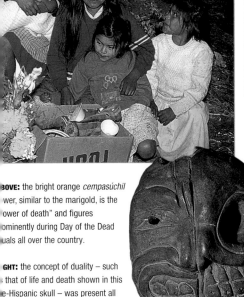

ABOVE: the bright orange *cempasúchil* flower, similar to the marigold, is the "flower of death" and figures prominently during Day of the Dead rituals all over the country.

RIGHT: the concept of duality – such as that of life and death shown in this pre-Hispanic skull – was present all over Mesoamerica, and is apparent in this ritual today.

TOP: it is a festive occasion for the whole community, but also deeply spiritual; a time of personal contemplation, of shared memories, and for reuniting the living with their dead relations.

LEFT: Mexicans dread death but also laugh at it. The ritual is neither morbid nor mocking, but an effort to laugh at the tragically inevitable.

ABOVE: some people prepare an altar at home, others visit the cemeteries to share the festivities with the spirits of their loved ones.

MÚSICA MEXICANA

Salsa is the essence, while *cumbia, quebradita, danzón* and others are not formation showpieces, but everyday dances in bars and *barrios*

Music is everywhere in Mexico, and just like the people, the music is a rich, varied mix of influences, cultures, and languages. Wherever you happen to be, whether it's in a restaurant, on the beach, on the subway, or a crowded bus in the rush hour, somebody is likely to produce a guitar and strike up a song. Tourists often balk at paying 20 or 30 pesos (or sometimes more) for a song but take a moment to look around and you'll see Mexican families paying the same: in Mexico, music matters.

But you won't hear the same rhythms from Chihuahua to Chiapas. In Mexico the music is as varied as the food, the culture and the country itself; it is as mestizo as the Mexican people and has absorbed traditional and popular music from all over the world: Spain, Argentina, Colombia, Cuba and Africa, as well as the more recent influence of rock music from Europe and the USA.

Música popular

In the north of Mexico (and the south of the United States), hugely popular Western-style *norteña* bands pump out Tex-Mex *corridos* on guitars, accordions, contrabass and drums. The *corrido* always tells a story and its hero is usually on the wrong side of the law; in the old days, the ballads would extol the virtues of the likes of Pancho Villa and Emiliano Zapata; these days, they may tell of an illegal immigrant, the fate of the *mojado* (wetback) across the border. Banda, often a group of 10 swaggering men in cowboy hats and accordions, is a frenetic version of this same hallowed theme, but with a polka-like sound, and often with a tuba as the main keeper of the beat.

Canción ranchera is another all-time favorite; it is Mexico's version of country music, which dates back to Spanish romances or chivalric ballads. Mexican *ranchera* music is passionate by definition; the emotions are up-front and the action is melodramatic: heroes and villains, *bandidos* and *pistoleros*, politics, current affairs and, most of all, tragic and heartrending love.

Tropical bands play salsa music in the dance halls with a selection of percussion instruments – bongos, *tumbas, güiros*, rattle-gourds, *timbales* and cowbells – as well as guitars, trumpets, flutes, pianos and even *marimbas*. Salsa, or *música tropical*, generically includes a whole range of rhythms from *mambo* and *cumbia* (as popular in

Mexico as in its native Colombia) to the frenetic *merengue* and the sedately seductive *danzón*.

The *marimba* itself is most popular in the southern states of Chiapas, Oaxaca, Tabasco and Veracruz. This large wooden xylophone-type instrument is played by up to four musicians, using rubber-tipped batons. The soloist carries the tune; the other three divide the secondary melody in counterpoint. Traditionally all players came from the same family and could play waltzes, *paso dobles, boleros* and even excerpts from operas.

The nostalgic, romantic *bolero* is probably the most popular type of music in urban Mexico.

differ greatly from region to region or state to state. In Jalisco, the *son* is the music of the *mariachi* bands and is often considered the most representative of Mexican music. In the region known as the Huasteca, the *son* or *huapango huasteco* is sung in falsetto while in southern Veracruz the *son jarocho* (of which *La Bamba* is the most famous example) includes harp, *jarana* (small guitar) and sometimes tambourine along with its guitars and violins.

Mexicans, masters of improvisation, come into their own with the *son* and, although the lyrics of many *sones* date from 16th-century Spain, many more verses concerning a particu-

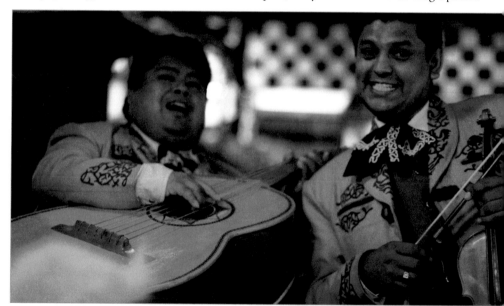

Its origins go back to Andalusia, but it was enriched by the tropical beat that came over from Cuba. Agustín Lara, the most famous composer of *boleros* in the 20th century, is a household name in Mexico, and in Veracruz there is a museum dedicated to his life.

But probably the most Mexican of all is the ubiquitous *son* which is interpreted in many regions and with a variety of instruments throughout Mexico. These blends of improvisation using local instruments or melodies rapidly developed into unique local dances that

The name mariachi *comes from either* mariage, *the French for wedding, or* mariagero, *the Galician for a musician who performs at a wedding. The costume is based on the* charro *suit, traditional cowboy attire from Jalisco state.*

lar event or person are ingeniously invented by the *soneros* on the spur of the moment. Other rhythms may be less well known – the *jarabe* of Jalisco, the *sandunga* of Oaxaca, the *jarana* of the Yucatán, the *pirecua* of Michoacán, and many more – but are still popular in their specific regions and are accompanied, like the *son*, by dances.

LEFT: rubber batons on wooden keys produce the mellow *marimba* tone.
ABOVE: *mariachi* music hails from Jalisco state.

Noble musical traditions

Musical tradition in Mexico has its roots in both pre-Hispanic and Spanish cultures. Before the arrival of the conquistadors, music was an integral part of religious rituals and was unexpectedly energetic and varied. Like the dance, it had to be performed in a plaza, on a platform, or on a pyramid. Priests, nobles and even kings took part.

Netzahualcóyotl, king of Texcoco, was a poet and a fine singer who encouraged the composers in his court to narrate the glories of his lineage and the history of his kingdom. Many of the songs dedicated to the gods have survived. Manuscripts and codices with rhythmic annotation

were set down by the Spanish friar Bernardino de Sahagún in the 16th century and are the first examples of scored music in the Americas.

The songs were generally accompanied by the *huehuetl* and the *teponaztli*, both percussion instruments, as well as by rattles, flutes, conch shells and grooved bones. In some villages of Hidalgo, Veracruz and Tabasco both the *huehuetl* and the *teponaztli* are considered sacred instruments and are still used to accompany ancient rituals.

Pre-Hispanic wind instruments were sophisticated: reed and clay flutes, multiple flutes, ocarinas, whistle jugs and conch-shell trumpets. In funerary rites, the sound of conch shells was associated with mourning.

Fray Juan de Torquemada left an excellent description of pre-Hispanic song and dance that were incorporated into religious rites. Musical instruments for ceremonial use in Mexico-Tenochtitlán were kept in a sacred place called Mixcoacalli. A large number of musicians were employed in the service of the temples; men dedicated themselves to the study of song and dance. So important was music to the indigenous peoples that a missionary claimed conversions came about more readily through music than through preaching.

Colonial influences

After the Spanish Conquest, musicians who had served in Aztec temples were employed in churches. The earliest school to teach music to the indigenous people was founded just three years after the Conquest by Fray Pedro de Gante. It was not long before New Spain started making its own organs and other secular instruments. Some, such as guitars, violins and harps, became the specialty of certain villages. The Aztecs were a musical people. One early missionary marveled "at the beginning they did not understand anything nor did the old instructor have an interpreter. In a short time they understood so well that they learned not only plain chants but also the songs of the organ and now there are many choirs and singers who are skillful in modulation and harmony, learning everything by heart."

The secular music of the Renaissance arrived aboard the galleons from Spain. Out of the Caribbean came rhythms and musical forms that mixed Latin, Mediterranean, Arab, African and indigenous music. From all these came the exciting rhythms of the tango, the rumba, the fandango, the *chaconne*, the *saraband*, the *cumbé*, the *habanera*, the *bolero* and the *danzón*.

During its 300 years as a colony, Mexico was treated to all kinds of music. In 1711, Mexico City played host to the first opera composed and performed in the New World, *La Parténope*, by Manuel de Zumaya. During late colonial times, the *corrido*, accompanied by guitar and harp, became the most popular musical form.

Mariachi music, often thought of as the quintessential "Mexican" music, originated in the 18th century. It is still played all over the country but is most popular in Jalisco and central Mexico. At first the players used only stringed instruments but trumpets were added later for pizazz.

During the 19th century the waltz became popular. The new music spoke of the triumph of the War of Independence. Major composers such as Juventino Rosas gave form to the Mexican version of the waltz combining originality, nostalgia and melodic imagination.

Música moderna

Recently, stars such as Luis Miguel, with his hit CD "Mexico en mi Piel," have brought a resurgence in more traditional songs and in Mexican pride, while other Mexican muscians

the music here reflects the unique mix of influences and cultures. It's hard to characterize. What's easier to state is that no matter where you go, be it in quiet Chihuahua in the north or crazy Cancún in the south or anywhere in between, pop into any disco and you'll see it packed with young people all enjoying the same thing at the same time: a beat and a place to see and be seen. You won't find a universal music that encompasses all of Mexico. But you will find that music here is inescapable. Don't be afraid to toss a few pesos to a passing troubadour or to kick off your sandals and put on your dancing shoes. ❑

have dominated the pop charts and club scene. Thalía, a stunningly beautiful Mexican singer with a voice to match, has done well not only within Mexico but also in the US, crossing the musical border with English albums, tours, a fashion clothing line. She became a US citizen in 2006. Another beauty, Belinda, has wooed listeners and viewers with success in both the film and music industry. Modern Mexican music is hard to characterize, in part because it means so many different things to so many different people, and much like the country's people,

LEFT: *norteña* blends musical styles from both sides of the Mexico-US border. **ABOVE:** *marimba* band guitarists performing in Veracruz.

REGIONAL VARIATIONS

As you travel through Mexico you'll find that the differences from state to state are often stark: a mountain range will separate lush tropics from dry plains and desert and the styles of clothing, customs and food will change. Similarly, the music you'll hear may vary substantially as you journey from place to place. *Banda* is big in Sinaloa and Zacatecas; *norteño* in Baja, Chihuahua, Nuevo Leon; *son* in Oaxaca. In Jalisco, the birthplace of *mariachi* music, being a *mariachi* is a time-honored, respected profession. Just about everything makes its way to Mexico City including Cuban-influenced *danzón* and even Argentine tango.

omate

+chico+

5.00

CHICO

MEXICAN FOOD

Mexican cuisine goes far beyond chips and salsa:
rich culinary traditions make dining as much about
understanding Mexican culture as about flavor or taste

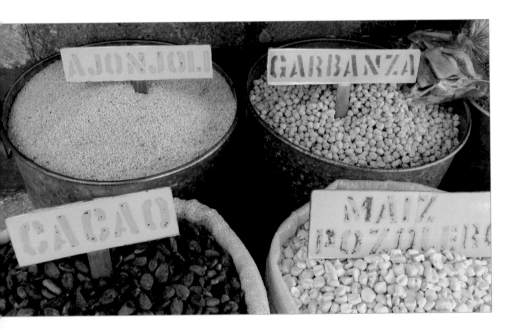

Like so many other things in Mexico, the cuisine is the result of centuries of encounters and mixings of cultures and peoples. Along with the essential staples of chilies, beans and corn, the pre-Hispanic peoples enjoyed a varied diet that included turkey, wild pig, *itzcuintli* (a plump, hairless dog), fish and iguana, as well as avocados, tomatoes, the green *tomatillos*, nopal cactus, tropical fruits like pineapple and papaya, vanilla, pumpkins, herbs and cacao.

The Spanish conquistadors and settlers, wanting to maintain their own eating habits, brought to the New World their Mediterranean-style foods with chickens, pigs and cows, cheese and wheat, olive oil and wine, citrus fruits, onions and garlic. New methods of cooking were adopted to integrate the European and native ingredients, although, for the vast majority of Mexicans, the staples of corn, beans and chilis have remained unchanged for centuries.

During the colonial period, rice and spices arrived on the galleons from China and the Philippines, and potatoes were brought from South America. Even the brief French occupation is responsible for the addition of several cakes and sweet dishes such as *crème caramel*. Over the centuries, the blending of all these different foods, methods and styles of cooking has become

PRECEDING PAGES: tomatoes and sweet potatoes piled high in Guanajuato. ABOVE: pulses and maize for sale in Oaxaca. FAR RIGHT: breakfast in Baja California.

accepted as Mexico's own cuisine, making it one of the most varied in the world.

The spice of life

Eating can be one of the chief pleasures in Mexico, where the cuisine is as varied as the country itself. Generally speaking, food in the south is much spicier than in the north. Some dishes, although native to certain regions, can be found all over Mexico, while others are found only locally. A trip to a market is the perfect way to see or sample the huge variety of unusual fruits, vegetables, chilis and other strange or exotic ingredients. Mexico City is the culinary melting pot, with many restaurants specializing in regional dishes. As in most big cities, the capital also has plenty of international cuisine as well as good vegetarian restaurants.

North to south

The characteristically simple, unspicy food of northern Mexico – usually grilled meats – is accompanied by wheat-flour rather than corn tortillas. *Cabrito* (baby goat) is the specialty in Monterrey; grilled and greasy but very tasty, it is washed down with another local favorite, cold Carta Blanca beer. But even the sparse northern cooking offers such delicacies as *caldillo*, which is as close as Mexico gets to chili con carne.

Cooking in the Central Highlands is more adventurous and includes many traditional dishes, such as *pozole*, a hearty soup made of hominy (large maize kernels) with pork or sometimes chicken. Much of the flavor of a good *pozole* lies in the extravagant garnishing of chili sauce, oregano, avocado, lettuce, onion,

radish and lime juice. Other exquisite dishes include the delicate *flor de calabaza* (squash blossom) soup, or the tacos and crêpes filled with *huitlacoche*, a blackish fungus that grows on corn and which has been savored since the days of the Aztecs. These smoky mushrooms are an acquired taste but are well worth sampling for anyone interested in true Mexican cuisine.

Chile relleno is another favorite. The large green *poblano* chili peppers are stuffed with cheese or a mixture of ground meat and spices, dipped in batter, fried and served with a tomato sauce. Chilis in Puebla are traditionally served *en nogada* – filled with meat, covered with a

CHILI PEPPERS

Chili peppers, far from being alike in taste or spiciness, are almost endless in variety, depending on the climate in which they are grown, the chemical composition of the soil and the geographical characteristics of neighboring plantings. The Aztecs and the Incas domesticated chilis about 7,000 years ago, but now these picant fruits are found all over the world, and in many kinds of cuisines.

• **Serrano** is a thin green pepper added to sauces and stews and soups for a touch of piquancy.

• **Ancho**, a full-flavored but mild and sweetish chili, is a dried version of the green Poblano, often served with a tomato sauce as *chile relleno*.

• **Chipotle** is the same variety as a jalapeño, only in this version it is first ripened, then smoked and finally dried.

• **Guajillo**, the dried version of the Mirasol chili, adds bite as well as a yellow color to dishes in which it is cooked.

• **Pequín**, known in other cultures as "cayenne," is very hot in flavor, generally exceeded only by Yucatan's Habanero, which is said to be the hottest in the world.

What to do if you find most Mexican food far too hot? If it's already in your mouth, reach for the bread, not the water. If you're ordering a meal, the key word is *picante* (spicy) not *caliente*, which means hot only in temperature.

white walnut sauce, and garnished with red pomegranate seeds, echoing the three colors of the Mexican flag. Though traditionally from Puebla, it is a common offering throughout Mexico and is often served on Independence Day, as a way of showing Mexican pride.

Puebla is the home of the famous *mole poblano*, the curiously rich sauce said to have been invented by a nun during colonial times. *Mole* is, in fact, one of the most obvious Spanish-indigenous combinations on any menu. As many as 40 ingredients go into its preparation, including chilis, spices, tortilla, nuts and even chocolate. The sauce, served with chicken or the native tur-

key and accompanied with corn tortillas and rice, is often eaten at parties or wedding feasts. Every variation of *mole* can be sampled at the yearly *mole* festival held in San Pedro Atocpán (Mexico City), including the spicier and more robust Oaxaca version of the dish, and the milder and easier to digest *piplán*, as well as *mole verde* (green *mole*), which is made with pumpkin seeds.

Almost 10,000km (6,200 miles) of coastline provides Mexico with an abundance of seafood. Two of the most popular fish dishes are *ceviche*, (raw fish marinated in lime juice and mixed with onions, chilis, tomatoes and cilantro) and *huachinango a la veracruzana*, a classic of red snapper

VERSATILE TORTILLAS

Tortillas, the thin round patties made of cornmeal or wheatflour, are the very soul of Mexican food, and they're also in peril: use of corn for ethanol has caused a huge rise in the cost of cornmeal, once the cheapest and most common tortilla. Now you will often be asked if you'd like corn or flour tortillas, or they'll choose for you depending on which is less costly. Tortillas are used as a form of bread with just about everything and are the basic ingredient of many of Mexico's wonderful *antojitos* (snacks). Here are some of the most widely available:

• *Tacos:* warm tortillas rolled around any sort of filling; *tacos al pastor* is meat rolled in a tortilla and served with chopped coriander onion and a chunk of pineapple.

• *Flautas:* tortillas rolled very tightly around chicken then fried and served topped with lettuce and cream.

• *Enchiladas:* tortillas folded around meat, cheese, or fish and covered in sauce; *enchiladas suizas* are always served with chicken, a spicy sauce, cream and cheese.

• *Quesadillas:* tortillas folded around cheese (or other fillings) and fried or cooked on a griddle.

• *Chilaquiles:* fried tortilla chips in a spicy red or green sauce, sometimes served topped with sour cream and cheese.

• *Tostados:* crispy fried tortillas spread with refried beans and topped with lettuce, chicken, tomato, onion, avocado, chili, sour cream, or any other combination.

• *Sopa de tortilla:* soup with fried tortilla strips.

with olives, capers and tomato sauce. As well as the Spanish influence, there is a strong Cuban element in the food from Veracruz, with its characteristic black beans and giant tropical *macho* banana (plantain), eaten fried. Veracruz also has the most delicious fruit in Mexico – huge pineapples, exquisite mangoes, and juicy oranges and other citrus fruits are sold at the roadside.

Oaxaca is renowned for its *mole negro* and banana-leaf tamales, which are bigger and more elaborate than the others *(see below)*. Oaxaca cheese, not unlike mozzarella, is the best kind to use in quesadillas as it melts beautifully when grilled or fried inside a tortilla.

try – both the light Montejo, and the dark and rich Negro León. *Queso relleno*, another Yucatecan specialty is, surprisingly, Dutch cheese stuffed with spicy minced meat. In comparatively recent times Lebanese immigrants have dipped their own spoon into Mexican cuisine and some of the best restaurants in Mérida offer both Yucatecan and Lebanese dishes.

Antojitos

Similar to the Spanish tapas, *antojitos* are the Mexican answer to fast food. These mouthwatering snacks or light dishes can be bought – and eaten – almost anywhere, from north to

The inspiration of cooking in the Yucatán dates back to the pre-Hispanic Maya people. Yucatecan cuisine claims such outstanding dishes as *cochinita pibil*, a sweet and spicy pork dish cooked in banana leaves, and *papadzules* (tortillas filled with egg and pumpkin seeds). Sopa de Lima, similar in many ways to Sopa Azteca of northern Mexico, is delicious – named for its use of the juice from Mexican limes. The salsas are often made with simple lime juice, tomatoes, and habanero peppers. Beer aficionados rate Yucatán's beer as the best in the coun-

south and from the best city restaurant or most elegant hacienda to the village plaza, the market, and even on the bus or train.

A whole range of Mexican food is classed as *antojitos*, from succulent corn on the cob, to tortilla chips with guacamole and the delicious *tortas*, or filled bread rolls. Tamales are also popular; these little parcels made from corn husks (or banana leaves in Oaxaca) wrapped around a cornmeal mix are stuffed with highly seasoned meat, cheese or chili sauce, and then steamed. Tamales can also be sweet, the meat replaced with strawberries, pineapple, pecan nuts or raisins. But whether it is tacos, tostadas, quesadillas or enchiladas, most *antojitos*, like Mexican food in general, rely on the tortilla. ❑

FAR LEFT: a winning *antojito* combination – guacamole, tortilla chips, and salsa. **LEFT:** shrimp fresh from the Pacific. **ABOVE:** lunch in Mérida.

ARTESANÍA

After sampling the endless variety of crafts in Mexico, your ideas of beauty and color may never be the same again

The craft tradition in Mexico dates back to long before the arrival of the Spanish, and many of the colorful and decorative *artesanías* can be traced to their pre-Hispanic origins. Often the materials and techniques have survived too, although synthetic fibers and colors have taken over much of the market and mass production is threatening some of the more laborious but infinitely more beautiful, authentic creations.

When the Spaniards came to Mexico, they found the native artisans well organized and selling their wares at great markets called *tianguis*. The Náhuatl word is still in use today, as are the pots, baskets, toys, clothes, sandals, hats, hammocks and other everyday objects made by the modern craftsmen of Mexico.

Among the profound changes wrought by the Spanish newcomers were the introduction of the wheel in pottery making and the use of metal tools. The Spaniards needed items which

Artisans often learn their craft from their parents, who have learned from their parents – the skills and techniques are traditions that span generations.

were too expensive to import from Spain: saddles and bridles, woolen weavings, furniture and other household items. So, on the heels of the conquistadors came Spanish craftsmen who

PRECEDING PAGES: natural dyed wool from Teotitlán del Valle. **LEFT:** a mask from Guerrero reflects both Spanish and indigenous influences. **RIGHT:** religious folk art in a Michoacán shop.

taught their specialties to indigenous apprentices. In 1529, a lay brother, Pedro de Gante, established an arts and crafts school in Mexico City for the indigenous, and in Michoacán Bishop Vasco de Quiroga introduced new techniques for working copper and for producing iron and lacquerware.

Changing fashions

Initially, native craftsmen were scorned and everything Spanish was considered superior. It was not until the early 20th century, with the new spirit of nationalism that arose from the Revolution, that the pendulum began to swing the other way.

In 1921, President Alvaro Obregón opened a crafts exhibition, the first such official recognition given to the native artisan. Diego Rivera, his wife Frida Kahlo, and other artists of the time praised the artisans and became collectors of their crafts. All of this hype had its effect. Indigenous handicrafts became fashionable and middle-class Mexicans started to buy them; so did visitors from the US. They still do, although the picture is not as rosy as it might seem: so many middlemen get their cut that the craftsman seldom fares well.

The majority of artisans in Mexico are peasant farmers or laborers who work at their craft

Zapata

part-time to supplement their income, and generally make objects for everyday domestic use. Then there are full-time craftsmen, who either have their own shops or work for someone who does. They fashion items that are both decorative and useful, but also supply the souvenir trade with cheap stuff that appeals to visitors. Next come those engaged in mass-production, and finally there is the unemployed city worker who lives by his wits and, with great ingenuity and skill, fashions toys and trinkets out of factory offcuts and cheap materials such as paper, tin, wire, wood and cork.

Buying crafts

Each region and, in some cases, each town or village in Mexico specializes in one or more particular craft (*see page 109*). Sometimes the same village has made the same item since pre-Hispanic times. In many state capitals there is a *Casa de las Artesanías* where you can admire and buy the particular crafts of the region, although prices may be higher than in the marketplace. Some major cities will have a Fonart shop, too – which are run by a government agency that promotes the work of craftsmen and preserves the quality of the crafts. These, or any of the better tourist shops, will provide a good overall view of what is available as well as an idea of the prices.

However, when possible, it is infinitely more interesting to buy the crafts from their region of origin. Markets all over the country are an important source of handicrafts. The daily or weekly *tianguis* usually have a few stalls selling craft items for everyday use such as pots

---

STATES OF THE ARTS

Crafts produced in villages around Oaxaca are both beautiful and collectable. Visiting these villages is easy using public transport.

• **San Bartolo Coyotepec** is known for its surprisingly light and highly polished black pottery.

• **San Martín Tilcajete** is the center for fancy, carved and brightly painted wooden animals.

• **Ocotlán de Morelos** is the home of many renowned pottery artists. Friday is market day and occasionally it is possible to find outstanding baskets.

• **Santo Tomás Jalieza** is the center of backstrap weav-

ings in the form of belts, bags, place mats and napkins, usually decorated with plant and animal designs.

• **Santa María Atzompa** is famous for intricate pottery renditions of La Virgen de la Soledad along with other raw clay figures. Much of the pottery is glazed with a green finish, which, owing to its lead content, is unsafe for cooking.

• **Teotitlán del Valle** is famous for its blankets, rugs, *serapes* and other woven goods. Motifs range from traditional geometric shapes to portraits of Che Guevara, copies of pre-Hispanic sculpture, or even of paintings by Picasso or Miró.

and baskets, while some towns have markets devoted exclusively to the crafts of that region. Often the most exciting buys of all, though, are the crafts stumbled upon on a street corner or at the roadside in the middle of nowhere.

Regional specialties

Although many of today's handicrafts combine pre-Hispanic, Spanish and contemporary influences, the majority of wonderful *obras de artesanías* are in the areas with a significant indigenous population like Michoacán, Puebla, Oaxaca, Guerrero and Chiapas.

Northern Mexico is not known for crafts, but exceptions include the ironwood animal carvings of the Seri; woolen baskest, belts and dolls of the Tarahumaras and the *serapes* (ponchos) from Coahuila and Zacatecas.

The Cora and Huichol travel to Tepic and Guadalajara to sell their woolen belts and bags, superb beadwork, embroidered clothing and yarn paintings. Tlaquepaque, a suburb of Guadalajara, is a center for ceramics – including fine copies of pre-Hispanic pieces – blown glass and furniture. The nearby town of Tonalá specializes in pottery and glass and has a large street market on Thursdays and Sundays.

The best time to buy the delicate *deshilados* (drawn threadwork) and embroidery of Aguascalientes is at the Festival de San Marcos, from April to early May each year. The silk *rebozos* (shawls) of San Luis Potosí are famed for being so fine you can slip them through a wedding ring. In the area known as La Huasteca, the native people weave the traditional white *quechquémetl* (cape for women) with cross-stitch embroidery. They also make rough and inexpensive wool bags and items out of cactus fiber.

Guanajuato has sophisticated Talavera-style pottery, while San Miguel de Allende sells *serapes*, tinware, *piñatas* (a papier-mâché figure filled with sweets and toys for fiestas and children's parties) and masks. Querétaro is famous for its semi-precious stones and silver jewelry, and in Tequisquiapan, craftsmen make baskets, folding stools, and *serapes*. It can all be bought in the colonial town of San Juan del Río. In the valley of Mezquital (Hidalgo), the Otomí use backstrap looms to weave *rebozos* (scarves or shawls

used as baby slings) and belts, while the town of Ixmiquilpan, also in Hidalgo state, is renowned for bird cages in the shape of cathedrals.

Michoacán probably has the greatest variety of crafts in all Mexico. Many of the artisans live near Lake Pátzcuaro and most of the crafts are available in Pátzcuaro town. On November 2, the Plaza Vasco de Quiroga becomes a center for craftsmen. Some artisans work year-round in the nearby Casa de los Once Patios (the House of the Eleven Patios), which used to be a convent.

Some Michoacán towns specialize in particular crafts: Santa Clara del Cobre, copperware;

FUNDACIÓN BANAMEX

The Arte Popular program, funded by the Fundación Banamex, aims to preserve and protect unique parts of Mexico's cultural heritage by identifying and supporting certain native traditions, crafts, and artwork. Masters of these arts are contacted and urged to take direct steps, such as teaching others, to ensure that the some 250 different art forms do not die out completely. Once these masters have begun to instruct others in the particular trade, publicity and exhibitions are phased in so as to promote the craft and explain its value to the world. Tourists can play a role in this process too: that souvenir you bring home may help keep that particular tradition alive.

FAR LEFT: colorful bags printed with Mexican icons.
RIGHT: hand-crafting a garment in Zacatecas.

Paracho, guitars; Tzintzuntzán, burnished ceramics; Quiroga, painted wood bowls and household items; Ihuatzio, reed mats and basketry; Patambán, exquisite green-glazed pottery; and Uruapán, masks and lacquerware. In Morelia, capital of Michoacán, some of the state's best handicrafts can be bought at the Casa de las Artesanías, located in the former Convento de San Francisco.

The state of Mexico produces warm wool serapes, colorful baskets from Lerma, and the polychrome ceramic "trees of life" in the town of Metepec. In Ixtapán de la Sal, household utensils and decorative animals are carved out

of orange-tree wood. Toluca, the state capital, is known for silverware, and also for chess and domino games made of leather, bone or wood.

The town and state of Tlaxcala, where wool was first woven in New Spain, is still a center of weaving. *Serapes* are again a specialty of the house, and hand-carved, brightly painted walking sticks are also popular.

Puebla state is one of the richest in the variety and quality of its crafts. Talavera ceramics (*see page 167*), household crockery and faïence tiles are made in the capital, while onyx is cut in Tehuacán and Tecali. The Baroque ceramic "tree of life" decorations, often seen on travel posters, are made in the town of Acatlán, especially by Herón Martínez, and in Izúcar de Matamoros, by the Flores and Castillo families. Puebla is also famed for its thick, tree-bark *amate* paper and for its textiles and traditional clothing; embroidered *huipiles* (tunics) and the wall-hangings and bead-decorated blouses of Cuetzalan and San Pablito Pahuatlán are the best examples. Reed baskets, made in Puebla, are the items most tourists buy.

To the south of Mexico City, the state of Morelos concentrates the sale of its craft production in Cuernavaca. Here, locally made, colonial-style furniture, wooden bowls, *serapes*, palm-leaf strip basketry and jewelry are for sale. The village of Hueyapan, situated in the municipality of Tetela del Volcán, produces wide, embroidered shawls.

The adjoining state of Guerrero specializes in pottery but also produces, in Olinalá, Mexico's most beautiful lacquerware: gourd bowls, trays, boxes and jaguar masks. Taxco, also in Guerrero,

RELAXING IN STYLE

If you haven't yet taken the time to lounge in one of those colorful, banana-like hammocks you've seen, you're missing out on some of the most comfy siestas around. Made from cotton, nylon, or *seda* (literally "silk" but now a mix of silk and nylon fibers), the Mexican or Mayan hammock has been around since before the conquistadors arrived. If you'll be sleeping, lie crossways; if you're napping, lengthwise. Here are some pointers if you're thinking of getting one:

• **Cotton** – Light, airy, great in dry climates; more expensive and less durable than nylon.

• **Nylon** – Brightly colored, durable, cheap; heavier and harder to dry if it gets wet.

• **Seda** – Lightest and most beautiful; often fake – buy seda hammocks only from trusted sources.

• **Single** – One person hammock, usually around $100 to $150.

• **Double** – Two people if you don't mind a squeeze, $150 to $250.

• **Family** – Two people will fit comfortably in the family-size hammock, $200 to $300.

• **Weave should be dense**, even, and there should be at least 10 edge strands (cheap hammocks will only have five to seven).

• **Look for hammocks** in Yucatán, especially Tixcocob, Campeche, Michoacán.

is famous for silverware. In the tropical southern towns Huapanec use bright, even fluorescent colors to paint stories and abstract designs on *amate* bark paper.

Over the border in Oaxaca, the Zapotec villagers make elaborate blouses with tiny flowers and miniature dolls which hold the pleats together. The blouses and wrap-around skirts of Yalalag are dyed with natural colors.

In the town of Oaxaca, artisans create exact copies of the intricately beautiful Mixtec jewelry found in the tombs of Monte Albán. The Mixtec coast of Oaxaca is known for its carrying nets, whereas Cuilapan and San Martín

The indigenous woven woolen clothing worn in the highlands of Chiapas is sold at the Sna Jolobil weavers' cooperative, in San Cristóbal de las Casas; alternatively, there are Sunday markets in San Cristóbal and most of the surrounding hill villages. The Tzotzil village of San Juan Chamula makes much of the woolen clothing sold throughout the state, as well as guitars and harps. The town of Chiapa de Corzo is known for its lacquerware, especially the masks used in the festival of San Sebastián, while Amatenango produces traditional pottery, which is fired without an oven.

The Yucatán Peninsula produces quality

Tilcajete produce wooden *animalitos* (little animals) in bright colors and assorted shapes; the village of San Bartolo Coyotepec is famous for its traditional burnished black pottery, and Santa María Atzompa makes ceramic animal figures and green glazed pottery; Teotitlán del Valle produces Mexico's best *serapes*, either in traditional pre-Hispanic designs or as copies of famous modern art paintings. Oaxaca's handicrafts can be found in the many shops and markets (where the prices are cheaper) and especially during the fiestas in December.

LEFT: painting ceramics needs a steady hand.
ABOVE: a variety of bright and cheerful handmade dolls for sale on Cerro de la Bufa, Zacatecas.

mahogany and cedar furniture as well as the county's best hammocks – made either from sisal or cotton – and the best Panama-style hats come from Becal in Campeche.

Capital crafts

Many of Mexico's wonderful crafts can be found in the capital city, which also has plenty of its own gifted jewelers and artisans. The work of the Linares family, for example, who produce fantastical figures they call *alebrijes*, has become extremely popular in recent years. But there are also the skillful and often ignored urban artisans who create art objects and toys from remnants, such as bottle caps and wire. ❏

MURALISTS

Mural painting has been Mexico's greatest contribution to contemporary art, with its origins dating back to pre-Hispanic times

tant than José Guadalupe Posada (1852–1913), whose powerful yet humorous engravings reached the very essence and vitality of Mexico's rich tradition of popular art; indeed, they represent the fullest and most penetrating view of Mexican social life in the years before the Revolution. Posada, whose skeletons were authentically Mexican (a far cry from the foreign models used by artists of his era), laid the groundwork for a whole school of artistry that was vigorous and obsessively nationalistic. The muralist movement remained close to the folk tradition – the so-called *Mexicanidad* – of Posada's wonderful, popular engravings.

The first murals

In 1921, members of President Alvaro Obregón's new cabinet were keen to spread awareness of Mexico's history and culture. None more so than the radical education minister José Vasconcelos, who commissioned murals for the walls of a number of centrally located public buildings. And so the Mexican *Muralismo* movement began and Diego Rivera (1886–1957) painted his first mural at the Escuela Nacional Preparatoria in Mexico City.

Dramatic artworks adorn the walls of public buildings all over Mexico. Murals have been painted in Mexico since pre-Hispanic times although many, such as those at Bonampak *(see page 297)* and Cacaxtla *(see page 170)*, have only recently been discovered by historians and archeologists.

The explosive murals of the post-Revolution were a new departure; the works of Diego Rivera, David Alfaro Siqueiros and José Clemente Orozco were to become the most powerful visual expression of the emerging modern Mexico, and were to astound the world.

Of the Mexican artists who influenced *Los Tres Grandes* (the three great Mexican muralists), none appears to have been more impor-

Rivera was a contradictory painter who aroused deep feelings and controversy. Though an ideologist (he was a Communist, but was expelled from the party), his work is less political than sensual in style, in the tradition of Paul Gauguin, Henri Rousseau and even Pieter Brueghel the Elder. Rivera's formative artistic influences were by no means exclusively Mexican. In Europe, he had been in touch with avant-garde movements, and the influence of Cubism is apparent in much of his work from that period. However, as a result of the Russian

Revolution, and his stated belief in "the need for a popular and socialized art," Rivera distanced himself from the Cubists and sought a more direct and functional artistic style. It is often said that the most important influence on Rivera was not contemporary at all, but came from the frescoes and paintings of the Italian Renaissance. In

The majority of the most famous murals can be seen in Mexico City, although Orozco's finest works were made in Guadalajara, and others in the US.

draftsman and watercolor artist, he created an idealized and sentimental image of a primitive Mexico, inhabited by brown-skinned girls and dreamy children carrying huge bouquets of exotic flowers.

Rivera himself was a colorful character, a constant source of gossip who loved to shock. One of his works, entitled *Dream of a Sunday Afternoon in Alameda Park*, originally flaunted the words *Dios no existe* (God does not exist), causing such an uproar among Catholics and Church authorities that they had to be removed from exhibition and were expunged (Museo Mural Diego Rivera – *see page 142*).

fact, Uccello's *La Battaglia di San Romano* is said to have been one of the most important influences on Mexican mural painting.

Notwithstanding all these European influences, Rivera acknowledged his debt to José Guadalupe Posada by including the engraver's portrait in some of his most important murals. Rivera was deeply Mexican in his love of color and soft shapes, and in his strong identification with the Mexican native; he was also profoundly influenced by pre-Hispanic architectural form and sculpture. An excellent

PRECEDING PAGES AND LEFT: details from Rivera's *Dream of a Sunday Afternoon in Almeda Park* and *Mexico Through the Centuries*. ABOVE: Siqueiros' self-portrait.

The ideologue

David Alfaro Siqueiros (1899–1974), like Rivera, continued his training in Europe. Unlike Rivera, he had been a combatant in the Mexican Revolution; he was a strong man of action, a political activist who volunteered for the Spanish Civil War, took part in labor struggles, was involved in a failed attempt to assassinate Leon Trotsky, and was imprisoned several times. His paintings reflect his ideological drive, his taste for bold action, even for violence. Massive and muscular, they become a kind of imprisoned sculpture.

Siqueiros experimented with a combination of painting and sculpture which he called *esculto-pintura*. A great innovator, Siqueiros was constantly trying new materials and techniques. Perhaps his best murals are in Mexico City's Chapultepec Castle *(see page 145)*, which offer a powerful interpretation of Mexican history. At the Palacio de Bellas Artes *(see page 140)* are displayed the best of his easel paintings, but he is best known for the vast, three-dimensional mural in the city's Poliforum Cultural Siqueiros *(see page 151)*.

The satirist

José Clemente Orozco (1883–1949), a tragic and passionate artist, is often considered the best of the big three. He was a political skeptic, a bit-

ing satirist, but also an idealist who was deeply disturbed by the sordidness of history. Orozco used the mural to convey his troubled feelings; his message transcends the national picture and can be understood by everyone. He has been compared to such German artists as Max Beckmann, Otto Dix, and Käthe Kollwitz. Orozco, always an outspoken man, denounced the tendency to convert the Mexican Revolution into a bloody farce that would result in new servitude for the masses.

The first important Orozco mural was painted in the early 1920s at the Escuela Nacional Preparatoria *(see page 138)*. Stark and simple, it showed some influence from early Italian Renaissance painting. At the Escuela

Preparatoria, Orozco does achieve moments of grandeur, especially in *The Trench*, a powerful image of war and human struggle. On the staircase of the same building, he painted *Cortés y la Malinche*, depicting the naked bodies of the Spanish conquistador and Malintzin, his native guide, interpreter and mistress. The painting makes a clear statement about the relationship between Spain and Mexico, between conqueror and conquered, a theme to which Orozco returned many times.

From 1927 to 1934, Orozco lived in the US and painted murals for Pomona College, California, the New York School for Social Research and Dartmouth College, New Hampshire. He described the cultural life of the times in his bitter autobiography, and in letters to his friend and fellow artist Jean Charlot.

Back in Mexico, at the Palacio de Bellas Artes, Orozco painted *Catharsis*, whose central figure is a colossal prostitute, the symbol of corruption. Orozco produced many paintings, drawings and watercolors on the subject of prostitution, viewing the brothel as a place of ultimate horror.

Orozco's greatest works were produced in the late 1930s in Guadalajara – in the Palacio de Gobierno *(see page 234)*, the University *(see page 236)* and on the walls and ceilings of the Hospicio Cabañas *(see page 235)*. Here he is at the peak of his power, covering straight and curved surfaces with fiery reds and stark blacks, paying homage to Padre Hidalgo, denouncing political manipulation and searching for deep and universal symbols.

Other muralists

Jean Charlot (1898–1979) was born in Paris and is another of the early muralists. His *Massacre in the Main Temple*, a mural completed in 1923 on the stairway of the west court of the Escuela Nacional Preparatoria in Mexico City, is generally regarded as the first fresco painted in Mexico since colonial times. Before his move to Hawaii, Charlot painted in the US, where he helped, with his art, but most of all with his writings, to popularize mural painting during Franklin D. Roosevelt's early years as president.

Juan O'Gorman, a painter and architect of Irish ancestry born in Mexico, transformed the mural into a kind of panorama of miniature scenes. Although they are modern, his paintings are anchored in Mexico's 19th-century popular art. He is famous chiefly for the murals decorating the Biblioteca Central (Central Library) of Mexico City's Ciudad Universitaria *(see page 154)*. Constructed with colored stone, these giant mosaic-murals describe the culture of the world in a Baroque texture that is surprisingly innocent and fresh.

There had grown up a second generation of muralists, one of whom was Rufino Tamayo, a Zapotec from Oaxaca who died in 1991 at the age of 92. Never political, Tamayo soon abandoned realism for poetically simplified forms. His decorative murals deal with cosmic and domestic sym-

Contemporary murals

The Mexican muralist movement sprang out of the Revolution and, in reality, that emotion is gone and done with. In the second half of the 20th century, the new generations of muralists reacted against the movement that they accused of being too obviously didactic and obsessively nationalistic. But disciples of the great muralists continue to cover the walls of public buildings throughout the country. Visitors will be well-served by meandering the grounds of Mexico City's UNAM (Universidad Nacional Autónoma de México), where many of the buildings display stunning murals for all to see. ❑

bology (stars, cats, women) and are indifferent to the direct interpretation of history.

Zacatecas-born artist Pedro Coronel (1922–85) explored much the same ground as Tamayo. His murals are perhaps the best of those painted in recent years. Other mainstream Mexican muralists, whose work is never far removed from realism, include Fernando Leal, Xavier Guerrero, José Chávez Morado, Roberto Montenegro, Raúl Anguiano, Manuel Rodríguez Lozano, Alfredo Zalce and Jorge González Camarena.

LEFT: Orozco's portrait of Hidalgo, Guadalajara.
ABOVE: detail from *Niña atacada por un pájaro extraño* (Girl attacked by a strange bird), by Rufino Tamayo.

FRANCISCO TOLEDO

Francisco Toledo – probably Mexico's greatest living painter – has produced numerous important pieces during his lifetime. Born in Oaxaca where he trained as a graphic artist, Toledo was instrumental in regenerating the art scene in his home state after returning to Mexico from Paris, where he spent a formative part of his artistic career. His works are prolific and include oil paintings, charcoal drawings and assemblages composed of seashells, textiles, crushed eggshells, and household objects. He was awarded the Mexican National Prize in 1998 and the Right Livelihood Award in 2005.

PLACES

Step-by-step through Mexico from the Río Grande
to the Yucatán, with cross-references to a
comprehensive series of maps

There's no way to see all Mexico on one vacation. Not only is it far too big, it's also too diverse. Consider just a few highlights: the world's most remarkable train ride through the Copper Canyon from Chihuahua to the Pacific, bigger even than the Grand Canyon; tumultuous Mexico City and the ancient pyramids of Teotihuacán; the Maya ruins of the south, and the coral reefs off the Riviera Maya.

From the arid deserts of Baja California to the mountains of Chiapas, and from the northern border to the mangrove lagoons of the Yucatán and the turquoise waters off Cancún, Mexico has 9,650km (6,000 miles) of coastline. Nearly half the country is more than 1,500 meters (5,000ft) above sea level, and mountain ranges are dotted with still-smoking volcanoes. Mexico's rugged mountain landscapes are breathtaking; its waters – from the Sea of Cortés in the northwest to the Caribbean – are filled with spectacular marine life.

The most practical plan is to settle for one region per visit and explore it thoroughly. Or concentrate on one theme – colonial architecture, Maya ruins, wildlife. If you want to be more adventurous, possibilities include mountain trekking and white-water rafting, as well as some of the world's best diving.

And Mexico is a year-round destination. The entire Pacific coast, including the giant Baja Peninsula, is bathed in sunshine for at least three-quarters of the year, and even in the tropical south the summer rains conveniently fall mostly in the afternoons, often leaving the rest of the day clear and sunny. Many of the beautiful colonial cities of the Central Highlands such as San Miguel de Allende, Guanajuato or Morelia may feel a little chilly at night in mid-winter, but in compensation the air is wonderfully crisp and fresh, and moderate temperatures even on the hottest days of the year provide an ideal setting for exploration. In the sultry Yucatán, winter months are generally the best time to scramble over Maya pyramids, but the powdery soft white beaches of Tulum or Cozumel beckon irresistibly at any time. ❏

PRECEDING PAGES: Popocatépetl looms above the cornfields; riding a Pacific wave; Campeche's Iglesia Dulce Nombre de Jesús. FAR LEFT: dome of the Church of Santa María, Guadalajara. FROM TOP: Presidencia Municipal, Guadalajara; folk dancers.

Mexico

0 ___ 200 km
0 ___ 200 miles

1 Aguascalientes
2 Distrito Federal
3 Colima
4 Morelos
5 Tlaxcala

MEXICO CITY AND ITS SURROUNDINGS

An overview of the giant capital and its surrounding region, Mexico's teeming, sometimes overwhelming but always fascinating core

Commonly referred to by Mexicans simply as México, the Distrito Federal (Federal District) or just the DF (De-efe), Mexico City is one of the most populous places on earth – the city proper officially had 8,836,045 inhabitants in 2008, but the whole Zona Metropolitana or Greater Mexico City area has close to 20 million, a fifth of Mexico's population. At 2,250 meters (7,380ft) above sea level, it is also one of the world's highest cities – new arrivals may feel a little tired and short of breath – and, despite big steps taken to improve air quality, still heavily polluted. *DF*-lovers get used to occasional coughs and stinging eyes, but visitors may prefer to avoid the busiest areas at peak times.

Many beach lovers choose to fly directly to Cancún or the Pacific resorts, but Mexico City is the first stop for anyone wishing to explore the center of the country, and an essential transport hub, with connections to every part of Mexico. It is also fascinating in itself, and far less forbidding than its size and reputation can suggest. There are plenty of calm corners among the giant avenues, and superb museums. For anyone planning to visit any of Mexico's pre-Hispanic sites, a few hours browsing through the magnificent Museo de Antropología is a must.

Most of Mexico City's major sights are in a central area that stretches west from the Zócalo (main square) to Chapultepec Park, with the anthropology museum. North and south of the park are the fashionable districts of Polanco, Roma and Condesa, with many of the best restaurants and most stylish nightlife. Further south are the charming old *colonias* (neighborhoods) of San Angel and Coyoacán, with their Bohemian feel and memories of Diego Rivera and Frida Kahlo, and the floating gardens of Xochimilco.

Mexico City makes a base for all kinds of day and weekend excursions: to pre-Hispanic ruins at Teotihuacán and Tula, colonial towns, and Baroque churches in sleepy villages; or to shop for silver in Taxco, relax at spa resorts in the lush hills of Morelos or sail on a mountain lake at Valle de Bravo. ❑

FAR LEFT: Palacio de Bellas Artes. **FROM TOP**: a view of Pirámide del Sol, Teotihuacán; interior of Palacio Central, Mexico City; *chacmool* figure at Templo Mayor.

MEXICO CITY

The statistics of Mexico's capital often beggar the imagination, but there's a wealth of life and spectacular attractions within its sometimes crazy urban fabric

México City

The vast megalopolis of Mexico City is a love it *and* loathe it kind of place. Much of the nation's wealth and power is concentrated here, and the finest in music and the arts. If Mexico is the country of surprises and contradictions *par excellence*, then most of them can be found here, all jumbled up together within its vast capital: stylish modernity next to ancient, apparently bizarre traditions, grand monuments beside sprawling markets, hectic highways a few steps from placid squares. It is a huge, exciting, unpredictable city, full of discoveries, where people are friendly and adventure seems to linger on every street corner. Being one of the largest and most populous cities in the world naturally has its disadvantages too: traffic congestion and pollution can be appalling, and the petty crime of pickpockets and thieves is rife *(for some security tips ` page 134)*. Like any giant city, it is a place you need to adapt to, but, pace yourself, work out how to walk around its multilane traffic junctions, and when to find a place to sit and let the crowds pass by, and its multicolored verve becomes richly enjoyable.

The Historic Center: along Calle Madero

The Centro Histórico or old town corresponds roughly to the old colonial capital, centered like all the cities of Spanish America around a main square, the giant Zócalo, which was built on top of the former center of the Aztec capital Tenochtitlán. A great way to begin a tour is with breakfast at the charming **Casa de los Azulejos ❶** or "House of Tiles" between calles Madero and 5 de Mayo. First built in the late 16th century, it was extensively rebuilt in the 1730s for the Condesa del Valle de Orizaba, with ornate carvings and facades covered in blue and white Puebla tiles, and is one of the best-

Main attractions
THE ZÓCALO
CATEDRAL METROPOLITANA
TEMPLO MAYOR
PALACIO NACIONAL
ANTIGUO COLEGIO DE SAN ILDEFONSO
PLAZA GARIBALDI
LA ALAMEDA
PALACIO DE BELLAS ARTES
CASTILLO DE CHAPULTEPEC
MUSEO NACIONAL DE ANTROPOLOGÍA
MUSEO-ESTUDIO DIEGO RIVERA
MUSEO FRIDA KAHLO
XOCHIMILCO

LEFT: the view from Torre Latinoamericana.
RIGHT: children phoning home.

preserved of Mexico City's colonial mansions. Since 1917 it has housed the flagship branch of Sanborns restaurant. Californian brothers Frank and Walter Sanborn created a sensation when they opened their first American-style soda fountain, café and drugstore in Mexico City in 1903, and Sanborns – long-since Mexican-owned – has become an institution, with branches all over the city and the country. In the days of the Revolution the ragged soldiers of Pancho Villa and Emiliano Zapata were famously photographed sampling unfamiliar luxuries at an earlier Sanborns, just along Calle Madero on the site now taken by the Librería Madero, one of Mexico City's best bookstores.

The glass-roofed patio is the most striking part of the Casa de los Azulejos, with a mural on the staircase by José Clemente Orozco *(see page 116)*, titled *Omnisciencia* (Omniscience). The traditionally dressed waitresses are quietly attentive, and a while spent observing the regulars, many of whom seem to have been coming here for decades, is a fine introduction to Mexico City life by itself.

Opposite Sanborns, the **Torre Latinoamericana** ❷ (daily 9am–11pm; charge) was, in 1956, Mexico's first skyscraper. The panoramic views from the 44th-floor observation platform and its cafés (on the 42nd, 43rd, and 44th floors) are clearest at night. There is a small museum of the building's history on the 37th floor, and even an aquarium on the 38th. Below, busy **Calle Francisco Madero** leads east to the Zócalo. Its landmarks include the sinking church of **San Francisco** ❸, once part of a Franciscan monastery founded by Cortés himself three years after the Conquest, in 1524. Most of the structure, including the stone portal and Churrigueresque facade, is 18th-century.

The heavily adorned baroque **Palacio de Iturbide** ❹, built as an aristocratic residence in the 1780s, is so-named because "Emperor" Agustín

Detail on the facade of the cathedral.

BELOW: the cathedral provides a dramatic backdrop for an Aztec dance performance in the Zócalo.

The Sinking City

Walking around the old center of Mexico City it is possible to feel a little dizzy, and not just because of pollution. Some streets don't look quite right, their sidewalks seem to buckle. You haven't been drinking: many buildings *do* lean at weird angles, especially the massive Spanish stone palaces and churches. They have been quietly sinking for centuries.

Aztec Tenochtitlán was built on a low island in the shallow Lake Texcoco. The Spaniards cut down many trees around the Valley of Mexico, causing most of the lake to silt up. This led to catastrophic flooding at times of heavy rain, a problem solved by building giant drains and aqueducts, from the 1600s to the early 1900s, to take the water away. As the natural water was drained away, however, Mexico City's subsoil got more and more powdery, and softer and softer. Subsidence became especially acute when added to the effects of the 1985 earthquake. The cathedral, especially, was on the verge of collapse. Raising the worst-affected part, the apse, was impossible, so the emergency rescue program actually involved taking away soil from beneath the main facade to lower it, so that the whole building would at least be relatively level. The cathedral was declared out of danger in 2000. It was first built on a platform above the Zócalo; it is now several feet below it.

TIP

The basic security precautions here are the same as in any big city – with perhaps a little extra alertness. Keep cameras and jewelry out of sight, never leave bags on the floor or the back of a chair in restaurants or cafés, and always keep a hold of your possessions, especially on buses and the metro. If you need a taxi, try to use an authorized *sitio* one (based at a taxi rank, which can be phoned). Avoid dimly lit, empty streets at night. Only use ATMs in safer areas, and never after dark.

BELOW: military parade at the flag lowering ceremony in the Zócalo.

de Iturbide briefly made it his palace in 1821. It is now owned by the Banamex cultural foundation, and as the **Palacio de Cultura Banamex** (daily 10am–7pm; free) hosts wide-ranging art exhibitions in its sumptuously restored rooms.

Nearing the Zócalo, the somber **Templo de la Profesa** has sunk considerably since it was built in the 1720s. Across the same intersection is a brighter attraction, the **Museo del Estanquillo ❺** (Wed–Mon 10am–6pm; free), with thousands of old postcards, photos, calendars, paper Day of the Dead dioramas and other Mexican ephemera from the personal collection of author Carlos Monsiváis (an *estanquillo* is the kind of stall where such things were sold). It is in a lovely 19th-century building, and the roof terrace café has a great view. A brief detour one block down Avenida Isabel la Católica from there to the corner of Calle 16 de Septiembre will take you to another idiosyncratic corner, the **Bazar de Fotografía Casasola** (Av. Isabel la Católica 45; Mon–Fri 9.30am–7.30pm, Sat 10.30am–3.30pm). Agustín Victor

Casasola was a pioneer of Mexican photography, and took many of the iconic images of the Revolution (including those of the revolutionaries in Sanborns; *see page 67*). His main archive is now in a museum in Puebla, but the fourth generation of his family still run a photo "bazaar," where you can browse through vast stocks of fascinating pictures or even pose for a souvenir photo dressed as a revolutionary.

Around the Zócalo

Once the ceremonial center of Aztec Tenochtitlán, with pyramids, palaces and wide-open spaces, the **Zócalo** has been transformed many times. The second-largest city square in the world (beaten only by Red Square in Moscow), over the years it has housed executions, markets, palm trees and a tram terminal. Today the center is free of trees or permanent structures except for the pole that supports what is said to be the world's biggest flag. The hub of the city – and at times the whole country – throughout its history, the Zócalo is used for many official ceremonies, but also hosts massive rallies, protests, and concerts and performances. At any time there is nearly always some kind of political demonstration somewhere on the square, as well as "Aztec" folk dancers and other street performers. The best view of the Zócalo is from the rooftop restaurant of the **Hotel Majestic** (entrance on Madero), and photographs and models of how the square used to be can be seen in Zócalo metro station. The west side of the square is filled by long colonnaded buildings known as the **Portal de Mercaderes**, which have housed jewelers since colonial times.

Filling the block on this side of the Zócalo north of Calle 5 de Mayo, the **Nacional Monte de Piedad** ❻ is an enormous pawnshop and loan bank, founded in 1775. Run as a charity, it has become an important part of local life, especially at holiday time, when people queue up to hock their possessions.

The vast, towering **Catedral Metropolitana** ❼, is an encyclopedia of Mexican colonial art. The building took around three centuries to complete, beginning in Spanish Renaissance style and finishing in the neoclassical style of the early 19th century. Most of the lower walls were built between the 1570s and the 1650s; the upper portion of the elegant facade and the unusual bell towers were added in the 1790s by the Mexican-born José Damián Ortiz de Castro, and the dome and the clock were finally finished by the Spanish neoclassical architect Manuel Tolsá in 1813.

Huge and impressive, the cathedral's somber but magnificent interior is illuminated through contemporary stained-glass windows that give a mellow, golden light. The 100-meter (328ft) long and 46-meter (151ft) wide interior is divided into five naves. Close to the main entrance, the **Altar del Perdón** (Altar of Forgiveness) with its huge altarpiece was the work of the 17th-century architect and sculptor Jerónimo de Balbas. Both the altar and the adjacent choir, with its intricately carved stalls, were severely damaged by fire in 1967 but have been restored.

Dominating the view at the end of the central nave is the magnificent **Altar de los Reyes** (Kings' Altar) –

EAT

One of the most atmospheric places to eat and drink in the center is the Cantina La Opera, at the corner of Calle 5 de Mayo and Calle Filomena Mata, opened in 1876. The gleaming wood and velvet decor is magnificent, and the story goes that Pancho Villa once shot a hole in the ceiling.

BELOW:
pedi taxis in front of the cathedral.

Danzón in the street.

BELOW: Diego
Rivera's mural
depicting life before
the Conquest,
Palacio National.

also by Jerónimo de Balbas – one of the masterpieces of the elaborate, ultra-Baroque, Churrigueresque style (*see page 58*). Completed in 1737, the altar is drenched in gilt carvings, moldings, angels, saints and cherubim. In the center, two paintings represent the Assumption of the Virgin and the Adoration of the Magi. A massive engineering program has put a halt to the subsidence that long threatened the cathedral with collapse (*see box page 133*), but the strange angles of its walls and giant columns, and the slope of the floor, stand out to any visitor. Monitors around the cathedral check constantly on the state of the building, and a giant pendulum hanging down in the middle allows you to verify just how off-level it is.

The cathedral's neighbor the **Sagrario Metropolitano** ❽ is in fact an entirely separate church, built in 1740–68. It has the most extravagant of all Churrigueresque facades, an explosion of red and white stone. The Sagrario had a special subsidence problem of its own, in that the sinking of the cathedral was pulling it

down, and it has only been possible to stabilize the building by separating it from the cathedral wall against which it was built. Hence it has only recently been reopened to worshippers and visitors. Just in front of the cathedral and the Sagrario, glass panels in the pavement allow you to see remains of the Temple of the Sun of Tenochtitlán, on the site on which both were built.

Ruins of Tenochtitlán

The **Templo Mayor** ❾ (Tue–Sun 9am–5pm; charge) in the northeast corner of the Zócalo stood at the center of the Aztec universe, the exact spot where the eagle was sighted on the cactus (*see page 41*). Today it is the largest surviving relic of Tenochtitlán. Remarkably, its existence was virtually unknown until 1978, when electricity workers laying cables chanced upon the 8-ton stone disc of Coyolxauhqui, Goddess of the Moon, showing her dismembered body after her defeat by her brother the Sun God Huitzilopochtli. Excavations began soon afterwards, and revealed the structure of the great pyramid and many other treasures. The pyramid was divided into two, with temples at the top dedicated to Huitzilopochtli and Tlaloc, God of Water. A pathway round the site reveals the multiple levels of construction. The beautifully designed **museum** exhibits artifacts found here, including the original Coyolxauhqui stone, and helpful models of what Tenochtitlán and the Templo Mayor looked like before the Conquest.

Looming up along the Zócalo's east side is the **Palacio Nacional** ❿ (daily 10am–5pm; free), built on the site of Moctezuma's palace and the official seat of power in Mexico, although nowadays the president generally only comes here on ceremonial occasions. The Baroque heart of the palace was begun in 1562, but it has been added to and altered countless times. As well as government offices, preserved within the giant building are Mexico's first Congress chamber and the office of revered President Benito Juárez, but most visitors come to admire the astonishing murals by Diego Rivera *(see pages 114–15)* that adorn the main staircase and first-floor gallery. Painted between 1929 and 1935, they dramatically illustrate the history of Mexico, from an idealized pre-Hispanic past through the horrors of the Conquest to Independence and the 1910 Revolution, with Karl Marx and Zapata pointing to the future.

On the night of September 15, the president of Mexico appears on the balcony of the palacio to ring the bell with which Hidalgo summoned the people of Dolores *(see page 56)*, thus starting the War of Independence. *El Grito* (The Shout) is a short but emotional ceremony.

Behind the Palacio along Calle Moneda, the **Museo Nacional de Las Culturas** ⓫ (Tue–Sun 9.30am–6pm; free), occupies an impressive edifice first built as the colonial mint (*La Moneda*, or the House of Money), with a flower-filled patio around a fountain. The collection itself is less special, with

anthropological artifacts from around the world.

South of the Zócalo

One block south of the Zócalo down Calle 20 de Noviembre, the **Palacio de Hierro** department store is worth visiting just to see one of the most gorgeous stained-glass ceilings in existence. Nearby on Calle Pino Suárez, the **Museo de la Ciudad de México** ⓬ (Tue–Sun 10am–5.30pm; charge), in the magnificent colonial palace of the counts of Santiago de Calimaya, provides an excellent overview of the history of the city from prehistoric origins to contemporary problems.

Across the street is the fort-like **Hospital de Jesús** ⓭, established in 1524 by Hernán Cortés himself. It is the oldest hospital in the New World, and said to be located at the very spot where Cortés first met Moctezuma. The

*Making the most
of a visit to the
Aztec site
of Templo Mayor.*

Marketing

Every neighborhood in Mexico City has a market of some kind. A Mexican city market is an immense warren of activity, with an overpowering variety of sounds and smells: chickens frying, radios blaring, men with loudspeakers peddling unusual remedies alongside girls heating fresh *tortillas* and exuberant heaps of pineapples, cactus leaves, and chilies. Every kind of human need is catered for.

One of the largest central markets is the **Mercado de la Merced**, near Merced metro station. A couple of blocks south is **Mercado de Sonora**, famed for its arrays of medicinal herbs and the alleged witch doctors who sell them. One of the most famous markets is **La Lagunilla**, north of Plaza de Garibaldi. During the week it is another general market, with a huge, noisy food section and another where you can look over embroidered *charro* hats, children's party dresses and all sorts of other gaudy or useful things, including pirated DVDs and other electronics. On Sundays, the Lagunilla becomes a massive **flea market**, with hundreds of stalls selling treasures, trash and anything in between. Note that this is a place to be on your guard for pickpockets.

aggressively plain facade on Pino Suárez is part of a modern addition: walk through it to reach the lovely 16th-century patio and the hospital church. The remains of Cortés are in a tomb beside the altar, and the vaulted ceiling is decorated with a mural on *The Apocalypse* by Orozco *(see page 116)*.

North of the Zócalo

The bustling streets north of the Zócalo, the university area before the vast modern campus was built in the south of the city, house a fascinating mix of museums and other attractions. Right behind the Templo Mayor, the former church of Santa Teresa has been turned into **Ex-Teresa Arte Actual** (daily 10am–6pm; free), a hip contemporary arts center. Two blocks away, **Museo José Luis Cuevas** ⓮ (Tue–Sun 10am–6pm; charge), founded by one of Mexico's best-known living artists, has a wide-ranging collection of mostly Latin American contemporary art, including a *Sala de Erótica*, and presents many temporary shows.

Just across Calle Justo Sierra from the Templo Mayor is one of the area's prime sights, the **Antiguo Colegio de San Ildefonso** ⓯ (Tue 10am–7.30pm, Wed–Sun 10am–5.30pm; charge, free on Tue), also known as the Escuela Nacional Preparatoria (National Preparatory School), where some of the most dramatic revolutionary-era murals cover three floors around the patios of a former Jesuit college. The main work here is by Orozco, but Siqueiros, Rivera and others also feature *(see pages 114–17)*. San Ildefonso also hosts important temporary exhibits. On the next block west is the **Museo de la Caricatura** ⓰ (Mon–Fri 10am–6pm, Sat–Sun 10am–5pm; charge), in the 18th-century former Colegio de Cristo. The Cartoon Museum engagingly covers the history of Mexican cartoons and related arts since Independence.

Some of the finest of Diego Rivera's work is two blocks north in the twin patios of the **Secretaría de Educación Pública** ⓱ (Education Ministry; Mon–Fri 9am–5pm; free), painted between 1923 and 1928 with more than 120 mural panels on Mexican life, history and the Revolution. Outside is an

BELOW: printers and stationers on Plaza Santo Domingo.

immense statue of José Vasconcelos, the revolutionary education minister who commissioned many of Mexico City's murals. The Secretaría can sometimes, rather unpredictably, be closed to visitors for official reasons.

Delightful **Plaza Santo Domingo** ⓲ is one of the most traditional in the capital. Under the colonnade on the west side, the **Portal de los Evangelistas**, public scribes known as *evangelistas*, who used to write letters for the illiterate, today mainly fill out government forms on ancient typewriters. Street printers with old-fashioned hand-presses also vie for trade. At the north end of the plaza is the beautiful Baroque **Iglesia de Santo Domingo**, while across the road is the **Palacio de la Inquisición**, once the local headquarters of the dreaded institution, but now the **Museo de la Medicina Mexicana** (daily 9am–6pm; free). Behind Santo Domingo, the remains of its former monastery have been turned into another striking new contemporary arts center, the **Centro Cultural del México Contemporáneo** (Tue–Sun 10am–6pm; free). By way of con-

trast, close by is a noisier cultural hub, the **Arena Coliseo**, the number one venue for *Lucha Libre*, the crazy Mexican style of wrestling. Wrestlers, usually masked and with bizarre names, have cult status, and fights attract huge, raucous crowds.

If the Coliseo is Mexico City's wrestling center, a few blocks to the west in **Plaza de Garibaldi** ⓳ is the traditional home of its *mariachis*, where costumed musicians stand around with their instruments until someone pays them for a song, or hires them for a wedding or a party. With *mariachis*, *jarochos* and other musicians playing all day long, this is one of the most characterful parts of the city, but since it is also Mexico City's foremost tourist trap it's also a place to visit with care. Many of the restaurants around the plaza have a bad reputation for exaggerated prices and scams such as unannounced *cubiertos* (cover charges), and it has a higher-than-average number of pickpockets. The atmosphere is fine during the day, but it is best not to wander around the main plaza at night.

The gallants of this city shew themselves daily, some on horseback, and most in coaches, about four o'clock in the afternoon in a pleasant shady field called La Alameda… where do meet as constantly as the merchants upon our exchange about 2,000 coaches, full of gallants, ladies, and citizens, to see and be seen, to court and to be courted.

English traveler Thomas Gage, who visited Mexico City in 1625.

BELOW: open-air audition in Plaza Garibaldi.

Carlos IV on the well-traveled El Caballito statue.

Around the Alameda

In early colonial times, the stretch of open land west of the old center known as **La Alameda** ⑳ was both a site for the burning of heretics and, according to the Englishman Thomas Gage, who visited in 1625, a place where local "gallants" showed themselves off on horseback to young ladies driving by in their carriages. Around 1700 a reforming viceroy began to make it more orderly, and in the 19th century it was transformed into a romantic park full of trees, fountains, sculptures, and the inevitable bandstand. It is a welcome refuge in the noisy and chaotic capital. Among the park's monuments is the **Hemiciclo de Juárez**, a tribute, in white Italian marble, to the great president; a statue of Beethoven; and two women, also in marble, called, in French, *Malgré Tout* (In Spite of Everything) by Jesús F. Contreras and *Désespoir* (Despair) by Agustín Ocampo.

At the east end of the Alameda is the huge and extravagant **Palacio de Bellas Artes** ㉑ (Palace of Fine Arts; Tue–Sun 10am–6pm; free except for special exhibits), commissioned by Porfirio Díaz in 1905. The original design was by Italian architect Adamo Boari, but building was interrupted by the Revolution and it was finished 30 years later by the Mexican architect Federico Mariscal. This time-lapse helps to explain the blend of styles: the Italian marble exterior is a combination of neoclassical with Art Nouveau, full of flying sculpture and florid decoration, while the interior is a sort of Aztec Art Deco. The structure is so massive and heavy that it has sunk noticeably.

Its four auditoria and other rooms are used for concerts, dance performances, and art exhibitions, and the building has yet more fine murals. Most notable is Diego Rivera's replica of a controversial mural commissioned in 1934 for the Rockefeller Center in New York; the subject matter was deemed too left-wing, and the original was destroyed. There are also other works by Rivera, in addition to murals by Orozco, Siqueiros, O'Gorman and Tamayo. The stained-glass mosaic curtain, designed by Gerardo Murillo, "*Dr Atl*," was made by Tiffany of New York. Showing the volcanoes Popocatépetl and Iztaccíhuatl, it is a masterpiece of high-class kitsch, and is lit up for public viewing on Sunday mornings and before evening performances.

Behind Bellas Artes is the almost equally elaborate Venetian-style **Palacio Postal** (Central Post Office), also by Adamo Boari. Nearby, on a small plaza at the western end of Calle Tacuba, is a well-loved monument, **El Caballito** (The Little Horse). This statue, which is not little at all, depicts the Spanish king Carlos IV on horseback. Sculpted by Manuel Tolsá in 1803, El Caballito has galloped all over Mexico City in search of a home; at different times it has adorned the Zócalo, the old university patio, and the busy Reforma–Juárez crossroads, where increasing traffic meant it became a nuisance, until in 1979 it was moved to this square, renamed Plaza Manuel Tolsá in its creator's honor. Across the street is the **Palacio de Minería** ㉒ (Wed–Sun 10am–6pm; free), also by Tolsá and one of the best neoclassical buildings in Mexico. Behind the statue on the plaza is the **Museo Nacional de Arte** ㉓ or MUNAL (Tue–Sun 10.30am–5.30pm; charge, free on Sun). Occupying a beautifully restored neoclassical edifice built as a government ministry in 1904–11, it displays a comprehensive collection of paintings, sculptures and graphics tracing the history of Mexican art from pre-Hispanic times to the mid-20th century, with interesting 19th-century landscapes as well as the better-known modern Mexican artists.

Tilting churches and moving murals

Avenida Hidalgo runs along the north side of the Alameda. Two small colonial churches face tiny, peaceful **Plaza de la** **Santa Veracruz**, which preserves some of the atmosphere of old Mexico City. Next door to the severely tilting Templo de San Juan de Dios, in a beautifully restored 16th-century hospital, is the remarkable **Museo Franz Mayer** ㉔ (Tue–Sun 10am–5pm; charge).

A German-born financier who moved to Mexico in 1905, Mayer assembled a fantastically rich collection of paintings, furniture, ceramics, rugs, silverware and every other kind of applied art from around the world. The 10,000-piece collection is beautifully exhibited in rooms around a garden courtyard, and the Cafetería del Claustro adds to its charm.

The **Museo Nacional de la Estampa** (Tue–Sun 10am–6pm; charge, free on Sun), on the same plaza, specializes in graphic arts, with a superb collection of the work of José Guadalupe Posada. Another leaning church next door, the

Shoeshine and the daily news.

BELOW: handicrafts on sale from all over Mexico.

18th-century **Santa Veracruz**, has a fine Churrigueresque facade. Farther west, near the corner of Puente de Alvarado and Paseo de la Reforma, the small church of **San Hipólito** stands on the spot where the Spaniards and Aztecs fought most savagely in July 1520 during the so-called *Noche Triste* (Sad Night – *see page 51*). This was then the landward end of one of the causeways to the island-city across Lake Texcoco. A church was first built here by the Spanish shortly afterwards, to celebrate their eventual victory, but it has since been greatly altered.

There are two more artistic attractions on the western side of the Alameda. Nearest to Hidalgo is the **Laboratorio Arte Alameda** ㉕ (Tue–Sun 9am–5pm; charge, free on Sun), a dynamic contemporary arts center housed in the former San Diego church, specializing in very of-the-moment, multimedia work. Alongside, the **Museo Mural Diego Rivera** ㉖ (Tue–Sun 10am–6pm; charge) houses Rivera's famous mural *Sueño de una Tarde Dominical en la Alameda* (Dream of a Sunday Afternoon in Alameda Park), which portrays more than 100 historical characters – including himself, Frida Kahlo and the engraver Posada – under the trees of the Alameda. After the 1985 earthquake, when the Hotel del Prado, its original location, collapsed, a mammoth operation was mounted to transport the wall and mural to its present site.

Seine in cement: Paseo de la Reforma

Modern Mexico City owes one of its most emblematic features to poor, sad Emperor Maximilian and his Belgian Empress María Carlota. When they arrived here in the 1860s, they decided their new capital needed a tree-lined avenue to link their favorite residence in Chapultepec Castle with the old city, running across what were then open fields to the Alameda. After his demise in 1867, the leaders of the Republic took to the new boulevard, definitively named **Paseo de la Reforma**, with enthusiasm, and in the Díaz era it developed into a grand promenade, full of shade trees and monuments and lined by the homes of Mexico's elite.

Zona Rosa and Chapultepec

The great writer Octavio Paz called the Paseo Mexico City's river, a sort of Seine in cement, majestically crossing the best part of town. But, alas, the horses and carriages were replaced by torrents of automobiles, and many of the French-looking mansions were torn down and replaced by skyscrapers. Nevertheless, the Paseo is still a spectacular avenue; extended well beyond Maximilian's original conception, nowadays, like any river, it brings together every aspect of the city at some point along its length.

At the hectic intersection of Reforma, Juárez and Bucareli is the tall tower of the Art Deco **Lotería Nacional** (National Lottery Building), where public draws take place several times a week. From the crossroads, Reforma marches grandly towards Chapultepec, while Avenida Juárez heads up to the massive **Monumento a la Revolución ㉗**. Some consider this the biggest Art Deco building in the world.

It began as the central dome of a never-completed legislative palace, part of Porfirio Díaz's plan to make Mexico City a Latin American Paris.

The Revolution interrupted that grand scheme, and the gigantic structure was left to rust until an enterprising architect transformed it into the imposing, if ugly, monument it is today. The **Museo Nacional de la Revolución** (Tue–Sun 9am–5pm; charge, free on Sun), in the basement, tells the story of the revolution in detail.

Three blocks northeast on Calle Puente de Alvarado is the **Museo de San Carlos ㉘** (Wed–Mon 10am–6pm; charge, free on Sun), in an 18th-century mansion by Manuel Tolsá. Descended from one of the oldest academies of art in the Americas, it houses Mexico's finest collection of European art up to the 19th century, from medieval altarpieces to works by Goya and Ingres.

Back on Reforma, the paseo's flow is interrupted by giant traffic circles or Glorietas, each with a special monument. The **Glorieta Cristóbal Colón** has a statue of Christopher Columbus. Further south, at the Insurgentes

Benches in a variety of playful forms line Paseo de la Reforma.

BELOW: *Puerta 1808,* a sculpture by Manuel Felguerez, in front of the Lotería Nacional building.

The Museo Nacional de Antropología's fine Huastec figure is believed to be of the young Quetzalcóatl.

BELOW: shopping in the hip Condesa neighborhood.

crossing, is the monument to **Cuauhtémoc**, last Aztec emperor and first Mexican hero. Cuauhtémoc, who defended Tenochtitlán against Cortés *(see page 52)*, became the perfect romantic figure, valiant and doomed; he stands erect and proud like a Roman senator, wearing a feather headdress.

The **Ángel de la Independencia** is perhaps the most beautiful of all the monuments. Poised gracefully atop a tall and elegant column, the golden angel commemorates Mexico's Independence.

Zona Rosa, Roma and Condesa

South of Reforma below the Ángel is the famous **Zona Rosa** ㉙ or "Pink Zone," which in the 1960s became modern Mexico City's most popular area for hotels, restaurants, window-shopping and nightlife. It still has plenty of hotels and places to eat, which, with a relaxed atmosphere and good communications, makes it a convenient base for many Mexico City visitors. However, it is now less fashionable than other areas further south,

especially for nightlife, and many of its shops have become increasingly shabby as more upscale stores have moved out to neighborhoods such as Polanco and San Ángel.

The areas that have displaced it in fashion are south of Avenida Chapultepec, beginning with **Colonia Roma**. Its main attraction for visitors, apart from the unhassled atmosphere, is its architecture. Around 1900 its streets filled with ornate residences in French Beaux-Arts and other European styles, many of which have been beautifully restored since the 1985 earthquake, especially around **Plaza Rio de Janeiro** ㉚. More specific attractions include the **Casa Lamm** (daily 11am–6pm; free), a prestigious private contemporary art center and one of several galleries on or near Avenida Obregón.

Roma cannot compete in trendiness today, however, with **Condesa** just to the south (although it is often unclear where one ends and the other begins). If the core of Roma is from the 1900s, most of Condesa dates from the 1930s and 1940s, and is full of spectacular examples of Art Deco. The Art Deco

Parque México is one of the city's most attractive parks. Outside **Parque España**, another pretty park, is the **Plaza Condesa**, a giant 1950s building that contains movie theaters, restaurants, bars and music venues. Nearby on Avenida Tamaulipas, at No. 202, an Art Deco 1942 cinema has been converted into the **Centro Cultural Bella Epoca**, with a gallery and Latin America's largest bookstore. **Avenida Michoacán** is Condesa's main thoroughfare for gallery-browsing, shopping, and people-watching, and on or around it are many of Mexico City's hippest restaurants, bars, and clubs, and some of its sleekest boutique hotels.

Chapultepec and Polanco

At the western end of the main stretch of Reforma, where the paseo bends north, a footbridge leads conveniently over the traffic to six vast columns, the **Monumento a los Niños Héroes**, commemorating the "Boy Heroes," the six young cadets who died defending Chapultepec Castle during the Mexican–American war in 1847. This also marks the entrance to the **Bosque** de **Chapultepec**, the largest green area in Mexico City, a great green lung that is the best place in the downtown area to relax in the open air. It is also a place of great historical importance. It is believed the poet-king Nezahualcóyotl had a palace here, and in pre-Hispanic times the city's drinking water came from the springs of Chapultepec, which means "hill of the grasshopper" in Náhuatl.

The **Castillo de Chapultepec ㉛**, built as a residence for the Spanish viceroy in the 1780s, is said to be inhabited by the ghosts of Maximilian and María Carlota, who lived here during their short reign. Nowadays the castle – a steep 20-minute hike up from Paseo de la Reforma – houses the **Museo Nacional de Historia** (Tue–Sun 9am–5pm; charge, free on Sun), which chronicles Mexican history from the Conquest to the Revolution. Maximilian and María Carlota's rooms are decorated with period furniture, and artifacts on show include the emperor's carriage. Several rooms contain impressive murals by Siqueiros, O'Gorman and Orozco, and, smog

TIP

There is a lot to see in the Anthropology Museum – seeing it all without rushing can easily fill a whole day. If you don't want to spend this much time there, head straight for the rooms dealing with the parts of Mexico and the archeological sites that you are planning to visit. Guided tours are also available in Spanish, English and French: phone ahead to book a time.

LEFT: dog training in Parque México.
BELOW: Argentinian restaurant mural, Condesa.

Discovered at Chichén Itzá, the Maya figure Atlantes *(c. AD 1000–1250), is on display at the Museo Nacional de Antropología.*

BELOW: inner courtyard of the Museo Nacional de Antropología.

permitting, there is a fantastic view over the city.

Just down the hill is a lighter alternative, the **Museo del Caracol** (Tue–Sun 9am–4.15pm; charge), the "Snail Museum," so-called because of its spiral shape, which portrays Mexico's modern history through child-friendly dioramas.

The Museo de Antropología

But most of all, Chapultepec Park is home to one of the world's great museums, the **Museo Nacional de Antropología** ㉜ (tel: 5553 8381; www.mna.inah.gob.mx; Tue–Sun 9am–7pm; charge). The main entrance is marked by a vast statue probably representing the Rain God Tlaloc, although it could be another water deity, Chalchiuhtlicue. The 7.5-meter (25ft) monolith was brought here in the 1960s when the museum opened, amid heavy downpours interpreted by some as the god's protest at being moved.

Pedro Ramírez Vásquez, its architect, found his inspiration in Maya architecture, especially Uxmal (*see pages* *309–11*). The museum is a giant quadrangle, with exhibition halls opening separately onto a central patio shaded by an immense rectangular fountain-canopy, held up, amazingly, by a single central pillar.

The different halls cover every one of Mexico's many historical cultures, providing a stunning vision of their sheer variety. It is possible to visit in any order, but they are arranged counter-clockwise around the great patio as follows: first there is an Introduction to Anthropology, and then the *Sala Orígenes*, telling the complex story of the first movement of peoples into the Americas from Asia. The Preclassic hall deals with the region's early cultures, followed by the spectacular halls on central Mexico (*Culturas del Centro*) – Teotihuacán, the Toltecs, the Mexica or Aztecs. Oaxaca (Mixtecs and Zapotecs) has a hall to itself, followed by another on the Gulf of Mexico (Olmecs, Totonacs and Huastecs), a large *Sala Maya* and finally the halls on western (*Culturas de Occidente*) and northern Mexico. While the main archeological exhibits are on

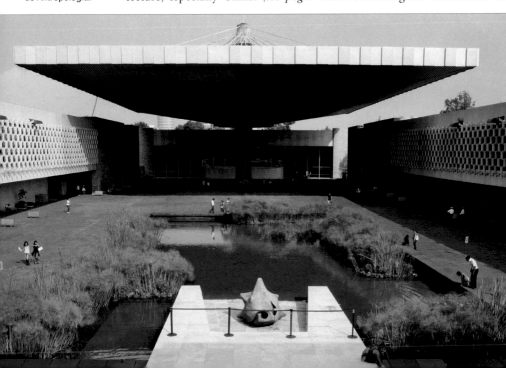

ground level, the floor above has displays on the rich indigenous cultures that survive in the same regions today, emphasizing the continuity between past and present.

Every hall has its treasures. Exhibits in the marvelous **Sala Mexica**, on Aztec art and history, include the famous Sun Stone or Aztec Calendar, and a fascinating model of Teotihuacán. The **Culturas del Golfo** hall has two astonishing Olmec basalt heads from San Lorenzo in Veracruz, and the **Sala Maya** has a model of the tomb of King Pakal from Palenque. Even the less celebrated halls have superb ceramics. For a rest between *salas*, the museum has a relaxing terrace café.

Chapultepec contains many more attractions. The **Museo de Arte Moderno** ③③ (Tue–Sun 10am–5.30pm; charge, free on Sun), in two circular glass buildings, is Mexico's main depository for the non-mural work of its greatest 20th-century artists: Frida Kahlo, Rufino Tamayo, *Los Tres Grandes* – Orozco, Rivera and Siqueiros – and more. As well as paintings, there is an impressive sculpture garden. The **Museo**

Rufino Tamayo ③④ (Tue–Sun 10am–6pm; charge, free on Sun) has a fine collection donated by the great Mexican artist Rufino Tamayo, housed in an ingenious modern building. As well as his own vibrant works, the great highlight is his personal collection of international contemporary art, including works by Léger, Tàpies and Warhol. Further west into Chapultepec, the park's facilities include the Auditorio Nacional, the city's foremost concert hall, three lakes beloved by locals for boat rides, botanical gardens, an amusement park, and Mexico City's zoo.

North of Chapultepec, **Polanco** is the wealthiest residential district in the city, and so contains many of its most upscale shops, fine restaurants and luxury hotels. Just outside the park on the south side, by Constituyentes metro station, is the **Casa Luis Barragán** (tel: 5515 4908, www.casa luisbarragan.org; visits by appointment Mon–Fri 10am–2pm, 4–6pm, Sat

A single central umbrella (paragua) column supports the Museo Nacional de Antropología's vast fountain canopy.

BELOW: taking a moment to reflect during a visit to the museum.

México Distrito Federal

10am–1pm; charge), an extraordinary avant-garde house, making fabulous use of light and color, created by the architect of the same name in 1947. The requirement for visitors to book is not always adhered to, but it is still best to phone ahead.

Outside the center: Guadalupe and Tlatelolco

The image of the **Virgen de Guadalupe** *(see page 29)* is everywhere in Mexico: in homes, places of work, even buses and taxi cabs. On December 12, tens of thousands make the pilgrimage to the **Basílica de Nuestra Señora de Guadalupe**, in the north of the city, for the anniversary of her 1531 apparition.

When the beautiful 18th-century **Antigua Basílica** became too small to accommodate the crowds (and began to list noticeably due to subsidence), it was decided to build a new one next door. By the same architect as the Anthropology Museum, Pedro Ramírez Vásquez, the vast concrete **Basílica Nueva** was completed in 1976, and accommodates as many as 10,000

worshipers at a time. All around it are shops and stalls selling religious images, incense, food, toys and lottery tickets.

There is almost always a service in progress in the basilica, while a slow-moving mechanical walkway carries an endless stream of pilgrims past the image of the Virgin. Behind the basilica a path winds uphill to the **Capilla del Pocito**, a small but ornate circular Baroque chapel beside a well.

Back toward the center, the **Plaza de las Tres Culturas ㉟** is hailed as a symbol of modern Mexico, with the fusion of two previous cultures (pre-Conquest and Spanish) to create a third, the mestizo Mexican synthesis. In the center of the square are the ruins of **Tlatelolco**, site of Tenochtitlán's biggest marketplace. Today the square is also remembered for the hundreds massacred here in October 1968, when police opened fire on student protesters.

The upsweeping modern steeple of the Basílica de Nuestra Señora de Guadalupe.

BELOW: *gorditas*, a specialty from La Villa de Guadalupe.

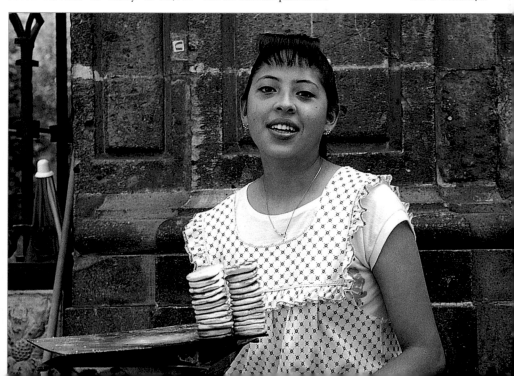

Los Toros

The "fiesta brava" may not be everybody's idea of fun, but the bullfight has been a part of Mexican culture for nearly 500 years.

Ernest Hemingway claimed there were two kinds of spectators at a bullfight: those who identify with the bull and those who prefer the bullfighter. But there is no denying its popularity: in Mexico, there are 225 permanent arenas and around 500 improvised ones, hosting rough-and-ready fights during country fiestas. There are big differences between the kind of bullfights you can see in Mexico, for small-town *corridas* are often pretty chaotic affairs, where the "bullfighters" may be local boys with no experience, and the bull may be too valuable to kill, so that instead it is just chased around for a while.

The traditional Spanish-style bullfight seen in cities is a much more formal, stately ritual. The Plaza México in Mexico City is the biggest bullfighting arena in the world, seating 50,000 spectators. The season runs from late November to March or April. This combines easily with the season in Spain, which runs through the summer, so every year the most famous Spanish bullfighters come to Mexico to compare their skills with those of local stars.

A bullfight starts promptly at 4.30pm, even if the clock has to be turned back. The opening parade is led by a bailiff, followed by three *toreros* resplendent in their *trajes de luces* – suits of light – all shiny silk, brilliant colors and gold embroidery. Behind them come their assistants, the *picadors* (horsemen armed with lances), and lastly attendants with mules, to haul away the dead bulls. The ring *presidente* waves his handkerchief, and the first bull rushes in. Weighing over 500kg (1,100lbs), he is a raging muscular combatant, itching to fight. The drama unfolds in three acts.

Act 1: The *torero* watches while his assistants handle the bull with their capes. Then he takes a few turns himself to test the animal's behavior. The *picadors* ride in, and push their lances into the muscular hump on the bull's back to expose the "cross" where the bullfighter will thrust his sword in the death stroke. Exit *picadors*, leaving a raging but weakened bull.

Act 2: The *torero's* assistants, or in some cases the bullfighter himself, plant three pairs of *banderillas* (barbed darts) into the bull's hump. The *banderillero* runs to the bull, plants the darts, and dexterously gets out of the way of the charging animal, which by this time is bleeding profusely.

Act 3: *La Hora de la Verdad* (The Moment of Truth). The *torero* asks permission to kill the bull and dedicates the kill to a lady friend or anyone else he chooses. He then has 16 minutes to dispatch it, or be ordered from the ring in disgrace. He first works his magic on the bull with his heavy cape, working ever closer to the horns, before switching to a smaller flannel cape. When the bull has been so weakened that its head droops, the *torero* plunges his sword between the shoulder blades, going over the horns and into the "cross," where the sword can penetrate cleanly and sever an artery or puncture a lung. The bull drops to its knees and usually dies at once, although sometimes a *coup de grâce* has to be delivered.

Depending on his performance, the *torero* can be awarded an ear, two ears, two ears and the tail, and sometimes even a hoof. He does not always win though; many *toreros* are gored, and many are crippled or even die. If a bull puts up a particularly good fight, he can be pardoned and retired to stud, in the hope his sons will inherit his courage. ❑

LEFT: a *torero*, or matador wearing the traditional *traje de luces* (suit of light).

Outside the center: south along Insurgentes

Avenida Insurgentes runs for 25km (15 miles) from the north of the city across Reforma to the south, where the colonial suburbs of San Ángel and Coyoacán offer a more tranquil side of Mexico City. The first landmark to look out for on Insurgentes Sur is the 50-story **World Trade Center**, which has a revolving restaurant on the top floor.

Attached to it is the unusual and seemingly haphazard **Polyforum Cultural Siquieros** (daily 10am–11pm), a multi-faceted building designed by David Alfaro Siqueiros *(see pages 115–16)*. Inside the vast main hall is a mural – said to be the world's largest – entitled *The March of Humanity*, which is combined with a light and sound presentation. Another record breaker, just a few blocks further south, is the **Plaza México**, Mexico City's bullring *(see page 150)*.

The huge mosaic covering the **Teatro de los Insurgentes 🟢**, is by Rivera. Taking the history of theater in Mexico loosely as its subject, it includes many characters from Mexican history books, but pride of place goes to Cantinflas, the national hero of popular comedy, who appears Robin Hood-like, with outstretched arms, taking from the rich and giving to the poor.

San Ángel

The fashionable "village" of **San Ángel** lay outside the city until well into the 20th century; it has now been encompassed by its sprawl, but has retained much of its charm. The delightful **Iglesia del Carmen**, with its tiled domes, serene cloister and Churrigueresque altar, was once part of one of the wealthiest monasteries in the area. The convent buildings, now the **Museo del Carmen 🟢** (Tue–Sun 10am–5pm; charge, free on Sun), retain most of their frescoed walls, furniture and paintings. However, most people head for the crypt to glimpse the eerie group of naturally mummified bodies of monks, in glass-topped cases.

The coyotes of Coyoacán in the Jardín Centenario.

LEFT: cool drinks in the shade.
BELOW: the Museo del Carmen is housed in a former convent.

Up the hill, the 18th-century **Casa del Risco** (Tue–Sun 10am–5pm; free) is a lovely example of the district's old mansions, with a fountain composed of hundreds of gaily colored plates, cups, and vases. The house contains an eclectic collection of colonial art, and hosts contemporary art shows.

You can still escape the city's bustle along these quiet, bougainvillea-shrouded streets. On Saturdays, crowds descend on San Ángel for the **Bazar Sábado**, a handicrafts market with brightly colored stalls on normally sleepy Plaza San Jacinto.

A short walk away on Calle Altavista, the **San Ángel Inn** *(see page 355)* is one of Mexico's most seductively pretty restaurants, in the stunning patios and gardens of the 18th-century Goycoechea hacienda, once an aristocrat's ranch. Around the corner is an essential visit, the Modernist, box-like twin buildings designed by Juan O'Gorman *(see page 116)* in 1931 that make up the **Museo Estudio Diego Rivera** ❸ (Tue–Sun 10am–6pm; charge, free on Sun), where the artist and his equally celebrated partner Frida Kahlo worked

in their separate homes, connected by a precarious-looking bridge, and where Rivera died in 1957.

The house will delight any Rivera admirer. On show are some of his later portraits and objects including his characteristic denim jacket, painting materials, newspaper cuttings and his collection of masks. It is a five-minute walk back to Avenida Revolución and the **Museo Carrillo Gil** (Tue–Sun 10am–6pm; charge, free on Sun), an airy modern building that houses another of Mexico City's fine collections of modern art.

Coyoacán

After the fall of Tenochtitlán, Cortés set up his headquarters in Coyoacán, east of San Ángel. Still a separate town in the 1940s, it has long been a desirable neighborhood for artists, intellectuals and bohemians. On the corner of Londres and Allende, the **Museo Frida Kahlo** ❸ (Tue–Sun 10am–6pm; charge, ticket also valid for Museo Diego Rivera-Anahuacalli) is the bright "blue house" where Frida was born, where she later lived with

Rivera, where she returned whenever their relationship fell apart and where she died in 1954. Beautifully intimate, it contains some of her work, an inspirational kitchen and all kinds of memorabilia, including the couple's letters and Frida's dresses.

Three blocks away, the **Museo Casa de León Trotsky** ❿ (Tue–Sun 10am–5pm; charge), home of the exiled revolutionary in 1939–40, is surrounded by a high wall and watchtowers; inside, it is kept almost exactly as when he worked here, with his library containing books in several languages. Bullet holes remain from a failed assassination attempt in 1940 (led by the Communist muralist Siqueiros); three months later, Trotsky was assassinated at his desk with an ice-pick by a Spanish Stalinist agent. His small tomb, by Juan O'Gorman, stands in the gardens, and there is an informative video on Trotsky's life in Mexico.

In the center of Coyoacán, the attractive **Plaza Hidalgo** and adjoining **Jardín del Centenario** have the feel of a real Mexican small-town plaza. They buzz with activity at weekends, and it is worth standing in line at the kiosk in the garden, which sells some of the best ice creams in Mexico City. The 16th-century **Casa de Cortés**, now containing the tourist office, lines the north side of the plaza. This is said to be where the Spanish tortured the defeated Aztec emperor Cuauhtémoc – by burning his feet – to persuade him to reveal the whereabouts of his treasure. Opposite is the church of **San Juan Bautista**, begun in the 1560s. One block to the east is the **Museo Nacional de Culturas Populares** (Tue–Thur 10am–6pm, Fri–Sun 10am–8pm; free), a friendly museum with imaginative, multicolored exhibits on all aspects of Mexican folk culture.

Detail from a painting in the Museo Frida Kahlo.

Gardens and weddings

To the west of Plaza Hidalgo, running away towards San Ángel, **Avenida**

Frida and Diego

Diego Rivera (1886–1957) was already a major artistic figure when he married Frida Kahlo (1907–54) in 1929. In her lifetime he largely overshadowed her, but since the 1980s she has become an international cult figure probably even better known than the great Diego himself.

Rivera's art was very public. After studying in Paris, he returned to Mexico to become the most flamboyant figure in the Muralist movement which, given spectacular spaces to work on by the revolutionary government, deployed distinctively Mexican imagery to create a new sense of cultural identity. Frida's paintings, in contrast, were intensely personal. Aged 18 she nearly died in a bus accident, as a metal rail almost went through her body. She survived, but suffered near-constant pain and needed medical attention for the rest of her life. Her self-portraits often include nightmarish references to her accident,

her miscarriages and operations. A remarkable feature of Frida's work is the way it combines the experience of pain with a vivid energy, expressed in the rich colors that have themselves become part of Mexico's cultural backdrop.

Diego and Frida's tempestuous relationship is inseparable from their mystique. They were both leaders of Mexico's bohemian intelligentsia. Her personal style – her traditional clothes, jewelry, and hairstyles, her untrimmed thick eyebrows – was even more radical at the time. He was always unfaithful, and she also had many affairs, with men and women. They tormented each other, but also adored each other. In 1931 they had their "twin houses" built in San Ángel (now the Museo Estudio Diego Rivera), linked by a bridge. In 1939 they divorced, but soon married again, although while he stayed in San Ángel she went back to her family's "Blue House" in Coyoacán. When she died, he was utterly devastated.

Detail from Diego Rivera's mural, Dream of a Sunday Afternoon in Alameda Park, *showing a young Rivera and Frida Kahlo.*

BELOW: the fabulous facade of the Bilbioteca Central.

Francisco Sosa is one of the best-preserved colonial streets in Mexico City, lined with (now much-desired) 17th-century residences. Just to the north is another special feature of Coyoacán, the **Víveros**, a huge area set aside as nursery gardens, where flowers and trees are grown for sale and for use in parks, and where many locals grow their own produce in cooperative gardens. It is also a much-loved park, and a favorite with joggers.

East of Plaza Hidalgo is the picturesque **Plaza de la Conchita**, where the Capilla de la Concepción, with a rare Mudéjar-style facade, is a favorite for weddings. Overlooking the square is the Casa Colorada, said to have been built for La Malinche, Cortés' interpreter and mistress.

The **Museo Nacional de las Intervenciones** ④① (Tue–Sun 9am–6pm; charge), in the fortified former Convento de Churubusco, in the northeast of Coyoacán, traces the history of foreign interventions in Mexico's affairs since independence – by Spain, France and above all the United States. Special tribute is paid to the *San Patricios*, Irish soldiers who deserted the US Army in 1847 to fight on the Mexican side, calling themselves St Patrick's Battalion.

About 3km (2 miles) south of central Coyoacán is the unusual **Museo Diego Rivera-Anahuacalli** ④② (guided tours only Tue–Sun 10.30am–5pm; charge, ticket also valid for Museo Frida Kahlo), conceived by Rivera himself to house his personal collection of pre-Hispanic art. The somber building of dark volcanic rock is reminiscent of an Aztec temple; apart from the ancient treasures, there are examples of his own work, and a superb view of the city and volcanoes.

Ciudad Universitaria

Farther south again, Insurgentes Sur crosses the vast 1950s campus of Mexico's National University (UNAM), the

Ciudad Universitaria ⑬, with its bold use of color, murals and sculpture. The **Biblioteca Central** (Central Library) is an extraordinary 10-story block with walls entirely covered by a Juan O'Gorman stone mosaic, and there is another mural by Siqueiros behind the nearby **Rectoría** building. Across the road, a Rivera mural adorns the **Estadio Olímpico**. Built for the 1968 Olympics and designed to resemble a volcano, the stadium holds up to 80,000 people.

South of the university Insurgentes meets the Anillo Periférico, a giant highway around the city. Near the intersection is the oldest ceremonial center in the Valley of Mexico, the round pyramid of **Cuicuilco** ⑭ (daily 9am–5pm; free), occupied as early as 1000 BC but buried when the Xitle volcano erupted around AD 100. A little further to the west is the **Estadio Azteca**, one of the world's biggest soccer stadiums.

Floating gardens

The famous floating gardens of **Xochimilco** ⑮ (take the light rail line to Embarcadero from Tasqueña Metro) are the only remnant of the pre-Hispanic lake towns. They are a favorite place for a Sunday outing for local people, who come to eat, drink and be serenaded by *mariachis* on the flowery *trajineras* (boats). Weekdays are not half as lively, but can be cheaper (the hourly rate for a *trajinera*, around US$10 per hour for a whole boat or US$1.50 per person, is posted, but there's room for negotiation).

Just off the district's main plaza is the lovely 16th-century church of **San Bernardino**. At Avenida México 5843 is the **Museo Dolores Olmedo Patiño** (Tue–Sun 10am–6pm; charge, free on Tue; light rail to La Noria). The late Dolores Olmedo was one of Rivera and Kahlo's foremost patrons, and her magnificent house, another former hacienda, displays an outstanding collection of their work and other 20th-century art. ❑

The Xochimilco trajineras are very distinctive little boats.

BELOW: the floating gardens at Xochimilco.

AROUND MEXICO CITY

Massive pyramids, ornate Baroque buildings, snow-capped volcanoes, subtropical gardens; whoever chooses Mexico City as a base will find interesting options in every direction

México City

Although sprawling suburbs have engulfed much of the area around Mexico City, an hour or two's drive in almost any direction will introduce you to the heart of the country – a mosaic of peoples and characterful towns, and geography that ranges from cool, stately pine forests and snow-capped volcanoes to hot, humid valleys bursting with plant life.

North to Tepotzotlán and Tula

Though now on the city fringes, the town of Tepotzotlán is about 35km (22 miles) north of central Mexico City, along the Querétaro road (Mexico Highway 57), which is a continuation of the Anillo Periférico boulevard that runs through the Bosque de Chapultepec. This passes through the **Ciudad Satélite**, a vast area of modern housing initially planned in the 1950s. Its main landmarks are the **Torres de Satélite**, a sculptural group of brightly colored modern towers by German-born artist Mathías Goeritz.

The magnificent Jesuit church and monastery of **Tepotzotlán ❶** are jewels of Mexican colonial art in themselves. The college of San Francisco Javier was founded in the 1580s as a school for indigenous children, but had been left in decay for years when it was made a museum in 1964. As the **Museo Nacional del Virreinato** (Viceroyalty Museum; tel: 55-5876 0245; Tue–Sun 10am–6pm; charge, free on Sun) it contains Mexico's foremost collection of colonial art.

The church of **San Francisco Javier** is one of the finest examples of Churrigueresque (*see page 58*) architecture in Mexico. The main nave dates from the 1670s, but the lavishly decorated stone facade and the carving on its

Main attractions
TEPOTZOTLÁN
TULA
TEOTIHUACÁN
PARQUE NACIONAL IZTACCÍHUATL-POPOCATÉPETL
PUEBLA
CHOLULA
CUERNAVACA
TEPOZTLÁN
XOCHICALCO
TAXCO
MALINALCO
VALLE DE BRAVO

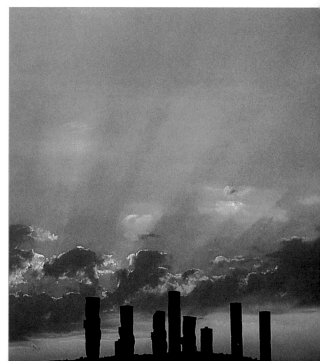

PRECEEDING PAGES: the magnificent Pirámide de la Luna, Teotihuacán.
LEFT: gilded interior, Tepotzotlán.
RIGHT: the Atlantes of Tula once supported the roof of the Temple of the Morning Star.

Pre-Hispanic anthropomorphic ceramic figure displayed in the museum at Teotihuacán.

single, graceful belfry were added in 1760–2. Inside, golden altarpieces appear to multiply like exotic tropical plants, transforming the walls into a mysterious, glittering curlicued mass. It provides an inspiring frame for sculpture and paintings such as Miguel Cabrera's retablo of Our Lady of Guadalupe.

Baroque ornamentation reaches its dazzling extreme in the **Camarín de la Virgen**, a small octagonal side room that was used for dressing an image of the Virgin of Loreto, where every inch is covered in a riot of archangels, cherubim, fruit, flowers and shells. It is reached through the Casa de Loreto, a little chapel said to be a "replica" of the house where the Virgin Mary lived in Nazareth. It has been said that Baroque style – especially in its most extravagant forms – goes hand in hand with the Mexican psyche: the lavish use of color and movement and the excesses and unbounded imagination are seen as the soul of Mexican art.

The rest of the monastery, with graceful cloisters and delightfully shady gardens, houses ornaments, jewelry, furniture, clothing and other objets d'art from the colonial period, as well as displays on life in Mexico under Spanish rule.

Tula and the Toltecs

The ruins of ancient **Tula ❷** (daily 9am–5pm; charge), capital of the Toltecs, are about 50km (30 miles) north of Tepotzotlán. Founded around AD 800–850, the city played a major role in Mesoamerican history. According to local chronicles Topiltzin, Tula's semi-legendary founder, was expelled by followers of the warrior god Texcatlipoca, who dominated the city until it was destroyed 300 years later. As well as skilled artisans the Toltec seem to have been a particularly warlike culture – even for ancient Mexico – and Tula was the most powerful city in the Central Highlands for around 250 years, with trading links over a huge area. However, many of its main buildings were destroyed by fire – due to an invasion, or perhaps internal conflicts – and its power dwindled rapidly after about 1170.

The main pyramid is the **Tlahuizcalpantecuhtli** (Temple of the Morning

Star), on top of which stand, 4.6 meters (15ft) tall, the **Atlantes**. These massive basalt figures, which once supported a wooden temple roof, are Tula's most distinctive contribution to Mexican art. They are giant images of Toltec warriors, armed with javelins and wearing pectoral adornments in the form of butterflies; on their backs are round shields in the form of the setting sun, with a human face at the center. The box-like headdresses are decorated with vertical feathers.

Of the other surviving structures, perhaps the most interesting is the **Coatepantli** or "Wall of Serpents," along the north side of the pyramid; 40 meters (130ft) long and over 2 meters (6.5ft) high, its reliefs show snakes devouring human bodies. Nearby is the **Palacio Quemado** (Burnt Palace), once an exceptionally large palace complex, with in front of it the *chacmool*, the characteristic reclining figure holding a receptacle on which the hearts of sacrificial victims were placed.

Teotihuacán

Leaving Mexico City in another direction, northeast along Insurgentes Norte and then Highway 132, you will come to one of Mexico's unmissable sights, the immense ancient city of Teotihuacán, "the place where men become gods," 50km (31 miles) from the capital. For once, the over-used description "awe-inspiring" is really unavoidable.

On the way, look out for the fortress-like **San Agustín Acolman** ❸ (Tue–Sun 9am–5pm; charge), an imposing church with a fine plateresque facade from 1562. The monastery it served was one of the oldest in Mexico, founded in 1536, and like many missionary monasteries has in front a huge open atrium or square, built to hold open-air services for hundreds of recently converted indigenous people.

The setting of **Teotihuacán** ❹ (tel: 594-956 0052; daily 7am–5pm; charge), in a bare, dusty valley, seems perhaps less exotic than those of Maya cities further south, shrouded in tropical green-

ery. It impresses most by its majestic geometry and sheer scale, with vast pyramids and structures lined up along the nearly 2km (1½ miles) of the "Avenue of the Dead." Teotihuacán began life several hundred years before the Christian era, and the building of its first large structures began around 200 BC. At its zenith, from around AD 150 to 600, Teotihuacán was one of the biggest cities in the world, with a population of around 150,000 – some estimates go up to 250,000 – and an area of 20 sq km (8 sq miles), more extensive even than its contemporary, Imperial Rome. Its influence in politics, culture and trade extended over a huge area, and, in the same way that ancient Rome contained communities from every part of the Mediterranean, Teotihuacán appears to have had areas inhabited by Maya, Zapotecs and other peoples from many parts of Mesoamerica. Even so, Teotihuacán was also a

Step by step to the top of Pirámide del Sol.

BELOW: view of Pirámide de la Luna across fields of cacti and wild flowers.

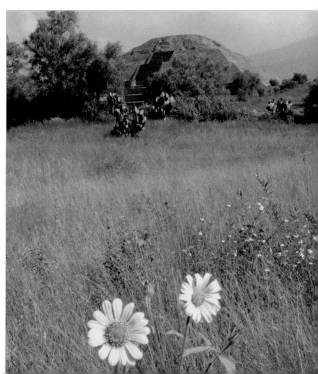

BELOW:
architectural crenelation representing a bird, on view at the Teotihuacán Museum.

virtually illiterate culture, so a great deal about it remains mysterious.

One of the principal "mysteries" of Teotihuacán is just how and why this city declined so rapidly, around 650. The most likely explanation, as in the case of the Maya, is a combination of agricultural collapse due to overpopulation, drought, invasions by newer, competing cities, and internal revolt – several of Teotihuacán's major buildings seem to have been sacked and burnt around the same time. The shock waves of its collapse were felt throughout ancient Mexico. Teotihuacán's population dwindled away over the next centuries, but it was regarded with awe by all the later cultures of the Central Highlands, especially the Mexica and the Aztecs, who considered it almost the birthplace of civilization.

Around the site

Buses from Mexico City drop you at **Gate 1**, in the southwest corner; drivers can continue north around the perimeter to several more gates and parking areas. At Gate 1, you walk up past

stalls selling clothing and souvenirs, and a small restaurant (there is also a delightful restaurant outside the site to the south, in the Villas Arqueológicas hotel). The site is so huge it can rarely ever feel crowded.

Beyond the Gate 1 entrance you emerge at the south end of the **Calzada de los Muertos** (Avenue of the Dead), the main axis, which stretches 3km (2 miles) north, past the Pyramid of the Sun to the Pyramid of the Moon. In front of you is a broad, sunken square that the Spaniards called the **Ciudadela** (Citadel), because it looked to them like a fortress, and which probably was indeed the primary residential area of the rulers of Teotihuacán. Within it is the **Templo de Quetzalcóatl**, a tiered temple decorated with alternating motifs of the feather-collared Serpent God, and the goggle eyes of the Rain God Tlaloc. The temple was discovered in the 1920s, hidden beneath a cruder later pyramid probably added by the Toltecs in the 9th century.

To the north the Avenue of the Dead is lined by smaller pyramids and temples, nearly all in a similar squat,

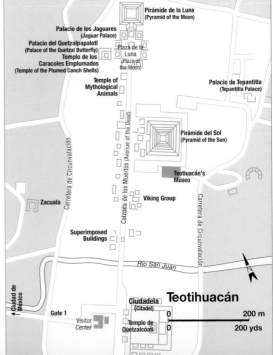

square-sided style. Unmissable around halfway up on the east side is the gigantic **Pirámide del Sol** (Pyramid of the Sun), Teotihuacán's foremost landmark. Most of it had been built by around AD 100. The entire structure, with a base measuring almost 225 meters (738ft) square, was at one time covered in stucco and brightly painted. For an impressive overview of the city, a steep 248-step climb will take you up the 75 meters (246ft) to the top, where a temple once stood.

Below the pyramid on its south side is Teotihuacán's **museum**, which contains a fascinating scale model of the site, plenty of explanatory displays, and artifacts found here, although many others have been taken to the Anthropology Museum in Mexico City. There is also a restaurant and a shady botanical garden, ideal for a break in the tour.

On the northeast side of the site, the **Palacio de Tepantitla** contains Teotihuacán's finest surviving fresco, the *Paradise of Tlaloc* mural. A reproduction can also be seen in the Mexico City museum.

The **Pirámide de la Luna** (Pyramid of the Moon), though smaller than the Sun Pyramid, is built on higher ground and so their tops stand at the same level. It is also easier to climb. Overlooking a plaza at the northern end of the avenue, the Moon Pyramid is surrounded by a dozen small temples. Nearby, in the **Palacio del Quetzalpapalotl** (Palace of the Quetzal Butterfly), one of the largest residential complexes, there are well-preserved murals and stylized reliefs of creatures that are part bird and part butterfly. Also part of this complex are the **Palacio de los Jaguares** (Palace of the Jaguars), named for its feline mural painting, and the **Templo de los Caracoles Emplumados** (Temple of the Plumed Conch Shells) which still bears traces of the red, green, yellow and white symbols representing birds, maize and water.

It's easy to spend a whole day at Teotihuacán, and any decent visit requires at least two hours (more than some bus tours allow). The pyramids are at their most impressive first thing in the morning or towards sunset. Like most great Mesoamerican cities,

One of the many ceramic masks found in the vast ancient city of Teotihuacán, and now on display in the site museum.

BELOW: well-preserved fresco in the Palacio de los Jaguares.

Pachuca is the cradle of Mexican soccer. Its team C.F. Pachuca is the oldest professional club in the country, and was founded in 1901 by miners brought from Cornwall in England to work in the silver mines. Pastes, a local delicacy, are another product of Cornish influence – a kind of meat pie based on Cornish pasties.

Teotihuacán was aligned with the heavens, and the Avenue of the Dead points precisely 15.5º east of north – just why, is another source of argument. Thousands flock here to greet the dawn on the Spring Equinox, March 21, when the site opens especially early.

The surrounding countryside is of interest too. Just to the west is **Otumba**, where the Aztecs were defeated by Cortés in one of the major battles of the Conquest. The region is typical of central Mexico: desert plains and hills, and fields of maguey plants, from which *pulque*, one of Mesoamerica's oldest alcoholic beverages, is extracted. Strong, frothy, beer-like and loaded with vitamins, *pulque* is said to be very nourishing (the best excuse in the world for a favorite drink). In the 19th century *pulque* plantations were developed, but it is now far less common than beer, which is much easier to produce and to transport.

Hidalgo

Tucked-away Hidalgo is one of Mexico's least visited yet most beautiful states. The capital **Pachuca ❺**, 94km

(58 miles) northeast of Mexico City, makes a good base. Its history is closely linked to its silver mines, worked at different times by Spanish, British, Mexican and US mine owners. All have left their mark on Pachuca and the quaint town of **Mineral del Monte**, especially the miners who came here from Cornwall in the 19th century. Not far from the attractive Plaza de la Independencia, the 16th-century former Convento de San Francisco is now the **Centro Cultural Hidalgo** (tel: 771-713 1977; Tue–Sun 10am–6pm; free), which contains Mexico's Museo Nacional de Fotografía (National Photography Museum), the core of which is the extraordinary archive of pioneer photographer Agustín Víctor Casasola, who took many famous images of the Mexican Revolution. There is also a collection of work by Tina Modotti, the Italian photographer who was inspired by Mexico in the 1920s.

Some 20km (12 miles) north of Pachuca, pine forests, lakes and spectacular rock formations in the **Parque Nacional El Chico ❻** provide great hiking and climbing terrain. Within

BELOW: open for business.

the park is **Mineral El Chico**, a picturesque old mining town.

Monday is market day in **Ixmiquilpan**, 75km (47 miles) northwest of Pachuca along the Highway 85 Querétaro road, and the chief town of the Otomí people, Hidalgo state's original inhabitants. This is the best day to see the beautiful Otomí textiles and fine inlaid woodwork; on the way, stop off at **Actopan** to see the 16th-century monastery. Further on beyond Ixmiquilpan are the waterfalls, hot springs and caves of the **Grutas de Tolantongo**, a spectacular box canyon.

East of Mexico City

The road to Puebla and the east coast is a continuation of the great avenue called **Calzada Ignacio Zaragoza**, the backbone of proletarian Mexico City. It runs eastward through the sprawling suburb of **Ciudad Nezahualcóyotl** (also known just as Neza), with a population of nearly 3 million, and sometimes called Mexico's third-largest city.

Once the road leaves the urban area behind, it enters the beautiful pine-forested mountains near the **Parque Nacional Iztaccíhuatl-Popocatépetl** ❼. The volcanoes loom very close, and the climate becomes cooler. The road to these magnificent snow-capped wonders is reached via a turn-off through the pleasant hill town of **Amecameca**, in a green, pastoral landscape.

Puebla: City of the Angels

After crossing the mountains, the road descends into the ample valley of **Puebla** ❽, culturally one of the richest of Mexico's colonial cities, known both for the uniquely colorful style of its historic buildings, many clad in Talavera tiles, and the special qualities of its cuisine. In spite of being a growing industrial center, with an enormous Volkswagen car plant, Puebla has preserved a good deal of its old character, and possesses some of the most impressive colonial art and architecture in Mexico.

One such gem is the elegant cathedral ❹, the second-largest in

Spanish colonial coat of arms on the facade of a Puebla house.

Popo and Izta

Mexico City's valley is a volatile place, surrounded by volcanoes – most famously the majestic Popocatépetl (5,465 meters/17,926ft) and Iztaccíhuatl (5,230 meters/17,155ft), affectionately known as *El Popo* and *Izta*. In the past these enormous snow-capped peaks formed a backdrop to the city, 60km (40 miles) away; nowadays, it's a talking point if they are not obscured by smog, but they still make an impressive sight when traveling east towards Puebla or the Gulf – or coming in to land at Mexico City airport. According to legend, Popocatépetl (Náhuatl for "Smoking Mountain") was a warrior in love with Iztaccíhuatl ("White Lady" or "Sleeping Woman"), a beautiful Aztec princess. Fearing her lover had been killed in battle, Iztaccíhuatl died of grief, and when Popo returned alive, he laid her body on the hill where he stands, the eternal sentinel, beside her.

El Popo has been quite active recently, so access has been closed. Izta is much quieter, and can still be explored.

The road from Amecameca is open as far as the Paso de Cortés, the saddle over which the conquistadores entered the Valley of Mexico in 1519, from where footpaths lead around the lower levels. Going further should only be attempted by experienced climbers with a guide: several Mexico City agencies offer treks. Mexico's highest mountain is the Pico de Orizaba (5,635 meters/18,490ft) east of Puebla, also known as Citlaltépetl or "Star Mountain."

Between 11am and noon you can climb one of Puebla's cathedral belltowers for a superb view of the city and nearby volcanoes. They only let you up, however, if you're accompanied.

the country. Overlooking, naturally, the main square, it was consecrated in 1649, and combines the refined architecture of the Spanish Renaissance with more ornate Baroque styles. The exterior is severe and somber, while inside the main altar, another work by Manuel Tolsá, is like a miniature Roman temple. The angel statues around the atrium are symbols of the town, the original name of which was "Puebla de los Angeles."

The tourist office is beside the cathedral, almost next door to the **Casa de la Cultura** (tel: 222-246 6922; Tue–Sun 10am–5pm, later for concerts; free). Occupying the former Bishop's Palace from 1646, with a lovely Puebla facade in brick and tile, the center has a sculpture garden and an open-air theater. Up the stone stairs is the splendid **Biblioteca Palafoxiana B**, the oldest library in America, with 50,000 volumes on ornately carved wooden shelves.

Two blocks west, the **Museo José Luis Bello y González C** (tel: 222-232 9475; Tue–Sun 10am–5pm; charge, free on Tue) contains a fascinating collection of decorative art amassed by a local industrialist in the 19th century, displayed in ornate rooms in his former home. Back to the south of the cathedral, the untypically high-tech **Museo Amparo D** (tel: 222-229 3850; Wed–Mon 10am–6pm; charge, free on Mon), in an 18th-century former hospital, has interactive, multilingual displays to complement its beautifully presented collections of pre-Hispanic artifacts and colonial art and furniture. On the corner of calles 2 Sur and 3 Oriente – behind the cathedral – is the **Casa del que Mató al Animal** (House of the Man who Killed the Animal), a 16th-century house, now a newspaper office, which retains a spectacular Renaissance carved portico with images of a hunter and his dogs.

The 18th-century **Casa de los Muñecos E** (House of Puppets), now the University Museum (tel: 222-246 2899; Tue–Sun 10am–4pm; charge) has the most amusing of Puebla's tiled facades, with panels portraying 16 apparently dancing figures, allegedly caricatures of the first owner's enemies. On the ground floor there is also an elegant restaurant.

One block eastward along Avenida Juan de Palafox y Mendoza, the **Templo de la Compañía F**, with its elaborate facade, is said to be the last resting place of the celebrated **China Poblana**, a 17th-century Asian princess who was adopted by a local merchant, and whose statue surmounts a fountain at the east side of town. Her costume of frilly blouses atop embroidered, sequinned skirts have become part of local tradition. Adjoining the church, bordering a cobbled alley, is the 16th-century Puebla University building, first built as a Jesuit college. A short walk up Calle 4 Norte leads to the **Museo Poblano de Arte Virreinal G** (tel: 222-246 6618; Tue–Sun 10am–5pm; charge, free on Sun), another fine collection of colonial art in the former Hospital de San Diego, dating from 1647, with a beautifully restored cloister.

The stalls of Puebla's main tourist market, **El Parián H** (daily), sell everything Mexican, from *serapes* to *piñatas*, but are naturally especially strong on Puebla ceramics. If it's pictures you're after, cross the road and wander through the open studios of the **Barrio del Artista I**.

Puebla's traditional architecture is a very Mexican adaptation of Spanish Baroque, with the characteristic addition of color, and expressed in a profusion of tiles and plaster decoration. Perhaps the finest example is the sugar-icing stucco, set off against red walls, of the **Casa del Alfeñique J** (an *alfeñique* is a kind of sugar-and-almond meringue). Now the **Museo Regional** (tel: 222-232 0458; Tue–Sun 10am–5pm; charge), it contains fine Puebla ceramics, and memorabilia from the 1862 Battle of Puebla against the French. Just beyond the "artists' quarter," the **Teatro Principal K** was almost 150 years old – one of the oldest in the Americas – when it suffered a disastrous fire in 1902, after which it had to be rebuilt.

Calle 6 Oriente is a fascinating street, renowned for its *dulcerías*, sweet shops with beautiful displays of exquisite handmade confections. There are

TIP

Since 1996 the name of Puebla's main avenue, east of the Zócalo, has been Avenida Juan de Palafox y Mendoza, in honor of the town's most distinguished Spanish bishop. However, some maps and leaflets still refer to it by its old name, Avenida Maximino Ávila Camacho.

BELOW: distinctive Talavera tiles are used in houses and buildings throughout Mexico.

The Talavera of Puebla

Talavera pottery is everywhere in Puebla: there are tiles, bowls, vases, flowerpots, jugs and sculptures. The technique, combining earthenware with a tin-based enamel glaze, takes its name from Talavera de la Reina in Spain, and was introduced into Mexico around 1550, probably by craftsmen from Talavera brought here by Dominican friars to teach new skills to the indigenous people. The original pottery was cobalt blue and white, with strong Moorish motifs, but the Mexican potters added their own touches and also received influences from China and Renaissance Italy. This led to the introduction of new designs and colors, particularly greens, yellows and oranges. Using the original technique, it takes six months to produce one piece of authentic Talavera pottery, and it is fairly easy to distinguish the earthy mineral colours of these items from the bolder hues of mass-produced copies (there is also a difference in price).

There are naturally plenty of shops around Puebla selling local ceramics. The historic Uriarte factory, on Calle 4 Poniente, has a beautiful shop and also offers tours (Mon–Sat 11am, noon, 1pm; charge) that explain the process from beginning to end: first the clay is left to stand for three months, and then wedged underfoot until it is well kneaded; after another month, the piece of pottery is made and left to dry before it is fired, painted, glazed, and fired again.

EAT

Puebla's traditional cuisine, cocina poblana, is celebrated throughout Mexico: among its most popular specialties are chile en nogada, green chili stuffed with meat, white walnut sauce and red pomegranate seeds – the colors of the Mexican flag – and mole poblano, a rich savory chocolate and chili sauce. The Fonda Santa Clara, almost opposite the Museo Bello, has long been renowned for its typical Puebla dishes.

BELOW:
the splendid ornamentation on the dome of Santo Domingo church.

camotes (sweet potatoes with pineapple and sugar), fudge-like dulce de leche, limes filled with sweet coconut, and rompope, a sort of eggnog, often a child's introduction to alcohol.

The church of **San Cristóbal ⓛ** has sumptuous stucco carvings. One of the first battles of the 1910 revolution took place next door; this was then the house of Aquiles Serdán, a leading liberal conspirator, and in November 1910 he and his family were besieged here by the troops of Porfirio Díaz, firing back from the balconies (the bullet-holes have been preserved). It now houses the **Museo de la Revolución Mexicana Ⓜ** (tel: 222-242 1076; Tue–Sun 10am–5pm; charge). Looking west up Calle 6 Oriente you can see the cast-iron structure of the **Mercado de la Victoria**, transformed into a modern shopping mall.

Two ex-convents north of the center are worth discovering. The austere **Ex-Convento de Santa Mónica Ⓝ** (tel: 222-232 0178; Tue–Sun 10am–5pm; charge, free on Sun), founded in 1606, was officially closed by the Reform Laws of 1857, but a community of nuns lived

on here in secret until 1934. Today, as the **Museo de Arte Religioso**, it is particularly focused on the life of women in religious houses. Nearby, the **Ex-Convento de Santa Rosa Ⓞ** (tel: 222-232 7792; Tue–Sun 10am–5pm; charge), also 17th-century, is now a **Museo de Artesanías**, with a wonderful display of the many crafts of Puebla state. A highlight is the beautiful vaulted kitchen of the convent itself, covered with traditional Puebla tiles. Mexico's famous mole sauce (made from, among other ingredients, chocolate, almonds and chili) is said to have been invented by nuns in this very room.

The pride of Puebla's religious architecture, however, is on the way back to the center, tucked away inside the 16th-century **Santo Domingo** church: the breathtaking **Capilla del Rosario Ⓟ**, to the left of the main altar, is a dazzling mass of Baroque gilt decoration, with a host of angels and a heavenly chorus.

Cholula and the villages of Puebla

Cholula ❾ is now almost a suburb of Puebla, but it was a major center from around AD 600 up until the Conquest, when it was one of the largest cities in the Central Highlands after Tenochtitlán. In 1519, Cortés, claiming to fear an ambush, made an example of Cholula by massacring some 3,000 of the city's elite. Then, after being depleted by plague, Cholula rapidly dwindled in size.

Modern Cholula is famous for its many churches; according to tradition, the conquistadors vowed to build one for every pagan temple they found or, alternatively, one for each day of the year. The fortified **Convento de San Gabriel** is the most impressive, its massive walls lining the east side of the attractive **Zócalo** (main square). On one side of the convent atrium is the **Capilla Real**. Originally an open chapel for holding Mass services, its roof, with 49 little domes, was added in the 18th century.

Most people come to Cholula to see what looks like an ordinary hill with a church on top. In fact, this is the **Gran Pirámide** (tel: 222-247 9081; daily 10am–5pm; charge), the largest pyramid and largest man-made structure anywhere in the world, with the Náhuatl name *Tlachihualtépetl*, or "handmade mountain." Like all pre-Hispanic pyramids it was built up over centuries; in the final phase, the entire pyramid was covered with a thick layer of adobe, which over time became covered in vegetation. Only part of the pyramid has been excavated, but you can enter tunnels within it, and there are remains of fine murals. From the top, beside the earthquake-battered church of **Nuestra Señora de los Remedios**, there's naturally a superb view.

The villages around Puebla state are rich in folk traditions. **Huejotzingo ⑩**, about 14km (9 miles) northwest of Cholula, is a small town known mainly for its cider, woolen *serapes* and its **Carnaval**, usually in February, highlights of which are masked dances that re-enact a battle against the French. Just off the main square is the impressive 16th-century **Convento Franciscano** (Tue–Sun 10am–5pm; charge, free on Sun), with original frescoes, and artifacts that illustrate life in the early Spanish missions. **Santa María Tonantzintla ⑪**, just south of Cholula on the old road to

The queen of one of Puebla's many fiestas poses in full regalia.

BELOW: lunchtime in Cholula.

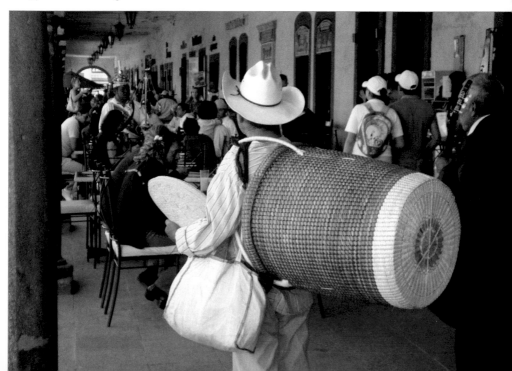

TIP

Archeologists have excavated as much as 8km (5 miles) of tunnels inside the Great Pyramid of Cholula, revealing some of the many stages of its construction. Before entering this well-lit warren, have a look at the large cut-away model of the pyramid in the museum opposite the tunnel entrance.

Oaxaca, has a remarkable folk-Baroque church with an interior entirely covered with colorful, vibrant carvings. The decor took 200 years to complete, and is a wonderful example of the way indigenous artisans adopted Spanish iconography. The dazzling tiled facade of the church of **San Francisco Acatepec**, a couple of miles farther south, is one of the region's unmissable sights. Damaged by fire in the 1930s, it was restored in every detail.

Into Tlaxcala

In the neighboring state of Tlaxcala, 18km (11 miles) west of the state capital is **Cacaxtla** ⑫ (tel: 246-416 0000; daily 8am–5pm; charge), "the place where the rain dies in the earth." Once the chief center for a people called the Olmeca-Xicalanca, it flourished between around AD 400 and 1000. It was virtually unnoticed until 1975, but excavations of the huge, 200-meter (660ft) platform known as the *Gran Basamento* have revealed some of the best-preserved ancient murals in Mexico, notably the 22-meter (72ft) *Mural de la Batalla*, which vigorously depicts

a battle between jaguar and eagle warriors. Only 2km (1½ miles) away is **Xochitécatl**, a smaller but older site that may have been a subordinate community to Cacaxtla.

The town of **Tlaxcala** ⑬, capital of Mexico's smallest state, is one of its hidden colonial treasures. The center has been beautifully restored, and thanks to a traffic control scheme its plazas are unusually tranquil. Although they lived only 115km (70 miles) from the Aztec capital, the Tlaxcalans always managed to maintain their independence. When Hernán Cortés arrived in 1519, they became crucial allies in the conquest of Tenochtitlán. A mural by local artist Desiderio Hernández Xochitiotzin, in the **Palacio de Gobierno** on the Zócalo, tells the story.

A steep walk uphill leads to the **Convento de San Francisco**, with a beautiful view over the city and its bullring. The church – which is now the city's cathedral – has a Moorish-style wooden ceiling, and the font used to baptize the four Tlaxcalan chiefs; the monastery buildings now house the **Museo Regional** (tel: 246-462

BELOW: the Cholula pyramid towers in the background behind the domes of the Capilla Real.

0262; Tue–Sun 10am–5pm; charge), with a fascinating collection of local pre-Hispanic pieces.

Also worth discovering is the **Museo Vivo de Artes y Tradiciones Populares** (tel: 246-462 2337; Tue–Sun 10am–6.30pm; charge), a "living museum" where local craftspeople demonstrate the intricate work involved in producing Tlaxcala's wonderful handicrafts, which are on sale in the museum shop.

Perched on a hill above Tlaxcala, in the village of **Ocotlán** ⓮, is a twin-towered church that seems as lightly spun as sugar candy. This is the 18th-century **Basílica de Ocotlán**, another of Mexico's most ornate Churrigueresque churches, and built in honor of an apparition of the Virgin said to have occurred here in 1541. The explosion of Baroque giltwork inside is dazzling.

To the east, **Huamantla** ⓯ is famed for its celebration of the Feast of the Assumption (August 15), when the town is covered in flower carpets, which are destroyed in the following days by the *huamantlada*, when bulls run through the streets Pamplonastyle. The **Museo Nacional del Títere** (Puppet Museum; tel: 247-472 1033; Tue–Sat 10am–2pm, 4–6pm, Sun 10am–2pm; charge) on the main square houses an interesting collection of puppets. Beyond Huamantla a lonely road leads back into Puebla state to a dirt-track for **Cantona** ⓰ (daily 8am–5pm; charge), an archeological site that may have been one of the largest Mesoamerican cities, extending over 12 sq km (5 sq miles). It was at its peak in the late Classic era, about AD 700–1000.

South: Cuernavaca and Morelos

Mexico City's Insurgentes Sur joins the road to **Cuernavaca** ⓱. After an initial climb, the road descends in 75km (47 miles) to an altitude substantially lower than that of the capital. Cuernavaca, capital of Morelos state, is also a weekend resort where *capitalinos* go

for clean air, a pleasant climate and relaxation. It has always attracted the capital's elite: Aztec emperors built temples here, and Cortés a palace; artists, retired North Americans and even the fugitive Shah of Iran have also chosen to settle in this flower-filled "city of eternal spring." In the 1930s, writer Malcolm Lowry (using its Náhuatl name, *Quauhnahuac*) made it one of Mexico's mythical cities in his novel *Under the Volcano*, as the place where his British Consul drinks himself to death. More recently – in contrast – exhilarating landscapes, the fine climate and fast-flowing rivers have made Cuernavaca and Morelos one of Mexico's most popular areas for adventure and health tourism. The city itself has grown rapidly, but a weekend here still comes as a welcome escape from the cacophony of the metropolis.

In the center of town, the **Plaza de Armas** is flanked by the **Palacio de Cortés** (tel: 777-312 6996; Tue–Sun 9am–6pm; charge, free on Sun), which the conqueror had built on the ruins of a pre-Hispanic temple. It now houses the **Museo Cuauhnáhuac**, a substantial

On August 14, known as "the night when nobody sleeps," the people of Huamantla create beautiful carpets of flowers and colored sawdust along 12km (7 miles) of streets, in readiness for the Feast of the Assumption on the 15th.

BELOW: the richly decorated San Francisco Acatepec.

Pulque *has been made and drunk in central Mexico since at least AD 200, and many beautiful* pulque *jars have been found at archeological sites. Like everything in ancient Mexico it had special rituals attached to it: as well as Tepoztécatl, the* pulque *god whose shrine was in Tepoztlán* (see page 173), *it was associated with rabbits, symbols of the gods of drunkenness.*

BELOW: detail from Rivera mural in the Palacio de Cortés, Cuernavaca.

collection of pre-Hispanic and colonial artifacts from the surrounding area. There is also a series of murals by Diego Rivera *(see pages 114–15)* depicting 400 years of Mexican history, from the Conquest to the Revolution. For decades, teachers have been challenging Mexican children to identify the heroes and villains of their national saga.

Jardín Juárez, off the square's northwest corner, has a bandstand designed by Gustav Eiffel, who designed the famous Paris tower, where you can buy fresh fruit juice or *licuados* to sip in the shade of the flame trees.

Two blocks west up Calle Hidalgo, the imposing **cathedral** stands in a high-walled, fortified garden. Like the palacio it was begun in the first years after the Conquest, in a massive, plain style. Inside, some curiously Oriental frescoes were discovered during renovation work in 1959. They seem to depict the mass crucifixion of missionaries in Japan, and are believed to have been painted in the 17th century by a Japanese Christian convert. The Sunday Mass (11am) with *mariachi* musicians is famous all over Mexico.

Also part of the *recinto* or cathedral compound is the **Museo Casa Robert Brady** (tel: 777-318 8554; Tue–Sun 10am–6pm; charge). Brady, a wealthy US artist and collector, lived and worked in Cuernavaca until his death in 1986, and the museum exhibits his extraordinary collection of art, antiques and crafts from Mexico and other parts of the world. Nearby, in the **Palacio Municipal** (daily 9am–6pm; free), paintings around the courtyard give a romantic vision of local history.

A great deal of Cuernavaca's beauty lies behind high walls in private gardens. However, the prettiest of them, the **Jardín Borda** (tel: 777-312 9237; Tue–Sun 10am–5.30pm; charge, free on Sun), created in the 1780s around the home of Taxco's richest silver magnate, is public. Inside its walls, there are fountains, terraces, an artificial lake with row boats for rent and an outdoor theater. The museum, in part of the old house, has exhibits from the time when this was the summer residence of Maximilian and María Carlota, and their favorite place in all Mexico.

Apart from the large **market** (north-east of the center) and the not very impressive **Teopanzolco Pyramid** (daily 8am–5pm; charge), in a park further east (a bus or taxi ride), these are the specific attractions of Cuernavaca. It is also known, though, for its excellent luxury hotels. The **Hacienda de Cortés** and **Las Mañanitas** are two of the most opulent. If you've ever dreamed of staying in a place with a beautiful, flower-filled garden where fountains tinkle and peacocks strut; of sleeping in a room filled with period furniture and eating first-rate food, now is the time to indulge. The restaurants are open to non-guests too.

Morelos state

Morelos is the sugar bowl of Mexico. The conquistadors brought sugar cane here, and during the dictatorship of Porfirio Díaz local *hacendados* seized huge areas of land to plant sugar for export. This laid the seed for agrarian revolution, and Morelos was also home to the Mexican Revolution's most legendary leader, Emiliano Zapata, born in Anenecuilco, a village near Cuautla. Villages around the state still display his portrait: the huge bristling moustache, the *charro* jacket, the sombrero, and the deep, sad look that is ever present in his eyes.

Spiritual support offered by a statue in colonial church niche.

Tepoztlán ⓲ is an attractive town nestling at the foot of the Tepozteco mountain, 26km (16 miles) northeast of Cuernavaca. Its center is dominated by a massive **Dominican** Monastery (Tue–Sun 10am–5pm; free) and church built in a near-medieval style in the 1560s. Behind the church, the small Museo Arqueológico Carlos Pellicer (Tue–Sun 10am–6pm; charge) has a remarkably good collection of pre-Hispanic pieces. It is a strenuous one-hour hike up to the **Tepozteco Pyramid** (daily 9.30am–6pm; charge), a temple dedicated to Tepoztécatl, Aztec god of fertility and *pulque*. The climb is rewarded with an awe-inspiring view of the Tepoztlán valley. With a special atmosphere and balmy climate, Tepoztlán has become an

BELOW: girls' talk.

BELOW: interior detail, Santa Prisca.
RIGHT: one of the steep, cobbled streets in the pretty town of Taxco.

ecotourism and New Age travel hub. A craft market draws the crowds on Sundays, as do the Carnival celebrations in February and a *pulque* festival in September.

Heading south from Cuernavaca on the old road to Taxco, a short detour leads to the spectacular archeological site of **Xochicalco** ⑲ (daily 9am–5pm; charge), "place of the house of flowers" in Náhuatl. One of the most significant sites in the Highlands, covering 25 hectares (62 acres), it flourished between the 7th and 10th centuries, bridging the gap between the decline of Teotihuacán and the rise of later cultures. Sometimes called the crossroads of Ancient Mexico, Xochicalco was declared a Unesco World Heritage site in 1999. The most striking monument is the **Pirámide de Quetzalcóatl** (Temple of the Plumed Serpent), with superb bas-reliefs, at the summit of the terraced platforms. The **Grutas de Cacahuamilpa** ⑳ (guided tours every hour, daily 10am–5pm; charge) caves are unmissable: enormous, intriguing, but forbidding for the claustrophobic. The main tour

takes you through just 2km (1 mile) of well-lit paths, past vast chambers with extraordinary rock formations.

Silver town: Taxco

Taxco ㉑, Mexico's most famous silver-working town, is 72km (45 miles) south of Cuernavaca and about a third of the way between Mexico City and Acapulco. It is truly picturesque: red-roofed whitewashed houses, pretty plazas, cascading bougainvillea and narrow, cobbled streets twist up and down the steep hills. All tend to lead to the **Zócalo** or main square, overlooked by the pink stone Baroque church of **Santa Prisca**. Completed in 1758, with twin, 40-meter (130ft) towers, its elaborate Churrigueresque facade and tiled dome are more than matched by the dazzling gilded interior. Take special notice of the fine German organ and delicately carved woodwork. The church was entirely paid for by José de la Borda, a Spaniard who redeveloped Taxco's silver mines in the 18th century and became one of the richest men in Mexico.

To the right as you leave the church

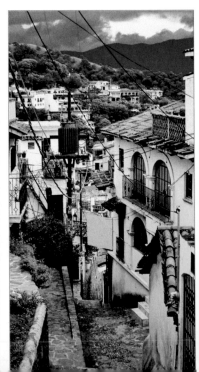

is the **Casa Borda** (tel: 762-622 6634; Tue–Sun 10am–5pm; free), a humble house built in 1759 by the town's wealthy patron for the church priest. It is now a cultural center, with exhibits on local themes. An adjoining arcade and a set of stairs leads to the **Museo de la Platería** (Silverware Museum; tel: 762-622 0658; Tue–Sun 10am–5pm; charge), with a rich selection of local work. It was William (Guillermo) Spratling, an architect from New Orleans, who sparked off Taxco's modern jewelry boom when he opened the first silver workshop here in the early 1930s, after silver-working had been neglected in the town for centuries. Spratling's apprentices went solo, and today there are more than 300 shops in Taxco, selling an enormous variety of silver work, including some of the finest in the world.

Behind Santa Prisca church, the **Museo de Taxco Guillermo Spratling** (tel: 762-622 1660; Tue–Sun 9am–5pm; charge, free on Sun), Spratling's home until his death in a car accident in 1967, houses his private collection of pre-Hispanic art and antiquities. There is also a small section on local history.

The **Casa Humboldt**, on Calle Juan Ruiz de Alarcón, is one of Taxco's oldest colonial houses, and so-named because the German explorer-scientist and traveler Baron Alexander von Humboldt (1769–1859) stayed a night there in 1803. With an exquisitely ornate facade, this beautiful Moorish-style house now contains the **Museo de Arte Virreinal** (tel: 762-622 5501; Tue–Sun 10am–5pm; charge), a miscellaneous collection of religious artifacts and other items. Easter is a major festival in Taxco, when hotels are often booked early.

West to Toluca

Many roads connect Mexico City with **Toluca ㉒**, capital of Mexico state and only an hour's bus journey west of the capital, climbing through surprising countryside with pine forests reminiscent of Germany, before typical Mexican landscapes reassert themselves in dry, golden fields, cacti and adobe houses. Toluca's proximity to the capital has aided its industrial growth, and its airport is now promoted as an alternative entry point for Mexico

SHOP

Many shops and stalls around Toluca sell local handicrafts – woven goods, carved wood, ceramics of many kinds, metalware, basketwork, papier-mâché and more – but a comprehensive range can be found in one place at the state-run Casart store, at Paseo Tollocán 700, outside the city center on the main road toward Mexico City.

BELOW: Nevado de Toluca.

Modern architecture in Toluca.

BELOW: the Cosmovitral stained-glass mural.

City, 60km (38 miles) away. Toluca's Friday **open-air market** (in the outskirts, near the bus station), reputedly the largest in Mexico, draws huge crowds.

The center of Toluca is typically provincial with colonial churches, a large square (Plaza de los Mártires) and 120 *portales* (arcades). Look out for the local specialties – fruit jam, spicy *chorizo* sausages and *moscos*, orange-based liqueurs served from bottles with long spouts that are known for being *muy traidores* (very treacherous).

One block north of the square, in a magnificent old Art Nouveau former market on Plaza Garibay, is the **Cosmovitral** (Tue–Sun 9am–5pm; charge), a beautiful indoor botanical garden, lit by brilliantly colored stained-glass panels. The best of the area's traditional arts and crafts can be found in the **Museo de Culturas Populares**, one of three museums in the **Centro Cultural Mexiquense**

(tel: 722-274 1131; Tue–Sun 10am–6pm; charge), 8km (5 miles) west of the city. This ambitious center also contains museums of anthropology and modern art.

Mexico State

Metepec ㉓, now almost a suburb of Toluca, is famed for its craftworkers and especially its colorful ceramic trees of life, offering a very Mexican interpretation of the story of Adam and Eve. Farther south, above Tenango del Valle, are the hilltop ruins of **Teotenango** ㉔ (daily 9am–5pm; charge) a fortified center first built up around 750, and later taken over by a people called the Matlatzincas, who were conquered in turn by the Aztecs. Across to the west is the majestic extinct volcano the **Nevado de Toluca**, 4,680 meters (15,354ft) high.

Not far from Teotenango is the site of **Malinalco** ㉕ (daily 9am–5pm; charge), in a spectacular location high up on a rocky crag. First built by the Matlatzinca culture, it was soon taken over by the Aztecs, and the Emperor Ahuitzotl began large-scale building here in 1501 that was still unfinished when the Spaniards arrived. The main temple, the **Cuauhcalli** (House of the Eagle Warriors), was carved into the face of the mountain itself, and used for initiation ceremonies of young Aztec nobles into the warrior elite. The entrance has the form of the tongue and giant mouth of a fanged serpent, and images of sacred eagles, serpents and jaguars abound throughout the site. The nearby town of Malinalco has become a fashionable weekend getaway, with a golf club and plenty of shops and restaurants.

Several times a year pilgrims swarm to the village of **Chalma** ㉖, 12km (7 miles) farther east, to worship the Santo Señor de Chalma, an image of Christ said to have appeared miraculously in 1533. It is one of Mexico's most revered shrines, after Guadalupe.

Farther south on the main Taxco road (Mexico 55) is the spa resort of **Ixtapan de la Sal** ㉗, semitropical and flowery, whose mineral waters are said to have rejuvenating properties. On the outskirts of town is the **Parque Acuático Ixtapán** (tel: 01 800 4932 726; daily, water park 9am–6pm, spa 8am–7pm; charges depending on activities). Here you can head for the slides and wave machines, swim in the Olympic-sized pool, or relax in Roman-style baths with massage, mud and beauty treatments. There are also several hotel spas.

One of the state's most popular destinations is away to the west at **Valle de Bravo** ㉘, a picturesque colonial town 80km (50 miles) from Toluca, which acquired a beautiful lake due to a 1940s hydroelectric scheme. Weekend visitors, including many foreigners, enjoy the idyllic mountain scenery and the attractive hotels and cottages overlooking the lake. Watersport enthusiasts are well catered for, while other popular activities include paragliding, horseback riding, golf and hiking.

To the west and northwest, the remote mountains of Piedra Herrada and **Cerro Pelón** contain valleys that are wintering-grounds for Monarch butterflies, and are less exploited than similar locations in Michoacán (*see page 239*). ❏

LEFT: Parque Alameda, Toluca.
BELOW: unwinding at a bathhouse at Ixtapan de la Sal.

THE NORTH

South of the border is not just a buffer zone;
this often bypassed region has natural and
cultural gems all of its own

The fact that most of northern Mexico is not tourist country is one of its main attractions. This rugged land is starkly beautiful, a region of desert landscapes with huge and varied cacti, lofty mountains and high plateaus. Renowned for its vast cattle ranches, it is Mexico's Wild West. It also contains some of the country's most fertile agricultural land. Sadly, recent drug-related crime has overshadowed the many reasons tourists should take the time to come here: ancient ruins, peaceful towns, and beautiful architecture make it well worth visiting, and crime is rarely directed at tourists. In fact, you're far more likely to make friends here.

Baja California is becoming a destination in its own right, and for good reason. One of the world's longest peninsulas, Baja stretches more than 1,600km (1,000 miles) with two of the world's prettiest ocean bodies on either side: to the west, the Pacific, which surfers have long known as paradise; to the east, the Sea of Cortés, with placid lagoons and stunning vistas; in the middle, some of the most curious plant and animal life on the planet; visit parts of Baja and you'll feel like you're visiting the moon. Some of the towns, such as Todos Santos and Loreto, once quiet one-horse villages, are developing fast with big hotels and resort-style development on the horizon; others feel more like American suburbs, albeit with much better food. Much of Baja's fame rests now on the beaches and the massive Californian gray whales cavorting in their breeding waters at Scammon's Lagoon.

The far north of mainland Mexico – the vast and monotonous Sonora Desert, the imposing Sierra Madre, and the sprawling industrialized cities – is usually visited en route to somewhere else. But the interminable, barren landscape also conceals some outstanding surprises: the pre-Hispanic Paquimé ruins at Casas Grandes or – the highlight of any trip to northern Mexico – the world's most spectacular train journey, from Chihuahua to Los Mochis, through the breathtaking scenery of the Copper Canyon. And Chihuahua, with its cathedral and broad plazas and friendly smiles, seems like a stopover in yesteryear. ❑

PRECEDING PAGES: granite rock shoreline at Cabo San Lucas, Baja California Sur. **LEFT**: taking the long way up. **FROM TOP:** Mushroom Rock at Bahia Balandra, La Paz; divers encounter a manta ray.

The North

0   100 km

0   100 miles

BAJA CALIFORNIA

Mountains, deserts and thousands of kilometers of coastline for exploring, snorkeling, whale-watching, diving, and some of the best deep-sea fishing in the world

México City

Highway 1, the 1,690km (1,050-mile) road that spans the peninsula from Tijuana to Los Cabos, didn't even exist until 1973 and although there are half a dozen shorter subsidiary routes, hundreds of kilometers of Baja's coastline and almost all the interior can be comfortably reached only by four-wheel-drive vehicles. While some people deplore this inaccessibility, the majority of Baja fans rejoice in their knowledge of a land that – though a very close neighbor to California and its teeming millions – remains largely unexplored.

The peninsula was opened, Christianized and depopulated by the Spanish missionaries; in just a few decades, the missions – intended to spread salvation – spread plagues and diseases that depleted the native populations, and with it, their culture. Most missions were subsequently abandoned; their ruins, remote and slowly eroding, make for wonderful photos and interesting side treks, but only a few, such as the one in Loreto, still function today. Pre-European Baja culture is found in intricate, ethereal paintings on cave walls, on pottery, and in legends and lore.

Baja's population and its economy are both concentrated in the north. Bumper crops are produced in the irrigated lands around Mexicali: cotton, alfalfa, wheat, tomatoes and grapes.

Recently Baja's wineries have received international recognition, and there's even a Wine Country route north of Ensenada that tourists can follow, tippling as they go. Workers in northern Baja get the highest minimum wage in the country.

On the border

There are three major crossings into Baja at the California border – **Tijuana**, **Tecate** and **Mexicali** – all connected by Highway 2. These places are fun but be aware that staying out after midnight,

Main attractions
TIJUANA
ENSENADA
WINE COUNTRY
SAN PEDRO MÁRTIR
   NATIONAL OBSERVATORY
CATAVIÑA
GUERRERO NEGRO
SANTA ROSALIA
MULEGÉ
LORETO
LA PAZ
ESPIRITU SANTO
BARRILES
SAN JOSÉ DEL CABO
CABO SAN LUCAS
TODOS SANTOS

LEFT: a towering Baja cactus.
RIGHT: *Blue Ocean* mural, La Paz.

TIP

Don't forget to get your passport stamped at the border if you plan to travel south beyond the "free zone" (Ensenada/San Felipe) either by bus or by car. Currently, anyone crossing the border – including US citizens – will need a passport to enter Mexico and re-enter the US by land.

purchasing drugs or other illegal items, or being rowdy or obnoxious can lead to problems with the police. Drug-related crime is unfortunately on the rise; the best way to avoid trouble is to pass on offers of illicit goods.

Tijuana

Once a rip-roaring, shoot 'em up, anything-goes border town and still living up to its reputation in some ways, **Tijuana ❶** is now one of Mexico's busiest and most prosperous cities. It also claims to be the most-visited border city in the world, with more than 2 million people crossing each year.

Because Tijuana is a duty-free zone, imported goods can be surprisingly cheap and there are bargains to be found in Russian caviar, Spanish leather, French perfume and even Cuban cigars (shoppers should not plan on buying anything illegal here that they plan to bring into the United States: you may be arrested and illegal goods will be confiscated, including non over-the-counter medicines for which you do not have a doctor's prescription). The city's main drag, Avenida Revolución,

BELOW: craft market in Tijuana.

is lined with popular bars, nightclubs, craft stores and clothing and jewelry stores mixed among those selling *serapes* and sandals, but shoppers will find even more variety in the Plaza Río Tijuana (www.plazariotijuana.com.mx; daily 10am–9pm) near the river, the largest shopping center in northwestern Mexico. For a massive selection of footwear, head for the Plaza del Zapato (www.plazadelzapato.com.mx; Mon–Sat 10am–8.30pm, Sun until 6pm) within the Plaza Fiesta. While TJ has seen a lot of bad press due to a resurgence of drug-related crime, it's unlikely you'll have problems if you're moderately careful. Caution is advised after 9 or 10pm.

The distinctive red **Tijuana Trolley** runs between the city's main sightseeing attractions (there is also a San Diego trolley link), but it's a pleasant stroll back northward on Via Poniente along the river. It will bring you to an older, funkier shopping center, **Pueblo Amigo**, which comes alive at night.

Tijuana Attractions

Behind the Plaza Revolución is the **Museo de Cera** (Wax Museum; tel: 664-688 2478; Tue–Sun 10am–5.45pm; charge, children under 6 free), whose motley inhabitants range from Madonna, Mahatma Gandhi and the Pope to Mexican revolutionary heroes and a gray-haired lady known as **Tía Juana** (Aunt Jane), the legendary *cantina* owner after whom the city was named. The ultra-modern **Centro Cultural** (Cultural Center; tel: 664-687 9600; www.cecut.gob.mx), with its comprehensive survey of Mexican history, adjoins a building that resembles a giant golf ball. This is the concert hall and 26-meter (85ft) high **Omnimax Theater** where movies about Mexico's history and culture are shown regularly, some in English.

Tijuana is in Mexico's wine-growing region, and the **L.A. Cetto Winery**, at Avenida Cañon Johnson 2108, tel: 664-685 3031, offers tours of the vast cellars and wine tasting. Call for an appointment. **Mundo Divertido** (Fun World;

tel: 664-701 7133; www.mundodivertido.com.mx; Mon-Fri noon–9pm, Sat–Sun noon–10pm; free park entry, ride prices vary), at Paseo de los Héroes and José María Velasco, in Zona Río, is a family-oriented amusement park with miniature golf, a roller coaster, miniature train rides, batting cages, video games, go-karts and more.

The highway west of Tijuana leads to the **Plaza Monumental** bullring, 10km (6 miles) away, beside the sea. Bullfights take place (either here or at the older bullring downtown) on Sundays at 4.30pm during the season, which runs from May to September. There are inexpensive motels along the seashore road and stalls selling coconut drinks and seafood.

Rosarito

The expensive *cuota* toll road to Ensenada includes stretches of fine scenery as it passes along a series of cliffs overlooking the Pacific Ocean (the *libre*, or free road, runs parallel most of the way). About 27km (17 miles) south of the border is **Rosarito** ❷, an over-commercialized town with a good swimming beach, which gained celebrity after 1927, when the newly opened Rosarito Beach Hotel began to attract the movie crowd and other famous faces. Pacific lobster is a favorite in the town's numerous restaurants and there is even a so-called "Lobster Village" – **Puerto Nuevo** – 10km (6 miles) to the south, where this dish is widely available and uniformly overpriced.

Ensenada

As you enter the big city of **Ensenada** ❸ (population 369,000), 113km (70 miles) south of the border, turn right off Highway 1 and drive up Avenida Alemán into the Chapultepec Hills, a high-rent district which offers a magnificent view of the city set around Todos Santos Bay.

A busy port, Ensenada is a regular stop for cruise ships and the farthest south that the vast majority of tourists penetrate. A favorite haunt of fishermen, it tags itself "the yellowtail capital of the world," with surf fishing along the rocky shoreline and organized trips from the sport-fishing

Robert Louis Stevenson penned part of his book Treasure Island *while in Ensenada.*

LEFT: young vendor with a selection of *ojos de dios* and other woolen handicrafts.
BELOW: emblem of the lively cruise-ship port of Ensenada.

Dolphins can often be seen in the Gulf of California.

BELOW: hiking in the national park of San Pedro Mártir.

piers off Boulevard Lázaro Cárdenas. In winter, whale-watching trips are also popular. The city stages various regattas and, in November, a noted off-road race.

Ensenada is the center of the area's wine industry, and there are winery tours every day except Sunday at the **Bodegas de Santo Tomás** (Miramar 666; tel: 646-178 3333; www.santo-tomas. com). The main tourist shopping zone is along **Avenida López Mateos**, a few blocks from the bay, but prices are lower around Avenida Ruíz and Calle 11, where every other store or bar seems to bear the name Hussong. The original Hussong's *cantina* (Avenida Ruíz 113; tel: 646-178 3210; www.cantinahussongs. com), with its dusty floor and time-polished wood, is a popular drinking place, and visitors from all over the world have been pinning samples of their currency to the walls for a century. Visit the fish market, at the end of Avenida Macheros, to sample the fish tacos.

South of town take the turn-off to **La Bufadora**, where incoming waves are forced into a narrow "V"-shaped wedge, causing great jets of sea water to spout over 18 meters (60ft) into the air, spraying amused spectators. Incoming tides are best, and it is a good idea to consult the *Baja Sun* for the tide timetable.

San Pedro Mártir

Back on Highway 1, at **San Telmo de Abajo**, just south of Colonet, a reasonably good road (in the dry season) heads east to the sprawling Meling Ranch (tel: 619-328 0386 from the US; www. melingguestranch.com). You can stay here in comfortable quarters, swim in the pool and ride horses into the mountainous **San Pedro Mártir** national park, with its beautiful oak and pine forests. The National Observatory is located near the highest peak, the **Picacho del Diablo** (3,090 meters/10,135ft).

Productive agricultural land surrounds **San Quintín,** a small town strung out along the highway. To reach the best place for an overnight stop, turn right off the highway just south of the military camp at Lázaro Cárdenas and drive 5km (3 miles) along the unpaved road to the **Old Mill**, a reminder that this area was once colonized by an English land company that went bankrupt;

the names of the almost forgotten pioneers are recorded on a group of lonely graves by the shore. The wild peninsula along **Bahía de San Quintín** ❹ is a well-loved camping area for the cognoscenti, whose favorite pastimes include fishing and digging for "chocolate-tipped" clams.

Cataviña

South of San Quintín the road veers inland and you will begin to see the spidery *cirio* trees (*Idria columnaris*) that bear tiny yellow flowers and are sometimes referred to as **boojum** after the mythical species described by Lewis Carroll in *The Hunting of the Snark*. Gigantic boulders carpet the landscape here. Heading southeast, past **Cataviña** (an unexpected oasis with a Pemex station) the road climbs over the summit of the sierra, then drops into the arid bed of **Laguna Chapala**. Near the south end of the boojum area, a paved side road branches east to **Bahía de Los Ángeles** ❺, on the calm waters of the Gulf of California. Protected by the aptly named **Isla Ángel de la Guarda** (Guardian Angel Island), the fishing and shelling here are great; dolphins can often be seen in the bay, and the waters teem with fish; the tiny island of **Isla de la Raza** is a wildlife refuge. The town itself still has few facilities – a minuscule museum, a store and a couple of hotels and trailer parks – but the views are splendid and the setting idyllic.

Guerrero Negro

Back on the main road, going south, you reach the 28th parallel, where a looming metal sculpture marks the boundary between Baja California Norte and Baja California Sur. Acres of shallow saltwater ponds lie just beyond this border, at **Guerrero Negro**, the largest salt plant of its kind, producing one-third of the world's supply, where guided ecological tours are available. The town has hotels, restaurants, stores and gas, although only from January to March is it of much interest to tourists, many of whom come to watch the whales in the **Laguna Ojo de Liebre** ❻. Scammon's Lagoon, as it is also known, is at the end of a dirt road several kilometers south of town, past the salt-evaporating ponds.

One of several powerful telescopes at The National Observatory in San Pedro Mártir national park.

Whale-Watching

For centuries, gray whales have traveled from Alaska's icy Bering Sea to mate and spawn in the warm, shallow waters off the coast of Baja California. It takes these gentle giants two or three months to complete the 9,500km (5,900-mile) journey, the longest migration of any mammal. They arrive between December and January and stay until March, or sometimes as late as June.

In 1857 the breeding ground was discovered by a rapacious whaling captain from Maine, Charles M. Scammon – hence Scammon's Lagoon. For the next 100 years the whales were hunted almost to extinction until, in 1972, the area became the world's first whale sanctuary, the Parque Natural de Ballena Gris. Nearby Guerrero Negro (Black Warrior) is named after a British whaling boat that was wrecked off the coast soon after.

Today's hunters come armed only with binoculars and cameras and the gray whale population has almost fully recovered. Early morning or late in the day are the best times for whale-watching, either from the shore (or observation tower by Scammon's Lagoon), or else from locally hired boats, which provide an even closer view of these magnificent, 15-meter (49ft) long leviathans.

You don't have to have a skiff to view these gentle creatures either. In peak season, simply pull over to the curb and scan the water for a while – chances are you'll see a whale, sometimes a whole pod, surfacing out there to breathe. Other behavior you may catch (if you're lucky) is full or partial breaching (where the animal leaps out of the water), fluke slaps (where it slaps the water with its tail), or flipper waves.

Abandoned trolley from the El Boleo copper mine.

From Guerrero Negro, the highway cuts across the peninsula to the Sea of Cortés. A mandatory stop should be made at tiny **San Ignacio ❼**, whose plaza, lined with shady laurel trees, is dominated by the San Ignacio mission. Built by the Dominicans in 1786, with 1.2-meter (4ft) thick walls and a vaulted ceiling, it replaced an earlier (1728) Jesuit mission. The church, with its perfect symmetry and Baroque facade, is a delightful example of what is left of colonial architecture in Baja California. An oasis of almost 100,000 date palms, sustained by an underground spring which surfaces here, has become the basis of the town's economy.

Remember to set your watches one hour earlier as you cross south into Baja California Sur.

The Sea of Cortés

After many dramatic curves, Highway 1 reaches the coast, 73km (45 miles) beyond San Ignacio, at **Santa Rosalía ❽**. In 1887, a French company opened the El Boleo copper mine here. The company left in 1954, but the small wooden houses from the French

era still give the town a curiously anomalous look; indeed, author John Steinbeck called it the "least Mexican-style city" he had seen. Unexpectedly, the church behind the plaza was built by Gustav Eiffel, the French engineer responsible for the famous Parisian tower. This prefabricated metal structure won second prize at the 1889 Universal Exposition in Paris; it was later acquired by the El Boleo company, shipped over from France and assembled here.

From Santa Rosalía, an overnight ferry crosses the Gulf to **Guaymas** on the Sonora coast. Otherwise you can follow the Transpeninsular Highway down the dry Gulf Coast to **Mulegé ❾**. Threatening US warships were frightened away from here by a locally orchestrated subterfuge during the Mexican–American war in 1847. In July and August the town is stiflingly hot, but usually the palm trees and plantings along the Río Santa Rosalía make Mulegé a pleasant oasis. There's a wonderfully situated 1766 mission church on the outskirts of town, and a fortress-like museum – a jail until 1975 – up

BELOW: view from the Old Mill Hotel, San Quintín.

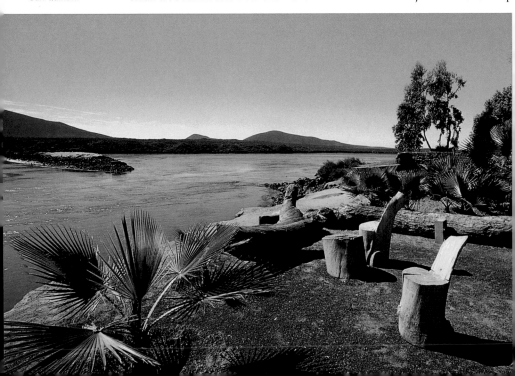

the hill. Snorkeling, diving and fishing are all popular activities, and there are ancient **cave paintings**, in the San Francisco mountain range, which are a Unesco World Heritage site.

South of Mulegé the highway skirts the shore, offering tantalizing glimpses of delightful coves and bays which are only accessible with a four-wheel-drive vehicle. Framed to the east by a north-ward-pointing peninsula, the 40km (25-mile) long **Bahía Concepción ⑩** is particularly renowned for its enticing camping beaches, all with at least a few facilities such as restrooms, trash cans and sheltering *palapas* (beach shacks). Most of the rocks between the beaches are occupied by morose pelicans gazing silently at the sea.

Loreto

Loreto ⑪, about 136km (85 miles) farther south, was the site of the first permanent mission and for 130 years the capital of Baja. After it was leveled by a storm in 1828, the capital was moved to the pearling center at La Paz. The twin towers on the restored mission were replaced using money won by the local priest in the national lottery. The town's main street is named after the Jesuit priest Juan María Salvatierra, who established and ran the mission here for 20 years. The tourist complex at **Nopoló**, 25km (15 miles) south of Loreto, has sports facilities such as golf and tennis, and a pleasant marina.

En route to La Paz

The scenery south of Loreto is spectacular; lovely beaches and the reddish-brown slopes of the Sierra de la Giganta sometimes distract attention from the dangerous curves and steep switchbacks on the highway. In the fertile Santo Domingo valley, **Ciudad Constitución** is a fast-growing, busy agricultural center with some of the ambiance of the old American West. Highway 22 heads west from here 57km (36 miles) to the Pacific port of **San Carlos**, a small fishing town overlooking Bahía Magdalena, the largest bay on Baja's Pacific coast, which shelters a commercial fishing fleet and, during the spawning season, Californian gray whales.

Early in the 20th century there were

Baja California is twice as long as Florida, but much skinnier. A great crack in the San Andreas fault created the Gulf of California millions of years ago; the water is 3,290 meters (1,800 fathoms) deep off La Paz.

BELOW: pelican on the green at Loreto Bay golf course.

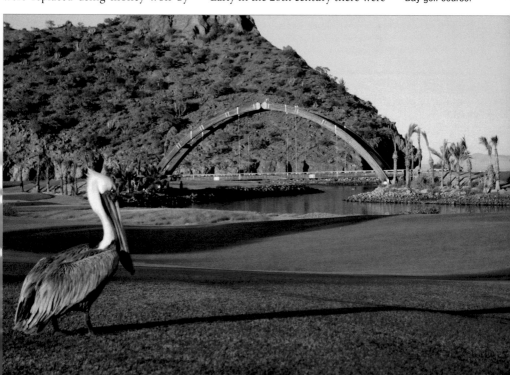

The unique rocks at Baja's southern tip have several names: "The Three Friars" and "Land's End" are the most common.

steamboat connections from **La Paz** ⑫ to other Baja ports; now there are daily ferries to Topolobampo on the Sonora coast. La Paz, the capital of Baja California Sur, is a delightful city with a population of almost 200,000. Its streets, with their old colonial buildings, are shaded by coconut palms and laurel trees and, in the spring, blossoming jacaranda, acacia and flame trees add to the splendor.

Apart from its celebrated sport fishing, La Paz is famous for its spectacular sunsets – best viewed from the terrace café of the popular Hotel Perla, on Paseo Alvaro Obregón (the local **tourist office** has a branch office on Alvaro Obregón, the seafront, about one block away). If you have the time, it is worth visiting the **Biblioteca de las Californias** (Library of California's History; Mon–Fri 9am–4pm) opposite the cathedral on the town square and the **Museo de Antropología** (tel: 612-125 6424; daily 9am–6pm; donation), on Altamirano, for information and exhibitions on Baja's history. There is also an aquarium, a serpentarium, and a cactus sanctuary to entertain and edu-

cate visitors. La Paz is a favorite vacation town for Mexicans, so prices are cheaper here and those seeking a more authentic Mexico may prefer this peaceful city to the resort-filled Cabos.

Northward out of La Paz, the road goes up the **Pichilingue** peninsula, past the ferry terminal to lovely bays and beaches at **Balandra** and **Tecolote**; there is a bus every hour from La Paz. Another popular destination is the island of **Espíritu Santo** (8km/5 miles offshore), uninhabited today, but once known as the "isla de perlas" after Cortés harvested black pearls here in the 16th century. After centuries of exploitation, the pearl trade finally came to an end in the 1940s when a mysterious disease wiped out the oyster beds of La Paz.

Though off the beaten path just south of La Paz, the towns of Barriles and Buenavista are excellent for anyone wishing to windsurf – at certain times of year the prevailing winds across the Sea of Cortés are so perfect that you can see hundreds of colorful sails zipping around in the water. Sport fishing and other water sports are also prime attrac-

BELOW: the golden sands of Los Cabos.

tions. Those wanting fewer people but similar trade winds can head to Ventana, less than an hour east of La Paz.

Los Cabos

Of the two famous *cabos* (capes) at Baja's southern tip, **San José del Cabo** ⑬ is by far the less glitzy and more typically picturesque. The 32km (20-mile) strip of highway between the two is filling up with resorts, golf courses and all the trappings of a developing tourist region, but San José itself, at the eastern end of the "corridor," remains relatively unspoiled. Rent a bicycle or car, or walk to the beach at **La Playita**, where you can dine on freshly caught seafood, go fishing in a *panga*, or just admire the estuary, home to thousands of birds.

The highway continues on down to the tip of Baja at **Cabo San Lucas** ⑭, a former supply station for the Spanish treasure galleons from Manila and now a major tourist center bulging with bars, cafés, nightspots and dozens of luxury hotels; some have private beaches and their own landing strips for small aircraft. On a Saturday night,

with two or three cruise ships moored in the bay, you'll find little difference between Cabo and a college fraternity party, and for many, that's all part of the attraction. Come here and plan on feeling like you've stepped into a Jimmy Buffet song.

The tides in the Gulf are powerful and tricky, and the wind is strong. This means small boats are difficult to handle and it can be very dangerous. You can rent a boat with an experienced local crew at the marina; this is also the place to take glass-bottomed boat trips to **El Arco**, the natural stone arch at the southernmost point of the peninsula.

From the town of Cabo San Lucas you can make your way back to La Paz along the Pacific coast on a good but partially unpaved road past some lovely lonely beaches, though the ocean is rough. The road leaves the coast near **Todos Santos**, a quaint, quiet, surfing and art community, which stands exactly on the Tropic of Cancer. Rumor has it that the "original" Hotel California is here. From Todos Santos, the road loops back across the peninsula to La Paz. ❏

Sailfish, marlin, roosterfish, swordfish, yellowtail, dolphin fish, cabrilla, tuna and sierra are among the many fish living in the waters off La Paz.

BELOW: adobe house fronts in Cabo San Lucas.

THROUGH THE SIERRAS

The mountainous north is different from the rest of the country; this is Mexico's Wild West, where men wear Stetsons not sombreros

México City

Heading south from the Texas border, you will be confronted by two great mountain ranges, the Sierra Madre Occidental in the west and the Sierra Madre Oriental in the east. The former is by far the more rugged of the two. Between Ciudad Juárez, on the US border, and Guadalajara, 1,600km (1,000 miles) farther south, there are only a few major ways to cross the mountains to the Pacific coast: the railroad from Chihuahua City to Los Mochis, the highway between Chihuahua and Hermosillo (and from there to Guaymas) or, much farther south, the road from Durango to Mazatlán.

State of Chihuahua

Ciudad Juárez ⓯ lies just across the border from El Paso, in Texas. It's an interesting town, the biggest in the state of Chihuahua, where you can watch the bullfights, go to the grayhound races, or even to the dentist (dental work is cheaper here than in the United States). However, the majority of travelers move on fairly quickly, in part because of recent drug-related crime, which has sadly overshadowed the tourism. While it's unlikely you will find trouble if you're not looking for it, Juárez and other border towns are less appealing than they were a few years ago.

About 300km (186 miles) south of Ciudad Juárez, **Paquimé** ⓰ (tel:

636-692 4140; Tue–Sun 10am–5pm; charge) also known as Casas Grande (the name of the surrounding township) is the most important archeological site in northern Mexico. A Unesco World Heritage site, the ruin is a series of beautifully eroded adobe walls and structures, many still preserved in clear detail. Key-shaped entryways and parrot cages are some of the intriguing legacy of the Paquimé, who lived here from around AD 900. Additionally, they knew how to irrigate the land and build three-story adobe houses. Once

Main attractions
CIUDAD JUÁREZ
PAQUIMÉ
CHIHUAHUA CITY
HIDALGO DEL PARRAL
CUAUHTÉMOC
CASCADA DE BASASEACHIC
BARRANCA DEL COBRE
MONTERREY
GRUTAS DE GARCÍA
SALTILLO
PARRAS
LA PESCA

LEFT: riding along the Copper Canyon tracks.
RIGHT: García Caves, Monterrey.

The beloved and reviled Chihuahua dogs do originate from this, the largest state in Mexico, though exactly why they appeared here remains shrouded in mystery. Explanations range from simple genetic inbreeding all the way to space aliens. We may never know, but the breed is here to stay.

BELOW: keeping watch in Chihuahua.

an important trading center, Paquimé combines elements of the Pueblo civilization from the southwestern United States along with Mesoamerican influences. The town was abandoned around 1300, possibly after attacks by Apaches. Paquimé-style pottery is made, using ancient techniques, in Mata Ortiz, a small town located 55km (34 miles) south of Nuevo Casas Grandes – about an hour's drive away. This small town has recently been rediscovered, and the pottery, created using a technique called burnishing which produces a highly polished surface without the use of traditional glaze, is a hot collector's item. Visits to Mata Ortiz can be done either through pre-arranged tours or by taxi from Nuevo Casas Grandes. You will tour the humble homes where the artisans work, and perhaps dine at one of the town's tiny restaurants. Despite the simple way of life and the apparent poverty, the pottery is quite expensive and collectors should plan on bringing plenty of pesos if they wish to take something home.

Founded in 1709, **Chihuahua City** ⑰, with a population of 670,000

and some fine colonial buildings, is worth more than a casual look. Quinta Luz, the 30-room mansion belonging to Pancho Villa, is now the **Museo de la Revolución** (tel: 614-416 2958; Tue–Sat 9am–1pm, 3–7pm; charge). Among the assorted memorabilia is the bullet-riddled Dodge car in which the bandit-turned-hero of the Revolution was gunned down in 1923. Señora Luz Corral de Villa, one of his many female companions, lived here until her death in 1981.

On the main plaza, the twin-towered Baroque **cathedral** is one of the few outstanding gems of colonial architecture to be found in the north of Mexico. It was financed by voluntary contributions from miners working in the nearby silver mines.

An aqueduct and the church of **San Francisco** (daily 7.30am–1pm, 4.30–8pm; free) also date from colonial times. Murals inside the **Palacio de Gobierno** (tel: 614-429 3596; 8am–8pm; free) tell the history of Chihuahua, while in the inner courtyard stands a monument to Father Miguel Hidalgo, hero of the War of

Independence, who was executed here. You can visit the grim dungeon in the Palacio Federal where he was imprisoned while awaiting his fate. Another mansion, **Quinta Gameros**, dates from the turn of the century and now houses the **Museo Regional** (tel: 614-410 5474; www.ccu.uach.mx; Tue–Sun 11am–2pm, 4–7pm; charge), with elaborate Art Nouveau exhibits and a display of Paquimé artifacts. The house was built as a gift from the owner to his fiancée, but during the construction she fell in love with the architect instead.

Hidalgo del Parral and Pancho Villa

Driving south from Chihuahua City you will see the state's richest agricultural regions. It is here that they grow many of Mexico's famous chili peppers. Silver was once the main support of the economy in the prosperous old mining town of **Hidalgo del Parral** ⓲. Nearby mines are still active although lumbering and commerce are now equally important.

The fine 18th-century church of **Nuestra Señora del Rayo** (Our Lady of the Lightning) is said to have been paid for in ingots by a local man who had struck gold but refused to reveal the location of the mine, even when beaten and tortured to death. Another fine church, **Nuestra Señora de Fátima**, is built entirely out of ore-bearing rock – gold, silver, copper, lead, zinc – right down to the pews inside.

Parral, as it is often called, is notorious as the town where General Francisco "Pancho" Villa was assassinated in 1923. There's a small museum (Museo Francisco Villa, tel: 627-525 3292; Tue–Sun 10am–5pm; charge) near the center, which contains old photos and a number of mementoes. Some years ago the government decided to rank Villa in with the country's other revolutionary heroes, and his grave was dug up, then the body reburied in the Monument to the Revolution in Mexico City.

The villages around the town of **Cuauhtémoc** ⓳, 95km (60 miles) southwest of Chihuahua City, are home to more than 15,000 members of the Mennonite sect, whose families moved here in the 1920s. Speaking their own

TIP

Residents of Chihuahua are not called Chihuahuaians or Chihuahuaese, they are Chihuahuenses. Don't confuse with Chihuahuenio either – that's for a dog!

BELOW: Mennonite gathering.

The Cuauhtémoc brewery and its parent company FESMA produce about 5.6 million barrels of beer annually.

dialect of old German, the Mennonites are farmers, best known for the mild cheese they produce *(queso menonita)*. They do not mix much and few speak Spanish. It is their custom to shun luxury and modernization, and most still drive around in horse-drawn carts (although nowadays you may see a pick-up truck or two).

Television is still taboo in most of the homes, and 10-children families are not uncommon. Some tours from Creel include sharing a simple lunch in a Mennonite household. Cuauhtémoc is the Mennonite center for commercial activity, though the people do not live here. During the day you will see them: overall-clad men, married women dressed in dark colors, and girls in bright floral dresses.

From Cuauhtémoc a paved road leads to the **Parque Nacional Cascada de Basaseachic** ⑳ and Mexico's highest waterfall. Be sure to enquire about road conditions before driving this route as access to the waterfall is difficult, especially during the rainy season. The falls plunge over 300 meters (1,000ft), but it's an easy

walk up the road to the top. If you are in good shape, walk about halfway down for a spectacular view. It is best to hire a local guide as the path is not clearly marked.

The Sierra Tarahumara

The **Barranca del Cobre** ㉑ (Copper Canyon; *see pages 202–3*), one of many canyons in the Sierra Tarahumara, southwest of Chihuahua City, is even deeper than the famous Grand Canyon of Colorado. This is Tarahumara country. Some 50,000 Tarahumara live in this region, typically in caves or wooden huts in the mountains. Although they are one of the largest indigenous groups left in Mexico, the Tarahumara are also one of the most reclusive, a condition that has exacerbated their dire poverty while at the same time enabling them to maintain many of their traditions.

The Chihuahua–Pacífico train ride, which has been called "the world's most scenic railroad," just might live up to its name. It winds up, over, around, under and through the Sierra Madre mountains, passing spectacular scenery the entire way. You can stop off at **Creel** ㉒ or **Divisadero** ㉓ and explore some of the canyon on foot (there are special trails to follow). Those not stopping should take care to disembark at the canyon for a 15-minute viewing. Poorly announced, it's easy to miss if you're not paying attention.

Northeast Mexico

Most foreign tourists cross the border into the northeast of Mexico at **Nuevo Laredo** ㉔. From here, it is less than a two-hour drive south to **Monterrey** ㉕, the third-largest city in the country and a center for industry and commerce. Old guidebooks refer to Monterrey as the "Pittsburgh of Mexico," but that description is outdated, for its huge steel industry was shut down years ago. *Regiomontanos* (natives of Monterrey) have an uneasy relationship with the government in Mexico City, and local businessmen often seem to have closer

BELOW:
Barranca del Cobre.

cultural ties with the US than with the rest of Mexico.

The capital of the state of Nuevo León, Monterrey produces about 25 percent of Mexico's manufactured goods, including half the manufactured exports. In the center of town, at the south end of the vast Macro Plaza, is the busy **Plaza Zaragoza**, with a Baroque-facaded **cathedral** on its east side and the modern Palacio Municipal to the south. Between the two is the **Museo de Arte Contemporáneo de Monterrey** (MARCO; tel: 81-8262 4500; www.marco.org.mx; Tue, Thur–Sun 10am–6pm, Wed until 8pm; charge), with its Latin American collection. Nearby stands a large free-form sculpture by Rufino Tamayo, one of Mexico's best-known 20th-century artists (*see page 117*).

Dominating the plaza is the Faro del Comercio, a concrete "beacon of commerce" designed by architect Luis Barragán, with a laser beam that sweeps the city every evening. Just northeast of the Macro Plaza, on Plaza Santa Lucía, the **Museo de Historia Mexicana** (tel: 81-2033 9898; www.museohistoriamexicana.org.mx; Tue–Fri

10am–7pm, Sat–Sun until 8pm; charge) is one of the best history museums in the country and has free guided tours.

Strategically situated on a hill 2.5km (1½ miles) west of the center, the 18th-century **Obispado** (Bishop's Palace), now the **Nuevo León Regional Museum** (tel: 81-8346 0404; Tue–Sun 10am–7pm; charge), affords an excellent overview of the city and an impressive mountain backdrop called **Cerro de la Silla** (Saddle Peak). The bullet holes and shellfire scars in the building's walls are souvenirs of the US invasion of September 1846; it was also attacked by the French in the 1860s and witnessed clashes between Villa's troops and Constitutionalists during the Revolution half a century later. A cheerful way to start or finish a tour of Monterrey, especially if you are thirsty, is with a visit to the **Cervecería Cuauhtémoc** (tel: 81-8328

Valley of the Mushrooms in Copper Canyon, near Creel.

LEFT: Monumento del Reloj (Clock Tower), Monterrey. **BELOW:** school music group.

5355; www.ccm.com.mx; Mon–Fri 9am– 4.30pm, Sat until 1.30pm; free), Mexico's biggest and oldest brewery, which produces Carta Blanca and Bohemia brands – fine Pilsner-type beers. The original brewery, also within the complex, has been converted into the **Museo de Monterrey** (Tue–Sun; free), one of the best museums of contemporary art in Mexico, with works by Murillo, Siqueiros, Orozco, Rivera and Tamayo, among others (*see pages 114–17*), as well as some excellent visiting exhibitions.

Out of town

It's worth spending some time exploring the area around Monterrey. A short drive up the pine-covered slope to the southwest of the city leads to **Chipinique Mesa**, Monterrey's most exclusive suburb, which also has a restaurant, hotel, picnic facilities and stunning views over the city and surrounding area. The **Grutas de García** ㉖ (tel: 81-8347 1533; daily 9am–5pm; charge), about 35km (21 miles) northwest of town, near Villa de García, are a spectacular series of caverns set high inside a mountain with astounding rock formations, stalactites and stalagmites. The drive from Monterrey is beautiful, although winding and narrow. You can take a little cable car up to the cave entrance.

Only a 15-minute drive from downtown Monterrey, outside suburban Santa Catarina, the **Cañón de la Huasteca** ㉗ is a dramatic 300-meter (1,000ft) deep canyon (the road is good only as far as the Gruta de la Virgen). The **Cola de Caballo** ㉘ waterfall is a 35km (22-mile) drive south of Monterrey. The area around the triple cascade called the **Tres Gracias** is an ideal picnic spot. En route you pass **La Boca** dam, where there is good fishing and water sports.

Mile-high city

The state of Coahuila is almost as big as neighboring Chihuahua. **Saltillo** ㉙, at 1,598 meters (5,245ft) above sea level, is the state capital, with a population of 600,000. This mile-high altitude with its sunny, dry climate has made Saltillo a favorite summer vacation spot, especially for visitors from the United States, for many years. There is also a fine university which runs Spanish courses for foreign students in summer.

Founded in 1575 by Captain Francisco Urdiñola, Saltillo became the Spanish headquarters for exploring and colonizing land to its north, and in the early 19th century it was the capital of a large area which included Texas. In 1847 one of the bloodiest and most decisive battles of the Mexican–American War took place at **Buena Vista** (half an hour south on Highway 54). A small monument marks the site. Soon after this battle the war ended and Mexico lost half of its territory to the USA. Nowadays, Saltillo is an interesting blend of colonial and modern; the city manages to maintain its charm despite being an important industrial center. The elaborate facade of the late 18th-century **Catedral de Santiago** (daily 9am–1pm, 4–7.30pm;

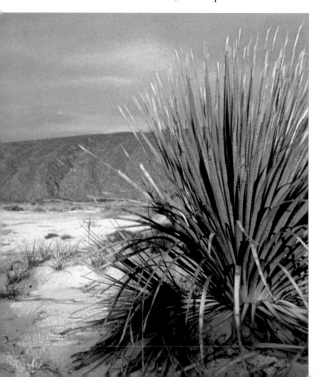

free) on the main plaza is one of the finest examples of Churrigueresque architecture in Mexico.

The elegant **Palacio de Gobierno** on the opposite side of the square is also worth visiting. Among the museums of Saltillo are the Museo del Desierto (tel: 844-986 9000; www.museodeldesierto. org; Tue–Sun 10am–5pm; charge), and the **Museo de las Aves de México** (tel: 844-414 0167; www.museodelasaves. org; Tue–Sat 10am–6pm, Sun and hols 11am–7pm; charge), an impressive museum devoted to the many birds of Mexico. The 2,000 specimens were collected by Aldegundo Garza de León over a period of 40 years.

Parras, a small town about 160km (100 miles) west of Saltillo, is an oasis in the Coahuilan desert and is also the birthplace of revolutionary leader Francisco Madero. An excellent local wine is bottled at nearby Casa Madero (tel: 844-132 0861; www.madero.com. mx; daily 8am–5.30pm; free) in San Lorenzo; this is Mexico's oldest winery, founded in 1626 (tours are conducted). Another specialty of the famous Saltillo vineyards is Brandy Madero.

South of Chihuahua and Coahuila, but still considered the north, the state of Durango is a cattle and lumber center which was once a popular location for Hollywood Westerns. Excursions to the film sets at **Chupaderos** and **Villa del Oeste** can be arranged by the local tourist office. The industrial city of **Durango** ③, with an attractive plaza, Baroque cathedral and other fine colonial buildings, is situated at a crossroads: to the southeast lies Zacatecas and the colonial heartland (*see pages 217–29*); to the southwest is Sinaloa and the Pacific coast at Mazatlán.

The Gulf Coast

People who cross the border at Brownsville or McAllen, in the east of Texas, enter Mexico through the towns of **Reynosa** ③ or **Matamoros** ③, in the state of Tamaulipas. The Gulf Coast of Mexico between the border and

Tampico, 619km (384 miles) farther south, has little to offer tourists except a scattering of hunting lodges and fishing camps. The roads are often poor and the coast is littered with oil refineries and tankers.

Most visitors choose to drive south through Monterrey and down to the colonial heartland of the central states. If you do choose the east coast route, the little town of San Fernando is a popular spot for a break, with good restaurants and hotels. It is also the center for hunting in the area.

About three hours southeast of Soto La Marina, **La Pesca** ③ is a sleepy little fishing village that was saved from being another tourist-trap like Cancún only by its lack of resources. In 1991 the government designated it a mega project; a small airport was built, plans were laid for building five-star hotels and land speculation became frantic. Fortunately, the project eventually fizzled out and the village, with its hotels, hunting lodges, and an RV park, retains much of its charm. From Soto La Marina to Tampico it's about a three-hour drive. ❏

Saltillo is famous for its colorful handwoven serapes which can be bought at the market on Plaza Acuña.

BELOW: a popular swimming spot at La Pesca.

THE WORLD'S MOST SCENIC RAILROAD

Riding on bridges over yawning chasms, viewing awesome scenery and age-old settlements – welcome aboard the Copper Canyon Railroad

Some of Mexico's most spectacular scenery is found in Chihuahua – the massive canyons and gorges in the Sierra Madre known as the Barranca del Cobre. It has taken millions of years for rivers and wind to mold what is actually a series of five interconneted canyons, covering 64,000 sq km (25,000 sq miles) of rugged land, that ranges from below sea level to more than 3,046 meters (10,000ft) at its peak. Mexico's tallest waterfall, the 300-meter (1,000ft) Cascada de Basaseachic, is found here, as well as a variety of plant life and one of the world's most interesting indigenous tribes. It is a living museum of natural history – except for animals. Although you may see buzzards and bald eagles flying overhead, the majority of animal life has disappeared.

The Ferrocarril Chihuahua al Pacífico, called "the world's most scenic railroad," hauls timber and tourists through this spectacular setting. This extraordinary feat of engineering – 661km (410 miles) in all – was begun in 1881 and not completed until 1961, at a total cost of more than US$100 million. It passes through 87 tunnels (one almost a mile long) and crosses 35 bridges. The train ride from Chihuahua to Los Mochis takes anywhere from 12 to 15 hours with short stops along the way to enjoy the splendid views – from alpine forests and rushing rivers to dusty gorges studded with Tarahumara settlements, and the remains of old missions and mining towns.

BELOW: if you prefer your views from the comfort of your own hotel room, try the Posada Barrancas Mirador in Divisadero, where everyone gets a look in.

LEFT: if you have a head for heights, enjoy the canyon view from one of the lofty scenic outlooks.
RIGHT: the Chihuahua-Pacífico Railroad is renowned for big vistas and small lunches. Tortillas and other local snacks fill a gap in the market.

ABOVE: the railroad project was conceived by US idealist [Alb]ert Owen, who came to Mexico to form a utopian colony [on] the Pacific coast.

BELOW: clothing for Tarahumara women and girls is usually [a s]ack-shaped tunic. Sometimes a woolen skirt is wound [aro]und their waist and held by a belt.

THE TARAHUMARAS

Long before the advent of the railroad, the highlands and deep gorges of the Copper Canyon were inhabited by the Tarahumara indians. Exploited for centuries by the Spanish colonists and the mestizos, these unique people give Copper Canyon part of its character. While some visitors may balk at the obvious poverty (begging at train stops is common), these people have carved a living out of these rough mountains for centuries, despite modern progress, the advent of the train, and missionary zeal. In church, their ancient gods *Raiénari* (Sun) and *Mechá* (Moon) happily exist side by side with images of Christ and the Catholic saints.

ABOVE: a Tarahumara woman in a bright cotton costume vends handmade baskets by the railroad line at the edge of the canyon.

BELOW: a variety of handicrafts are on sale at the Copper Canyon train stop, many of them following the same traditions that have been passed down from generation to generation for centuries.

THE NORTHWEST COAST

From the great desert of Sonora to the tropics of Nayarit, the northwest of Mexico offers fantastic beaches, good fishing, delicious seafood and spectacular birdlife

Main attractions
PUERTO PEÑASCO
MAGDALENA
BAHÍA KINO
ISLA DEL TIBURÓN
GUAYMAS
ALAMOS
EL FUERTE
MAZATLÁN
SANTIAGO IXCUINTLA
MEXCALTITÁN
SAN BLAS
IXTLÁN DEL RÍO

Northwest Mexico's vast stretches of barren yet beautiful desert, plateaus, and unique plants, animals, and birds was neglected by European invaders until the missionaries started to work among the tribes in the 17th century. The Jesuit priests introduced domestic animals, showed the indigenous peoples new crops and taught them farming and building techniques, as well as introducing less desirable things, like European diseases. Problems arose when Spanish colonists arrived and tried to take the most fertile lands and force local people into hard labor. The locals resisted and, as they were split into many tribes and spread out over great distances, they could not be conquered in one blow. Rebellion flared, on and off, for many years, particulary with the Yaqui (see page 211).

La Familia Revolucionaria

This areas was already fiercely independent and cut off, both culturally and geographically, from the rest of Mexico. Thus, by the time the Revolution broke out in 1910, the northwest had developed muscle and conscience and was ready to take part wholeheartedly in ushering in change, providing both troops and the general (Alvaro Obregón) who emerged after the inevitable internal power struggle. For a decade, Mexico was ruled directly or indirectly by one of Sonora's Familia Revolucionaria, first Obregón, then Generál Plutarco Elías Calles.

The Yaqui deal

The Yaquis, who had joined Generál Obregón's forces, wanted their tribal lands back, and when Cárdenas became president in the 1930s, he ordered a dam to be built on the upper Yaqui River for irrigation, setting aside some 4.5 million hectares (1 million acres) for the Yaqui tribes.

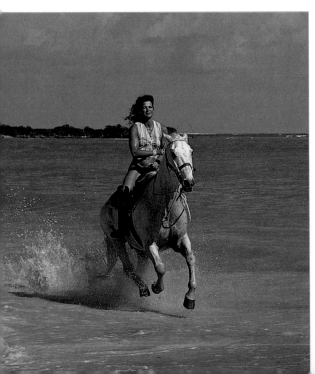

LEFT: saddle and surf.

It included the whole north bank of the river and part of the south. Setting up a reservation, the Yaquis took over their own tribal lands, which they control to this day. Other northwest natives did not fare so well. The Seris, for example, were either killed or died of European diseases and their population dropped from 5,000 to less than 200. The Opatas, on the other hand, disappeared due to assimilation: they learned Spanish, intermarried and cooperated in the battles against the Apaches.

The northwest is a highly productive region: Sonora leads the nation in cotton, wheat and soybean production; Sinaloa tops the other states in tomatoes – most of which go to the US – and also raises a hefty crop of wheat, cotton, sugar cane and chickpeas, which are exported chiefly to Spain and Cuba. Although the silver mines of the northwest are practically exhausted, the mines of Cananea make Sonora the country's leading producer of copper. (The 1906 miners' strike at Cananea was critical in the lead up to the Revolution.)

Mexicali to Mazatlán

The Pacific beaches are the main attraction of the route from the Arizona border to Mazatlán, but there are also interesting mountain towns and historical sights along the way. An excellent, though expensive, super-highway stretches down most of the coast. The alternative *libre* (free) route is longer and the traffic is predictably heavier.

Many people who come south from the US, either through **Mexicali** ❸❹ or **Nogales** ❸❺, begin with a jaunt to **Puerto Peñasco** in the far northwest corner of Sonora. This funky fishing village is a popular weekend retreat for Arizonans. Fishing and enjoying the beach are the main reasons for going there. If you are thinking of taking a boat out, be extremely careful as tides are hazardous and winds are strong in the shallow waters at the head of the Gulf of California. Like most of the resorts in the north, Puerto Peñasco offers good trailer facilities, with water and power hook-ups.

El Gran Desierto

There is precious little to break the beautiful monotony between the border and

"Familia Revolucionaria" *is not a term reserved only for the Sonora area, but includes all families throughout Mexico who were connected to the Revolution.*

BELOW:
colorful homes on a hillside adjacent to Mazatlán.

Waiting for a wave? Not all waves are surfable. To be "good surf" the waves have to be created by storms far out at sea, called swell, and have long intervals between them. Waves, the higher the better, are improved by a stiff offshore wind, which holds them up and shapes them nicely.

BELOW: passing time with friends.

Hermosillo. In the small town of **Magdalena**, 20km (12 miles) northeast of the junction at Santa Ana, a glass shrine contains the mortal remains of Padre Eusebio Kino, the Jesuit priest who helped establish missions along the coast, and later in Arizona and California. Often crippled with arthritis, Kino, a mathematician, astrologer, architect and economist, died in 1711 but his grave was only discovered in 1966. Gold is mined in the hills around Santa Ana but neither it nor Sonora's capital **Hermosillo ③⑥**, a thriving city with a Ford automobile plant, have much of interest to tourists.

Seri ironwood carvings

The next worthwhile stop is **Bahía Kino ③⑦**, which just about clings on to its unsophisticated fishing-village atmosphere, despite the many *norteamericanos* who choose to spend the winter months there. The local Seri sell wonderful handicrafts such as baskets and ironwood carvings, so-called

because they are made out of an exceptionally hard local wood. The Seri, a nomadic people, were moved to this part of Sonora from nearby **Isla del Tiburón ③⑧** (Shark Island), which is now a wildlife sanctuary.

Cool winter nights

You can rent a boat for fishing in most of the resort towns along the coast. It is easy to acquire a permit, and most come complete with tackle, crew and cold beer, though prices do vary, so you would be wise to shop around. Winter nights can get chilly along the coast of Sonora, and although it is sunny during the day, the water is cold for swimming. The ocean can get rough and swimmers should be careful of the big waves and powerful undertow, except in protected bays. There are ocean breezes even when it does warm up, and the Pacific beaches seldom get as muggy as the Gulf Coast.

A gringo oasis

Though many people call **Guaymas ③⑨** a beach resort, it is not. It is a fishing town and Sonora's main port, with ferries to Santa Rosalía in Baja California. The beaches are pretty and you can easily spend an afternoon just watching the sun sink to the sea as the pelicans glide by in formation. While drivers headed toward Baja won't save any money by taking the ferry, they will save time, and those without cars will find that the cost per passenger is still very reasonable. But don't plan your trip too closely as the ferry times and days change frequently.

Nearby **San Carlos** ⓴ is the beach resort; it is a gringo oasis inhabited by many retired Americans and Canadians. There are dozens of hotels and restaurants, and it has one of Mexico's largest marinas, with sailing vessels from all around the world. The 1970 movie *Catch 22* was shot nearby.

Navojoa, south of **Ciudad Obregón**, is the center of a major cotton-producing area and the home of the Mayo people. A detour from Navojoa takes you 53km (33 miles) inland to the beautiful old town of **Alamos** ⓵ in the foothills of the sierras. This was a rich mining center in the 18th century, with dozens of fabulous residences lining its cobblestone streets. After the Revolution, the mines were closed down and the town was practically abandoned. In the late 1940s, Alamos was rediscovered by wealthy Americans who bought up many of the colonial mansions and restored them. The beautiful central plaza is dominated by the Baroque-facaded church of **Nuestra Señora de la Concepción**. The town, which has some of the best examples of colonial architecture on the West Coast, is a national monument, and visiting it is like stepping back in time.

Los Mochis

From Navojoa, the main highway continues through some of the richest farmland in Mexico to **Los Mochis** ⓶, a pleasant and friendly town. Most people spend a day or two here while waiting for the **Copper Canyon train** *(see pages 202–3)*, which traverses the rugged mountains of the Sierra Madre to Chihuahua, offering one of the most spectacular train rides in the world. It leaves early in the morning and arrives in Chihuahua around nine at night. Los Mochis has become a boom town,

Alamos is the capital of the Mexican jumping bean, which is in fact a seed pod whose restlessness is due to the tiny larva of a moth growing inside it.

BELOW: there are splendid sea views from the popular resort of San Carlos.

The beach at Mazatlán, the closest Mexican resort to the US.

BELOW: washing by hand at a Mexcaltitán laundry.

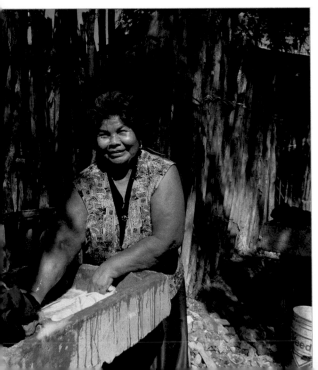

with rice, cotton, winter vegetables, sugar cane, and marigolds all produced nearby. Tourists will find it quiet, laid back, without a lot to offer aside from a pretty plaza. Hunting and beach-going are other options.

The ferry from La Paz in Baja California docks south of Los Mochis in **Topolobampo**. Just off the coast, the rocky island of **Farallón** (sometimes called Isla las Animas) is a breeding ground for sea lions and attracts flocks of sea birds. The underwater marine life around the island is colorful.

El Fuerte, an important Spanish settlement during colonial times, and once capital of the state of Sinaloa, is a picturesque town 78km (48 miles) northeast of Los Mochis. Apart from the plaza, the museum (tel: 698-893 1501; daily 9am–7pm; charge) and the church, it is worth visiting the Posada del Hidalgo (tel: 698-893 1194;

www.hotelposadadelhidalgo.com), a 19th-century mansion which has been converted into a beautiful hotel. Fishing for catfish and carp is possible in the nearby Presa Miguel Hidalgo, one of the best bass-fishing lakes in the country. El Fuerte is far more picturesque than Los Mochis, and many tourists taking the Copper Canyon railway may want to overnight here. The train stops briefly to pick up passengers but doesn't wait. Anyone not there at the station will have to wait 24 hours before getting another chance.

From Los Mochis to Mazatlán, the highway cuts through **Culiacán**, capital of Sinaloa, known for its bumper crops of tomatoes and opium, both destined for the US (some opium is legally exported for medicinal purposes). Marijuana is another crop grown in the complex landscape of the Sierra Madre Occidental. Culiacán, along with Sinaloa, are current centers of the Mexican drug trade, and visitors are strongly warned against using or dealing; Mexican anti-drug laws are very strict, and looking for drugs is one of the quickest ways to get mixed up in the usually non-tourist crimes connected with warring gangs.

The toll road from Culiacán to Mazatlán, the most expensive stretch, saves about 1½ hours, while traffic on the old free route is congested, although the road surface is usually quite good. About halfway between the two, you can make a detour to **Cosalá**, an old mining town with hot springs nearby.

The Pearl of the Pacific

Mazatlán ❹ (meaning "Place of the Deer" in Náhuatl) is a booming resort town about 15km (9 miles) south of the Tropic of Cancer. It is also one of the most important ports on Mexico's west coast and home to the country's largest shrimp fleet. Unlike most Mexican towns, Mazatlán's first plaza, Plaza Zaragoza, was not built around a church and government offices because the city's richest and most influential people were merchants. Only later was the Plaza de la República built. Both plazas are worth visiting. Much of the action occurs along the long Malecón, a pedestrian avenue that follows the white sand beaches. Golf carts, often souped up to suit the driver's tastes, are as common as taxis.

The old part of the city, situated on a peninsula, centers around the Plaza Principal and the 19th-century twin-towered cathedral, whose unusual facade is decorated with intricately carved volcanic rock. Towering over this old part of town, the **Cerro de la Nevería** (Icebox Hill) has panoramic sea views. Most tourists spend their time in the so-called **Zona Dorada** (Golden Zone), a long stretch of hotels, restaurants and shops about 3km (2 miles) north of the old town. Here, close to the biggest hotels, is the well-stocked **Centro de Artesanías** (Arts and Crafts Center).

A little farther south, near Playa del Norte, the **Acuario Mazatlán** (tel: 669-981-7815; www.acuariomazatlan.gob.mx; daily 9.30am–5.30pm; charge), with nearly 200 species of fish, is worth a visit. Local travel agencies organize city and jungle tours. There are also boat trips around the harbor and to the nearby islands.

Winter is the most popular season here, though any time of the year is pleasant. Summer is the "rainy" season, but unless there is a hurricane nearby it will not greatly inconvenience you. *Carnaval* in Mazatlán (the week before Ash Wednesday) is one of Mexico's liveliest fiestas; hotel reservations are essential then, as they are between Christmas and New Year, and for the week before Easter, when all beach resorts are jam-packed. There is plenty in the local area to explore, including the countryside and nearby swamp areas. There is also a popular Tequila Tour (contact Vista Tours; tel: 669-986 8610.)

On a cloudy day you may want to take a short detour east up Highway 40 into the foothills of the Sierra Madre for a pleasant day trip from Mazatlán. The colonial town of **Concordia** ❹, set in lush, tropical vegetation with hot springs nearby, is known for its pottery and hand-carved furniture. Picture-postcard **Copala** ❺, 25km (16 miles)

The best views in Mazatlán are from El Faro, the lighthouse at the southern tip of the peninsula; at 157 meters (515ft) above sea level, it is said to be the world's second highest (after Gibraltar).

BELOW: gentle sunset over the water.

Mexico's national symbol originated from an Aztec legend.

farther on, with its cobblestone streets, red-tiled roofs and wrought-iron balconies, is an old silver-mining town. Keep your eyes peeled for wild parrots; sightings are not unusual.

The Huichol

Craftwork from all over the Republic can be found in Mazatlán, but particularly beautiful is the beaded artwork and weavings of the Huichol people. However, if you are on your way south, it is more helpful to them –and more interesting for you – if you wait until you reach **Santiago Ixcuintla** ㊻. Here there is a Huichol Center for Cultural Survival and Traditional Arts (tel: 323-235 1171; www.huicholcenter.org), where you can watch Huichol families making their crafts; any money you spend here goes directly to the tribe, and much of it to the nearby hospital (tuberculosis, malnutrition, and other ailments mean Huichol children suffer a 50 percent infant mortality rate).

The Venice of Mexico

The small island village of **Mexcaltitán** ㊼ has been nicknamed the "Venice of

Mexico," because, during heavy rains, the streets are frequently flooded and you have to pole your way around town in a canoe. But in recent years more and more of the streets have been filled in, so Mexcaltitán's waterlogged days are probably limited. The seafood here is excellent, but don't look for luxury hotels; the town is a bit run down. Some historians believe that Mexcaltitán is the legendary island of Aztlán, the original home of the Aztec people and the place where they first had the vision of the eagle perched on a cactus with a serpent in its claws; this symbol of their promised land was eventually found in Tenochtitlán, now Mexico City.

Surf City

San Blas ㊽ is a quiet fishing town noted for the ferocity of its gnats, known as *jejenes*. The insects are at their worst early in the morning, in the evenings and during a full moon, so be sure to stock up on insect repellent. Surfers flock to San Blas to ride its famous long waves, and ornithologists come to watch the many

BELOW: aerial view of the island village of Mexcaltitán, Mexico's Little Venice.
RIGHT: Mexcaltitán sisters at play.

species of migrating and native birds that take refuge here. Birdwatching trips to the **Santuario de Aves** (Bird Sanctuary) can be arranged. Another popular pastime is to take the jungle boat-ride up the San Cristóbal estuary, through a green tunnel of vegetation to **La Tovara** springs, where you can swim in crystal-clear water, picnic, or eat at one of the *palapa* (shack) restaurants.

Although it is hard to believe now, San Blas was once a ship-building center and the point of departure for Spanish exploration of the Pacific Northwest. Vestiges of this period include the old **Aduana** (customs house) by the port and the **Fuerte de Basilio**, a counting house built in 1768. It was the church here that inspired 19th-century US poet Henry Wadsworth Longfellow to write the poem entitled *The Bells of San Blas*.

The journey to Ixtlán

About 70km (44 miles) inland, **Tepic ㊾**, the capital of the state of Nayarit, has a pleasant square, flanked by a cathedral with impressive neo-Gothic towers, though overall the city does not cater much to foreign tourists and is better as a lunch stop on the way to Tequila or Guadalajara rather than as a destination all its own. The **Museo Regional de Nayarit** (tel: 311-212 1900; Mon–Fri 9am–6pm, Sat and hols until 3pm; charge) houses a collection of pre-Hispanic ceramics and the **Museo de Artes Populares** (tel: 311-212 1705; Mon–Sat 9am–2pm, 4–7pm; free) exhibits handicrafts by Huichol, Cora, Náhuatl and Tepehuano people which can be bought far more cheaply here than in the resort boutiques.

Just outside the town of **Ixtlán del Río ㊿** – made famous by Carlos Castaneda's *Journey to Ixtlán* – is an extensive and largely restored archeological site, **Los Toriles** (daily 9am–5pm; charge), which flourished in the 2nd century AD. The main structure is an unusual circular stone temple with cruciform windows, dedicated to Quetzalcóatl. ❑

Carved coconut heads make an unusual souvenir.

The Yaqui Indians

When the Jesuits were expelled from Mexico in 1767, the missions disintegrated and the colonists brazenly encroached on tribal lands. The Yaquis, a fighting race, reacted angrily and the Spanish dealt with them harshly. For centuries the tribes of the northwest were isolated in a remote corner of Mexico. They took little part in the life of the nation and were marginal to the Independence movement of the 1810s. The region was weak and unprotected and practically invited invasion. The French, led by Gaston Raousset de Bourbon, captured Hermosillo in 1852, and in 1857 Henry Crabb, an American from California, tried to capture northern Sonora. In both instances, the Mexicans reacted vigorously, defeating the invaders and executing the leaders.

The largest campaign against the Yaqui was in the 1880s–90s, under Porfirio Díaz, when large numbers of Yaqui were taken to Yucatán. But several decades later the Yaquis, in exchange for their help during the Revolution, requested their lands back. When Cárdenas became president in the 1930s, he set aside 485,000 hectares (1 million acres) for the Yaqui tribes. It included the whole north bank of the Yaqui River and part of the south.

CENTRAL MEXICO

Famous for its Pacific beaches, tequila and
Unesco World Heritage sites; above all this is
the heartland of colonial Mexico

The Central Highlands were a source of wealth for the Spanish colonists, as the silver route from Zacatecas to Mexico City passed through the magnificent towns of the so-called colonial heartland. The cathedrals, monasteries, chapels and mansions that can be visited today are the exquisite legacy of Spanish prosperity, on the one hand, and of the extreme exploitation of indigenous labor, on the other. In the 19th century the Independence movement was ignited in El Bajío – the triangle formed by the towns of Querétaro, San Luis Potosí and Aguascalientes. El Bajío's San Miguel de Allende has become one of the most important tourist towns in all of Mexico.

To the south are the rolling hills of Michoacán, one of the most beautiful states in the Republic. Visitors can ride up to the crater of a smoldering volcano or else witness the spectacular sight of the Monarch butterflies that arrive from Canada in their millions each year. For anyone traveling in November, nowhere is Mexico's unique Day of the Dead celebrated more fervently than in the delightful town of Pátzcuaro and on the nearby island of Janitzio.

Fields of blue-green agave surround the world-famous town of Tequila. Among other things, Jalisco is home to the Cora and Huichol people who live in the sierra and make yearly pilgrimages to San Luis Potosí – a 1,600km (1,000-mile) round trip – to collect the hallucinogenic peyote cactus that is central to their ancient rituals. Guadalajara, the "City of Roses" is a rose itself, a magnet for language students, artists, musicians, and cooks.

Jalisco is also the gateway to the Pacific coast, where mega-resorts of Puerto Vallarta, Ixtapa, and Acapulco attract sun-worshippers by the tens of thousands. Break-bound surfers will find the azure coastlines hold a wealth of waves at almost every corner, and anyone who wants to get away from the crowds will find there are still hundreds of kilometers of deserted coast fringed with vast plantations of bananas, mangoes and coconuts.❑

PRECEDING PAGES: a Guadalajara monument to illustrious Jalisco people.
FAR LEFT: statue of Papila, overlooking Guanajuato. **FROM TOP:** party people; a *charro* entering the rodeo ring; Voladores de Papantla performing in Zacatecas.

EL BAJÍO AND THE COLONIAL HEARTLAND

For centuries, the mines of central Mexico produced much of the world's silver; their legacy today is reflected in some of the country's finest colonial architecture

México City

Less visited than the coastal resorts and some parts of southern Mexico, the five states of the central highlands, to the north of Mexico City, have much to offer any traveler who has the time, patience and curiosity to explore. Zacatecas, Aguascalientes, San Luis Potosí, Guanajuato and Querétaro are the colonial heartland of Mexico. Some of the most impressive colonial architecture can be seen in the cities of this region, which grew and flourished under Spanish rule as a result of the huge quantities of silver and other metal extracted from the local mines. Several of these areas have earned Unesco World Heritage status.

Crown in 1546. Soon after, enormous quantities of silver were being mined and shipped off to Spain. Fortunes were rapidly amassed and Zacatecas, as a result of this prosperity, has some of the finest colonial architecture in Mexico. Declared a Unesco World Heritage site in 1993, the city is one of the cleanest and friendliest in Mexico, and combines the vigor and roughness of the north with the architectural refinement of the Central Highlands. The elegant stone mansions have fancy wrought-iron balconies and window

Main attractions

CHALCHIHUITES
ZACATECAS
MINA EL EDEN
TEATRO HINOJOSA
LA QUEMADA
AGUASCALIENTES
SAN LUIS POTOSÍ
REAL DE CATORCE
GUANAJUATO
FESTIVAL CERVANTINO
LA VALENCIANA
DOLORES HIDALGO
SAN MIGUEL DE ALLENDE
QUERÉTARO
SAN JUAN DEL RÍO
TEQUISQUIAPAN

Zacatecas, the pink city

The state of **Zacatecas** is the gateway between the huge, barren and empty north and the richer, more fertile and more densely populated highland region of central Mexico. The fortified archeological site at **Chalchihuites ❶**, in the northwest of the state, which flourished from AD 900 to 1200, has yielded ceramic treasures that suggest contact between the Mesoamerican style of the Central Highlands and the simpler geometric art style of the American West.

The city of **Zacatecas ❷**, spectacularly sited between arid hills at an altitude of 2,500 meters (8,200ft), was declared the property of the Spanish

LEFT: a Zacatecas neighborhood at night.
RIGHT: indigenous dance group.

Central Mexico

0 — 100 km

0 — 100 miles

grilles. Meandering the streets, camera or sketchbook in hand, is an agreeable way to discover the city's charm. The main sights are mostly concentrated in a small area of 12 blocks, easily explored on foot. To the north of this area, on the Plaza de Armas, the **cathedral**, with its delicately carved pink stone facade, is considered one of the masterpieces of Mexican Baroque. Also on the plaza are two colonial mansions: the **Palacio de la Mala Noche** and the **Palacio de Gobierno**.

Around the cathedral

Just south of the cathedral are the 19th-century **Teatro Calderón** and the **Mercado González Ortega**, a turn-of-the-20th century cast-iron structure that has been converted into a shopping center. Uphill from the Plaza de Armas, behind a sober facade, the 18th-century **Santo Domingo** church holds some fine gilded altarpieces. The 17th-century monastery next door, now the **Museo Pedro Coronel** (Fri–Wed 10am–5pm; charge), exhibits an enviable collection of both ancient and modern art and artifacts from all over the world (including works by Picasso, Braque, Chagall and Miró), which this noted Zacatecan artist bequeathed to his home town. The artist's brother also donated a collection, this one of masks, 19th-century marionettes and pre-Hispanic pottery. These are displayed in the magnificently restored Convento de San Francisco, now the **Museo Rafael Coronel** (tel: 492-922 8116; Thur–Tue 10am–5pm; charge).

Perhaps the most fascinating local attraction is a trip into the heart of the **Mina El Eden** (tel: 492-922 3002; daily10am–6pm; charge), one of Mexico's richest mines, which was worked from 1586 until the 1950s. As the tour passes dramatically lit shafts, subterranean pools and chasms, the guides describe the deplorable working conditions that existed for the miners in the colonial era. For a thrilling view of the city, a cable car will take you from the entrance to the mine up to the top of the **Cerro de la Bufa**. On weekends there's dancing in a discotheque that has been installed near the entrance of the mine.

Large quantities of grapes are harvested in Aguascalientes, most of which go to make a local brandy.

BELOW: a horse takes a well-earned break.

The early 18th-century **Convento de Guadalupe** (tel: 492-923 2386; daily 9am–6pm; charge, free on Sun), 10km (6 miles) southeast of Zacatecas, is a remarkable museum and monastery with one of the most elaborately decorated chapels and an impressive collection of colonial paintings. Viewed on a bright day, the majestic exterior, with its pink stone walls and cupola, is postcard perfect. Inside, it seems almost fantastical with its scooped out ceilings, high arches, and pastel blues and golds.

About 45km (28 miles) to the west of Zacatecas, through the best cattle-raising country in Mexico, in the attractive colonial town of **Jerez**, is the horseshoe-shaped **Teatro Hinojosa**, a replica of Ford's Theatre in Washington, DC.

Just off the road to Guadalajara, about 50km (30 miles) south of Zacatecas, the ruins of **La Quemada** ❸ (daily 9.30am–5pm; charge) spread over the hillside. It is thought to have been part of a trade network, and was inhabited between AD 300 and 1300, when it was destroyed by fire. It is one of the largest sites of that era ever discovered, and it is well worth a detour to see it. Like many Mexican archeological sites, La Quemada remains shrouded in mystery – some theorize that this was a temporary settlement used en route to elsewhere, others point to the establishment of defensive walls and additional indicators and claim it was a settlement in its own right. Either way, it's an interesting spot to explore, and some of the ruins are sensitively preserved.

Aguascalientes

The city of **Aguascalientes** ❹ regards itself as Mexico's grape capital. Until recently the small state of Aguascalientes, south of Zacatecas, was an important wine-producing region but the local vintners could not compete with imported wines, either on price or quality. Today most of the grapes wind up in Mexican brandy, which bears only a slight resemblance to Spanish brandy or French cognac. The **San Marcos Winery** north of the city conducts tours. Also north of town are the hot springs from which the town takes its name.

Aguascalientes' **Jardín San Marcos**, west of the town center, hosts one of Mexico's biggest annual festivals. During the end of April and early May, thousands of visitors flock to the **Feria de San Marcos** for the parades, exhibitions, bullfights, singing, dancing and brandy drinking.

On the main Plaza de la Patria is the impressive 18th-century **Palacio de Gobierno**; brightly colored murals by Chilean artist Oswaldo Barra Cunningham decorate the patio walls inside. The 18th-century Baroque **cathedral** and the religious picture gallery next door both contain paintings by colonial artist Miguel Cabrera. There are several museums in Aguascalientes, but the highlight is the **Museo José Guadalupe Posada** (tel: 449-915 4556; Tue–Sun 11am–6pm; charge, free on Sun), next door to the Templo del Encino. Posada, most famous for his satirical (skeleton) prints *(see page 114)* and a great social and political critic during the *Porfiriato*, inspired many later artists, including Diego Rivera and José Clemente Orozco *(see pages 114–17)*. The museum houses over 200 works by this local artist. A new **Museo de los Muertos** (tel: 449-139 3258; Tue–Sun 10am–6.30pm; charge, free on Wed) offers a close, intimate, fun look at the fate that awaits us.

San Luis Potosí

The state of San Luis Potosí is large and diverse: the east is hot and tropical; dry plains stretch across the center; while the west, like neighboring Zacatecas, is mountainous and rugged. The industrial city of **San Luis Potosí ⑤** is the state capital and was the seat of Juárez's government before the defeat of Maximilian. The attractive city center has many beautiful plazas, elegant mansions and pedestrian walkways. The city's pre-eminent jewel is the **Templo del Carmen**, a Churrigueresque church completed in 1764 and adorned with shells on the facade, multicolored tiles on the dome and a wonderfully intricate retablo inside. The adjacent **Teatro de la Paz** was built in the 19th century, during the dictatorship of Don Porfirio Díaz. Across the street the **Museo Nacional de la Máscara** (tel: 444-812

The lyrics for the Mexican national anthem were composed by San Luis Potosí poet, Francisco González Bocanegra.

LEFT: the Museo Rafael Coronel in Zacatecas is housed in the restored Convento de San Francisco. **BELOW:** a swimming hole near San Luis Potosí.

Statues of Don Quixote and Sancho Panza at the Museo Iconográfico del Quijote in Guanajuato.

3032; Tue–Sun 10am–5pm; charge) displays over 2,000 ceremonial masks, both pre-Hispanic and modern, from all over Mexico. The **Museo Regional de Arte Popular** (tel: 444-814 3572; Tue–Sun 10am–7pm; charge, free on Sun) is a regional handicrafts museum housed in a former Franciscan monastery; the richly decorated 18th-century Capilla de Aranzazú is on the second floor.

Shopping is a popular pastime here in San Luis Potosí, and you'll find an abundance of handiwork and crafts, especially textiles and fabrics, often handwoven by craftsmen whose families have been doing similar work for decades or even centuries.

Real de Catorce

Once a thriving silver-mining center housing a royal mint and 40,000 inhabitants, **Real de Catorce ❻** is practically a ghost town today. It is located in the mountains west of Matehuala. You have to go through a 2.5km (1½-mile) tunnel – a former mine shaft – to reach this extraordinary town where street after street of once sumptuous mansions stand eerily in ruins. However, the 1,000-strong population provides rooms to rent, as well as stores, restaurants, silversmiths and (why not?) mystics.

Guanajuato

The city of **Guanajuato ❼**, which in the local tongue translates to "Hill of Frogs," is the capital of the state and one of Mexico's most famous tourist spots. In colonial days it was the center of a rich mining area and one of the greatest producers of silver in the world. The mines were flooded during the wars for Independence, but reopened again under Porfirio Díaz. Abandoned again in the Revolution, they reopened recently as the price of silver escalated.

A Unesco World Heritage site, Guanajuato is charming, romantic and sometimes eerie. This well-preserved city is built in a ravine and on the banks of a river; no street runs in a straight line; all go their crooked ways, up and down steep hills, some falling into an abyss; in some houses the entrance is through the roof. Tunnels and streets wind their way along the basements of the town's old buildings, with steps intermittently leading to a square or winding alley. Buildings new and old are brightly colored and give the vistas a fiesta-like feel even when nothing in particular is going on.

Central Guanajuato

At the heart of Guanajuato is the **Jardín de la Unión Ⓐ**, a cool, shady wedge-shaped plaza surrounded by cafés. Across the road is the churrigueresque church of **San Diego Ⓑ**, next door to the magnificent **Teatro Juárez Ⓒ** (Tue–Sun; charge), inaugurated in 1903 by the dictator Porfirio Díaz himself, and with a "French-Moorish" interior.

Almost all of Guanajuato's sights are to the west of the Jardín de la Unión, with the exception of the **Museo Iconográfico del Quijote Ⓓ** (tel: 473-732 3376; Tue–Sat 10am–6.30pm, Sun 10am–2.30pm; charge), a few blocks to the east. Dedicated to Cervantes's *Don Quixote de la Mancha*, the collection –

ranging from dime-store junk to works by Picasso and Dalí – was donated by a rich advertising executive and avid Quixote-phile.

Two blocks west of Jardín de la Unión, near **Plaza de la Paz Ⓔ**, are some of Guanajuato's richest colonial buildings. The **Supreme Court**, which was designed by the 18th-century architect Eduardo de Tresguerras, was the home of the Condes de Rul y Valenciana, owners of Mexico's richest silver mine. On the east side of the plaza is the **Basílica de Nuestra Señora de Guanajuato Ⓕ**, which houses the image of the city's patroness, a gift in 1557 from King Philip II of Spain and said to date from the 7th century.

The **University Ⓖ**, a huge white building, is an outstanding example of Moorish-inspired architecture only half a century old, relatively new in comparison to its ancient surroundings. It is the pride of Guanajuato and the centerpiece of the **Festival Cervantino**, an important international arts festival which is celebrated in Guanajuato every October. The pink stone baroque **Templo de la Compañía Ⓗ**, is the grandest

Once a year, on October 4, Real de Catorce comes back to life when thousands of pilgrims arrive to celebrate the feast of St Francis.

LEFT: collecting peyote in Real de Catorce.

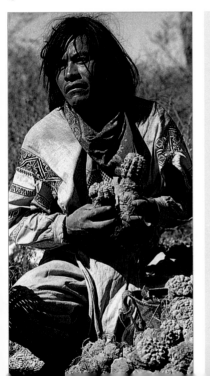

Guanajuato's Festival Cervantino

Originally a casual university production of Cervantes' farces (from whence the name), the Festival Cervantino, held each October, has grown in size and scope and now is one of Mexico's largest and grandest performance art festivals. Tourists from all over the world flood the city (and the streets) to watch the various events, which include all kinds of dramatic and performing arts, such as plays, music, opera, concerts, recitals, stage events, and so on. Each year the focus is on a particular Mexican state, and a different foreign country is honored, making this truly a uniquely multicultural experience. In 2009, for example, Quebec and Zacatecas were given the seat of honor. Other locales of honor have included Catalonia and Campeche (2008), China and San Luis Potosí (2007), Japan, Spain, and Yucatán (2005).

Recently there has been a bit of controversy surrounding the problematic and excessive use of drugs and alcohol. In response, city officials have taken steps to regulate drinking, as well as beef up the police presence during the festivities, which has helped keep things from getting out of hand. This is still considered "one big party" by many twentysomethings, so despite prohibitions on drinking alcohol openly in the streets, visitors should keep in mind that there's plenty of craziness and cavorting mixed in with the culture.

church in town with an impressive 19th-century dome and paintings by Miguel Cabrera inside. One block west of the university, the **Museo Casa Diego Rivera ❶** (tel: 473-732 1197; Tue–Sat 10am–6pm, Sun 10am–2pm; charge) exhibits a collection of works by the famous muralist, who was born in this house in 1886.

Plaza San Roque ❶ is renowned for its presentations of *Entremeses Cervantinos*. These light-hearted theatrical sketches by 16th-century Spanish writer Miguel de Cervantes have become a tradition in Guanajuato and are central to the Festival Cervantino. Nearby, in a French wrought-iron structure, **Guanajuato's Market ❶** is large, noisy and full of good and bad smells.

Other Attractions

Originally a granary, the impressive **Alhóndiga de Granaditas ❶** (tel: 473-732 1112; Tue–Sat 10am–5.30pm, Sun 10am–2pm; charge) was used as a fortress for the Spanish and Royalists during the War of Independence before being captured by the rebels after the

famous Pípila incident. Carrying a slab of stone on his back for protection, a local miner known as the Pípila rushed the door of the Alhóndiga, set it on fire, and the rebels poured in. Today the building houses a museum with murals by Chávez Morado and a collection of paintings by the 19th-century Guanajuato artist, Hermenegildo Bustos. A grandiose monument to **Pípila ❶** stands on a ridge overlooking the city; it's a steep climb, but the view from the top is superb.

The best panoramic view of Guanajuato is from **La Valenciana** (daily 10am–7pm; charge), the mine which under its Spanish colonial masters produced a large quantity of the world's silver. The elaborate church of **San Cayetano**, next to the mine, is a masterpiece of churrigueresque style and the interior is quite dazzling. On the way you may want to stop at Guanajuato's most famous attraction, the **Museo de las Momias** (tel: 473-732 0639; daily 9am–6pm; charge). The museum exhibits over 100 grotesque mummified corpses mostly found when the public cemetery was extended in 1865

The Cry of Independence

On the morning of September 16, 1810, in the town of Dolores, the parish priest Padre Miguel Hidalgo rang the church bells. He addressed the congregation with an impassioned speech and ended with his famous *Grito de Dolores*: "Death to the Spaniards" *(Que mueran los gachupines)* – the "shout" for independence from Spanish rule, and the most famous outcry in Mexican history.

Hidalgo, a creole, soon became the moral and political leader of the Independence movement. He had no military training but with the help of men like Ignacio Allende, his forces – creoles, mestizos and Amerindians – took control of a large part of western central Mexico and came close to taking the capital itself. Ten months later Hidalgo was imprisoned and executed by firing squad in Chihuahua. After Independence was finally won 11 years later the town was renamed Dolores Hidalgo.

Every year, on the night of September 15, enormous crowds gather to hear the president and politicians in the squares of every town across the whole country repeat *El Grito*: "¡Viva México!" marking the beginning of Independence Day celebrations; and that is the one night of the year when the church bell still rings out in the colonial town of Dolores Hidalgo.

(the combination of mineral-rich soil and exceptionally dry air can mummify bodies in as little as five years).

The beautiful 17th-century **Hacienda San Gabriel Barrera** (daily 9am–6pm; charge), about 2km (1 mile) out of town on the road to Marfil, may not be completely authentic, but it does give visitors an idea of the opulence of the wealthy during the colonial era.

Dolores Hidalgo

Dolores Hidalgo ❽, 45km (28 miles) northeast of Guanajuato, is known as the cradle of Mexican Independence. The beautiful 18th-century **Parroquia** on the main square, where Hidalgo uttered his famous *Grito (see page 224)*, is lovingly preserved. The **Museo Casa de Hidalgo** (Tue–Sun 10am–5.30pm; charge), at the corner of Hidalgo and Morelos, is where Hidalgo lived and plotted the uprising with Ignacio Allende and Juan de Aldama. The museum displays personal items and documents related to the life of the priest. Dolores is a typical Mexican town: the houses are solid and secretive, and there are many simple churches. Several workshops in town produce Talavera-type pottery and the ice-cream stands round the square are famous for the unusual flavors they offer.

San Miguel de Allende

The pretty colonial streets and buildings of **San Miguel de Allende ❾** have been protected since 1926, when the whole town was declared a National Monument. Initially a native settlement, owing to the natural spring, the town grew exponentially after mining began in Zacatecas and other places north. In 1938, US artist Stirling Dickinson founded an art school here. Soon after, the town began to attract foreign artists, writers and, eventually, tourists, and even now it is easy to see the attraction. The **Instituto Allende** is still a popular arts and language center and one of the town's chief attractions, housed in what was the 18th-century home of the Conde de Canal. It offers a wide range of courses, including photography, sculpture, painting and weaving. San Miguel de Allende now has a large

TIP

It is still possible to see people doing laundry in the local spring, one of the traditions that has endured in San Miguel de Allende for centuries.

BELOW: relaxing at a viewpoint overlooking the Unesco World Heritage site of Guanajuato.

The Cerro de Cubilete, a mountain between Guanajuato and León, marks the geographical center of Mexico. On the summit stands a 20-meter (65ft) statue of Christ with open arms, blessing the valley below.

BELOW: dome of the parroquia, San Miguel de Allende.
RIGHT: a bride-to-be arrives at church.

community of US expatriates, including many artists and writers.

On the main plaza and dominating the entire town, the neo-Gothic **Parroquia** (parish church) was designed in the late 19th century by self-taught stonemason, Zeferino Gutiérrez who gained inspiration from postcards of French churches, which is why the rest of the building is so different in construction from the wild facade.

Across the road from the parroquia, the **Museo Histórico de San Miguel de Allende** (tel: 415-152 2499; Tue–Sun 9am–5pm; charge) occupies the elegant house where Independence hero Ignacio Allende was born. Exhibits relate to local history, particularly that of the Independence movement and its heroes. Also on the plaza is the **Casa de los Condes de Canal**, one of the palatial mansions of the aristocratic Canal family, the devout "Medici" of San Miguel. It now houses the offices of Banamex, one of Mexico's largest banking institutions. It was Canal money in the 1730s that paid for the **Santa Casa de Loreto**, part of the multi-towered, 18th-century

Oratorio de San Felipe Neri, a few blocks northeast. Dedicated to the Virgin Mary, the chapel is a replica of one in Loreto, Italy, and contains a lavish *camerino*, or dressing chapel. The main church contains more than 30 oil paintings depicting the life of San Felipe, some by Miguel Cabrera.

Two blocks west of the Jardín on Calle Canal, is the church and monastery of **La Concepción** whose huge dome (added in the late 19th century, again by Zeferino Gutiérrez) was inspired by that of Les Invalides in Paris. The former monastery now houses **Bellas Artes** (tel: 415-152 0289; daily 9am–7pm; free), a state-run fine arts education and cultural center. Like the Instituto Allende, Bellas Artes runs arts and crafts courses, although usually only in Spanish. One room contains an unfinished mural by David Alfaro Siqueiros (*see pages 114–17*) who taught at the institute in the 1940s.

One of San Miguel's major attractions is the excellent shopping. In fact, it's hard to walk for more than 60 seconds without passing a gallery, shop, or store. Many of the businesses around the main square sell beautiful handmade items, including the finely woven tablecloths and the tin and brass ware produced in the region. You can also hop in a horse-drawn carriage for a scenic bump over the cobblestones.

El Charco del Ingenio (daily sunrise–sunset; charge) is a 65-hectare (160-acre) botanical garden mainly devoted to the cultivation of cacti, and other plants and wildlife native to this semi-arid region of Mexico. Situated on a hill just 1.5km (1 mile) northeast of San Miguel, the view of the town in the valley below is spectacular.

There are several resorts with hot springs and mineral waters in the area surrounding San Miguel. Taboada, 10km (6 miles) northwest, is probably the most popular. A little further on, in the village of Atotonilco ❿, is a Baroque pilgrimage church filled with a huge variety of artwork including frescoes by the colonial artist Miguel Antonio Martínez de Pocasangre.

Cities of El Bajío

The colonial cities of León, Irapuato, Salamanca and Celaya, also in the state of Guanajuato, are growing rapidly and not much favored by tourists. Lively León is an important industrial and commercial center; it is Mexico's shoemaking capital and a good place to buy leather goods of any kind.

Salamanca, once a sleepy agricultural town, has become prosperous and chaotic since it became the site of a huge oil refinery. A redeeming feature is the church of San Agustín, which possesses some of the most beautiful retablos in Mexico. South of Salamanca, the farming village of Yuriria is the site of a 16th-century Augustinian monastery with an ornate plateresque facade.

Celaya has some late-colonial architecture and the neoclassical Templo del Carmen, designed by Francisco Eduardo Tresguerras.

Querétaro

Alongside Guanajuato is the state of Querétaro whose capital, also called Querétaro ⓫, is known for its colonial art. It also has a good bullring and its festival attracts famous *toreros* and enthusiastic fans from afar. Querétaro has staged some of the greatest episodes

Nopal cactus leaves are tasty grilled, boiled and in tacos – *but don't forget to remove the spines!*

BELOW: horse awaiting its rider outside a San Miguel cantina.

Querétaro's statue of St James, the patron saint of the city.

BELOW: Querétaro street performers.

in Mexican history, including the events that accelerated the proclamation of Independence. The Treaty of Guadalupe Hidalgo, which ended the Mexican–American war and handed over half of Mexico's national territory, was signed in Querétaro in 1848. It was here that Maximilian was executed in 1867 and that the Constitution was signed in 1917.

The outskirts of Querétaro are sprawling and industrial, but the preserved historic center has been declared a World Heritage site. The main plaza, Jardín Obregón, is dominated by the church of **San Francisco**, one of the city's earliest. The dome's colored tiles were imported from Spain in 1540. The cloister of the adjoining monastery now houses the **Museo Regional** (Tue–Sun 10am–6pm; charge) displaying local archeological finds as well as some fine colonial paintings.

One block north of the square is the 19th-century **Teatro de la República** (daily 10am–8pm; free). This was where Emperor Maximilian faced the tribunal in 1867 and where the Mexican Constitution was signed in 1917.

Facing the attractive Plaza de la Independencia, the **Casa de la Corregidora** (now the Palacio de Gobierno) was once the residence of Doña Josefa Ortiz de Domínguez, wife of the local governor. In 1810 Doña Josefa, *La Corregidora*, sent a message alerting the Independence conspirators to the fact that her husband had discovered their plot; her action triggered Father Hidalgo's *Grito de la Independencia* (see page 224).

Curiously enough, the monument in the square is not dedicated to Father Hidalgo or Ignacio Allende, but rather to a colonial aristocrat, Don Juan Antonio Urrutia y Aranda, who built the magnificent 1,170-meter (3,840ft) **aqueduct** with its 74 towering arches more than 250 years ago. The aqueduct, which can be seen from the *mirador* (viewpoint) in the east of Querétaro, still carries water into the city.

The **Museo de Arte de Querétaro**

(Tue–Sun 10am–6pm; charge) is housed in a late-Baroque Augustinian monastery with fantastically carved columns and arches. The leering gargoyles are said to be uttering the Ave Maria in sign language. The museum also exhibits a fine collection of paintings from the 16th to the 20th centuries.

Santa Clara

Behind a deceptively austere facade, the church of **Santa Clara**, one block north on the corner of Madero and Allende, is wildly Baroque: the interior walls are covered with overflowing gilt retablos, and the grille separating the choir from the congregation is a masterpiece. Outside, the fountain dedicated to Neptune was designed in 1797 by one of Mexico's greatest architects, Francisco Eduardo Tresguerras. **Santa Rosa de Viterbo**, southwest of the center at Arteaga and Montes, contains grand altarpieces and a splendid organ. It has a more flamboyant exterior with buttresses that seem more Chinese than European in style.

East of the center, the **Convento de la Santa Cruz** (daily 9am–6pm; donation requested) is built on the site of the Otomí defeat in 1531, and is said to be inhabited by the ghost of Emperor Maximilian, who was imprisoned here before his execution.

To the west of Querétaro, the **Cerro de las Campanas** is a low, barren hill where Maximilian went before the firing squad. Nearby is a humble chapel dedicated to the emperor and a huge statue of Benito Juárez.

Provincial Querétaro

About 60km (38 miles) south of Querétaro, **San Juan del Río** ⑫ is a popular place for a weekend outing from the capital. A market town with narrow streets and solid provincial houses, it is not as aristocratic as Querétaro, but offers the atmosphere of rural Mexico. Some of the country's best fighting bulls are raised near here, and the town is known for basket-weavers and lapidaries (dealers in opals and amethysts).

Nearby, on Highway 120, is the picturesque village of **Tequisquiapan** ⑬, another weekend resort with thermal springs, fine climate, water sports and a popular wine and cheese festival in the summer. ❑

Eyewitness accounts inspired the French Impressionist Edouard Manet to produce his famous painting of the execution of Emperor Maximilian.

LEFT: the 18th-century Querétaro aqueduct.
BELOW: colorful Querétaro restaurant interior.

JALISCO AND MICHOACÁN

Guadalajara and Morelia are very Spanish cities,
but indigenous traditions and culture are still
alive in many of the Purépecha and Huichol
villages of Michoacán and Jalisco

Jalisco, northwest of Mexico City and the Central Highlands, is one of the most important states in the country. It has agriculture, a booming industry, and popular coastal resorts. Its capital, **Guadalajara** ⑭, is the second-biggest city in Mexico, with a population of more than 4 million. Jalisco is also the home of tequila, the hat dance, and *mariachi* music.

Perched on a "mile-high" plain (actually 1,524 meters/5,000ft high), Guadalajara has been called "the biggest small town in Mexico;" it is a busy metropolis that manages to retain a provincial atmosphere. The city has a pleasant climate, with temperatures averaging 20–25°C (68–77°F) all year round, although the days can be hot in summer (July–August).

Pearl of the west

Mexico's second-largest city is in many ways one of its most pleasant. The numerous universities, the cooking schools, the language institutes mean a constant influx of foreigners and Mexican youth, and the expansive parks and plazas with fountains and monuments make it an attractive and communal city perfect for strolling and watching the world go by. It has a big-city bustle with all the benefits of great restaurants, delightful B&Bs, and

fancy hotels, while the calm markets, local vendors, and quiet back streets keep it from feeling overwhelming. It is also large enough to attract vibrant cultural events, yet small enough to avoid soaring crime rates of larger urban centers. Guadalajara has the kind of easy ambience that encourages visitors to linger.

Founded in 1532 by Nuño de Guzmán, Guadalajara was not recognized by the Spanish Crown until 10 years later. A cruel and ambitious conquistador, Guzmán, who intended

Main attractions
GUADALAJARA
CATHEDRAL
MERCADO CORONA
PLAZA DE LOS MARIACHIS
TLAQUEPAQUE
TONALÁ
LAGO DE CHAPALA
MORELIA
CASA NATAL DE MORELOS
MUSEO DE LA MÁSCARA
MONARCH BUTTERFLY SANCTUARY
PÁTZCUARO
TZINTZUNTZÁN
URUAPAN
TZARARÁCUA WATERFALL

LEFT: a *campesino* shapes a hat from a rolled cactus fiber called *ixtle*. **RIGHT:** farmers gather blue agave for tequila production.

Guadalajara is at its prettiest in March, when the jacarandas are flowering. However, the liveliest time of year is during the Fiestas de Octubre (October), when there are mariachis, charros, processions and fireworks every night.

Guadalajara to be the capital of the kingdom of New Galicia, was sent back to Spain in disgrace. Guadalajara managed to remain independent of Mexico City, and its archbishopric was as rich and powerful as that of the capital itself.

Guadalajarans are uniquely proud of their city and their role in shaping Mexico's historical past. The city played a key role in the Mexican War of Independence: it was here that Hidalgo spoke about the importance of ending slavery, and numerous Mexican leaders of the 19th and 20th centuries have visited or lived here. Guadalajara was also one of the largest cities to avoid invasion by American forces during the Mexican–American War.

The city has long been an important commercial center and it always retained some political and judicial autonomy; it is strategically situated near one of the few passages leading through the mountains to the fertile Pacific coast. Its university was founded very early on, and students were drawn from as far away as southern Texas, then part of New Spain; the university remains one of Mexico's best and most popular to this day.

The cathedral

Most of the interesting sights in Guadalajara are downtown. Its landmark, the huge **cathedral Ⓐ**, with its yellow-tiled spire, exhibits a mixture of styles, from neo-Gothic to Baroque and neo-classical. Surrounded by four plazas, it provides a welcome oasis amid the bustle of the big city.

Don't miss the tombs beneath the altar, where several religious figures are buried. The cathedral's many exhibits are worth visiting as well – religious artifacts dating back hundreds of years are on public display on the walls and in side rooms. Tipping a local person 20 or so pesos for a short tour is worth it, as he or she can point out many details of the place that you would otherwise miss, and currently there is little to no literature about the cathedral aimed at tourists.

Two blocks west of the cathedral is an interesting market, the **Mercado Corona Ⓑ**, with stalls selling every kind of herbal tea and natural remedy imaginable. These narrow side streets, with their brightly painted walls, street vendors, and little stores are great for exploring. You'll find orange trees, and houses with pretty wrought-iron grilles leading into patios overflowing with bougainvillea, jasmine and songbirds. Be sure to bring the camera.

Two often-overlooked churches in this area are the **Templo de Santa Mónica C** and **Templo de San Felipe Neri D**; the former, a convent church, has a prodigiously carved, late-Baroque facade. Inside, women still pray to St Christopher to help them find a husband (or to get rid of the one they've got). Nearby, 18th-century San Felipe is a very grand church with an exotic belfry and well-proportioned dome.

A fountain in the **Plaza de los Laureles E**, in front of the cathedral, commemorates the founding of the city and serves as a good base for people-watching or as a landmark for a meeting point; along its north side is the porticoed Presidencia Municipal (City Hall). Some of Jalisco's most distinguished men are buried beneath the Greek-style **Rotonda de los Hombres Ilustres F**, which stands, surrounded by Doric columns, in the center of another plaza to the north of the cathedral. Statues of famous *jalicienses* are dotted along the plaza's shady paths. The **Museo Regional G** (tel: 33-3614 9957; Tue–Sun 9am–5pm; charge, free on Sun) occupies an attractive 18th-century building, a former seminary, on the east side of the square. The museum has galleries dedicated to archeology, colonial history, painting and ethnography.

To the south of the cathedral is the pretty **Plaza de Armas H**, originally Guadalajara's main market square and ancient execution site. The French bandstand in the center hosts concerts every Thursday and Sunday evening. Facing the plaza, the late-Baroque **Palacio de Gobierno I** (daily; free) houses a magnificent mural by **José Clemente Orozco** (*see page 116*). The mural is a striking homage to Padre

A horse-drawn carriage passes along the street outside the Museo Regional.

LEFT: Belle Epoque figure detail on the bandstand in Plaza de Armas.
BELOW: the dome and twin spires of Guadalajara's cathedral.

Tequila & Co.

Straight, with salt and lime, or in a *margarita*: chances are you won't leave Mexico without a taste of this venerable spirit.

Like Jerez in Spain, famous for its sherry, or Champagne in France, the Jalisco town of Tequila has achieved a reputation far out of proportion to its size. Millions of drinkers who would otherwise never dream of going to this small town will wax rhapsodically about its name, though they are of course referring to the eponymous liquor.

Less than an hour's drive northwest of Guadalajara, Tequila lies almost under the shadow of an extinct 2,950-meter (9,700ft) volcano. It is surrounded by thousands of acres of bluish-green, spear-like, cultivated agave plants.

Although there are hundreds of different species of the maguey plant, under Mexican law at least 51 percent of any tequila must be from the *Tequilana weber* agave, which grows only in this region. The best kinds of tequila use pure maguey (or agave) juice; cheaper brand liquors are supplemented with cane juice.

After growing for eight to 10 years, the tequila maguey is trimmed down to its 50kg (110lb) heart, the *piña*, which is steamed, then shredded and squeezed. Sugar is added and it is allowed to ferment for four days before undergoing two distillations. Most of this colorless liquid is then bottled; the rest is aged in oak casks for up to seven years, during which time it assumes the golden color and mellow flavor of *tequila añejo*.

Mezcal and *pulque* are also derived from the maguey cactus. *Pulque* is fermented rather than distilled (the distillation process was unknown before the Conquest) but it is becoming hard to find these days. Mezcal, primarily produced in Oaxaca but made here in Jalisco as well, is a fiery, flavorful, high-proof alcoholic drink, which, like tequila, is distilled, although the methods used are different.

The small worm in the *mezcal* bottle is considered a delicacy but does not indicate the quality of the liquor. Many excellent brands opt to forgo the hapless larvae, which do not possess hallucinatory qualities *(see pages 280)*.

Tequila is the only one of the three liquors to have taken its place on the top shelf, especially in the US, which annually imports several hundred thousand dollars' worth from its southern neighbor. There are three common varieties: *blanco*, *reposado*, and *añejo*. They are primarily distinctions of color, flavor, and age. *Blanco*, as the name suggests, is white and young, and strong. *Reposado* has been aged and has a golden color and a medium taste. *Añejo* has been aged for at least four years and will have lost a lot of the punch that most people attribute to tequila. For someone who prefers cognac to tequila, *añejo* will be the best choice, while hardened tequila afficionados may prefer a shot of *blanco*.

The ritual of correct tequila drinking begins with placing salt on the fleshy area between the thumb and forefinger. After licking the salt, take a shot of the tequila and then suck on a slice of lime. The idea is to establish a precise and satisfying balance of strong flavors in which the tequila's pure, sweet fire is complemented by the acidity of lime, and the relief given by those grains of salt. It is also fine simply to sip tequila straight as one would a fine cognac, while many prefer their tequila mixed with Sangrita, a spicy concoction containing tomato and orange juice, or in the ever-popular and ubiquitous *margarita*. ❑

LEFT: pouring a stiff shot of *blanco*.

Miguel Hidalgo, the "father of Mexican Independence."

The **Plaza de la Liberación** ❶, to the east of the cathedral, is the largest of the four squares. Designed by contemporary Guadalajara architect Ignacio Díaz Morales, the plaza blends with the buildings framing the rear of the cathedral and the facade of the 19th-century **Teatro Degollado** ❶ (Mon–Fri 10am–2pm and during performances). The recently restored theater has a sumptuous red velvet and gilt interior and a ceiling painted with a scene from Dante's *Divine Comedy*.

Hospicio Cabañas

Behind the theater, the **Plaza Tapatía** is a long pedestrian precinct which leads down to the elegant **Instituto Cultural Cabañas** ❶ (Tue–Sun; charge, free on Sun) in the Hospicio Cabañas, which was founded and financed by one of Guadalajara's great benefactors, Bishop Juan Ruiz de Cabañas. More than 20 patios interconnect the different sections of this neoclasssical building, which was designed by Manuel Tolsá in 1805. At the center is the Capilla

Tolsá, whose walls and ceiling were decorated in the late 1930s with what are considered to be Orozco's finest murals. These dramatic, symbolic works depict, among other things, the destruction and suffering caused by the Spanish Conquest. As the city's most important cultural center, the institute also organizes many other artistic activities such as plays, concerts and films. The odd bronze statue rising up near the fountain is actually a headless snake. The head, which fell off in the 1980s, lies on the ground nearby, a testament to creative – if unsuccessful – engineering.

Market stalls and *mariachis*

Guadalajara has a host of great shopping opportunities for just about anyone with a few pesos to burn, so many in fact, that shoppers will find themselves overwhelmed with the possibilities. Bargaining is commonplace, and in crowded areas it isn't a bad idea to keep some change in a separate place, away from your wallet, just in case a pickpocket comes along. While this kind of crime is rare, a little caution can

TIP

A huge range of leather goods, including belts, bags and *huaraches* (rough leather sandals) are on sale in the Mercado Libertad. Traditional handmade sweets are another specialty; try the ones made of tamarind fruit and the ultra-sweet coconut, *cocada envinada*.

BELOW: the Plaza de los Laureles fountain and Presidencia Municipal building at night.

Jalisco is the home of the Mexican cliché: the mustachioed macho wearing a broad-brimmed sombrero and riding a horse (although these days it is just as likely to be a pick-up truck).

make a big difference in the long run. Just south of the Hospicio Cabañas, at the core of Guadalajara's traditional center, the **Mercado Libertad** ⓜ is a vast, colorful, covered market. Better known as San Juan de Dios after the nearby church, the market sells everything from herbal remedies, fresh food and handicrafts, to imported jeans and stereo systems. Beside the church, the **Plaza de los Mariachis** comes alive in the evening when the musicians gather in the square to play traditional songs and *corridos* (ballads) outside the cafés and restaurants. If you stop for an *helada* (ice-cream cone) and sit on a park bench as the musicians play, you'll find yourself fitting right in with the easy pace of life here.

In the southern part of the downtown area, **San Francisco** ⓝ and **Aranzazú** ⓞ are two remarkable colonial churches built by the Franciscans in their ambitious attempts to extend their missions all the way to the Californias. Now located in a busy financial district, these churches, with their attractive gardens, were once at the heart of one of the city's best

neighborhoods. The Templo de Aranzazú has a highly elaborate interior with three golden Churrigueresque altarpieces. The retablos in the older San Francisco church were destroyed by arson in the 1930s.

Farther south, toward the train station, the large, well-kept **Parque Agua Azul** (tel: 33-3619 0328; Tue–Sun 10am–6.30pm; charge) offers relief from the city noise with an aviary, butterfly dome and orchid house. The **Casa de las Artesanías de Jalisco** (Mon–Fri 10am–6pm, Sat 10am–5pm Sun 10am–3pm), on the north side of the park, sells excellent handicrafts from all over the state.

The university and beyond

Farther west, on Avenida Juárez, is the **Universidad de Guadalajara** ⓟ, whose central building dates from the 1920s. More impressive Orozco murals decorate the dome and back wall of the *Paraninfo* (main hall). The building also houses the **Museo de las Artes** (tel: 333-134 1664; Tue–Sun 10am–6pm, Sat–Sun until 4pm; free), which exhibits a permanent collection

BELOW: vegetable market stalls, Mercado Libertad.
RIGHT: sculptures along Plaza Tapatía.

of mainly local modern art, and temporary shows from farther afield. Behind the university, the neo-Gothic church, modeled on the cathedral of Orvieto in Italy, is known as the **Expiatorio**. The area just beyond the university, along Vallarta and Chapultepec, offers relief from the downtown noise and traffic with its broad, tree-lined streets and inviting sidewalk cafés.

Calzada Independencia is the backbone of popular Guadalajara. It is not a beautiful street, but it is busy and full of life. Due north along the street is a huge soccer stadium, the **Estadio Jalisco**, a shrine to Mexico's most popular – some might say fanatical – sport. A few kilometers farther north is the **Barranca de Oblatos**, a superb 600-meter (1,970ft) canyon whose dramatic stone walls are softened by lush vegetation, and which has an impressive waterfall, the **Cola de Caballo**. At the bottom of the canyon the Santiago River slides into the tropics and toward the distant Pacific. There's a great view of the Barranca from the nearby zoo (tel: 363-674 4488; www.zooguadalajara.com.mx; Wed–Sun and hols 10am–5pm;

charge) at **Huentitán Park**, which has more than 1,500 animals and also features an amusement park and planetarium.

In the northwestern suburbs of Guadalajara, **Zapopán** (tel: 333-633 0141; daily) is visited for its basílica, a Baroque church that houses the miraculous image of the Virgen de Zapopán. Every summer, the Virgin is paraded from church to church through the streets to Guadalajara; then, on October 12, in what must be among the best-attended pilgrimages in the world, the image is brought back to Zapopán. Next door to the church is the small but interesting **Museo Huichol** (tel: 333-636 4430; Mon–Sat 9.30am–1.15pm and 3–5.45pm, Sun 10am–2pm; charge), with displays that relate to the art, crafts and traditions of the Huichol people.

Tlaquepaque and Tonalá

San Pedro Tlaquepaque, in the southeastern suburbs, is famous for pottery

Getting a shoeshine in downtown Guadalajara.

BELOW: street life and view of the church in the pottery-manufacturing town of Tonalá.

Religious-themed postcards for sale.

BELOW: sculptures along the Malecón, Puerto Vallarta.

and craftwork, though it pays to be careful, as the quality varies. Many pieces are now mass-produced; however, there are still many beautiful, handmade crafts to be found and the **Museo Regional de Cerámica** (tel: 333-635 5404; Mon–Sat 10am–6pm, Sun 9am–4pm; free) is worth visiting for its display of local pottery and to get a sense of the range of quality that's out there. Then wander along Tlaquepaque's cobbled streets and browse around the 19th-century houses that have been turned into shops and restaurants, looking for deals (or meals) that suit your fancy. **El Parián**, the covered market on the central Jardín Hidalgo, is especially favored by *tapatíos* – the nickname given to people from Guadalajara – who flock here at weekends to drink beer, eat *birria* (a local dish of barbecued kid/young goat) and listen to the *mariachis*.

Much of the pottery and glassware sold in Tlaquepaque and Guadalajara is produced in the *fábricas* (factories) of nearby **Tonalá**. On Thursdays and Sundays practically the whole town becomes a street market, although many of the stalls sell factory seconds, and sometimes it is better to go directly to the shops.

Chapala, Tapalpa and beyond

Southeast of Guadalajara is **Lago de Chapala**, Mexico's biggest (although fast shrinking) lake, renowned for its glorious sunsets. The comfortable weekend homes of wealthy *tapatíos* and retired *norteamericanos* line its north shore. The town of **Chapala** ⑮, only 40 minutes from Guadalajara, can get crowded at weekends; you can hire a boat to take you to one of the tiny islands for lunch. Farther west along the shore is the attractive, sleepy village of **Ajijic** ⑯, largely populated by US expatriates, and the thermal spa at **San Juan Cosalá**.

The town of **Tapalpa** ⑰, with its delightful old wooden-balconied houses in the cool pine-forested hills southwest of Lake Chapala, offers a complete change of scenery, and makes a delightful weekend escape from the city.

But for anyone seeking a few leisurely days at the beach, **Puerto Vallarta** – Jalisco's sophisticated Pacific coast resort – is just minutes away by plane and three hours by car (see page 247). For those who prefer less activity and more privacy, there are long stretches of creamy-colored sand beaches such as Sayulita north of Puerto Vallarta, and romantic rocky coves to the south (see pages 247).

Michoacán

With its lakes, rivers, indigenous villages, volcanoes and colonial cities, Michoacán is like a miniature model of Mexico. In the northeastern part of the state, the capital, **Morelia ⑱**, formerly known as Valladolid, was renamed in 1828 for José María Morelos, one of the heroes of the Independence movement. The roads (toll and free) from Mexico City are marvelously scenic. The slow but beautiful free road passes **Mil Cumbres** (Thousand Peaks), through shady pine forests, mountain vistas, cool waterfalls, and rural villages. Those taking the coastal route from Puerto Vallarta to Acapulco along Mexico 200 will find a beautiful shoreline, remote beaches, banana and coconut plantations, and laid-back locals.

The climate is mild and life moves at a slow tempo in Morelia, a pretty colonial town built of rose-colored stone. The **cathedral ⒶΑ**, which took over a century to build (1640–1744) is a grand combination of Herrerian, Baroque and neoclassical styles. Sadly, much of the Baroque relief work inside was replaced in the 19th century. However, there is a magnificent German organ, and a corn-paste statue of Christ wearing a 16th-century crown, a gift from Felipe II of Spain. In the **Palacio de Gobierno Ⓑ**, a former seminary on the other side of Avenida Madero, local artist Alfredo Zalce has painted colorful murals which reflect the beauty of Michoacán and its rich history.

The **Casa Natal de Morelos** (tel: 443-312 2793; Tue–Sun 9am–7pm; free) on the corner of Corregidora and Obeso, was the birthplace (in 1765) of José María Morelos y Pavón, who studied under Padre Hidalgo and also became a priest. One block east, the **Museo Casa de Morelos Ⓒ** (tel: 443-313 2651; daily 9am–5pm; free), where Morelos lived from 1801, has

BELOW: a Tarascan market.

Butterfly Sanctuary

One of nature's most spectacular sights is the annual Monarch butterfly migration, which begins in the United States and Canada and ends here in the mountains near the village of Angangueo. Though threatened by severe frosts, logging, and climate change, there are still between 30 and 100 million Monarch butterflies which breed in the eastern part of Michoacán. Not far from the Mexico City–Morelia highway is the **Santuario de Mariposas El Rosario ⑲** (Nov–Mar daily; charge). It is best to visit the sanctuary in the morning when the butterflies flutter from the trees to the humid ground as the day becomes warmer. The butterflies blanket the entire landscape: covering trees, bushes, the ground, everything. Blur your eyes slightly and they look like flakes of fluttering orange snow.

*Ice-cream bar in
Morelia.*

BELOW: graveside
Day of the Dead
observances
include food,
flowers, candles
and other offerings.
RIGHT: El Sagrario
church, Pátzcuaro.

exhibits on his life along with memorabilia, such as the blindfold he wore when he was executed in 1815.

Just off the square, the **Museo Regional D** (tel: 443-312 0407; Tue–Sat 9am–7pm, Sun 9am–2pm; charge, free Sun) has exhibits on archeology, history, ethnology, and, most interestingly, a complete pharmacy dating from 1868.

The elegant **Palacio Clavijero E**, a former Jesuit seminary founded in 1660, now houses the **tourist information office**. It was named in honor of Francisco Xavier Clavijero, a Jesuit who taught here and who wrote what many believe to be the best historical account of Mexico. The nearby **Colegio de San Nicolás F**, where Morelos studied as a young man, is one of the oldest universities in the Americas. One block north, facing a peaceful plaza with a statue of Miguel de Cervantes, is the pretty Baroque church of **Santa Rosa G** and the adjoining 18th-century **Conservatorio de las Rosas**, which still functions as a major music academy and arranges classical music concerts from time to time.

Marvelous masks

A small but fascinating collection of ceremonial masks associated with dances from different regions of Mexico is on display at the **Museo de la Máscara H** (tel: 443-313 1320; Tue–Fri 9am–2pm, 4–8pm; free). The museum is part of the Casa de la Cultura, a lively cultural center in the converted **Convento del Carmen** which hosts arts workshops, performances and temporary exhibitions.

Three blocks east of the square, in the converted Convento de San Francisco, the **Casa de las Artesanías I** (tel: 443-312 2486; daily 10am–6pm; free) has devoted separate rooms to handicrafts from different Michoacán villages, whose dazzling craftsmanship is rivalled only perhaps by that of Oaxaca. Farther east, beyond the beautiful **Templo de las Monjas J**, on Avenida Madero, is the 18th-century **Aqueduct**, with 253 arches. South of the aqueduct, in Morelia's largest park – the Bosque de Cuauhtémoc – is the **Museo de Arte Contemporáneo** (tel: 443-312 5405; Tue–Fri 10am–8pm, Sat–Sun 10am–

6pm; free), which has very good exhibitions of contemporary art.

Lake Pátzcuaro and Janitzio

The very Spanish city of Morelia is uncharacteristic of the rest of Michoacán, which has remained strongly indigenous. Directly west of Morelia, surrounded by native villages, is **Lago de Pátzcuaro** ㉟, where the fishermen use distinctive butterfly-shaped fishing nets, and *pescado blanco*, a white fish unique to the lake, is a common menu item. There are boat trips to the island of **Janitzio**, in the middle of the lake, with its giant 40-meter (130ft) sculpture of Independence hero, José María Morelos. You can climb inside the statue, right up to the clenched fist, for a wonderful panoramic view.

Janitzio is especially known for its **Day of the Dead** celebrations (*see pages 92–3*) on November 1–2, when local people cross the lake in a procession of candlelit canoes, bringing flowers, food and other offerings to the cemetery in commemoration of their loved ones. In order to preserve the intimacy of

the occasion, tourists are discouraged from attending the all-night vigil in Janitzio, but there are other cemeteries in the region where visitors are more welcome to observe the celebrations.

Pátzcuaro

The town of **Pátzcuaro** ㉑, on the south side of the lake, has whitewashed adobe houses with overhanging red-tiled roofs, colonial mansions with balconies and coats of arms, cobbled streets, and the smell of wood smoke in the air. This is the heart of Purépecha country; the Friday market is especially lively, although indigenous wares are being overtaken by imported goods.

All the main sights of Pátzcuaro, or Tarascan, are on or near the two central squares: first, the shady **Plaza Vasco de Quiroga**, which is named after the 16th-century bishop who dedicated his life to the welfare of the Purépecha, or Tarascan people – his statue stands in the center. On the east side of the square is the 17th-century **Casa del Gigante** (House of the Giant), former residence of the Counts of Menocal and still a private home. Other

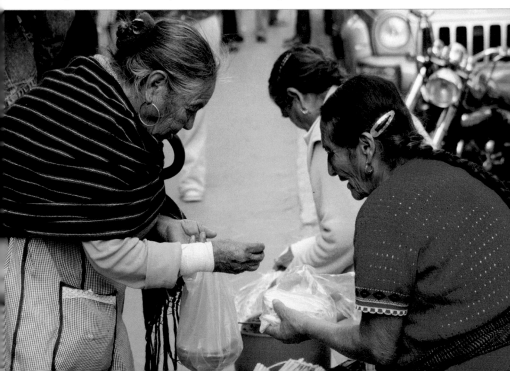

BELOW: selling fresh corn tortillas on Plaza Vasco de Quiroga.

Performing in Pátzcuaro on the Day of the Dead.

BELOW: the Tzintzuntzán site contains many *yacatas*, a type of rounded temple platform.

mansions have been converted into hotels, restaurants and craft shops.

The **Plaza Gertrudis Bocanegra**, one block north, is named after an Independence heroine. The busy town market is on the west side, while on the north side, the 16th-century biblioteca (library) occupies the former church of **San Agustín**. Inside, murals by the celebrated Juan O'Gorman illustrate the history of Michoacán. East of the plaza is the **Basílica de Nuestra Señora de la Salud**, a shrine for health-seekers from all over Mexico, who come to revere the statue of Our Lady of Health. Quiroga planned the basilica to be a majestic and enormous, five-nave cathedral, but unfortunately the majority of his plans were never completed.

The **Museo Regional de Artes Populares** (tel: 434-342 1029; Tue–Sat 9am–7pm, Sun until 3pm; charge), south of the basilica, on Alcantarillas, was founded in 1640 as the Colegio de San Nicolás by Don Vasco de Quiroga. The museum has a fine collection of regional handicrafts, including lacquerwork, pottery, textiles and copperware from Santa Clara. The **Casa de los Once Patios** (House of Eleven Patios; daily 10am–7pm) southeast of the main square, is a craft center, with workshops and boutiques set around the courtyards of an old Dominican convent built in the 18th century.

The villages of Michoacán

On the eastern shore of Lake Pátzcuaro the village of **Tzintzuntzán** (Place of Hummingbirds) is the ancient capital of the Purépecha, or *tarascos* as they were called by the Spanish. The Tarascans, unconquered until the Spanish arrived with their armor plate and cannons, have preserved their traditions, language and way of life to this day, especially in the mountain redoubts. The ruins, also called **Tzintzuntzán** (daily 9am–5.30pm; charge), and one of the chief ancient sites in Michoacán, consist mainly of a group of five *yácatas*, or round-based temples, on a reconstructed terrace that offers wonderful views of the lake and surrounding countryside. In the village, there is a large 16th-century Franciscan monastery in peaceful gardens; the olive trees are deemed the oldest in Mexico, said to have been brought from Spain by Quiroga himself.

The area is dotted with indigenous villages, each known for its own special handicraft. Many of these are sold in the market town of **Quiroga**, which itself produces brightly painted wooden furniture and masks. South of Pátzcuaro, for instance, **Santa Clara del Cobre** (sometimes called Villa Escalante) is famous for its copperware, although no ore is now extracted from local mines. Guitars and all sorts of wooden handicrafts are made in the workshops of **Paracho**.

The town of **Uruapan** ㉒, 62km (39 miles) west of Pátzcuaro, marks the beginning of another Michoacán – the *tierra caliente*, or tropical lands. It is the center of a rich agricultural area known for its avocados. The town itself is famous for its lacquered trays and boxes; there is a good display of this craft in the **Museo Regional de Arte Popular** (tel: 452-524 3434; Tue–Sun 9.30am–1.30pm, 3.30–6pm; free), which is housed in one of the oldest buildings in Uruapan, the 16th-century

Huatapera (built as one of the first hospitals). A few blocks west of the Zócalo (square), along Calle Independencia, is the entrance to the delightful **Parque Nacional Eduardo Ruiz** (daily 6am–6pm), a luxuriant tropical park that surrounds the source of the Río Cupatitzio. The country around Uruapan is remarkable. One very popular excursion, just 10km (6 miles) south, is to see the Río Cupatitzio cascading 25 meters (82ft) through lush tropical forests, over the **Tzararácua** waterfall.

Even more impressive is a trip to the still smouldering **Paricutín**, a volcano whose eruption in 1943 lasted until 1952, leaving whole villages buried. Miraculously, there were no fatalities. It is an extraordinary moon-like landscape, which is slowly sprouting with green life again. You can walk or hire a pony and guide in the Purépecha village of **Angahuan**, 30km (18 miles) northwest of Uruapan. ❏

Fountain at the entrance to the Parque Nacional Eduardo Ruiz.

BELOW: the church, San Juan Parangaricutiro, was trapped in the lava slide following Paricutín's eruption.

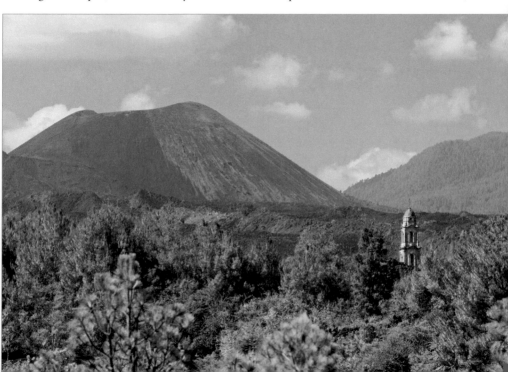

MEXICAN ICONS: CHARROS

Nostalgic, romantic, the charros with their sombreros, embroidered jackets and daring feats with horse and lasso are an abiding symbol of Mexican tradition

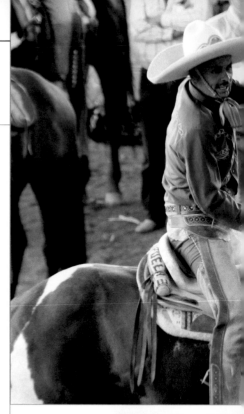

To describe a *charro* as just a Mexican cowboy is an injustice. He has become perhaps the country's most instantly recognizable symbol, an image of Mexican identity.

In the first decades of Spanish rule, only Spaniards were allowed to ride horses. However, when cattle ranches spread across central and western Mexico, they needed workers, and as well as Andalusians – prized by landowners for their riding skills – mestizos and indigenous horsemen were employed on the haciendas. The traditional Andalusian short riding jacket was adapted, with added Mexican ornament for special occasions; the Andalusian flat-brimmed hat evolved into the *charro*'s sombrero. Haciendas and the *charro* way of life extended over large areas, but are most associated with Jalisco state, also home to two other Mexican icons, tequila and *mariachis*; the latter, of course, also adopted *charro* dress.

Horsemanship displays had long been a feature of country fiestas, and the structure of such contests (*charrerías*) had become more formal. However, it was really only after the Revolution that the *charro* became an inescapable feature of Mexican popular entertainment, and *Lienzos Charros* (rings for *charrerías*) spread across the country. As Mexico urbanized, the *charro* became a nostalgic symbol of a simpler way of life. The great actor-singers of the golden age of Mexican cinema celebrated *charro* heroes: brave, passionate, loyal to friends and fierce with enemies, fun-loving, macho, endlessly flirtatious with women but irresistibly charming. Nowadays, many Mexicans see this as a tired, kitsch stereotype, but the *charrería* still has a hold as Mexico's "national sport."

RIGHT: *charro* skills are based in country traditions and often passed from father to son; the earlier you start, the more you learn.

BELOW: *mariachi* bands, like *charro* shows, developed out of older traditions around the end of the 19th century, and their outfits became more elaborate too.

TOP: musicians are a part of every *charrería*.
LEFT: a Mexican *vaquero*, or cowboy, on a 19th-century hacienda, in an early form of *charro* dress.

THE CHARRERÍA PROGRAM

The biggest *Lienzos Charros* are in Mexico City and Guadalajara, where competitions are held on most Sundays, but there are rings in nearly every city. Full of music and color, *charrerías* are spectacular.

The show starts with a *desfile* or parade, as the competitors ride in to salute judges and public. The first *suerte* (event) is the *cala de caballo*, when each rider demonstrates his mastery over his horse by going full gallop across the ring, then coming to an abrupt stop inside a precisely marked rectangle and executing a series of movements before walking his horse out backwards. Some of the most thrilling events are the *coleadero*, when a *charro* on horseback tries to throw a charging bull off balance and roll it over by pulling on its tail; and the *paso de la muerte* (pass of death), when a *charro* jumps from his saddle onto a bareback colt at full speed.

The last *suerte* is for women, who perform as a team, an *escaramuza charra*. They carry out intricate maneuvers that could be compared to dressage, except that they ride very fast, and no one could suggest it's an easy option. Plus, to remain feminine, *charras* must ride side-saddle, and in long skirts.

ABOVE: a *charro* demonstrating his impressive roping skills at the *Lienzo Charro* in Zacatecas.

RIGHT: showing off one's finery is an essential part of the show.

BELOW: beautifully crafted boots of the finest leather are only one part of the *charro* costume.

TOP: a *charro* makes his entrance at full speed.
ABOVE: cowgirls of an *escaramuza charra* twist and turn in complex patterns in the ring.
LEFT: basking in the acclaim of the crowd.

ACAPULCO AND THE PACIFIC BEACHES

The Pacific coast has glamorous beach resorts with luxury hotels and all the facilities, but there are still secluded bays where you can just slip into a hammock and watch the tequila sunrise

Acapulco, with its dramatic mountains sweeping down to the Pacific, was the first of the coastal resorts to achieve international fame as a mecca for the "beautiful people." Later, when the value of tourism as a major industry became apparent, Ixtapa was developed some 257km (160 miles) northwest. Puerto Vallarta comes next, and in between it's just miles of beautiful coastline. Several major surf breaks, such as Sayulita and Pascuales, draw wave worshippers from around the globe.

Romantic Vallarta

Puerto Vallarta ㉓ owes its fame to Hollywood. It came to prominence with John Huston's 1964 filming of Tennessee Williams' *Night of the Iguana* on Mismaloya beach, just south of town. Richard Burton, who starred in the movie, subsequently bought a home nearby; his relationship with bride-to-be Elizabeth Taylor attracted much media attention, and it wasn't long before the tourists started arriving. Their house – at Zaragoza 445 – is now a bed and breakfast establishment, Casa Kimberley, and still has its original furnishings (tel: 322-222 1336; www.casakimberley.com; Mon–Sat; charge). Many other movies have also been filmed in the town since, including *Predator* with Arnold Schwarzeneg-

ger in 1987 and *Puerto Vallarta Squeeze* starring Harvey Keitel in 2002.

Vallarta lines the shore of **Bahía de Banderas**, one of the world's 10 largest bays, where migrating whales gather each spring; it is also a breeding ground for dolphins, and not surprisingly, there's good deep-sea fishing as well. Straddling the **Río Cuale**, the relatively unspoiled **Old Town** has white adobe houses with red-tiled roofs, donkey traffic, and cobblestones.

The **Templo de Guadalupe**, a central landmark, is topped by an

Main attractions
PUERTO VALLARTA
BAHÍA DE BANDERAS
YELAPA
BARRA DE NAVIDAD
MANZANILLO
COLIMA
VOLCÁN DE FUEGO
IXTAPA
ZIHUATANEJO
PLAYA TRONCONES
ACAPULCO

LEFT: Puerto Vallarta's *Boy on a Seahorse.*
RIGHT: the beach and skyline of Acapulco.

Manzanillo claims to be "the sailfish capital of the world." The fishing season runs from November to March.

imposing crown, a replica of that worn by Maximilian's wife, María Carlota. Attractive bridges cross the river to an island, where there are art galleries, shops, restaurants, and a small **archeological museum** (Mon–Fri 10am–7pm; donation requested).

North of the old town, the **Zona Hotelera** is a long stretch of coast lined with luxury hotels which appears never-ending: almost as soon as a hotel finishes, construction begins on a new one close by. **Marina Vallarta**, a 178-hectare (440-acre) upscale resort area, has even more luxurious hotels, condos and an 18-hole golf course. Parasailing, an easy and spectacular parachute ride behind a speedboat, is a popular pastime on several of Vallarta's beaches. Other water sports include snorkeling, scuba diving, jet-skiing, windsurfing, sailing and deep-sea fishing for marlin, dorado and tuna.

BELOW AND RIGHT: parasailing on the Puerto Vallarta shore, and the city's cathedral, Our Lady of Guadalupe.

Playa Olas Altas and **Playa de los Muertos**, on the south side of Río Cuale, are the most crowded beaches, but there are several others farther south, beyond the city limits at **Mismaloya** or **Boca de Tomatlán**.

Boat or catamaran excursions can be arranged from Los Muertos pier to **Las Animas**, a tiny community with inexpensive hotels; **Quimixto**, where movie director John Huston built a house, and which is popular with divers; or **Yelapa**, farther on, which is a nice choice for those who want to escape the all-inclusive experience and try for something more low-key. You can choose between staying in a palm-thatched *palapa* or a small hotel, and (finally) there is internet at the cafés. It is also possible to rent a horse or *burro* (donkey) and venture into the jungle to the nearby waterfalls.

South of Vallarta

Those wanting a road trip will find that the route from Puerto Vallarta to Acapulco is worth the trip. It follows some of Mexico's finest stretches of coastline – with unspoiled beaches and some great surf spots – and passes through quaint villages. However, unless you plan on getting up before dawn and driving until midnight, you'll want to stop overnight somewhere along the way. It is long drive,

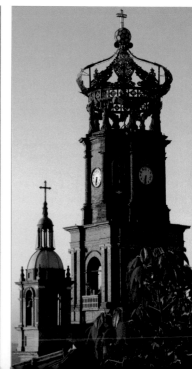

but those making the effort will really be rewarded with seeing what Mexico once was, before the boom of development hit so much of the coastline. Towns still primarily depend on fishing and agriculture, and you will see numerous palm, mango, and pineapple farms. There is a plethora of *buteos* (buzzards), songbirds, and waterfowl so it's great for birderwatchers.

The road runs inland for a while and then passes **Playa Blanca**, a loud and busy Club Med facility, and **Pueblo Nuevo**, a budding US-style resort community. Then comes **Bahía Chamela**, upscale **Costa Careyes**, and the **Costa Alegre ㉔**, a 96km (60-mile) strip of relatively undeveloped coastline where the delightful bays have changed little since the Spanish galleons sailed these waters more than 400 years ago.

The next resort along the coast is **Barra de Navidad ㉕**, a sleepy town aimed mainly at vacationers from Guadalajara. It's worth stopping here to enjoy the views or even surf if the waves are right. Deep-sea fishing is big, and for those wanting the beach but not quite ready for the boondocks,

Barra de Navidad will fit the bill nicely. There's a nice tourist zone with hotels and restaurants, but very little of the push and brass of the big places – no touts, no hawkers. It's easy to sit and watch pelicans glide by as children beachcomb or play in the gentle waves. The same vacationers also head for **San Patricio Melaque**, just 2km (1¼ miles) along the beach. It was from this bay that Miguel López Legazpi sailed in 1564 to conquer the Philippines.

Manzanillo ㉖, just an hour away in the state of Colima, is a busy railhead and port, with narrow, traffic-choked streets, though sport fishermen may find rates are cheaper here (both for hotels and for fishing services) than in the more touristy destinations. There are a few good hotels in town, although the resort hotels and the best beaches are to the west of the bay around the **Santiago Peninsula**.

For the affluent, Las Hadas (The Fairies) complex, built by a Bolivian

Snorkeling is just one of the many water sports available at Puerto Vallarta.

BELOW: a rococo Beetle.

Selling colorful woven bags, made of ixtle fiber.

BELOW: a hotel infinity pool in Ixtapa-Zihuatanejo.

tin magnate, is a mixture of pseudo-Moorish, Mediterranean and Disney styles. For those on a budget, look for the tiny ecotourism spots that have sprung up: a hammock and a parking spot right on an unblemished beach are hard to beat when you're paying only a fraction of the cost of an ordinary hotel. Surfers should make sure not to miss Pascuales, south of Manzanillo near the small town of Tecomán.

Colima

A short ride inland through lemon groves is the colonial city of **Colima ㉗**, the state capital and first Spanish city to be built in the west of Mexico. There are two worthwhile museums in Colima: the **Museo Regional de Historia** (tel: 312-312 2298; Tue–Sat 9am–6pm, Sun 5–8pm; charge, free on Sun); and the even better **Museo de las Culturas de Occidente** (tel: 312-313 0608; Tue–Sun 9am–6.50pm; charge), which exhibits a large and varied col-

lection of pre-Hispanic pottery from the cultures of western Mexico. Most notable are the pot-bellied Itzcuintli dogs for which Colima is renowned. Colima is a pleasant city of parks and gardens and the surrounding countryside is dramatically dominated by two volcanoes: the still rumbling **Volcán de Fuego**, and its larger, extinct neighbor, the often snow-capped **Nevado de Colima**, which is popular with climbers.

Ixtapa and Zihuatanejo

As they are served by the same airport and are only a few kilometers apart, Ixtapa and Zihuatanejo tend to be listed and lumped together as a unit, and indeed their boundaries have almost blended; but the characters of these two resort towns are wildly different. **Ixtapa ㉘**, like Cancún in the Yucatán and Huatulco, is the result of government-planned tourism. It came into existence in the 1970s, but now attracts almost half a million visitors each year, three-quarters of whom are Mexican, giving it slightly more authenticity than its Yucatecan counterpart,

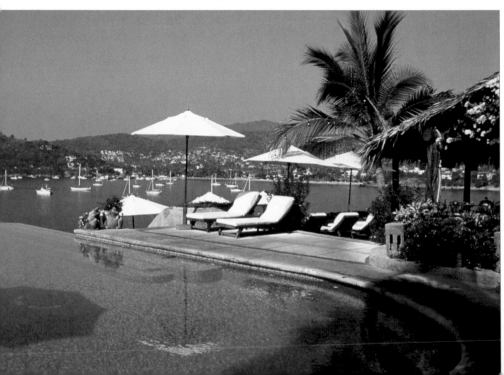

which caters primarily to foreigners. Here you'll find a nice mix of guests from all over, and a much quieter vibe. There's also none of the March spring break madness that the "other" resort is famous for. Ixtapa's luxury high-rise resort hotels are strung out along the dramatic Playa del Palmar and around the Punta Ixtapa. The beach is beautiful and the sunsets sublime; however, there are numerous small pebbles which make barefoot walks less fun. As with any Pacific location, be cautious about undertow and errant waves.

Across a manicured roadway that runs past the hotels is a cleverly constructed mall that feels a little more like a village than just a strip shopping center. There are restaurants and juice shops interspersed with stores offering necessities and fripperies of all kinds. Shopping here is a major activity; there are more than 1,000 stores in these two resort towns, including trendy boutiques, silversmiths, goldsmiths, folk art and handicraft markets.

In addition to its hotel zone, Ixtapa has luxury condominiums, several immaculate golf courses (one designed by Robert Trent Jones), a sheltered marina and all the most popular water sports. Boats leave from Playa Quieta (and less frequently from Zihuatanejo) for **Isla Ixtapa**, an island wildlife sanctuary lying a couple of kilometers offshore, with good swimming, excellent snorkeling, and a handful of beach restaurants.

Zihuatanejo ㉙ – or "Z" or even Ziwa, as it's known to anyone who has been there for any longer than a few hours – does more than merely cater to tourists: it is a real town with real people engaged in real activities. Getting around in either Zihuatanejo or Ixtapa, or from one to the other, is fairly easy; the hotels know what the prices for cabs are likely to be, and the drivers very rarely take advantage of unsuspecting tourists. The larger hotels often have shuttle services to and from the beaches or to their other satellite locations.

Unlike the sport fishing in the waters off Ixtapa, fishing is still a livelihood in Zihuatanejo as it provides food for both locals and visitors, although tourism is creeping in at a steady pace. Avid fishermen may want to try striking a deal with one of the local fishermen and tag along for the ride; most of the boats leave from the beach in the center of town, and a tasty lunch may be included in the overall price.

Facing the sea, on Paseo del Pescador in the center of town, is the small **Museo Arqueológico de la Costa Grande** (tel: 754-544 7552; Tue–Sun 10am–6pm; charge), which offers an insight into the interesting culture and archeology of the coast of Guerrero. Ziwa is full of little restaurants of all kinds, and not surprisingly, those serving seafood are particularly popular.

Many of the hotels in Ziwa qualify as "budget" (Villas Miramar and Bungalows Ley are both good value), with a few notable exceptions such as La Casa Que Canta (tel: 755-555 7030; www.lacasaquecanta.com), a stunning building that cascades down the hill overlooking **La Ropa** beach; and the

Bronze hands and cross at the Chapel of Peace in the exclusive Acapulco neighborhood of Las Brisas.

BELOW: the light fades over Ixtapa.

In the late 1950s Acapulco became known as "The Riviera of the West."

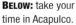

BELOW: take your time in Acapulco.

older, beautifully maintained and exquisitely landscaped Villa del Sol. For a change of pace, the tiny village and beach of **Playa Troncones** is half an hour's drive northwest of the resorts, and has recently garnered much attention among the surfing set. The beach runs for 5.5km (3½ miles) with several unspoiled, secluded coves at the southeastern end. There are a few properties to rent, and surfers will want to head to Saladita, a prime reef break nearby which offers excellent surf; beginners should watch out for the sea urchins, or, better yet, leave this break to the more experienced.

Acapulco

Very recently, the press coverage here has not been good: drug wars and even beheadings have plagued this once-glittering tourist mecca, and even though the crime is almost never directed specifically toward tourists, the city is seeing fewer international visitors than it once did. It's unfortu-

nate, but Acapulco is undeniably less popular these days. That said, it is not a place to be afraid of. Crimes likely to affect tourists are usually the petty kind, rarely violent, and even these are unlikely – though corrupt policemen have set up shop on rental cars heading toward the airport, threatening tourists with an expensive ticket and then offering to make a deal *(see page 334)*.

While its golden years may be behind it, **Acapulco** ❸ is still a fun spot to visit and is increasingly affordable, too. The economy here depends on tourism, so downturns are an excellent opportunity to take in what resorts have to offer at a bargain price. Stylish crowds of all ages and backgrounds come here to mix and mingle, hang out on the beaches during the day, and spend the nights dancing and drinking in the various bars and clubs. On the beach or off, the vibe is casual and relaxed. Everyone here is looking for the same thing: fun.

Bahía de Acapulco

At the west end of the large, sheltered Bahía de Acapulco is the traditional

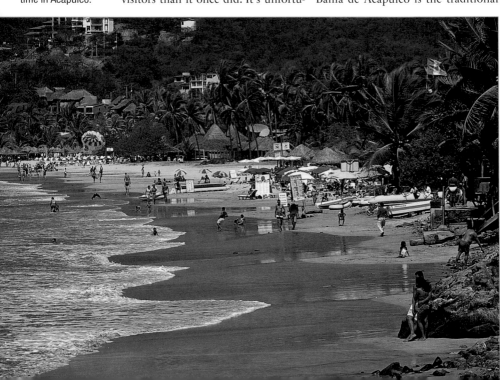

Old Town. Clustered around **Playa Caleta Ⓐ**, the original resort beach, some of the older hotels (reliable, but not luxurious) are still in operation. The rocky promontory of **La Quebrada Ⓑ** and the traditional Hotel El Mirador (tel: 744-483 1155; www.hotelel miradoracapulco.com.mx) rises above the Old Town before the bay sweeps past the *malecón* (seafront promenade) and east toward the strip of modern resort hotels. The views are still stunning, and on a calm day you can look down from the mountains at the flat, silvery water, so still it has become a mirror. It's easy to find a spot to sit, order a beer, look out at the beach or watch the activity on the white sand, and realize why this harbor became the mega-resort that it did. Acapulco continues to grow every year, and its rapid expansion eastward, in an area not far from the airport, has been influenced by the arrival of a toll road from Cuernavaca and Mexico City. In place of foreign tourists, Mexicans now flood the bars and discos, especially during Semana Santa (Easter), when nightclubs can be so packed you can stand for hours just trying to get in. Few Acapulco experiences are as authentic as dancing all night in the middle of a packed club, listening to the music and watching the smiles as favorite songs come on.

The **zócalo** (square), situated in the heart of town, is a reminder that this is Mexico and not just resortland. There are parks with benches and shade, a 1930s **cathedral** (tel: 744-482 1848; www. arquidiocesisacapulco.org/ catedral_soledad.htm; free) with a mosque-type dome, open-air cafés, inexpensive restaurants, plenty of stores and the town's largest **craft market**. There are also many small eateries that serve up wonderful fresh fish; they mostly cater to local people and Mexican tourists: be sure to ask for the catch of the day. Situated across the boulevard is the **Malecón Ⓒ** and the docks where the deep-sea fishing vessels moor.

One event that sticks in the

A margarita cocktail served with limes.

memory of all visitors to Acapulco is the emotion of watching the **high divers** at La Quebrada, an amazing spectacle that still hasn't lost its allure. For many tourists, cliff divers symbolize everything that makes Acapulco great: drama, danger, and flair. Every hour, beginning at 7.15am and ending just after midnight, young men execute dazzling swallow dives from a 40-meter (130ft) cliff into a narrow channel below; split-second timing is imperative for the divers to hit the water on the swell and not get dashed on the jagged rocks. Many divers train from boyhood, starting their jumps at the bottom of the cliff and working their way higher and higher as they gain experience and skill.

Acapulco's most historic landmark, the **Fuerte de San Diego** ❶, was built in 1616 to protect the port from mainly Dutch and English pirates. The fort was leveled by an earthquake in 1776, but was quickly rebuilt and has now been restored to house the small but interesting **Museo Histórico de Acapulco** (tel: 744-482 3828; Tue–Sun 9.30am–6.30pm; charge).

Leaving the warren of streets in old Acapulco, most tourists head along the 11km (7-mile) **Costera Miguel Alemán** ❷, a broad boulevard that stretches along the bay and is lined with high-rise hotels, restaurants and little thatch-roofed bars advertising *la hora feliz* (happy hour) with drinks priced at three for the price of one. You can't miss the giant bungee jump tower or the Palladium disco, both landmarks that overlook the bay.

Hotel prices vary greatly with the time of year. The peak season with the best weather and highest prices is between mid-December and Easter and reservations should be made well ahead of time. The best fishing months are from November through May. Boats for big- and small-game fishing can be chartered for $300 or so a day through the hotels or directly at the downtown Malecón (promenade). Sailboats, motor boats, pedal boats and canoes can all be rented too.

Some sections of the beaches in Acapulco can be polluted, although generally the sea is cleaner toward the east end of the bay; however, many

RIGHT: tequila served in generous measures.

The Changing Face of Acapulco

In the 16th century, the large natural harbor of Acapulco was the only port authorized by Spain to receive the treasure-filled galleons arriving from China and the Philippines. The goods were transferred overland via Mexico City to the Gulf Coast port of Veracruz, from where they were shipped on to Spain. Over the next couple of centuries, something like 200 million pesos worth of silver was shipped out of Acapulco as payment for the silk, porcelain, spices and ivory of the Orient.

Naturally, the flourishing trade and rich shipments attracted pirates, freebooters and the enemies of Spain. The Mexican War of Independence brought an end to the galleon trade and the town of Acapulco was forgotten until it was rediscovered as a resort during the 1930s. Over the next 70 years, Acapulco grew into one of the glitziest vacation spots in the world, rivaled (perhaps) only by Las Vegas or Rio.

Nowadays, everybody has heard of Acapulco, even if they have never been there, and despite the recent increase in drug crime, it remains a popular tourist destination both within Mexico and abroad. The beaches, nightlife, and the food keep people returning for more, and few sights are as iconic – here and indeed all over Mexico – as its bronzed cliff divers plunging into the water from their bird-like perches on the rocks.

tourists prefer to stick to the hotel swimming pools. All the usual water sports, from water- and jet-skiing to "bananas" and parasailing (easier than it looks), are readily available, while snorkeling is best in the shallow waters near **Isla de la Roqueta**. A glass-bottomed boat to the offshore island leaves from playas Caleta and Caletilla; en route you can see a huge diversity of aquatic plants and animals as well as the **Capilla Submarina** (Underwater Chapel), which is a wonderful submerged statue of the Virgen de Guadalupe (see page 29) placed here by local fishermen.

Sunset at Pie de la Cuesta

Some 8km (5 miles) north of town is **Pie de la Cuesta**, a fishing village. It is the best place to spend the day listening to the waves and watching the spectacular sunsets, but is not a good place to swim, as the undertow is vicious. A long sand-bar peninsula sheltering the **Laguna de Coyuca** (abounding in catfish, snook, and mullet) is gradually filling up with modern villas and hotels catering to tourists. The fresh water lagoon is also very popular for water-skiing, sailing and fishing trips.

Luxury hotels

Taxis are reasonable and most hotels list the prices for the usual destinations. Make sure you agree on a price in advance as taxis don't have meters. If you're on a budget, there are buses that run regularly along the Costera (see page 331–2).

On the way southeast to another popular beach at **Puerto Marqués**, in the next bay, you'll pass some of Acapulco's fanciest hotels, such as **Elcano**, **Las Brisas**, **Quinta Real**, and the **Camino Real** located at the bottom of a villa-studded hill. Each of these high-class resorts enjoys views of its own small bay, but people pay plenty for the privacy. Other high end luxury hotels are spread out further on, though they thin out eventually, leaving essentially unblemished coastline (often inaccessible) all the way to Puerto Escondido. ❑

A sunset stroll along the Pie de la Cuesta shoreline.

BELOW: young fiesta-goers.

SLICES OF PARADISE: MEXICO'S BEACHES

With all of 10,000km (6,200 miles) of coastline, Mexico offers an irresistible range of beach locations to escape to, from big, glitzy resorts to empty palm-lined bays, as well as surf beaches and stunning coral reefs

Surrounded by the warm waters of the Pacific, the Gulf of Mexico and the Caribbean, Mexico has some of the most enticing tropical coastal scenery in the world: long, silky-soft beaches, soaring cliffs and crystalline waters full of a dazzling array of marine life, from giant whales to kaleidoscopic shoals of tiny fish.

On both sides of Mexico there are big, multicolored resorts with every entertainment on hand, beginning with the two biggest, Cancún and – the favorite with Mexico City weekenders – Acapulco, followed by Cabo San Lucas, Mazatlán, Puerto Vallarta, Ixtapa-Zihuatanejo and Huatulco on the Pacific, and Cozumel and Playa del Carmen on the Caribbean "Riviera Maya." Around them, many beaches have been snapped up by giant all-inclusive resort complexes, with every activity on-site. If you prefer to evade the crowds, however, look further – around Baja California, south of Puerto Vallarta, along the coast of Oaxaca, on the southernmost part of the Riviera Maya – and you can find intimate, chic retreats with pampering spas and whole beaches all to themselves, or low-key, still scarcely developed hideaways.

Different places naturally have special attractions. The Pacific coast draws surfers from around the world, especially to Baja, Troncones, near Ixtapa, and Puerto Escondido, in Oaxaca. On the Caribbean, the exquisite waters are more suited to swimming and relaxing, and a big draw is the seductive sand of the Yucatán's beaches itself, always soft, white and cool. Offshore, though, magnificent coral reefs make this area the prime magnet for divers and snorkelers.

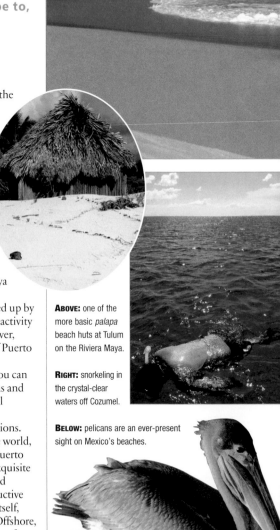

ABOVE: one of the more basic *palapa* beach huts at Tulum on the Riviera Maya.

RIGHT: snorkeling in the crystal-clear waters off Cozumel.

BELOW: pelicans are an ever-present sight on Mexico's beaches.

LEFT: catching a break at Puerto Escondido, the foremost surf center on the coast of Oaxaca.

ABOVE: strolling across the sands of one of the many beautiful bays of Huatulco, a Pacific resort with both well-developed beachfronts and quiet hideaways.

ABOVE: palms, turquoise sea and plenty of lounging-space at one of the Riviera Maya's many boutique resorts.

ABOVE: Cancún's beach stretches for 23km (14 miles), lined with resort hotels and other attractions.

BEACH PARTYING

Big and buzzing, Mexico's main resorts naturally all have plenty of places to continue the fun after dark – but with differences in style. Specialties of the giant resorts are huge mega-clubs – in Cancún, the biggest venues in Latin America – where once inside you have a whole assortment of bars, terraces, live shows, dance spaces and music styles to choose from. Lines are long to get in and costs quite high – often around US $45 – but all drinks and entertainments are included (although you still need to keep your waiter happy with frequent tips). For an older audience, in the same resorts there are also usually a few sunset or moonlight cruises available, often on "pirate ships," with dinner and show all-in.

Smaller, more hip resort towns, in contrast – such as Puerto Escondido, or Playa del Carmen – tend to have smaller, less expensive venues, with a less cheesy, more fashion-conscious style and music range, and all-night beach parties on the sand. In really small places, you'll usually have to be content with chatting in the local bar or stretching back in a hammock to gaze at the stars, although even the quietest beach village sometimes holds a fiesta at weekends.

TOP: Cancún's Coco Bongo is one of the world's biggest nightclubs, with spectacular live shows.
ABOVE: the party gets going at Señor Frog's in Playa del Carmen
BELOW: a more rustic style of music can also be found in Mexico's seaside resorts.

THE GULF COAST AND THE SOUTH

With their beautiful beaches, lush forests, relaxed feel and ancient cultures, Mexico's southern states have something for everyone

The east and south of Mexico offer perhaps more for the visitor in variety of landscape, cultural attractions and outdoor activities than any other part of the country. Hugging the Gulf Coast, Veracruz is one of Mexico's greenest states. Its beaches are not a scratch on those of the Caribbean or Pacific, but the state has much to offer, including the awe-inspiring ruins of El Tajín, the thrill of whitewater rafting, and the historical trail of Cortés. For music, dance and fiestas, head for Veracruz itself, the most atmospherically appealing of Mexico's coastal cities.

The rugged landscapes of Oaxaca are very different, providing a home for more indigenous peoples than any other state in Mexico. Many live in severe poverty, but Oaxaca's peoples are highly resilient, and they and their handicrafts and traditions form a remarkable cultural tapestry. There is also the cosmopolitan colonial city of Oaxaca, dramatic ruins at Mitla and Monte Albán, and a beautiful Pacific coastline with surfers' hang-outs, such as Puerto Escondido and a new mega-resort at Huatulco.

Humid, oil-rich Tabasco, home to the oldest Mesoamerican cultures, is the threshold of the Maya world. Chiapas is an extraordinarily varied state, changing in a few hours' drive from rain forest to pine-clad mountains. There are quaint colonial towns, traditional Highland Maya villages, the dramatic Sumidero Canyon, glittering lakes, and Palenque, Yaxchilán and Bonampak, most sensational of all the Maya ruins.

After Chiapas, the flatness of the Yucatán comes as a shock. Visitors can easily alternate the azure colors of the Caribbean with visits to a spectacular variety of Maya ruins. Offshore, the Caribbean coast offers some of the finest diving and snorkeling in the world, while inland the Yucatán limestone is riddled with caverns, many of which form *cenotes* (water holes) exquisite for swimming. The Yucatán is also known for the special charm of its colonial towns – from Mérida and Campeche to sleepy Izamal – and for its mangrove and forest reserves, which protect a fantastic diversity of flora and fauna. ❑

PRECEDING PAGES: early morning light over the central Oaxaca Valleys. FAR LEFT: a toucan native to Veracruz. FROM TOP: textiles for sale; fishing boat moored at Playa Manzanillo, Puerto Escondido; native Veracruz angel fish.

THE GULF COAST

There's plenty to see in Mexico's greenest state: the highest mountain, the fastest rapids, the oldest civilization, the best museum outside the capital and the liveliest plaza in the country

Veracruz is a long, narrow, tropical state that extends down the Gulf of Mexico. Its coast, including the historic port of Veracruz, is hot, humid and still relatively untouched by large-scale tourism.

As well as being a center for three major pre-Hispanic cultures – Olmec, Totonac and Huastec – Veracruz was Spain's gateway to the wealth of its Mexican empire. It was near the modern port of Veracruz that Hernán Cortés and his men first landed in 1519, and a short way to the north they founded the first permanent Spanish settlement in mainland America, the *Villa Rica de la Vera Cruz* or "Rich Town of the True Cross," before marching on to conquer the Aztecs in Tenochtitlán *(see page 50)*.

Nowadays it is "black gold" that sails out of Veracruz; some of Mexico's biggest oil fields are in the north and south of the state, in Tampico, Minatitlán and Coatzacoalcos. However, with a population of over 7 million, including some 650,000 indigenous people, Veracruz is also an important agricultural state, growing much of the country's sugar cane, vanilla, tropical fruits, and coffee.

The oil country and La Huasteca

The northern third of the state, between **Tampico** and Poza Rica –

both oil-refining towns – has little to detain most tourists. Tampico, with its huge new harbor complex, has a sometimes-abrasive seaport atmosphere and excellent seafood. South of town is the **Laguna de Tamiahua**, where the islands and mangrove swamps can be explored in rented boats.

Far more enticing to most visitors is **La Huasteca ❶**, a fertile region west of Tampico that extends into the states of Tamaulipas, Hidalgo and San Luis Potosí as well as Veracruz. It is home to the Huastecs, one of the most

Main attractions
LAS POZAS, XILITLA
PAPANTLA
EL TAJÍN
RÍO FILOBOBOS
CEMPOALA
VERACRUZ
MUSEO DE ANTROPOLOGÍA DE XALAPA
PICO DE ORIZABA
TLACOTALPAN
LAGUNA DE CATEMACO

LEFT: the *voladores* could show bungee jumpers a trick or two.
RIGHT: all dressed up for Mardi Gras.

The South and the Gulf Coast

intriguing Mesoamerican cultures. Their language is related to Mayan languages, and there are competing theories on when and why they migrated to La Huasteca from the far south of Chiapas or Guatemala, probably as long ago as 1000 BC. Huastec culture was at its strongest from about AD 1000 to 1500. In some ways they appeared very sophisticated, producing exceptional stone sculptures and ceramics, but their buildings were relatively simple, and Huastec men and women usually went naked, which led the Aztecs and the Spaniards to consider them primitive. The main Huastec archeological site is south of Ciudad Vallés in San Luis Potosí, at **El Consuelo**, also known as **Tamuín** or **Tamtoc** (daily 8am–5pm; charge). The best places to see Huastec art work are the anthropology museums of Xalapa *(see page 270)* and Mexico City.

The Huastecs were subjugated by the Aztecs around 1450, and later by the Spaniards, but many towns and villages maintain Huastec language and customs today (although the missionary friars eventually got them to wear clothes, including brilliantly embroidered smocks). One of the most characterful Huasteca towns is **Tamazunchale,** known for its Sunday market. Equally colorful are the local Day of the Dead celebrations *(see pages 92–3),* when streets are carpeted with confetti and petals. Rainfall is heavy in La Huasteca, and the result is tropical vegetation of astonishing lushness and beauty. Many rare birds and butterflies are found here, attracting nature enthusiasts, and local shops sell mounted butterflies.

South of Ciudad Valles is one of the most extraordinary sights in all Mexico. A road leads through jungles of bamboo and banana plants to the remote village of **Xilitla,** where English eccentric Edward James built his Dalíesque retreat at **Las Pozas ❷** (daily 9am–6pm; charge, *see box, page 267).*

Flying men and El Tajín

The little Totonac town of **Papantla,** a favorite stopover for visitors to the ruins of El Tajín, has two claims to fame: it is Mexico's main vanilla-growing center, and the home of the **Voladores de Papantla.** Their

BELOW: statue of a Voladores de Papantla musician.

famous "dance" involves five "flying men," dressed in bird-like costumes.

With ropes attached to one leg, four of the men, representing the cardinal points, launch themselves backwards in a kind of slow bungee-jump from the top of a 32-meter (105ft) pole. The *voladores* revolve slowly around the pole and the rope unwinds until they gracefully reach the ground. Meanwhile, on a tiny platform at the top, the fifth man plays a reed flute and a little drum.

Originally this spectacular performance was a solemn fertility ritual. These days it provides a means of economic survival, and *voladores* perform daily outside El Tajín ruins, and can be seen at many other touristic venues throughout Mexico.

El Tajín ❸ (daily 9am–5pm; charge) was the most powerful center of the Classic-era Veracruz civilization, whose people may have been ancestors of the region's later Totonac inhabitants. Most of the city was built after about AD 600, and its period of splendor continued until around 1100–1200, when, possibly after attacks by primitive invaders, El Tajín declined quite rapidly.

The luxuriant surroundings and the way the site is almost hidden in the jungle make El Tajín all the more wonderful to visit. The lower part of the site – the first area beyond the entrance – seems to have been mainly used for ceremonial purposes, and feels almost like a forest of massive, awe-inspiring step-pyramids. The finest work of Tajín architecture is the oriental-looking **Pirámide de los Nichos**, with its 365 square insets or niches, one for each day of the solar year. The ancient ball game was extraordinarily important in the lives of El Tajín's people; there are 17 ball courts around the site, and relief panels along the walls of the **Juego de Pelota Sur** illustrate the ritual sacrifice of ball players.

To the northeast of the main area is the Plaza de Oriente, leading to the giant walls of the **Gran Xicalcoliuhqui**, which was probably a residential complex. The main residential area for El Tajín's elite was above the ceremonial center at **El Tajín Chico**, while higher up still, with a superb view over the entire city, was the palace of its rulers, the **Building of the**

El Tajín

0 ——— 200 m
0 ——— 200 yds

Columns. There is a site museum, and many other treasures can be seen in the Xalapa Museum (see page 270).

Rafting and Beaches

Not far south of El Tajín is the foremost center for adventure tourism in Veracruz, along the **Río Filobobos** ❹. The river descends close to 1,000 meters (3,280ft) in around 65km (42 miles) to reach the sea at Nautla, passing through tree-shrouded canyons, whitewater rapids, placid pools suitable for swimming and waterfalls like the 80-meter (262ft) -high *El Encanto*. **Tlapacoyán** is the main departure point for trips on the river. Some itineraries include visits to the remote archeological sites within the Filobobos Ecological Reserve, **El Cuajilote** and **Vega de la Peña** (both daily 8am–5pm; charge).

The beaches of Veracruz are less outstanding. The **Costa Esmeralda** ❺ – in spite of its enticing name – is a stretch of very straight coastline between Tecolutla and Nautla, with palm-lined sands that fill up on local holidays. It can be an enjoyable base for visiting the area,

but be prepared for modest beach towns with typical Mexican seafood restaurants along the sand, not any upscale resorts.

There are dozens of small archeological sites along this coast, such as **Quiahuiztlán** (daily 8am–5pm; charge), overlooking the Gulf, which has a remarkable "Totonac Cemetery," with over 100 tombs. Below it, the village of Villa Rica was the site where Cortés first founded Veracruz. Of particular historic significance is the fortified center at **Cempoala** ❻ (tel: 297-971 4335; daily 8am–5.30pm; charge), which was the largest Totonac city when the Spaniards arrived in 1519, with around 30,000 people. Cortés and his men were initially well received by the Totonacs of Cempoala (sometimes spelled Zempoala), and their chief struck an alliance with the Spaniards against the Aztecs, who had been

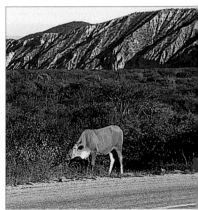

Highway maintenance in operation.

An Englishman's Castle: Las Pozas

Salvador Dalí described Edward James (1907–84) as "crazier than all the Surrealists put together." The son of a millionaire and a socialite, he was charming, refined, eccentric, and a prominent figure in British bohemia. He wrote poems himself, but was better known for using his wealth to sponsor the projects of his many friends – books, exhibitions, ballet companies – and collect art by Picasso, Magritte, Klee, and others. In the 1930s James discovered Surrealism, and was hooked. Dalí's famous sofa in the shape of Mae West's lips was first created for James' "dream house" at West Dean, near Brighton.

In 1940 James moved to the USA, and then Mexico. In Cuernavaca he met a young man called Plutarco Gastelum, and hired him as his "manager." He first visited the remote Huasteca in 1945, drawn by its astonishing varieties of orchids and birdlife. James bought land in Xilitla and made it into a spectacular orchid garden and zoo, while Plutarco – who could be pretty eccentric himself – built a large house, *El Castillo*, where he and his family all lived with the man the children called "Uncle Edward." In the 1960s, after a cold snap damaged many flowers, James decided to work in more solid form, imagining ever more bizarre – and larger – sculptures and fountains in concrete and metal. Between them he and Plutarco created a unique dream landscape, its surreal inventions intertwining unforgettably with the Huasteca forest.

On his death James left Las Pozas to the Gastelum family, but with nothing for its upkeep, as his fortune had finally run out. It decayed for years, but in 2007 a foundation, Fondo Xilitla (www.xilitla.org), took over the estate to ensure its survival. The Castillo is now a very special guesthouse.

Statue commemorating the city's development, on the Malecón in Veracruz.

BELOW RIGHT: holding the True Cross in a church courtyard in Veracruz.

exacting hefty tributes from the Cempoalans for years.

South of Cempoala, **Antigua ❼**, founded in 1525, was the second location of Veracruz, and remains a little museum of early colonial architecture; the tiny **Ermita del Rosario** church dates from the 1520s, as does the ruined **Casa de Cortés** – although the conquistador never actually lived here.

El Puerto de Veracruz: city of song and dance

When it comes to atmosphere, effervescence and music, Mexico's largest port, **Veracruz ❽** – often called *El Puerto de Veracruz* to tell it apart from the state – is the place to be. Its *zócalo*, the **Plaza de Armas,** is the liveliest in Mexico. By day, and for much of the night, it vibrates with *trios, marimbas*, salsa and *danzón*. The palm-shaded square is lined with elegant white 18th-century buildings, and *portales* filled with restaurants and cafés. There is organized music and dance several evenings a week, and itinerant musicians play at other times. Merrymaking reaches a crescendo in February during **Carnaval**, the week before Ash Wednesday. Veracruz has the biggest, loudest, most colorful Carnaval in Mexico, and people stream into the city to watch and take part.

In 1519 Cortés first landed on the Isla de Sacrificios, just off present-day Veracruz, but when he founded his new "town" shortly afterwards he initially preferred a spot further north at Villa Rica. Six years later he moved it south to Antigua, but it was not until the 1590s that Spanish governors transferred Veracruz to its definitive location, with the best harbor of all. The city, nevertheless, proudly traces its ancestry back to the first foundation in 1519.

Malecón and museums

A stroll along the waterfront promenade, the **Paseo del Malecón**, is an essential pastime in Veracruz. Ships

Old World Tlacotalpan

Little Tlacotalpan is a gem of Veracruz. Set beside the vast Papaloapan River, it was an important port under Spanish rule and in the first decades of independence, when it acquired its special colonial architecture and well-shaded plazas. Then, when steamships and railroads came, Tlacotalpan was bypassed, and so the center of the town has scarcely changed since then. Although most of Tlacotalpan's old houses are modest in size, many have impressive facades of colonnades or arabesque portals; as a very Mexican touch, these European-looking neoclassical columns are painted in bright yellows, blues and other tropical shades. Since 1998 the town, beautifully restored, has been a Unesco World Heritage site. Arriving in Tlacotalpan is like stepping into the past; though discovered by a fair number of visitors, it has retained its elegance and charm.

Tlacotalpan is exceptionally peaceful most of the time, but is by no means a museum. As well as for its buildings it is known for its fiestas leading up to La Candelaria or Candlemas on February 2, one of the most colorful in Mexico. There are parades through the streets and on flower-decked boats on the river, plenty of food, drink, dancing and the local *jarocho* folk music, and even Pamplona-style bull-running through the town. Local hotels get booked up well ahead.

come and go, and you can take a boat trip round the harbor; stalls and street vendors sell toys, cigars, amber jewelry, leather belts and souvenirs. No trip to Veracruz is complete without a visit to the **Gran Café de La Parroquia**. An institution, this unpretentious café has been the city's prime location for socializing for two centuries. A much-discussed family feud meant that in 1994 the Parroquia had to move from its traditional location on the *zócalo* to its present site on the Malecón; fortunately, the waiters, regulars and beautiful Italian coffee machines moved too.

Traditional sightseeing in Veracruz is somewhat limited. The **Museo Histórico Naval** (tel: 229-931 4078; Tue–Sun 9am–5pm; free) on Calle Arista houses exhibits on Mexico's naval history and the port itself. One block south, the **Baluarte de Santiago** (tel: 229-931 1059; Tue–Sat 9am–6pm, Sun 9am–5pm; charge) is the only remaining bastion of the Spanish fortified wall that surrounded the city until the 1880s. Its main exhibit is a collection of beautifully intricate

pre-Hispanic gold jewelry, the *Joyas del Pescador* (Jewels of the Fisherman). Lost in a shipwreck centuries ago, they were discovered by a fisherman in 1976.

The small **Museo de la Ciudad** (tel: 229-989 8872; Wed–Mon 10am–6pm; free) has a thought-provoking section on slavery and the caste system in colonial Mexico. Two kilometers (1 mile) south along the *Malecón* above **Playa de Hornos** beach is the fine **Acuario de Veracruz** (tel: 229-932 8324; Mon–Thur 9am–7pm, Fri–Sun 9am–7.30pm; charge), a state-of-the-art facility with spectacular tanks containing every kind of marine life.

Fortress island

Across a causeway, on what was once an island, forbidding **San Juan de Ulúa** (tel: 229-938 5151; Tue–Sun 10am–5pm; charge) guards the mouth of Veracruz harbor; the past 500 years of Mexican history can be told from the forbidding walls of this fortress, which has borne the brunt of many attacks – from the likes of Sir Francis Drake and 17th-century pirates to the navies of France, Britain and the United States.

EAT

Try fresh oysters on the half-shell, exotic shrimp soup, or *huachinango* (red snapper) *a la veracruzana* in one of Boca del Río's lively seafood restaurants.

BELOW: the cool and elegant Plaza de Armas, Veracruz.

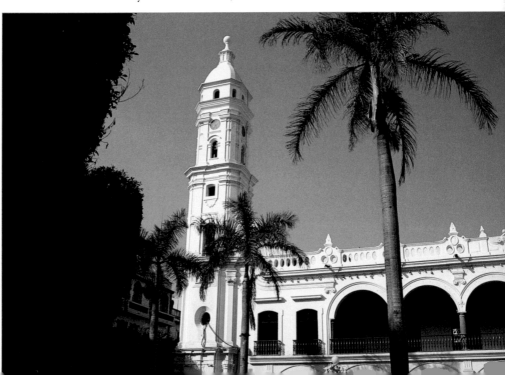

During the dictatorship of Porfirio Díaz (see page 64), this was a notorious high-security prison, and its formidable, damp cells can be visited. A little further south is the smaller island of **Isla de Sacrificios**, where Cortés first landed in 1519.

The beaches popular with *Veracruzanos* are south of the city at **Playa de Oro** and **Mocambo**. While the ocean water is warm, and the Gulf waves leisurely, they are really no match for the sands of the west coast or the Riviera Maya. For seafood, though, Veracruz is hard to equal. About 10km (6 miles) south of downtown Veracruz, **Boca del Río** is famed for its seafood restaurants (open for lunch only, to about 6pm).

Xalapa and its Museo de Antropología

Although *El Puerto* is much larger, the state capital of Veracruz is actually the attractive university city of **Xalapa ⑨**, sometimes spelled Jalapa, in the hills 135km (84 miles) inland. Its climate is cool and damp, and the city is often shrouded in mist. Nevertheless, Xalapa

enjoys a privileged setting: from the central **Parque Juárez** there are spectacular early-morning views of the **Cofre de Perote** volcano and, more distant, the Pico de Orizaba (see page 271). Just below the square, **El Agora** is a lively, multi-purpose arts center, and nearby is the **Pinacoteca Diego Rivera** (tel: 228-818 1819; Tue–Sun 10am–7pm; free), with some of Rivera's own work and contemporary art shows. Uphill from the park, the old neighborhoods have cobbled streets of colorful houses, with sloping tiled roofs and wrought-iron balconies.

Xalapa's great highlight is in the northwestern suburbs, the outstanding **Museo de Antropología de Xalapa** (tel: 228-815 4952; Tue–Sun 9am–5pm; charge). The best anthropology museum outside Mexico City, it is spacious and light, with halls and sunny patios displaying priceless treasures of the pre-Hispanic cultures of the Gulf Coast.

The first rooms are dedicated to the Olmecs, the "mother culture" of Mesoamerica. The most striking pieces are naturally the celebrated colossal

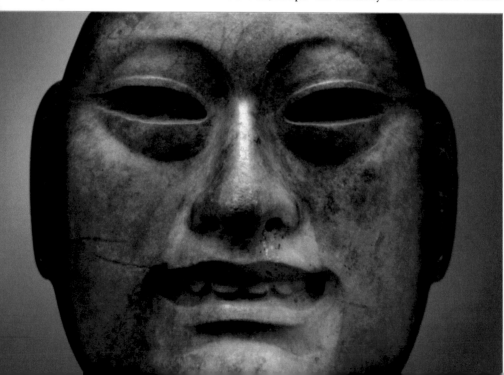

heads, dating from 1200–600 BC. The museum has seven of the 17 heads discovered so far, and the largest **El Rey** (The King), from San Lorenzo, dominates the first patio that you enter.

The next group of galleries is devoted to the Totonacs and other cultures from Central Veracruz. These include the haunting Cihuatéotl – terracotta figures of women deified after dying in childbirth – and the enchanting smiling figures, the most characteristic products of Classic-era Veracruz. The last rooms contain finely delineated **Huastec** sculptures and terracotta figurines.

The towns and countryside around Xalapa are also worth exploring. On the road toward Veracruz is the **Museo Ex-Hacienda El Lencero** (tel: 228-820 0270; Tue–Sun 10am–5pm; charge), the former estate of the dictator Santa Anna, which is now a delightful museum of colonial hacienda life. South of Xalapa is the colonial town of **Coatepec**, known for its fine coffee and orchid gardens, restaurants and enticingly peaceful hotels, notably the Posada de Coatepec, a converted

hacienda. The picturesque village of **Xico** is a short but beautiful drive away, through coffee plantations; an easy 2km (1¼-mile) walk leads to the spectacular **Cascada de Texolo** waterfall, featured in several movies.

Xalapa is also a base for rafting and adventure sports. As well as the Río Filobobos to the north *(see page 267)*, **Jalcomulco** on the **Río Pescados**, 30km (18 miles) south of Xalapa, is another popular center.

The highest peak

Mexico's highest mountain, the **Pico de Orizaba** ❿ (5,635 meters/18,490ft) is the third-highest peak in North America. Known to the Aztecs as Citlaltépetl, or "Star Mountain," this extinct volcano last erupted in 1687. The main start-point for climbers is **Tlachichuca**, on the Puebla side. Only two of the 16 climbing routes are suitable for inexperienced climbers, and first-timers should always climb with a local guide.

Industrial **Orizaba** ⓫, on the Mexico City–Veracruz highway, has some fine colonial architecture, and

Orizaba is one of Mexico's oldest beer-making towns – the Cervecería Cuauhtémoc Moctezuma, makers of Sol, Carta Blanca, Dos Equis and other labels, began production here in 1896, only six years after the company was founded in Monterrey. The brewery is still Orizaba's largest employer.

BELOW: the cloud-shrouded slopes of the Pico de Orizaba.

Countless varieties of orchids grow in the Veracruz region.

BELOW: traditional weaving skills are adapting to modern demands, as with these colorful belts.

the former **Palacio Municipal** is an extraordinary Art Nouveau construction in iron that was shipped over from Belgium in the 1890s. Also worth seeing are the 1926 mural by José Clemente Orozco *(see page 116)* in the current Palacio Municipal, and the paintings, colonial to contemporary, at the **Museo de Arte del Estado de Veracruz** (tel: 272-724 3200; Tue–Sun 9am–6pm; charge).

A few miles farther east, busy **Córdoba** ⓬ is one of the centers of Mexico's coffee industry. Its most interesting buildings are on or near the Plaza de Armas, the main square; best of all are the arcades of the **Portal de Zevallos**, along the north side, where several cafés serve the aromatic local coffee.

Southern Veracruz

Many of the rivers that divide up the hot, humid plains south of Veracruz city flow into the Río Papaloapan or "Butterfly River," which is 300 meters (985 ft) wide by the time it reaches the Gulf. Beside it is the most atmospheric of the region's colonial towns, at **Tlacotalpan** ⓭ *(see page 268).*

The small town of **Santiago Tuxtla** ⓮ nestles in the foothills of the **Sierra de los Tuxtla**. It was in these hills more than 3,000 years ago that the Olmecs found the hard basalt stone they used for their extraordinary sculptures, even though the main Olmec centers were all many kilometers away to the east. At one end of Santiago's Zócalo, standing 3.5 meters (11ft 6in) high and weighing almost 50 tons, is the largest of the Olmec colossal heads yet found. The **Museo Tuxteco** (tel: 294-947 0196; Tue–Sat 9am–6pm, Sun 9am–5pm; charge) has another head and fine pieces from nearby Olmec sites. A road leads 23km (14 miles) southwest to the largest of them at **Tres Zapotes** (Tue–Sat 9am–5pm, Sun 9am–6pm; charge). There is little left at the ancient site itself, but there are fascinating artifacts in the adjacent museum.

Not far from **San Andrés Tuxtla**, a sprawling cigar-making center, is the turn-off for the **Salto de Eyipantla ⓯**. The road passes through fields of papaya, sugar cane and tobacco before reaching this stunning waterfall, amid a perpetual cloud of mist.

The **Laguna de Catemaco ⓰** is a picturesque lake, 16km (10 miles) long, in the crater of an extinct volcano. Boat trips and other facilities can be found at the town of Catemaco, on the north bank. This is also a land of *brujos* (witch doctors), as you will soon see from the witch-related souvenirs on sale everywhere. The dividing line between authentic *brujos* and charlatans cashing in on tourists is very fine, but the tradition is real and goes back centuries. The annual gathering of *brujos* on the first Friday of March on Mono Blanco (White Monkey) hill outside Catemaco is now a tourist attraction itself.

Farther around the lake is **Nanciyaga** (tel: 294-943 0199; daily 9am–5pm; charge depending on activities), a 40-hectare (100-acre) ecological reserve. Guided walks take you through pristine rain forest, and attractions include hanging bridges, traditional steam baths, pools of spring water to swim in, cabins and a campsite. Boat trips from Nanciyaga and Catemaco also go around the **Isla de los Monos**, which is inhabited by a colony of macaque monkeys brought here from Thailand for research purposes.

Some 37km (23 miles) beyond Acayucán are the remains of the oldest of all the pre-Hispanic "cities," at **San Lorenzo Tenochtitlán ⓱** (daily 8am–6pm; free). This was the first great Olmec center, which flourished from around 1300 to 900 BC. As at Tres Zapotes, the site mainly consists only of grassy mounds, and many sculptures found here have been taken to Xalapa and other museums, but there is still one colossal head and some remarkable carvings in the village museum. ❑

Spooky figures bearing plants and herbs used for medicinal purposes and in witchcraft "haunt" the Jauregui traditional market, Xalapa.

BELOW: saddled up and ready to go.

OAXACA

This southern state is rich in history, from the archeological magnificence of its pre-Hispanic cultures to its native-born leaders, Benito Juárez and Porfirio Díaz

axaca is indigenous country par excellence. Though the Zapotec and Mixtec indigenous peoples dominate the state, 16 other linguistically and culturally distinct groups live here too. No other Mexican state is as diverse. There's so much to see in the wild and wonderful state of Oaxaca: major archeological sites, tiny rural villages where people actually produce many of the country's best handicrafts, and the exquisite seashore that lies over the mountains from the high valley of the capital, which is also called Oaxaca. While recent increases in crime here have got lots of press, incidents are rarely directed toward tourists; as in most places in Mexico, tourists are welcomed and the vast majority will find they have few, if any, problems.

Mountain vistas

The city of Oaxaca is 548km (341 miles) from Mexico City and you can fly, go by train, or take the excellent and reasonably inexpensive toll road. The drive through the mountains is beautiful whichever road you take. If you don't want to take the toll road and go through Puebla you can stop at **Atlixco**, known for its bandstand and tiled benches and a dance festival held in September. The "tree of life," often thought to be from Metepec near Toluca (*see page 373*), originated

in **Izúcar de Matamoros**, which is a center for ceramics located a little farther south.

The state of Oaxaca was also the birthplace of two of Mexico's most prominent leaders: Benito Juárez, the country's first liberal president, was a Zapotec born in the hill village of San Pablo Guelatao, about 65km (40 miles) north of Oaxaca; and Porfirio Díaz, who seized the presidency in 1877 and stayed in power until the Revolution in 1910 was born here in 1830.

The Spanish city of Villa de

Main attractions
ATLIXCO
OAXACA CENTRO
SAN FELIPE NERI
BASÍLICA DE NUESTRA SEÑORA DE LA SOLEDAD
INSTITUTO DE ARTES GRÁFICAS DE OAXACA
MONTE ALBÁN
MITLA AND THE TULE TREE
PUERTO ESCONDIDO
PARQUE NACIONAL LAGUNAS DE CHACAHUA
PUERTO ANGEL AND HUATULCO

LEFT: church of Santo Domingo, Oaxaca city
RIGHT: Atlixco's Huey Atlixcayotl festival.

A cup of chocolate caliente, *the Mexican version of hot chocolate, which mixes chocolate and cocoa beans.*

BELOW:
a masked penitent in a Holy Week procession, Atlixco.

Antequera de Guaxaca, now known simply as **Oaxaca** ⓲ (pronounced *wa-ha-ca*), was founded in 1529 near an indigenous settlement called Huaxyacac, which means "Place of Gourds." At an altitude of about 1,500 meters (4,920ft) high, its mountain climate is splendid – never too hot and never too cold. Oaxaca's center received Unesco World Heritage status in 1987 and still retains much of its old world charm, and eco-tourism trips to remote ruins are growing in popularity.

The city has a population of just over 500,000 inhabitants and an unexpectedly cosmopolitan atmosphere. The indigenous influence is stronger here than in any other state capital, the Spanish colonial architecture is superb and well-preserved and there are some fine museums and a thriving artistic community.

Oaxaca is justly famous for its markets. The **Mercado de Abastos**, the Saturday market, is where the locals come to do their weekly shop. The buying frenzy takes place on a huge plot of ground next to the second-class bus station south of town, on the Periférico (ring road). The fruit, vegetables and pottery sections are particularly interesting. Otherwise, there's a hodgepodge of furniture, clothing and kitchen equipment.

The **Benito Juárez market** and the adjacent **Mercado 20 de Noviembre** Ⓐ, both open daily, are more varied and attractive to visitors. Located on Calle 20 de Noviembre, just a few blocks south of the main square, they offer crafts (many of which are found in stalls on the street outside the market), souvenirs of all sorts, flowers and food, both raw and prepared. Photographers and cooks will find it particularly interesting for its huge mounds of dried peppers in a range of subtle colors and not-so-subtle flavors.

A shady bench in the beautifully planted **Zócalo** Ⓑ (plaza), the social hub of Oaxaca, is an excellent place to start a tour of the city. Alternatively, you can watch the world go by from the tables outside the many cafés and restaurants under the *portales* (arcades) around the square. The history of Oaxaca is illustrated in a mural that adorns the staircase inside the imposing 19th-century **Palacio de Gobierno** ●, on the south side of the plaza.

To the north of the square, facing the adjacent **Alameda**, the vast **cathedral** has a fine Baroque facade; building started in 1554 but was only completed in the 18th century. In addition to its regular services, the cathedral is often used for concerts; dates and details are available from the **tourist office** on the corner of Independencia and García Vigil.

Baroque churches

Two blocks west of the cathedral, on Independencia, the church of **San Felipe Neri** ●, with its green stone Baroque facade, is where Benito Juárez got married. Farther along the same street, the 17th-century **Basílica de Nuestra Señora de la Soledad** ● (daily 7am–2pm, 4–9pm; free), also

of green stone, has a lavish Baroque interior and houses a bejeweled statue of Oaxaca's much-revered patron saint, believed to possess miraculous healing powers. There is a small religious museum behind the basilica (daily; donation), and delicious ice creams for sale on the plaza in front.

Ancient and modern art

Concentrating on esthetic rather than historical value, it took the 20th-century artist Rufino Tamayo (*see page 117*) more than 20 years to assemble his superb collection of pre-Hispanic artifacts. He then donated the pieces to his native city in the select **Museo Rufino Tamayo** ● (tel: 951-516 4750; Wed–Mon 10am–7pm, Sun 10am–3pm; charge), and they now make up one of the most important collections in the country.

The Baroque facade of Oaxaca's cathedral.

BELOW: a quiet backstreet in Oaxaca.

A more recent donation to another building was made by Francisco Toledo, arguably Mexico's greatest living artist, who is also from Oaxaca. Housed in his elegant former home, the **Instituto de Artes Gráficas de Oaxaca** ❼ (tel: 951-516 6980; Wed–Mon 10am–8pm; donation requested) displays a small but important collection of prints by internationally famous artists as well as the prominent Mexican muralists Rivera and Orozco (*see pages 114–16*). The institute also has temporary exhibitions of graphic art.

Just north of the plaza, the **Museo de Arte Contemporáneo de Oaxaca** (tel: 951-514 2228; Wed–Mon 10am–8pm; charge) is in a beautiful 18th-century building, with work mostly from the state of Oaxaca, along with some international exhibits.

The **Museo Regional de Oaxaca** ❽ (tel: 951-516 2991; Tue–Sun 10am–7pm; charge), housed around the handsome cloisters of a Dominican monastery, is most noted for its spectacular collection of intricate Mixtec jewelry and other objects in gold, turquoise, obsidian, amber, conch

shell and glass. The pieces, dating from approximately AD 500, were found in Tomb 7 at nearby Monte Albán when it was uncovered in 1932. (They are often faithfully copied by local jewelers in gold or gold-washed silver, and sold in several of the city's better shops.) The museum also has interesting displays of textiles, clothing, household implements and archeological relics.

The adjacent 16th-century former monastery of **Santo Domingo** ❶, one of Oaxaca's noteworthy churches, has two handsome bell towers and a magnificent gilt and colored stucco interior. The exquisite giltwork reaches its crescendo in the dazzling 18th-century **Capilla del Rosario.**

Shopping opportunities

Oaxaca is a wonderful and exciting town for shopping. It is possible to buy handicrafts directly from the indigenous craftsmen and women, who come to town to sell their wares, chiefly handwoven rugs or *serapes*. A certain amount of bargaining is expected, although prices are often so low that it would seem insulting to beat them down any further.

From Santo Domingo, it is a short five-block walk back to the plaza along **Macedonio Alcalá**, a street lined with beautifully maintained colonial buildings and excellent shops selling crafts and jewelry, such as **La Mano Mágico** or **Yalalag de Oaxaca**. On nearby García Vigil, **Artesanías Chimalli** has authentic folk art and is reliable for shipping purchases.

It costs very little to join the **Biblioteca Circulante de Oaxaca** (tel: 951-518 7077; Mon–Fri 10am–2pm and 4–7pm, Sat 10am–1pm; charge), a private library with a fine selection of books in English and Spanish, many of them on Oaxaca and Mexico; the resident librarian, Ruth González, is an invaluable source of information and is also helpful if you just drop in to read a magazine.

Probably the most colorful of Oaxaca's legendary religious festivals is the

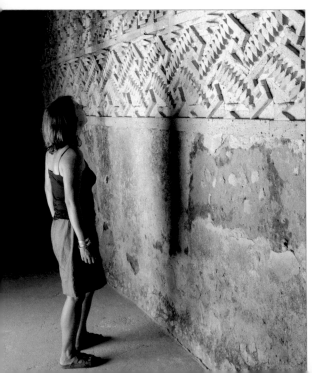

BELOW: geometric mosaics in Templo de las Columnas at Mitla.

Guelaguetza, which takes place in the Cerro del Fortín amphitheater on the first two Mondays after July 16. On December 23, the **Noche de los Rábanos** (Night of the Radishes), the plaza is filled with an extraordinary display of sculptures (often scenes of the birth of Jesus) which are made out of these intricately carved vegetables.

Monte Albán

What draws many people to Oaxaca is the proximity of its archeological wonders. The best time to see the ruins of **Monte Albán ⑲** (daily 9am–5pm; charge) is when it first opens in the morning. The grand Zapotec ceremonial center stands, about 10km (6 miles) west of the city, on an artificially leveled mountain top commanding compelling 360-degree views. These majestic ruins were also listed as a Unesco World Heritage site in 1987.

Monte Albán was established around 500 BC although the city did not peak until 1,000 years later when the population reached 25,000. The entrance to the **Gran Plaza** is at the northeastern corner located between the **Ball** **Court** and the **Plataforma Norte**. In the center of the plaza, **Edificio J** is known as the Observatory, while at the south end is the towering **Plataforma Sur**, Monte Albán's tallest building.

The **Palacio de los Danzantes** is on the west side of the square. Archeologists have not yet agreed upon the meaning of the strange low-relief "dancers" carved on the walls of this building; the figures, which bear definite Olmec influence, have been interpreted variously as ball players, medical specimens, deformed persons, sacrificial victims, or slain enemies.

It is possible to go down into some of the tombs to see the ancient frescoes. In **Tomb 104**, in the northwest, there is a fine figure of Cocijo, the Rain God, whose forked tongue represents lightning; the treasures of **Tomb 7**, which belonged to a 14th-century Mixtec dignitary, can be seen in the **Museo Regional de Oaxaca** (see page 278).

Pottery made in Atzompa, near Oaxaca city.

BELOW: Ball Court at Monte Albán.

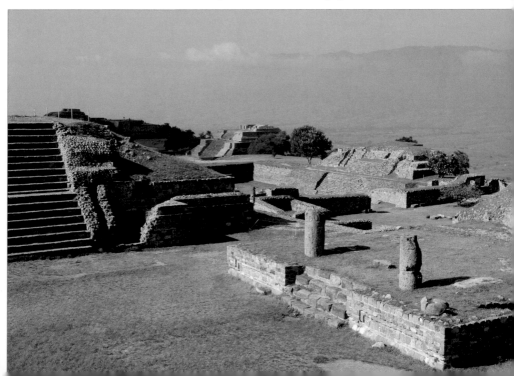

Mitla and the Tule tree

About 10km (6 miles) from Oaxaca, on the road to Mitla, is the village of **Santa María de Tule ⑳**, which has a small craft market, a pretty church and an enormous, 2,000-year-old *ahuehuete* tree (daily 9am–5pm; charge) which, with a girth of 50 meters (164ft), is thought to be the widest in the Americas. Also known as the Montezuma Cypress, it is famous for the animals one can find in the gnarled bark.

Following the decline of Monte Albán, **Mitla ㉑** (daily 9am–5pm; charge) became one of the most important Zapotec centers. The site's main structures, however, are Mixtec in style. The buildings, with their complex technique of inlaid stone, are reminiscent of the geometric friezes of the ancient Greeks.

The most intricate of the "mosaics" are in the **Patio de las Grecas**. In the **Patio de las Tumbas** there are two underground, cross-shaped tombs, one of which contains the **Columna de la Vida**; it is said that if you embrace this Column of Life, the gap left between your hands represents the years you have left to live. Unlike most ceremonial centers, Mitla was not abandoned after the Spanish Conquest, but remained inhabited well into the 16th century.

The church next to the site is built of stones taken from the ceremonial center. Outside the site entrance there is an extensive craft market with some white, lacy handwoven shawls. Just off the plaza, the **Museo de Arte Zapoteca** (daily 10am–5pm; charge), a research center for the University of the Americas, has an excellent collection of Zapotec artifacts on display and handicrafts for sale. The trip to Mitla can be combined with visits to other, less extensive, but nonetheless impressive ruins at **Dainzu**, **Lambityeco** and **Yagul.**

Several tour companies run minibuses with English-speaking guides to the various archeological sites. The one to Monte Albán operates from the Mesón del Angel, and to Mitla from the Camino Real, Victoria and Marqués del Valle hotels. People who prefer to explore on their own can drive, negotiate an hourly rate with

RIGHT: detail on Preciosa Sangre de Cristo church in Teotitlán del Valle.

Magical Mescal

Mescal and tequila are often confused, but if there's a worm floating in the bottom, chances are good that you've found yourself a bottle of *mescal* but not necessarily a good bottle. The worm – often mistaken as an indicator of quality – really makes little or no difference to the taste or strength, and some brands add a worm just for show. *Mescal* differs from its more famous cousin (tequila) in several ways, but primarily by taste. It is stronger, more complex, and more varied than tequila (which by law may *not* have a worm in it!). Hollywood (and college students) make much out of the effects of eating the worm, but aside from a bit of flavor, the worm does not have hallucinatory or other "magical" side effects. Drinkers of *mescal* primarily opt to have it neat (without ice or other mixers) and it is most often drunk as a shot, sometimes with salt or a lime chaser. Unlike tequila, it is rarely an ingredient in other cocktails. In Oaxaca, many people drink *mescal* while nibbling at fried worms, the way other cultures might injoy beer nuts. The city of Oaxaca holds a *mescal* festival annually each July, highlighting its own liquor as well as that produced in other Mexican states.

a taxi driver, or take a local bus that goes near but not directly to the sites. Many hotels and city bookstores sell specific guidebooks providing background and directions to the more established locations.

Exploring the area

For an insight into life in this mountainous region, you could travel on one of the second-class buses to villages, several jolting hours away, where many indigenous groups live in relative isolation. Oaxaca is one of the poorest states of Mexico; erosion is devastating and the farm laborers do not have enough land to support themselves. To supplement what they earn from farming, many Oaxacans have become craftsmen, and villages in the area surrounding Oaxaca offer opportunities to see the artisans at work. Prices are much the same as they are at city market stalls, but much less than in Mexico City or other tourist towns.

In **Teotitlán del Valle** ㉒, a couple of kilometers off the main road to Mitla, it is sometimes possible to watch weavers creating designs from wool spun and dyed by the women of the household. Some people also come to the village specifically to eat at **Tlamanalli** (tel: 951-524 4006; Tue–Sun 1–4pm), a restaurant featuring updated versions of traditional Zapotec food.

The fine Dominican church at nearby **Tlacolula** was built in the 16th century; particularly note the indigenous influence in the riotously decorated interior and the antique, tubular pipe organ. The town also has the best Sunday market in the region and is the place to get top-quality *mezcal*, sometimes flavored with herbs; bottles often include the coveted worm that lives in the maguey plant.

South of Oaxaca, in the Mixtec town of **Cuilapan**, are the ruins of an early Dominican church and monastery. Independence hero Vicente Guerrero was executed here in 1831. Cuilapan was once a center for the production of cochineal, the scarlet dye made from female insects that feed on cactus. Used as a base for magenta hues in Europe, and even in the red coats of the British army, this dye was once so highly

TIP

B. Traven's short stories make excellent reading for anyone traveling in Oaxaca or southern Mexico. *(See Further Reading, page 391.)*

BELOW:
Maundy Thursday procession leaving a church in Teotitlán del Valle.

Hand sculpture at Zicatela beach, Puerto Escondido.

RIGHT: pelicans in Parque Nacional Lagunas de Chacahua.

prized that its export was strictly controlled under Spanish rule.

Oaxaca's coast

Oaxaca has 480km (298 miles) of Pacific coastline with excellent beaches, quiet lagoons and good surfing. The highway from Acapulco (in neighboring Guerrero) to Salina Cruz (in Oaxaca) has been resurfaced, although it is still rough in many places. Puerto Escondido, Puerto Angel and now Huatulco are the three best-known destinations. Although all were badly hit by hurricanes in recent years, they were quickly repaired.

Of these three resorts, **Puerto Escondido** ㉓ has been in the business of tourism the longest, although it is by no means a sophisticated destination. Fishing is still an important source of revenue and the daily catch turns up fresh in the marketplace and on the table in local seafood restaurants.

The atmosphere in Puerto Escondido is low-key and relaxed with little to do but enjoy the sun, sea and surf. The **old town** is on a hill above the

bay. The main tourist area stretches from **Playa Principal**, where the fishing boats are berthed, to **Playa Marinero**, the swimming beach. Around the curve is the long, sandy beach at **Zicatela**, a magnet for surfers who come to ride the famous "Mexican Pipeline." Luckily for surfers, Playa Zicatela has a lethal undertow which keeps swimmers away.

Most tourist facilities are on or near the beach. The pedestrian walkway that parallels the bay through the tourist part of town is lined with shops selling silver, jewelry and other trinkets.

There are simple but excellent seafood restaurants, such as La Perla Flameante and Junto al Mar, as well as bars that have live jazz and dance music starting at about 10pm and continuing far into the night. The most outstanding hotel in Puerto Escondido, the **Santa Fe**, stands at the point where the surf beach and the swimming beach converge. On the hill at the other end of town, **El Aldea del Bazar** is a handsomely designed hotel, although a taxi is needed to get to or from anywhere else.

Playa Zicatela: the Mexican Pipeline

Surfers have always drifted south from California into Baja's remote beaches, but the mainland has made a name for itself as well. With the resurgence in popularity of the sport, towns along the Pacific coast with good breaks have become more popular as well. Nowhere is that more true than at Puerto Escondido. Once a quiet fishing community known primarily for seafood and a few places to stay, this town is now synonymous with a break rivaled only by Oahu's North Shore: the Mexican Pipeline. While the town still retains a quiet, low-key, relaxed tourist atmosphere, the surfing is anything but placid. Playa Zicatela, is one of Mexico's greatest – and most dangerous – surfing breaks, in part because large waves break in shallow water. This is not a beach for swimmers, as strong currents run along the shore, making for undertows and rips that can pull even the strongest swimmer far from shore. Though famous, it is not for inexperienced surfers either: broken boards, separated shoulders, and other injuries are common. Use care and caution if you head out. On heavy surf you'll need a jet ski tow-in, but the rewards are adrenalin rushes and glassy glides down some of the most powerful, and perfect, wave faces Mexico can offer. Those who don't feel comfortable surfing, can enjoy just hanging out and watching some of the world's greatest surfers strut their stuff on some of Mexico's best and biggest waves.

Spectacular wildlife

Anyone with an interest in birds and other wildlife should consider a 60km (37-mile) detour west of Puerto Escondido to the **Parque Nacional Lagunas de Chacahua** ㉔. *Lanchas* (small motor boats) can be rented in the village of Zapotalito to tour the lagoons and their mangrove-edged islands.

It is best to come in the early morning or late afternoon to see the ibis, spoonbills, parrots, alligators, turtles and many other creatures that inhabit the lagoons. There are also fine sandy beaches and sheltered coves; but bring insect repellent as the mosquitoes can be fierce.

Puerto Angel and Huatulco

Even more than Puerto Escondido, **Puerto Angel** ㉕ is a sleepy resort with a tropical setting and superb sheltered beaches for people who want to relax, swim and lie in the sun. The fishing village is on the east side of the bay, while swimming is better at **Playa del Panteón**, on the west side. Fresh seafood abounds and there are several comfortable, though not luxurious, hotels in the town. And if you want

to get right back to basics, the long, sandy, palm-fringed beach of Zipolite is only 5km (3 miles) along the coast.

In contrast, **Huatulco** ㉖ has become a mega-resort, with marina, golf courses, scuba diving and horseback-riding, somewhat overshadowing the emerald islands and sandy coast that made it famous. Beaches still sprawl along 35km (22 miles) of glorious coastline. Numerous resort hotels have been completed, including the Barceló, the Dreams Huatulco, the Camino Real Zaashila, the Quinta Real and Las Brisas. The Punta Celeste archeological site just south of Tangolunda Bay is currently under excavation and access is limited.

There are boat trips from the harbor in the main Bahía de Santa Cruz to some wonderful beaches with excellent snorkeling. The purpose-built town of **La Crucecita**, 2km (1 mile) inland, is an integral part of the development, complete with a central plaza, restaurants, some inexpensive hotels, crafts markets, and a delightful marketplace. ❏

Playa Zicatela is the main surfing beach in Puerto Escondido.

BELOW: Playa La Entrega, Huatulco.

TABASCO AND CHIAPAS

The two states of Mexico's southeast offer extraordinary contrasts, from the flat, humid, tropical delta of Tabasco to the mountainous subcontinent of Chiapas

México City

The two very different states of Tabasco and Chiapas span the country from the Gulf of Mexico to the Pacific, just east of the Isthmus of Tehuantepec, Mexico's narrow waist. They are the westernmost part of the region occupied, in pre-Hispanic times and today, by the Maya.

Green, tropical **Tabasco** is often wrongfully dismissed as an oil state to pass through on the way to Chiapas and the Yucatán. Much of this steamy, low-lying area is the delta of two giant rivers, the Grijalva and the Usumacinta, and the state is crisscrossed with meandering tributaries and palm-lined creeks that were used as trading highways by the oldest of Mexico's civilizations, the Olmecs, who inhabited this land 3,000 years ago. The ever-presence of water and green vegetation makes Tabasco a vivid contrast to the arid states to the west.

Villahermosa

In March 1519, after rounding the Yucatán peninsula, Hernán Cortés won his first victory in Mexico at Centla in northeast Tabasco – one of the spoils of which was his interpreter and later mistress, *La Malinche* – before sailing north to Veracruz. He left behind a small outpost at the mouth of the Río Grijalva, which grew into a small town.

By the 1590s, however, it was being raided by French and English pirates, and it was decided to move it upriver. Now called **Villahermosa** ㉗, it is the capital of Tabasco and, with close to 700,000 people, one of the busiest cities in southern Mexico.

A sleepy river town until the 1950s, Villahermosa has been transformed by the arrival of cars, air conditioning and above all the oil boom of the 1970s, which led to it more than doubling in size and becoming a city of wide modern avenues (and sometimes

Main attractions
PARQUE-MUSEO LA VENTA, VILLAHERMOSA
COMALCALCO
CAÑÓN DEL SUMIDERO
CHIAPA DE CORZO
LAGUNAS DE MONTEBELLO
SAN CRISTÓBAL DE LAS CASAS
CHAMULA AND ZINACANTÁN
TONINÁ
AGUA AZUL AND MISOL-HA
PALENQUE
BONAMPAK
YAXCHILÁN

LEFT: masked performers at the fiesta of San Sebastián. **RIGHT:** Our Lady of Guadalupe church in Cupilco, near Villahermosa.

Tabasco sauce is from Louisiana, not Mexico, but a highlight of real Tabascan cuisine is the pejelagarto or lizard-fish, a type of river fish unique to the Grijalva-Usumacinta delta, with an almost sweet flavor. Some of the best places to sample it are the many riverside restaurants near Puerto Ceiba and Paraíso, north of Comalcalco.

BELOW:
Villahermosa's
Government Palace.

horrendous traffic). The biggest expression of Villahermosa's oil wealth is the area around the **Tabasco 2000** complex, with a convention center, a shopping mall, lakeside parks and gardens, and upscale hotels.

The "old" center of the city – which is mostly 19th- or early 20th-century – is down below, beside the Grijalva, and known as the *Zona Luz* or "Zone of Light." It doesn't have the historic charm of Mexico's colonial cities, but does offer plenty of bustle and streetlife. Like all of riverside Villahermosa the area was badly hit by massive floods in 2007, but reconstruction has progressed steadily.

The city's greatest attraction, which largely escaped the flood, is **Parque-Museo La Venta** (tel: 993-314 1652; daily 8am–5pm; charge), in an exquisite jungle setting alongside a lake near Tabasco 2000. This unique open-air museum is a showcase for superb sculptures from the Olmec center of **La Venta**, 130km (80 miles) west of Villahermosa, which flourished from about 900–400 BC, after the still-unexplained decline of San Lorenzo in Veracruz *(see page 273).*

Initial excavations at La Venta were made in the 1920s and 1940s. Then, in the 1950s, the original site was threatened by oil drilling, and Tabascan poet and anthropologist Carlos Pellicer Cámara came up with the radical proposal to transport 32 of its massive monuments to Villahermosa for their protection. The result is spectacular: visitors "discover" the powerful sculptures amid lush forest plants, along paths around the park. Most celebrated are the colossal Olmec heads, more than 2 meters (6ft) tall, but equally dramatic are the altars, often showing priest-lords emerging from alcoves representing gateways to the underworld. Another feature of Parque La Venta is that it is intertwined with a zoo entirely of local wildlife (entry included in the ticket), so that as you walk around the monuments you can also see parrots, toucans, jaguars and other exotic creatures.

The **Museo Regional de Antropología Carlos Pellicer** (tel: 993-312 6344; normally Tue–Sun 9am–8pm; charge), by the river, has a fine collection representing all Mexico's ancient cultures. However, restoration after flood damage has been protracted, so check it is open before visiting.

Comalcalco and Cacao

Just east of Villahermosa is a popular natural attraction, the park of **Yumká** ㉘ (tel: 993-356 0107; daily 9am–4pm; charge), which contains a large area of native tropical forest and a safari park with exotic animals such as lions and hippos. More adventurous ecotourism trips can be made to forest waterfalls near Huimanguillo, off the Tuxtla Gutiérrez road, and to caves and sulfur springs in the **Sierra de Tabasco**, south of Villahermosa.

Comalcalco ㉙ (daily 10am–5pm; charge), 62km (39 miles) from Villahermosa, is the westernmost ancient Maya city. It is also a remarkable demonstration of Maya adaptability. In most places, the Maya built in stone; in the soft, muddy delta this was impossible, so they built in stucco and brick. Most of its buildings date from AD 600–800. As you enter the site, you first come to the majestic **Plaza Norte**, surrounded by step-sided brick pyramids. Above it is the massive artificial mound of the **Gran Acrópolis**, with temples adorned with fine carvings; and the atmospheric **Palacio** that was home to Comalcalco's elite, with water-courses running through it to provide an early system of air conditioning.

As well as being the oldest Mesoamerican culture the Olmecs are also thought to have been the first people ever to cultivate cacao, or chocolate, in the Tabasco deltas in about 1000 BC. The area is still considered to produce some of the world's finest chocolate, and along the road south of Comalcalco town there is a modest *Ruta del Cacao*, with pleasant little cacao estates that are open to visitors, with tours, shops and (of course) tastings.

Into Chiapas

No state in Mexico offers such radical contrasts in landscape and climate as Chiapas. It has as many differences

as whole countries: from dense, sultry rain forest around Palenque or on the Pacific coast, to spectacular mountain peaks, pine forest, crystalline waterfalls and massive rock ridges in the Chiapas Highlands, another world where temperatures drop and the air feels completely different. The range of wildlife and vegetation is astonishing.

Like Oaxaca, Chiapas has a large indigenous population, making up about one third of the total. Long remote from the rest of Mexico, Chiapas has been known for chronic social problems, with many of its Maya communities, especially, living in severe poverty – the background to the Zapatista movement *(see page 288)*. One effect of this conflict has been to draw more official attention to Chiapas than has been seen in decades – reflected in huge investment in new roads, which has made many parts of the state a great deal easier to get to.

The inscrutable features of a massive Olmec stone head in the open-air Parque Museo La Venta.

BELOW: the still waters of the Sumidero Canyon.

The Zapatistas of Chiapas

The world news agenda may have moved on, but the Zapatista rebels remain in their Chiapas villages, a combination of Maya tradition and radical social experiment.

On January 1, 1994 Mexico's political world was shaken to its foundations when armed Maya rebels, wearing anonymous ski-masks and calling themselves the Ejército Zapatista de Liberación Nacional (EZLN, Zapatista National Liberation Army), emerged from the Lacandón forest and took over San Cristóbal de Las Casas and Ocosingo. President Carlos Salinas and his government appeared stunned. The supposedly ignorant Indians seemed constantly able to wrong-foot them, represented by their multi-lingual non-Maya spokesman Subcomandante Marcos, whose sharp jibes at the established order made him one of the anti-globalization movement's first heroes.

In the background was a long-simmering conflict. From the 1940s, poor Maya in Chiapas were encouraged to move down to farm in the "empty" forest east of Ocosingo. However, with no formal title, they could be thrown off this land whenever it became more valuable, as happened with the expansion of commercial ranching from the 1970s. Combined with this was the corruption of local Chiapas authorities.

After a few days the government agreed to a cease-fire, while the Zapatistas withdrew from the towns. The resulting standoff has lasted ever since. The government declared its commitment to negotiate, but also poured troops into Chiapas, to prevent any repetition of 1994. Local authorities often tacitly encouraged the emergence of paramilitary groups to oppose Zapatista land claims. The conflict carried on at a half-hidden level, with flashes of violence usually far from media attention, as when 45 Zapatista sympathizers were murdered in Acteal in 1997.

In 1996 government and Zapatistas signed a set of accords in San Andrés Larraínzar, which seemed to promise land rights and autonomy for indigenous communities, and since then have encapsulated the Zapatistas' core demands. However, nothing was done to put them into practice. Optimism revived in 2000 with the election of President Fox, but he failed to push a new agreement through Congress, and the Zapatistas again accused politicians of never negotiating in good faith.

There have been no negotiations since then. The Zapatistas, aware of their weakness in the face of all the military hardware now in Chiapas have proclaimed an almost Gandhi-like policy of non-violent resistance. In 2003 they announced that, rather than wait for a settlement, they would put the San Andrés accords into practice by themselves, linking the 2,000 villages they control across Chiapas to large "hub villages" or *caracoles* (snails), and developing their own system of participatory democracy.

Outposts of this network can be seen in Territorio Zapatista signs outside villages. In San Cristóbal, the Zapatistas seem part of the scenery. Economically the *caracoles* are weak, but supporters point to their achievements in building clinics and schools. However, the Army maintains a powerful presence, and there are still confrontations with anti-Zapatistas, usually in remote villages. Now largely ignored by the media, and politically isolated, the Zapatistas feel vulnerable.

One thing this situation does not create is special dangers for foreign visitors. Zapatistas are generally happy to have foreigners around, since they believe this deters aggressive actions by others. In 2008 the *caracol* of Oventic north of San Cristóbal actually began to invite visits, which can be arranged through local guides. ❑

LEFT: EZLN leader Subcomandante Marcos.

Tuxtla Gutiérrez and the Sumidero

The state capital, **Tuxtla Gutiérrez** ③⓪, is 290km (180 miles) south of Villahermosa. It is a modern city with a few specific attractions. The **Museo Regional de Chiapas** (tel: 961-613 4479; Tue–Sun 9am–6pm; charge), in Parque Madero, has superb artifacts from the state's exceptional range of archeological sites. The fascination of the **Zoomat** or **Zoológico Miguel Alvarez del Toro** (tel: 961-614 4700; Tue–Sun Sept–Apr 8.30am–4pm, May–Aug 8.30am–5pm; charge), on a hill south of the city, is that absolutely all of its more than 300 species are native to Chiapas, such as tapirs, jaguars, ocelots and a dazzling array of birds. Many smaller animals are allowed to run freely around the park.

The most popular destination around Tuxtla is the **Cañón del Sumidero** ③①, a giant gash over 1,000 meters (3,280ft) high and at times 2km (1¼ miles) wide, in the massive wall of rock north of the city. The Grijalva River used to become a whitewater torrent as it ran through it, but now, blocked by the dam at Chicoasén to the north, it is a broad, placid waterway. Boat trips run daily beneath the sheer cliff walls of the gorge, giving the opportunity to see a wide range of bird life and many bizarre rock formations. On one side of the gorge is the **Parque Amikúu** (tel: 961-600 6708; www.parqueamikuu.com; daily 9.30am–dusk; charge), an "ecopark" with jungle trails, kayaks for rent, a swimming pool, folkloric shows and other attractions.

Boats to the Sumidero and the Parque Ecoturístico leave daily (8am–4.30pm; charge) from **Cahauré** and the town of **Chiapa de Corzo** ③②, 15 minutes east of Tuxtla, where there is a line of riverside restaurants by the *embarcadero*. The first Spanish settlement in Chiapas, founded in 1528, Chiapa has all the colonial charm that is missing in Tuxtla Gutiérrez. The huge octagonal well in

Highland music features traditional flutes unchanged since ancient times.

BELOW: Tzeltal officials sharing a ritual drink, or two.

Still waters run deep in Parque Nacional Lagunas de Montebello.

BELOW: the church of Santo Domingo in San Cristóbal de las Casas.

the town plaza, dating from 1562 and called **La Pila**, is a remarkable example of Spanish Mudéjar or Moorish-influenced architecture, the finest in the Americas. The beautifully airy cloisters of a former monastery are now the **Centro Cultural ex-Convento de Santo Domingo** (tel: 961-616 0055; Tue–Sun 10am–5pm; free), with exhibition spaces and the **Museo de la Laca**, dedicated to the lacquerware for which the town is famous.

Chiapa de Corzo is also famous for its wild, spectacular fiestas around the day of San Sebastián, January 20. Men dress up as *parachicos*, in bright ponchos, fur hats and strange, pale-faced lacquered masks, which began as a way of satirizing the Spanish conquerors, while women wear elaborate, dazzlingly coloured skirts. They dance wildly around the town for days, and the fiesta culminates in a "battle of boats" on the river.

Another way to see the Sumidero is from the viewpoints *(miradores)* above the gorge, reached by a road from the west side of Tuxtla (signposted Chicoasén). *Combis* run there from central Tuxtla.

Pacific Chiapas

Southwest of Tuxtla are Arriaga and **Tonalá**, from where you can drive or get a *combi* to cover the 19km (12 miles) to **Puerto Arista** ㉝, so far the only "beach resort" in Chiapas. Crowds descend here from Tuxtla at Mexican holiday times, but the rest of the year the town, its huge beach and its cheap seafood restaurants are very quiet.

The capital of the long coastal plain of the Soconusco is hot, busy **Tapachula** ㉞, Mexico's "gateway to Central America." Nearby, almost at the Guatemalan border, is the oldest Maya site in Mexico at **Izapa** (Wed–Sun 8am–5pm; charge), dating back to 300 BC. Behind Tapachula the land rises extraordinarily steeply, to 2,000 meters (6,560ft) in just 60km (37 miles). Some of the coffee plantations on the high slopes, such as **Finca Hamburgo**, still

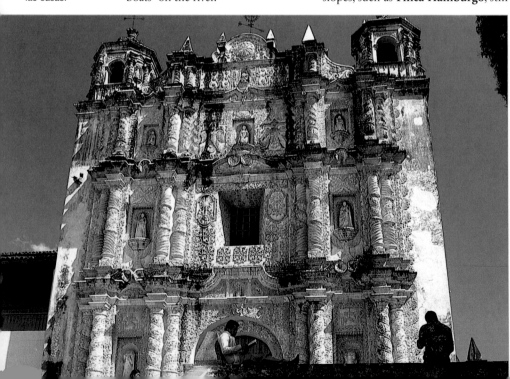

owned by descendants of German and Swiss families who came here in the days of Porfirio Díaz, have been made into very special hotels. Far above the plain, they feel like a different world.

From **Huixtla**, 42km (26 miles) north of Tapachula, the highway north begins an incredible climb, before dropping down to meet Highway 190 near the Guatemalan border crossing at **Ciudad Cuauhtémoc**.

Montebello and Comitán

From the border the Pan-American Highway (Mexican Highway 190) climbs steadily into the central highlands, with superb views east towards Guatemala's mountains, looming hazily in the distance. At Trinitaria, an eastward turn leads onto the Carretera Fronteriza or Highway 307, which now follows the border for some 450km (280 miles) all the way to Palenque. After about 38km (23 miles) it passes through the **Parque Nacional Lagunas de Montebello** ㉟. Between precipitious, pine-clad slopes there are some 60 jewel-like lakes; also known as the **Lagunas de Colores**, they range

spectacularly from turquoise and amethyst to dark emerald green and steely gray. Most people visit the lakes as a day trip, but there are rustic *cabaña* hotels in the largest village, **Tziscao**, right by a placid lake that extends into Guatemala.

Just west of the Montebello entrance, a road turns north to the Maya ruins of **Chinkultic**, astonishingly located on a near-vertical crag above a lake. However, access has become difficult owing to a dispute between local villagers and the state authorities, and before going there it's advisable to check on the situation at the Comitán museum. Back on Highway 190, a turning west leads 6km (4 miles) to the larger and more accessible site of **Tenam Puente** (daily 8am–5pm; charge), with massive stone pyramids on an immense hill, giving sweeping views. These centers were on the southern borders of Classic Maya civilization, and are believed to have survived after the more famous cities further north had collapsed.

Comitán ㊱ is known for its steep streets and broad plaza and as the

TIP

There are three main road crossings from Chiapas into Guatemala: at Ciudad Hidalgo and Talismán near Tapachula, and Ciudad Cuauhtémoc on Highway 190. Direct international buses run from Tapachula via Ciudad Hidalgo; on the other routes, you must get a Mexican bus to the border, then a Guatemalan bus on the other side. Most nationalities do not need a visa for tourist trips. It is not usually permissable to take a Mexican rental car into Guatemala.

BELOW: metal sculptures on a Comitán street.

Comitán students on the zócalo..

RIGHT: a finely carved perch.

home of Rosario Castellanos, Chiapas' greatest modern writer. As well as a charming small-town atmosphere, good restaurants and hotels it has an attractive **Museo Arqueológico** (tel: 963-632 5760; Tue–Sun 9am–6pm; charge), with many finds from Tenam Puente.

San Cristóbal de las Casas

North of Comitán the highway continues climbing into the heart of Los Altos, the highlands of Chiapas. This is also the heartland of living Maya culture in the state, where many communities speak Mayan languages – Tzotzil in some, Tzeltal in others – wear traditional dress and maintain beliefs that are a fascinating blend of ancient Maya tradition with Catholic elements brought by the Dominican friars. The women of **Amatenango del Valle**, on

Highway 190, specialize in making beautiful earthenware pottery, using an open fire instead of a kiln, employing a technique dating back over a thousand years. Older women from Amatenango are instantly recognizable by their red and orange woollen smocks, and long blue skirts.

At an altitude of 2,100 meters (6,890ft), **San Cristóbal de las Casas** ③⑦, capital of Los Altos, is many visitors' favorite town in Mexico. It is a city of immense colonial charm, with mostly one-story houses with red-tiled roofs and walls in blue, green and ochre around secluded patios, and the scent of wood smoke lingering in the air. The cool mountain air is sparkling, and plenty of likeable restaurants, surprisingly trendy cafés and attractive hotels make this a very relaxing place just to spend some time and soak up the atmosphere.

San Cristóbal was founded in 1528 as the first capital of Spanish Chiapas. Formerly *Ciudad Real de Chiapa*, the "Royal City" of Chiapas, its was given its current name in honor of Bartolomé de las Casas, first bishop

The Highland Weavers

Among the Highland Maya, gender roles have traditionally been very set. Men's first role is to grow corn and keep livestock; the quintessential art of women is to weave. Ixchel, the most important Maya fertility goddess, was also goddess of weaving. In traditional communities, all women and girls weave, from an early age. They do so using the Maya backstrap loom, examples of which can be seen on pots and figurines from the Classic era, before AD 800. It is made up essentially of two wooden rods, with the main threads stretched between them. One is attached, by a cord tied to both ends, to a post or tree, while the other is connected to a strap around the lower back of the woman, who works kneeling, moving backward and forward to stretch and relax the threads, and with a heavy wooden comb to pack down each row of colored cross-threads.

Each of the Highland communities has its own distinctive style of weaving, and some soon become familiar to any visitor. The bright flower-designs of Zinacantán are the most eye-catching and often the most popular, but in textile cooperatives you can also find the beautiful, extraordinarily intricate work of more remote villages such as San Andrés Larraínzar or Mitontic, the larger pieces of which are made with immense skill. And within each local style, each piece is also an individual creation of each weaver, using a great range of motifs, and no two pieces are ever the same.

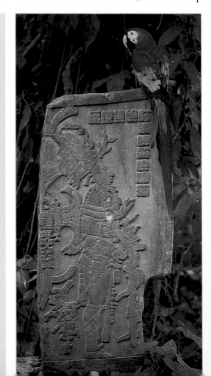

of Chiapas, who defended indigenous people against the excesses of the conquistadors. For centuries only Spanish-speaking people were allowed to live in the town, while the townspeople in turn rarely ever entered the Maya villages around them. This pattern has marked society in the Highlands ever since, but the last few decades have seen a vast change, as the Maya have flocked down to the city not only for the daily market, but to live in suburbs around it.

As in all Spanish colonial towns, there are fine churches. Alongside the zócalo (main square) is the cathedral, with a facade painted Highland-style in yellow and red ochre. Calle Real de Guadalupe, running eastwards from the square, has the highest concentration of restaurants and shops, many selling Highland weaving and jewelry of Chiapas amber. The finest of San Cristóbal's churches is the **Templo de Santo Domingo**, at the other end of Calle General Utrilla from the Zócalo, begun in 1547 but with a stunning 17th-century Baroque facade in yellow stone. The church is equally dazzling

inside, with an overwhelming display of Baroque gilt.

Around Santo Domingo is the Mercado Indígena or **handicrafts market**, an irresistible place to browse through brilliantly colored clothing, mats and other Highland products. Women from Maya villages come here every day to sell their own weaving and embroidery, as well as pottery, leather goods and more modern things like toys and T-shirts. Some of the finest-quality weaving can be found in the cooperatives near the market, at **Sna Jolobil** (which is Tzotzil for "Weavers House"), behind Santo Domingo, and **J'Pas Joviletik**, at Calle Utrilla 43.

One of the most distinctive products of Chiapas is fine amber, found especially in remote villages in the north of the state. San Cristóbal has a delightful **Museo del Ambar** (Tue–Sun 10am–2pm, 4–7pm; charge), in the former convent of La Merced, giving detailed information on how amber is formed, and with a lovely shop with original jewelry. There are many more shops with attractive amber jewelry around the town, especially on Calle Real.

EAT

San Cristóbal has some of Mexico's best vegetarian restaurants. La Casa del Pan, with two locations at Calle Dr Navarro 10 and Calle Real de Guadalupe 55, has delicious, imaginative variations on local dishes made with organic ingredients, and fabulous bread.

BELOW: brotherly love.

TIP

When visiting Chamula and Zincantán for the first time, it is always better to go with a tour. As well as explaining what you are seeing, tour guides have access to many places that are otherwise closed to outsiders. Some of the most satisfying, good-value tours are those of Alex y Raúl, who can be found with their bus every day in the Zócalo in San Cristóbal at 9.30am. On request they can also arrange trips to less-vistied areas, and Zapastista villages. .

BELOW: Templo de las Inscripciones at Palenque.

A walk east from Santo Domingo leads to **Na Bolom** (tel: 967-678 1418; tours daily 11.30am, 4.30pm; charge), the former home of the Swiss writer and photographer Trudi Duby-Blom (1901–93) and her Danish husband, the archeologist and anthropologist Frans Blom (1893–1963). It is now a center that continues their work with the Lacandón Maya and other indigenous peoples of Chiapas, with a library and a guesthouse, but a great attraction is the house itself, with its patios, herb garden and fascinating relics of the Bloms' life here.

The highland villages

No stay in San Cristóbal is complete without a visit to the Maya communities north of the city, at **San Juan Chamula ❸** and **Zinacantán**. They are very different. Chamulans keep sheep, and their traditional dress for men – nowadays worn over conventional clothes – is a coarse woollen smock in black or white; women wear long black woolen skirts and blue or white blouses bordered with embroidered strips. The people of

Zinacantán, in contrast, are the great color-lovers of the highlands, and men and women wear beautiful multicolored smocks with intricate flower motifs. *Zinacanteca* weaving is, consequently, the most popular buy for visitors.

Tours from San Cristóbal include both villages, beginning at Chamula, 10km (6miles) from the city, with a visit to the extraordinary church. As in all the highland villages, the religion of the Chamulans is a complex mix of Catholic and pre-Conquest Maya beliefs. Inside, there are no services or seats, but the floor is carpeted with pine needles and lit with hundreds of candles, and people come and go to consult traditional healers or *ilol*, sitting on the floor. At Zinacantán, typically, the church is more colorful, and the atmosphere less intense. As your guide will tell you, it is absolutely forbidden to take photographs in either of the churches.

Another village easy to get to is **Tenejapa**, 29km (18 miles) east. The road there passes through spectacular scenery, and there is a vibrant Thursday market.

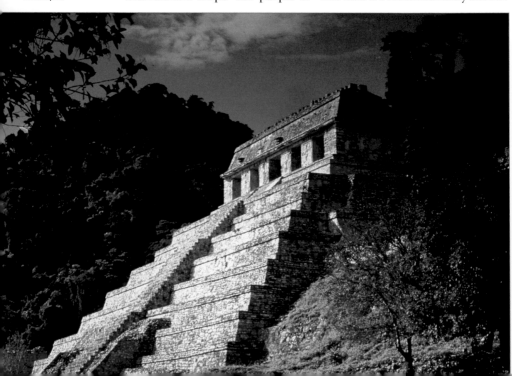

Toniná and the waterfalls

Highway 199 runs down from San Cristóbal to Palenque (in 192km/119 miles) and the steamy forests of northeast Chiapas. About halfway down is the market town of **Ocosingo**, where a turning leads 14km (9 miles) to one of the most extraordinary Maya creations at **Toniná** ❸ (tel: 919-673 1224; daily 8am–5pm; museum Tue–Sun only; charge). Instead of spreading over several pyramids like most Maya cities, Toniná is almost one giant structure, rising up a mountain side through seven levels and endless staircases, and looking more than any other Maya center like a work of science fiction. The excellent museum displays remarkable sculptures from the site. As a warrior state Toniná fought many battles with Palenque.

There are two more popular stops before Palenque. The 7km (4 miles) of breathtaking jungle waterfalls at **Agua Azul** ❹, on Río Tulijá, are 4km (2½ miles) off the main road. The most turbulent cataracts are – naturally – extremely dangerous, but if you walk up 1 km (½ mile) there are large, placid pools that are easy to swim in. A safer and often more enjoyable spot for swimming, which generally has a more relaxed atmosphere, is the pool beneath the 35-meter (115ft) waterfall at **Misol-Ha** ❹, 22km (14 miles) from Palenque. Apart from the dangers of the waterfalls, Agua Azul is also a black spot for petty crime. Keep an eye on your possessions when swimming, and do not walk alone on the apparently empty paths farthest from the entrance.

Palenque

Looming out of the Chiapas jungle, the Maya ruins at **Palenque** ❷ (museum tel: 916-348 3079; site daily 8am–5pm, museum Tue–Sun 9am–4.30pm; charge) are one of the great sights of Mexico. They inspire awe and wonder, and yet the main area visited today represents barely 10 percent of all the temples, palaces and other structures that graced Palenque in the 7th century AD, when it had a population of around 70,000. Palenque has been the site of many crucial discoveries in Maya archaeology, including the deciphering of Maya glyph writing.

Rising up beyond the entrance is the massive pyramid of the **Templo de las Inscripciones** (Temple of the Inscriptions), a majestic symbol of Classic Maya architecture. At the top of its giant steps is a temple, where in 1952 archeologist Alberto Ruz Lhuillier discovered a sealed passageway that led to a burial chamber 25 meters (82ft) down, which contained a richly adorned tomb of a man, beneath a superbly carved sarcophagus lid. This was the tomb of the greatest of Palenque's kings, Pakal, the first Maya

A glimpse of Agua Azul.

The Palenque Archives

Palenque has more Maya glyph inscriptions than any other city. The longest are the "king lists" around the walls of the temple at the top of the Temple of Inscriptions – now normally closed off, although some replicas are in the site museum. They give information on ten rulers of Palenque, from K'uk-Balam (Quetzal-Jaguar) who founded the dynasty in AD 431. They were made for the eleventh, Pakal "the Great," who became king aged 12 in 615 and died at 80 in 683, and who built the Inscriptions Temple as his monument and tomb.

Pakal had them carved for a reason. He had been born in a time of trial for Palenque: two kings had died without male heirs, and the city had twice been raided by Calakmul. He was only the nephew of the previous king, through his mother, who had ruled in his name while he was a child. Power in Maya cities normally passed only through the male line, therefore Pakal, despite his later victories, could still have been considered a usurper. The aim of his monument building was to restate emphatically his links to the dynasty and his right to rule. The point was made still more strongly by his son Kan-Balam II in the Cross Group carvings, which vividly portray the Maya concept of the shaman-king as an essential channel between his community and the heavens.

BELOW: Mayan stone discovered at Toniná, dating from 613 AD.

ruler identified by modern archeologists. Sadly, pyramid and tomb are now closed to visitors for their preservation, but there is a precise replica of the tomb in the Palenque museum. Another tomb in **Temple XIII** alongside, known as the **Tomb of the Red Queen** and believed to be that of Pakal's wife, is still open.

Opposite the pyramid is the **Palacio** of the kings of Palenque, a fascinating complex of rooms, courtyards, passages and tunnels, crowned by a unique tower which may have been an observatory or a watchtower. Around its walls and columns are carved stucco panels, stone sculptures and inscriptions, showing events in the life of the city and celebrating its victories.

On the north side of the Palacio is a **Ball Court** and more small pyramids, forming the **Groupo del Norte** (North Group), while to the east a path leads across a stream to the three spectacular pyramids of the **Cross Group**, the **Temple of the Cross**, **Temple of the Sun** and **Temple of the Foliated Cross**. Built by Pakal's son Kan-Balam

II, they have some of Palenque's finest carving, although again, nowadays they are often closed to visitors.

From beside the North Group a lovely path runs down through forest past waterfalls and the remains of residential areas to the museum (included in the site ticket), which as well as the replica of Pakal's Tomb has his jade death mask and other stunning treasures. The town of Palenque, 8km (5 miles) from the ruins, has a choice of hotels, restaurants and services, but the most attractive places to stay are on the ruins road.

Bonampak, Lacanjá and Yaxchilán

Two more spectacular Maya sites, Bonampak and Yaxchilán, are deep in the forest near the Usumacinta River, the frontier with Guatemala. They have become far easier to get to thanks to the Fronteriza highway around the Chiapas border to Comitán. One- or two-day tours are offered by many agencies in Palenque, but with a car it's easy to get there independently, staying over at **Lacanjá** near Bonampak, one of the villages of the Lacandón, the only Maya group never Christianized by the Spaniards. Nevertheless, discovering these remote sites still has a great feel of adventure.

Bonampak ❸ (tel: 961-345 2684; daily 8am–5pm; charge), shrouded in forest 148km (92 miles) southeast of Palenque, is quite small compared to the great Maya sites, but is of huge importance since it has, in one building, the one and only complete set of possibly hundreds of Maya mural paintings that has survived the ravages of the centuries. In vivid color and detail they show the presentation of the son and heir of the lord of Bonampak, Chan-Muaan, in AD 790, followed by a bloody battle and further extravagant ceremonies that took place in the following two years, giving a matchless image of Classic-era Maya court life. All of Maya life is there – Chan-Muaan's queen and her maids, prisoners waiting to be sacrificed, bored-looking nobles chatting during a ceremony.

Yaxchilán ❹ (daily 8am–5pm; charge), was much larger than Bonampak, with a commanding posi-

tion above the Usumacinta, and under Shield Jaguar II (reigned 681–742) and his son Bird Jaguar IV (752–68) was one of the most powerful cities along the river. There is still no access by road, and to get there you must take a boat from the little town of **Frontera Corozal**, 39km (24 miles) from Lacanjá, where there is also a boat crossing to Guatemala.

This all adds to the excitement of getting to Yaxchilán, first glimpsed through the trees on a crag above the river. Around its many temples there are superb relief carvings and stelae (standing stones), detailing milestones in the lives of Yaxchilán's kings. Another feature of the site is the many howler monkeys, heard (and often seen) booming through the trees. ❏

Pok-Ta-Pok, the ball game of the ancient Maya.

BELOW: replica of a wall painting from Chiapas.
FOLLOWING PAGES: beach at Tulum.

YUCATAN'S NATURAL WONDERLAND

The Yucatán Peninsula and its Caribbean coast harbor magnificent natural treasures – hundreds of species of birds, animals and colorful marine life, forming a diver's paradise

Visitors to the Yucatán Peninsula often spend their time clambering over its awe-inspiring Maya ruins, sunning themselves on its gorgeous beaches, or exploring old colonial towns, but many birders, divers and snorkelers flock here above all for its uniquely rich and diverse natural environment. The immense limestone slab that makes up the Yucatán is flanked for long kilometers by vast, virtually uninhabited fresh and salt water coastal lagoons, which as well as being home to a great many resident birds provide winter quarters for millions of migrants from across North America. The Yucatán's *cenote* water holes, beautiful and mysterious (*see page 317*), and the huge underwater rivers beneath them, filter minerals from the rock as they flow out to sea, providing rich nutrients for the Great Maya Reef, along the Caribbean coast. This is part of the second-longest coral reef system in the world, stretching for some 350km (218 miles) along the east coast of Yucatán and south past Belize to Honduras. Although narrower than the Australian Great Barrier Reef, this system reaches depths of over 40 meters (130ft) around Cozumel, and at times the remarkable transparency of the water provides visibility up to 27 meters (90ft).

The Caribbean is one of the richest regions on earth in coral formations. Reefs, in turn, harbor an incredible variety and density of marine life. Over 50 species of coral, 400 of fish and 30 gorgonians have been identified in the Yucatán reefs, along with hundreds of mollusks, crustaceans, sponges and algae.

TOP: the Great Maya reef is home to thousands of plant and animal species, from brilliantly colored exotic fish to rare sea turtles.
ABOVE LEFT: tiny jellyfish are quite easy to avoid when swimming in the perfectly clear sea.
RIGHT: pink conch provides the basis for many delicious local dishes.
BELOW: from turquoise to deep blue, the colors of the Caribbean waters are hypnotic by themselves.

RIGHT: pink flamingos breed in many of the shallow mangrove lagoons around the Yucatán coast, especially at Celestún and Río Largartos.

DIVING DESTINATIONS

There are many well-equipped locations from which to explore the Yucatán's underwater garden and coral mountains. Cozumel generally has the biggest variety of reefs, from shallow and ideal for beginners to giant wall dives, dropping sheer into the depths. Isla Mujeres, if sometimes crowded, also offers a good range of dives. On the mainland, friendly Puerto Morelos and busier Playa del Carmen are both excellent dive centers, while Akumal and Tulum, as well as having good open-water operators, are now major locations for cave diving in nearby *cenotes*. The small dive operations on the Costa Maya, near Mahahual and Xcalak, offer a complete escape from any crowds (for slightly higher prices), and the chance to explore the vast, pristine Banco Chinchorro reef.

In general, the further south, the better condition the reef will be in. Recent hurricanes, notably Wilma in 2005, have done considerable damage to the coral, especially on Cozumel's inshore reefs. More long-term damage is being done by over-development, particularly the constant building of resort hotels down the Riviera Maya. These often obstruct the natural flow of nutrients out to sea from the mangroves and underground rivers, causing rapid coral deterioration.

Only restrictions on building will halt this process.

ABOVE: the loggerhead is one of the five species of sea turtle that come to the Yucatán to nest on the beaches from May to September.
BELOW: pelicans taking wing above a mangrove lagoon.

ABOVE: divers in the upper caverns of the Dos Ojos *cenote*, near Tulum.
LEFT: snorkeler with a conch, a favorite food that also makes attractive ornaments.

THE YUCATÁN

Long separate from the rest of Mexico, the Yucatán Peninsula has special attractions: awe-inspiring Maya cities, a unique landscape, sultry colonial towns, sparkling Caribbean beaches, coral reefs and a distinctive tranquility

The Maya of the Yucatán were never subjugated by the Aztecs, nor by any of the cultures of central Mexico, and under Spain the peninsula, with its own governors, had little contact with the viceroys in distant Mexico City. There was not even a usable land link between the peninsula and central Mexico until the mid-20th century. In its isolation, the Yucatán got used to seeing itself as a world apart, with its own ways of doing things, its own particular synthesis of Maya and Spanish cultures. This blended with the uniqueness of the landscape – a giant, flat limestone slab, with no surface rivers but with mysterious rock pools called *cenotes* leading into vast underwater cave systems – to create a very special ambiance with a distinctive charm.

Conquest

The Maya of the Yucatán resisted the Spaniards longer than any other people in Mexico, despite being divided in traditional Maya style between some 19 small lordships. Cortés had sailed around the Yucatán without making any permanent landing, and it was not until 1526 that one of his former lieutenants, Francisco de Montejo, obtained from Emperor Carlos V the commission to be the *Adelantado* or "First Promoter" of the Yucatán. The

following year he landed at Xel-Ha on the Caribbean coast – now one of the Riviera Maya's most popular snorkel parks – and tried to march inland, but after six months had to withdraw, having conquered nothing and lost over half of his men to disease and Maya attacks. He tried again in 1531, landing near Campeche with his son, with the same name but known as Montejo *El Mozo* (The Boy), but this expedition failed as well. Finally, in 1540 *El Mozo* tried again with his cousin, yet another Francisco de Montejo, known

Main attractions
CAMPECHE
UXMAL AND THE PUUC ROUTE
MÉRIDA
CELESTÚN
IZAMAL
CHICHÉN ITZÁ
CENOTES
CANCÚN
ISLA MUJERES
COZUMEL
PLAYA DEL CARMEN
TULUM
CALAKMUL

LEFT: ruins overlooking the beach at Tulum.
RIGHT: colorful Campeche street.

The Yucatán

as *El Sobrino* (The Nephew). They took Campeche, then marched north to occupy the ruined Maya city of Ti'ho, where they resisted a bloody siege. They thought only divine intervention could explain their eventual victory, after a sudden collapse in Maya morale. In 1542, Mérida was founded at Ti'ho, as capital of the new colony.

The task of Christianizing the Yucatán was entrusted to Franciscan friars, led by Father Diego de Landa. The austere attitudes of the Franciscans can be seen in the plain, massive early colonial churches and monasteries across the Yucatán, with few architectural details. Another feature of colonial Yucatán was that, while in central Mexico the indigenous population fell disastrously after the Conquest, owing to European diseases, over-exploitation and the complete disruption of the traditional economy, in the peninsula this decline was far less marked, and the Maya continued to make up half or more of the population.

Nationalist feeling in this sleepy colony was limited, and the ending of Spanish rule was extraordinarily peaceful: in 1821, when news reached Mérida that Spain had lost control of Mexico, the last Spanish governor called a meeting of prominent local citizens, told them that it was impossible for him to continue on his own, shook hands and left. The Yucatán declared its sovereignty, together with a grudging, conditional adherence to Mexico. If the peninsula's criollo elite had had no great problems with Spanish rule, they were far more suspicious of "Mexicans." In 1839, in response to the authoritarian measures of Santa Anna, the Yucatán declared its independence, and in 1842 even succeeded in driving back an army sent to restore Mexican control.

Caste War

This, though, was the prelude to the most extraordinary event in Yucatecan history, the "Caste War" of 1847–50. To fight their wars the Yucatecan elite did something the Spaniards had never done, recruiting the Maya as foot soldiers, offering in return land rights and lower taxes. These promises were never kept, and pent-up Maya rage

Good-quality handwoven Panama hats, made near Campeche, can be rolled up and will immediately resume their shape.

BELOW: well-restored traditional houses near the church of San Francisco, Campeche.

reached boiling point. In 1847, the Maya rose up across eastern Yucatán, and attacked the old colonial center of Valladolid. Panic spread through Spanish-speaking Yucatán, as town after town fell to the rebels, and whites and mestizos were massacred. At one point, the governor of the Yucatán, Santiago Méndez, sent letters to Britain, Spain and the United States, offering the peninsula to whichever country would save its "civilized population" from certain death. The Maya came closer than any other native people in the Americas to regaining their land. Then, there was an equally astonishing turnaround. The Maya were village farmers, and would starve if they missed a planting season. In May 1848, as they prepared to assault Mérida, signs appeared that rains were going to come early that year; against protests from their chiefs, many went home, and lost their opportunity for ever.

While no foreign power wanted to get involved, Mexico sent troops, in return for the Yucatán rejoining the nation, and reprisals were as bloody as the earlier massacres. Nor did the war end simply. Some rebel Maya retreated into the empty southeast of the peninsula, where they established a "mini-state" around their new town of Chan Santa Cruz (now Felipe Carrillo Puerto) that remained outside Mexican control until 1901.

The war ended hopes of independence among white Yucatecans. The influence of the local elite was reduced further when Campeche became a separate state in 1863, and in 1902 when the eastern Yucatán was made a Federal Territory, which in 1974 became the state of Quintana Roo.

Their frustrations were compensated for by new prosperity. Yucatán was finally found to produce something that was very valuable, as demand rose worldwide for sisal rope, made from *henequén* cactus, the "green gold" of the Yucatán. Under Porfirio Díaz, Yucatecan *hacendados* made vast fortunes, and Mérida became the most modern city in Mexico after the capital. After the Revolution, large areas of land were redistributed to villages, but *henequén* had already begun to lose its market to other fibers. The economy did not really revive until the tourist transformation began in the 1970s.

Campeche State

One main road runs from central Mexico into the Yucatán: Highway 186 via Villahermosa and the shabby truck-stop town of **Francisco Escárcega**, from where 186 continues east to Chetumal and the Riviera Maya, while Highway 261 turns north for Campeche and Mérida. One other, much slower road, Highway 180, runs along the coast through the oil town of **Ciudad del Carmen**, once a pirate stronghold.

Highway 261 meets 180 just south of **Champotón ❶**, at the mouth of the northernmost river on this side of the peninsula, with the same name. The first two Spanish expeditions to Mexico led by Hernández de Córdoba and Grijalva both put in here in 1517 and 1518 looking for water, and both suffered in clashes with the Maya lord of Campeche, Moch-Cuouh. Champotón still has a Spanish fort, and a fishing harbor.

Walled Campeche

It is an easy 62km (40-mile) drive along the coast to **Campeche ❷**, the most complete Spanish fortified city in Mexico and one of the most romantic of its colonial cities. This was the first city founded in the Yucatán by the Montejos, and for centuries its only official port. Hence Campeche became an irresistible target for all the pirates who proliferated in the Caribbean from the 1580s. The city was attacked countless times, when its people had to take refuge in the monastery of San Francisco, north of the old town, while the buccaneers camped outside, demanding ransom to leave. Finally, the city's governors levied a special tax, and beginning in 1684 old Campeche was ringed with ramparts and *baluartes* or bastions, some of the most solid Spanish fortifications in the New World. In 1718, when the Spaniards expelled the last buccaneers from what is now

Ciudad del Carmen, Campeche's pirate era came to an end.

After independence Campeche became a backwater, despite being given its own state in 1863. Its economy only revived with the discovery of oil offshore in the 1960s. As the oil boom gathered pace, modernity was seen as the way forward, and a plan was adopted called the *Resurgimiento* (Resurgence) of Campeche, which involved knocking down large parts of the old walls – some of which had already gone in the 19th century – and building an all-new modernistic square, **Plaza Moch-Cuouh**. In the 1990s, as tourism grew, this policy was completely reversed. Whole sections of wall were even rebuilt. Within the walls, gracious colonial houses with iron window-grilles were beautifully restored, and repainted in traditional colors – blues, greens, ochre. Old Campeche thus regained a huge amount of its historic charm, and in 1999 was declared a Unesco World Heritage site.

A walk around the circuit of bastions is an enjoyable way of getting a feel of

TIP

Campeche has its own distinctive cuisine, *cocina campechana*, based on fish and seafood. Specialties include *pan de cazón* (hammerhead shark, chopped and baked in a tomato sauce between two tortillas), *camarón al coco* (shrimp in coconut), and *arroz con pulpo* (octopus and rice salad). Among the many enjoyable places to try it are the smart La Pigua, just outside the city walls at Av. Miguel Alemán 179A, and the long-established traditional café La Parroquia, off the main square on Calle 55.

BELOW: Spanish fortress Fuerte De San Miguel.

Yucatán license plate.

the old city, beginning at the main plaza or **Parque Principal**. Overlooking it is the twin-towered **cathedral**, built over the course of three centuries and so with elements of several styles. Opposite, a typical Campeche house, the **Casa Seis** (daily 9am–9pm; free), restored in the style of a 19th-century merchant's residence, contains the tourist office. On the landward side of the plaza is the **Portales** building, with graceful two-story arcades hosting a restaurant overlooking the square.

Near the square are the **Puerta del Mar**, the "Sea Gate" which once led out to the port, and the **Baluarte de la Soledad**, which contains the **Museo de la Arquitectura Maya** (daily 8am–8pm; charge), with Maya stone stelae and carvings from around Campeche state. The next stop, heading clockwise, is the **Baluarte de Santiago**, inside which is a tropical garden, the **Jardín Botánico X'much Haltún** (daily 9am–9pm; free). The longest surviving stretch of battlements is between the **Puerta de Tierra** or "Land Gate" and **Baluarte de San Juan**. You can walk along the top, and the Puerto de

Tierra is the backdrop to Campeche's regular sound-and-light show. Beside the gate there is also a fun museum on pirates, the **Museo de la Piratería** (daily 9am–5pm; charge). The large **Baluarte de San Carlos** in the northwest corner has cannons, dungeons and the **Museo de la Ciudad** (Tue–Sat 9am–8pm, Sun 9am–1pm; free), detailing the city's history.

Campeche's great museum treasures are not, however, in the bastions but some way outside the old city. The **Museo de la Cultura Maya** (Tue–Sun 9.30am–6pm; charge) is in the **Fuerte de San Miguel**, a dramatic Spanish fortress on a hilltop to the south. Campeche state has a wealth of archeological sites, and the museum has many superb exhibits: most spectacular are the jade funeral masks from Calakmul, but other highlights include small clay figurines from Isla Jaina on the Gulf Coast, which show a very human aspect of Maya culture. Another fortress north of the city, **Fuerte de San José**, contains the **Museo de Barcos y Armas** (Museum of Ships and Weapons; Tue–Sun

BELOW: heading to church. **RIGHT:** Campeche's twin-towered cathedral.

9.30am–6pm; charge), on post-Conquest and maritime history. There are superb views from both fortresses.

Some 55km (34 miles) southeast of Campeche is the large Maya center of **Edzná** ❸ (daily 8am–5pm; charge), which like many had its own building style, spectacularly represented by the Palace of Five Stories, the largest multi-level structure in Maya architecture. The temples around it have especially intricate carvings. The region east of Edzná is known as the **Chenes**, from the Yucatecan Maya for well, because water can only be obtained here from deep wells. There are several remote archeological sites around the little town of **Hopelchén**, notably **Santa Rosa Xtampak**, and on the road north in Bolonchén is the **Xtacumbilxunaan** or Great Well, an awe-inspiring cave used as a water source for centuries. Tourist facilities in this area are very limited.

Uxmal and the Puuc

The landscape rises into Yucatán state and the Puuc Hills, which stand out in the flat Yucatán (*Puuc* is Maya for hill).

Water here is even scarcer than in the rest of the peninsula, and in ancient times the supply was supplemented by collecting rainy-season water in *chultunes*, huge cisterns dug into the ground. Nevertheless, this was the setting for the emergence from around AD 650 to 950 of several Maya communities, around the great city of Uxmal, that developed the most refined of all Maya architecture, featuring an intricate interplay between natural and symbolic imagery and a dramatic rhythmic geometry. An unmissable part of the Maya world, the Puuc area can easily be visited from Mérida, 80km (50 miles) north.

The name **Uxmal** ❹ (daily 8am–5pm; charge) means "thrice built," but it seems major building here only began late in the Classic period. Uxmal was at its peak under a king known as Lord Chac, who completed many of its finest structures in about 890–910. Only a few decades later, from about 920, Uxmal and the other Puuc communities declined rapidly, owing perhaps to a combination of overpopulation, soil exhaustion, drought and defeat in war.

TIP

The best way to visit the Puuc region is by staying at least one night in the area, in order to arrive in Uxmal before the heat and the crowds. There are hotels at Uxmal itself, as well as in Ticul and Oxkutzcab, and guesthouses in the village of Santa Elena, between Uxmal and Kabah. If you do not stay nearby or have a car, a bus leaves the second-class bus station in Mérida every day at 8am and visits Uxmal and all the main Puuc Route sites, returning around 2.30pm.

BELOW:
Hacienda Uayamón.

The Yucatán Haciendas

Haciendas, aristocratic plantation houses, are emblematic of the Yucatán, with lofty ceilings and colonnaded terraces, ringed by exuberant tropical gardens. Built up from the 17th century to the *henequén* boom around 1900, most fell into atmospheric decline after the 1910 Revolution, but several have been reborn as very special hotels. A stay in a hacienda is one of the Yucatán's most seductive experiences. Several luxurious haciendas – at Temozón, Santa Rosa and San José around Mérida, and Uayamón and Puerta Campeche in Campeche – are run by the same group (www.thehaciendas.com), all with gorgeous pools and restaurants. Hacienda Xcanatún, just north of Mérida, has some of the area's best dining. More modest alternatives include the laid-back Hacienda San Antonio Chalanté, near Izamal.

There is no rudeness or barbarity in the design or propor- tions... If it stood on this day on its grand artificial terrace in Hyde Park or the Garden of the Tuileries, it would form a new order, I do not say equalling, but worthy to stand side by side with the remains of Egyptian, Grecian and Roman art.

Early explorer John Lloyd Stephens on his first visit to the Governor's Palace at Uxmal, in 1840

BELOW: carved masks of the Rain God Chac at Codz- Poop at Kabah.

The first structure beyond the entrance is the partially oval **Pyramid of the Magician**, facing you, with steep steps leading up to a dramatic "mon- ster-mouth" temple. Unfortunately, visitors are no longer usually allowed to climb them. Like most Maya pyra- mids, it was built up in many stages, but its name comes from a legend in which an *Alux* or Maya spirit or lepre- chaun, the "Dwarf of Uxmal," built it in a single night in a test of strength with a local king.

Behind the pyramid are the exten- sively restored **Cuadrángulo de los Pájaros** (Birds Quadrangle) and the superb **Cuadrángulo de las Monjas** (Nunnery Quadrangle), a square plaza composed of four buildings that are each different, yet form a harmonious whole. For the full effect, walk around to the left and enter through the arch in the south building. The visual imagi- nation of the Puuc builders is evident; carvings combine homely images – *Na* stick-and-palm huts that can be seen in Maya villages today – with intricate representations of vision serpents, chan- nels to the gods. A recurring image is

the Rain God Chac, recognizable by his long curved nose, who was especially important in the dry Puuc. Like many buildings at Uxmal the "Nunnery" was given its name in 1658 by a Spanish Friar, Diego López de Cogolludo, on the basis of Spanish equivalents.

To the south is Uxmal's main **Ball Court**, beyond which is another huge artificial platform, created for the **Palacio del Gobernador** (Governor's Palace), which the archeologist Syl- vanus Morley called "the most mag- nificent, the most spectacular single building in all pre-Columbian Amer- ica." The name was apt for once, as this does seem to have been the residence of the lords of Uxmal. A figure of Lord Chac sits in the center of the 100-me- ter (328ft) frieze, the rest of which is a complex representation of the Maya calendar. As at the Nunnery, the frieze was made up by separately carving individual panels – more than 20,000, on the palace – which were then fitted together in a giant jigsaw-puzzle.

Sharing the same platform is the neat **Casa de las Tortugas** (House of Turtles), adorned with carved turtles,

Mérida

Grupo Norte (North Group)

Hotel Hacienda Uxmal

261

Campoche

Platform of the Stelae

Cuadránglo de las Monjas (Nunnery Quadrangle)

Museo

Grupo del Cementerio (Cemetery Group)

Group of the Columns

Main Entrance

Juego de Pelota (Ball Court)

Pirámide del Adivino (Pyramid of the Magician)

Visitors' Center

Casa de la Palomas (House of the Pigeons)

Casa de las Tortugas (House of the Turtles)

Palacio del Gobernador (Governor's Palace)

El Gran Pirámide (Great Pyramid)

Templo Sur (South Temple)

Casa de la Vieja (House of the Old Woman)

Temple of the Centipede (Chimez Temple)

San Simon Road

Uxmal

0   200 m

0   200 yds

which the Maya associated with rain and creation. Beside the Palace platform are the older **Gran Pirámide** (Great Pyramid) and **Casa de las Palomas** (House of Pigeons), a large complex so-called because its roof comb, built as a base for long-lost sculptures, was thought to look like a dovecote. Down the path beyond it is a large arch, which stood at the end of a *sacbé* or Maya stone road to Kabah.

The Puuc Route

The smaller sites of the "Puuc Route" (all daily 8am–5pm; charge at each site) are spread along Highway 261 south of Uxmal and a road that turns east near Kabah. As well as their architecture, these sites are also beautiful places to explore, set in woods full of birds. **Kabah** ❺ has a fine **Palacio**, but its highlight is the extraordinary **Codz-Poop** or Palace of Masks, with a facade of some 250 curled-nose masks of the Rain God Chac. An **arch** across the highway was the southern end of the *sacbé* from Uxmal.

A short way after the turn east, **Sayil** has one of the most elegant Maya palaces, with more than 90 rooms spanning three levels, and typical Puuc "drum column" facades. Further along, **Xlapak** is a small site with one intricately carved temple, while **Labná** has the most beautiful of all Maya arches. Near the end of the route are the most remarkable caves in Yucatán, the **Grutas de Loltún** ❻ (guided tours daily 9.30am, 11am, 12.30pm, every hour 2–4pm; charge), which have the oldest evidence of human occupation in the peninsula, from 5000 BC, and have been used by the Maya in every era since then. The caverns are vast, with wonderful rock formations, bizarre changes in atmosphere, and underground gardens, as well as Maya relics.

The Puuc Route road ends by meeting Highway 184 at **Oxkutzcab**, one of several likeable towns along this road. **Ticul** is the largest, with good restaurants, and shops selling traditional ceramics. A detour east leads to **Maní**, with the massive, austere early Franciscan monastery where Father Diego de Landa burned hundreds of Maya manuscripts in 1562.

TIP

Mérida – especially the market area – is the best place in the whole of the Yucatán to buy any kind of traditional local product: men's *guayabera* shirts, embroidered blouses, leather sandals. Handwoven Panama-style hats are mostly made in Campeche state, but the best ones still usually go on sale in Mérida. The best places to buy good-quality hammocks are the specialist shops on Calle 65, especially La Poblana, between calles 58 and 60.

BELOW: a quiet street in Oxkutzcab.

Monumento a la Patria, *Maya-inspired modern art, Mérida.*

BELOW: catching up with the news in a Mérida park.

Mérida

Heart and hub of the Yucatán, **Mérida ❼** is a city with a special blend of fine colonial architecture, tropical languor and easy-going streetlife, dubbed *La Ciudad Blanca*, "The White City," for its streets of colonial houses with whitewashed walls, behind which there are often secluded patios with gorgeous gardens of coconut palms and papaya plants. Many are now lovely small hotels, which helps make Mérida a great base for exploring the Yucatán.

Founded in the 1540s as capital of the whole peninsula, Mérida remains its biggest market. At the end of the 19th century, the city revived after the Caste War through the *henequén* boom, when its new millionaires spent their wealth on lavish homes along the all-new Paseo de Montejo, based on the Parisian Champs-Elysées. These ornate buildings combine with Franciscan austerity in Mérida's architectural mix.

Plaza Mayor and the market

Central Mérida is compact, and easy to explore at a stroll. In line with Spanish colonial tradition, streets spread out in a grid from the main square; even-numbered streets run north–south, odd-numbered ones east–west.

With giant laurel trees giving shade, the broad **Plaza Mayor Ⓐ** (also known as the Plaza Grande, or the Zócalo) is a natural place to begin a walking tour. On the east side is the massive, rather stark **Catedral de San Ildefonso Ⓑ**, the oldest cathedral in mainland America, completed in 1598 (Santo Domingo, in the Dominican Republic, is the only older one in the Americas).

The spacious building beside the cathedral contains the **Museo de Arte Contemporáneo de Yucatán** or **MACAY** (Wed–Thur and Sun–Mon 10am–6pm, Fri–Sat 10am–8pm; free), with modern Yucatecan art and interesting temporary exhibits.

The first large Spanish building completed in Mérida, well before the cathedral, was the **Casa de Montejo Ⓒ** on the south side of the plaza, built as the home of the Yucatán's conquerors, the Montejos. In the 1980s most of it was rebuilt and is now a Banamex bank, but it retains its extraordinary plateresque portico, with the Montejo coat of arms, and flanked by two giant figures of Spanish conquistadors, their feet on screaming heads, presumably representing the Maya. On the west side is the **Ayuntamiento** or city hall, with an 18th-century loggia. Presiding over the north side are the colonnades of the 19th-century **Palacio del Gobierno D** (daily 8am–8pm; free), with powerful murals around its patios by Fernando Castro Pacheco, evoking the history of the Yucatán.

From the plaza a walk south down Calle 60 and east on Calle 65 leads to the **market**, Mérida's giant bazaar, which spreads over several blocks. In front of the main market, at the crossing of calles 65 and 56, is the **Museo de la Ciudad E** (Tue–Fri 8am–8pm, Sat–Sun 8am–2pm; free), with informative displays on the history of the city, and temporary exhibitions. A few blocks away on Calle 50 are two surviving gates from the Spanish city wall built around Mérida in the 18th century.

Calle 60 and Paseo de Montejo

After the Plaza Mayor, the other great hub of Mérida is the north stretch of Calle 60, which runs up from beside the cathedral. On the corner of calles 60 and 61 you can hire a horse-drawn carriage or *calesa*, for a ride up to Paseo Montejo. One block up from Plaza Mayor is **Parque Hidalgo**, one of the best squares for people-watching, beside which is the **Iglesia de la Tercera Orden F** (also called Iglesia de Jesús), originally built for the Jesuit Order in 1618, and more ornate than the Franciscan churches.

A five-block walk east along Calle 59 leads to another, more typically austere church, **La Mejorada**, on a quiet plaza. Nearby are two delightfully individual museums: the **Museo de la Canción Yucateca** (Calle 57; Tue–Fri 9am–5pm, Sat–Sun 9am–3pm; charge) on the Yucatán's traditional music; and the **Museo de Arte Popular de Yucatán** (Tue–Fri 9.30am–4.30pm, Sat–Sun 9am–2pm; charge), with beautiful handicrafts from around Mexico.

Back on Calle 60, at the corner of

EAT

Lunch in Progreso *(see page 314)* is a great way of sampling local food and getting a feel of local life. Seafront restaurants such as Los Pelícanos and Flamingos all have delicious fresh fish and *ceviches* of conch, shrimp and octopus, and are packed with family groups every weekend.

BELOW: contemporary and ballroom dance performances, as well as movies, can be seen at Teatro Mérida.

Food stand in Mérida.

Calle 55 is **Parque Santa Lucía**, one of the prettiest of Mérida's old squares and the venue for the Thursday night *Serenatas Yucatecas*, performances of local music and dance. Mérida provides a delightful range of free entertainment. Every Saturday night, Calle 60 is closed to traffic and taken over by salsa bands and food stands, the prelude to the all-day *Mérida en Domingo* every Sunday, which also features displays of the main Yucatecan folk dance, the *jarana*. Every night there are events, presented more for locals than tourists. The free English-language magazine *Yucatán Today* has the full program (*see page 383*).

A few blocks further up from Parque Santa Lucía, a turning right leads to the very different **Paseo de Montejo**, with broad, tree-lined sidewalks. Opulent French- or Italian-style mansions can be seen between more modern buildings. One of the grandest, the 1909 Palacio Cantón, is now the **Museo de Antropología e Historia G** (Tue–Sat 8am–8pm, Sun 8am–2pm; charge), which provides an excellent background to visits to the peninsula's Maya sites.

Day trips from Mérida

The mangrove lagoons at **Celestún 8**, 90km (56 miles) west of Mérida, provide breeding grounds for flocks of pink flamingos and other water birds. Boats to see them depart daily (6am–5pm) from the **Embarcadero** at the entrance to Celestún village; tours are also offered by many Mérida agencies. Carry on through the village and you will find a long, white beach.

North of Mérida, Maya **Dzibilchaltún 9** (daily 8am–5pm; charge) was one of the oldest continuously occupied sites in the Americas, dating back to 500 BC. One of the most striking structures is the **Templo de las Siete Muñecas** (Temple of the Seven Dolls), through the doors of which the sun pours on the morning of the Spring equinox, March 21. There is also a stunning *cenote* (water hole), **Xlacah** (open for swimming) and an excellent site museum.

Campeche was long the Yucatán's only port because the peninsula's northwest coast is a long sandbar, with very shallow sea beyond it; to compensate, the harbor at **Progreso 10** is at the end of a giant quay built out to sea, now 6km (4 miles) long. Behind it, Progreso's beaches make it a favorite weekending spot for *Meridanos*, with terrace restaurants along the seafront.

Izamal

A short detour east from Mérida leads to **Izamal 11**, known as *La Ciudad Dorada*, "The Golden City," because its old buildings are painted yellow-ochre: horse-drawn carriages clop through cobbled streets, and little disturbs the tranquil pace. Nowhere else in Yucatán are the Maya and Spanish traditions so closely intertwined. Izamal was a Maya pilgrimage center, and the remains of pyramids are scattered around the town, notably the immense **Kinich Kak Mo** (daily 8am–5pm; charge). Izamal is dominated, though, by the **Monasterio de San Antonio de Padua**, largest of the Franciscan monasteries, founded by Diego de Landa

The Two Sides of Father Landa

Father Diego de Landa (1524–79) is a very ambiguous figure in Yucatán and Maya history. Founder of the monastery at Izamal and first head of the Franciscans in Yucatán, Landa admired the virtues of courage and willpower which the Maya shared with Christianity and was awed by their accomplishments. In 1566 he wrote a report titled *Relación de las Cosas de Yucatán* (Relation of the Affairs of Yucatán), which is the most complete account we have of Maya life on the verge of the Conquest. Rediscovered in a Spanish library in the 19th century, the *Relación* also contained information that was indispensable for the deciphering of the Maya calendar and, later, Maya glyph writing.

However, it was also Landa who in 1562, after he discovered that many Maya were still holding their old rituals in secret, furiously ordered that a mass *auto-da-fe*, or religious trial for heresy, be held at Maní, where suspected pagan backsliders were beaten and tortured, and every Maya artifact the friars could find was destroyed. They included, as Landa wrote, "a great number of books written in their letters, and because there was nothing in them but superstitions and falsehoods of the devil we burnt them all, which had an extraordinary effect on the people, and caused them great sorrow." Today, only four Maya manuscripts survive.

in 1549. Huge and simple, in yellow and white, the monastery occupies an old Maya pyramid-platform, and has an equally huge atrium or courtyard, built to contain open-air services for the newly converted Maya.

Opposite the monastery an imaginatively renovated old house is now the **Centro Cultural y Artesanal** (Mon–Wed and Fri 10am–8pm, Thur, Sat 10am–10pm, Sun 10am–5pm; free), with beautiful exhibits of traditional craftwork, and a shop. It also provides information on artisans currently working in Izamal.

Chichén Itzá

Chichén Itzá ⑫ (daily 8am–5pm; charge), voted one of the "New Seven Wonders of the World" in 2007 in a global poll, is the most famous and most visited of all the Maya sites. It is often crowded, and visitors can no longer climb up most of its giant structures. Nevertheless, the extraordinary scale and ambition of Chichén Itzá cannot fail to be awe-inspiring.

It is paradoxical that Chichén should be the best-known Maya city, for its "Mayan-ness" has long been debated. The severe, flat-walled style of its Castillo pyramid and other major structures is very unlike other Maya cities, more reminiscent of central Mexico, and different from other more traditionally "Mayan" buildings at Chichén. It used to be widely believed that around the year 1000 the Yucatán was invaded by Toltecs from Tula in the Central Highlands, who took over an older Maya city of Chichén and added their own "Toltec-Maya" city.

This theory has been largely discredited, above all because it has been shown that the "Maya" and "Toltec" buildings at Chichén were built in roughly the same period, mostly from about AD 800 to 950. The argument is still open, but it seems fairly clear that Chichén Itzá was always an unusually mixed community, where Yucatán Maya and "Mexicans" (groups of migrants, not an "invasion") lived alongside each other. Chichén rose to splendor from about 700, and dominated northern Yucatán after defeating Cobá around 860. It also survived the "Maya Collapse" longer than other

TIP

At both Chichén Itzá and Uxmal there are sound-and-light shows at the ruins, every night at 7pm (Nov–Mar) or 8pm (Apr–Oct), which are included in the admission ticket, although there is an extra charge for headphone commentary in languages other than Spanish. To attend you must go back to each site after visiting during the day. The presentations are spectacular, and at Chichén Itzá the show recreates the "Descent of Kukulcán" effect on the stairway of the Castillo.

BELOW: stairway of the Castillo de Kukulcán at Chichén Itzá.

The road to the ruins.

BELOW: part of the Nunnery at Chichén Itzá.

major cities, but was finally abandoned around 1200.

The monuments of Chichén

Dominating the view as you enter the site is Chichén Itzá's "sacred mountain," the **Castillo de Kukulcán**. It is a giant representation in stone of two of the three Maya calendars, the *haab* and the *tzolkin*: its four staircases have 91 steps each, which, including the platform at the top, total 365, the number of days in a year; each side has 52 panels, representing the 52-year cosmic cycle.

It is also aligned, with extraordinary precision, with the movements of the sun. Every year, on the Spring equinox (March 21), thousands come to Chichén Itzá to witness the "Descent of Kukulcán," the astonishing play of sunlight on the northern staircase. As the afternoon progresses, the sun picks out the great feathered serpent carved beside the staircase, beginning at its tail, and moving down to its head,

"bringing it alive." On the Fall equinox (September 21), the "snake" appears to ascend the pyramid.

On the northwest side of the central plaza is the great **Ball Court**, the largest in Mesoamerica, and vastly bigger than the older courts in most Maya cities. Games must also have been played in a different style, with teams of around seven, who had to get the ball through the stone rings on each side. The superbly carved panels along the bottom of the walls shows headless figures with writhing snakes symbolizing blood coming out of their necks, suggesting that losing players were decapitated.

Beside the Ball Court a path leads to the **Cenote Sagrado** (Sacred Well), 60 meters (197ft) in diameter. It appears to have been used only for rituals (another *cenote*, the **Xtoloc**, was Chichén's main water source). Many rich offerings have been retrieved from it, but no solid evidence that people were thrown into it as human sacrifices.

Back at the plaza, on the east side is the squat **Temple of the Warriors**, with, at the top, the celebrated statue

Chichén Itzá

0 — 200 m
0 — 200 yds

Cenote Sagrado (Sacred Well)
Sacred Causeway
Mérida
N

Juego de Pelota (Principal Ball Court)
Tzompantli (Temple of the Skulls)
Plataforma de Venus (Temple of Venus)
Plataforma de Águilas y Jaguares (Platform of the Jaguars and Eagles)
Main Plaza
Templo de los Guerreros (Temple of the Warriors)
Parking
Juego de Pelota (Ball Court)
Main Entrance
Castillo de Kukulcán (Pyramid of Kukulcán)
Grupo de las Mil Columnas (Court of the Thousand Columns)
Visitors' Center
El Osuario (The Ossuary)
Juego de Pelota (Ball Court)
El Templo del Venado (Temple of the Deer)
Mercado
La Casa Colorado (Red House)
Xtoloc Cenote
Eastern Entrance
El Caracol (Observatory)
Hotel Mayaland
Templo de las Monjas (Nunnery)
La Iglesia (Church)
Hotel Villa Arqueológica
Hotel Hacienda Chichén
180
Chichén Viejo
Valladolid

of the reclining **Chacmool**, holding a receptacle for the hearts of sacrificial victims – although visitors are no longer allowed up to see it. The temple takes its name from the columns in front, carved with portraits of more than 200 warriors, priests and other figures. They lead to the **Court of the Thousand Columns**, once the main market area. The forest of columns once supported wood and palm roofs.

South of the plaza are the more "Maya" buildings of Chichén. The most prominent is the fascinating **Observatory**, known as the **Caracol** (Snail) because of its spiral-like drum tower, with slots for tracking the movements of the stars. Beyond it, the buildings the Spaniards called the **Nunnery** (Templo de Las Monjas) have Puuc-style carvings.

Some 5km (3 miles) east are the **Grutas de Balankanché** ⑬ (daily 9am–5pm; charge), another of the Yucatán's great cave systems. Like the Loltún caves, this labyrinth of chambers, leading down to a magical underground pool, was used by the Maya for centuries, and many relics have been found here.

Valladolid and Río Lagartos

Valladolid ⑭ gives an enjoyable taste of Yucatecan small-town life to anyone heading west from Cancún. As in all old colonial towns the hub of local life is the broad plaza, with the tall, white **cathedral**. A short walk west leads to the semi-fortified church and monastery of **San Bernardino Sisal**, begun in 1552.

In the middle of Valladolid is the town's original water source, **Cenote Zací**, but its water is now dirty. Around 5km (3 miles) west of the town, however, is the unmissable **Cenote Dzitnup** (daily 8am–5pm; charge), a subterranean cathedral, with a vast, arching cavern above a perfect pool of clear turquoise water that is irresistible for swimming. A short walk away is the almost equally spectacular **Cenote Samula**, which, though, gets fewer visitors.

North of Valladolid, Highway 295 leads to the coast. After 18km (11 miles) a turning leads to a remarkable Maya site at **Ek-Balam** ⑮ (daily 8am–5pm; charge), extensively excavated only since the 1990s. Its greatest feature is the extraordinary mouth-shaped tomb

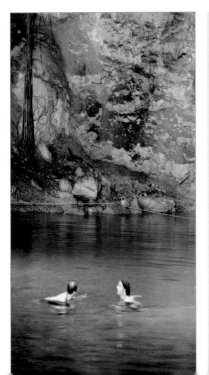

LEFT: the popular *cenote* Samula in Dzitnup, near Valladolid.

Cenotes: the Yucatán's Underground World

From the surface the Yucatán can appear to be a great, flat expanse of forest, with no rivers, hills or other natural landmarks. These are below ground. Rainwater runs straight through the limestone, forming an immense labyrinth of caves and underground rivers. Seven of the 10 longest underground rivers in the world have been discovered here, including the longest of all, the Ox-Bel-Ha system around Tulum, which so far has been explored to a distance of 180km (112 miles).

Any hole in the rock that allows access to underground water is a *cenote* (a Spanish version of Maya *dzonot*). They can be huge pools open to the sky (where a cave roof has fallen in, centuries ago) or dark tunnels leading down to subterranean cathedrals. Spellbinding to explore, they are magical places in which to swim and snorkel.

Among the most popular swimming *cenotes* is the magnificent Dzitnup near Valladolid. However, every village in the Yucatán once needed to have a *cenote* nearby, and many village *cenotes* are now open to visitors. Guides in Mérida offer *cenote* snorkel tours. Several famous *cenotes* are around Tulum, now the world's foremost center for cave diving. For beginners, a good place to get a taste of cavern diving or snorkeling is Hidden Worlds, north of Tulum, at one of the entrances to the Ox-Bel-Ha caves (www.hiddenworlds.com).

BELOW: turquoise waters off Cancún beach. **RIGHT:** Boulevard Kukulcán.

entrance of **El Trono**, with some of the finest Maya carving. The road ends at the laid-back fishing town of **Río Lagartos** ⑯, on a long lagoon that hosts flamingos and countless other water birds. Local boatmen offer trips, and there is also excellent fishing. Seeing birds at Río Lagartos is a more relaxed experience than it is at Celestún.

Cancún

Virtually every kind of modern architectural fantasy can be found in the Hotel Zone at **Cancún** ⑰; neo-Parisian mansions rub lawns with Las Vegas-Baroque and neo-Maya pyramids. Cancún provides luxuries on tap and on a big scale: glittering restaurants, eye-popping nightclubs, stunning pools with swim-up bars.

Now the biggest resort in Mexico – and the Caribbean – Cancún's legendary attractions are, naturally, its warm, turquoise sea and long, long beaches of wonderfully soft, powdery white sand that never gets hot underfoot. To take advantage of them, all sorts of water activities are on offer (although scuba

diving and snorkeling are better further south or on the offshore islands).

No one really noticed these beaches until 1969, when the Mexican government looked around for a location for a new resort on its then-empty Caribbean coast to match Acapulco on the Pacific, and the narrow sandstrip of Cancún was chosen. The first hotel opened in 1971, and building has gone on ever since. Cancún has had its setbacks, such as Hurricane Wilma in 2005, which stripped away sections of the beach, which then had to be "rebuilt" with sand dredged up from the sea bed nearby. Nevertheless, Cancún has a natural tendency to bounce back, and after every stumble – hurricanes, financial downturns – construction picks up again on a bigger scale.

Hotel Zone and Downtown

There are two parts to Cancún. The main beach hotels and biggest malls and nightclubs are all along the strip of Cancún island, often known just as the **Hotel Zone**, shaped like a "7" on the map, and with one road, the **Boulevard Kukulcán**, along its 23km (14½ mile)

length (places along it are identified by kilometer markers, Km 14, Km 16 and so on). The island encloses a mangrove lagoon, the **Laguna Nichupté**. The biggest hub of activity is around the bend in the "7," near Km 9, with the **Convention Center** and the loudest nightclubs, such as **Dady'O** and the **Coco Bongo**.

The biggest shopping zone is further south around Km 11–13, with the **Flamingo Plaza** and **Kukulcán Plaza** malls and the upmarket **La Isla** "shopping village." At Km 17 is the Maya site of **El Rey** (daily 8am–5pm; charge), a Postclassic-era trading settlement. Though small it gives a clear sense of having been a small town, with a main street and central plaza. Opposite is the best of Cancún's public-access beaches at **Playa Delfines**, with crashing surf. Beaches around the north side of the "7" have more tranquil waters for swimming, but tend to be more crowded.

The other part is **Ciudad Cancún** (or **Downtown**), the town at the north end of Boulevard Kukulcán first built as a dormitory area for Hotel Zone workers. After 40 years and with a population over 600,000, this is now a city in its own right. Its main streets of **Avenida Tulum** and **Avenida Yaxchilán** have attractive, reasonably priced restaurants, with plenty of Mexican atmosphere, and there's a busy market, Mercado 28. The bus station, banks, other services and more economical hotels are also here. As the Hotel Zone has filled up, resort development is spreading up the coast to the north, especially around a new marina, **Puerto Cancún**.

Isla Mujeres

Puerto Juárez, just north of Cancún, is the passenger ferry port for **Isla Mujeres** ⑱, site of the first Spanish landing in Mexico in 1517, when Hernández de Córdoba and his men saw figures of the Maya goddess Ixchel, and so gave it the name "Island of Women." No longer the remote backpacker paradise it once was, the little island is still a less glitzy alternative to Cancún. A narrow strip 8km (5 miles) long, Isla is easy to explore

Birds at Holbox island, part of Yum Balam ecological reserve, and separated from the mainland by the Yalahua lagoon.

BELOW: beachside bar, Cozumel.

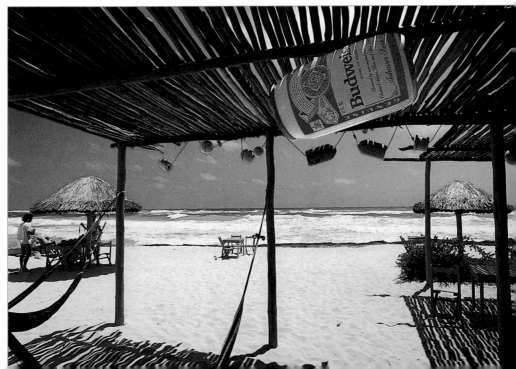

by rented bikes, scooters or, a local favorite, golf carts.

Isla town has kept its tiny, sandy streets, full of souvenir stores and dive shops, and some of its old wooden houses in candy-box colors. The best beach is **Playa Norte**, across the top of the town, and Isla is an excellent snorkeling, diving and fishing center, with the **Manchones** reef nearby. Boat trips to the bird sanctuary at **Isla Contoy** are also available. On the island's west coast is a family attraction at **El Garrafón** (daily 10am–5pm; charge), a natural lagoon with a dolphin pool and easy snorkeling (although the coral is now in poor condition), and the **Tortugranja** (daily 9am–5pm; charge), a turtle conservation center.

Cozumel

Mexico's largest island, **Cozumel** ⑲, the "Island of Swallows," was a place of pilgrimage for the Postclassic Maya, with a shrine to the goddess of fertility, Ixchel. In the 1960s French oceanographer Jacques Cousteau made it known that as well as fine, sheltered beaches it had some of the world's richest

offshore reefs, and Cozumel became a mecca for divers and snorkelers on Mexico's Caribbean coast.

Tourism thus began on Cozumel before Cancún existed, and the island and its little capital **San Miguel de Cozumel** retain a less hectic, cozy, family feel. San Miguel is now also a major cruise ship port, with two large terminals, and the waterfront **Malecón** (Avenida Rafael Melgar) is lined with handicraft and jewelry stores, where cruise passengers can buy tax free goods. Large resort hotels are mostly along the beaches north and south of the town.

From San Miguel a straight road runs to the east coast, passing the turn to the ruins of **San Gervasio** ⑳ (daily 7am–4pm; charge), the main town of Maya Cozumel, with large structures in quiet woods. Cozumel's east coast is empty and windswept, with a few sheltered coves. The road turns south to follow the shore down to **Faro Celarain Eco Park** (daily 8am–5pm; charge) at **Punta Sur**, with a lighthouse and lagoons with crocodiles, flamingos and other birds. Some of Cozumel's most popular beaches are along the southwest coast, such as **Playa San Francisco**. Only 8km (5 miles) before San Miguel is Cozumel's most popular (and often crowded) location at **Parque Chankanaab** (daily 7am–5pm; charge), a snorkel park around a lagoon in a botanical garden.

Cozumel's greatest jewels are in the seas around it. Sadly, Hurricane Wilma damaged the coral of inshore reefs near San Miguel, such as **Paraíso** or **Chankanaab**, although they are still full of fish. Other renowned reefs such as **Palancar** off the southwest coast are still in fine condition and offer a spectacular range of diving. Snorkeling is not an inferior option here, as you can still see a stunning range of marine life. There are around 60 dive operators on the island, which also offer snorkel trips.

The Riviera Maya

For many years, Cancún and Cozumel were the only tourist centers on the Mexican Caribbean. Since the 1990s, opulent retreat hotels and all-inclusive resorts have spread all the way along the 131km (81 miles) to Tulum, down the coastline now labeled the Riviera Maya. One consequence of this boom is that access to some of the finest bays is now difficult for non-hotel guests.

The first major stop south of Cancún, after 36km (22 miles), is **Puerto Morelos** ㉑, which before Cancún was actually the largest village on this coast. Mellow and relaxing, it has a fine long beach, excellent restaurants and a protected inshore reef for great diving and snorkeling. Another 25km (15 miles) south are some of the most exquisite palm-lined bays on the whole coast. Some, notably at **Punta Bete**, are still open to all, while others now contain the Riviera's most opulent resorts, especially **Hacienda Tres Ríos** and **Maya Kobá**, with its PGA-standard golf course.

From there it's not far to the phenomenon that is **Playa del Carmen** ㉒, the passenger ferry port for Cozumel and second-biggest center on the coast after Cancún. A tiny village in the 1980s, its

population is now over 100,000. So fast is its growth that it changes identity every few years: a backpacker hangout in the mid-1990s, it is now exploding with luxury condominiums. Playa still has a different style to Cancún: its main artery is a long pedestrian street, the **Quinta Avenida** (Fifth Avenue), giving much more of a sense of streetlife. Nightlife in Playa is also much more hip than in the mega-clubs of Cancún. Playa is another excellent diving center, with high-quality operators.

Just south of Playa is one of the Riviera's most popular attractions, the family friendly "eco-archeological theme park" of **Xcaret** ㉓ (daily Apr–Oct 8.30am–10pm, Nov–Mar 8.30am–9pm; charge). Created around a lagoon that was once the Maya port of **Polé**, it has a semi-underground snorkeling river, dolphins, a beach, a zoo, a live show and a dazzling butterfly garden.

Puerto Aventuras is a purpose-built marina surrounded by condos and large hotels, while at **Xpu-Ha** many of the fabulous bays are now occupied by large resorts. On the landward side of the highway are some *cenotes*, for

Swimming with performing dolphins at Xcaret.

BELOW: tourist train at Tulum.

The Nohoch Mul pyramid at Cobá.

BELOW: part of Tulum's fantastic beach.

a cooling swim. At 40km (25 miles) from Playa del Carmen, **Akumal** ㉔, famous for snorkeling and diving, has condos and medium-sized hotels well-spaced out around beautiful arching beaches, especially the enchanting **Media Luna** (Half Moon) bay. Akumal means "place of the turtles," and, carefully protected, they still breed here in the summer months. Shortly beyond Akumal, "snorkel heaven" signs lead to the very popular snorkel park at **Xel-Há** ㉕ (daily 8.30am–6pm; charge), around a gorgeous, if often crowded, coastal lagoon.

Tulum and Sian Ka'an

The Riviera ends at the ruins of **Tulum** ㉖ (daily 8am–5pm; charge), one of the most prominent Maya coastal trading towns in the Postclassic era, from around 1200–1530. One of few enclosed Maya settlements, architecturally it is relatively crude, but few sites have a more spectacular setting, on cliffs above a beach. It stunned the Spaniards of Grijalva's expedition when they first saw it, with a fiery beacon on top of the

Castillo pyramid, as they sailed down this coast in 1518.

Tulum gets many visitors, so most of its buildings are now roped off. The wall around the site on three sides – the fourth being the sea – probably only marked off the inner core of the city, the reserve of lords and priests, while a larger population lived outside. As well as the Castillo, other striking buildings at Tulum include the two-level **Temple of the Frescoes** and small **Temple of the Diving God**. Both have images of a god-figure diving into the sea, possibly related to fishing.

Tulum's other treasure is its fabulous beach, which runs for 11km (7 miles) all the way to the Sian Ka'an reserve. This is the foremost home of the palm-roofed beachside *cabaña* on the Riviera, a wonderful place for relaxation, with a wide choice of cabins, from luxurious to basic wood-and-palm huts. The growing village of Tulum Pueblo, 2km (1¼ miles) inland, has ATMs and other services.

Any extension to the Riviera is blocked off by the **Sian Ka'an Biosphere Reserve** ㉗, a vast swath of virtually uninhabited forest, savanna, mangroves, freshwater lagoons and reefs that is home to a huge variety of flora and fauna including monkeys, tapirs, crocodiles, and more than 400 species of birds. Tours – among the Riviera's best experiences – are available from Tulum. A very bumpy dirt road also runs down to the lonely fishing village of **Punta Allen**, where modest guesthouses offer total tranquility. The coastal lagoons of Ascension Bay are considered among the best fly fishing grounds in the world.

Cobá

From Tulum a road leads inland 45km (28 miles) to **Cobá** ㉘ (daily 8am–5pm; charge). This was one of the greatest Maya cities, the largest in northeast Yucatán from around AD 500–850. Its power was challenged by the rise of Chichén Itzá, and Cobá's defeat appears to have led to its decline

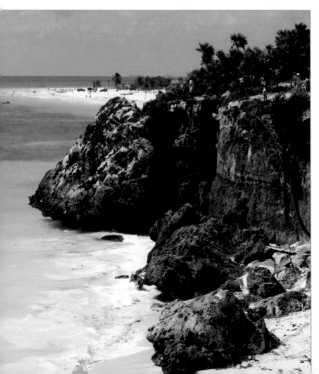

from about 860. It was an unusually dispersed Maya city, with centers spread between lakes and linked by *sacbeob* (*sacbé*, in singular) stone roads. Around 800 the longest of these roads ever found, nearly 100km (62 miles) long, was built from Cobá westward to Yaxuná, a strongpoint in the wars with Chichén.

Because the site is so spread out a visit to Cobá involves a real forest walk, with the chance to see plenty of birds (bikes can also be rented at the entrance). The largest area is the **Cobá** group, between two lakes, with a Ball Court and large pyramid. Save energy for the **Nohoch Mul** pyramid, which at 42 meters (138ft) high is the tallest in the Yucatán. Elsewhere in the woods there are finely carved stelae.

Costa Maya to Chetumal

South of Tulum, Highway 307 bends inland around Sian Ka'an. Another 76km (47 miles) south a road turns off east for the **Costa Maya**, the latest stretch of Yucatán coast opened up for tourism. The road meets the sea after 56km (35 miles) at **Mahahual**

29. Development here was set back by Hurricane Dean in 2007, but reconstruction has been fast, and a dock for cruise ships reopened a year later. Along the beach south of the town, there are Tulum-style beach *cabañas*, and stylish small hotels.

The paved road continues south just inland for 59km (37 miles) to end at **Xcalak 30**. Lacking Mahahual's cruise traffic, this sand-street village has a still more laid-back feel, and along the beach north of Xcalak are some of the Yucatán's most utterly tranquil small hotels. Some 20km (12 miles) offshore is a paradise for divers and snorkelers at **Banco Chinchorro**, a huge atoll with pristine coral. Operators in Xcalak and Mahahual have equipment for trips to the reefs.

Inland, Highway 307 continues past the lovely **Laguna de Bacalar 31**. A giant *cenote*, fed by underground rivers, it is wonderful for swimming. **Bacalar** town has lakeside hotels and restaurants, and the Fuerte de San Felipe Bacalar (Tue–Sun 9am–7pm; charge), a squat Spanish fortress built for protection against pirates in the 18th century,

Peaceful lookout, Laguna de Bacalar.

BELOW: stopping to shop in Chetumal.

BELOW: Laguna Bacalar.
RIGHT: inside Becán's walled city.
FAR RIGHT: Maya figurine.

which is now a museum. Farther south again, **Chetumal** ㉜, the state capital of Quintana Roo, is a small, very tropical, modern city with great waterfront restaurants. Nearby is the road crossing into Belize.

The Río Bec and Calakmul

Highway 186 heads west from Chetumal across the peninsula to Escárcega, completing the "Yucatán Loop." Along or not far off the road is a remarkable wealth of archeological sites. Around 60km (37 miles) west is the turn to one of the most beautiful Maya sites at **Kohunlich** (daily 8am–5pm; charge). Surrounded by giant fan palms, its greatest treasure is the Palace of the Masks, with a staircase lined by six serene *mascarones*, giant heads believed to represent the city's rulers.

As the road crosses into Campeche it enters the **Río Bec** region, which contains an extraordinary concentration of archeological sites with a distinctive style, often featuring monster-mouth temples combined with peculiarly steep, theatrical pyramids. Several are near the highway: **Chicanná** (daily 8am–5pm;

charge) has some of the most spectacular temples, but the highlight is **Becán** (daily 8am–5pm; charge), a walled city containing a maze-like complex of palaces and intimate plazas.

A separate but unmissable site is reached from a turning 45km (28 miles) west of Becán, from where there is another 60km (37 miles) to the ruins. **Calakmul** ㉝ (daily 8am–5pm; charge), extensively excavated only since the 1990s, is the most important recent discovery in American archeology. This was possibly the largest Maya city, and its wars with Tikal had a huge effect on Maya history. Looming up out of the forest, the site centers on the largest of all Maya pyramids, **Structure II**. It is within the **Calakmul Biosphere Reserve**, Mexico's largest rain forest reserve, so you may also see monkeys, coatis, an array of birds and even jaguars. Back on Highway 186, 5km (3 miles) west of the Calakmul turn is another small site, **Balamkú** (daily 8am–5pm; charge) which has one of the largest surviving Maya stucco friezes, an astonishing mass of strange imagery. ❑

☀ INSIGHT GUIDES TRAVEL TIPS
MEXICO

TRANSPORTATION ACCOMMODATIONS EATING OUT ACTIVITIES A – Z LANGUAGE

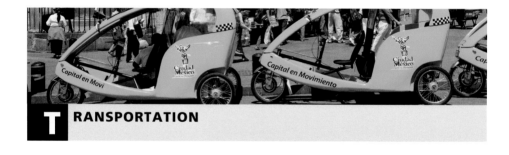

TRANSPORTATION

GETTING THERE AND GETTING AROUND

GETTING THERE

By Air

Mexico's main gateway airports are Mexico City and Cancún, which can be reached by direct flights from many US and Canadian cities, as well as several cities in Europe and Central and South America.

From the US and Canada: There are frequent scheduled flights from most large US and Canadian cities to Mexico City and Cancún; airlines include Aeroméxico, Air Canada, Alaska Airlines, American, Continental, Delta, Mexicana, North West, and United. Flights are most numerous from Los Angeles, Houston, Miami, Chicago, New York and Toronto, but there are also many from other cities. Some airlines, especially Aeroméxico, Continental and Mexicana, also fly to other Mexican cities, such as Los Cabos, Monterrey, Puerto Vallarta, Guadalajara, Villahermosa and Mérida.

From Europe: There are direct scheduled flights to Mexico City from Amsterdam, Frankfurt, London, Madrid and Paris, and to Cancún from Madrid. The main carriers are Aeroméxico, Air Europa, Air France, British Airways, Iberia, KLM, Lufthansa and Mexicana.

From Asia: Japan Airlines flies to Mexico City from Tokyo.

If you cannot fly directly to your destination in Mexico, connections can be made on domestic flights via Mexico City with Aeromar, Aeroméxico, Aviacsa, Mexicana, or Interjet, which between them provide flights all around the country.

Airline Numbers

Air Canada
Tel: 888-247 2262 (US and Canada); 0871-220 1111 (UK)
www.aircanada.com

American Airlines
Tel: 800-433 7300 (US and Canada); 020-7365 0777 (UK)
www.aa.com

British Airways
Tel: 0844-493 0787 (UK)
www.britishairways.com

Continental
Tel: 800-523 3273 (US and Canada); 0845-607 6760 (UK)
www.continental.com

Delta
Tel: 800-241 4141 (US and Canada); 0845-600 0950 (UK)
www.delta.com

Northwest
Tel: 800-225 2525 (US and Canada); 0870-507 4074 (UK)
www.nwa.com

United
Tel: 800-538 2929 (US and Canada); 0845-844 4777 (UK)
www.united.com

US Airways
Tel: 800-622 1015 (US and Canada); 0845-600 3300 (UK)
www.usairways.com

Mexican Airlines

Aeromar
Tel: 01800-237 6627 (Mexico)
www.aeromar.com.mx

Aeroméxico
Tel: 800-237 6639 (US and Canada); 01800-021 4000 (Mexico)
www.aeromexico.com

Aviacsa
Tel: 800-967 5263 (US and Canada); 01800-284 2272 (Mexico)
www.aviacsa.com

Interjet
Tel: 01800-011 2345 (Mexico)
www.interjet.com.mx

Mexicana
Tel: 877-801 2010 (US and Canada); 0870-890 0040 (UK); 01800-801 2030 (Mexico)
www.mexicana.com

Volaris
Tel: 01800-122 8000 (Mexico)
www.volaris.com.mx

There is a proliferation of **discount air fares** at different times of the year. Check out travel and airline websites for the best prices for both international and domestic flights. In addition to scheduled services, there are often low-cost direct **charter flights** available, especially to Cancún, from the US, Canada and many parts of Europe.

When you arrive at Mexico City, Cancún or any other airport, there are special taxis for getting to your final destination (see page 329 To and From the Airport). If you do not have any Mexican pesos when you arrive, change at a bureau de change desk or withdraw from an ATM only the amount you need for a taxi, and then get more cash near your hotel. Do not make it evident that you have any large amount of cash when passing through Mexico City airport.

By Sea

Cruise ships frequently include a Mexican port in their voyages, and from the US, a selection of 1- to 3-week cruises is available. Caribbean cruises departing from New Orleans, Tampa, Miami, Fort Lauderdale and some other ports regularly stop at Cozumel, and less frequently at Progreso and Mahahual. Numerous cruises along the west coast of Mexico start from Los Angeles or San Francisco, and some can be also be boarded in San Diego, Portland, Seattle, or Vancouver: they may stop at Ensenada or Los Cabos in Baja, Mazatlán, Puerto Vallarta, Manzanillo, Ixtapa-Zihuatanejo, and Acapulco. Cruises are a leisurely, comfortable way of getting to Mexico, but usually give you only one day in each port of call.

To travel to Mexico in your own boat you must have full documentation for the boat, including **registration** and **proof of ownership**, full insurance, and full passports for everyone on board. Fishing and radio licenses should also be obtained in advance; Mexican consulates and marine insurance brokers can advise on current requirements..

If, as many people do, you plan to sail down Baja to Mexico's west coast, and are doing so for the first time, it's naturally essential to get as much information as possible on charts, weather conditions, etc., and if possible to take a crew member who has sailed these waters before.

By Bus

Bus travel is an essential means of getting around in Mexico *(see page 331)*, and there are some direct long-distance bus services into Mexico from the US (notably from Brownsville, Texas), and many more from Mexican cities just south of the border. However, unless you live near the border or have more time than money, flying to the area you want to visit and then using buses is a better bet.

By Car

To drive a US or Canadian vehicle into most of Mexico you must get a **Temporary Import Permit**, which can be done at all main border crossings, at the *Módulo de Control Vehicular* desk in the Customs Post *(Aduana)*. To obtain one you must present the originals and at least two photocopies of these documents: your passport; current driving license; and the car registration papers, which must be in the name of the passport holder. You must also have a Mexican Tourist Card, which you should therefore get at Immigration before visiting the

Aduana. It is also best to have a credit card, to pay for the permit (around $27) and as a guarantee against overstaying your permit. There are higher charges for RVs and anything towed behind the main vehicle. You can pay for the permit in cash, but if so you must leave a large cash bond as the guarantee. The permit is valid for 6 months, during which you can enter and leave Mexico as you wish, but when you finally leave be sure to visit a **Mexican Customs Post** again at the border to have the permit cancelled; if you do not, you will be considered to have overstayed the permit and a fine will be charged against your credit card, or you will forfeit the cash bond.

Temporary Import Permits can also now be obtained from many Mexican Consulates in the US, for a slightly higher fee, and procedures can also now be initiated online, saving time, but the website (www.banjercito.com.mx) is mainly in Spanish, and the cost is again higher. AAA offices near the border also help with paperwork and advice.

Note that special conditions apply in Baja California, where Temporary Import Permits are not required for US and Canadian vehicles. Sonora state has an **"Only Sonora"** program, under which drivers are provided with permits for free (which also takes very little time) so long as they do not go beyond the state. Elsewhere along the border, Import Permits are often not strictly required in the **"Frontier Zone"** (roughly 20km/12 miles into Mexico), but since security and other procedures have been tightened up, in practice it's best to have one.

Details of these procedures can change, so check before you travel. You must also obtain **Mexican car insurance**, as US and Canadian policies are not valid in Mexico. There are several auto insurance offices at nearly every border crossing, and the AAA also provides advice for members. Better deals, though, can often be had by getting your insurance in advance, through services such as www.sanbornsinsurance.com or www.mexbound.com. Details of cover can vary widely, so shop around online, and always check the small print. For more on driving in Mexico, see page 334.

GETTING AROUND

Almost 250,000km (150,000 miles) of free and toll roads make Mexico's cities, towns, and most villages accessible by car. If you don't drive

yourself, buses provide a comfortable and economical way to see every part of the country, and for fast journeys there is an extensive domestic airline network. The only passenger trains left in Mexico are on tourist routes such as the spectacular Copper Canyon line from Chihuahua, but Mexico's long coastline and some frequent ferry services make going by boat an easy way to travel in some areas.

To and From the Airport

At most Mexican airports only special **authorized airport taxis** are allowed to take arriving passengers into town. Except at Cancún, there are not many airport buses. Airport taxis are more expensive than standard cabs but are well-regulated and safe. At Mexico City airport, *Taxi Autorizado* stands are easy to find just beyond the arrivals area. It's good to have an idea in mind of whereabouts your hotel or final destination is in the vast city; Mexico City is divided into various zones for airport taxis, and the fares for each of them are posted up at each stand. You buy a ticket at the stand, and then present it to a driver of the relevant company outside the building. There is usually a choice between standard cars, or vans for larger groups. A cab from the airport to the Zona Rosa, for example, location of many hotels, should cost around US$16–20. It is also usual to tip the driver. If you are not going to Mexico City itself, there are **buses** from the airport to some nearby cities such as Cuernavaca, Puebla and Toluca, which leave from near Area D.

When leaving Mexico City, any cab can take you to the airport, but as usual in the city *(see page 333)*, it is best to get a hotel to call a cab for you, and to be clear on the price first.

At Cancún, the main authorized transportation are the large *colectivo* **vans**, which wait outside Terminals 2 (used by Mexican airlines and many charters) and 3 (used by most US and European airlines). Fares are around US$15 per person; from the airport they drive all the way along the Hotel Zone to Ciudad Cancún, dropping passengers at their hotel, but if, for example, you are staying in Ciudad Cancún, this will take over an hour; also, they are not obliged to leave without a minimum of eight passengers, so at slack times you may have to wait. *Colectivos* also leave more or less hourly for Playa del Carmen, via Puerto Morelos. There are also, however, airport buses, which run from outside Terminal 2

Air Passes

If you have a set itinerary and expect to be taking a few domestic flights while in Mexico, the **Mexipass** system, operated jointly by Aeroméxico and Mexicana, can give savings of some 25–50 percent on some routes. You can arrive in Mexico with any airline, but must book the Mexipass tickets outside the country at the same time that you buy your main ticket, so the system is a little inflexible if you want to make last-minute changes of plan. Travelers must take at least three domestic flights per person on the same trip (or two, if traveling from Europe or anywhere else other than North America), and European travelers can also get reductions on long-distance Mexicana flights to the US, Canada and other parts of Latin America. For details contact, in the US and Canada, tel: 1-800-531 3585, in the UK, tel: 0808-101 7600.

(from Terminal 3, take the free shuttle bus), usually several times an hour to the bus station in Ciudad Cancún (not the Hotel Zone), and once or twice an hour to Puerto Morelos and Playa del Carmen. They are much cheaper than *colectivos* (around $3). Individual standard cabs are not available, but to get direct to any specific location on the Riviera it can be both quick and economical, especially for a family or a group, to book a **private van** transfer through services such as www.cancunvalet.com or www.cancuntransfers.net.

When leaving, again, any cab from Cancún or any of the Riviera towns will take you to the airport, but agree the price first. Regular buses run from the bus stations in Ciudad Cancún and Playa del Carmen.

Smaller airports all have their own local airport taxis, fares for which are generally reasonable, and there's rarely any need to wait. Again, any **local cab** can take you to the airport. Some airports have bus services from nearby cities, but they are often at very inconvenient times.

By Air

Getting between different parts of Mexico by land often involves long drives, but as a fast alternative there are plenty of **domestic airline services**. Recently, deregulation has led to the big traditional carriers Aeroméxico, Mexicana and Aviacsa

being joined by several low-cost operators. Every state capital has at least a few flights daily to Mexico City, and there are also airports near all the main tourist areas, such Los Cabos, Ixtapa-Zihuatanejo, and the main airport of southern Mexico: Cancún. One disadvantage of the network has been that since deregulation there have been relatively few direct inter-regional flights, so getting to many destinations has required changing flights in Mexico City's huge **Benito Juárez airport**. However, more options are becoming available.

Toluca, only 60km (38 miles) west of the capital, is being developed as an "alternative" airport for overloaded Mexico City, used particularly by the low-cost airlines Interjet and Volaris; and other regional hub airports are Guadalajara, Monterrey and Cancún. The two largest Mexican airlines each have lower-cost arms flying smaller aircraft that are intended to open up more regional routes, Aeroméxico Connect and MexicanaClick and MexicanaLink, so it's always worth looking around to see what routes are available, to save travel time. Flying via Toluca in particular can be much cheaper than going through Mexico City.

There is a good deal of fare competition on popular routes (such as Mexico City–Cancún), and airlines frequently announce **special offers**, including flight and hotel combinations, but prices are more static on routes with fewer operators. All Mexican airlines now take online bookings, but for complicated flight combinations you may find good deals in local travel agents.

In some parts of Mexico small airlines operate local **"bus flights"** with small turboprop aircraft. Aerotucán (www.aerotucan.com.mx) flies between Oaxaca and Puerto Escondido and Huatulco, Mayair (www.mayair.com.mx) runs a frequent shuttle between Cancún and Cozumel. En route, you naturally see much more than from a standard jet.

By Boat

Ferries run between Baja California and the mainland, and cover the short distances between the Yucatán mainland and the Caribbean islands of Cozumel and Isla Mujeres. The Baja ferries make long journeys across the deep Gulf of California, which gives the traveler the chance to appreciate both the peninsula and the mainland without making the extremely long and hot drive around the Gulf.

Baja California Ferries

Make sure you have the latest timetable as boats don't leave every day (visit www.bajaferries.com). Alternatively, ask at your hotel for ferry information. If you are coming from the US, ask a travel agent or insurance agent at the border for an up-to-date timetable.

The northernmost route, operated by **Ferry Santa Rosalía** (www.ferrysanta rosalia.com), connects the port of Santa Rosalía with Guaymas, leaving Santa Rosalía on Tuesday, Wednesday, Friday, and Sunday, and returning from Guaymas on Monday, Tuesday, Thursday, and Saturday. A similar schedule applies between Mazatlán and La Paz. There are cabins on the ferries running from Topolobampo to La Paz and from Guaymas to Santa Rosalía, as well as a public (not very comfortable) salon area. Food and drink are available on the ferries. Double-check schedule information as boats are sometimes delayed.

Yucatán Ferries

Reservations and schedules are not a problem for the frequent, short ferry trips from Cancún and the Riviera Maya to the offshore islands of Cozumel and Isla Mujeres. Passenger ferries to Isla Mujeres run from Puerto Juárez, just north of Cancún. They are run by two companies, **Magaña** and the newer **Ultramar**, but their docks (the Estación Marítima and the Gran Puerto Cancún respectively) are very near each other, and fares (around US$3 per adult) and schedules are also similar. Both companies have ferries to Isla every half-hour from around 6am–11.30pm; from Isla, Magaña generally has a last boat around 8.30pm, but Ultramar runs until 11pm–midnight. The crossing

BELOW: cruise ships dock in Cozumel, one of the Caribbean's busiest ports.

time is around 15–20 minutes. The car ferry to Isla Mujeres runs from Punta Sam, at the end of the road north of Puerto Juárez. There are usually five sailings daily in each direction, and fares are around US$25 for a car and two people.

Passenger ferries to Cozumel leave from Playa del Carmen, and journey time is around 30 minutes. Again there are two companies, Mexico and Ultramar, which both have sailings usually every hour on the hour (with less frequent services in the middle of the day) from Playa 6am–11pm, and from Cozumel 5am–10pm. Fares are around US$10, but special offers can often be had. Car ferries to Cozumel run from Puerto Calica, 10km (6 miles) south of Playa del Carmen, with from four to seven sailings daily in each direction. Fares are around US$30, for a car and two people.

By Train

Apart from a handful of up-market operations on limited lines, there is only one passenger train still operating in Mexico. This is the spectacular Chihuahua–Pacífico railroad, through the amazing Copper Canyon to Los Mochis on the Pacific coast, officially the Ferrocarril Chihuahua–Pacífico but known as El Chepe (www.chepe.com.mx).

By Bus

One can go virtually anywhere in Mexico by bus. Hundreds of bus companies crisscross the country, with vehicles ranging from big, modern, fast, air-conditioned models to small combis and vans for village routes. In virtually every part of Mexico, the bus system is the cheapest way to get around.

There are two basic categories of Mexican buses. First-class buses are air-conditioned, have comfortable reclining seats, videos showing movies, toilets at the back and often free coffee and soft drinks. Seats are assigned, and all baggage is carefully checked in and out. First-class buses run between cities and main towns, with only a few set stops on each route, have a pretty precise schedule, and are generally very punctual. There are also some more expensive "extra-luxurious" or "Executive Class" buses on busy routes, which generally means they have more leg-room and almost bed-like seats. Ordinary first-class fares are still very reasonable, and unless you take flights this will be the best

way to make any longer journeys in Mexico.

Second-class buses run on local routes and also often follow the same ones as first-class, but stop whenever anyone asks them to, and so take much longer. They are a good deal cheaper, tickets cannot be bought much in advance, seats are not assigned, and baggage is just put into overhead racks or the bus's side compartments rather than checked in (so you need to keep more of an eye on it). Second-class buses have also generally been more basic, but nowadays many – such as the buses that go up and down the Riviera Maya, which are described as Intermedios between the two classes – have comforts close to first class, including air conditioning. Using second-class buses is essential for getting to many places that do not have a first-class bus route, but using them for long journeys is usually not worth the saving, given how long they take.

The third element in the system is the mass of colectivos or combis, small vans of different sizes that ply the same routes as second-class buses (but are even cheaper) or serve places too small to justify even a second-class bus route. This is a very personal way of traveling: to find a colectivo to a particular place you often have to ask, and they leave when they have enough passengers, and stop when asked. Nevertheless, they are licensed, and have set fares for each route, and drivers are generally very punctilious about returning change. Even the remotest village in Mexico has some kind of colectivo service, so nowhere is inaccessible.

Buying Tickets

You can reserve and buy first-class, luxury-class and some second-class bus tickets in advance at bus stations, by phone, or, increasingly, online through the websites of the individual companies. Online bookings, however, are sometimes difficult with a non-Mexican credit card. In addition, **Ticketbus** (tel: 55-5133 2424, toll-free within Mexico 01800-702 8000, www.ticketbus.com.mx) sells tickets for many bus companies in central and southern Mexico, and has handy "Ticket Shops" in many areas of Mexico City and other cities, which, if you cannot book online, help you avoid an extra trip to the bus station. There is no extra charge for buying through Ticketbus. For busy times of the year, especially Mexican holiday seasons such as Christmas and Easter, make reservations well

ahead. If you make several stops, buy your seat for the next stage of your trip as soon as you arrive – otherwise you may have to stay longer than you intended.

In second-class bus stations, you generally line up on the day to buy a ticket at the relevant window in the second-class bus station. However, at the point of origin of the bus you must usually have your ticket before you get on the bus, rather than buy it on board. This does not apply if you join the bus later in the route.

Bus Stations

In most cities, there are separate first- (estación de autobuses de primera) and second-class (de segunda) bus stations, while combis run from squares or individual garages. Exceptions include Cancún, which has one station for all services. In some cities, notably in Oaxaca and Chiapas, individual second-class companies have kept their own, separate depots, which can be confusing.

Mexico City, as often, is an exception because of its huge size. There are four big stations for first- and most second-class buses to different parts of the country. Some buses stop at more than one station, but to save time it's best to know which one you need:
Terminal de Autobuses del Norte
Av. de los Cien Metros 4907
Metro: Autobuses del Norte, Line 5.
Buses for the north of the country – roughly beyond Manzanillo on the Pacific side, including Baja California, or beyond Poza Rica on the Gulf side.
Terminal Central de Autobuses del Sur
Av. Tasqueña 1320
Metro: Tasqueña, Line 2
Buses bound for points south and southwest of Mexico City, such as Cuernavaca and Morelos, Taxco, Acapulco, Oaxaca and Chiapas.
Terminal de Autobuses del Poniente (Terminal del Observatorio)
Av. Sur 122, Colonia Tacubaya
Metro: Observatorio, Line 1
For Toluca and Mexico state, Michoacán, Jalisco, Nayarit, Sinaloa and other points west.
Terminal de Oriente (TAPO)
Zaragoza 200
Metro: San Lázaro, Lines 1 and B
Buses to the east and southeast, including southern Veracruz, Tabasco, northern Chiapas and the Yucatán Peninsula.

All these bus stations are well away from Downtown to avoid traffic problems. As at the airport (see page 329), there are authorized taxi stands at each terminal for getting cabs into the city, and these are the most reliable option to use. The stations are well policed, but be careful with your bags while walking around the Mexico City stations.

Baggage

Officially, the amount of baggage each passenger can take with them is limited to 25kg (55lbs) on first-class buses, but this is not usually enforced. On second-class buses there is virtually no limit, although you will often have to load it yourself.

Bus Companies

There are many bus companies around Mexico, but the following are the major first-class companies, serving different parts of the country: **ADO**, tel: 55-5133 2424, 01800-702 8000, www.ado.com.mx
The largest company in southeast Mexico, particularly Veracruz, Tabasco, Chiapas and the Yucatán Peninsula, which also has services from Mexico City.
Enlaces Terrestres Nacionales (**ETN**), tel: 55-5277 6529, www.etn.com.mx
Mexico City and Mexico state, Aguascalientes, Michoacán, Jalisco and other areas of west-central Mexico.
Estrella Blanca, tel: 01800-507 5500, www.estrellablanca.com.mx
Large company with services in every part of Mexico except Tabasco, Chiapas and the Yucatán Peninsula.
Estrella de Oro, tel: 01800-900 0105, www.estrelladeoro.com.mx
Mexico City to Morelos, Guerrero, Ixtapa-Zihuatanejo, Veracruz.
Estrella Roja, tel: 01800-712 2284, www.estrellaroja.com.mx
Mexico City to Puebla and Cholula, and some other destinations.
Omnibus Cristóbal Colón, tel: 01800-822 2369, www.occbus.com.mx
Subsidiary of ADO especially serving Guerrero, Oaxaca and Chiapas, with connections to the Yucatán and Mexico City.
Omnibus de México, tel: 01800-765 6636, www.odm.com.mx
Mexico City, Jalisco, Zacatecas and many destinations in northeast Mexico.
Primera Plus, tel: 01800-375 7587, www.primeraplus.com.mx
Mexico City to Jalisco, Guanajuato, León, the Pacific coast

City Buses

City buses are a very cheap (under US$0.50) way of getting around, and

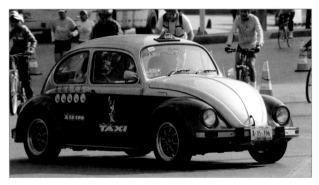

ABOVE: a VW Beetle taxi deftly navigates Mexico City.

in Mexico City can be an enjoyable means of getting to places not well served by the metro, seeing the city and getting close to local life. That is so long as you are prepared to be adaptable and try some Spanish, and so long as you only try to use them outside of peak times – after 10am in the morning, and before about 4–5pm in the afternoon. During the long peak hours, buses are incredibly crowded, slow, and often impossible to board.

Local buses in Mexico City come in different sizes, from rather more comfortable full-size buses to the hundreds of **peseros**, medium-sized minibuses, or small **combis**, known in the capital as **micros**. The easiest to handle is the **Metrobus** which runs up and down dedicated lanes on the Avenida Insurgentes, with big modern buses and set stops almost like metro stations; special tickets are required (not the same as metro tickets) which can be bought at the stops. Using any of the other city buses (especially peseros and micros) requires a little practice, and it helps a lot if you can ask for explanations (such as where a bus is going) in Spanish. One complication is that they do not usually have clear route numbers; instead, destinations are written on the windshield, so to get the right bus you need to know not only where you're going but the names of some places close to it. Also, you must be aware of the potential for pickpocketing and other petty crime on Mexico City buses (especially when they are crowded). Notice when people are close to you, and do not attract attention by showing that you have large amounts of money, or wear easily-stealable jewelry. Always have change when you use buses, and do not try to change large notes.

Other cities all have their own local buses. Similarly they do not generally have route numbers, but using them

is usually a much calmer business than in the capital, and in tranquil cities such as Mérida they provide an easy way to get around. In most cities there are also local combis, but again, it is difficult for newcomers to identify where they are going. Many tourist cities such as Puerto Vallarta and especially Cancún have bus services that are much easier for foreigners to use, and even have easy-to-identify route numbers.

By Metro

Mexico City has an excellent subway (metro) system, officially the **STC** (Sistema de Transporte Colectivo, tel: 55-5709 1133; www.metro.df.gob.mx), which for much of the day is a very quick as well as convenient way to get around the city. Stations are well-lit and the trains are very quiet, and a small free map of the network is available at most stations. All lines are open Mon–Fri 5am–midnight, Sat 6am–midnight, Sun 7am–midnight; tickets cost only around US15¢, and it's best to buy them in strips of five or 10, to avoid queuing each time you use the system. In the south of the city, the system is extended by the **Tren Ligero**, an overground light rail line that runs from Taxqueña metro to the gardens of Xochimilco.

There is a possibility of petty crime on the metro – as in any giant city – but so long as you are reasonably careful traveling on the system is pretty trouble-free in the middle of the day. However, stay away from it during rush hours (usually 7.30–10am, and 5.30–8pm), when like all Mexico City public transport it gets atrociously crowded, and the risk of pickpocketing is also naturally much greater (note, though, that at peak times there are also special **women-only carriages**, usually at the front or back of each train). It is also not advisable to use the metro in the center and east of the city late at night. Don't plan, either, on using the metro to get to the airport or bus station with all your luggage; no large bags are permitted, especially at peak traveling times.

By Taxi

Mexico City

As has been well-publicized, there have been particular problems with crime in Mexico City taxis, so special care is advisable; follow a few basic precautions, and you can travel without any difficulties. The city has a bewildering variety of taxis, and since 2008 the local authorities have relicensed all the thousands of taxi drivers in a bid to root out **"pirate cabs"** and increase passenger safety. All cabs except some hotel and airport taxis, which have set fares by zones, now have meters (taximetros).

If you are a newcomer to the city, and especially if you do not speak good Spanish, it will always be best to get a hotel to call a cab for you (larger hotels will have ranks outside) or to find an official taxi rank (called a sitio, and signposted in the street) and get a cab there. **Sitios** all have phone numbers, so it's a good idea to note down the number of a local rank and use it when necessary; there are also 24-hour phone cab services, such as **Taxi Mexico** (tel: 55-1495 3545) or **Servitaxis** (tel: 55-5516 6020). Hotel and phone taxis are more expensive than street cabs, but still cheap by international standards, and you have a guarantee of security.

If you cannot find a sitio and need to get a cab in the street, only hail one of the larger, more modern cabs, in white with a red stripe along the side or in burgundy and white or gold. A properly licensed cab should have a white license plate with a capital letter followed by five numbers. The old green and white cabs are the cheapest, but also have the most risk of crime, so it's best to avoid them.

Always look for the driver's photo ID which should be displayed on the dashboard of the cab. Also check that the driver has turned on the meter.

Other Towns and Cities

In other parts of Mexico traveling by taxi is far less problematic and this level of caution is not generally necessary, so there is rarely a problem in hailing cabs in the street. However, note that in most cities and towns taxis do not have meters. Instead, there is a set fare for the whole

town, or a system of fares by zones. It is a good idea to have an idea of the current local rates: hotels will tell you them, and in most tourist areas they are listed in free English-language magazines. As a general rule it is advisable to agree on the fare before you get in the cab – and reject anything exaggerated. Except in tourist areas drivers will usually only speak Spanish, so try, at least, to know your numbers.

In some cities (such as **Villahermosa**, **Tabasco**) it is customary for taxi drivers to cruise up and down popular routes, especially at peak times, and pick up several passengers on a colectivo basis, who each pay part of the fare. When you want a taxi to yourself to go to a specific location, you may have to phone for one (again, best done through hotels), or pay a bit more. Colectivo taxis naturally blend into colectivo minibuses, and in small towns and country districts the only difference between them is the size of vehicle. Small town and rural taxis will take passengers long distances, so long as you agree a price first. Similarly, Toluca airport taxis run to Mexico City, those in Villahermosa will happily take you to Palenque (a 2hr drive) and those from Tuxtla Gutiérrez will go up San Cristóbal de las Casas, for around US$40.

In Mérida, Yucatán, the city has introduced metered taxis, but there are also still taxis (generally white with a red stripe along the side) that are meter-less and use the old set

fare-zone system. Metered taxis are nearly always cheaper, especially for short journeys, so it's best to use them when possible. Local phone taxi services, such as **EconoTaxi** (tel: 999-945 0000) or **Taximetro** (tel: 999-982 2250) all use metered cabs.

Cancún and the Riviera Maya have thousands of taxis, mostly licensed from Cancún, Puerto Morelos, Playa del Carmen or Tulum. They do not have meters, but instead there are complicated scales of official rates for each area. Current rates are often posted up outside bus stations, and listed in free magazines such as Cancún Tips and on several local websites; hotels should also have lists of them. One peculiarity of the taxi rates in Cancún is that they are based on the idea that tourists should pay more than locals, so fares are higher for any journey to or from the Hotel Zone than in Ciudad Cancún. Taxis from any of the major centers will usually take you anywhere on the Riviera, for the right price. However, Riviera cab drivers – especially in Cancún – have a bad reputation for exploiting the confusion this system produces among recent arrivals, with exaggerated prices and other scams. Again, try to get an idea of current rates soon after you arrive, and always agree a price before you get into a cab.

Isla Mujeres and Cozumel each have unmetered local taxis with a fare scale for the whole of each island, not just the main towns. Current rates are posted up at the ferry landings.

Day Without a Car

In an effort to combat pollution, Mexico City and Mexico state operate a "Day Without a Car" (Hoy No Circula) program based on the last number of your license plate. The program restricts circulation between 5am and 10pm to cars with plates ending in 5 and 6 on Mondays; 7 and 8 on Tuesdays; 3 and 4 on Wednesdays; 1 and 2 on Thursdays; and 9 and 0 on Fridays. In addition, vehicles may not be used on one Saturday each month, depending on the last digit of the license number. Some vehicles that meet special low emissions standards are exempt. These regulations are quite strictly enforced. Also at times when pollution levels are becoming particularly high, an extra level of restriction comes into operation, which allows vehicles with plates

ending in odd or even numbers only to be used on alternate days. On certain public holidays, restrictions are lifted and all cars are allowed to circulate. This program has not met all the hopes that were placed in it – in part because locals have invented many ways to get around it – but is kept in force since it is thought that without it, pollution would return to its 1990s levels.

Hoy No Circula is also applicable to foreign-plated vehicles, and most rental cars and vehicles from other Mexican states, based in the same way on their license numbers. However, owners of foreign vehicles can obtain a **Pase Turístico**, giving exemption from the scheme, so long as their car is less than eight years old and passes a brief emissions test. Details are available from tourist offices.

Acapulco

Acapulco's airport is slightly south of the city, about 20 minutes by car from Downtown. Buses for Mexico City leave either from a station near the airport or from a location in the center of town. Those renting a vehicle should beware of unscrupulous police who target rentals (or foreigners) heading out of town towards the airport, stopping cars along the main road and asking for bribes. This is annoying, but be polite at all times. If you do not wish to pay the bribe, insist on paying the ticket at the station. They may remove your license plates and insist you pay... or they may just decide it's easier to let you go. Do not threaten or insult them at any time.

Most taxis are reasonable and Acapulco is so dense it only takes 20 minutes to go from one side to the other. Be sure to agree on the fee before entering the vehicle. In the Downtown area, it's often just as easy to walk.

Guadalajara

Guadalajara is served by air, buses, and several *cuota* (pay) highways that connect it to cities nearby. Streets are wide, though crowded, and much of the driving action is on Juárez or Vallarta. The cathedral fronts onto 16 de Septiembre, which parallels Independencia for a bit before the two diverge. Guadalajara is a "walking" city, with generally safe, easy to follow streets. Local buses are the cheapest way to get around – a 10- or 15-minute ride only costs a few pesos. Taxis for the same distance may cost about 50 pesos, but as with any place in Mexico it's vital to set a price before you hop in.

La Paz

La Paz is the biggest city in the southern part of Baja, served by air, bus, and good highways, as well as by ferry via the port in Pichilinque, which connects to Mazatlán and Topolobampo on the mainland. The airport is about 15 minutes' drive from the main city centers: the Zona Hotelera, a strip of stores and hotels along the scalloped bay; or the Centro, which is a largely developed, untouristy business area further back from the shore. Car rentals from a variety of companies can be done either at the airport or in the Zona Hotelera. Buses run frequently throughout the day in both directions: toward Los Cabos in the south or north to Tijuana and Mexicali. The latter two destinations take approximately 24 hours.

By Car

While buses, *colectivos* and local taxis can get you to just about every part of Mexico, if you want to explore with more freedom – and with more control over your time – it will be much better to have your own car. Major roads are mostly of a high standard, and there is a growing number of fast toll highways that cut journey times between major regions of the country. Their tolls *(cuotas)* are relatively high, and many local drivers do not use them, but this means that they are often empty, and so very fast. Among the most important **cuota highways** are those from Mexico City to Guadalajara, Acapulco and Veracruz (via Puebla), and that from Mérida to Cancún.

Local and village roads are often slow – above all in mountain regions – but in most parts of the country they are now paved, with bumps and potholes the further you go from main routes. Some remote places can only be reached by dirt track, notably in protected natural areas.

For the requirements needed to bring your own vehicle into Mexico from the US or Canada, *see page 329.*

Car Hire

It is straightforward to rent a car in Mexico. All the major international car rental agencies are represented here, and there are also many local agencies. Resort hotels often have recommended agencies, but you will often find better deals if you look around a little more. There is a big choice of agencies in resort areas and some larger cities; in smaller cities there may be only one or two, with a limited choice of vehicles, so if you expect to be driving any distance it is generally advisable to rent in one of the **regional car-rental centers** – such as Puerto Vallarta, or Mérida and Cancún in the Yucatán – rather than arrive in a small city such as Tuxtla Gutiérrez and expect to find a car available there.

Renting a car is especially popular in the Yucatán Peninsula since, because it is so flat, it is easy to drive around; in more rugged areas, driving is less attractive, so there may also be fewer agencies. Mérida agencies often have the Peninsula's best rental deals.

To rent a car you need to be **over 21** and have your **passport**, **driving license** and a **credit card**. Small agencies in particular often give discounts for payments in cash, but you still need a credit card for a deposit. Most car rental deals now include **unlimited mileage** (kilometraje ilimitado), and cheaper basic rates that are generally a false economy. During peak vacation times, it's advisable to book a car in advance. Nowadays, naturally, some of the best rental rates can be obtained by booking online, directly with an agency or through one of the international car-rental websites. It is usually costly to drop off a car in any place other than where it was rented.

When you collect your car, the agency should show you that the tires and spare wheel are in good condition, and that the car has the necessary jack. It should also have a fold-up red warning triangle, which you should place 50 meters (165ft) behind the car if you ever have to stop on a highway.

Insurance

Your car rental agreement will usually include **Collision Damage Waiver** (CDW) insurance. However, be aware that in Mexico this normally covers you only for the total loss of the car – in which case, you will still generally be liable for 10 percent of the value of the vehicle – and does not cover *daños parciales* or "partial damage," minor knocks and collisions such as a broken fender or windscreen. Additional, comprehensive cover is often available, but it can be expensive. When Mexican drivers have minor collisions with other vehicles, they usually settle the matter with an exchange of cash, without recourse to insurance. This is an added incentive to drive carefully.

If you bring a US or Canadian vehicle to Mexico, you must get a Mexican insurance policy *(see page 329).* It is advisable to get the most comprehensive one you can manage.

Fuel

All gasoline in Mexico is sold by the state oil company, Pemex. Some gas stations are now independently operated, but prices are generally the same throughout the country – more expensive than in the US, but still low by world standards. All **Pemex gasolineras** have diesel and unleaded *(magna)* fuel, and many also have a higher-grade unleaded gas called *Premium*. Gas stations rarely accept credit cards. When arriving at a *gasolinera*, check that the attendant sets the pump at zero before filling the car, to avoid being overcharged. Attendants will usually offer to clean your windscreen, check tires, check your oil, and so on, for a tip.

Pemex *gasolineras* are easy to find in cities and resorts, but in rural areas there may only be one in a district's main town, and on some highways they are spread out over long distances. When making long trips, fill up before starting out, and again every chance you get.

Safety Tips and Rules of the Road

In Mexico City, and some other cities such as Monterrey, traffic is hectic enough to deter any visitor from driving, and this is rarely the most convenient way to get around. Elsewhere, though, there are no special problems with driving in Mexico. The chief things to look out for, especially in small towns and villages, are *topes* or **speed bumps**. Children, old people and animals

ABOVE: open highway, Puuc region.

have priority on Mexican country roads, not vehicles, and *topes* are intended to slow traffic down as quickly as possible. They come in different styles and sizes, from large humps that can really batter a car if you hit them at speed to rows of ridges called *vibradores*. Many are signposted, with signs such as "*Topes a 100m,*" but others are not, so you always need to look out for them. It is best to avoid driving outside towns at night, because roads are rarely lit and *topes*, potholes, and other dips in the road are much harder to spot. Except when overtaking always keep an extra distance from vehicles in front of you, as they may have to brake suddenly for a *tope*.

Other things to bear in mind are that Mexican drivers rarely use blinkers (indicators) to indicate that they are about to turn left or right, but may put on hazard warning lights as an indication they're about to make a maneuver in either direction (buses and *combis* especially do this when they are about to stop). Also, drivers of slow trucks often put on their left

blinkers as a helpful sign to drivers behind them that it is safe to pass.

Breakdown Services

The **Green Angels** (*ángeles verdes*) are a free government-run drivers' assistance service who patrol Mexico's major highways in green-and-white radio-equipped vehicles. They can offer first-aid, minor repairs to your vehicle, or an emergency supply of gas and oil. You pay only for the parts used and for gas and oil. The Green Angels (emergency number: 078) operate daily 8am–8pm. Most speak some English. If you have more than a minor problem in a rented car, call your rental agency as soon as possible, and follow their advice.

Always carry water for the radiator, a jack, and spare tire (or two, in rugged, remote areas of the country), fuses, and any other spare parts that might need replacing – even if you're not prepared to do the repair yourself. You can count on the Green Angels for mechanical know-how but not for parts specific to your make and model (and away from the main roads you may well be on your own).

Nearly every village will have at least one mechanics' workshop (*mecánico*) – who, you may be surprised to find, can often handle repairs to any kind of vehicle – and a tire repair shop (a *llantera* or *vulcanizadora*). Due to country roads in bad condition and dirt tracks, flat tires can be quite common. If you have a flat and can then get to the nearest *llantera* on the spare, they will make an immediate repair to the burst tire for very little money, and if necessary you can then get a new tire in the nearest town.

Road Signs

Many road signs are international, others assume a knowledge of Spanish. If you don't understand a road sign, slow down and be prepared to stop.

Parking

Parking is restricted in the centers of most cities. Where parking is prohibited the curb is painted yellow or red. If you park illegally the police may tow the car away (or, in Mexico City, clamp the wheels) with surprising speed, and to get it released you must pay a fine. Where on-street parking is permitted, the stretch of street will often be "administered" by an **aparcacoches**, a man with a red rag who points out spaces to arriving drivers, stops traffic to allow them to park, and watches over the car while it is there, for a few pesos.

In all city centers there are plenty of paid parking lots (*estacionamientos*, marked with a large "E" sign) and, as charges are not huge, it will generally be better to find one rather than waste time driving around looking for a space on the street. For a tip, attendants will usually wash the car too. In central Mexico City, Monterrey and the modern areas of some other cities there are often giant multistory parking lots. If you are driving into any city, try to get a hotel with its own parking lot, and leave the car there while in the city.

In small towns finding parking space is rarely difficult, but you still need to avoid parking next to any painted curbs.

Distances and Driving Times

Driving times in Mexico will vary a lot depending on the kinds of roads you use. On *cuota* highways you can travel very fast; on country roads, because of the need to slow down for towns, villages and *tope* speed bumps, average speeds are much lower. The relationship of distance to driving time is also very variable. In the flat Yucatán or the Gulf Coast you can expect to get around fairly quickly at an average of around 90kph (56mph) between towns, but in the mountains of Oaxaca or Chiapas journeys will take far longer.

The following are only rough averages. All driving times are without any allowances for stops.
US Border (Brownsville, TX)–Mexico City: 964km (600 miles), 12hrs
US Border (Brownsville, TX)–Cancún: 2,333km (1,450 miles), 30hrs
US Border (San Diego)–Cabo San Lucás: 1,711km (1,063 miles), 24hrs
Mexico City–Puerto Vallarta: 906km (563 miles), 11hrs
Mexico City–Acapulco: 382km (237 miles), 4–5hrs
Mexico City–Veracruz: 406km (253 miles), 4–5hrs
Mexico City–Palenque: 930km (578 miles), 14hrs
Mexico City–Oaxaca: 452km (280 miles), 6–7hrs
Mexico City–Cancún: 1,630km (1,012 miles), 22hrs
Oaxaca–Puerto Escondido: 290km (180 miles), 5–6hrs
Oaxaca–Palenque: 815km (506 miles), 15hrs
Palenque–San Cristóbal de Las Casas: 191km (118 miles), 5hrs
Palenque–Mérida: 555km (345 miles), 7–8hrs
Mérida–Cancún: 320km (199 miles), 3–4hrs by *cuota* highway, 4–5hrs by ordinary road.

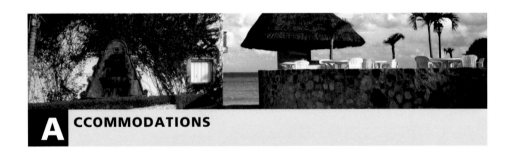

A CCOMMODATIONS

HOTELS, YOUTH HOSTELS, BED & BREAKFAST

Choosing Accommodations

Hotels in Mexico cover every option – from luxury grand hotels and chic design venues in cities, through opulent beach resorts and spas down to palm-roofed forest cabins and simple *posadas* and hostels with rooms for under 200 pesos per night. Around the main resort areas – Puerto Vallarta, Huatulco, the Riviera Maya – there are ever more all-inclusive resorts, with every facility on-site.

Virtually every kind of hotel in Mexico, except perhaps some of the most remote, can now be booked online, or at least by email. If you are going to stay in a large resort hotel, or one of the bigger city hotels, you will generally get better rates by booking them as part of a package through a travel website or tour operator, with flight included, than if you simply book a room direct from the hotel. Hotel costs naturally vary a great deal across the country – in the most popular resort areas and major cities they can be as high as US or European levels, but in other areas – Chiapas, Michoacán, cities not fully on the tourist track – even luxurious old colonial **haciendas** can be remarkably economical, with beautiful rooms for around US$60 or less.

Several kinds of Mexican hotel have distinctive attractions. Dotted along both the Pacific and Caribbean coasts, set apart from the bigger resorts, are exquisite, ultra-stylish **beach retreats** with everything you need for serious pampering, including acres of beach and pristine forest to themselves. In colonial towns such as San Miguel de Allende, Oaxaca or Mérida many characteristic old Spanish colonial houses, built around intimate patios, have become hotels with an irresistible charm. Other relics of an older Mexico are the aristocratic haciendas, with fabulous grounds and gardens, that have been made into seductively tranquil rural retreats, especially in Jalisco, Morelos and the Yucatán.

RVs and Camping

Facilities for camping and, particularly, traveling with an RV in Mexico have expanded a good deal since the 1990s, and there are RV parks with good hook-ups, laundries, showers, and other facilities in many parts of the country. They are most numerous along the peninsula of Baja California and along the Pacific coast around Puerto Vallarta, but there are also well-equipped sites in many other areas, such as around Lake Pátzcuaro in Michoacán, or at Paamul near Playa del Carmen on the Riviera Maya, where many RVers spend the winter.

If you do not wish to travel with an RV but simply to camp, many RV sites also offer camping space. Other popular camping sites include Palenque, near the ruins, and many backpacker hostels around Mexico offer camping space in their yards and gardens. It is not usually a good idea to try "wild camping" in open country, above all if you do not speak good Spanish. You may find that even remote parcels of land belong to an individual or a community, who will resent you camping without permission. For safety's sake, stick to campsites or beaches where others are already camping.

For more information on both RV travel and camping in Mexico, the most comprehensive one-stop guide is the *Traveler's Guide to Mexican Camping*, published by Rolling Homes Press (www.rollinghomes.com). Other handy sources include *On the Road in Mexico* (www.ontheroadin.com), *The People's Guide to Mexico* (www.peoples guide.com) and www.rversonline.org.

BELOW: Hotel Shangri-La Caribe at Playa del Carmen in the Yucatán.

MEXICO CITY AND ENVIRONS

Mexico City

Centro Histórico

Boutique Hotel de Cortés
Av. Hidalgo 85
Tel: 55-5518 2181
www.boutiquehoteldecortes.com
This historic hotel in a 17th-century former hospice on the Alameda has recently been given a very chic transformation, stylishly combining the original Baroque architecture with modern design, a spa, a gorgeous patio restaurant and a hip rooftop bar. **$$$**

Chillout Flat
Bolívar 8
Tel: 55-5948 7048
www.chilloutflat.com.mx
An exceptional and very imaginatively run "boutique B&B," between the Zócalo and the Alameda. Its four rooms are each different and very comfortable, and the owners, as well as providing excellent breakfasts, really take care of their guests, providing all sorts of information. Needs to be booked well in advance. **$$**

Hotel Catedral
Donceles 95
Tel: 55-5518 5232
www.hotelcatedral.com
An attractive traditional hotel one block from the Zócalo, a few steps from the Colegio de San Ildefonso and with cathedral views from some rooms. The comfortable rooms are great value for this central location. **$$**

Hotel Gillow
Isabel la Católica 17
Tel: 55-5510 0791
www.hotelgillow.com
One of the Historic Center's most popular hotels, the Gillow is known for reliable quality and very good value, with spacious, traditionally styled rooms that now have full modern fittings. It is often full, so book well ahead. **$$**

Hotel Majestic Best Western
Madero 73, on the Zócalo
Tel: 55-5521 8600
www.hotelmajestic.com.mx
This big veteran hotel is consistently in demand, for its fabulous location: right on the Zócalo, with unbeatable views from its best rooms and the lovely rooftop restaurant. Atmosphere is guaranteed but it can – inevitably – be noisy, and rooms looking out on Av. Madero are less attractive. **$$$**

Mexico City Hostel
República de Brasil 8
Tel: 55-5512 3666
www.mexicocityhostel.com
One of the best options for budget accommodation in central Mexico City, a bright modern hostel in an attractively renovated old building off the Zócalo. There's a choice of simple rooms with showers, or dorm beds. Staff are friendly, and it is very clean and well-run. **$**

Sheraton Centro Histórico
Av. Juárez 70
Tel: 55-5130 5300
US tel: 1-888 474 2122
www.sheraton.com.mx
The largest hotel in the old center, a spectacular modern tower beside the Alameda – opened only in 2003 – with more than 450 rooms. All fittings, the indoor pool, fitness center and so on are naturally state-of-the-art, and there's a choice of restaurants. Special deals make some rooms remarkable value. **$$$**

Zona Rosa and Reforma

Casa González
Río Sena 69
Tel: 55-5514 3302
The cozy style of this slightly old-fashioned, family-run hotel, in two old houses north of Paseo de la Reforma, has won it many return visitors. Breakfasts, served in a bright, convivial dining room, are delicious. It still does not have its own website, but can be booked through many travel sites. **$$**

Four Seasons Mexico D.F.
Reforma 500
Tel: 55-5230 1818
US tel: 1-800 819 5053
www.fourseasons.com/mexico
Just east of Chapultepec park, this ultra-luxurious hotel was designed to evoke Mexican traditional architecture, with its eight floors rising up around a patio garden to provide seclusion from the Paseo outside. The Italian-based cuisine of its Reforma 500 restaurant has a very high reputation. **$$$$**

Hotel Century
Liverpool 152
Tel: 55-5726 9911
www.century.com.mx
A well-equipped, good-value high-rise hotel, with an indoor pool, on the south side of the Zona Rosa. Rooms do not have much character, but many have fine views. **$$**

Hotel María Cristina
Río Lerma 31, Col. Cuauhtémoc
Tel: 55-5566 9688
www.hotelmariacristina.com.mx
The mansion-style architecture and patio of this veteran hotel give it added charm, although fittings are modern. In the Embassy area north of Paseo de la Reforma, this is a relaxing mid-range option. **$$**

Marquís Reforma Hotel
Reforma 465
Tel: 55-5229 1200
US tel: 1-800 745 8883
www.marquisreforma.com
This big and smart business hotel, in an original Art Deco-influenced building, has recently been upgraded, with a much-improved spa and health club. The restaurants have fine Mexican cuisine. **$$$$**

Sevilla Palace Hotel
Reforma 105, near Colombus Monument
Tel: 55-5705 2800
US tel: 1-800 732 9488
www.sevillapalace.com.mx
A modern high-rise hotel on a very busy part of Reforma with every kind of facility. Rooms are functionally comfortable, but the big attraction is the pool in a rooftop garden, with stunning views. **$$$**

Roma/Condesa

Casa Roma
Aguascalientes 174
Tel: 55-4006 9199
www.casaromadf.com
Actually in the south of Colonia Condesa rather than Roma – so some way from the center – this intimate guesthouse has just three beautiful rooms, and meals and the very personal service are exceptional. **$$$**

Hippodrome Hotel
México 188, Condesa
Tel: 55-5212 2110
www.thehippodromehotel.com
One of Condesa's most fashionable new hotels, in a great location next to the Art Deco Parque México, with luxurious facilities, suitably stylish decor in muted colors and a restaurant

PRICE CATEGORIES

Price categories are for a double room for one night in high season:
$ = under 500 pesos
$$ = 500–1,200 pesos
$$$ = 1,200–2,500 pesos
$$$$ = over 2,500 pesos

appropriately named the Hip Kitchen. Occasional offers soften the blow of the high prices. **$$$$**
Hostal Condesa
Tamaulipas 197
Tel: 55-5273 6851
www.hostalcondesa.com
A real bargain, this very attractive modern hostel has a choice of private rooms or four-bed dorm rooms, at very generous prices. Breakfast and Net access are included, the staff are very helpful, and it is a pleasant place to stay in a fashionable (and often expensive) area. **$**

Chapultepec and Polanco
Camino Real Polanco
Mariano Escobedo 700
Tel: 55-5263 8888
www.caminoreal.com
A huge modern complex just opposite Chapultepec park, which like all the hotels in the Camino Real has a whole range of facilities: bright, modern rooms, several large restaurants, a gym and a pool in a garden. **$$$$**
Casa Vieja
Eugenio Sue 45
Tel: 55-5282 0067
www.casavieja.com
A special small boutique hotel with just 10 suites in a finely restored former hacienda in a fashionable part of the city. Because of the traditional architecture, rooms do not have much natural light, but they're utterly comfortable, and the patio restaurant is delightful. **$$$$**
Habita
Presidente Masaryk 201
Tel: 55-5282 3100
www.hotelhabita.com
Mexico City's original boutique hotel, which attracts design fans from across the world to admire its unreservedly radical architecture and stunning pool and other features. If you like its hip style you'll love it: if you prefer more traditional opulence, it is better to look elsewhere. **$$$$**
W Mexico City
Campos Eliseos 252
Tel: 55-9138 1800

www.whotels.com
A branch of the New York-based W boutique arm of the Sheraton hotel group. Rooms and suites are, naturally, ultra-chic, and cutting-edge electronic extras are a hallmark; the restaurant – with eclectically modern menu – bars and spa are equally hip. **$$$$**

Coyoacán
Hostal Frida
Francisco Javier Mina 54, Coyoacán
Tel: 55-5659 7005
www.hostalfridabyb.com.mx
As an alternative to staying in the center, it is possible to settle in to the quiet streets of Coyoacán. There are several self-contained guest suites in this large, pleasant family home, all with twin beds and small

ABOVE: rooftop bar, W Hotel.

kitchens (so breakfast is not actually provided). Longer-term rates are available. **$$**

Cholula

Villas Arqueológicas Cholula
Calle 2 Poniente No. 601
Tel: 222-273 7900
www.villasarqueologicas.com.mx
One of the "archeological villas" hotels built at major pre-Hispanic sites *(see page 339 Teotihuacán)*, and right opposite Cholula's Great Pyramid. As at all the Villas hotels there's a lovely pool,

patios and gardens, and charming rooms in traditional Mexican style are combined with very reasonable prices. **$$**

Cuernavaca

Camino Real Sumiya
Jiutepec
Tel: 777-329 9888
US tel: 1-800 722 6466
www.caminoreal.com/sumiya
Once the home of millionairess Barbara Hutton, built in a unique semi-Japanese style, this magnificent estate is now the most opulent link in the Camino Real chain, but still has on display her fine collection of Oriental art and furniture. The rooms and terrace restaurant all have superb views, and the pool is fabulous. **$$$**
Casa Poezia
Río Panuco 23, Colonia Vista Hermosa
Tel: 777-322 5538
www.cuernavacainfo.com/casapoezia.html
A more intimate alternative to the big Cuernavaca luxury hotels, this boutique guest-house has just six delightful rooms in a colonial-style house, with a fine garden and pool. Service is personal, and delicious meals are available. **$$$**
Hacienda de Cortes
Plaza Kennedy 90
Tel: 777-315 8844
www.hotelhaciendadecortes.com.mx
Lush gardens surround this 16th-century estate – which actually was once the property of the family of Hernán Cortés – where history and comfort combine with Mexican traditions to provide magnificent, very special accommodations. Regular special offers make it a very accessible treat. **$$$**
Hostería Las Quintas
Blvd Díaz Ordaz 9
Tel: 777-362 3949
www.hosterialasquintas.com.mx
Although it has 85 rooms, they are spread around the lush gardens in several sections, giving it a more intimate feel than some Cuernavaca luxury hotels. The spa and restaurant are

stunning, and exceptional service leaves every guest feeling very pampered. **$$$$**
Las Mañanitas
Ricardo Linares 107
Tel: 777-362 0000
US tel: 1-800 735 2478
www.lasmananitas.com.mx
The grandest of Cuernavaca's mansion hotels, with a stunning spa for total indulgence as well as its gardens and gourmet restaurant. Rooms are all suite-sized, and the best face the garden. **$$$$**
Misión del Sol
Gral Diego Diaz González 31
Tel: 777-321 0999
US tel: 1-800 999 9100
www.misiondelsol.com.mx
This beautiful spa retreat is both luxurious and very mellow. The design and fine gardens are all inspired by ecological principles, there are no TVs in bedrooms, and no red meat is served in the restaurant, but it also offers sports facilities and exquisite rooms. **$$$$**

Ixtapan de la Sal

Bungalows Lolita
Blvd Arturo San Román 33
Tel: 721-143 0016
A long-standing, modest hotel popular with Mexican families, with a pleasant restaurant and a good-sized pool. Rooms are conventional, but good value. **$$**
Ixtapan Spa Hotel & Golf Resort
Blvd Arturo San Román
Tel: 721-143 2440
US tel: 1-800 638 7950
www.spamexico.com
There's plenty to do at this giant resort: golf on a full 18-hole course, thermal tubs and many other spa treatments, or just enjoying the two swimming pools and ample gardens. A variety of spa and sports packages make it good value. **$$$–$$$$**

Pachuca and Hidalgo

Hotel Real del Monte
Real del Monte

TRANSPORTATION

Tel: 771-715 5654
www.hotelesecoturisticos.com.mx
A comfortable, friendly little hotel in the silver-mining village of Real del Monte, just outside Pachuca. A range of activities are available in the magnificent mountain scenery (guided walks, climbing) and the same company also has two more beautiful hotels further into El Chico national park: Hotel El Paraíso and Posada del Amanecer. They can be booked through the same website. **$$**

Puebla

Camino Real Puebla
7 Poniente No. 105
Tel: 222-229 0909
US tel: 1-800 722 6466
www.caminoreal.com/puebla
This beautiful Camino Real hotel occupies the 16th-century former Convent of La Concepción, with a spectacular cloister-patio, and two blocks from the main plaza. Rooms are decorated to match, with colonial art and antiques, and the fine restaurant is similarly gracious. **$$$**
Hotel Royalty
Portal Hidalgo 8
Tel: 222-242 4743
www.hotelr.com
A good-value traditional mid-range hotel that puts you right in the middle of things, on the main square, and with a popular terrace restaurant for people-watching. Rooms on the square have a fine view, but can be noisy. **$$**
Mesón de Capuchinas
9 Oriente No. 16
Tel: 222-232 8088
www.mesondecapuchinas.com
Dating from the 17th century, this lovely colonial house has been sympathetically converted into a sumptuous boutique hotel, blending together modern fittings and antiques. The restaurant has fine *cocina poblana*, and the location is just as atmospheric, only a few steps from Puebla's main square. **$$$**

Mesón Sacristía de la Compañía
6 Sur No. 304,
Tel: 222-232 4513
www.mesones-sacristia.com
A gorgeous boutique hotel in a classic old Puebla house that has been restored with wonderful attention to every detail by the Espinosa family, who themselves deal in antiques. The equally beautiful restaurant showcases Puebla's refined cuisine, and cookery courses are available. The family has also begun the restoration of another historic house a few blocks away, the Mesón Sacristía de la Soledad (contact via La Compañía) which is due to have larger suites with luxurious fittings. **$$$**

Taxco

Hotel Los Arcos
Juan Ruíz de Alarcón 4
Tel: 762-622 1836
www.hotellosarcos.net
Beautiful rooms decorated with traditional Mexican colors and fittings in a stunning colonial patio house in central Taxco. No restaurant or pool, but there's plenty of charm and atmosphere, and very reasonable prices. **$$**
Hotel Victoria
Carlos J. Nibbi 5 and 7
Tel: 762-622 0004
www.victoriataxco.com
One of Taxco's oldest hotels, visited by many celebrities in the 1930s and 1940s, with a superb hilltop location, wonderful views over the town, and romantic gardens. Parts of it have seen better days (hence the low prices), but you have to forgive its faults for the atmosphere. Be sure to get a room with a balcony. **$$**
Posada de la Misión
Cerro de la Misión 32
Tel: 762-622 0063
www.posadamision.com
A large hilltop hotel, with superb views of Santa Prisca church and a celebrated mosaic mural by Juan

O'Gorman beside the pool. Some rooms are small and plain, but the best ones, naturally, have the best views. **$$$**

Teotihuacán

Villas Arqueológicas Teotihuacán
Periférico Sur, Tenochtitlán
Tel: 555-836 9020
www.villasarqueologicas.com.mx
One of a small group of very attractive, hacienda-style

ABOVE: breakfast on the terrace.

hotels created outside major archeological sites in central Mexico and the Yucatán. Rooms are pretty and comfortable, service is delightful, and the gardens with poolside bar are ideal for relaxing after a day spent exploring ruins. Prices are exceptional. **$$**

Tepoztlán

Hostal de la Luz
Carretera Tepoztlán–Amatlán Km4
Tel: 739-395 3374
www.hostaldelaluz.com
A holistic but very luxurious resort on a mountain top between Tepoztlán and the next village of Amatlán. A wide range of spa treatments, yoga, meditation and other activities are available, but it is tempting just to sit back and admire the pool, the gardens and the breathtaking natural setting. **$$$–$$$$**

Posada del Tepozteco
Paraíso 3
Tel: 739-395 0010
www.posadadeltepozteco.com
Staying at this beautifully peaceful hillside hotel is a great way to soak up the special atmosphere of Tepoztlán. Rooms offer an attractive mix of rustic style and comfort, and the gardens and views from the terrace restaurant are magnificent. **$$–$$$**

Tlaxcala

Posada San Francisco
Plaza de la Constitución 17
Tel: 246-462 6022
www.posadasanfrancisco.com
A reliable mid-range hotel right on Tlaxcala's main square (so some rooms can be noisy). Rooms are spacious and comfortable, and there's a very good-sized pool and terrace in an interior patio. **$$$**

Tula

Hotel Real Catedral
Zaragoza 106, Tula de Allende
Tel: 773-732 0813
www.tulaonline.com/hotelrealcatedral
Tula does not have many hotels, but this is the most enjoyable, in an attractively renovated old building and with charming, attentive service. There is no restaurant, but there are several nearby. **$$**

Valle de Bravo

Suites en la Montaña
Plaza de la Constitución 17
Tel: 726-266 1094
www.suitesenlamontana.com.mx
As the name suggests, the romantic suites at this hotel are spread around a mountain side above the lake at Valle de Bravo, in cottages with balconies and lovely views. **$$–$$$**

PRICE CATEGORIES

Price categories are for a double room for one night in high season:
$ = under 500 pesos
$$ = 500–1,200 pesos
$$$ = 1,200–2,500 pesos
$$$$ = over 2,500 pesos

ACCOMMODATIONS
EATING OUT
ACTIVITIES
A – Z
LANGUAGE

BAJA CALIFORNIA

Cabo San Lucas

Bungalows Breakfast Inn
Libertad and Herrera
Tel: 624-143 5035
www.cabobungalows.com
Cozy oasis with a beautiful pool, immaculate rooms, exquisite breakfasts, and very friendly staff. **$$$**
Las Ventanas al Paraíso
Carretera Transpeninsular Km 19.5
Tel: 624-144 2800
US tel: 888-ROSEWOOD (888-767 3966)
www.lasventanas.com
The ultimate in luxury. Suites feature fireplace, telescope for stargazing, and panoramic views. Other amenities include spa and fitness center, available yachts for fishing, and access to championship golf course. **$$$$**
Pueblo Bonito Pacifica
Cabo Pacifica S/N
Tel: 624-142 9696
www.pueblobonito.com
Luxurious and grand, this adults-only resort and spa has zen-inspired decor, unmatched views of the Pacific, and excellent service. **$$$–$$$$**

Ensenada

Desert Inn Ensenada
On the Ensenada highway
Tel: 800-026 3605
US tel: 1-800 542 3283
www.desertinns.com
Small hotel with restaurant and bar which organizes excursions to see the gray whales and salt mines. **$$**
Punta Morro
Transpeninsular, Km 106
Tel: 646-178 3507
US tel: 1-800 526 6676
www.punta-morro.com
Large hotel with great ocean views, pool, and bar on the outskirts of Ensenada. **$$$$**

Guerrero Negro

Desert Inn
Carretera Transpeninsular
Tel: 615-157 1304
US tel: 1-800 800 9632
www.desertinns.com
A hacienda-style inn with

restaurant, bar, and excursions to see the gray whales during the winter season. **$$**

La Paz

El Ángel Azul
Independencia 518
Tel: 612-125 5130
www.elangelazul.com
This historic monument in central La Paz was once the town's courthouse and is now a stylish hacienda-style B&B/hotel. **$$$**
Posada de las Flores
Alvaro Obregón 440
Tel: 612-125 5871
www.posadadelasflores.com
Beautiful hotel on the malecón with hacienda-style rooms, excellent breakfasts, and great views. **$$$$**

Loreto

Plaza Loreto
Hidalgo 2
Tel: 613-135 0280
www.loreto.com/hotelplaza
One block from the mission. Attractive rooms around a small patio, with bar/restaurant, pool. **$$**
Baja Outpost
Blvd López Mateos
Tel: 613-135 1134
www.bajaoutpost.com
Recently added swimming pool and plans for a restaurant. Baja Outpost offers posh *cabañas*, several hotel-style rooms, and a wealth of outdoor tours and activities. **$$$**

BELOW: sunset over Loreto, the former capital of Baja.

Mexicali

Crowne Plaza
Blvd López Mateos and Av. de los Héroes 201
Tel: 686-557 3600
US tel: 1-877 227 6963
www.ichotelsgroup.com
Nicely appointed modern low-rise with restaurant, bar, pool, gym. **$$$**

Mulegé

Hotel Las Casitas
Madero 50
Tel: 615-153 0019
www.historicolascasitas.com.mx
This cozy B&B has a beautiful patio with a lush, tropical feel and comfortable rooms, plus a restaurant and store. **$$**
Serenidad
La Playa s/n
Tel: 615-153 0530
www.hotelserenidad.com
Situated where the river meets the sea. Comfortable and attractive with bar, restaurant, and pool. Offers tours to cave paintings. **$$**

Rosarito

New Port Beach
Carretera libre Tijuana–Ensenada Km 45
Tel: 661-614 8000
US tel: 1-800 582 1018
www.newportbeachhotel.com
Beach front, family-oriented hotel, and, for a fee, pets are allowed. Pool, tennis, gym, restaurant, and bar. **$$$**
Rosarito Beach Hotel
Blvd Benito Juárez 31

Tel: 661-612 0144
US tel: 1-800 343 8582
www.rosaritobeachhotel.com
Legendary resort, equipped with pools, restaurant, spa, tennis, shops. The hotel has 230 rooms, all with ocean views. **$$$**

San Felipe

El Cortéz
Avenida Mar de Cortés
Tel: 686-577 1055
This has been the main hotel in San Felipe for 50 years and, although it is slightly out of the center, it is located right on the beach front. The many rooms are modern, and there are bungalows dotted around the grounds. It has two bars, a restaurant, and a pool. **$$$**

San Ignacio

Desert Inn
Tel: 615-157 1305
US tel: 1-800 800 9632
www.desertinns.com
Colonial-style hotel with pool and restaurant. **$$**

San José del Cabo

Casa Natalia
Blvd Mijares No. 4
Tel: 624-146 7100
www.casanatalia.com
Downtown, right on the plaza. Beautiful boutique hotel with terraces, bar, restaurant, tasteful decor, pool, and a magical margarita. **$$$$**
Presidente Inter-Continental
Blvd Mijares
Tel: 624-142 9229
US tel: 1-800 424 6835
www.ichotelsgroup.com
All-inclusive resort on a secluded beach next to the lagoon. **$$$$**

Westin Resort and Spa Los Cabos
Transpeninsular Carretera Km 22.5
Tel: 624 142 9000
US tel: 1-800-WESTIN 1
www.starwoodhotels.com/westin
A spectacular resort with restaurant, bar, pool, and tennis. **$$$$**

San Quintín

Desert Inn
Playa Santa María
Tel: 616-165 9008
US tel: 1-800 800 9632
www.desertinns.com
Charming hotel on the beach. Restaurant and

cocktail lounge. Rooms with balconies and sea view. **$$**

Santa Rosalia

Hotel Francés
Jean M. Cousteau 15
Tel: 615-152 2052
Situated in a French colonial building that is a national historic monument. Dominates the hill near the mining office at the north end of town. **$$**

Tecate

Rancho La Puerta
Highway 2, 5km (3 miles) west of

Tecate
Tel: 858-764 5500
US tel: 1-800 443 7565
www.rancholapuerta.com
Luxurious all-inclusive health spa and resort with restaurant, pool, massages, and tennis. Seven-day minimum stay. **$$$$**

Tijuana

Camino Real
Paseo de los Héroes 10305
Tel: 664-633 4000
US tel: 1-800 722 6466
www.caminoreal.com
Deluxe, with 250 rooms, restaurants, bars, and a

gym. **$$$-$$$$**
Grand Hotel Tijuana
Blvd Agua Caliente 4500
Tel: 664-681 7000
US tel: 1-866 GRAND TJ
www.grandhoteltijuana.com
Modern skyscraper with 422 rooms and suites. Restaurant, nightclub, pool, tennis, gym, spa, and movie theaters. **$$$**
Lucerna
Av. Rodríguez & Paseo de los Héroes
Tel: 644-633 3900
www.hoteleslucerna.com
Situated near the river, away from the crowds. With restaurant, attractive coffee shop, pool, tennis. **$$$**

THE SIERRAS

Chihuahua

San Felipe El Real
Ignacio Allende 1005
Tel: 614-437 2037
www.sanfelipeelreal.com
Charming boutique hotel in the center of the city, with antiques, excellent breakfasts, and attentive, friendly staff. **$$$$**
Westin Soberano
Barranca del Cobre 3211
Tel: 614-429 2929
US tel: 1-800 363 5997
www.westinsoberano.com
A beautiful hotel about 15 minutes from Downtown, with upscale rooms, nice views of the city, and a smallish pool. **$$$**

Ciudad Juárez

Holiday Inn Express Hotel & Suites
Paseo de la Victoria 4202
Tel: 656-692 5100
US tel: 1-800-315 2621
A clean hotel in a safe area that's near the US Consulate. **$$**

Copper Canyon (Barranca del Cobre)

Hotel Posada Barrancas Mirador
El Divisadero
Tel: 635-578 3020
US tel: 1-888 528 8401
www.mexicoscoppercanyon.com
Country inn with fireplaces,

ABOVE: spectacular views on the road to Monterrey.

restaurant, bar. Guided horseback trail rides. **$$$**
Mansión Tarahumara
Posada Barrancas station
Tel: 614-415 4721, in Chihuahua
US tel: 1-888 790 5264
www.lasierratarahumara.com.mx
Fifteen cabins in the heart of the Copper Canyon with a restaurant and bar. Recreational vehicles can park here. Rate includes meals. **$$$**
Riverside Lodge
Batopilas
US tel: 1-800 776 3942
Restored 19th-century hacienda in the heart of the Copper Canyon. **$$$-$$$$**

Monterrey

Colonial
Hidalgo 475 Oriente
Tel: 81-8380 6800
US tel: 1-877 663 9246

www.hotelcolonialmty.com
Six-level Downtown hotel across from Ancira. Reasonably priced but sometimes a bit noisy. **$$**
Gran Hotel Ancira
Ocampo 443 Oriente
Tel: 81-8345 1060
US tel: 1-800 833 3333
www.hotel-ancira.com
Monterrey's most famous landmark hotel: Pancho Villa stabled his horse in the lobby in 1913. Distinguished, five-story building with restaurants, bar, and pool. **$$$**
Quinta Real
Diego Rivera 500
Tel: 81-8368 1000
US tel: 1-800 457 4000
www.quintareal.com
A stunning property in the Garza García district. Restaurant, bar, spa. **$$$$**

Nuevo Laredo Saltillo

Camino Real
Blvd Los Fundadores 2000
Tel: 844-438 0000
US tel: 1-800 722 6466
www.caminoreal.com
Very good motor inn on top of knoll on Highway 57 southeast of town. Pool, restaurant, bar, tennis, and putting green. **$$-$$$**
Rancho El Morillo
Prolongación Obregón & Echeverría
Tel: 844-417 4078
www.elmorillo.com
Popular guest ranch 3km

México City

(2 miles) southwest of town. Beautifully landscaped grounds around old hacienda. **$**

Tampico

Camino Real
Hidalgo 2000
Tel: 833-229 3535
www.caminoreal.com/tampico
Set in a lush garden. Restaurants, bar, gym, pool. Access to tennis and golf. **$$$**
Posada del Rey
Madero 218 Oriente
Tel: 833-214 1024
Downtown hotel, the oldest in town, which has been renovated. It has 60 rooms with ceiling fans and air conditioning. No elevator. Inner rooms are quiet. **$**

PRICE CATEGORIES

Price categories are for a double room for one night in high season:
$ = under 500 pesos
$$ = 500-1,200 pesos
$$$ = 1,200-2,500 pesos
$$$$ = over 2,500 pesos

TRANSPORTATION — ACCOMMODATIONS — EATING OUT — ACTIVITIES — A - Z — LANGUAGE

THE NORTHWEST COAST

Alamos

Casa de los Tesoros
Alvaro Obregón 10
Tel: 647-428 0010
www.tesoros-hotel.com
Romantic, converted 18th-century convent with restaurant, bar, and pool. $$

Bahía Kino

Kino Bay
Tel: 662-242 0216
Six two-story units (with kitchenettes) at north end, combined with a nice RV park. Restaurant across the street. $
Posada Santa Gemma
Mar de Cortés and Rió de la Plata
Tel: 662-242 0026
A 14-unit air-conditioned motel: two-bedroom split-level units with bath, kitchen and fireplace. $$$

ABOVE: many resorts offer meditation and yoga lessons.

Bucerías

Royal Decameron
Lázaro Cárdenas 150
Tel: 329-298 0226
www.decameron.com
All-inclusive colonial-style beach front hotel. $$$

Guaymas/San Carlos

Playa de Cortés
Bacochibampo Bay
Tel: 622-221 1047
www.hotelesgandara.com.mx/playas.html
Famous hotel with restaurant, bar, pool, tennis, boat ramp. $$

Hermosillo

Kino
Pino Suárez Sur 151
Tel: 662-213 3131
www.hotelsuiteskino.com
Comfortable hotel with restaurant and pool. Rooms have refrigerator and TV. $

Los Mochis

Plaza Inn
Leyva and Cárdenas
Tel: 668-816 0809
US tel: 1-800 862 9026
www.plazainnhotel.com.mx
Modern and friendly air-conditioned hotel with restaurant, bar, pool, disco. $$–$$$

Mazatlán

Las Moras
Reservations: Avenida Camarón Sábalo 204–6
Tel: 669-916 5045, in Mazatlán
A former 19th-century tequila ranch at the foot of the Sierra Madre mountains, 48km (30 miles) inland from Mazatlán. No TVs, clocks, or phones. Rate includes all meals. Pool, tennis. $$$$
Playa Mazatlán
Av. Playa Gaviotas 202
Tel: 669-989 0555
US tel: 1-800 762 5816
www.hotelplayamazatlan.com
This beach front hotel is a Mazatlán institution. Restaurant, swimming pool, bar. $$–$$$
Pueblo Bonito
Camarón Sábalo 2121
Tel: 669-989 8900
US tel: 1-800 990 8250
www.pueblobonito.com
Beautiful beach front property with full amenities. The **Pueblo Bonito Emerald Bay** (tel: 669-989 0525) is located 15 minutes north of town on a secluded bay, and has recently opened a fantastic luxury spa. Guests of either Pueblo Bonito or Emerald Bay can use either location's facilities. $$$–$$$$

Nuevo Vallarta

Allegro Resort
Paseo de los Cocoteros 18
Tel: 322-226 9800
US tel: 1-800 858 2258
www.occidentalhotels.com
All-inclusive hotel on Banderas Bay. Non-stop activities plus restaurant, bar, tennis, kids' club, and land and water sports. $$$$
Paradise Village
Paseo de los Cocoteros 001
Tel: 322-226 6770
US tel: 1-800 995 5714
www.paradisevillage.com
Unusual self-contained holiday resort built in the style of a Mayan village but with pools, tennis, spa, golf course, and other leisure facilities. $$$$

Puerto Peñasco

Costa Brava
Malecón Kino & 1ero de Junio
Tel: 638-383 4100
Small, clean Downtown hotel. $$
Hotel Peñasco Del Sol
Paseo de las Glorias
Tel: 638-383 0302
US tel: 1-800 259 6976
Beautiful colorfully decorated, newly remodeled beach front hotel with a restaurant and pool. $$$

Punta Mita

Four Seasons
Carrera a la Cruz de Huanacaxtle-Punta Mita Km 11.5
Tel: 329-291 6000
US tel: 1-800 332 3442
www.fshr.com
Overlooks a rocky bluff and a sand beach; this luxurious beach front resort features signature Jack Nicklaus golf course. Outstanding amenities and service. $$$$

Rincón de Guayabitos

Royal Decameron Los Cocos
Retorno Las Palmas
Tel: 327-274 0190
www.decameron.com

All-inclusive resort on seafront. $$

San Blas

Garza Canela
Paredes Sur 106
Tel: 323-285 0112
www.garzacanela.com
The nicest place in town, with 50 air-conditioned rooms and swimming pool. $$$

San Carlos

Fiesta Real Hotel
Carr. San Carlos Km 8.5
Tel: 622-226 0229
www.fiestareal-hotel.com
Three-story air-conditioned motel in Mayan temple-style, on the beach, with pool. Breakfast included. $
Las Playitas
Carr. Varadero Nacional Km 6 by the naval base
Tel: 622-221 5696
Thirty air-conditioned cottages on Las Playitas peninsula in conjunction with RV facility of same name. Boat ramp. $
San Carlos Plaza
Mar Barmejo 4
Tel: 622-225 3000
US tel: 1-800 854 2320
www.sancarlosplaza.com.mx
This is as luxurious as San Carlos gets, complete with marble-floor atrium. $$$

San Francisco

Costa Azul Adventure Resort
50km (30 miles) north of Puerto Vallarta in San Francisco (known as San Panchito), Nayarit
Tel: 311-258 4210
www.costaazul.com
Ecologically friendly resort with water sports, biking, hiking, and horseback riding. $$$$

EL BAJÍO AND THE COLONIAL HEARTLAND

Aguascalientes

Fiesta Americana
Calle Laureles s/n
Tel: 449-910 0500
US tel: 1-800 FIESTA-1
www.fiestamericana.com
This well-equipped hotel has 192 air-conditioned rooms, a swimming pool, restaurant, gym, and obliging staff. **$$$**

Quinta Real
Av. Aguascalientes Sur 601
Tel: 449-978 5818
US tel: 1-866 621 9288
www.quintareal.com
Beautifully appointed suites, set around a pretty courtyard, restaurant, and swimming pool. **$$$**

Guanajuato

La Casa de Espíritus Alegres
Ex-Hacienda de la Trinidad 1, Marfil
Tel: 473-733 1013
www.casaspirit.com
An artist couple have converted an 18th-century mansion into this charming B&B. **$$–$$$**

Quinta Las Acacias
Paseo de la Presa 168
Tel: 473-731 1517
US tel: 1-888 497 4129
www.quintalasacacias.com.mx
A French-style mansion overlooking a park. The nine guest rooms are individually decorated with antiques. Gourmet breakfasts, coffee shop, outdoor jacuzzi, lovely gardens. **$$$$**

León

La Estancia
Blvd López Mateos 1311 Oriente
Tel: 477-716 3939
www.estancia.com.mx
A colonial-style hotel conveniently located near the convention center and Downtown. Pool, restaurants, bar, business center. **$$–$$$**

Querétaro

Fiesta Americana Hacienda Galindo
Carr. Amealco Km 5
Tel: 427-271 8200

www.fiestainn.com.mx
Sprawling yet attractive resort, with comfortable rooms and suites. There are also restaurants, pools, tennis and horses. **$$$**

La Casa de la Marquesa
Madero 41
Tel: 442-212 0092
www.lacasadelamarquesa.com
A unique luxury hotel housed in an 18th-century mansion. **$$$$**

Sol y Fiesta
H. Colegio Militar 4
Tequisquiapan
Tel: 414-273 1504
www.geocities.com/hotelsolyfiesta/hotel.htm
Small hotel with jacuzzi, pool, hot springs, and restaurant. **$$**

San Luis Potosí

Fiesta Inn San Luis Potosí Oriente
Carretera 57, Hotel Zone
Tel: 444-834 4900
www.fiestainn.com.mx
Comfortable rooms situated around a large central pool. **$$–$$$**

Holiday Inn
Carr. 57, near the Industrial Zone
Tel: 444-834 4100
US tel: 800 HOLIDAY
www.ichotelsgroup.com
Ten minutes from Downtown. Excellent facilities and services, lovely grounds, pool, tennis courts, gym. **$$–$$$**

María Cristina
Juan Sarabia 110
Tel: 444-812 9408
www.mariacristina.com.mx

BELOW: panoramic view of Guanajuato.

Close to the sights. Good value. **$**

San Miguel de Allende

Casa de Sierra Nevada
Hospicio 46
Tel: 415-152 7040
www.casadesierranevada.com
Perfect location and gracious, professional staff. The exquisitely furnished units are divided among several colonial mansions. Fine restaurant, pool, and spa. **$$$$**

Casa Quetzal
Hospicio 34
Tel: 415-152 0501
www.casaquetzalhotel.com
Stylish boutique hotel with just six suites, all different and ranging from calming simplicity to vibrant Mexican color schemes – so make sure you get the right one to suit your mood. **$$$$**

Casa Rosada
Hotel Quinta Loreto
Loreto 15
Tel: 415-152 0042
A good budget choice that is central but in a quiet spot with a relaxing garden and simple but spotlessly clean rooms. **$–$$**

La Puertecita
Santo Domingo 75
Tel: 415-152 5011
www.lapuertecita.com
Charming, small hilltop hotel, exquisitely furnished with wonderful views. Some 25 minutes from Downtown. 25 suites (two with jacuzzi). Pool, gardens, good

México City

restaurant, music room. **$$$–$$$$**

Rancho El Atascadero
Prolongación Santo Domingo
Tel: 415-152 0206
Former hacienda converted into 51 units, in extensive grounds about 2km (1 mile) east of town. Rooms have fireplaces. Tennis, pool, excellent restaurant. Popular with families. **$$–$$$**

Zacatecas

Hotel Emporio Zacatecas
Hidalgo 703
Tel: 492-925 6500
US tel: 1-866 936 7674
Situated on the main plaza, facing the cathedral, with Baroque style architecture and nice amenities. Restaurant, bar. **$$$**

Mesón de Jobito
Jardín Juárez 143
Tel: 492-924 1722
www.mesondejobito.com.mx
A beautifully renovated 19th-century building. Restaurant, bar, pool. **$$$**

Posada de la Moneda
Av. Hidalgo 413
Tel: 492-922 0881
Clean budget hotel, centrally located. No credit cards. **$**

Quinta Real
Rayón 434
Tel: 492-922 9104
www.quintareal.com
Stunning hotel built around the remnants of an old bullring. Restaurant, bar. **$$$$**

PRICE CATEGORIES

Price categories are for a double room for one night in high season:
$ = under 500 pesos
$$ = 500–1,200 pesos
$$$ = 1,200–2,500 pesos
$$$$ = over 2,500 pesos

JALISCO AND MICHOACÁN

Chapala

Lake Chapala Inn
Ramón Corona 23
Tel: 376-765 4786
Right on Lake Chapala is this intimate inn which has just four rooms, all of them large and three of them facing the lake. **$$**
La Nueva Posada
Donato Guerra 9, Ajijic
Tel: 376-766 1344
www.hotelnuevaposada-ajijic.com
With 19 spacious suites in a colonial-style inn overlooking the lake. Pool, excellent restaurant. Rate includes a hot breakfast. **$$$**

Costa Alegre

Las Alamandas
Carretera Melaque–Puerto Vallarta Km 83, Quemaro
Tel: 322-285 5500
US tel: 888-882 9616
www.alamandas.com
The ultimate in understated luxury. Just six exclusive villas tastefully decorated with Mexican art and crafts. Impeccable service. Facilities include restaurant, beach club, bar, pool, tennis, gym, horseback riding. **$$$$**
El Careyes
Carretera Puerto Vallarta–Barra de Navidad Km 53.5, Las Huertas
Tel: 315-351 0000
US tel: 1-888 433 3989
www.elcareyesresort.com
A stunning hotel situated on its own private bay. El Careyes has a health club, pool with jacuzzi, tennis, restaurant, bar, gourmet deli. Polo and horseback riding November to April. **$$$$**
The Tamarindo
Carretera Melaque–Puerto Vallarta Km 7.5, Cihuatlán
Tel: 315-351 5032
US tel: 1-866 717 4316
www.tamarindoresort.com
An exquisite luxury resort in a rustic beach front setting with 29 villas and an 18-hole golf course. Facilities include restaurant, bar, tennis. **$$$$**

Guadalajara

Casa Venezuela
Calle Venezuela 459
Tel: 333-826 6590
US tel: 832-519 1904
www.casavenezuela.com.mx
Only a 15-minute walk from the central plaza, the Casa Venezuela will quickly feel like home. It offers great breakfasts, cozy patios, beautiful decor, and friendly, gracious staff. Nahual the dog is the welcoming party. **$$$**
Crowne Plaza
López Mateos Sur 2500
Tel: 33-3634 1034
US tel: 1-800 365 5500
www.ichotelsgroup.com
Ample rooms, first-class amenities, beautiful grounds, and an excellent location. **$$$–$$$$**
Hotel Francés
Maestranza 35
Tel: 33-3613 1190
www.hotelfrances.com
Attractive colonial building in the center of the city. Restaurant, bar, and good atmosphere. **$**
Presidente Inter-Continental
López Mateos Sur and Moctezuma
Tel: 33-3678 1234
US tel: 1-800 327 0200
www.ichotelsgroup.com
A 14-story glass pyramid with atrium lobby and outstanding facilities. **$$$$**
Quinta Real
Av. México 2727
Tel: 33-3669 0600
US tel: 1-866 621 9288
www.quintareal.com
Intimate, well-located hotel with 76 luxurious suites. Excellent restaurant, pool. **$$$$**

Morelia

Hotel de la Soledad
Zaragoza 90
Tel: 443-312 1888
www.hsoledad.com
Spacious rooms surround the flower-filled courtyard of a beautifully restored colonial monastery. One block from the main plaza. Good restaurant. **$$$**

Villa Montaña
Patzimba 201
Tel: 443-314 0231
US tel: 1-800 223 6510
www.villamontana.com.mx
On a hill overlooking town, with 36 units, all individually decorated. Private patios, pool, outstanding view. **$$$$**
Virrey de Mendoza
Av. Madero Pte. 310
Tel: 443-312 0045
www.hotelvirrey.com
The first floor dates from the 16th century. Perfect location on the main square. Restaurant. **$$$**

Pátzcuaro

Hacienda Las Mariposas
Carretera Pátzcuaro-Sta Clara Km 3
Tel: 434-342 4728
US tel: 1-800 573 2386
www.haciendamariposas.com
Hacienda resort and spa set amidst 7 hectares (18 acres) of wooded meadows, run by archeology professor Rene Ocaña and his wife. Rate includes breakfast and some rooms include gratis horseback riding. Spanish immersion courses are available. **$$$–$$$$**
Los Escudos
Portal Hidalgo 73
Tel: 434-342 1290
The 16th-century home of the Count de la Loma is now a pleasant hotel with a restaurant, right on the main square. **$–$$**

Puerto Vallarta

La Jolla de Mismaloya
Zona Hotelera Sur Km 11.5
Tel: 322-228 0660
www.barcelo.com
This all-suite property on beautiful Mismaloya Bay consistently gets rave reviews. Numerous restaurants, bars, pools. Excellent water sports. All-inclusive plan optional. **$$$–$$$$**
Marriott Casa Magna
Paseo de la Marina 5, Marina Vallarta
Tel: 322-226 0000
US tel: 1-888 236 2427
www.casamagnapuertovallarta.com
Bayfront property with 433

rooms and suites, excellent restaurants, and fine service. Pool, tennis, gym, children's activities. **$$$$**
Quinta María Cortéz
Calle Sagitaro 126
Tel: 322-221 5317
US tel: 1-888 640 8100
www.quinta-maria.com
Eccentric accommodations cluttered with antiques, interesting junk, and paintings. Great baths, no TVs, pool. Rate includes breakfast. **$$$**
Velas Vallarta/Casa Velas
Av. Costera
Tel: 322-226 9500
US tel: 866-847 4609
www.velasvallarta.com
Very classy hotel and nearby boutique "casa" which offer luxury, relaxation, excellent service, and fine food. Velas Vallarta is right on the beach; the more intimate Casa Velas is tucked around the corner. **$$$$**
Verana
Boca de Tomatlan, Yelapa
Tel: 322-222 2360
US tel: 1-800 530 7176
www.verana.com
At Boca de Tomatlan, the last beach you can reach by car, it is a 30-minute boat ride to Yelapa. A mule ride can be arranged to take you to this exquisite hillside hotel which has an infinity pool, a spa, and an excellent restaurant. Fashionable decor and a jungle setting complete the picture. **$$$$**

PRICE CATEGORIES

Price categories are for a double room for one night in high season:
$ = under 500 pesos
$$ = 500–1,200 pesos
$$$ = 1,200–2,500 pesos
$$$$ = over 2,500 pesos

ACAPULCO AND THE PACIFIC BEACHES

Acapulco

Las Brisas
Carretera Escénica 5255
Tel: 744-469 6900
US tel: 1-866 427 2779
www.brisas.com.mx
Secluded *casitas* (cottages) set on a hillside with individual or shared pools. Superb service. Restaurants, tennis, beach club. **$$$$**

Boca Chica
Punta Caletilla
Tel: 744-483 6741
US tel: 1-800 337 4685
UK tel: 0800-3746 8357
A small hotel on a private swimming cove, with pool, restaurant, and beach club. Rate includes breakfast and dinner. **$$$**

Elcano
Av. del Parque y Las Palmas
Tel: 744-435 1500
US tel: 1-800 917 4901
www.hotel-elcano.com
Across from the municipal golf course, this high-rise hotel has cool white modern bedrooms, all with ocean view, air conditioning and cable TV. Pool and beach. **$$$**

The Fairmont Acapulco Princess
Playa Revolcadero
Acapulco Diamante
Tel: 744-469 1000
US tel: 1-800 441 1414
www.fairmont.com/acapulco
The largest hotel in Acapulco, with two 18-hole golf courses, seven tennis courts, and five pools. Rate includes breakfast and dinner. **$$$$**

ABOVE: having fun in a wave machine pool, Acapulco.

Los Flamingos
Av. López Mateos
Tel: 744-482 0690
www.hotellosflamingos.com
Almost a historical landmark – the favored hang-out of the "Hollywood gang" in the 1950s. Stunning views, restaurant, and pool. **$$**

Mayan Palace Acapulco
Av. Costera de las Palmas 1121
Acapulco 39000
Tel: 744-469 6002
US tel: 1-800 292 9446
www.grupomayan.com
Stunning Maya-style architecture including thatched roofs and glass pavilions. Large complex with 18-hole golf course, 12 tennis courts, and canals connecting facilities. **$$$**

Misión
Calle Felipe Valle 12
Tel: 744-482 3643
A charming budget hotel, Downtown. No air conditioning, but ceiling fans and plenty of hot water. No credit cards. **$$**

Quinta Real
Paseo de la Quinta 6
Tel: 744-469 1500
US tel: 1-800 457 4000
www.quintareal.com
Spectacular luxury all-suite hotel and spa, overlooking its own secluded beach. Fine restaurant. Exceptional service. **$$$$**

Ixtapa/Zihuatanejo

Barceló Ixtapa Beach
Blvd Ixtapa s/n, Ixtapa
Tel: 755-555 2000
US tel: 1-800 227 2356
www.barcelo.com
Soaring lobby atrium with glass elevators. Close to Ixtapa golf course. **$$$$**

Las Brisas Ixtapa
Playa Vista Hermosa, Ixtapa
Tel: 755-553 2121
US tel: 888-559 4329
www.brisas.com.mx
Private rooms and suites cascade down a hillside to a private beach. Excellent resort amenities. **$$$$**

La Casa Que Canta
Camino Escénico Playa la Ropa, Zihuatanejo
Tel: 755-555 7000
US tel: 1-888 523 5050
www.lacasaquecanta.com
Luxurious, low-key, intimate tropical retreat. Exquisite decor, exceptional service, fine restaurant. **$$$$**

Emporio Ixtapa
Ixtapa Blvd s/n
Tel: 755-553 1066
US tel: 1-866 936 7674
www.hotelesemporio.com
A large hotel with several restaurants, pools, and beach front

México City

looking out on the bay. **$$$**

Villa del Sol
Playa La Ropa
Tel: 755-555 5500
www.tideszihuatanejo.com
Totally remodeled, high-end rooms with private terraces, Wi-fi, yoga, and tasteful Mexican decor. **$$$$**

Manzanillo

Barceló Karmina Palace Hotel
Av. Vista Hermosa No 13
Tel: 314-334 1300
US tel: 1-888 234 6222
www.karminapalace.com
Deluxe all-inclusive resort on the beach. Spa, gym, 10 tennis courts, access to golf, pools, excellent restaurants, child care. **$$$$**

Las Hadas Manzanillo Golf Resort and Marina
Avenida de los Riscos & Vista Hermosa
Tel: 314-331 0101
US tel: 1-866 221 2961
www.brisas.com.mx
Gorgeous location next to the beach. The building is fantastical and resembles a giant wedding cake overlooking the sea. Restaurants, pools, tennis, golf. **$$$$**

THE GULF COAST

Acayucán

Hotel Kinaku
Ocampo Sur 7
Tel: 924-245 0410
www.hotelkinaku.com
Well located for anyone interested in the Olmec ruins of San Lorenzo and Tres Zapotes or driving through to the Yucatán, this modern hotel has comfortable rooms,

a pool and a relaxing restaurant. Service is friendly too, and it is a handy stop-off in an area without many hotels. **$$**

Catemaco

La Finca
Carretera 180 Km 147
Tel: 294-947 9700
www.lafinca.com.mx
A big, modern, family-

oriented resort hotel on the lake shore, with a large pool and beautiful views, especially at sunrise and sunset. There's also a simple spa. **$$$**

Coatepec

Posada Coatepec
Hidalgo 9
Tel: 228-816 0544
www.posadacoatepec.com.mx

México City

The rooms at this former colonial hacienda are

TRANSPORTATION ACCOMMODATIONS EATING OUT ACTIVITIES A – Z LANGUAGE

positively baronial, with giant roof beams, and around the lounges and restaurant there are antiques and traditional ceramics. The gardens and pool are relaxing, and it makes a very agreeable base for exploring Veracruz state. Superb local coffee is a specialty. **$$$**

Papantla

Hotel Tajín
José Núñez y Domínguez 104
Tel: 784-842 0121
www.hoteltajin.com.mx
There are no special traditional features here, but a large pool in a patio is one thing that makes this big hotel a pleasant base for visiting Papantla and El Tajín. Rooms are plain but comfortable, and there's a pretty restaurant. **$$**

Tlacotalpan

Casa del Río
Miguel Z. Cházaro 39
Tel: 288-884 2947
www.tlaco.com.mx/casadelrio
The location of this mellow little nine-room hotel immediately gives any visitor a sense of calm – right by the slow-moving Plapaloapan river, with a riverside terrace café. The restored 19th-century building has plenty of Tlacotalpan's celebrated charm, and birdwatching trips, demonstrations of local crafts and bicycle rental are all available. **$$**

Hostal El Patio
Puerto de Alvarado 52
Tel: 288-884 3197
www.hostalelpatio.com.mx
Bright traditional colors make the six rooms at this small hotel especially attractive, while the beds have giant traditional wooden headboards. It also has Wi-fi and plenty of other modern extras, and great fresh breakfasts are included – so it is excellent value. **$$**

Tlapacoyan

Filobobos Camp
Tlapacoyan
Tel: 225-315 1784
www.filoboboscamp.com.mx
The most popular and best-equipped rafting and adventure sports center on the Río Filobobos, with accommodations in simple cabins with good shared bathrooms, camping space, a restaurant and a pool for relaxing after a day on the river. Many other activities are offered including hikes, ruins visits, and rafting, and cabins are usually taken as part of good-value packages, with activities included. **$$–$$$**

Veracruz

Gran Hotel Diligencias
Independencia 1115
Tel: 229-932 0280
www.granhoteldiligencias.com
Guests get an instant taste of the life of Veracruz at this historic hotel right on the city's Zócalo. Recently comprehensively updated,

with full modern services. Despite the bustle outside, the hotel is quiet inside and has a terrace pool. **$$$**
Hotel Mocambo
Calzada A. Ruiz Cortines 4000,
Boca del Río
Tel: 229-922 0200
www.hotelmocambo.com.mx
A fixture on Mocambo Beach near Boca del Río, 10km (6 miles) south of the city, this giant resort hotel is very popular with local families. A beautiful pool surrounded by a mock-colonial colonnade is one of its best-appreciated features. **$$$**

Xalapa (Jalapa)

BG Hotel
Avila Camacho 60
Tel: 228-817 3433
www.hotelesenxalapa.com/bg
An unusual modern hotel in the center of Xalapa that aspires to a chic "style hotel" look, but at low prices,

BELOW: dancing in the Zócalo, Veracruz.

making it a great bargain. Rooms are spacious and comfortable, and there's a café-restaurant specializing in crêpes. **$$**
Mesón del Alférez Xalapa
Sebastián Camacho 2
Tel: 228-818 0113
www.pradodelrio.com
One of Xalapa's historic houses, the residence of one of the town's last Spanish colonial officials, is now a pretty and tranquil small hotel, with a lovely patio. Delicious traditional local breakfasts are included. The same owners also have another hotel nearby, also pretty but slightly simpler and so cheaper: the Posada del Cafetó (Cánovas 8, tel: 228-817 0023, same website). **$$**

Xilitla

El Castillo
Ocampo 105, Xilitla, San Luis Potosí
Tel: 489-365 0038
www.junglegossip.com/castillo.html
The rambling house built by Plutarco Gastelum, the general assistant and helper of Edward James (see page 267), is as eccentric as the two men themselves, combining Mexican, English, Spanish and Moorish styles and all sorts of quirky features. Each of the eight rooms is different (and differently sized), but have recently been modernized without losing their unique appeal. A fascinating and memorable place to stay. **$$–$$$**

OAXACA

Huatulco

Barceló Huatulco Beach
Paseo Benito Juárez
Tel: 958-581 0055
www.barcelo.com
All-inclusive beach front resort with an extensive range of amenities. **$$$$**
Camino Real Zaashila Huatulco
Blvd Benito Juárez 5,

Tangolunda Bay
Tel: 958-583 0300
US tel: 1-800 722 6466
www.caminoreal.com
A spectacular resort with all amenities. **$$$$**
Casa del Mar
Balcones de Tangolunda 13
Tel: 958-581 0203
US tel: 1-800 537 8483
Beautiful suites set on a cliff. Steps lead to the beach. **$$$**

Quinta Real
Paseo Benito Juárez 2
Tel: 958-581 0428
US tel: 866-621 9288
www.quintareal.com
Hilltop tropical resort featuring spectacular views, luxurious suites, fine restaurant, beach club, tennis. **$$$$**
Villablanca
Blvd Benito Juárez and Zapoteco
Tel: 958-587 0606
www.hotelesvillablanca.com

Colonial-style hotel with a restaurant, bar, and pool. **$$**

Oaxaca

Camino Real Oaxaca
5 de Mayo 300, north of Zócalo
Tel: 951-501 6100
US tel: 1-800 722 6466
www.camino-real-oaxaca.com
A former 16th-century convent with cloisters and courtyard. The Camino Real is now a national monument. $$$$

Casa Oaxaca
García Vigil 407
Tel: 951-514 4173
www.casaoaxaca.com
This 18th-century home has been converted into an exclusive inn. Conveniently located within walking distance of the main plaza, it features tastefully decorated rooms, excellent service, pool, *temazcal* (pre-Hispanic sauna), fireplace, patio, cocktail hour, and breakfast service. $$–$$$

Hacienda Los Laureles
Hidalgo 21, San Felipe del Agua

Tel: 951-501 5300
www.hotelhaciendaloslaureles.com
Very attractive colonial-style hotel, with excellent breakfasts and a lush inner courtyard replete with hummingbirds and bougainvillea. $$$

Hacienda de la Noria
Avenida Eduardo Mata 1918
Tel: 951-514 7555
www.lanoria.com
Well-run hotel, about a 15-minute walk from the main square, with a restaurant and pool. $$$–$$$$

Hostal de la Noria
Hidalgo 918
Tel: 951-501 5400
www.hostaldelanoria.com
The more centrally located establishment under the same ownership as the Hacienda de la Noria. Hostal de la Noria is located just one block from the main square in a colonial building, with a good restaurant. $$–$$$

ABOVE: idyllic sunset viewed from Playa Zicatela.

Puerto Escondido

Aldea del Bazar
Avenida Benito Juárez 7
Tel: 954-582 0508
US tel: 1-800 325 2525
www.aldeadelbazar.com
Set on a bluff over Bacocho Beach, the Aldea del Bazar has rooms in a pre-Hispanic style, with eucalyptus sauna

and massages, Moorish-style restaurant, bar, and pool. $$–$$$

Arco Iris
Calle del Morro
Tel: 954-582 1494
www.oaxaca-mio.com/arcoiris.htm
Simple clean rooms, some with kitchenettes. Pool, restaurant. $$

Best Western Posada Real
Blvd Benito Juárez
Tel: 954-582 0133
US tel: 1-800 528 1234
www.posadareal.com.mx
Perched on a hill at the edge of the sea. Comfortable rooms, restaurants, bars. Beach club with pool, restaurant, bar. $$$

Santa Fe
Calle del Morro
Tel: 954-582 0170
US tel: 1-888 649 6407
www.hotelsantafe.com.mx
A delightful hotel on Zicatela beach. Excellent restaurant with seafood and vegetarian specialties. $$$

TABASCO AND CHIAPAS

Chiapa de Corzo

Hotel La Ceiba
Domingo Ruíz 300
Tel: 961-616 0389
www.laceibahotel.com
A delightful hotel in a big, colonial-style house, with pretty rooms – some with much more light than others – around a pool in a tree-filled patio. The big restaurant is known for its local specialties, and is very popular. $$

Lacanjá/Bonampak

Campamento Río Lacanjá
Lacanjá village
Tel: via Explora Agency, San Cristobal, 967-674 6660
www.ecochiapas.com/lacanja
The most comfortable and best-run of the Campamentos set up by the Lacandón Maya in Lacanjá, in the forest near Bonampak. There are cabins sharing good-standard showers, and slightly more expensive ones (called Ya'axcan) with

their own. The owners provide simple meals and give advice on local tours, and it is in a gorgeous setting by the Lacanjá River, where you can swim in a forest pool. $–$$

Palenque

Camping Maya Bell
Carretera Palenque
Zona Arqueológica Km 6
Tel: 916-348 4271
www.mayabell.com.mx
This long-running operation has developed considerably, and there's now a choice of comfortable cabins with showers and others sharing facilities, as well as camping and RV space. There's also a pool and a vegetarian restaurant, and it is within walking distance of Palenque ruins. Depending on the humidity, there can be a lot of bugs around. $–$$

Chan-Kah Village
Carretera de las Ruinas Km 3
Tel: 916-345 1134
www.chan-kah.com.mx
One of the most enjoyable

places to stay at Palenque, beside the road to the ruins, with rooms in bungalows spread around a wonderfully lush, bird-filled tropical forest-garden. They are a little old, but it has plenty of attractions to make up for this, especially a fabulous pool that's a delight after few hours climbing pyramids, and overlooked by a charming terrace restaurant. $$$

Hotel Chan-Kah Centro
Juárez 2, on the main square
Tel: 916-345 0318
www.chan-kah.com.mx
The owners of the Chan-Kah village *(see above)* also have a likeable hotel in the middle of Palenque town. Rooms are again a little elderly, but staff are friendly, prices are low, and from the restaurant and the best rooms you can watch whatever is happening in the town plaza. $$

Hotel Maya Tulipanes
La Cañada 6
Tel: 916-345 0201
www.mayatulipanes.com.mx

A very popular hotel in the tranquil La Cañada area, on the west side of Palenque town. The rooms don't have much character, but they are comfortable, with efficient air conditioning, and as well as a garden pool there are excellent replicas around the entrance of the Tomb of Pakal and other carvings from the Palenque ruins. $$

PRICE CATEGORIES

Price categories are for a double room for one night in high season:
$ = under 500 pesos
$$ = 500–1,200 pesos
$$$ = 1,200–2,500 pesos
$$$$ = over 2,500 pesos

TRANSPORTATION

ACCOMMODATIONS

EATING OUT

ACTIVITIES

A – Z

LANGUAGE

San Cristóbal de las Casas

Casa Felipe Flores
Dr Felipe Flores 36
Tel: 967-678 3996
www.felipeflores.com
A beautiful 18th-century house that has been very carefully restored by its American owners to become a quite sumptuous B&B, with antiques and individual fittings throughout. Guests are given every assistance to make the most of their stay, and it is a real home from home, as well as being another of Chiapas' amazing bargains. **$$$**

Casa Mexicana
8a Av. Sur No. 19
Tel: 967-678 0698
www.hotelcasamexicana.com
One of San Cristóbal's most characteristic mansions, with a magnificently lush patio, has been imaginatively renovated as a hotel filled with artworks, subtle colors and traditional Chiapas textiles and other crafts. As in many such old houses rooms don't have much natural light, but they're very appealing. **$$$**

Hotel Posada El Paraíso
5 de Febrero 19
Tel: 967-678 0085
A stylish conversion of an old patio house, incorporating a little modern design as well as bright traditional textiles, and with

ABOVE: Hacienda Puerta Campeche

an excellent restaurant, El Edén. As is common in San Cristóbal hotels, rooms are of a standard that would cost a lot more in most other towns. **$$**

Tapachula

Casa Mexicana
8 Sur No. 19
Tel: 962-626 6605
www.casamexicanachiapas.com
A remarkable place to find in hot, busy, Tapachula, this snug hotel really is run in boutique style, with individual attention to detail. Rooms are beautifully and imaginatively decorated using traditional craftwork, there's a tiny pool, and the Tapachtlan restaurant provides astonishingly refined cuisine. **$$**

Finca Hamburgo
Carretera por Zaragoza
Tel: 962-625 1812
www.fincahamburgo.com
One of the coffee estates founded in the 1880s high in the mountains behind Tapachula is now a true Shangri-La of a luxury retreat, with snug guest cabins with balconies and jaw-dropping views over the Soconusco and the Pacific Ocean, 1,250 meters (4,100ft) below. Hikes and activities are available, and the restaurant is excellent. Booking is essential, as the Finca must collect guests at the nearest highway and take them to the estate. **$$$**

Tuxtla Gutiérrez

Hotel María Eugenia
Central Oriente 507
Tel: 961-613 3767
www.mariaeugenia.com.mx
Hotels in Tuxtla Gutiérrez tend to be functional, but this is the most attractive in the center, with large, bright rooms with good modern facilities, a comfortable restaurant and – rare in central Tuxtla – a pool. **$$$**

Villahermosa

Best Western Hotel Madan
Madero 408
Tel: 993-312 1650
www.madan.com.mx

Low rates make this a decent mid-range choice in the Zona Luz, Villahermosa's bustling center. Some rooms are dark, others can be noisy, but they're comfortable, and the restaurant is an enjoyable local meeting point. **$$**

Hyatt Regency Villahermosa
Av. Juárez 106,
by Paseo Tabasco
Tel: 993-310 1234
http://villahermosa.regency.hyatt.com
Villahermosa's most luxurious hotel doesn't offer any local character but naturally has all the comforts and facilities associated with the Hyatt brand, plus a pretty garden pool and a choice between a Mexican restaurant and a more international lobby bar. **$$$**

Quality Inn Villahermosa Cencali
Av. Juárez 105,
by Paseo Tabasco
Tel: 993-313 6611
www.qualityinnvillahermosa.com
One of the more individual of Villahermosa's big hotels on Paseo Tabasco – and so within walking distance of Parque-Museo La Venta – with a particularly lush garden around the pool and a striking Maya-themed mural in the lobby. The restaurant has some interesting Tabascan specialities. **$$$**

THE YUCATÁN

Akumal

Villas de Rosa
Aventuras Akumal
Tel: 984-875 9020
US tel: 1-866 619 9050
www.cenotes.com
Distinctive hotel on one of Akumal's finest beaches, with spacious condos, a pool and rooftop bar. Diving is a specialty. **$$–$$$**

Bacalar

Villas Ecotucán
Highway 307, 5km (3 miles) north of Bacalar town
Tel: 983-834 2516

www.villasecotucan.info
A very pleasant little "ecohotel" on the shores of Laguna Bacalar, with pretty low-impact, palm-roofed cabins around a natural botanical garden that's great for walks. At other times you can take kayaks out on the lake, and there's a pleasant restaurant. **$$**

Campeche

Best Western Hotel del Mar
Av. Ruíz Cortines 51
Tel: 981-811 9191
www.bestwestern.com

One of two big 1970s hotels that dominate Campeche's seafront, the Del Mar's great selling point is the panoramic sea views from its best rooms (those facing the town are far less attractive). There's also a nice pool and bright restaurant, and large, modern rooms. **$$–$$$**

Hacienda Puerta Campeche
Calle 59 No. 71, between calles 16 and 18
Tel: 981-816 7508
www.thehaciendas.com
The same group that has restored several haciendas

around the Yucatán as luxury hotels has also converted this gracious town house in Campeche's old city in similar style. With just 15 rooms, it has a very intimate feel, and the company's characteristic

flair can be seen in the restaurant and pool. **$$$$**
Hotel Francis Drake
Calle 12 No. 207, corner Calle 65
Tel: 981-811 5626
www.hotelfrancisdrake.com
Comfortable rooms with good modern facilities and pleasant staff have made this old-town hotel one of Campeche's most popular. The main square and other attractions are just a short stroll away. **$$**

Cancún

Ambiance Villas Kin-Ha
Blvd Kukulcán Km 8.5
Tel: 998-891 5427
US tel: 1-866 340 9082

ABOVE: many resorts crowd right on to the beach.

www.kinhabeach.com
An attractive family-oriented complex with suites in three-story villas around a garden and a pool, facing the beach on the north side of the Hotel Zone. Prices are very reasonable. **$$**
Fiesta Americana Grand Coral Beach
Blvd Kukulcán Km 9.5
Tel: 998-881 3200
US tel: 1-800 343 7821
www.fiestaamericana.com
A candidate to be the grandest of all the eye-popping luxury hotels in Cancún's Hotel Zone, with an unrivalled location at Punta Cancún, every imaginable luxury facility, excellent restaurants and a stunning pool winding through a garden. **$$$$**
Hotel Alux
Av. Uxmal 21

Tel: 998-884 0556
www.hotelalux.com
Bargain rates and a location right next to the bus station have made the Alux a big favorite with travelers who only pass through Cancún. Despite the prices, rooms are comfortable, with air conditioning, TVs and other extras: book well ahead. **$**
Hotel Antillano
Av. Tulum, corner of Calle Claveles
Tel: 998-884 1532
www.hotelantillano.com
A long-running, reliable mid-range hotel in the middle of Ciudad Cancún, well placed for the bus station and other services. Rooms are plain but bright, well-equipped and comfortable, and there's a small pool. **$$**
Hotel El Rey del Caribe
Av. Uxmal 24, corner of Av. Nader
Tel: 998-884 2028
www.reycaribe.com
Ciudad Cancún hotels don't generally have much character, but this one stands out a little with its pleasant rooms around a leafy patio with a pool. A location a block away from Avenida Tulum makes it quieter than many, and rates are generous. **$$**

Celestún

Eco Paraíso Xixim
Camino Viejo a Sisal Km 10
Tel: 988-916 2100.
www.ecoparaiso.com
A wonderfully secluded "ecoretreat", with 15 palm-roofed but luxurious *cabañas* (cabins) on a huge beach facing the Gulf, with fabulous sunsets, at the end of a track through the dunes 10km (6 miles) north of Celestún. Guests can choose from an individual range of birdwatching and other tours. **$$$$**

Chetumal

Holiday Inn Chetumal Puerta Maya
Avenida Héroes 171-A
Tel: 983-835 0400
US tel: 1-800 HOLIDAY
www.ichotelsgroup.com
There are no special features at Chetumal's

biggest hotel, but all the comforts and modern facilities to be expected from a Holiday Inn, at unusually low rates. The buffet breakfast sets you up for the whole day. **$$**

Chichén Itzá

Hacienda Chichén
Eastern entrance to the ruins, off Highway 180
Tel: 999-925 3952
www.haciendachichen.com
The most charming hotel at Chichén Itzá, in the old hacienda that was used as a base by archeologists excavating the site in the 1920s. Recently, it has been imaginatively renovated to recapture some of its hacienda elegance while implementing sustainable ecological practices, and there's now a seductive holistic spa as well as a delightful garden pool. **$$$**
Hotel Dolores Alba
Highway 180 Libre Km 122
Tel: 985-858 1555
www.doloresalba.com
Off the highway 3km (2 miles) east of the ruins, near Balankanché caves, this is the best of the lower-cost hotels around Chichén, with pretty rooms with good air conditioning, a garden, pleasant restaurant and two pools. Free transportation is provided to the ruins. The owners also have a hotel of the same name in Mérida. **$–$$**
Hotel Mayaland
Eastern entrance to the ruins, off Highway 180
Tel: 01-800 235 4079
www.mayaland.com
Largest of the upscale hotels just outside the Chichén Itzá site, with traditional opulence rather than individual charm. However, the ample facilities include a giant pool, and the best rooms have a great view of the ruins. **$$$**
Villas Arqueológicas Chichén Itzá
Eastern entrance to the ruins, off Highway 180
Tel: 985-856 6000

www.villasarqueologicas.com.mx
One of the most popular branches of the Villas Arqueológicas (also found at Teotihuacán and other Maya sites) an easy walk from the ruins and with delightful, airy rooms, and a garden restaurant beside the pool. Generous prices make it outstanding value. **$$**

Cobá

Villas Arqueológicas Cobá
Cobá village
Tel: 984-206 7001
www.villasarqueologicas.com.mx
Cobá is another archeological site that has a Villas Arqueológicas right outside to provide instant relaxation after a steamy jungle walk. As at the group's other hotels, there are pretty rooms, a lovely garden with a terrace restaurant and fine pool, and very friendly prices. **$$**

Costa Maya

Balamkú Inn on the Beach
Carretera Mahahual–Xcalak Km 5.7
Tel: 983-839 5332
www.balamku.com
This lovely small hotel meets the highest ecological low-impact standards, using solar and wind power. The nine rooms are in palm-roofed cabins right on the beach, and it is ideally relaxing. Guests have free use of kayaks, as well as fine fresh breakfasts. **$$**
Casa Carolina
Beach road, 4km (2½ miles) north of Xcalak
Tel: 983-831 0444
www.casacarolina.net
Four large, pretty rooms, all with small kitchens, right on a beautiful placid beach. Owners Bob and Caroline are very welcoming, and high-standard diving, diving

PRICE CATEGORIES

Price categories are for a double room for one night in high season:
$ = under 500 pesos
$$ = 500–1,200 pesos
$$$ = 1,200–2,500 pesos
$$$$ = over 2,500 pesos

instruction and snorkeling are available, including trips to Banco Chinchorro. **$$**

Sin Duda
Beach road, 11km (7 miles) north of Xcalak
Tel: 983-831 0444
www.sindudavillas.com
A remarkable guesthouse created by architect Robert Schneider and Margo Vorheis. The house and delightful rooms combine Mexican style ecological principles and inventive design and are full of surprises – and it is right on an idyllic beach far from any crowds. **$$–$$$**

Cozumel

Casa del Mar Cozumel
Carretera a Chankanaab Km 4
Tel: 987-872 1900
www.casadelmarcozumel.com
One of Cozumel's best-value family resort hotels, south of San Miguel, and with 98 attractively decorated rooms facing the beach. There is a very pleasant restaurant beneath a *palapa* roof, and an excellent on-site dive and snorkel shop. **$$$**

Casa Mexicana Cozumel
Avenida Melgar 457, between calles 5 and 7, San Miguel
Tel: 987-872 9090
www.casamexicana.com
An architecturally striking modern hotel on the San Miguel Malecón, with great views from its best rooms. Despite being in a busy part of town it is peaceful inside, with an attractive terrace pool. **$$$**

Hotel Flamingo
Calle 6 Norte, off Av. Melgar, San Miguel
Tel: 987-872 1264
www.hotelflamingo.com
Combining stylish modern decor and a laid-back feel, this imaginatively run hotel stands out in San Miguel. The Aqua bar-restaurant is lively, and there are good-value dive and fishing packages. **$$–$$$**

Tamarindo Bed & Breakfast
Calle 4 Norte 421, between Av. 20 and 25, San Miguel
Tel: 987-872 6190

ABOVE: a close encounter in the Yucatán.

www.tamarindocozumel.com
A delightfully tranquil guesthouse a few blocks from central San Miguel, with very pretty rooms around a garden, where generous breakfasts are served. Two large suites have their own small kitchens. **$$**

Isla Mujeres

Cabañas María del Mar
Av. Carlos Lazo 1
Tel: 998-877 0179
www.cabanasdelmar.com
A long-standing, popular hotel on Playa Norte, Isla town's main beach. The nicest rooms are in *cabañas* by a pool right behind the beach; "tower" and "castle" rooms are more conventional, but have good views, and hammocks. **$$$**

Hotel Secreto
Playa Secreto
Tel: 998-877 0390
www.hotelsecreto.com
Isla's award-winning boutique hotel, with nine very chic, minimalist rooms overlooking a gorgeous pool and with an equally stylish spa. It is on Playa Secreto, a tranquil cove just beside Isla town. **$$$**

Hotel Villa Kiin
Calle Zazil-Ha 118
Tel: 998-877 0045
www.villakiin.com
An individual hotel with colorful rooms in a main building, or bungalow-style *cabañas*, on Secreto beach. Rooms are in many different

sizes, so prices vary too; low-season rates are a real bargain. **$$–$$$**

Izamal

Macan Ché
Calle 22 No. 305, x 33 & 35
Tel: 988-954 0287
www.macanche.com
Waking up at this lovely B&B-hotel it is hard to believe you're in a town, but that's typical of Izamal's tranquility. Rooms are in individually decorated cottages around a garden, with a little rock pool for cooling off. The American owners are extra-hospitable. **$$**

Mérida

Cascadas de Mérida
Calle 57 No. 593C, x 74A & 76
Tel: 999-923 8484
www.cascadasdemerida.com
This very individual bed and breakfast is in an entirely new house built by owners Jesús and Ellyne Basto, with four ideally comfortable rooms, each at a corner of the pool. Abundant, convivial breakfasts sum up the generosity of the operation. **$$**

Hacienda Xcanatún
Calle 20, Xcanatún
Tel: 999-930 2410
www.xcanatun.com
A gracious 18th-century estate in the village of Xcanatún, just north of Mérida off the Progreso road, with 18 luxurious suites, with jacuzzis, around luxuriant gardens with two pools. The Casa de Piedra restaurant is one of the Yucatán's best. **$$$$**

Hotel Marionetas
Calle 49 No. 516, x 62 & 64
Tel: 999-928 3377
www.hotelmarionetas.com
A very attractive small hotel in a classic old Mérida town house, with patio enclosing a neat pool, that has been imaginatively renovated with subtle colors and traditional fittings. Delicious breakfasts are served by the pool, and the owners run it with individual verve. **$$$**

Hotel MedioMundo
Calle 55 No. 533, x 64 & 66

Tel: 999-924 5472
www.hotelmediomundo.com
One of the prettiest of the small hotels that make the most of Mérida's traditional architecture, with 12 delightful rooms around tropical-blue patios that catch the light wonderfully. At the back is the essential patio-pool, where fresh-fruit breakfasts are served. **$$**

Nómadas
Calle 62 No. 433, x 51
Tel: 990-924 5223
www.nomadastravel.com
The most attractive and reliable of Mérida's budget hostels, with helpful staff, free Internet, an agency offering low-cost tours, a pretty patio – and even a pool. It's well-kept, and there's a choice of dorms or private rooms with or without bathrooms. **$**

Playa del Carmen

Casa Tucán
Calle 4, between Av. 5 and 10
Tel: 984-873 0283
www.casatucan.de
One of Playa's best low-cost options, with colorful, comfortable rooms, and a lush garden with a good-sized pool. Next door is one of the best local dive shops, and joint packages are available. **$**

Deseo
Av. 5, corner of Calle 12
Tel: 984-879 3620
www.hoteldeseo.com
The most chic hotel in Playa del Carmen, part of the same group as the renowned Mexico City design hotel Habita. They also have another Playa Hotel, Basico (www.hotelbasico.com). Both are very trendy, but not recommended for a quiet stay. **$$$–$$$$**

Hotel Cielo
Calle 4, between Av. 5 and 10
Tel: 984-873 1227
www.hotelcielo.com
A friendly, excellent value small hotel with 18 pretty rooms with an imaginative blend of Mexican colors and materials. Breakfast is included, and there's both a ground-floor restaurant and a top-floor bar. **$$**

Playa Palms
Av. 1, between calles 12 and 14
Tel: 984-803 3966
www.playapalms.com
This suite hotel is on the beach just up the street from some of Playa's most buzzing nightclubs, but inside it is nicely quiet. The studios and suites have small kitchens, and share great beach views. $$$

Shangri-La Caribe
Calle 38 Norte
Tel: 984-803 2804
www.shangrilacaribe.net
Some of the Yucatán's most seductive beach *cabañas* can be found at this lovely resort hotel at the north end of Playa beach, combining palm roofs and charming Mexican design with luxury fittings. There's also a lovely pool, and excellent dive shop. $$$$

Puerto Morelos and Punta Bete

Maroma Resort & Spa
Highway 307 Km 305, at Punta Bete
Tel: 998-872 8200
www.maromahotel.com
One of the most luxurious and secluded retreats on the Riviera, with 80 hectares (197 acres) of forest and a magnificent beach to itself. There are three fine restaurants, and the indulgent spa treatments are a specialty. $$$$

Maya Koba
Highway 307 Km 298
Tel: 984-206 3000
www.mayakoba.com
The Riviera's most ambitious, sophisticated development, with four different luxury resorts in different styles around a huge property landscaped with careful attention to local ecology, and a PGA-standard golf course. $$$$

Rancho Sak-Ol
By the beach at the south end of town, Puerto Morelos
Tel: 998-871 0181
www.ranchosakol.com
A very relaxing hotel on the beach in mellow Puerto Morelos, with simple

---

cabaña-style rooms, some with great views. Breakfast is included, and there's an open kitchen, Wi-fi, and free use of bikes and snorkels. $$-$$$

Río Bec

Río Bec Dreams
Highway 186 Km 142, near Chicanná ruins
No phone
www.riobecdreams.com
The best and most welcoming accommodations in the Río Bec area are to be found at this jungle clearing off Highway 186, with a choice of attractive cabins with bathrooms or shared facilities. Canadians Rick Bertram and Diane Lalonde also have a fun bar-restaurant, and provide all kinds of information on Calakmul and other nearby ruins. $$

ABOVE: Bacalar Lake in the Costa Maya region.

Río Lagartos

Hotel Punta Pontó
Calle 9 (Malecón), No. 140
Tel: 986-862 0509
www.riolagartos.com
A pleasant little hotel on the waterfront in Río Lagartos, with great sunset views from its 10 simple, well-kept rooms. Get there in the evening to book a lagoon trip for the next morning. $-$$

Tulum

Hemingway
Carretera Tulum–Boca Paila Km 5.5
Tel: 984-114 2321

---

www.hemingwaytulum.com
Very large and spacious cabins with Caribbean decor and equally spacious terraces, around a palm grove on the beach. Enjoyable, eclectic dishes are cooked to order at the restaurant. $$$

Tita Tulum
Carretera Tulum–Boca Paila Km 8
Tel: 984-877 8513
www.titatulum.com
Ten very pretty, individual beach *cabañas*, with terraces and surrounded by palms, make up one of Tulum's most relaxing hotels. Prices are reasonable, and the little restaurant has fine fresh seafood. $$$

La Zebra
Carretera Tulum–Boca Paila Km 8.5
Tel: 984-115 4728
www.lazebratulum.com
One of the trendiest spots in Tulum, with beautiful luxury cabins of different sizes running back from an exquisite beach. There's an equally hip cantina restaurant and beach lounge, with salsa parties on some nights. $$$-$$$$

Uxmal and Puuc Region

Flycatcher Inn B&B
Calle 20 No. 223 (off Highway 261), Santa Elena
Tel: 997-102 0865
www.flycatcherinn.com
The local knowledge of the American-Yucatecan owners allows guests to get a true feel of village life in this distinctive guesthouse in Santa Elena, between Uxmal and Kabah. There are several very comfortable rooms and one self-contained cottage, and a special range of nature and cultural tours and excursions ensure a memorable stay. $$

Hacienda Temozón Sur
8km (5 miles) east of Highway 261, 43km (27 miles) south of Mérida
Tel: 999-923 8089
www.thehaciendas.com
A sumptuous retreat in the countryside between Mérida and Uxmal, but ideally placed for exploring the

---

whole region. The enormous main house, terrace restaurant and pool are magnificent, the spa is delightful, and rooms are opulently romantic. A very seductive place. $$$$

Hotel Sacbé
Highway 261 Km 159, Santa Elena
Tel: 997-978 5158
www.sacbebungalow.com.mx
The best budget accommodations in the Puuc region, with seven pretty cabins, with showers, fans and porches, around a garden just south of Santa Elena village. Solar-powered electricity is available 24 hours, and the French-Mexican owners are very helpful. $

Villas Arqueológicas Uxmal
By Uxmal ruins entrance, Highway 261 Km 76
Tel: 997-974 6020
www.villasarqueologicas.com.mx
Like its sister hotels at other major archeological sites, the Villas Arqueológicas at Uxmal offers pretty, traditionally themed rooms, a lovely pool and other comforts at much lower prices than some of the similar big hotels nearby. Service is friendly and welcoming. $$

Valladolid

El Mesón del Marqués
Calle 39 No. 203, between calles 40 and 42
Tel: 985-856 2073
www.mesondelmarques.com
The classic hotel in Valladolid, in a grand old colonial house right on the town plaza. In the first patio is the lovely restaurant; continue further and there is another with a garden and pool. Some rooms are dark, but others have light and charm. $$

PRICE CATEGORIES

Price categories are for a double room for one night in high season:
$ = under 500 pesos
$$ = 500–1,200 pesos
$$$ = 1,200–2,500 pesos
$$$$ = over 2,500 pesos

E ATING OUT

RECOMMENDED RESTAURANTS, CAFÉS & BARS

What to Eat

Breakfast in Mexico

Breakfast is traditionally a major meal in Mexico, often eaten early, in the cool of the morning around 7am, which sets you up for the day. Eggs feature in most of the classic breakfast favorites, found all over the country, such as, most famously, *huevos rancheros* (tortillas topped by refried beans, a spicy tomato sauce and fried eggs). *Huevos revueltos* means scrambled eggs, but in Mexico this is often served with something else mixed in, such as ham or onion; *huevos a la mexicana* means scrambled eggs with chorizo sausage, onion, peppers and chili. If a menu says *huevos al gusto* this means "as you like," so you have a choice of fried *(estrellados)* or *revueltos* with various optional additions, such as *con jamón* (with ham).

One hefty breakfast staple without eggs is *chilaquiles*, fried tortilla strips in a cheese sauce with tomato, chili, peppers and chicken or turkey. Different areas also have their own specialties, such as *huevos motuleños* in the Yucatán, tortillas topped by beans, peas, a chili-tomato sauce, ham, grated cheese and fried eggs. Restaurants and hotels commonly offer **breakfast "packages,"** with coffee and fresh juice (usually superb) included. Many places also now offer "American breakfasts," with such things as hot cakes and waffles.

Later in the Day

Mexico is a huge country and its cuisine is immensely varied. The staples commonly identified as "Mexican food" abroad – and which are now also found across the country itself – such as fajitas, burritos, enchiladas and so on form only part of the range, and mainly originate from northern Mexico, near the US border. A "trinity" of ingredients has formed the historic basis of cooking across Mexico since pre-Hispanic times, and turn up in most states in all kinds of dishes – **beans**, **chili peppers** and **corn tortillas**. Nevertheless, this still leaves great room for invention, and every region has its specialties.

Apart from the familiar tortilla-based snacks, northern Mexican food is often fairly simple, hearty and meat-and-barbecue based, favorites including *puntas de res* (chargrilled strips of beef, usually served with tomatoes and onions) and *arracheras*, thin-cut steaks. In general, the further south you go, the more complex dishes become, with a more intricate use of herbs and chilis. One of the real "must-tries" of Mexican cooking – rarely done well in Mexican restaurants outside the country – is *pollo con mole*, chicken in a thick savory chocolate sauce; traditionally, the richest *moles* come from Oaxaca. A delicious specialty of Puebla – now also found elsewhere is *chile en nogada*, a large green chili stuffed with beef and herbs, and in a walnut and pomegranate sauce. The Yucatán has a very distinctive cuisine of its own, making great use of tropical fruits, spices and cilantro; specialties include *pollo pibil*, chicken marinated in *achiote* spices and bitter orange juice and baked in banana leaves.

Anywhere near the coast a wide range of generally-excellent fish and seafood will be available. Popular varieties of fish are gray mullet *(mojarra)* and red snapper *(huachinango* or *pargo)*, and they're often served quite simply, either plain-grilled, breaded *(empanizado)* or pan-fried in oil and garlic *(al mojo de ajo)*. A favorite way to serve seafood – generally shrimp *(camarón)*, conch *(caracol)*, octopus *(pulpo)* or lobster *(langosta)* is in a ceviche, marinated in lime or lemon juice and served cold with onion, tomato and cilantro. A good *ceviche* with a beer makes an ideal light lunch by the beach.

In resort areas and most cities there is also now a choice of eating-places offering wholefood-style cooking, with an international or a Mexican flavor. One standby for vegetarians in Mexico is the **100% Natural** wholefood chain, which while not wholly vegetarian always has an enjoyable range of meat- or fish-free options.

See "Mexican Food" pages 100–103.

Drinks

Mexicans tend to drink copiously at fiestas and in times of great calamity or great good fortune. At other times, men tend to have a few drinks whenever they get together socially, but women still drink alcohol much less.

Beer

Beer *(cerveza)* is Mexico's most popular drink, and a cool beer is an ideal accompaniment to Mexican food, complementing the flavors and helping take the bite out of strong chilis. The best-known brands are light *(clara)* beers such as Corona, Carta Blanca, Sol, Victoria, and Dos Equis lager, but there are also satisfying dark *(negra)* beers such as

Negra Modelo and León Negra. In tourist areas foreigners are commonly served beers just in the bottle with a slice of lime in the top, but you may notice Mexicans generally drink beer straight in a glass. Some mixes are popular, such as a *chelada* (or *chela*), beer with a dash of lime in a salted glass, or a *michelada*, which is similar but with shots of spicy sauce and other seasonings.

Wines and Spirits

Wine is relatively scarce in Mexico, and does not go particularly well with much Mexican food. There are some large Mexican vineyards, notably in Baja California, but their wines are rarely impressive. Upscale restaurants frequently do have fairly extensive (and quite expensive) wine lists, often of quality Spanish, Chilean or Argentinian wines.

Mexico's own deservedly most famous liquor is **tequila**, made from the agave or maguey plant, of which there are hundreds of labels. There are also some other liquors made from different varieties of maguey plants, most notably **mezcal** and **pulque** (see pages 234 and 280).

Soft Drinks

Non-alcoholic beverages are easy to find, as a range of sodas (all called *refrescos*) will be on sale even in small shops and cafés that do not have any beer. A cola of any brand is generally referred to as *una coca*.

There are also plenty of more natural alternatives. **Fresh fruit juices** *(jugos)* are among Mexico's treasures, and make a great counterbalance to the meat-heaviness of some local food. They can be ordered in several ways, as straight *jugos*, as *licuados* (a shake, put through a blender and mixed with a little water or milk), an *agua*, diluted with water and ice, or even *raspados*, with crushed ice. Some tropical fruits such as the *guanábana* (soursop) are much better juiced than they are to eat. There are also some combinations that are only available as *aguas*, such as the deliciously refreshing *agua de jamaica*, a specialty of the Yucatán, an infusion of hibiscus flowers. The best juices and the biggest choice are found in specialist *juguerías*, juice shops (which often double as ice-cream stands, *see below*), but many restaurants and hotels also offer *jugos*, *licuados* and *aguas*.

In areas with large indigenous populations, especially, you can try some traditional drinks dating back

centuries before the Conquest, such as *atole* or *posol*, based on diluted cornmeal with different flavorings. More easily enjoyable is a Spanish introduction, typical of the Gulf Coast, *horchata*, made from ground rice, cinnamon and water.

If you ask for water in any but the most backwoods restaurant it will always be bottled *(agua purificada)*. Similarly, juice stands now nearly always use bottled water to make *licuados* and other combinations.

Coffee

Some parts of Mexico have a traditional love of coffee – above all the Gulf Coast, Veracruz and Tabasco – so coffee there is particularly good. Elsewhere, coffee is generally quite good in cities, and international-style cafés are proliferating, but in many small towns and villages you may find that only cheap instant coffee is available. A straight black coffee is a *café americano*, with which you can ask for some milk *(leche)*; a *café con leche* can be mostly milk with just a little coffee in it.

Where to Eat

Street Food and Market Cocinas

One of the great attractions of eating in Mexico is the sheer range and quality of "street food" available. Mexicans are enthusiastic snackers, and every town, even every village, has a selection of small hole-in-the-wall shops and stands selling tacos, *tortas* (filled bread rolls), treats for kids like *marquesitas* (waffle-like cones filled with *cajeta* sweet toffee or cheese) and other specialties, and at weekends and during fiestas there are even more. Hence, you're never short of alternatives if you don't feel like a full meal. Some visitors shy away from all street food for hygiene reasons, but if you take reasonable care to avoid the most basic or badly tended stands you can try some of Mexico's most distinctive (and economical) dishes without any great risk. One other peculiarity of Mexico is that the food at some simple **street-stands** can be as good or better than that of many restaurants, and good taco-stands have a high local reputation, so look out for ones that draw a crowd.

Some of the biggest and most varied clusters of street-food outlets are those in and around markets, which open early in the morning and often close in mid-afternoon. Inside town markets there are usually rows of simple restaurants called **cocinas económicas** (cheap kitchens) which

again are great places to get a very economical full meal of local specialties, with plenty of atmosphere included.

Restaurants and Loncherías

In cities and most towns there will be a choice of restaurants, which, since many people eat out for breakfast, generally open early and stay open all day. In villages there may only be one or two simpler, cheap **loncherías** (from the English lunch), which often blend into **taquerías**. They close quite early (around 7–8pm) and generally do not serve any alcohol. Also, one feature of some of the best traditional Mexican restaurants is that they are not open in the evenings, closing around 6pm, as after breakfast the second main meal of the day has traditionally been a big, leisurely *comida fuerte* or "strong meal" from about 2pm through the afternoon, followed only by a snackish meal at night. Hence, a late lunch is often the best time to sample some of the most interesting Mexican cuisine. In all cities and tourist areas there are also plenty of restaurants with a more flexible, international timetable. Mexican restaurants of all kinds – even *cantinas*, at weekends – admit children, and make them welcome.

Bars and Cantinas

In addition to the usual international-style drinking places found in cities, resorts and hotels there are some with a distinctively Mexican flavor, notably the *cantina*. The cheapest *cantinas* are very basic, male places for heavy drinking, but there are also many more refined, less rough-edged *cantinas* often with beautiful traditional decor – especially in Mexico City – where women can feel comfortable, particularly at weekends. *Cantinas* serve a special kind of food, small snacks similar to Spanish tapas called *botanas*, of which there is a vast variety. One is served with each drink, and traditionally they get bigger with each successive drink, but by tradition you also pay only for the drink, not the *botana*, so this is an amazingly cheap as well as convivial way to eat.

Ice-Cream Stands

Another feature of the Mexican street is the number of ice-cream stands, often called a *Paletería-Nevería*. The best offer a big range of made-on-the-spot fresh fruit *paletas* (ice lollipops) or *nieves* (ices in a tub). Most also have a selection of juices, and so double as a *juguería* (see above).

MEXICO CITY AND ENVIRONS

Mexico City

Centro Histórico

Café Tacuba
Tacuba 28
Tel: 55-5521 2048
A historic restaurant that first opened in 1912, and retains its lovely tiled interior and eccentric accumulation of hand-painted murals. Rivera, Kahlo and many others ate or drank here over the years, and it remains a genuine, bustling local favorite. There's also a huge menu of classic Mexican dishes covering every option. $–$$

La Casa de las Sirenas
Guatemala 32
Tel: 55-5704 3345
The upstairs terrace at this charming restaurant, in a distinguished 16th-century town mansion, has a superb view of the cathedral and the Templo Mayor. The menu features both refined Mexican cuisine and French-influenced dishes, and the tequila salon has more than 250 labels. Prices are, predictably, higher than average. $$$

Los Girasoles
Tacuba 8, on Plaza Tolsá
Tel: 55-5510-0630
Traditional Mexican cuisine with creative modern touches, from inventive, beautifully refreshing salads to rareties such as *chapulines* (fried grasshoppers, typical of Oaxaca) are served in this very pretty restaurant. A great range of different fruit margaritas makes for an irresistible aperitif. $$$

El Huequito
Bolívar 58
Tel: 55-5521 0207
www.elhuequito.com.mx
A star among Mexico City's thousands of *taquerías* – try the *taco al pastor* special, with great meat and two sauces, one of guacamole

and another of chili, orange juice and onion. Having celebrated their 50th anniversary in 2009, the Huequito's now have three more branches. $

La Ópera
Cinco de Mayo 10
Tel: 55-5512 8959
One of the city's most historic *cantinas*, opened in 1876, the Ópera is unusually plush, with glorious decor of dark wood booths, velvet drapes and Baroque chandeliers. There's supposed to be a bullet hole in the ceiling, left by Pancho Villa; while taking in the atmosphere, you can enjoy the house specialty, red snapper *a la veracruzana* (with onions and tomatoes) or other tasty dishes. $–$$

Restaurante El Cardenal
Palma 23
Tel: 55-5521 8815
A traditional city center restaurant with an easy-going feel, a home-from-home for its regulars, that nevertheless takes its cooking very seriously. Menus vary by season to get the best ingredients, and the rich traditional specialties from many parts of Mexico are wonderful value. $$

Sanborn's Casa de los Azulejos
Madero 4
Tel: 55-5512 1331
Mexico City's most famous restaurant, in the magnificent "House of Tiles" just off the Alameda, Sanborn's is an institution, but service remains friendly, the atmosphere welcoming and unfussy. Breakfasts here are excellent, and other things to go for include the specialty *enchiladas suizas*, with *mole* chocolate sauce. There are many more Sanborn's branches around the city. $$

Zona Rosa and Reforma

Bellinghausen
Londres 95
Tel: 55-5207 6149
The snug, discreet atmosphere in this comfortable restaurant, opened by European migrants in the 1900s, is a reminder of an older time in the city. Classic Mexican dishes feature on the menu, but the specialties are steaks, seafood and Central European fare such as *chucrut* (sauerkraut) and wiener schnitzel. Very busy at lunchtime. $$$

Cicero-Centenario
Londres 195
Tel: 55-5533 3800
Consistently one of Mexico's best restaurants, with quirky, slightly hacienda-like decor and dishes devised by celebrated chef Patricia Quintana. One specialty is a delicious variation on *mole poblano*, but there are many others to be sampled. Booking essential. $$$

Círculo del Sureste
Lucerna 12
Tel: 55-5535 2704
A little out of the way in the southeast corner of the Zona Rosa near the Mercado Juárez, this simple restaurant is one of the best in the city for Yucatecan food. Tortillas are made right in front of you, and Yucatecan favorites such as *sopa de lima* (lime and chicken soup) and *papadzules* (chopped hard-boiled eggs in a pumpkin-seed sauce, served in rolled tortillas) are full of good flavors. $$

Fonda El Refugio
Liverpool 166
Tel: 55-5525 8128
The decor of white walls, bright colors and a selection of craftwork might seem so "typically Mexican" as to suggest a tourist trap, but this cozy restaurant has also kept going for more

than 50 years because its Mexican regional dishes are also well-prepared and full of flavor, and service is friendly but unfussy. Dishes from Puebla such as *chile relleno* (stuffed chilis) are particularly good. $$

Tezka
Hotel Royal Zona Rosa, Amberes 78
Tel: 55-9149 3000
A spacious, stylishly modern hotel restaurant with some of the city's best fine dining. The creative menu, based on Basque cuisine, is designed by Juan Mari Arzak of San Sebastián, in Spain regularly voted one of the world's finest chefs by critics. Seductive and luxurious. $$$

Yug Vegetariano
Varsovia 3
Tel: 55-5525 5330
One of the city's longest-running vegetarian restaurants, a favorite with non-carnivores since the 1960s. As well as delicious fresh salads and fruit juices, you can pick from an imaginative range of vegetarian tacos, enchiladas and other Mexican standards. $–$$

Roma/Condesa

Café La Gloria
Vicente Suárez 41
Tel: 55-5211 4180
One of the most popular of Condesa's hip-hang-out café-restaurants, with sidewalk tables just off Avenida Michoacán. People-watching is a main attraction, but there is also a fashionably global menu mixing Asian and Italian dishes with more Mexican options. Staff are equally trendy, but often slow. $$

El Califa
Altata 22
Tel: 55-5271 6285
A bright, trendy modern *taquería* in Condesa that many say has the best tacos in town – a pretty big claim.

Tortillas are fresh and hand-made, meats wonderfully juicy, chili salsas are perfectly seasoned. Be prepared to wait in line. $

Covadonga
Puebla 21
Tel: 55-5533 2701
This combination of Spanish restaurant and Mexican *cantina* was opened by Spanish Civil War refugees in the 1940s, and retains much of its rather grand original decor. In recent years it has become a hugely popular part of the Colonia Roma social scene, especially the ground floor *cantina*. The food range still mixes Spanish tapas and classics dishes such as paella with Mexican *botanas* and other local dishes. $–$$

Specia
Amsterdam 241
Tel: 55-5564 1367
In the heart of fashionable Condesa is this suitably stylish restaurant showcasing Polish cuisine. Its renowned specialty of *pato tin*, crisp-roast duck with baked apple and blueberry sauce and mashed potatoes has won so many fans that the restaurant is regularly full, especially for lunch. $$$

Chapultepec and Polanco

Águila y Sol
Molière 42, Polanco
Tel: 55-5281 8354
The cutting edge of modern Mexican cuisine, where chef-owner Marta Ortiz presents superb creations inspired by traditional dishes and ingredients, such as shredded duck with *mole poblano*, or a completely original range of *ceviches*. Both the restaurant and the food are beautiful to look at, and care is taken of every detail – the fabulously subtle fresh-fruit *aguas* are worth a trip in themselves. Prices, by international standards, are a gift. $$$

Au Pied de Cochon
Hotel Presidente Intercontinental,
Campos Eliseos 218
Tel: 55-5327 7756

Traditional French luxury in a plush luxury hotel in the heart of Polanco; this restaurant is very popular with wealthy locals. The menu focuses on equally traditional French haute cuisine, with the namesake leg of pork and blanquette of beef among the specialties. $$$

La Hacienda de Los Morales
Vazquez de Mella 525

ABOVE: a generous street-stand meal to set you up for the day.

Tel: 55-5283 3054
This exquisite hacienda, much of which dates from early colonial times, surrounded by large gardens, is now a beautiful city restaurant, greatly in demand for weddings and special celebrations. The menu features well-prepared steaks and international dishes as well as an ample choice of Mexican classics. $$$

Izote de Patricia Quintana
Presidente Masaryk 513
Tel: 55-5280 1671
The flagship restaurant of Mexico's most admired and influential modern chef, where Quintana herself presents the best of sophisticated Mexican cuisine, making inventive use of traditional ingredients such as pumpkin, tamarind and *huitlacoche* or corn truffle. It's small and intimate, so booking is an absolute necessity. $$$

L'Olivier
Presidente Masaryk 49
Tel: 55-5545 3133
A touch of the

Mediterranean in Polanco, this bright, airy French bistro is very popular. Southern French standards such as foie gras, salade niçoise and couscous are intriguingly blended with Mexican ingredients, and there's a good wine selection. $$–$$$

Sir Winston Churchill's
Avila Camacho 67, Polanco
Tel: 55-5280 6070
Curiously, wealthy locals love this very deliberately English (as the name suggests) restaurant, in a Tudor-style mansion with pretty gardens, and a snug, gentleman's-club-like atmosphere. On the menu are beef Wellington, and even roast beef and Yorkshire pudding. $$$

Insurgentes Sur

Bellini Piso 45
World Trade Center, 45th floor,
Insurgentes Sur
Tel: 55-9000 8305
The big attraction of the revolving restaurant at the top of the giant World Trade Center is, naturally, the view. The varied menu, which includes global options (Italian, Thai, American) as well as Mexican dishes, is not as exciting, but still satisfying. $$$

Suntory
Torres Adalid 14
Tel: 55-5536 9432
Sushi is as popular in Mexico City as anywhere else in the world, and this main branch of a small but select Japanese-owned chain is always busy, always

reliable. The decor includes both traditional Japanese-style private rooms and a more conventional dining room. $$–$$

San Ángel and Coyoacán

Cantina La Guadalupana
Higuera 2, Coyoacán
Tel: 55-5554 6253
Frida Kahlo was once a regular visitor here, at Coyoacán's most popular *cantina*. Recent refurbishment has been a little disrespectful of its historic character, but it's still a welcoming, genuine place, and the generous *botanas* are delicious. $

Los Danzantes
Plaza Jardín Centenario 12
Tel: 55-5554 1213
A bright, attractive restaurant on Coyoacán's main square that's one of the best places to try new, inventive Mexican cuisine – *nueva cocina* – at very accessible prices. *Huitlacoche* (corn truffle) ravioli is one of its most delicious specialties; another, since the food is based on that of Oaxaca, is a range of fine *mezcal*. $$

San Ángel Inn
Diego Rivera 50, by Calle Altavista
Tel: 55-5616 1402
One of the grandest of the old haciendas around Mexico City, dating from the 17th century – but almost next door to the eccentric former home of Diego Rivera – has long been one of the city's landmark restaurants. You can choose to eat in plush dining rooms inside, or in gracious, plant-lined patios; service, the wine list and the varied Mexican and international cuisine are impeccable. $$$

La Taberna del León
Altamirano 46, in Plaza Loreto
Tel: 55-5616 2110
An elegant, finely

PRICE CATEGORIES

Price categories are for a meal for one person without drinks:
$ = under 130 pesos
$$ = 130–280 pesos
$$$ = over 280 pesos

refurbished old house in the tranquil streets of San Ángel, not far from the university, where Mónica Patiño presents her imaginative cuisine, Mexican-based but eclectically blending in a range of international influences. The setting is delightful, and service very pleasant. **$$$**

Cuernavaca

Las Mañanitas
Ricardo Linares 107
Tel: 777-362 0000
The opulent restaurant in this seductive spa hotel has long been the most prestigious in Cuernavaca. Its quite old-fashioned, prices are high and the atmosphere is often formal, but the garden setting is beautiful, and the refined Mexican cuisine is exquisitely presented. **$$$**

Restaurante Los Arcos
Jardín de los Héroes 4
Tel: 777-312 1510
The foremost people-watching spot in the center of town, with a big sidewalk terrace just off the Plaza de Armas that's regularly full of foreign and local students. There's a reliable mix of Mexican favorites, and great fresh ice cream. **$**

La Strada
Salazar 38, near the Palacio de Cortés
Tel: 777-318 6085
A fine old colonial house in the heart of town is the setting for a mellow, romantic restaurant with first-rate Italian food. Pastas and breads are all own-made, and dishes are assembled from deliciously fresh, often organic ingredients. There's also a superior wine list. **$$**

Pachuca

Don Horacio
Hidalgo 24
Tel: 771-716 0525
An institution in Pachuca, Don Horacio's has been pleasing local diners ever since 1927. The highlights of the menu are local

specialties rarely seen elsewhere in Mexico, such as *mixiote* (varied meat, vegetable, herb and chili combinations baked in maguey leaves), as well as even rarer options such as dishes featuring *chinicuiles* and *gusanos* (different kinds of worms). **$$**

Puebla

Las Bodegas del Molino
Calzada del Bosque 12, San José del Puente
Tel: 222-248 2262
A short way outside Puebla (so best reached by cab), this restaurant occupies a finely restored 16th-century hacienda beside a mill. The menu features all the traditional Puebla specialties, and there's an above-average wine list to match the splendid setting. **$$$**

Casa de los Muñecos
2 Norte No. 2
Tel: 222-248 4825
This historic building with the most extravagant of Puebla's colonial tiled facades – which is also home to the University Museum – now hosts a sophisticated restaurant in its distinguished ground-floor rooms and patio. The menu includes international dishes – magret of duck, Kobe-style beef – as well as Puebla specialties and fine seafood. **$$$**

Fonda de Santa Clara
3 Poniente No. 307
Tel: 222-242 2659
A celebrated restaurant that has a long-established reputation as a showcase for Puebla's traditional cuisine, such as its celebrated *chile en nogada* (served especially around Independence Day, in September) or *mole poblano*. Other restaurants would now say they can do these dishes equally well, but it's good to try the definitive version. **$$–$$$**

La Guadalupana
5 Oriente No. 605 (Callejón de los Sapos)
Tel: 222-482 5136
An attractively modest

ABOVE: sweet refreshment for a hot day.

traditional restaurant with two patios, just off one of Puebla's best streets for handicraft hunting. The fresh *fajitas* are exceptional, and there are also good *moles* and other local specialties. **$–$$**

El Patio de la Pileta
Hotel El Sueño, 9 Oriente No. 12
Tel: 222-232 6489
The restaurant in this innovative, boutique-style Puebla hotel has a similarly fresh approach, combining modern design with the patios of a gracious 18th-century building. Menus feature light, creative variations on traditional *poblana* cuisine. **$$–$$$**

Restaurante La Compañía
Mesón Sacristía de la Compañía, 6 Sur No. 304
Tel: 222-232 4513
The restaurant in Puebla's most renowned hotel is often credited with having revitalized the standard of *poblano* cuisine across the city, with its attention to detail and revival of traditional recipes. The setting is beautiful, and the list of specialties – from original salads to substantial dishes such as pork in a nutty *pipián* sauce – is always enticing. A place to savor a very leisurely lunch. **$$$**

Taxco

Café Sasha
Juan Ruíz de Alarcón 1
Tel: 739-627 6494

American-owned Sasha's combines a bohemian-trendy atmosphere, great cocktails and a lovely view, from its rooftop terrace. The menu is particularly strong on vegetarian options – particularly good crêpes – but there's also a range of other Mexican and international dishes. **$–$$**

Del Ángel Inn
Celso Múñoz 4
Tel: 739-622 5525
Del Ángel is firmly established on Taxco's tourist itineraries, but for good reason: the views over the cathedral and the town from the rooftop terrace, and even from the dining rooms just below, are unbeatable. Service is also pleasing, and there's an extensive menu – international favorites like steaks and pasta are included, but the things to go for are Mexican classics like *fajitas, arracheras* or enchiladas with *mole*. **$$**

Sotavento
Benito Juárez 12
Tel: 739-627 1217
A more modern, chic alternative in Taxco, but located in a lovely colonial house, with the essential attractive patio. The food range is fashionably eclectic, featuring Italian-based as well as Mexican dishes, with some lively choices for vegetarians. **$$**

Tepoztlán

Axitla
Av. del Tepozteco
Tel: 739-395 0519
A refined little restaurant with the finest setting in town, in gardens below the Tepozteco pyramid. Favorite local dishes such as chicken in *chipotle* chili sauce or enchiladas are all prepared with a sophisticated touch, and the owners are very

PRICE CATEGORIES

Price categories are for a meal for one person without drinks:
$ = under 130 pesos
$$ = 130–280 pesos
$$$ = over 280 pesos

pleasant. A stroll around the garden is a great prelude to a meal. **$$**

El Ciruelo
Zaragoza 17
Tel: 739-395 1203
With the same owners as the Posada del Tepozteco hotel, this is another innovative restaurant with a perfectly relaxed feel and great mountain views from its intimate patio. Inventive specialties include *filete de res*, Mexican-cut

steaks, with sauces of mango and chili, or tequila and herbs. **$$**

Luna Mextli
Revolución 16
Tel: 739-395 1114
A hip and very good value restaurant in Tepotzlán, with a variety of artwork around the walls, a garden, occasional live music and excellent fresh salads and other light dishes. A good place to spend a relaxing afternoon. **$–$$**

Toluca

El Risco
Árbol de Capulín 101
Tel: 722-214 7821
On the hill of Lomas Altas on the north side of Toluca city, this pretty restaurant benefits from sweeping views of the Nevado de Toluca volcano from its garden terrace. On the menu are hefty Argentinian steaks as well as Mexican dishes,

and there's a good range of wines. **$$**

La Vaquita Negra
Portal Reforma 124
Tel: 722-215 6847
Occupying a prime spot on Toluca's main square since the 1950s, this humble place is known for some of the best *tortas de chorizo*, Toluca's characteristic spicy sausage served hot in a crusty roll. When you've tried that, other local meats are also available. **$**

BAJA CALIFORNIA

Cabo San Lucas

Mi Casa
Avenida Cabo San Lucas
Tel: 624-143 1933
www.micasarestaurant.com
Fresh seafood and an unusual range of subtle Mexican dishes make this one of the town's favorite places for sophisticated diners. **$$–$$$**

The Giggling Marlin
Matamoros at Marina
Tel: 624-143 1182
www.gigglingmarlin.com
Lively bar with dancing, fun, and games. **$$**

Nick-San
Blvd Marina
Tel: 624-143 4484
Zen-like atmosphere and heavenly sushi. **$$–$$$**

The Office
Playa El Medano
Tel: 624-143 3464
On the beach with a Mexican menu and a fiesta on Thur and Sun at 7.30pm. **$$**

Ensenada

La Embotelladora Vieja
Miramar 666
Tel: 646-174 0807
Fine Mediterranean-Mexican cuisine in a room that was once used

to age wines. **$$$**

La Hacienda del Charro
Av. López Mateos 454
Tel: 646-178 2114
Chickens roasted over a wood fire are the specialty. **$**

El Rey Sol
Av. López Mateos 1000
Tel: 646-178 1733
French and Mexican dishes in an attractive setting. A favorite for years. **$$–$$$**

La Paz

Bismark
Santos Degollado and Avenida Altamirano
Tel: 612-122 4854
Excellent Mexican dishes and seafood. Friendly, family-style ambiance. **$$**

La Boheme
Calle Esquerro 10
Tel: 612-125 6080
www.laboheme-lapaz.com
Historic building, great food, and candlelit ambiance in this French-fusion spot. **$$**

Loreto

Cafe Olé
Madero 14
Tel: 613-135 0496
Located just off the plaza. Cafe Olé is perfect for breakfast and people-watching. **$**

El Nido
Salvatierra 154, opposite the bus station
Tel: 613-135 0284
Cozy atmosphere, with oak beams and an open fireplace/grill. Good food, mostly steak and seafood. **$$**

Mexicali

Mandolino
Reforma 1070
Tel: 686-552 9544
A varied menu of Italian dishes. **$–$$**

Misión del Dragón
Blvd Lázaro Cárdenas 555
Tel: 686-566 4320
A beautifully decorated Chinese restaurant. **$–$$**

Mulegé

Las Casitas
Hotel Las Casitas, Callejón de los Estudiantes
Tel: 615-153 0019
Seafood specialists, and great BBQ from the garden grill. A *mariachi* band plays on Friday night. **$–$$**

Los Equipales
Moctezuma, near Zaragoza
Tel: 615-153 0330
An attractive restaurant with a large menu and a cool airy terrace upstairs. **$**

San José del Cabo

Damiana
Mijares 8
Tel: 624-142 0499
Romantic ambiance and outstanding food. **$$**

Mi Cocina
Hotel Casa Natalia, Blvd Mijares 4
Tel: 624-142 5100
Tasty Mexican and international cuisine. **$$$**

Tijuana

Casa La Especial
Revolución 718
Tel: 664-685 6654
One of the genuine Mexican places in Tijuana, serving good food in a bustling atmosphere. **$**

Hard Rock Cafe
Revolución 520
Tel: 664 685 0206
A classic spot to have a great burger before heading out on the town. **$$**

Todos Santos

Cafe Santa Fe
Calle Centenario 4
Tel: 612-145 0340
One of Baja's finest Italian restaurants. Some people travel all the way from the mainland to dine here. **$$$**

THE SIERRAS

Chihuahua

La Casa de los Milagros
Victoria 812
Tel: 614-437 0693
A colonial-style restaurant

with a bohemian ambiance and very tasty food. **$–$$**

Rincón Mexicana
Cuauhtemoc 3208
Tel: 614-411 1510
Exuberant Mexican

atmosphere with *mariachi* bands, a wide range of good, authentic Mexican dishes, and a mix of locals and Copper Canyon visitors. **$$**

Monterrey

Luisiana
Av. Hidalgo 530 Oriente
Tel: 81-8343 1561
www.restaurantluisiana.com.mx

TRANSPORTATION · ACCOMMODATIONS · EATING OUT · ACTIVITIES · A–Z · LANGUAGE

Old-time favorite with elegant, modern decor. International cuisine, including steaks, game, and seafood, with top-notch service. **$$$**
Regio
Av. Gonzalitos and Insurgentes
Tel: 81-8346 8650
Regio is one of a chain of good restaurants, which are open late and well known for their tasty charcoal grilled steaks and cabrito (kid). **$$**

Señor Natural
Vasconcelos 143
Tel: 81-8378 4815
Good assortment of healthy dishes including fruit salads, yogurt, granola, natural juices, and soy dishes. **$**
El Tío
Hidalgo 1746 Pte and México, Col. Obispado
Tel: 81-8346 0291
www.eltio.com.mx
Very popular for charbroiled steak, cabrito (kid), and other Mexican dishes. **$$**

Saltillo

Mesón del Principal
Blvd V. Carranza and Egipto
Tel: 844-415 0015
www.mesonprincipal.com
This restaurant is an excellent choice for cabrito (kid), roasted northern style. **$$**
El Tapanco
Allende Sur 225
Tel: 844-414 0043
Downtown restaurant in a converted 17th-century

house, serving excellent international and Mexican cuisine. **$$**

Tampico

Diligencias
H. del Cañonero & López de Lara, one block off Plaza de la Libertad
Tel: 833-213 7642
Absolutely the best seafood in town. Diligencias' delicious, inventive house specials are very good value. **$–$$**

THE NORTHWEST COAST

ABOVE: a light fruit parfait to round off the meal.

Mazatlán

Angelo's Gourmet Restaurant
Pueblo Bonito Hotel
Tel: 623-914 3700
Outstanding food and decor. Extensive wine list.

The best northern Italian cuisine in Mazatlán. **$$–$$$**
Jungle Juice
Av. de las Garzas 102
Tel: 669-913 3315
Restaurant, bar, and dance hall with excellent meats and seafood at reasonable prices. **$–$$**
Papagayo
The Inn at Mazatlán Hotel
Tel: 669-913 4151
Fine international and Mexican cuisine served in a romantic seaside setting. **$$–$$$**
Pastelería Panamá
Av. Camarón Sábalo and Av. de las Garzas
Tel: 623-985 7517
www.panama.com.mx
Good food and pastries. **$**
Sr Pepper
Av. Camarón Sábalo opposite the Camino Real Hotel
Tel: 669-914 0101
Steaks, lobsters, and shrimp, all delicious. **$$$**

Vittore
Rodolfo T. Loaiza 100
Tel: 623-986 2424
Chic Italian grill with indoor or terrace seating. Excellent pastas. **$$**

Guaymas

Baja Mar
Av. Serdán & Calle 17
Tel: 622-224 0225
Downtown restaurant with great seafood, and wonderful clam and fish soups. Prime cuts from Sonora. Cocktails. **$–$$**

Kino Bay

Kino Bay
On the beach
Tel: 622-222 0049
One of the few spots open for breakfast. Mexican food in a pleasant atmosphere. **$**
El Pargo Rojo
Av. del Mar 1426, across from beach

Tel: 622-222 0205
Pleasant seafood and steak restaurant. **$–$$**

San Blas

Garza Canela
Paredes Sur 106
Tel: 323-285 0307
About as elegant as San Blas gets. Good international fare. **$$**

San Carlos

Jax Snax
Carretera San Carlos
Tel: 622-226 0270
Good Mexican-US fast and not-so-fast food. **$**
Rosa's Cantina
Carretera San Carlos
Tel: 622-226 1000
A casual place, popular with young people, serving cabrito (kid), steak, and enchiladas. Bulletin-board for buying, renting, or local events. **$**

EL BAJÍO AND THE COLONIAL HEARTLAND

Guanajuato

Casa del Conde de la Valenciana
Carretera Guanajuato–Dolores Hidalgo Km 5
Tel: 473-732 2550
Beautiful 18th-century building housing a fine restaurant as well as wonderful crafts shop. **$$–$$$**
La Casona del Cielo
Pastita 76
Tel: 473-731 2000

La Casona serves up tasty international fare with a Mexican touch in very pleasant surroundings. You can dine inside or on the lovely patio. **$$**
La Hacienda del Marfil
Arcos de Guadalupe 3, in the suburb of Marfil
Tel: 473-733 1148
Traditional French dishes and nouvelle Mexican cuisine served in an elegant yet rustic restaurant and bar in a former hacienda. **$$–$$$**

Querétaro

Josecho's
Dalia 1, next to Plaza de Toros Santa María
Tel: 442-216 0229
Hefty portions of steak and seafood in a real macho atmosphere. **$$**
La Mariposa
Av. Peralta 7
Tel: 442-212 1166
La Mariposa has been serving tasty Mexican food for over 50 years. **$–$$**

Zacatecas

La Cuija
Mercado González Ortega
Tel: 492-922 8275
Zacatecas specialties, very well prepared. **$–$$**
Quinta Real
González Ortega, at the aqueduct
Tel: 492-922 9104
This beautiful restaurant offers fine Continental cuisine. **$$–$$$**

JALISCO AND MICHOACAN

Guadalajara

La Fonda de San Miguel
Donato Guerra 25
Tel: 33-3613 0809
www.lafondadesanmiguel.com
The best dining in the Centro Histórico, in a courtyard with a fountain and folk art on display, and sublime versions of Mexican favorites. **$$**
Galatea
Mexicaltzingo No. 1958
Tel: 33-1201-3932
A bit out of the center, this intimate restaurant has very casual decor and superb food, at very reasonable prices. **$$–$$$**
El Sacromonte
Pedro Moreno 1398
Tel: 33-3825 5447
A little expensive but worth

it for the divine food as well as the elaborate presentation. They have a lively bar next door, too. **$$$**

Morelia

Fonda Las Mercedes
León Guzmán 47
Tel: 443-312 6113
Restored colonial mansion with a varied menu including soups, crêpes filled with squash, and pastas. **$$**
San Miguelito
Avenida Carmelinas, at Ventura Puente
Tel: 443-324 2300
Restaurant-bar-bazaar. Beautiful setting and tasty food. Almost all the furnishings and decor are for sale. The tradition of

walking around the upside-down statue of St Anthony, considered the marriage saint in some parts of Latin America, is alive here. Women sometimes pray to St Anthony, telling him that they will only turn their statues right-side-up after finding a good husband. The restaurant staff are happy to lead curious visitors in a simple ceremony to attract a husband. **$$–$$$**

Puerto Vallarta

Café des Artistes
Guadalupe Sánchez 740, Downtown
Tel: 322-222 3229
www.cafedesartistes.com
French cuisine with a

Mexican accent prepared under the direction of award-winning chef Thierry Blouet. Outstanding. **$$$**
Don Pedro's
Sayulita town beach, north of Puerto Vallarta
Tel: 329-291 3090
www.donpedros.com
A huge *palapa* (beach hut) serving an array of fish, seafood, and poultry grilled over *mesquite*. Worth the trip. **$$**
Hacienda San Ángel
Miramar 336
Tel: 322-222 2692
Hotel dining room open to non-residents and worth it for the city views as well as fine dining, including the signature dish of *cabreria*: steak with a three-chile sauce. **$**

ACAPULCO AND THE PACIFIC BEACHES

Acapulco

100% Natural
Costera Miguel Alemán 200 and several other locations
Tel: 744-485 3982
www.100natural.com.mx
Chain restaurant that's open 24 hours for vegetarian dishes, fondues, and juices. **$**
El Amigo Miguel
Benito Juárez 31
Tel: 744-483 6981
A favorite with the locals, serving excellent seafood and fish. **$–$$**
Baikal
Carr. Escenica 16–29, Costera
Tel: 744-446 6867
www.baikal.com.mx
Fusion cooking in one of Acapulco's most fashionable dining places, with a romantic ambiance and a small but high-quality menu. **$$$**
El Cabrito
Costera Miguel Alemán 1480
Tel: 744-484 7711
www.elcabrito-acapulco.com
Real Mexican food and ambiance. *Cabrito* (kid) is a specialty. **$–$$**
Carlos and Charlie's
Boulevard de las Naciones 1813, inside La Isla Shopping Village

ABOVE: red and green salsas add just the right touch.

Tel: 744-462 2105
www.carlosandcharlies.com
Always a lively, noisy crowd, as at all restaurants in this chain. **$$–$$$**
Kookaburra
Carr. Escénica Las Brisas
Tel: 744-446 6020
Magnificent views and international dishes, with an emphasis on shellfish. **$$$**
Madeiras
Carretera Escenica 33-B
Tel: 744-446 5636
Excellent fixed-price menu, good value, and a great

view. Reservations are essential. **$$$**
Zorrito's
Costera Miguel Alemán and Antón de Alaminos
Tel: 744-485 3735
Specialty of *pozole*, a pork and hominy (ground maize) stew served with fresh vegetables. **$–$$**

Ixtapa/Zihuatanejo

Beccofino
Marina de Ixtapa
Tel: 755-553 1770
Stunning Italian preparation of local ingredients, specializing in fish and seafood. Reservations recommended. **$$–$$$**
Casa Elvira
Paseo del Pescador 32, Zihuatanejo
Tel: 755-554 2061
An old favorite serving seafood and Mexican dishes. **$–$$**
La Casa Que Canta
In the hotel of the same name in Zihuatanejo
Tel: 755-555 7030
Perfectly prepared traditional Mexican cuisine served in romantic surroundings. **$$$**
Coconuts
Paseo Agustín Ramírez 1

Tel: 755-554 2518
The oldest building in town with an excellent menu of fish, seafood, and choice meats. Fun bar. **$$$**
Villa de la Selva
Paseo de la Roca, Ixtapa
Tel: 755-553 0362
www.villadelaselva.com
Good international menu and a spectacular view. Great spot for watching the sunset. **$$$**

Manzanillo

Benedetti's Pizza
Las Brisas
Tel: 314-333 1592
A local institution. Informal Italian restaurant. **$**
Legazpi
Las Hadas Hotel
Tel: 314-331 0101
White-gloved service and continental cuisine with a Mexican touch. Dinner only. **$$$**

PRICE CATEGORIES

Price categories are for a meal for one person without drinks:
$ = under 130 pesos
$$ = 130–280 pesos
$$$ = over 280 pesos

TRANSPORTATION · ACCOMMODATIONS · EATING OUT · ACTIVITIES · A – Z · LANGUAGE

L'Recif
Cerro del Cenicero
Tel: 314-335 0900
www.lrecif.com
Restaurant set on a cliff overlooking the ocean, open from November to April. Don't miss the fish in black butter. **$$–$$$**
Toscana
Costero Miguel de la Madrid 3177
Tel: 314-333 2515
Open evenings only. People start to dance after dipping into the Mediterranean seafood specialties. Right on the beach. **$$**

San Miguel de Allende

Casa de Sierra Nevada
Hospicio 42
Tel: 415-152 7040
Fine dining at one of Mexico's most beautiful hotels. Brunch is exquisite and not to be missed. **$$$**
Nirvana
Mesones 101
Tel: 415-150 0067
Fusion cooking, with a menu that ranges from the Caribbean to Asia to the Pacific Rim. **$$**

Olé Olé
Loreto 66
Tel: 415-152 0896
Meaty and hearty grilled Mexican dishes, with a colorful decor. Great place for a fun night. **$**

Taxco

Hostería el Adobe
Plazuela de San Juan 13
Tel: 762-622 1416
Original decor and excellent food. Wait for a window seat to view the busy plaza below. **$–$$**

El Mural
Posada de la Misión, Cerro de la Misión
Tel: 762-622 0063
The mural of the name is by Juan O'Gorman and there is indoor and outdoor seating at one of the best dining spots in town. International cuisine as well as superior Mexican dishes. **$$$**
Sr. Costillas
Plaza Borda 1
Tel: 762-622 3215
Casual, fun spot on the main square, famous for its ribs and Mexican dishes. **$$**

THE GULF COAST

Catemaco

Hotel Catemaco
Carranza 8
Tel: 294-943 0203
This modest hotel in the center of Catemaco town has one of its most enjoyable restaurants, with a view of the lake from the dining room. Service is friendly, and the menu includes regional dishes such as egg tortillas as well as those with a variety of fish and seafood ingredients. **$$**

Coatepec

Casa Bonilla
Juárez 20, corner of Cuauhtémoc
Tel: 228-816 0374
A local institution, renowned for its classic Veracruz fish and seafood dishes such as *langostinos huérfanos* (langoustines cooked in a pre-Hispanic style, grilled in a chili paste), snook *a la veracruzana*, crab claws and much more. Wel worth a detour. **$–$$**
El Tío Yeyo
Santos Degollado 4
Tel: 228-816 3645
Coatepec's second famous bar-restaurant has a slightly different range of specialties, particularly focusing on river fish such as mountain trout, served 21 different ways. The airy dining room is decorated with an exuberant range of plants. **$–$$**

Papantla

Sorrento
Enríquez 105
Tel: 784-842 0067
A big, cheerful place with plenty of open-air tables on the plaza in Papantla village, which is a fine place to regain energies after a visit to El Tajín. For snacks there are local *molotes* (fried dough balls with a variety of fillings), but there are also plenty of more substantial dishes. **$$**

Tlacotalpan

Doña Lala
Venustiano Carranza 11
Tel: 288-884 2580
This big, pink-painted hotel restaurant right on the town square is an excellent place to take in the special atmosphere of Tlacotalpan. Fresh river fish is one of the strong points of the menu, but there's also a wide range of other dishes. **$–$$**

Veracruz

El Gaucho
Colón 642
Tel: 229-935 0411
A long-running restaurant with a curious history, founded by an Argentinian soccer player who finished his career in Veracruz. Giant-sized, perfectly grilled Argentinian steaks are a

specialty, but there is also a good selection of Mexican and seafood dishes. **$$–$$$**
Gran Café de La Parroquia
Valentín Gómez Farias 34, on the Malecón
Tel: 229-932 2584
Founded in 1810, and a national institution: according to a local saying, if you haven't been to La Parroquia and sipped a *café lechero* (a small amount of strong coffee served in a tall glass, to which you then ask the separate "milk waiter" – the *lechero* – to add however much milk you want from a steaming hot kettle) you haven't been to Veracruz. **$–$$**
Gran Café del Portal
Independencia 1187, by Zamora
Tel: 229-931 2759
This is one of Veracruz's historic coffee house-restaurants although it doesn't have the same fame as La Parroquia. Nevertheless, it does enjoy a fine location in the *portales* (arcades) in front of the cathedral. All the regional favorites and Mexican classics are on the menu and served up in generous quantities. The traditional *lechero* (see listing above) is highly recommended. **$–$$**
Mariscos Villa Rica
Calzada Mocambo 527, Mocambo beach
Tel: 229-922 2113

A large, lively restaurant, part open-air beneath a big palm-thatched roof, beside one of Veracruz's most popular beaches. The mostly seafood menu includes fine shrimp cocktails and *ceviches*, but also less common specialties such as pompano in a fragrant pepper-leaf sauce. **$–$$**

Xalapa (Jalapa)

Churrería de Mis Recuerdos
Francisco Javier Clavijero 17
Tel: 228-817 3390
Very popular with Xalapa's many students, this bright, lively place in the center of town has something for everyone – generous fresh breakfasts, a varied menu of enchiladas, Veracruz-style fruit-filled tamales and other dishes, fine coffee, and an unusual specialty for a restaurant – *churros*, fritters of sweet batter to dunk in hot chocolate. **$–$$**
La Casa de Mamá
Avila Camacho 113
Tel: 228-817 3144
A cozy, old-fashioned restaurant in the heart of Xalapa known for its succulent chargrilled steaks, excellent fish and seafood, and indulgent, creamy desserts, often flambéed in a little alcohol. Be ready for big portions. **$$**

OAXACA

Huatulco

Avalos
Bahía Santa Cruz
Tel: 958-587 0128
Also known as Doña Celia, this beach front restaurant serves fresh seafood. **$–$$**
Casa del Mar
Balcones de Tangolunda 13
Tel: 958-581 0203
Good Continental and Mexican fare and a lovely setting. Beautiful view. **$$–$$$**
El Sabor de Oaxaca
Guamuchil 206, Crucecita
Tel: 958-587 0060
Try the Oaxaca Special, a plate for two which gives you tastings from across the menu, including pork *mole*, in this popular spot which pleases locals as well as

visitors with its excellent local dishes. **$$**

Oaxaca

El Asador Vasco
Portal de Flores 10
Tel: 951-514 4755
Located on the second floor facing the Zócalo, specializing in Basque and Paxacan dishes. Reserve a front-row table on the balcony – the view makes up for the notoriously bad service. **$$–$$$**
La Asunción
Hostal de la Noria Hotel
Tel: 951-514 7844
Nouvelle Oaxacan cuisine beautifully presented. **$–$$**
Cocina del Mar Los Jorge
Pino Suárez 806
Tel: 951-513 4308

Outstanding fish and seafood. A real treat. **$–$$**
Como Agua Pa' Chocolate
Av. Hidalgo 612
Tel: 951-516 2917
Oaxacan and international dishes. **$$**
Flamanalli
Av. Juárez 39, Teotitlán del Valle
Tel: 951-562 0255
Charming village restaurant serving Zapotec food (somewhat overpriced) and also selling attractive hand-woven rugs. **$$**
Los Pacos Restaurante
M. Abasolo 121
Tel: 951-516 1704
A wonderful place to try some of the delicious regional *mole*. If you want to try two or three, they can be arranged on the same plate. The house *mezcal* is also an

excellent choice. **$$–$$$**
Restaurante Casa Oaxaca
Constitución 104-A
Tel: 951-516 8889
Classic dishes like black *mole*, and delicious fresh seafood platters. **$$$**

Puerto Escondido

Banana's
Av. Pérez Gazga
Tel: 954-582 0005
Casual beach front restaurant specializing in Mexican and Italian fare. **$$**
Santa Fé
Calle del Morro
Tel: 954-582 0170
Restaurant of the Sante Fé Hotel with a great view. Serves excellent Mexican, seafood, chicken, and vegetarian dishes. **$$$**

TABASCO AND CHIAPAS

ABOVE: guacamole and tacos make an ideal snack.

Palenque

Restaurante Maya Cañada
Merle Green, La Cañada
Tel: 916-345 0042
Generous margaritas and other cocktails are some of the things that make this romantic open-air restaurant a likeable place to rest after pyramid-climbing. The menu features reliable Mexican classics, and good tamales and other Chiapanecan dishes. **$$**

San Cristóbal de las Casas

La Casa del Pan
Dr Navarro 10

Tel: 967-678 5895
One of Mexico's best vegetarian restaurants, with great fresh breads, invigorating juices and a delicious range of meat-free dishes based on traditional local cuisine. There is also now a branch at Real de Guadalupe 55. **$–$$**
El Edén
Hotel-Posada El Paraíso, 5 de Febrero 19
Tel: 967-678 0085
Subtle color schemes combine with the traditional architecture of this old San Cristóbal town house to make El Paraíso Hotel's restaurant one of the most attractive in town. The

European owners design varied menus combining French, Italian and Swiss influences as well as those of Chiapas. **$$**
La Paloma
Inside Casa de Mazariegos, Hidalgo 3
Tel: 967-678 1547
This restaurant's style is bright and modern, but it occupies the patio of the Casa de Mazariegos, a 16th-century house built by Chiapas' first conquistador. Traditional dishes are carefully prepared, and *chipotle* and other traditional local seasonings are imaginatively combined with international touches. **$$**
TierrAdentro
Real de Guadalupe 24
Tel: 967-674 6766
This cultural center in a big old house in the center of town, which provides a home for Zapatista cooperatives and other social organizations, also has an excellent, mellow café in its broad patio. The organic coffee is first-rate, and the salads and other light meals are fresh and full of flavor. **$**

Tapachula

Tapachtlán
Casa Mexicana Hotel, 8 Sur No. 19
Tel: 962-626 6605
Proof that Mexico can always surprise you: out-of-the-way Tapachula has one of the best restaurants in southern Mexico, in the delightful patio of the Casa Mexicana Hotel. The French chef produces highly creative dishes using local ingredients.Excellent value. **$$**

Villahermosa

Los Tulipanes
Carlos Pellicer Cámara 511
Tel: 993-314 5469
By the banks of the Grijalva, this is one of the best places to explore Tabasco's little-known cuisine, several *pejelagarto* (local freshwater fish) dishes included. Break-fast and lunch only. **$$$**

PRICE CATEGORIES

Price categories are for a meal for one person without drinks:
$ = under 130 pesos
$$ = 130–280 pesos
$$$ = over 280 pesos

THE YUCATAN

Campeche

Casa Vieja
Calle 10 No. 319
Tel: 981-811 8016
Location is the big draw of this friendly restaurant – it's on the first floor of the *portales* overlooking the Parque Principal, with a great view of whatever's going on. The *campechano* fish dishes are enjoyable too. **$$**

La Pigua
Miguel Alemán 197-A
Tel: 981-811 3365
A snug, air-conditioned restaurant just outside the circuit of Campeche's old walls that has a high reputation as a showcase for Campechano cuisine. Local dishes with a lovely range of flavors such as *arroz con pulpo* – octopus and rice salad – make a

ABOVE: dining out options are numerous and varied.

great opening to a meal, and the main dishes are equally as good. **$$–$$$**

Marganzo
Calle 8 No. 267
Tel: 981-811 3898
Just off Campeche's main Parque Principal, and long popular with visitors to the city, the Marganzo is not as refined in its cooking as some of the city's restaurants, but is very pretty, with waitresses in traditional dresses, and good value. **$$**

La Parroquia
Calle 55 No. 8

Tel: 981-816 2530
Not nearly as grand as the (unconnected) Parroquia in Veracruz, but this ultra-relaxed old café, with its whirring ceiling fans, is almost as much of a local institution. Open 24 hours daily, it's an excellent standby, and to eat there are local dishes like *pan de cazón* (hammerhead shark baked between two tortillas and with a tomato-chili sauce) as well as Mexican standards. **$–$$**

Cancún

100% Natural
Av. Sunyaxchén 62, corner Av. Yaxchilán
Tel: 998-884 0102
Cancún outlet of a very attractive wholefood chain that's much enjoyed by anyone looking for a change from standard local fare. Imaginative vegetarian options are a mainstay, but there are also meat and fish dishes. Don't miss out on the fabulous fruit juice combos – try a different one every day. **$–$$**

Los Arcos
Av. Yaxchilán, corner Calle Rosas
Tel: 998-887 6784
One of the best of several big, busy terrace restaurants on Avenida Yaxchilán in Downtown that are the best places to go in Cancún for a less touristy atmosphere and lower

prices than in the Hotel Zone. Grilled meats, *fajitas* and other Mexican classics are great value. **$–$$**

La Destilería
Blvd Kukulcán Km 12.5
Tel: 998-885 1086
The Mexican-rancho decor at this big restaurant is a bit cheesy – as is usual in the Hotel Zone – but its classic northern Mexican cooking is of a high standard, with especially good steaks. Another attraction is a vast tequila selection, in the very plush "cantina." **$$$**

La Dolce Vita
Blvd Kukulcán Km. 14.6
Tel: 998-885 0161
A stylish Italian restaurant, with tables on a terrace overlooking the Nichupté lagoon. The wine list is one of the best in Cancún, and the modern Italian cooking incorporates Caribbean ingredients. **$$$**

La Habichuela
Margaritas 25
Tel: 998-884 3158
Just off the quiet Parque de Las Palapas square in Ciudad Cancún, this is one of the resort's prettiest, most romantic restaurants, with tables in a garden that is beautifully lit at night. Classic Yucatecan dishes are very finely presented. **$$$**

La Joya
Fiesta American Grand Coral Beach Hotel, Blvd Kukulcán Km 12.5
Tel: 998-881 3200
One of Cancún's grandest hotels has one of its most spectacular restaurants, with soaring three-story windows providing stunning views. The fare features traditional Mexican dishes with refined original elements. **$$$**

Laguna Grill
Blvd Kukulcán Km. 15.6
Tel: 998-885 0257
A very impressive, and attractive modern restaurant in a lovely lagoon-side garden, with an international menu focusing on steaks and seafood and incorporating Asian and Mediterranean touches. One of the Hotel Zone

restaurants that best delivers on its promises. **$$$**

Chetumal

Sergio's
Av. Obregón 182, corner of Av. 5 de Mayo
Tel: 983-832 2355
Chetumal's best restaurant is eccentrically cozy (with excellent air con for this very hot town). There are pizzas on the menu, but it's much better to go for the excellent local seafood dishes. It's very enjoyable for breakfast, too. **$$**

Chichén Itzá

All the big hotels at Chichén Itzá have large restaurants open to non-guests: the one in the Villas Arqueológicas is particularly pretty, the Hacienda Chichén has the most refined food.

Hotel Dolores Alba
Highway 180 libre Km.122
Tel: 985-858 1555
This attractive hotel on the Highway 3km (2 miles) east of Chichén Itzá also has one of the most attractive restaurants in the area, set in a garden. *Sopa de lima*, *pollo pibil* and other Yucatecan favorites make up the menu. **$–$$**

Las Mestizas
Calle 15 (Highway 180), Pisté village
No phone
The little village of Pisté, just next to the ruins, has an ever-growing number of restaurants along its main street. Their quality varies a lot, but this is one that kept its Yucatecan village charm, and traditional dishes are very nicely done. **$$**

Cobá

Villas Arqueológicas Cobá
Cobá village
Tel: 984-206 7001
Like the other Villas Arqueológicas hotels next to major archeological sites, the one at Cobá has a delightfully relaxing garden

restaurant, open to non-guests. Yucatecan favorites such as *cochinita pibil* are excellently presented, for very reasonable prices. **$$**

Costa Maya

The Leaky Palapa
Xcalak village
No phone
Every season (usually from November to July) for the last few years two Canadian women have come down to remote Xcalak and turned this little sand-floored hut into an ideal beachcomber's restaurant. Timings vary, so ask. **$$**

Cozumel

Casa Denis
Calle 1 Sur, off main plaza
Tel: 987-872 0067
Cozumel's oldest restaurant is still in the same little wooden house as when it opened in 1945. With outside tables near the plaza, it has plenty of atmosphere, and the Yucatecan and Mexican dishes are reliably enjoyable. **$–$$**
Chi
Av. Rafael Melgar, corner of Calle 3 Sur
Tel: 987-869 8156
A chic option on Cozumel, on a terrace above the waterfront with great sunset views. The suitably sophisticated menu is "Pan-Asian," with Thai, Chinese and Japanese dishes, some with a Mexican twist. **$$–$$$**
La Choza
Calle R. Salas 198 and Av. 10 Norte
Tel: 987-872 0958
A big, long-established and very popular place that consistently has some of the best traditional Mexican food on Cozumel – seafood-stuffed *poblano* chilis are only one of the specialties. **$$**
Las Palmeras
Av. Rafael Melgar, corner of Av. Juárez, on the main plaza
Tel: 987-872 0532
Right opposite the main ferry landing in San Miguel, this big, bright and buzzing

restaurant is ideal for mingling and people-watching. Seafood grills are impressive, if a little pricey, and the cocktail list is worth exploring. **$$–$$$**
Restaurante Chen Río
Carretera Costera, on Chen Río beach
No phone
A reason to visit the windblown east coast of Cozumel, a wonderfully laid-back restaurant on the beach in a lovely sheltered cove, one of this coast's best spots for swimming. Giant seafood platters invite you to take your time. **$–$$**

Isla Mujeres

Brisas del Caribe
Av. Rueda Medina, across from ferry dock
Tel: 998-877 0372
With its palm-thatched roof, this big restaurant by the ferry landing is almost a symbol of Isla. The *ceviches*, grilled fish and other Mexican standards are fairly conventional, but the view is great. **$–$$**
Casa O's
Carretera al Garrafón
Tel: 998-888 0170
Isla's prettiest restaurant, on a terrace beneath a *palapa* palm roof on the southeast coast, with a view of Cancún in the distance. The lobster and other seafoods are excellent, and it's ideal for romantic dinners watching the sunset. **$$–$$$**
French Bistro Français
Av. Matamoros, by Av. Juárez
No phone
A Boho survivor from the first days of backpacker tourism on Isla, this colorful place almost invented the idea of laid-back. The food, like the name, is an eccentric mix – veggie burgers, French bistro dishes such as onion soup, Mexican-style grilled fish and more. **$–$$**
Zazil-Ha
Na-Balam Hotel, Calle Zazil-Ha 118
Tel: 998-877 0279
This mellow restaurant inside a hotel right on Isla town's main beach

specializes in wholefood and vegetarian dishes, inventively combining culinary traditions. Gracious service adds to the relaxing feel. **$$–$$$**

Izamal

Restaurante Kinich
Calle 12, corner of Calle 11
Tel: 988-954 0489
On a leaf-shaded terrace a short walk from the Kinich-Kakmó pyramid, this is one of the region's best restaurants for complex traditional dishes like *queso relleno* (pork in melted cheese). Very popular with locals at weekends; go mid-week to be sure of a table. Closed in the evenings. **$$**

Mérida

Los Almendros
Calle 50 No. 493, by Calle 57
Tel: 999-928 5459
Mérida's most famous restaurant, long-considered the main showcase for Yucatecan cuisine such as *poc-chuc* (pork marinated in garlic and bitter oranges). It's now very touristy, but an evening here can still be fun. **$–$$**
Amaro's
Calle 59 No. 507, between calles 60 and 62
Tel: 999-928 2451
One of the prettiest restaurants in central Mérida, with a lovely patio dominated by a giant orchid tree. The menu is very original, around half of it being made up of vegetarian versions of traditional local dishes. Musicians play live on many nights. **$–$$**
Café-Club
Calle 55 No. 496A, between calles 58 and 60
Tel: 999-923 1592
A relaxing spot for breakfast, opposite Santa Lucía church, with a varied mix of salads, sandwiches and Mexican dishes later in the day. Vegetarians are well catered for. **$**
La Casa de Frida
Calle 61 No. 526A, between calles 66 and 68
Tel: 999-928 2311

ABOVE: sit back and relax with a rum cocktail.

While traditional Yucatecan cooking dominates the range in Mérida, this attractive patio restaurant, decorated in colors that evoke the work of Frida Kahlo, takes a different tack with excellent central Mexican dishes, including stuffed *poblano* chilis. Service is very pleasant. **$$**
Casa de Piedra
Hacienda Xcanatún, Calle 20, Xcanatún
Tel: 999-930 2410
Just outside Mérida, the restaurant in Hacienda Xcanatún is a place for a special meal: the setting is stunning, and the menu offers refined creations mixing Yucatecan, French and Caribbean traditions. **$$$**
Eladio's
Calle 59 No. 425, at Calle 44
Tel: 999-823 1087
Eladio's is a local chain that has rejuvenated the old *cantina* concept, and made them more family-friendly – although in traditional fashion you still only pay for drinks, not the food. With dance bands playing most days, they're fun places to sample great local dishes

PRICE CATEGORIES

Price categories are for a meal for one person without drinks:
$ = under 130 pesos
$$ = 130–280 pesos
$$$ = over 280 pesos

and local life at the same time. **$–$$**
Marlín Azul
Calle 62 No. 488, between calles 57 and 59
Tel: 999-928 1606
Another demonstration that the quality of Mexican restaurants can never be judged by appearances. This looks just like a street-side bar (and is very cheap), but its seafood cocktails and ceviches are among Mérida's best **$**

Playa del Carmen

La Cueva del Chango
Calle 38 Norte, off Av. 5
Tel: 984-876 2537

ABOVE: hot, deep-fried stuffed jalapenos with a cool salad.

Some way from the center of Playa – near the Shangri-La Hotel – this friendly, original restaurant is worth finding: it's one of the best on the Riviera Maya for modern, inventive Mexican cooking, with ultra-refreshing salads and subtly-flavored seafood combinations. **$$**
Glass Bar
Calle 10, off Av. 5
Tel: 984-803 1676
Of all the chic, stylish restaurants in Playa, Glass Bar is one of those most worth visiting for its food – another eclectic European-Mexican mix as well as the design and the people-watching opportunities. There's a range of Spanish-style tapas as well as main dishes, and a refined wine list. **$$$**

Restaurante-Coctelería Las Brisas
Calle 4 Norte, off Av. 5
No phone
A good example of the Mexican rule that good restaurants don't need to be fancy or expensive. Local seafood favorites are the things to go for: great shrimp and conch ceviches, with lashings of plump seafood. **$–$$**
Yaxché
Calle 8 Norte, off Av. 5
Tel: 984-873 2502
The most renowned restaurant in Playa del Carmen, where the Lizaola family have created original dishes combining Maya traditions with refined culinary skills. Just reading the menu feels like an adventure, and the combinations of subtle seasonings are richly enjoyable. **$$$**

Progreso

Flamingos
Malecón, corner of Calle 72
Tel: 969-934 4050
Many places could claim to offer the Yucatán's best ceviches, but Flamingos is certainly a candidate, and the location on Progreso seafront makes it a very enjoyable place to spend an afternoon. **$$**

Puerto Morelos

Los Pelícanos
Town plaza, by the beach

Tel: 998-871 0014
With a prime position above Puerto Morelos beach, the big terrace of this traditional restaurant makes this one of the most enjoyable on the coast – sampling a ceviche while watching the pelicans hang in the wind is one of the Riviera's best experiences. **$$**

Río Bec

Río Bec Dreams
Highway 186 Km 142, near Chicanná ruins
No phone
www.riobecdreams.com
The best hotel in the Río Bec area also has its best bar-restaurant for miles, open to all. The Canadian owners present an untypical menu: pastas, salads, English dishes, curries and other options may all turn up. **$$**

Tulum

Don Cafeto
Av. Tulum, by Calle Orion, Tulum Pueblo
Tel: 984-871 2207
Don Cafeto has been in Tulum since before the village had paved streets, and has adapted to every change since then. It's now a big sidewalk terrace, with satisfying breakfasts and classic Yucatecan and Mexican fare. **$–$$**
Paris de Noche
Av. Tulum, by Calle Osiris, Tulum Pueblo
Tel: 984-871 2532
As the name tells you, this lively sidewalk restaurant in Tulum village is a Mexican-French combination – so there's a big range of crêpes and other French favorites as well as Mexican-based creations. **$$–$$$**
La Zebra
Carretera Tulum–Boca Paila Km 8.5
Tel: 984-115 4728
The "beach cantina" attached to some of Tulum's most hip cabañas is run with a lot of verve – the seafood grills and salads are ideal for a lunch by the beach, and the margaritas are first-rate too. **$$–$$$**

Uxmal and the Puuc Region

As at Chichén Itzá, the large hotels beside the ruins all have attractive restaurants, and the Hacienda Temozón hotel not far away has one of the region's finest.
Hacienda San Pedro Ochil
Highway 261 Km 176, 32km (20 miles) north of Uxmal
Tel: 999-924 7465
Though owned by the same group that runs Temozón and other hacienda-hotels, this smaller hacienda north of Uxmal is only a restaurant. The gardens are a lovely place to sample refined Yucatecan dishes – with especially good salads – and afterwards you can wander through craft workshops, a pretty shop and a museum. **$$**
The Pickled Onion
Highway 261, just south of Santa Elena village
Tel: 997-111 7922
Food options on the Puuc Route have been extended with this little café opened by English/Canadian Valerie Pickles. Menus mainly follow local tastes; there's a swimming pool, and she also offers sandwiches and box lunches – very handy in this often restaurant-free area. **$$**

Valladolid

El Mesón del Marqués
Calle 39 No. 203, Plaza Principal
Tel: 985-856 2073
Valladolid's most famous and atmospheric hotel also has its most enjoyable restaurant, in a lovely colonial patio. The town's own specialties are highlights of the menu, such as the roasted chicken dish, pollo oriental de Valladolid. **$$**

PRICE CATEGORIES

Price categories are for a meal for one person without drinks:
$ = under 130 pesos
$$ = 130–280 pesos
$$$ = over 280 pesos

A CTIVITIES

FESTIVALS, THE ARTS, NIGHTLIFE, SHOPPING AND SPECTATOR SPORTS

FESTIVALS

Listed here is just a small selection of Mexico's hundreds of fiestas and fairs, month by month, but every town has at least one special event during the year, and cities have several. Information on upcoming fiestas can be found at local tourist offices and in the local press. Check dates before you go, too, as many vary slightly from year to year. (See pages 9 and 89–91.)

January

6: Día de Reyes, Feast of Epiphany or "Three Kings": the traditional day for children to receive Christmas gifts. There are parades led by "The Kings" in most cities across Mexico.

February

late January or February: Carnaval, during the week before Lent: among Mexico's biggest carnival fiestas are those in Huejotzingo, Puebla; Tepoztlán, Morelos; Acapulco, Guerrero; Mazatlán, Sinaloa; Veracruz; Campeche city; and Mérida, Yucatán, all with several days of parades, floats, eating and dancing. A very special Carnaval takes place in San Juan Chamula, Chiapas, an extraordinary mix of Maya and Catholic traditions.

March

March or April: Semana Santa (Holy Week) sees a wide variety of celebrations and processions all over Mexico.

March: Festival del Centro Histórico, a three-week cultural extravaganza in Mexico City's Historic Center, with opera, rock, movie screenings and other events, often in open-air venues and including an international range of artists.

April

April–May: Feria Nacional de San Marcos, Aguascalientes: the largest of Mexico's ferias or fairs, given "national" status: for nearly four weeks Aguascalientes hosts stock sales, food displays, parades, charro shows, bullfights and cockfights, a beauty pageant, many other shows and daily parties.

May

5: Cinco de Mayo: holiday commemorating the Mexican victory over the French army at Puebla in 1862; in Mexico (in contrast to parts of the US with large Mexican populations) this is a relatively minor holiday, and the only big celebrations are in Puebla.

June

24: San Juan Bautista (John the Baptist): especially colorful fiestas are held in San Juan Cosalá, on Lake Chapala, Jalisco; Coatetelco, Morelos; San Juan Chamula, Chiapas; and on Cozumel.
29: Día de San Pedro y San Pablo. As with most saints' fiestas, celebrations go on for several days around the actual date; among the most attractive are the big street fiesta in Tlaquepaque, near Guadalajara, Jalisco, and the processions in Pochutla, Oaxaca.

July

16: Nuestra Señora del Carmen. Festivals in the San Ángel district of Mexico City, Catemaco, Veracruz, and Ciudad del Carmen, Campeche.
Last two Mondays in July: La Guelaguetza, or Lunes del Cerro (Mondays on the Hill), a stunning display of the dances, music, crafts and other traditions of all the many cultures of Oaxaca state, held on a hill outside Oaxaca city.

August

Usually 5–20: Feria de Huamantla, Huamantla, Tlaxcala. The most spectacular of many celebrations across Mexico around the Feast of the Assumption (August 15), culminating in "the night no-one sleeps" on **10:** San Lorenzo: the patron of many towns and notably Zinacantán, Chiapas, which marks the occasion with some of the most intriguing Highland Maya ceremonies, accompanied by the community's own, almost unearthly music.

September

14: Día del Charro. A special day to celebrate Mexico's horse-riding traditions: the biggest events are in Guadalajara, but there are also charro parades in Mexico City and many other cities.
15–16: Independence Day. Major celebrations begin on the night of the 15th, commemorating Hidalgo's Grito or call for Mexican independence, and are followed by other events and a national holiday on the 16th.

October

Mid-October–November: Festival Internacional Cervantino, Guanajuato: Mexico's première arts festival, with a prestigious range of international participants.

November

October 31– November 1–2: All Saints' Day and Día de los Muertos (Day of the Dead). The dead are commemorated in slightly different ways all over Mexico. Some of the most impressive events are at Pátzcuaro and Isla Janitzio, Michoacán, at San Andrés Mixquic, near Xochimilco in Mexico City, and in Oaxaca.
20: National Holiday commemorating the start of the 1910 Revolution.

December

12: Nuestra Señora de Guadalupe. The most important religious festival of the year: vast crowds visit the shrine of Our Lady of Guadalupe in Mexico City, and all over the country groups of *guadalupano* pilgrims can be seen in the days up to December 12 running along roads to the capital or to their local shrine to the Virgin.
24–25: Navidad (Christmas): the night of Christmas Eve (La Noche Buena) is the heart of Christmas celebrations, with Midnight Masses followed by very late family dinners, and Christmas Day itself is a very quiet holiday.

THE ARTS

Mexico's vibrant cultural scene is concentrated, predictably, in the capital, but opportunities to hear classical and other live music, especially, are expanding in other cities, notably Guadalajara and Mérida. There are also many fine arts festivals that bring very varied programs to different cities around the country during the year, of which Guanajuato's Cervantino each October is the most important.

Music, Dance and Theater

Mexico City

The capital's traditional main venues for all kinds of music and dance have been the two auditoria of the historic **Palacio de Bellas Artes** on the Alameda and the giant 1950s **Auditorio Nacional** in Chapultepec park. Both venues host classical

concerts and ballet, and Bellas Artes, in the past a major opera venue, also regularly presents Mexican folk dance shows by the Ballet Folklórico de México, while the Auditorio is now a prime venue for big-scale pop and rock concerts by international artists such as Gloria Estefan or the Pet Shop Boys. Since the 1990s classical music performances (including the regular seasons of Mexico's *Orquesta Sinfónica Nacional*) have tended to move to the **Auditorio Blas Galindo** in the vast **Centro Nacional de las Artes** (CENART), built on the site of the former Churubusco film studios in the south of the city, to the east of Coyoacán (metro General Anaya). Another major center for classical music is the **Centro Cultural Universitario** in the vast university complex (UNAM) in the south of the city, which has its own orchestra (the *Orquesta Filármonica de la UNAM*) and three fine-quality concert halls. The last of Mexico City's three full orchestras, the *Orquesta Filarmónica de la Ciudad de México*, generally performs at the **Centro Cultural Ollin Yoliztli**, a city-run cultural center near the university in the south of the city, but tours frequently.

CENART also hosts a whole complex of arts schools and a range of other performance spaces, which are increasingly the main venues for adventurous theater and ballet and contemporary dance, as well as classical music. Next to the Auditorio in Chapultepec, the **Centro Cultural del Bosque** also contains the **Teatro de la Danza**, an intimate venue for classical and contemporary dance. For theater, the **Teatro de la Ciudad** in the city center (metro Allende) is a major venue, but its eclectic program also includes many concerts. Mexico City has a very vibrant modern theater scene – virtually all, naturally, in Spanish – which can be seen mainly in the Cenart venues and many small theaters around town, best found by checking current listings magazines and websites. One of the most imaginative independent theaters is the **Foro Shakespeare** in Condesa (metro Chapultepec).

As well as at the Auditorio Nacional, pop and rock concerts are held in the **Teatro Metropólitan**, in the center near the Alameda (metro Juárez), which also co-hosts the city's Jazz Festival each September with the Auditorio, and the **Auditorio Plaza Condesa**. Many Mexican and big touring acts also play at the **Foro Sol**, an adapted baseball stadium near the airport, and the nearby **Palacio de los**

Deportes, the 1968 Olympic basketball hall. Both are much criticized for their acoustics, but continue to host many concerts. A few really huge acts also play the **Estadio Azteca** soccer stadium. At the other end of the scale, there are also plenty of small venues around the vast city, especially in Condesa, and many of the finest – but often scarcely known – Latin musicians from Cuba, the Dominican Republic and other countries play regularly in the city's salsa and dance clubs; for these, see Nightlife, page 369.
Auditorio Nacional, Paseo de la Reforma 50, tel: 55-9138 1350, www.auditorio.com.mx.
Auditorio Plaza Condesa, Juan Escutia 4, corner of Tamaulipas, Col. Condesa. Bookings via Ticketmaster.
CENART, Río Churubusco 79, tel: 55-4155 0000, www.cenart.gob.mx. Look under "Cartelera del Mes" for upcoming programs in music, dance and other fields.
Centro Cultural Ollin Yolintzi, Periférico Sur 5141, tel: 55-5606 3901, www.cultura.df.gob.mx.
Centro Cultural Universitario, Insurgentes Sur 300, telephone numbers vary for each venue; www.musicaunam.net.
Foro Shakespeare, Zamora 7, Col. Condesa, tel: 55-5553 4642, www.foroshakespeare.com.
Foro Sol, Viaducto Río de la Piedad, Ciudad Deportiva. Bookings via Ticketmaster.
Palacio de Bellas Artes, Av. Hidalgo 1, tel: 55-5512 2593, www.bellasartes.gob.mx.
Palacio de los Deportes, Av. Río Churubusco, Ciudad Deportiva. Bookings via Ticketmaster.
Teatro de la Ciudad, Donceles 36, tel: 55-5518 4926, www.cultura.df.gob.mx.
Teatro de la Danza, Centro Cultural del Bosque, Paseo de la Reforma & Campo Marte, Chapultepec, tel: 55-5280 8771, www.bellasartes.gob.mx.
Teatro Metropólitan, Independencia 90, tel: 55-5510 1035. Bookings via Ticketmaster.

Around Mexico City

Of the cities around the capital, **Puebla** has the most extensive cultural program. The 250-year-old (but much rebuilt) **Teatro Principal** makes an excellent venue for concerts, dance and theater performances, and many other events are presented in the **Centro Cultural Universitario** (University Cultural Center). In **Cuernavaca**, the **Teatro Ocampo**, off Jardín Juárez in the town

center, hosts music of various kinds, theater, folk and contemporary dance, and movie screenings.
Teatro Ocampo, Jardín Juárez 2, Cuernavaca, tel: 777-318 6385, www.teatroocampo.com.
Teatro Principal, Calle 6 Norte by 8 Oriente, Puebla, tel: 222-232 6085.

Other Areas
Yucatán and Riviera Maya
Founded only in 2004, the *Orquesta Sinfónica de Yucatán* is an ambitious young orchestra whose fast-rising standards have been widely admired. Concert programs often feature international guest performers, and are presented in the ornate **Teatro Peón Contreras** in Mérida. The orchestra also tours around the state and plays a major part in the Otoño Cultural festival each October– November, with concerts and arts events all over Yucatán.

Opportunities to hear other kinds of live music – beyond traditional musicians and the salsa bands ubiquitous at every fiesta – are fairly scarce. Mexican and other Latin stars regularly play at the **X'matkuil** state fair near Mérida in November– December, and there are a few jazz and rock clubs. In Cancún and the Riviera many clubs have cover bands, but the original acts rarely play here, except during the brief **Riviera Maya Jazz Festival** in **Playa del Carmen** in November, which is seeking to attract a sophisticated range of international artists to play on the beach (www.riviera mayajazzfestival.com).

Orquesta Sinfónica de Yucatán, Teatro Peón Contreras, Mérida, tel: 999-923 7354, www.sinfonicadeyucatan. com.mx.

Traditional Music and Dance

Virtually every part of Mexico has its own distinctive – but also distinctively Mexican – style of music, and traditional music and dance are very much a part of everyday life. *Mariachis*, guitar trios and other traditional musicians often play in hotels and restaurants, but they can also be seen and heard in *cantinas* and for free at every fiesta. Many state capitals present free displays of their own local dances and often other styles at some time, usually every weekend. Some cities, such as Oaxaca and Mérida, have particularly extensive programs which are not to be missed. Alternatively, since Mexican strolling musicians play for hire, you can also contract a *mariachi*

or other band for a personal serenade, wherever you wish.

Mexico City
The classic place to get into the *mariachi* spirit in the capital is **Plaza Garibaldi** *(see page 139)*, although it's now very "tourist-ized," and at night can be pretty seedy. A better alternative than just wandering around the square is to head straight for the **Salón Tenampa** just beside it, a legendary *mariachi cantina* with an irresistible atmosphere, where the musicians are always first-rate. *Mariachis* are not the only musicians who play in Garibaldi, as there are often bands from other traditions such as the sweet *jarochos* of

ABOVE: dancing in the street at night in Veracruz.

Veracruz or the accordion polka bands from the north.

Away from Garibaldi, some of the best places to catch traditional music in the right atmosphere are *cantinas*, of which **El Centenario** in Condesa and the **Guadalupana** in Coyoacán are two of the most enjoyable. In the Zona Rosa, **El Lugar del Mariachi** is a big bar-restaurant where a *mariachi* and dance show goes with the meal – again, touristy, but fun.

Another city plaza is a favorite venue for a gentler style of music and dance. The **Plaza de la Ciudadela**, five blocks south of the Alameda down Av. Niños Héroes (metro Balderas) has been dubbed the *Plaza del Danzón*, as every Saturday afternoon couples go there to practice the elegant, sinuous, very Caribbean *Danzón* dance beloved of older Mexicans.

Mexico's most admired and

professional folk dance company is the **Ballet Folklórico de México**, which when not touring generally performs twice each week in the **Palacio de Bellas Artes** *(see page 140)*. Shows commonly feature a mixture of dances from around the country.
Cantina El Centenario, Vicente Suárez 42, Condesa, no phone (metro Juanacatlán).
Cantina La Guadalupana, Higuera 2, Coyoacán, tel: 55-5554 6253 *(see Eating Out, page 355)*.
El Lugar del Mariachi, Hamburgo 86, Zona Rosa, tel: 55-5207 4864.
Salon Tenampa, Plaza Garibaldi 12, tel: 55-5526 6176, www.salontenampa. com.

Jalisco and Michoacán
Guadalajara
Casa Bariachi, Avenida Vallarta 2221, tel: 523-615 0029. A good *mariachi* and steak restaurant, with colorful *piñatas* hanging from the ceiling. A bit touristy, but the sing-along of waiters and diners is a crowd-pleaser, and the place couldn't be more fun.
La Maestranza, Maestranza 179, Centro Histórico, tel: 333-613 5878. This is a *cantina* as well as a bull fighting museum. Very nice atmosphere with an old 1940s era building that hasn't changed much since yesteryear. The walls are covered with bull fighting pictures, posters and art.

The Gulf Coast
Veracruz has some of Mexico's strongest and most distinctive musical traditions, with light, very Caribbean and Cuban-influenced rhythms like the *jarocho* and the *son* or *huapango*, played on guitars with the special addition of a harp (as heard in one of the most famous of all Mexican songs, La Bamba). Local music can be heard in the streets, in many city cafés and during the spring Carnaval and other fiestas, and a fine band usually provides music for *danzón* dancing in the **Zócalo** every Tuesday, Thursday, Friday and Saturday night, while on Sunday evenings there are *son* performances in the **Callejón de La Lagunilla**, one of the most attractive streets of the old town, just off Calle Arista.

This is also the location of **El Rincón de la Trova** (Callejón de la Lagunilla 59, Veracruz, no phone), one of the city's most time-honored music bars, where languid tropical music is enjoyed by crowds of every age. It's open daily, but there are usually live bands only from Thursdays to Saturdays.

TRANSPORTATION
ACCOMMODATIONS
EATING OUT
ACTIVITIES
A – Z
LANGUAGE

Oaxaca

La Candela, Murgía 413, Oaxaca City, tel: 951-514 2010. Good salsa and other Latin music live bands. Nice courtyard style ambiance, and it is open in the early evening as a restaurant, too.

Chiapas

The most treasured musical instrument in non-Maya Chiapas – as in Guatemala – is the marimba, and in towns like **Comitán** and **Tapachula** marimba bands play in the main squares every Sunday, and often on other evenings as well. **Tuxtla Gutiérrez** has a pretty square set aside for marimba recitals, **Parque de la Marimba**, where there are performances several evenings a week.

Many of the Highland Maya communities of Chiapas have their own special festival music, with a structure completely unlike any European-based music and a unique, unearthly sound, even though it is now played mainly on European based instruments. Each piece is played continuously during the major fiestas, such as the Carnaval in **Chamula** or San Lorenzo in **Zinacantán**, and rarely at any other time, so a chance to hear this unnervingly strange music is not to be missed.

Yucatán and Riviera Maya

The Yucatán Peninsula is another region very attached to its special traditions in music and dance. *Mariachis* and other "Mexican" musicians can be heard here, but more distinctive are the musicians of the Yucatecan trios, the *Trova Yucateca*, with a tradition going back well over a century, and the rapid rhythms of the *jarana*, an intricate dance performed by graceful couples, men all in white, women in exquisitely flower-embroidered dresses called *ternos*.

Campeche is equally proud of its own variations on Yucatecan tradition, which are showcased in several regular events (all free). The delightful **Casa Seis** cultural center on Campeche city's **Parque Principal** hosts the *Jueves de Música Campechana* sessions of traditional music, every Thursday from 8pm, and *Viernes Folclórico*, with dances as well as music, every Friday at the same time. In the middle of the square there are free concerts and folk dance shows every Saturday from 6pm, and all day on Sundays.

It's **Mérida**, however, the heart of Yucatecan culture, that has the most extensive free program, with events

The English-language paper *The News* has a limited "What's On" section on Fridays and Saturdays, but to really explore the options in this vast city you have to handle at least some Spanish. Tourist offices have a fairly limited free guide, *Chilanguía*, which highlights city-sponsored events, and the daily newspaper *Reforma* has a useful entertainments supplement every Friday, "Primera Fila." For full information there are also several comprehensive listings guides available at newsstands, which can also now be consulted online: *Tiempo Libre* is the most established

(www.tiempolibre.com.mx), but the hip *Dónde Ir* (www.donde-ir.com) and *Chilango* (www.chilango.com) both cover music, nightlife and independent arts well.

Ticketmaster (tel: 55-5325 9000, www.ticketmaster.com.mx) is well established in Mexico and is now the most convenient way to book tickets in advance, for the main public and independent venues. Tickets can be bought at Ticketmaster desks in several stores as well as online, and at some you can collect tickets previously bought by phone or online. Details are given (mostly in Spanish) on the website.

every night of the week that blend together purely local traditions with an eclectic mix of other styles. The usual schedule is as follows:

Monday: Vaquería Regional (country fiesta) in the city, with *Jarana* dancing and music, from 9pm in front of the Palacio Municipal on Plaza Mayor.

Tuesday: Remembranzas Musicales, nostalgic big-band music from 9pm in Parque de Santiago.

Wednesday: A variety of concerts, exhibitions and other events are presented in the Centro Cultural Olimpo, Plaza Mayor, from 9pm.

Thursday: Serenatas Yucatecas, in Parque de Santa Lucía from 9pm; an absolute must, held every Thursday for over 40 years and a wonderful, utterly charming showcase for the whole world of Yucatecan music, dance, poetry, dress and folklore. Enthusiastically enjoyed by locals, but very welcoming to visitors.

Friday: Serenata Universitaria, traditional dances and music from all over Mexico performed in the patio of the Universidad Autónoma de Yucatán, Calle 60 by Calle 57, from 9pm.

Saturday: A choice of two events: in Corazón de Mérida, calles 60 and 62 in the city center are closed to traffic from 8.30pm and taken over by dance bands, salsa, food stalls and wandering crowds; while the Noche Mexicana on Paseo de Montejo, at Calle 49, celebrates everything strictly "Mexican" (rather than Yucatecan) – *mariachis*, *rancheras*, and other classic Mexican songs, from 7pm.

Sunday: Mérida en Domingo: the streets on and around the Plaza Mayor are again closed to traffic, for a weekly, all-day fiesta. Events include *jarana* displays at the Palacio Municipal (around noon), and salsa,

danzón and other dances in Parque Hidalgo and Parque Santa Lucía, and there are also clowns, kids' shows, and a whole array of street stalls.

In **Cancún** and on the **Riviera Maya**, *mariachis*, Yucatecan trios and other musicians can be seen in many hotels and restaurants, but folklore shows have become less common. *Voces y Danzas de Mexico*, a colorful anthology of classic Mexican folk dances, is still sometimes presented at the **Teatro de Cancún**, but the theater's program is now more made up of concerts and plays primarily appealing to local audiences. A Mexican folk dance spectacular is also part of each day's show at **Xcaret** Eco Park.

Teatro de Cancún, El Embarcadero, Blvd Kukulcán Km 4, tel: 998-849 5580.

Movies

Mexico has a long and rich tradition in cinema. The 1940s and 1950s were the "Golden Age" of Mexican cinema, when the country produced more films than most European countries, and the movies of singer-action heroes like Pedro Infante and Jorge Negrete, screen goddess María Félix and comedian Cantinflas were hugely popular throughout the Spanish-speaking world. Vintage movies from that era are still favorites on Mexican TV today. The Churubusco studios in Mexico City (now the site of the CENART arts complex) were also admired for their high technical standards, and technicians, such as the great cinematographer Gabriel Figueroa, were in high demand in Hollywood.

There followed many years in the doldrums, but Mexican film-making revived in the 1990s with the so-called *Nuevo Cine Mexicano* or "New Mexican Cinema," spearheaded by independent productions such as María Novaro's enchanting **Danzón** in 1991 and **Como agua para chocolate** (*Like Water for Chocolate*, 1992). One of the films with the biggest impact worldwide has been Alejando González Iñárritu's fierce vision of Mexico City **Amores Perros** (2000), the first Mexican movie nominated for an Oscar. Mexican directors such as González Iñárritu, Alfonso Cuarón (**Y tu mamá también**, **Children of Men**) and Guillermo del Toro (**Pan's Labyrinth**) are also now well established internationally, and Mexico continues to produce an exciting range of new talent and new productions.

Movie-going is also very popular, and Mexico City especially has hundreds of movie theaters showing a very wide range of Mexican, Hollywood and international pictures. An essential stop for film-lovers is the **Cineteca Nacional** in Coyoacán, with six screens showing a constantly changing repertoire of classic and new movies. Other cities also have at least a few movie theaters, although in small towns they are now quite rare. More and more screens, in Mexico City and other cities, are in giant new multiplexes attached to shopping malls.

It is very common for Hollywood and other international films to be shown in English with Spanish subtitles on at least one screen in multiplexes. Where this is so, it is usually indicated with *En Inglés* (rather than *En Español*) or sometimes *VO* (for *Versión Original*) in advertising and listings, but it's often worth double-checking when you buy the ticket. In Mexico City, the best listings of current movie showings are in the Friday "Primera Fila" supplement with *Reforma* newspaper and *Tiempo Libre* magazine. In other cities, check local papers, where listings are usually easy to find.

Cineteca Nacional, Av. México–Coyoacán 389, Col. Xoco, tel: 55-4155 1190, www.cinetecanacional.net. Located to the north of central Coyoacán, near the Museo-Casa de Trotsky (metro Coyoacán).

NIGHTLIFE

The vast metropolis of Mexico City is, as in so many things, a place apart in the scale, variety and intensity of its life and entertainment after dark. Beyond the capital, Mexico's other big nightlife centers are the major resort areas such as Puerto Vallarta, Ixtapa-Zihuatanejo, Acapulco and the Riviera Maya, all of which have an ample choice from hotel lounge-bars and traditional tourist discos to, in the more hip spots, beach parties with international DJs.

Other cities – and even small towns – all have their own crop of discos and clubs, but their style tends to be far more conventional than that of the trendier venues in the capital. Latin music lovers, though, will always find something energetic to dance to. In state capitals most big hotels have nightclubs that are popular with an up-market local crowd, generally with unadventurous musical tastes.

Cantinas, Bars, and Nightclubs

Mexico City

A city this size naturally has a huge variety of nightlife venues spread over its many *colonias* or districts – keeping track of them is a major task in itself – but most visitors find it easier to limit themselves to certain more attractive areas. The **Centro Histórico** has some of the city's most buzzing streetlife around the Zócalo and Plaza Garibaldi, many historic *cantinas* and some lively clubs and music venues. The **Zona Rosa**, the main nightlife area from the 1960s to the 1990s, has now faded from fashion and many of its big clubs look fairly shabby, although it remains a hub of the Gay scene. The liveliest areas nowadays to explore by night are **Roma** and chic **Condesa** to the south, which have scores of restaurants, hip and more basic clubs and bars, and pavement cafés. In Condesa, a good place to begin is the junction of avenidas Michoacán and Vicente Suárez, where crowds gather and mingle every weekend, and from where a whole range of venues is within strolling distance. North of Chapultepec park, **Polanco**, the wealthy district par excellence of Mexico City, is also the setting for some of its most glitzy nightclubs.

Areas such as the Zona Rosa, Roma, Condesa and Polanco are also much safer to wander around at night than the center, where more care is necessary. Even there, though, always take a taxi from an official rank to get back to your hotel, or get a venue to call one for you.

Each area – naturally – has some high-class salsa and Latin dance venues, but in Condesa especially there are also places offering hip-hop, techno, 1940s retro, tango and virtually every other kind of music. In general, bars with a dance space are more common than nightclubs as such, and many host live acts on at least a few nights a week, giving way to DJs as the night goes on. To find out more about Mexico City's rapidly changing nightlife scene, the best sources are, again, magazines and websites (in Spanish) such as *Dónde Ir* and *Chilango* (look under *Bares y Antros*). As well as permanent venues and special events put on during fiestas, there are also many one-off events, which are advertized on websites such as http://thecitylovesyou.com. The list below can only be a sample of the city's best.

Acanto, Bosque de Chapultepec, 2a Seccíon, tel: 55-5515 9585. One of the city's most luxurious bar-nightclubs, beside one of the lakes in Chapultepec Park with a gorgeous view of the fountains. Dress to impress.

Área, Hotel Habita, Presidente Masaryk 201, Polanco (metro Polanco), tel: 55-5282 3100. The rooftop bar-lounge in Mexico City's most chic hotel is a stunning display piece of contemporary design, and a perennial favorite with some of the capital's most beautiful people. Music is suitably cool.

Bar Fly, Presidente Masaryk 393, Polanco, tel: 55-5282 2906. Intimate and elegant, but still with energy to spare, this Polanco salsa bar hosts fine Cuban and other musicians every night except Monday, with romantic *boleros* to start the evening before the dancing starts. Perhaps the city's most plush Latin dance venue.

Cafeína, Nuevo León 73, corner Calle Juan Escutia, Condesa, tel: 55-5212 0090. One of the coolest of Condesa's bar-lounges, attracting a very stylish, sexy crowd. The cocktails are a real indulgence, and the music is a hedonistic electro-Brazilian and lounge mix. The Monday night Brazilian parties, with live bands, are a big hit.

Mamá Rumba, Querétaro 230, Roma, tel: 55-5564 6920. Open for two decades, this Cuban restaurant is a huge favorite with local *salseros*, with superb live bands keeping up the energy till closing time. It's usually packed; many of the local dancers may seem intimidatingly good, but the atmosphere is infectious, and the *mojitos* and other cocktails are great.

La Maraka, Mitla 410, Colonia

Narvarte (metro Eugenia), tel: 55-5682 5479. The area is off the beaten track – some way south of Colonia Roma – but this Latin dance club consistently attracts some of the best salsa, *merengue* and *cumbia* musicians from Cuba, the US and around the Caribbean.

Mesón Triana, Oaxaca 90, Roma, tel: 55-5525 3880. The city's most long-established Spanish bar, with flamenco shows featuring visiting performers from Spain, fine wines and a very enjoyable range of tapas.

Pata Negra, Tamaulipas 30, corner Calle Juan Escutia, Condesa, tel: 55-5211 5563. Very popular with Condesa Bohemians, this big, friendly bar-venue has a choice of live music on its two levels on most nights of the week, followed by DJs into the small hours. The wonderful music menu typifies Mexico City's eclecticism: at different times you can hear salsa, jazz, rock, techno, samba, or Mexican folk styles such as *son*, and all first-rate. It particularly favors young, inventive bands.

Pasaje América, 5 de Mayo 7, Centro Histórico (metro Bellas Artes), tel: 55-5521 0870. A funky club that attracts some of the best Mexican and international DJs and live acts in varied styles, in a decadent setting in a distinguished 19th-century building, with plenty of original fittings and plush lounges as well as dance spaces. Open Thur–Sat.

Pervert Lounge, Uruguay 70, Centro Histórico (metro Zócalo), tel: 55-5510 4454. House, techno, trance and other dance music; the stone-walled decor is pretty plain, but it's a very popular fixture in the center of town. Open Wed–Sat.

Rioma, Insurgentes Sur 377, Condesa (metro Chilpancingo), tel: 55-5584 8540. A former restaurant with a mix of its original 1940s decor and slick modern touches that is now one of Condesa's most fashionable clubs, with largely techno and electro music and especially popular as an after-hours call in (from 4am). Open Wed–Sat.

La Terraza a Condesa DF, Veracruz 102, Condesa, tel: 55-5241 2600. The rooftop terrace bar of the ultra-chic Condesa DF hotel is another of Mexico City's most stunning spaces, and a seductive spot for late-night lounging or a romantic rendezvous under the stars.

Baja California

Cabo San Lucas is a prime spot in Baja to party. Tijuana, despite the problems caused by the drug trade,

remains a fun spot on the California border that's well worth visiting.

Cabo San Lucas

Cabo Wabo, cnr Cardenas and Guerrero, tel: 624-143 1188. This club, opened by rock and roll legend Sammy Hagar, remains a supreme place to drink, party, and have fun. Pool tables, a rock stage, and all the legends that go along with it are part of the fun here.

El Squid Roe, Cardenas and Marina, tel: 624-143 0655. A Cabo institution, this place is popular with all ages, young and old, provided you're willing to get wild and crazy in the congo line. Waiters dance on tables and stand ready with tequila shots. Plan on being thirsty when you arrive.

Acapulco

El Alebrije, Costera Miguel Alemán 3308, tel: 744-484 5902. This enormous club caters to an under-30 crowd but is standing room only on a Friday or Saturday night, with the party raging on until the sun comes up.

Paladium, Escénica Las Brisas s/n, tel: 744-446 5490. Perhaps the best view of the city, and with one of Mexico's best laser light shows, Paladium simply rocks. Well worth visiting, assuming you can wait for an hour or more to get inside.

Yucatán and Riviera Maya

In **Mérida**, the free fiestas and other entertainments in the street (see *Traditional Music and Dance, page 367*) often provide the most attractive way to spend an evening, but there are other options too. In the center, **Pancho's**, Calle 59 No. 509, between 60 and 62 (tel: 999-923 0942) is a fun bar-restaurant with classic Mexican food, live Latin bands and a tiny dance floor. The more modern clubs and bars popular with locals are all further north near Prolongación de Montejo, a continuation of Paseo Montejo; the sleek **El Cielo**, Prolongación de Montejo by Calle 25 (tel: 999-944 5127) is much the most elegant.

These attractions, though, are of course only small-scale compared to those on the coast to the east. Each of the Riviera Maya's three nightlife hubs – Cancún, Cozumel, and now Playa del Carmen – has a slightly different style. Many of the big resort complexes along the Riviera have their own nightclubs, and Isla Mujeres and other places along the coast also have a few night bars and discos, but the scene is much more low-key than in the main centers.

Cancún

The Hotel Zone was built on a big scale, and its multispace clubs are accordingly some of the biggest in the world. Taxis are often necessary for getting up and down the Hotel Zone strip, but conveniently the really giant, most popular venues are clustered together around Boulevard Kukulcán Km 9, near the bend in the "7" of Cancún island, and the Forum by the Sea mall. These big clubs can be expensive – they usually have an all-in-one entry charge of around $45, with all drinks included, but to keep drinks coming you must keep your waiter happy with frequent tips. Two-for-one nights and other promotions are worth taking advantage of. There are also smaller, more casual night bars along the strip, and in downtown Cancún there are more basic, more Mexican-style bars and discos, especially along Avenida Yaxchilán.

One way to get a sample of Cancún nightlife without spending too much money is to take the **Cancún Party Hopper Tour** (www.partyhoppercancun. com). This takes you around a selection of clubs for an all-in fee of around $65.

Azúcar, Dreams Cancún Resort, off Blvd Kukulcán at Km 9, tel: 998-848 7000. This elegant club beside the Dreams resort is Cancún's best Latin dance venue, and many big names in Latin music play here. A favorite with local dancers, who dress sharp. Entrance is free for Dreams guests. Open Thur–Sat.

The City, Blvd Kukulcán Km 9, tel: 998-848 8380. A truly vast multi-space with four dance floors and nine bars, and an adventurous music policy featuring international DJs. There are theme nights through the week, and a beach club for pool parties.

Coco Bongo, Blvd Kukulcán Km 9.5, tel: 998-883 5061. Cancún's most celebrated venue is a show as well as a club, with eye- and ear-boggling presentations nightly featuring acrobats, dancers and convincing lookalikes of Madonna and other superstars. A choice of hip-hop, salsa, rock and more in several dance spaces.

Congo Bar, Blvd Kukulcán Km 9.5, tel: 998-883 5061. This smaller, high-energy bar-club is a popular alternative to the big venues nearby. There's no cover, three dance floors (including one under the stars) and a lively music mix.

Dady'O, Blvd Kukulcán Km 9.5, tel: 998-883 3333. The traditional biggest rival to the Coco Bongo across the street, which offers a choice of spaces: Dady'O itself is a huge disco;

TRANSPORTATION

Dady Rock is a slightly smaller, even louder club with frequent bikini and wet T-shirt contests; the **XX Terrace** is a more casual, raucous party bar; the **O Ultra Lounge** is more stylish, with trance and house music; and **Terrasta** has reggae, R&B and similar. **Pat O'Brien's**, Plaza Flamingo, Blvd Kukulcán Km 11.5, tel: 998-883 0832. Giant American-style sports bar and restaurant, with games (including English soccer) on the screens and rock, jazz and country music. **Señor Frog's**, Blvd Kukulcán Km 9.7, tel: 998-883 1092. One of the foremost outlets of a chain that's ever-popular with its mix of Mexican rancho-themed decor, mostly-Mexican food and all-out party atmosphere, with often-cheesy disco, Latin and rock favorites to go with it.

Cozumel
In line with its easy-going, family-resort style, nightlife on Cozumel is

sushi, great cocktails and a fabulous view (especially at sunset). Guest DJs raise the energy level late-night. **Viva Mexico**, Av. Rafael Melgar, corner Calle 3 Sur, tel: 987-872 0799. Another roof terrace with a different style: a big, rumbustious Mexican restaurant-dance club, popular with locals and tourists, with an irresistible mix of Latin pop, salsa and *merengue*.

Playa del Carmen
With its rapid growth, Playa has emerged as the area's main "alternative" nightlife center to Cancún. One difference is that most of its venues are spread out along the promenade of the Quinta Avenida or the nearby beach, so you can get between them on foot, not by taxi – the best known are even around the same spot, at the crossing of Avenida 5 and Calle 12. Playa venues are also mostly smaller, with lower (or no) cover charges, so you can check out

competition, but it still has one of the best beach dance floors, mostly with pop and hip-hop. The bar itself is a perennially popular mingling spot, and there's a big lounging area (with sand floor) under a giant *palapa* palm roof. **Coco Maya**, Av. 1 Bis, corner Calle 12 Norte, tel: 984-111 9361. A cheeky competitor with the Blue Parrot next door, with a more adventurous slate of Mexican and international DJs hosting parties till sunrise. The view from the raised chill-out deck is another plus. **Deseo Lounge**, Hotel Deseo, Av. 5, corner Calle 12 Norte, tel: 984-879 3620. The pool-deck bar in Playa's sleekest designer hotel is the town's pinnacle of cool, with ambient music and giant divans to lounge on. **Mambo Café**, Calle 6 Norte, between Av. 5 and 10, tel: 984-803 2656. One of a chain of clubs with branches in Cancún, many cities and most of Mexico's main resorts that are a must for salsa and Latin dance fans. First-rate musicians play here each week, and there are also salsa classes. **Mamita's Beach Club**, Playa Tukan, end of Calle 28 Norte, tel: 984-803 2867. Open through the day, this hip, sexy beach club often stays open for all-night beach parties, with international DJs. **La Santanera**, Calle 12 Norte, between Av. 5 and 10, tel: 984-803 2294. The wildest, most imaginative club in Playa, with a very original Mexican take on club culture (including DJs dressed as masked wrestlers). Music is an equally eclectic mix.

ACCOMMODATIONS

EATING OUT

Dinner Cruises
Baja California
Several tours run catamarans out around Lands End on Cabo San Lucas, offering all-you-can-drink specials as well as breathtaking vistas. **Ecocat** (tel: 624-158 2647) is one of the largest, offering dinner options as well for those who want more than just snacks on the ride.

Tabasco and Chiapas
In Villahermosa, Tabasco, the **Capitán Beulo II**, (tel: 993-358 0102, www. olmecaepxress.com) is a pleasant local institution. This river boat sails up and down the River Grijalva from the city center on one- or two-hour tours, with a menu of local specialties included in the longer tours, and dance band on board at weekends.

The Yucatán
Floating dinner cruises, combining eating out with a romantic cruise or

ACTIVITIES

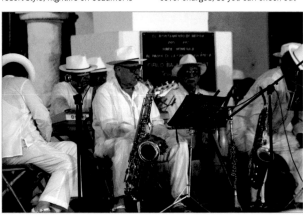

ABOVE: local band performing at Mérida's Serenatas Yucatecas.

much less intense, more restrained and smaller-scale than in Cancún or Playa. Most venues are within an easily walkable area in San Miguel town – especially along the waterfront Malecón, Avenida Melgar – but the big resorts to the north and south also have their own discos. **Hard Rock Café**, Av. Rafael Melgar 2A, corner Calle 1 Sur, tel: 987-872 5271. Handily easy to find right by the ferry dock, Cozumel's Hard Rock sticks to the chain's familiar style – with the addition of a coral-reef painting on the ceiling – and is very popular. Rock bands keep the dance floor busy. **1.5 Tequila**, Av. Rafael Melgar, corner Calle 11 Sur, tel: 987-872 4421. A stylish departure for Cozumel, a chic upstairs lounge bar with soft seating,

several in an evening. The foremost Playa venues also have a much newer hip style, more conscious of trends from Mexico City and abroad, in place of the giant spectaculars of Cancún. However, along the Quinta there also many unfussy dance bars, left over from less trendy days. **Alux**, Av. Juárez, between Av. 65 and 70, tel: 984-803 0713. Playa's remarkable cave bar, a labyrinth of romantically intimate spaces deep down in a real cave. However, it's a bit far from the main Playa scene, inland of Highway 307, so you need a cab to get there. **Blue Parrot**, Av. 1 Bis, corner Calle 12 Norte, tel: 984-206 3350. Playa del Carmen's original beach bar-club was once the only show in town. Nowadays it has a lot more

A – Z

LANGUAGE

more boisterous entertainment, are a long-standing Cancún attraction. The following are some of the fixtures; it is often easier to book them through agencies or hotels rather than direct. **Cancún Lovers Cruise**, tel: 998-883 1488, www.cancunloverscruise.com. An emphatically romantic (obviously) cruise on the "galleon" *Columbus* across Nichupté lagoon, with dinner of steak or lobster.
Cancún Queen, Aquaworld, tel: 998-848 8327, www.aquaworld.com.mx. A riverboat-style paddle steamer that cruises Laguna Nichupté every evening.
Caribbean Carnival Cruise, tel: 998-884 3760. Often known as the "booze cruise," an 4–5 hour party cruise across to Isla Mujeres and back, with plenty of food, an open bar, a live show and Latin bands to keep up the mood. Book through agencies and hotels.

Gay and Lesbian Nightlife

Mexico City

Despite all the stereotypes of Mexican machismo and traditionalism, Mexico City has an extensive gay and lesbian scene. The Zona Rosa remains its unquestioned hub, but there are also gay venues, from luxurious to very basic, in other parts of town.
Blackout, Amberes 11, Zona Rosa, tel: 55-5511 9973. Slick, stylish all-black restaurant, bar and club, known for inventive food and its 6-meter (18ft) -long bar, that's as popular with young lesbians as gay men.
Butterflies, J.M. Izazaga 5, Centro Histórico, tel: 55-5761 1861. Giant, very loud multi-space gay club with a high-tech sound system that also attracts a big non-gay audience for its extravagant drag shows. It's on the south side of the old center (by metro Salto de Agua).
Lipstick, Amberes 1, Zona Rosa, tel: 55-5514 4920. One of the smartest clubs in the Zona Rosa, with several striking spaces attracting a well-dressed crowd. There are usually women's nights on Thursdays.
El Viena, República de Cuba 2A, Centro Histórico (near Bellas Artes), tel: 55-5512 0929. Considered the city's only gay *cantina*, although it's now more comfortable than a really traditional *cantina*, and has a dance floor. It still has a uniquely Mexican atmosphere.

The Yucatán

The **Riviera Maya** has a small but growing gay scene. There are only a few specifically gay venues, but many

other clubs, especially in Playa del Carmen, are generally pretty gay-friendly.
Karamba, Av. Tulum 9, by Av. Uxmal, Ciudad Cancún. No phone. Cancún's longest-established gay disco, with drag shows and plenty of party nights. Loud and very popular. Open Tue–Sun.
Playa 69, Av. 5, between calles 4 and 6, Playa del Carmen. No phone. Like the Karamba, Playa's only 100 percent gay venue has a full-on party style.

SHOPPING

What to Buy

The sheer range of Mexican traditional handicrafts is stunning: every part of Mexico has its own distinctive traditions, and some areas are especially rich in the quality of their work – such as Puebla, Taxco in Guerrero, Oaxaca or Chiapas (see pages 108–11). Few visitors can resist shopping in Mexico, and for some, hunting for original craftwork and similarly distinctive items can be the primary purpose of their visit. The price range is nearly as wide as the range of items available, so take your time and choose wisely. Serious craftwork enthusiasts should plan to travel extensively in the countryside – the best work will often be found closer to where it is made. You may also be lucky enough to watch craftsmen and women (*artesanos* or *artesanas*) at work. If you're particularly interested in any type of craftwork, it's best to do some research before traveling on the best towns and villages to head for, and the kind of work they do; otherwise, check around in the nearest city to get an idea of the most distinctive local products.

Some large stores, and some-times even market traders, will pack and ship large purchases to your home for a reasonable charge.

Basketry

Plain but very attractive and practical baskets in a wide range of shapes and sizes can be found in Tequisquiapan in Querétaro, and more varied styles in the villages around Lake Pátzcuaro in Michoacán, such as Ihuatzio. **Cane** and **reed** containers are a specialty of Guanajuato, Puebla, and Guerrero, and among the indigenous communities, the Tarahumara of Copper Canyon and the Otomí of the

Mezquital valley, Hidalgo also make fine basketry.

Intricate **bark paintings** are among the many distinctive crafts of Xalitla, a Náhuatl-speaking community between Taxco and Chilpancingo in Guerrero, another of the remote towns in Mexico where most of the population seems to have some rare craft skill. In the Veracruz coastal area **palm-leaf mats** can be bought, while the Mixteca area of western Oaxaca produces palm-leaf mats, hats, bags, baskets and many decorative items.

Ceramics

Beautiful original ceramics are available all over Mexico, but the most renowned centers are Puebla and its surrounding region, for its multicolored glazed Talavera pottery and tiles, and Oaxaca, for entirely different black- and green-glazed pottery. In some areas, such as San Luis Potosí and Chiapas, ceramic styles are largely unchanged since pre-Hispanic times. Note that except for stoneware, many items may not be lead-free, so use them for decoration or for storing dry goods. If the empty article rings like a bell when flicked with the fingernail, it is safe; if it sounds as if you've tapped on wood, it probably contains lead. Glaze and paint may contain lead, as well.

Painted ceramics are used to produce many other items as well as **pots**, household **crockery** and **tiles**. Many areas in the Central Highlands, such as Acatlán in Puebla or especially Metepec in the state of Mexico, make intricate **"trees of life"** (which, however, are very hard to transport successfully). Tlaquepaque and Tonalá in Jalisco, now both effectively suburbs of Guadalajara, produce a fascinating range of ceramic figures and other pieces, in innovative and traditional designs.

In Tzintzuntzan and Morelia in Morelos, San Miguel de Allende in Guanajuato, and San Bartolo Coyotepec in Oaxaca, you will find burnished black ceramics, while the characteristic work of Santa María Atzompa, also in Oaxaca, is green, and very adaptable for many household uses. In Amatenango, Chiapas, Maya women make large earthenware pots using an open-fired technique believed to date back over 2,000 years.

Conventional Clothing and Shoes

The big Mexican resorts such as Acapulco or – especially – Cancún are major shopping centers, with a choice of giant malls that are local landmarks, but the products they stock are often familiar international brands, so unless you have left something behind there is rarely much that's very distinctive to look for. Leather belts and *huarache* **sandals**, however, are a good buy, and can be found in every market.

Hammocks and Hats

Hammocks are almost a symbol of the Yucatán, and an excellent buy to take home. The best place to find them is the market in **Mérida**, and the specialist hammock shops in the same area, on Calle 65. **Panama hats** are also typical of the peninsula, made especially in Becal in Campeche, but Mérida market is again the best place to find a big selection.

Jewelry and Metalwork

The silver jewelry of Taxco is now world-renowned; it can be found in stores all over Mexico – and especially in every resort – but the workshops and stores of its home city still have a special attraction. In Mexico City and other cities there are also plenty of shops with innovative modern as well as traditional jewelry designs.

It is always best to buy jewelry from an established store, not from a street vendor, and make sure it has a "plata de ley" ticket guaranteeing it is genuine silver.

Central Chiapas is one of few areas in the world producing high-quality amber, mined there for centuries, and in San Cristóbal de las Casas there are several shops with an attractive range of jewelry in amber and jade, another material prized by the ancient Maya. In Veracruz and on the Riviera Maya, coral jewelry is also made. Make sure you do not buy black coral, as this is now protected and its use in jewelry is prohibited.

Cruise passengers visiting Mexican ports such as San José del Cabo, Manzanillo, Acapulco or Cozumel enjoy certain duty-free privileges, and consequently many of these towns have a clutch of famous-name international jewelry stores, with Mexican and foreign designs. For non-cruise passengers, their prices are not especially advantageous.

Mexican artisans also work with plain as well as precious metals. In Michoacán, copper is worked into pots, plates and many decorative items. In Oaxaca, lovely small items, **picture frames** and **boxes** are made out of painted tin.

Textiles

Symbols of the country, Mexico's wonderfully colorful traditions in **weaving** and **embroidery** are generally centered in indigenous communities, and virtually always carried on only by women. These techniques were once only used for making traditional clothing such as the *huipil* **blouses** and **smocks** of women in Oaxaca and Chiapas, but in response to tourist demand craftswomen now apply their skills to many other items, such as decorative pieces, table mats and wearable blouses and shawls. Equally, most pieces were once made only with pure cotton (*algodón*) or wool (*lana*) and with natural dyes, but many weavers now use at least some synthetic threads, since they give bright colors with much less effort. Nevertheless, handmade items can still shrink, and colors can run, so be very careful when first washing any traditional textiles (if in doubt, wash only by hand, in cold water).

It is only possible to mention here just a few of the places with textile traditions. Good places to find distinctive **serape** blankets, rugs and other woolen items include Coahuila, Tlaxcala, Hueyapan in Morelos, Saltillo in Coahuila, San Miguel de Allende in Guanajuato, Zacatecas, Ometepec and its surrounding villages, Guerrero, and Teotitlán del Valle near Oaxaca city. In Temoaya, Mexico state, rugs are now made that combine Mexican indigenous imagery with Middle Eastern styles and techniques. Other communities, however, stick strictly to their own traditional weaving styles, such as the Otomí of the Valle del Mezquital, Hidalgo, the Tarahumara of Copper Canyon, or the Cora and Huichol of Nayarit, who often incorporate beadwork into their designs. In the Highlands of Chiapas around San Cristóbal de las Casas, each of the Maya communities has its own, instantly recognizable style of weaving and embroidery, incorporating intricate imagery founded in Maya beliefs. The bright weavings of women from Zinacantán are often the most attractive, and adaptable, for outside buyers, but the more remote communities also produce beautiful work.

In hotter, more lowland areas embroidery is a more prominent skill than weaving. In Oaxaca, the multicolored blouses, skirts and accessories of the towns around Tehuantepec – made famous by Frida Kahlo – have a special, tropical beauty. The villages of Oaxaca, in

general, produce a huge variety of attractive embroidery and weaving. In the Yucatán, traditional **flower embroidery** has customarily been used mainly for the white *huipil* smock dresses worn by Maya women and the dazzling *ternos* for special occasions, but, again, can now be found on more adaptable items.

Toys and Alebrijes

Among the most popular – and easy to carry – Mexican handicrafts is the infinitely variable range of brightly painted and **handmade toys**, animals, dolls, **Day of the Dead figures** and other, often bizarre, objects that are among the best expressions of the Mexican capacity for fantasy and imagination. They can be made in wood, metal or, very often, papier-mâché, and include the bizarre, fantastical creatures known as *alebrijes*, particularly associated with the Linares family of Mexico City. Charming, always surprising pieces can be found in many parts of the country, but the areas with the richest, most fascinatingly imaginative traditions are Mexico state and, once again, Oaxaca, especially the village of San Martín Tilcajete.

Woodworking

Wood is worked across Mexico in its plain state and as a base for varnishing and lacquerwork, and again areas specialize in different styles and techniques. The Seri Amerindians in Bahía Kino, Sonora make ironwood animals, while Ixmiquilpan, Hidalgo is known for its bird cages. In Uruapan, Michoacán, masks and lacquerware are the local products, while in nearby Quiroga painted wooden bowls and household items are common. Ixtapan de la Sal in Mexico state also specializes in household items as well as carved animals. Colonial-style furniture and wooden bowls can be found in Cuernavaca, Morelos. In Olinalá, Guerrero, you will find jaguar masks, gourd bowls, wooden trays, and fine lacquerware.

In Chiapas you can often find the masks and ornate lacquerware pots, cabinets and boxes traditionally made in Chiapa de Corzo. Wooden musical instruments can also be a good buy. Guitars are made especially in Paracho, Michoacán.

Where to Shop

Many cities and resort towns have dedicated **Craft Markets** (*Mercados de Artesanías*), where you can find a whole range of local and often other

TRANSPORTATION

ACCOMMODATIONS

EATING OUT

ACTIVITIES

A – Z

LANGUAGE

handicrafts under the same roof. Mexican **general markets** – of which there is at least one in every city – are also fascinating places to explore, whether or not you eventually find anything to buy. As well as more handicrafts stalls, they contain everything imaginable anyone could want – clothes, electrical goods, car parts, religious images, party *piñatas*, and plenty of places to eat. Away from the towns, many villages with distinctive craft traditions have their own markets where some of the best local work can be found, but these are generally only on one day a week – often at weekends – so ask around on the best days to visit.

Historic colonial cities, especially, have a range of attractive craft and **souvenir shops** spread around their streets. Some of the best places for browsing are naturally those at the center of areas with big craft traditions, such as Tlaquepaque in Guadalajara, San Miguel de Allende, Oaxaca or San Cristóbal de las Casas. In state capitals and some other towns there are also official state-sponsored handicrafts stores. Their prices tend to be a little above average, but they are good places to visit to get an idea of the range of work produced in each area, and of prices, before visiting the markets. The **Fomento Cultural Banamex** *(see page 109)* has also set up various exhibits of its own superb collection of Mexican folk art, especially in the Yucatán, which all have lovely shops attached. In the major craft centers there are also frequently **cooperative stores** set up by groups of local craftspeople, which is where you will often find the very best work; prices again are higher than in the markets, but one of the objects of these cooperatives is to ensure that local artisans, especially women weavers, get a fair price for their work.

Markets
Mexico City
The capital's markets are endlessly fascinating. The best (and cheapest) for handicrafts and souvenirs is **Artesanías de la Ciudadela** (metro Balderas) displaying items from all over Mexico and harboring neat cafés in its sunny central plaza. The second major handicraft option is a walkable distance away in the same area, the **Mercado de Artesanías de San Juan**, a few blocks east along Calle Ayuntamiento (metro San Juan de Letrán).

The biggest general market is probably the immense **Mercado de la Merced** (metro La Merced), where

there is as much going on outside as under cover, while three blocks south on Fray Servando Teresa de Mier is the **Mercado de Sonora**, famous for its magical and herbal remedies. Almost as large as the Merced is **La Lagunilla** market, off Calle Rayón near Plaza Garibaldi, which becomes a giant flea market on Sundays. This is also known as the "Thieves Market," so be very careful with your bags if you visit.

Around Mexico City
In **Puebla** the **El Parián** market (Calle 6 Norte, between calles 2 and 4) is a crafts market that is calmer than those in the capital, with, naturally, huge arrays of local Talavera pottery. In Morelos, **Cuernavaca** has a small *mercado de artesanías* just off the Zócalo, but more spectacular is the Sunday market in **Tepoztlán**. The famous artisan center of **Metepec** outside Toluca, known especially for its "trees of life," has a market every Monday, and many shops and workshops open through the week. The **Mercado Benito Juárez** in **Toluca** itself (east of the center, near the Mexico City road) is also huge, with handicraft and general stalls, and busiest on Fridays.
Guadalajara
Mercado Libertad, one of Latin America's largest markets, is a great place to find silver, gemstone jewelry, fruits and foods, and colorful textiles from the indigenous tribes nearby.

Acapulco
El Mercado de Artesanías Parasal is a huge market that draws thousands of shoppers, but one should be careful here. Be aware that some items are fakes or forgeries and pay attention to your wallet if you're in thick crowds. Discerning shoppers will find good quality wooden masks and other carvings, beadwork, hammocks, and real and faux religious items. Avoid prohibited items such as turtle shells.

Oaxaca
20 de Noviembre Market, located a few blocks from the zócalo, is one of Mexico's classic emporiums where a bit of everything can be found. Look out for *mole* sauces and reasonably priced Oaxacan crafts, textiles, tools, and clothing.

Chiapas
The **Mercado Indígena** or "Indian Market" beside the church of Santo Domingo in **San Cristóbal de las Casas** is an essential stop for seeing all kinds of weaving and other work of

the Maya communities of the Chiapas highlands, and close by there are also the shops of the main weavers' cooperatives. San Cristóbal's general market, reached by continuing north along Av. General Utrilla, is one of Mexico's most extraordinary giant bazaars, with all kinds of foods, handicrafts and other items, spreading over several blocks. The main market day in the Maya villages of **Chamula** and **Zinacantán** is Sunday, so this is the best day to visit.

Yucatán and Riviera Maya: The vast, sprawling market in **Mérida**, spreading over several blocks but with its core around the junction of calles 65 and 56, is the commercial heart of the whole peninsula and the best place to search for all kinds of Yucatecan products. There is a special handicrafts section, the **Bazar de Artesanías**, on an upper level and reached by a ramp at the crossing of calles 67 and 56, while the main market is great for sandles and bags, among many other things. The small specialist shops in the market area, especially along Calle 65 around Calle 58, are also the best places for hammocks and Panama hats.

In **Cancún**, the **Mercado 28** in downtown Cancún (off Av. Sunyaxchén) is a general market that also has plenty of souvenir and above all jewelry stores, of very variable quality.

Shops and Shopping Areas
Mexico City
Among the most attractive (if more expensive) places to find varied craftwork in the capital are those of the state-run **Fonart** organization, which has two in the center, as well as an outlet in the **Palacio Nacional** on the Zócalo:

Fonart, Juárez 89, Centro Histórico (near the Alameda), tel: 55-5521 0171, www.fonart.com.mx

Fonart, Paseo de la Reforma 116, Colonia Juárez (near Tlatelolco), tel: 55-5328 5000

The streets around the Centro Histórico are also great for browsing, especially avenidas 5 de Mayo, Madero and Isabel la Católica. Out of the city's thousands of shops, some to look out for are:

Arte Mexicano para el Mundo, Monte de Piedad 11, Centro Histórico, tel: 55-5518 6992, www.arte-mexicano.com.mx. Delightful shop right by the Zócalo, which also has the attraction of an attractive terrace restaurant above it.

Artesanos de México, Londres 117, Zona Rosa, tel: 55-5514 7455. Lovely old shop that's irresistible for browsing.

Víctor Artes Populares Mexicanas,

ABOVE: a pause in loom weaving in Oaxaca.

Madero 10, 3rd floor, Centro Histórico, tel: 55-5512 1263, http://artespopulares victor.com. The Fosado family are real experts in Mexican folk arts, and many items in their stock are real collector's pieces, but prices are still very reasonable. Open Mon–Fri 12.30–7pm, and at other times by appointment.

Puebla
Uriarte, 4 Poniente 911, by 11 Norte, Puebla, tel: 222-232 1598, www. uriartetalavara.com.mx. The most renowned maker of Puebla's Talavera pottery is naturally a good place to begin looking for fine work.

Cuernavaca
Artesanías Villamil Romero, Hidalgo 32, Cuernavaca, tel: 777-318 7158. By the cathedral, this little shop has a variety of woodcarvings and other craftwork mainly from villages around Morelos.

Toluca
Casart, Paseo Tollocan 700, Toluca, tel: 722-217 5144. Mexico State's huge official handicrafts showcase has a spectacular display of varied craftwork of all sizes.

Tijuana
Avenida Revo is a great spot for buying souvenirs, as almost anything from the entire country can be purchased in the multitude of shops. However, much of the gold and silver is fake and don't be enticed by the signs advertising things that are illegal elsewhere. Bargainig is fine, but it is better to find tourist-friendly stores like **Emporium** between 4th and 5th streets, where items are marked with a price tag.

Chihuahua
Cowboy boots and hats can be found at very reasonable prices in the side alleys around and behind the cathedral. From there, walk down the pedestrian avenue for several blocks where you will find clothing stores, pushcarts and a plethora of shoes. Brides-to-be may want to head southwest from the Plaza down to Victoria and look for the bridal boutiques with gowns for any dressy occasion. In nearby Cuactemoc, look for cowboy hats and Mennonite cheese.

Xalapa
Galería de Artesanías, Xalapeños Ilustres 3, Xalapa de Méndez, tel: 228-841 1202. Palm-leaf basketwork, ceramics and other work from Veracruz state.
San Cristóbal de las Casas
Amanecer–Casa de las Artesanías de Chiapas, Av. Miguel Hidalgo, corner Av. Niños Héroes, San Cristóbal de las Casas, tel: 967-678 1180. The official state handicraft store, with a small museum attached.
El Encuentro, Real de Guadalupe 63A, San Cristóbal de las Casas, tel: 967-678 3698. Charming old shop, slightly chaotic but with a huge stock of Mexican and Guatemalan textiles.
J'pas Joviletik, Av. General Utrilla 43, San Cristóbal de las Casas, no phone. Best of the cooperatives, run by Maya women themselves, with superb work spread through several tiny rooms.
Sna Jolobil, Convento de Santo Domingo, Calzada Lázaro Cárdenas, San Cristóbal de las Casas, tel: 967-678 2646, www.snajolobil.com. In the former convent beside Santo

Domingo, the "house of the weavers" is the most permanent and organized of the local craft cooperatives.

Palenque
Amanecer–Casa de las Artesanías de Chiapas, Museo del Sitio, Carretera de las Ruinas Km 6.5, Palenque, tel: 916-348 3511. Located inside the museum at Palenque ruins, this is another branch of Chiapas' official state handicrafts organization.

Campeche
Casa de las Artesanías Tukulná, Calle 10 no. 333, between calles 59 and 61, Campeche, tel: 981-816 9088, www.tukulna.com. A delightful, airy shop in an old Campeche house that is an excellent showcase for the state's traditional crafts.

Mérida
Alma Mexicana, Calle 54 No. 476, between calles 55 and 57, Mérida, tel: 999-924 5717, www.folkart-mexico. com. A dazzlingly colorful collection of folk art from all over Mexico, in a lovely old Mérida house.
Casa de las Artesanías de Yucatán, Calle 63, between calles 64 and 66, Mérida, tel: 999-928 6676, www.casade lasartesaniasdeyucatan.com. The official state handicrafts store, which also has branches at the Museo de Antropología and at Uxmal ruins.

Izamal
Centro Cultural y Artesanal, Calle 31 No. 201, on Parque Itzamná, Izamal, tel: 988-954 1012, www.centrocultural izamal.org.mx. A project of the Fomento Banamex, in a fine old house on the main square, this cultural center has beautiful craftwork in its shop, and also produces a free map of the town with a guide to local craftspeople whose workshops can be visited.

Cancún
In Cancún shopping is naturally a more conventional process than in more traditional parts of Mexico, and handicrafts, which are all shipped from other regions, are relatively expensive. Of the big Hotel Zone malls, **La Isla** at Blvd Kukulcán Km 12.5 – a "shopping village" rather than a single mall, is the most attractive, with some pretty souvenir stores as well as the best choice of top-line international brands. **Plaza La Fiesta**, Blvd Kukulcán Km 9, is almost a handicrafts mall by itself, with some fine items as well as a lot of junk. There are branches in Cozumel and Playa del Carmen, but if

TRANSPORTATION

ACCOMMODATIONS

EATING OUT

ACTIVITIES

A – Z

LANGUAGE

you travel on to Mérida you will find better goods at lower prices.

Cozumel
Los Cinco Soles, Avenida Rafael Melgar 27, by Calle 8 Norte, San Miguel de Cozumel, tel: 987-872 0132, www.loscincosoles.com. A big, uncluttered store that generally has the best array of all Mexican handicrafts on the Riviera Maya.

SPORTS

Outdoor Activities

Many hotels resorts around Mexico's coasts have in-house dive shops and other facilities, and/or can arrange packages with local fishing operators, golf courses and so on.

Diving and Snorkeling

There is fine diving off many places on the Pacific coast, such as around Baja California, Ixtapa-Zihuatanejo and Puerto Escondido, but the great paradise for divers is the Great Maya Reef south from Isla Mujeres past Cozumel and down the east coast of the Yucatán, one of the richest reef systems in the world. There are dive sites of every grade of difficulty, and the region's dive operators offer a complete range of services, from "resort courses" (a one-day introduction to scuba) and instruction, to complex night dives. For beginners, the best locations are generally Isla Mujeres, Cozumel, Puerto Morelos or Playa del Carmen. Most operators and hotels also offer much cheaper snorkel tours, and without tanks and just a snorkel you can still see a great deal, especially off Cozumel and Puerto Morelos where the reefs are close inshore.

Inland, the freshwater *cenote* caves of the Yucatán are fascinating to explore, and have made the southern Riviera Maya around Akumal and Tulum the world's most important area for cave and cavern diving and snorkeling. To undertake a full cave dive you must have an open-water dive certificate, but without this you can still snorkel in the upper chambers of the caverns *(see page 317)*.

The following is a brief selection from the many reliable dive and snorkel operators.

La Paz
Palapas Ventana (www.palapasventana. com), near La Paz, offers a variety of diving and outdoor tours.

Isla Mujeres
Carey Dive Center, Av. Matamoros 13-A, Isla Mujeres, tel: 998-877 0763, www.careydivecenter.com.

Cozumel
Deep Blue, Calle Adolfo Rosado Salas 200, by Av. 10, San Miguel de Cozumel, tel: 987-872 5653, www. deepbluecozumel.com. One of the best-equipped Cozumel dive operators, covering every option in local diving.
Dive Cozumel, Calle Adolfo Rosado Salas 85, by Av. 5, San Miguel de Cozumel, tel: 987-872 4567, www.dive cozumel.net. Highly regarded operator with advanced technical facilities.

Puerto Morelos
Almost Heaven Adventures, Av. Rojo Gómez, Puerto Morelos, tel: 998-871 0230, www.almostheavenadventures.com. Friendly, flexible operators that is very good for beginners, which also has expert fishing guides.

Playa del Carmen
Phocea Riviera Maya, Av. 1 Norte, between calles 10 and 12, Playa del Carmen, tel: 984-873 1210, www. phocearivieramaya.com. Excellent tuition, good-value packages and also tours to see whale sharks.
Yucatek Divers, Av. 15 Norte, between calles 2 and 4, Playa del Carmen, tel: 984-803 2836, www.yucatek-divers.com. Expert international team who also offer good dive+hotel packages.

Akumal
Aquatech-Villas de Rosa, Aventuras Akumal, tel: 984-875 9020, www.cenotes.com. Cave-diving and snorkeling experts who also offer all kinds of open-water activities, based in a very attractive beach hotel.

Tulum
Hidden Worlds, Highway 307 Km 242, 11km north of Tulum, tel: 984-873 1210, www.hiddenworld.com. Next to the vast Dos Ojos *cenote*, this family-friendly center offers a great introduction to cavern diving and other adventures.

Fishing
On the Pacific coast, Mazatlán is a major deep-sea fishing center, although fishing trips with expert captains can be arranged at many of the other ports along the coast. On the Riviera Maya, Cozumel, Puerto Morelos and Puerto Aventuras are particularly good fishing centers. Inshore, the mangrove lagoons around the coast of the Yucatán, from Celestún and Río Lagartos round to

the Riviera Maya, are excellent for fly fishing, and the shallow waters of Ascension Bay, south of Tulum, are considered the best bonefishing grounds in the world.

All of the Pacific resorts have a range of specialist fishing captains and guides, and on the Riviera Maya many dive operators will also arrange fishing trips. For deep-sea fishing a license is required, which can be arranged by fishing captains and agencies. If you aim to fish in any of the more remote fishing grounds, such as Ascension Bay, then it's best to arrange a trip in advance with local centers or one of the many US-based specialist fishing tour companies.

Surfing and Windsurfing
The beaches all along the Baja peninsula nearly all have fine surf, but the real targets for surfers are those near the southern tip. Across on the mainland, the biggest draws are the spectacular breaks at Troncones, near Ixtapa-Zihuatanejo, and Puerto Escondido, but the beaches around Mazatlán and Manzanillo also have plenty of potential.

The beach of Los Barriles, also near the southern tip of Baja California, is a mecca for experienced windsurfers due to the strength and quirks of its winds, but windsurf boards are also available to rent in most of Mexico's beach resorts. In Tulum on the Riviera Maya kitesurfing is now popular, and several places on the beach offer training and boards for rent.

Sailing
Exploring the Pacific coast and especially the Sea of Cortés by boat is ever more popular. There are good marinas and harbor facilities at many points along the coast, but especially at La Paz, Loreto, Mazatlán, Puerto Vallarta, and Zihuatanejo, while on the Caribbean, Cozumel and Puerto Aventuras are good sailing centers. A useful guide to every aspect of sailing in Mexico is www.latitudemexico.com.

Whale- and Shark-Watching
The Sea of Cortés and the seas of the Pacific shore of Baja California form one of the world's great meeting grounds of whales and dolphins of many different species, and whale-watching trips are offered by nearly all dive and adventure sports operators in Baja, and also from Puerto Vallarta. A lesser-known phenomenon is the gathering of whale sharks from July to September off Cabo Catoche, in the northeast corner of the Yucatán Peninsula.

Approved trips to see these rare creatures are operated from the tiny island of Holbox, on the north coast of Quintana Roo.

Rafting and Kayaking

In the last few years there has been a rapid growth in the possibilities for whitewater rafting and kayaking on Mexico's spectacular mountain rivers. The Río Filobobos in Veracruz, reached from Tlapacoyan, is one popular center, but another is the Río Amacuzac in Morelos, a short distance from Cuernavaca. In Chiapas, rafting and kayak trips of several days can be organized through La Venta gorge or the rivers of the Lacandón rain forest.

For very tranquil kayaking, most of the guide agencies that provide tours of the Sian Ka'an Biosphere Reserve from Tulum also offer tours by kayak. **Aventura Extrema**, Sánchez Tagle 973, Veracruz, tel: 229-202 6557, www.aventuraextrema.com. A variety of options around Veracruz.
Explora, 1 de Marzo 30, San Cristóbal de las Casas, Chiapas, tel: 967-674 6660, www.ecochiapas.com. Excellent small operator with some of the best rafting, kayaking and adventure options in Chiapas.
Terra 3 Expediciones, Júpiter 7, Cuernavaca, tel: 777-121 2017, www.t3expediciones.com. Rafting and other adventures in Morelos.

Hiking

Chihuahua's spellbinding Copper Canyon is Mexico's most established hiking destination, with well-established hiking and bike trails and well-prepared guides from the Tarahumara community. However, more areas are becoming more easily accessible all the time, particularly in the mountains around Mexico City, so in any area it's worth checking on what routes may be available. One popular region to explore is around the Ixtaccihuátl and Popocatépetl volcanoes east of the capital, and some ecotourism companies in the capital provide tours. Another place where formerly remote areas now have accessible hikes is Oaxaca, information on which can be found (in Spanish) on www.ecoturismoenoaxaca.com.

Cycling

Copper Canyon is, again, already a popular mountain biking destination, with well-established facilities. However, mountain bike routes, like hiking trails, are rapidly increasing in number, and bikers are exploring new possibilities. Two companies that

provide exciting bike tours are listed below. In addition, bikes can be rented in most resorts.
Mountain Bike Mexico, Mexico City, tel: 55-5846 0793, www.mtbmexico.com. Tours around Mexico City and the Central Highlands, in Jalisco and made-to-measure itineraries.
Solo Montaña, Mexico City and Cuernavaca, tel: 55-2145 6247, www.ruedapormexico.com.mx. One-day trips mostly around Morelos, Puebla and Mexico State, and longer trips.

Participant Sports

Golf

Golf course building has been accelerating fast in Mexico, and there is now a choice of courses around most of the major resort areas, and some cities. Many resort hotels now offer golf packages. On the Riviera Maya, the Camaleón Course at the Maya Koba resort near Playa del Carmen is Mexico's first PGA-standard golf course. For a full list of courses across the country, check www.golfinmexico.net.

Tennis

Public-access tennis courts are very rare in Mexico, but many big resort hotels have courts. There are also a few dedicated tennis resorts, especially in Baja California and around Mazatlán and Puerto Vallarta.

Spectator Sports

Baseball

In the border states, around the Gulf Coast, in much of southern Mexico and in the Yucatán baseball is actually more popular than soccer. The Mexican League is the only official Minor League outside the US; the main season runs from March to August. Full information can be found on http://web.minorleaguebaseball.com.

Bullfighting

Spanish-style bullfights or *Corridas de Toros* have long been popular in Mexico (see page 150). The vast Plaza México in the capital (www.lamexico.com) is naturally the country's bullfighting hub, but Aguascalientes, Guadalajara and San Luis Potosí are also bullfighting centers, and many cities have bullrings (plazas de toros). The main season is from November to April. Tickets for some plazas can be bought through **Ticketmaster** (tel: 55-5325 9000, www.ticketmaster.com.mx).

More rough-and-ready corridas also form part of many small town and village fiestas, which take place throughout the year (see page 365–6).

Horse Racing

In Mexico City, horse races are held at the **Hipódromo de las Américas** (tel: 55-5387 0600, www.hipodromo.com.mx) on Avenida Industria Militar, to the west of the Polanco district. There are races all year on Saturdays, Sundays and Tuesdays, and sometimes on Thursdays. Tickets can, again, be bought through Ticketmaster.

Jai Alai

The exciting, high-speed Basque game of pelota or jai alai is popular in some parts of Mexico, as an occasion for heavy betting. The biggest Frontones or Jai-Alai courts are in Tijuana and Acapulco, at Costera Miguel Alemán 498, where there are games every evening from Tuesday to Sunday. Though closed, the jai alai stadium in Tijuana is a local landmark. Look for the pink building near Sanborns as you wander down Avenida Revolución.

Soccer (Football)

Most of Mexico – especially the Central Highlands – is mad about soccer. In Mexico City, the biggest teams are **Club América** – the biggest of all Mexican clubs, who play home games in the vast **Estadio Azteca** – **UNAM** (known as Los Pumas) and **Cruz Azul**; outside the capital, other strong teams include **Guadalajara** (Los Chivas), **Toluca** and **Pachuca**, Mexico's oldest football club. The Mexican League has a complicated structure, with the season divided into two halves, the Apertura competition from August to December, and Clausura from January to May, and a separate champion for each. Games are played on Sundays, and now on other days midweek. Information on upcoming games can be found through listings websites and Ticketmaster, which is also now the best way to book tickets in advance.

Wrestling (Lucha Libre)

Mexican wrestling, fought by masked wrestlers with crazy super-hero like identities, is one of the wildest, most characteristic and most popular Mexican entertainments. The best place to see fights is at the historic **Arena Coliseo**, República de Perú 77 (tel: 55-5526 1687), near the church of Santo Domingo in Mexico City (metro Allende), but the city also has a larger hall, the Arena México, Dr Lavista 189 (tel: 55-5588 0266), near Colonia Roma (metro Cuauhtémoc), and there are bouts in other cities. Upcoming programs (in Spanish) are on www.cmll.com, and tickets are, again, available through Ticketmaster.

A – Z

A HANDY SUMMARY OF PRACTICAL INFORMATION, ARRANGED ALPHABETICALLY

A ddresses

Most Mexican cities have a grid street system, bequeathed by the Spaniards, with straight streets spreading out from a Zócalo or main square. In Mexico City and many other cities streets have names, which makes finding addresses fairly simple, although since streets are long it is very useful to have the name of the nearest cross-street as well as the building number. In the vastness of Mexico City and some other cities the name of the official district or *colonia*, attached to addresses, is also important in finding one's way around. Note that some popular area names do not have official status; the Zona Rosa, for example, is divided between colonias Cuauhtémoc and Juárez.

Puebla and many cities in southern Mexico have a much more confusing system that identifies streets by numbers. Streets running east–west are often (but not always) called *Avenidas*, those north–south are *Calles* (Streets). The two big streets that form the axis of the grid, running through the Zócalo, are generally the Avenida Central and Calle Central;

Avenidas north of Central may be numbered evenly Av. 2 Norte (North), 4, 6, etc., while to the south they will be Av. 1 Sur (South), 3, 5, etc. Streets west of Calle Central may be Calles 2 Poniente (West), 4, 6, etc.; to the east they will be Calle 1 Oriente (East), 3, 5, etc. There are also other number variations, without splitting odd and even numbers. This system produces combinations like "Avenida 5 Sur Oriente," (5 South, East), which will be in the southeast corner of the grid. This takes some time to get used to.

In the Yucatán most towns use a simpler street-numbering system: even numbers generally run north–south, odd ones east–west. Since streets are, again, very long, cross-streets are customarily given with addresses in the following style, Calle 55 No. 533, x 64 y 66 (Calle 55 No. 533, between calles 64 and 66).

Admission Charges

All archeological sites and most museums in Mexico are administered by the *Instituto Nacional de Antropología e Historia* (INAH). The INAH has set scales of admission charges for its sites: smaller sites cost around US$2.40 per person; medium-sized sites and museums around $3–4; the largest and most famous sites (Teotihuacán, Chichén Itzá, Uxmal and some others) are around $8.50, plus about $1 per vehicle to park. The charges at privately owned museums and attractions are generally around $3 or less. Admission is free on Sundays to INAH sites only for Mexican citizens and residents. Everyone else must pay at all times.

B udgeting for Your Trip

As in any country, there are variations in average price levels across Mexico, which can very roughly be divided into four – although within each area there can also be big price differences. The major resort areas are generally the most expensive, especially if you stay in the most "touristed" areas; Mexico City is a zone by itself, with the biggest range, from very high to very cheap; most other cities are, overall, a bit less expensive; and in many small towns, rural areas and some states such as Chiapas, prices are much lower.

Taking this into account, an attractive mid-range hotel in the third of these areas – most cities other than Mexico City, including the colonial cities like Oaxaca – can cost around $80–90 for a double room, sometimes with breakfast; below $40, rooms in the capital and resort areas will tend to be pretty basic, although elsewhere you can find great bargains. A decent full meal will cost around $15–18 or less (although there is always plenty of cheap food available), a beer about $1.50–2. Added to this are transportation costs: a first-class bus ticket for a long trip (for example, Mexico City–Oaxaca) will be around $30, a taxi ride in most cities will be about $1.50–2 (more in Mexico City and resort towns). Renting a car will cost from $40 a day.

Overall, therefore, in most parts of Mexico you can travel around very comfortably spending about $60–70 a day per person, but it's also possible to travel for much less taking advantage of budget options.

C hildren

Mexico is a very family-oriented society, and there are few places that do not admit children. Mexicans often travel in family groups, and most hotels have some big family rooms (habitaciones familiares) with several beds, which are very economical. Children are seen in most restaurants, including the very plush ones in Mexico City (although there they will be expected to sit at table and behave), and even many cantinas, where kids are not admitted during the week, have "family days" at weekends. Restaurants do not often have special children's menus but will often try hard to meet special requests, and many menus are so varied that there is nearly always something children will like. If children are picky about food, in all resort areas and most towns there are pizzerias and outlets of international fast-food chains. Familiar drinks brands are always available, but for more natural treats the local juguerías and paletería-nevería stands with fresh juices and own-made ice creams are ideal.

Entertainments for kids are naturally easiest to find in the big resort areas, where as well as hotel pools and beaches there are plenty of rides and water parks. Especially popular attractions are the "eco-parks" such as Xcaret on the Riviera Maya, which give a family-friendly introduction to the tropical environment, and the chance to

snorkel in complete safety. Elsewhere, rides and other kids' entertainments often appear in city centers and plazas at weekends. Mexican fiestas, big and small, are often magnetic for kids – so long as they get over the crowds – and always include more rides and children's activities.

Climate and Clothing

Central Mexico

Mexico City, Guadalajara, and many other cities lie in the Central Highlands where the climate is pretty temperate year-round. Most of this area is also south of the Tropic of Cancer, which runs across Mexico just north of Mazatlán and Zacatecas, so as well as summer (verano) and winter (invierno) an equally important distinction is the tropical one between the rainy season – roughly June–October – and the dry season during the rest of the year, which is the most popular time to visit. In July and August, Mexico City has rain nearly every day, usually for a couple of hours in the afternoon.

High altitude keeps these cities from becoming really hot at most times; in an average year, Mexico City's highest temperature will be around 31°C (88°F); Guadalajara's around 35°C (95°F). In Mexico City, the hottest months are April and May, towards the end of the dry season, but even then average temperatures are in the upper 20s°C (low 80s°F). However, because of the altitude temperatures drop noticeably at night at all times and winters can be chilly, with night-time temperatures around 0°C (32°F) in January–February. Altitude and mountainous terrain also create impressive local climate variations, and some areas are known for especially cold winters, notably Toluca, Mexico's highest state capital.

CLIMATE CHART

Mexico City

Maximum temperature
Minimum temperature
Rainfall

Baja California

Baja is mostly north of the Tropic and has very low annual rainfall, mostly in late autumn and winter. Temperatures are more comfortable where the land is cooled by sea breezes on the southern tip of the peninsula and along the Pacific coast. In an average year Ensenada's temperature will not rise above 35°C (95°F); but San Felipe, on the Gulf of California, may soar to 48°C (118°F). Desert areas are cold at night.

Northern Mexico

Northern Mexico is largely desert. The days are exceptionally hot in summer – well over 38°C (100°F). Mountainous areas are cooler. In winter, temperatures may drop below freezing at night.

As you head east toward Monterrey, the climate becomes wetter and more moderate, but remains very hot in summer. However, even on the tropical Gulf Coast, temperatures can fall quite low in winter as cold air plunges south from the US.

The Pacific Coast

Along the Pacific coast, temperatures are cooler at night than in the south, but otherwise similar. In an average year, the maximum temperature in Mazatlán or Puerto Vallarta is in the mid-30s°C (mid-90s°F). North of Mazatlán, the coast becomes desert, and summer weather is extreme, with temperatures frequently above 38°C (100°F). South of Puerto Vallarta, the climate conforms more to the tropical rainy and dry season pattern the further south you go. Acapulco has daily highs of 27–32°C (80–90°F) year-round, seldom falling much below 21°C (70°F) at night, and Pacific breezes keep temperatures bearable. There is little rain in winter.

Southern Mexico and the Yucatán Peninsula

The southern area has some of the most variable weather in Mexico – some regions are dry while others have nearly 5 meters (16ft) of rainfall a year. Terrain has a huge effect on climate, and so, for example, the cool mountain climate of San Cristóbal de las Casas is completely different from the steamy rain forest weather of Palenque, 190km (118 miles) to the north. In Oaxaca, over 1,500 meters (5,000ft) above sea level, the night-time temperature in January can fall below freezing but at the end of the dry season in May or June, at midday, it can rise to nearly 38°C (100°F).

On the Yucatán Peninsula, weather is entirely tropical. Daytime temperatures are generally in the upper 20s°C (low 80s°F) year-round, and night-time temperatures seldom go below 16°C (60°F). In the main winter tourist season (December–March) temperatures are ideal, rising to a peak towards the end of the *seca* (the dry season) in May–June again around 38°C (100°F). On the Riviera Maya temperatures are generally a little more moderate than in the interior. One consequence of climate change is that around the Gulf of Mexico the distinction between dry and rainy seasons has become less clear than it once was, and occasional rain storms are now more common in the first months of the year, while months such as August can be rain-free for days at a time.

Hurricanes

Both the Gulf and Pacific coasts are vulnerable to hurricanes, with the Yucatán region most at risk. The official hurricane season runs from June to November, but whether any major storms will develop during that time is unpredictable beyond a few days. Mexico, especially the Yucatán and Riviera Maya, has some of the best hurricane precautions in the Caribbean, and visitors are warned well ahead of any dangers. The best source of information on hurricanes, including current conditions, is the **US National Hurricane Center**, www.nhc.noaa.gov.

What to Wear

Mexico's climate is very diverse, and you need to be at least minimally prepared for the weather of every area you pass through. Pack a sweater, a fleece or a jacket if you are visiting mountain or desert areas, including those in the south such as the Chiapas highlands. If you are traveling any-where in the June to October rainy season, you may want to take some kind of waterproof coat. Even in the hottest regions, it's good to have some long trousers and at least one long-sleeved shirt or top, to protect against sunburn, insect bites and scratches from bushes whenever you explore archeological sites and forest paths. A sunhat is also an important accessory, but ideal ones can be bought in Mexico. Always bring sturdy, comfortable, walking shoes.

In cities and in provincial towns, casual clothes are all you need at most times, but note that it is not usual even in hot cities to walk around public places in beach wear or (for men) very short shorts, and most

especially not when visiting churches. At most times a shirt and long trousers or Bermuda-style shorts should be adequate for men, and women can wear anything reasonably respectable. For upscale restaurants, especially in Mexico City, a man will need smart casual clothes and a jacket, and sometimes even a jacket and tie, and a woman a smart dress or trousers. In hot areas, light chino-style trousers are ideal, and adaptable to most situations.

Standards are naturally different in resort areas such as Acapulco, Ixtapa-Zihuatanejo, Puerto Vallarta, the Riviera Maya, and the beach towns of Baja, where shorts and beach wear are often acceptable on the street, and even in restaurants (except the more formal ones). Beyond that, a shirt and smart pants for men and long, loose, cotton dresses for women are pretty much all you need.

Crime and Safety

As has been well-publicized, there has been a serious upsurge in violent clashes between the Mexican authorities and drug cartels in parts of Mexico, especially since President Calderón launched his offensive against the cartels in 2007 *(see page 75)*. However, this violent crime mainly affects certain areas – border cities such as Tijuana, Ciudad Juárez and Nuevo Laredo, Culiacán in Sinaloa – and the truth is it has very rarely had any direct effect on tourists. There is a certain greater risk in Acapulco, but other resort areas have been pretty peaceful. Overall, foreign visitors – unless they actually go looking for danger – are far less likely to be affected by this sort of violence than the more "traditional" problems of petty crime, bag-snatching and so

BELOW: the long arm of the law.

on. And the risks of these can be greatly reduced by following a few sensible precautions.

The risk of petty crime is, in general, highest in parts of Mexico City, but even there it's easy to have a trouble-free trip by following a few ground rules. Special care is needed when using taxis *(see page 333)* and you should avoid using the metro during peak times. Be especially aware of people around you in the Centro Histórico, and in any markets. Elsewhere and in most other cities it's much easier to drop your guard, but it's always best to keep to these rules:
• don't walk around dark, empty streets at night.
• in any crowd, always keep your bag in front of you with your hand on it, and be aware of anyone standing especially close.
• whenever you sit in a restaurant or café, always keep your bag in view and close to hand, preferably on your lap, an empty chair or on the table in front of you. Never leave bags on the floor or hanging from a chair back.
• use ATMs at banks only during business hours. Try to use them only where there are plenty of people around.
• don't carry all your credit cards or large amounts of cash with you.
• lock your bags whenever you leave your hotel room, and do not leave valuables lying around in the room.
• if you have a car, try to park in hotel or other attended parking lots.
• if you use second-class buses, try to put your bags in the overhead racks nearest to you, and keep an eye on them.

Police Forces and Military Checks

If you are the victim of any kind of crime, report it as soon as possible to the nearest police post. If you have been robbed it is unlikely the items can be recovered, but you will need a police statement for an insurance claim. In many resorts there are special tourist police (*Policía Turística*) units, with English-speaking officers.

On many roads drivers may be stopped by military checkpoints. They are checking for shipments of drugs or weapons, and are rarely ever interested in tourists, who are usually waved on their way. If, however, you are discovered in possession of any illegal drugs you can expect severe penalties.

Customs Regulations

All visitors arriving in Mexico must fill in a customs form (usually given out on incoming flights). When you hand it in at the airport, after clearing immigration, you will be asked to press a button by a kind of traffic light. If it comes up green, you go straight through; if red, your bag will be searched. The purpose of this system is to ensure that customs checks are random. As well as their personal effects visitors entering Mexico are allowed certain amounts of some goods *(see below)*; other items may be subject to duty and require an import permit. For specific requirements for taking US or Canadian vehicles into Mexico, *see page 329*. When leaving Mexico, it is expressly forbidden to take out any pre-Columbian artifacts without authorization, and there are severe penalties for doing so, with very little chance of appeal.

Customs Allowances

These include the following; for a full list, see www.aduanas.gob.mx, which has the relevant pages in English.
Cigars and cigarettes: For each visitor aged over 18, up to 400 cigarettes, or 50 cigars or 1kg (2.2lbs) of tobacco.
Currency: Up to US$10,000 or the equivalent in cash. Amounts over this level are not liable for duty but must be declared.
Alcohol: Visitors over 18 can bring in up to 3 liters (100 fl. oz) of wine or liquor.
Electrical equipment: One laptop computer and one CD or other music player, and two still or video cameras, per person, as long as they are for personal use and not re-sale.

D isabled Travelers

Traveling around Mexico has its problems for people with mobility problems, but facilities have been improving, albeit from a very low level. Many streets in Mexico City and other cities now have wheelchair ramps cut in pavements, and many state museums now have access ramps. In many situations, it's necessary to rely on the great helpfulness of Mexican people – ask for assistance on buses, ferries, or in public buildings, and great efforts will usually be made to find a lift, fit in a chair or otherwise accommodate you. Archeological sites tend to have stony paths that are difficult to negotiate, but the larger ones now tend to have smoother walkways.

To make the most of a trip to Mexico it's best to plan ahead carefully, and costs will unavoidably be higher than for other travelers. The best places to stay will be the big

beach resorts, where some hotels have fully adapted rooms, and even those that do not are more easy to get around. In the colonial cities, some hotels have attractive ground-floor rooms. A rented car or taxis will be the best way to get around.

Cancún Accessible, tel: 998-843 7702, www.cancunaccessible.com. Mexico's first specialized disabled travel company, which can provide tours, accessible transport, accommodation and other services around the Riviera Maya and Yucatán. The website is Spanish-only, but emails will be answered in English.

E lectricity

Mexico uses the same 110 volt electrical system as the USA and Canada, with the same flat two-pronged plugs. Anyone from areas with other systems should bring plug adaptors with them, as they are very difficult to find in Mexico.

Embassies and Consulates

Mexican Embassies Abroad

Australia
14 Perth Avenue, Yarralumla, ACT 2600, Canberra, tel: 02-6273 3963, www.mexico.org.au
Canada
45 O'Connor Street, Suite 1000, Ottawa, Ontario K1P 1A4, tel: 613-233 8988, www.sre.gob.mx/canada
UK
16 St George Street, London W1S 1FD, tel: 020-7499 8586, www.sre.gob.mx/reinounido
US
1911 Pennsylvania Avenue NW, Washington DC 20006, tel: 202-728 1600, http://portal.sre.gob.mx/eua

In Mexico City

Canada, the UK and especially the US also have consulates in various other parts of Mexico, details of which will be on the Embassy websites.
Australia
Rubén Darío 55, Col. Polanco, tel: 55-1101 2200, www.mexicoembassygov.au.
Canada
Schiller 529, Col. Polanco, tel: 55-5724 7900, www.canadainternational.gc.ca/mexico-mexique
Ireland
Blvd Ávila Camacho 76, 3rd Floor, Col. Lomas de Chapulpetec, tel: 55-5520 5803, www.irishembassy.com.mx
New Zealand
Jaime Balmes 8, 4th Floor, Los Morales, Col. Polanco, tel: 55-5283 9460, www.nzembassy.com/mexico

UK
Río Lerma 71, Col. Cuauhtémoc, tel: 55-5242 8500, http://ukinmexico.fco.gov.uk
USA
Paseo de la Reforma 305, Col. Cuauhtémoc, tel: 55-5080 2000, www.usembassy-mexico.gov

Emergency Numbers

General Emergencies: 060 is the shared number most commonly used for the police and all emergency services, but in some parts of Mexico the number used is **066**.

Health Emergencies: 080 (in Mexico City; in other areas, just try **060 or 066**).

However, rather than use the common emergency number it can be more efficient to call the service you need direct, particularly the local Red Cross (Cruz Roja) if you have a medical emergency: numbers of local police departments and ambulance services are in the phone book, and hotels should have them.

Etiquette

Mexicans, traditionally, lay great emphasis on courtesy. This has nothing to do with social class, and in country areas poorer people actually tend to be more polite than the wealthier members of the community. Indigenous people, especially, value traditional courtesies highly, and can appear positively ceremonious in the way they deal with strangers; if you respond in a casual manner this will appear contemptuous and aggressive rather than informally friendly.

An essential aspect of courtesy is to make at least some effort with Spanish, even if it is only with a simple greeting like *buenos días* (good day) or a *por favor* (please). When entering a shop, a restaurant or any other business it is usual to say *buenos días* (or *buenas tardes*, good afternoon, after around 1pm) first before saying what you want. Among country and especially indigenous people, it will also be appreciated if you follow this with an introductory question – *¿Le puedo hacer una pregunta?* or "Can I ask you a question?" – before, for example, asking directions in the street. When you have finished, always say *gracias* and *adios* clearly and with emphasis. Getting brusquely to the point and going about one's business is not highly valued. When introduced to someone by name, Mexicans shake hands, and do so again whenever they meet again, and when they take leave of one another. Women (but not many Indigenous women) nearly always greet anyone they are on friendly terms with, men or women, with a kiss on the cheek.

Mexicans believe it is less rude to accept an unwanted invitation, and fail to appear, than to refuse it. Equally, notions of punctuality are pretty vague, and any appointments are kept to only roughly.

Around Tulum and Playa del Carmen on the Riviera Maya, and Puerto Escondido and some other locations on the Pacific, topless and sometimes nude bathing are now effectively permitted, but in general Mexicans are not very tolerant of nudity or too much exposed flesh. In towns and above all in churches you should avoid any public exposure that might offend – for example, men walking around shirtless, and anyone wearing very short shorts.

G ay and Lesbian Travelers

Mexican attitudes to homosexuality are, like those to many things, contradictory. There is a strong strain of homophobia in parts of Mexican culture, but also a good deal of tolerance, and an assertive gay rights movement that enjoys some protection from the political left. A series of laws against anti-gay discrimination have been passed since 2000, and Mexico City and the border state of Coahuila both recognize civil partnerships for gay couples.

Mexico City has an energetic gay scene, centered in the Zona Rosa, and elsewhere there are sizeable gay communities in Monterrey, Mérida and, especially, Guadalajara. Of the beach towns, the hub is Puerto Vallarta, close to Guadalajara, followed by Cancún. In some cities and small towns, however, gay life may remain more underground. On the other hand, among Mexico's many, many surprises are the Zapotec communities such as Juchitán and Tehuantepec in eastern Oaxaca, where society is essentially matriarchal and women prize having gay sons, as being more help to them in their old age.

Of the gay websites on Mexico, the most extensive listings are probably on www.gaymexicomap.com.

H ealth and Medical Care

No one should travel in Mexico without a comprehensive travel insurance policy, covering loss or theft of their belongings, cancellations, and all medical eventualities, including

Medical Treatment

If you need medical assistance, the best place to call on will be one of the modern private clinics that are found in Mexican cities and resort areas, and then claim on your insurance. Such clinics have high-quality facilities, and near-invariably have some English-speaking staff. Hotels should be able to recommend one, and/or provide a list of local English-speaking doctors (or dentists). If you call the embassy or consulate of your home country (see page 381) they will also have a list of multilingual doctors. In small towns and country areas the only facilities will usually be a local public health center (Centro de Salud), which can handle basic emergencies perfectly well, but anyone with a more serious problem will need to be moved to the nearest private hospital.

emergency repatriation by air if necessary. Mexico's public health system is fairly limited, and for foreigners it is essential to have private health insurance. Many credit card companies provide some coverage for medical and/or legal emergencies for trips paid for with their card, but check whether this is sufficient for your needs. If you intend to try out any adventure sports activities – such as scuba diving – you may need additional cover or a specialized sports insurance policy, so check carefully how far your policy extends, and shop around to find the best options.

Health Precautions

At most times – that is, except during exceptional crises such as the 2009 swine flu outbreak – there are no inoculations that are obligatory for travelers to Mexico. However, it is advisable to be inoculated against polio, tetanus, and hepatitis A, and, if necessary, to have a typhoid booster shot. Cholera is also present in some areas, so to be sure you may wish to be immunized against that too. There is a very slight risk of malaria in forest areas of the Gulf Coast, Campeche and Chiapas, so some travelers take a course of anti-malaria tablets, but discuss the risks with your doctor before taking any such pills, as they can have strong side-effects. Dengue fever, another fly-born infection, affects local people in some areas, but the best way to avoid it is to steer clear of any pools of stagnant water.

If you fly into Mexico City, the combination of altitude and air pollution can leave some new arrivals weak and listless, with headaches and other symptoms. Take it easy during the first days you are there, to get acclimatized.

It's a good idea to bring a basic medical kit, including medication for diarrhea and stomach cramps, insect repellent, aspirin or an equivalent, antiseptic wipes and cream, plasters, sunscreen, and any prescription drugs you may need.

Drinking Water and Hygiene

The risks of ingesting any tap water in Mexico are often exaggerated, but in general, the essential rule is still to drink only bottled, purified water (agua purificada). This is guaranteed clean water, not mineral water (agua mineral), which is a lot more expensive. Purified water is sold in all grocery stores, supermarkets and pharmacies, and in all restaurants, and all hotels of mid-range level and up provide it free for their guests. Travelers in Mexico have commonly been advised to refuse to have ice in their drinks or to buy anything at street juice stands, but nowadays virtually every restaurant and stand also uses agua purificada to make ice and fruit-juice mixes, so there is very little risk in this either. At the same time, the standard of mains water in most parts of Mexico has also been improving, so you are unlikely to catch anything by swallowing a little water while in the shower.

Overall, the best ways to reduce the likelihood of getting any stomach complaints while in Mexico are simply to avoid the most basic lonchería restaurants and any street-food stands with obviously poor hygiene standards, and to be reasonably sensible about eating any high-risk foods such as seafood that is not clearly fresh. If you buy any fruits or vegetables yourself, rinse them with purified water, or peel them. If you are camping out or traveling in any remote areas, where you may run out of purified water, be prepared to purify water yourself: either boil it for 20 minutes or more (depending on altitude), or use purification tablets.

Hospitals

Private hospitals will be listed in the local phone book under Centros Médicos or Hospitales, and will normally have large ads making clear the services they offer and whether they have English-speaking staff. The following are some reliable

options around the country:
Mexico City: Centro Médico ABC, Avenida Observatorio, Colonia Américas, tel: 55-5230 8000, emergencies 55-5230 8161, www.abchospital.com.
Guadalajara: Hospital México-Americano, Colomos 2110, Guadalajara, Jalisco; tel: 33-3642 3333, www.hma.com.mx.
Acapulco: Hospital Magallanes, Wilfrido Massieu 2, Acapulco, Guerrero; tel: 744-469 0270, www.hospitalmagallanes.com.
Mérida: Clínica de Mérida, Av. Itzáes 242, Mérida, Yucatán; tel: 999-942 1800, www.clinicademerida.com.mx.
Cancún: American Hospital, Plaza Las Américas, Av. Bonampak, Cancún, Quintana Roo; tel: 998-881 3400, www.amerimed-hospitals.com. This same US-owned group also has hospitals in Puerto Vallarta and Cabo San Lucas.

Pharmacies

Well-stocked pharmacies (farmacias) are plentiful in Mexican cities, and there is usually one in every small town. In cities, there is nearly always at least one that is open 24 hours daily, often on or near the main square. Pharmacies stock a wide range of products as well as prescription drugs, such as cosmetics, condoms, purified water, and telephone cards (see page 385).

I nternet

Internet access is very widely available across Mexico, and has made up for the inadequacies of the mail system. Internet cafés are abundant in cities and there is even usually one at least in small towns, so

BELOW: embracing wireless internet in Querétaro.

checking email is never a problem. Charges are usually around $1 an hour, or more in resort areas. In addition, many hotels, even mid-range or budget ones, now offer Wi-fi connections, often for free (in remoter areas connections may be very slow, but they usually work). Email is now the most reliable way of keeping in touch while in Mexico, and of making hotel reservations.

L eft Luggage

There are left-luggage lockers in each of the main terminals at Mexico City airport and at most other airports, usually near the Departures area. In Mexico City, they are often in great demand. First-class bus stations (including all the Mexico City terminals) often have staffed left-luggage counters, and if you have a bus ticket for the next few days you can often check bags into the bus company's own luggage storage (guarda equipajes) room.

M aps

Completely accurate maps are oddly hard to obtain in Mexico. Many states have ongoing road-building schemes, and many maps are not updated frequently enough to catch them all, so you can find new roads not marked on any map. Tourist offices and free local English-language magazines commonly provide free maps, which are useful, although often a little sketchy. The most thorough maps are those of each state produced by the official Secretaría de Comunicaciones y Transportes (SCT), but some are now seriously out of date. The maps and road atlases of Mexico's main commercial map publishers, Guía Rojí and Editorial Independencia, are good for the capital, most cities and areas around them but sometimes less so for rural areas. If you intend to tour around, and haven't brought enough maps with you, stock up in Mexico City or in any shop that has a good map stock.

Media

Newspapers and Magazines

Mexico has a great many daily newspapers. Mexico City papers that are also distributed around the country include the prestigious Reforma, Excelsior, El Universal, the more popular-style UNO más UNO, the erudite left-wing La Jornada and business-oriented El Financiero, and every state has two or more papers of

its own. In Mexico City there are also several good entertainments guides (see Activities page 368). In English, The News (www.thenews.com.mx) is a fairly limited daily published in Mexico City, and the Miami Herald has a Cancún edition which is distributed around the Yucatán.

Major international magazines such as Time and Newsweek are readily available on newsstands in the capital, major cities and the big resort areas, but are scarce elsewhere. Sanborn's restaurant branches generally have a newsstand with a selection of the foreign press.

In many tourist areas, inland and especially around the coasts, there is at least one local free magazine published in English, such as Baja Times in Baja, Tourister in Ixtapa-Zihuatanejo, Yucatán Today in Mérida and Cancún Tips and several others on the Riviera Maya. They are distributed in hotels, tourist offices, restaurants and other venues, and while they are advertising-led they are handy to pick up, since as well as basic maps they also contain other useful information (such as current taxi rates).

For websites with news and information on Mexico, see page 387.

Television and Radio

Except for those in really remote areas, or boutique retreats that deliberately avoid it, nearly every Mexican hotel has TV, and a great many, even in lower price ranges, now have cable or satellite systems offering a variety of channels from a great many Mexican ones with their favorite mix of soap operas (telenovelas), entertainment spectaculars, chat shows, sensationalist news, classic Mexican movies and soccer, to a choice of channels in English. In addition, US and British TV shows and movies are often shown even on Mexican channels in English with Spanish subtitles. Anyone with some knowledge of Spanish can also get insights into local life by flicking around the many small-scale local channels.

There is an even bigger number of radio stations, most of them broadcasting Mexico's own music, of different kinds.

Money

Mexico's currency, the peso, comes in denominations of 20, 50, 100, 200, 500 and 1,000 peso bills, and there are coins for 1, 2, 5, 10, and 20 pesos, as well as flimsy coins of 10, 20, and 50 centavos of a peso. Since the global financial crisis of 2007 – 8

TRANSPORTATION ACCOMMODATIONS EATING OUT ACTIVITIES A – Z LANGUAGE

the peso has generally stood at around 12–14 pesos to the US dollar.

Along the US border and in big resort areas many shops and businesses accept US dollars, and prices may be labeled in both currencies. However, if you pay in dollars you will usually end up paying slightly more than if you had changed your money into pesos.

When getting spending money in Mexico it is best to be able to use a variety of methods – US dollar travelers' checks for extra security, some dollars in cash, and through ATM cash machines. If you are traveling from Britain or most other countries, always take cash or travelers' cheques in US dollars, as Mexican banks generally give very bad rates for non-dollar currencies (Euros and Canadian dollars may be less of a problem). Credit cards are widely used in Mexico, especially in hotels, big stores and dive shops, and effectively essential for renting a car. It is much less common to use them in restaurants, and in markets and street stores you must have some cash (in pesos). ATMs are also plentiful in cities, and there is usually one at least in the main town of each district. Given the time it can take to change money in Mexican banks, and the fact that withdrawing money through an ATM can be cheaper than paying bank commissions, this is often the most convenient way to get money, but it is not advisable to rely on ATMs completely. There may be none in remote areas, so check on the local situation – hotels will be able to advise you. For this reason it is good to have some dollar cash or travelers' cheques (which many hotels will exchange).

Note that owing to security concerns you should always notify your credit card company before traveling to Mexico, as otherwise you can find that your card is blocked without warning.

Changing travelers' cheques or cash can involve standing in long lines, and some bank branches do not change money at certain times (such as during the afternoon). This is a big reason why it's often much easier just to use an ATM. Before joining a line, always check if there is a special currency exchange (cambio) counter. It will always be quicker to change money in bigger branches than smaller ones. All banks are closed on Sundays and public holidays.

Outside of banking hours, in any tourist area there will be several small casas de cambio (money exchanges), where rates are sometimes quite reasonable. Avoid changing money in hotels, which habitually give very poor rates. There are also exchange desks at all airports, which nearly always give bad rates. If you have no pesos, change only as much as you need for a taxi to your hotel, and then get cash from an ATM.

Whenever you change money, avoid being left with only big-denomination notes (especially 500 or 1,000 pesos), which will be hard to break in most shops and restaurants.

Taxes

Airline passengers leaving Mexico must pay a departure tax, generally of around 550 pesos ($40). This is now nearly always included in the ticket price, but with a very few flights you may have to pay (in cash, not by card) at check-in. Mexico has a sales or value added tax (IVA) of 15 percent (10 percent in some border states) which is charged on most transactions, and most states charge a 2 percent accommodations tax which is added to hotel bills.

Tipping

Many Mexicans depend on tips to make up for low wages, so it is a good principle to follow to tip generously and often. In restaurants and bars in most parts of the country, the usual rate is around 10 percent of the bill; in resort areas this rises to around 15 percent. Some restaurants add around 10 percent to the check, but if the service has been good it will be appreciated if you also leave some cash.

Hotel porters and bellboys are usually tipped around 4–10 pesos, for chambermaids about 10 pesos per night. Tour guides are tipped according to the tour price and the quality of their performance. It is not, however, usual to tip taxi drivers, unless they have been especially helpful, for example with luggage.

There are also many people who are customarily given small tips for a range of small services. At gas stations there will often be a boy who will clean your windscreen for a few pesos, and it's usual to tip the main gas attendant if they provide any extra services such as checking your tires or oil. Boys or old men who guard areas on a street, guide you into one of "their" parking places and then watch over your car till you come back are given 2–5 pesos. More formal parking attendants are tipped 5 pesos or more.

O pening Hours

Opening hours vary a little around the country, with a greater tendency to get everything done in the morning, and then take a long siesta break through the afternoon, the further you go south. Office hours are widely variable, but in most areas they open 9am–2pm, then close for lunch, reopening from 4–6pm. In cities, many stores may also observe a long lunch break, opening from around 8.30–1 or 2pm and again from 4–8pm, but there are also plenty that stay open all day, 9am–9pm. In small towns and especially villages things are often just open through the day, for whenever there's any business. Markets generally begin business early, around 7am or earlier, and may be shutting down by about 2 or 3pm. Most city shops are closed on Sundays, but in small towns and villages this can be a busy market and shopping day.

Banks are traditionally open Mon–Fri 8.30am–1pm and Saturdays 9am–1pm, but many now stay open much later, often through the afternoon to 5–6pm or later.

Cathedrals and major city churches have their own timetables, and are often open all day, but village churches commonly open their doors early, at sunrise, and are nearly always closed in the afternoons, roughly from around 1pm to 4 or 5pm. They are then left open until after dark.

Except in beach resorts, business throughout Mexico slows to a near-standstill during Easter week, between Christmas and New Year, and around the major fiestas.

P hotography

All the major types of camera equipment, memory cards, and so on are available in Mexico, in resort areas and the main cities, where there are often specialist stores that should be able to provide any more technical equipment. However, they are relatively expensive, so bring everything you need with you if you can.

There are a few restrictions on photography at archeological sites and museums administered by the Instituto Nacional de Antropología e Historia (INAH). Tripods cannot be used without a permit, and an extra fee must be paid to use a video camera, but there are no limitations on the use of hand-held still cameras. At the larger archeological sites these controls are keenly enforced.

Indigenous peoples often resent being used arbitrarily as photographic subjects by wandering tourists. This is not because, as is often said, they think cameras "steal their souls," but because they greatly value courtesy (see Etiquette, page 381) and find it insultingly impersonal for a complete stranger to take their picture without asking. If you wish to take any pictures in indigenous communities, always greet people and ask first (¿Le puedo hacer una foto?); where there are plenty of tourists around, you may also be asked for money. There is a complete ban on picture-taking in many indigenous churches and other buildings in villages in highland Chiapas and many other areas. If you take any tours into indigenous areas your guide should make clear when it is acceptable to take photos.

Postal Services

Main post offices (oficinas de correos) are found in all main towns and are usually open Mon–Fri 9am–6pm, and often Saturday 9am–1pm. Offices in small towns and villages commonly open for shorter hours, and close for lunch. Stamps (estampillas) are sold in post offices and any shop with the sign Expendio de Estampillas. Mail boxes are generally small metal boxes attached to walls in two shades of blue and marked Servicio Postal Mexicano. In towns and outside some main post offices there are often large red boxes marked Buzón Expresso, but mail posted in them goes only marginally faster.

The Mexican mail service is cheap but erratic, and often very, very slow. Hence email is now a much better means of maintaining any kind of communication – postcards and letters will generally arrive, but it's hard to say when. If you have anything important you need to send, a good alternative to standard post is to use MEXPOST, a courier service that is run by the post office but is quite efficient:

Public Holidays

The following are Mexico's official holidays, when all businesses throughout the country are closed for the day.
January 1 New Year's Day
February 5 Constitution Day
March 21 Birthday of Benito Juárez
March/April Maundy Thursday, Good Friday, Easter Monday
May 1 Labor Day
May (Last Monday) Spring Bank Holiday
September 16 Independence Day
November 20 Revolution Day
December 12 Virgin of Guadalupe
December 25 Christmas Day

packages sent within Mexico usually arrive the next day, to the USA within two days, and to Europe in about a week. Available at most main post offices (but not small ones), it is still cheaper than most commercial courier companies. However, all the main international courier services (FedEx, UPS, etc.) are available in most Mexican cities.

You can also receive mail at Mexican post offices, although if possible it will be better to have the item sent to a hotel. Letters sent for general delivery/poste restante should be clearly addressed to your name (in capitals, underlined) and then Lista de Correos followed by the postcode and the name of the relevant town and state, as in CP 77510 Cancún, Quintana Roo, México. When you go to the post office where you are expecting mail, ask for the Lista de Correos, and take your passport.

R eligious Services

Mexico remains a predominantly Catholic country, but a wide variety of evangelical Protestant groups is also active, especially among indigenous people. In many cities and resort areas there is at least one Catholic church that holds services in English some time each week, and there are also expatriate Protestant churches and church groups. Local free magazines (see Media, page 383) will have details of services in English in each area. There is also a large Jewish community in Mexico City, particularly in Roma, Condesa and Polanco.

S moking

Officially, smoking is only permitted in outside spaces, such as patios or terraces.

Student Travellers

At some museums and other public buildings there are small discounts on admission for students. In most cases they are intended for Mexican students only, but since the situation is not clear, if you have an international student card you may be able to get the corresponding discount.

T elephones

White Lada public phones of Telmex, Mexico's main phone company, can be found easily in all but the remotest spots in the country. They work with phone cards (tarjetas lada), which are available for 30, 50 or 100 pesos from Telmex shops and any store with a

blue-and-yellow Ladatel sign (pharmacies nearly always sell them). Instructions are posted up in different languages in each phone box, and when you insert the card the display on the phone will tell you how much credit you have left on the card. By pressing a button you can also change the display from Spanish to English.

In villages that still do not have Lada phones there is always a local Caseta or phone office, identified by a blue-and-white Telmex Teléfono Público sign. At these you write down the number you want to call and it is dialed for you, and you then take the call from a booth. In cities there are also many private phone centers (locutorios) that use the same system.

Telmex charges are quite low for local calls but can go up sharply for anywhere outside your immediate area, and are high for international calls. If you need to make an international call, rather than watch a phone card running out very quickly, it will be better to make the call from a caseta or phone center, and then pay in one go when you have finished. This will also work out a little cheaper. Making any phone call from a hotel is generally particularly expensive.

The number of mobile/cell phones has been growing prodigiously in Mexico, as it has everywhere else in the world. Signal coverage is now good around cities and most towns, although the more remote rural areas remain "holes" in the network. Mexican cell phones operate on the same 1900 frequency band as in the US, so phones from Europe or elsewhere must have a quad- or triband facility. The cost of using a foreign cell phone in Mexico is steep, so if you expect to use a phone much it can be more economical to get a cheap model pay-as-you-go Mexican phone. In all cities there are plenty of phone shops of Telcel, Movistar and other companies that have frequent competitive offers.

Phone Codes

To make any call within Mexico but outside your immediate area, you must first dial an access code (**01**), followed by an area code (often called el Lada). In some big cities the area code has two digits (Mexico City 55, Monterrey 81, Guadalajara 33), followed by an eight-figure number; everywhere else the area code has three digits (Cuernavaca 777, Puerto Vallarta 322, Acapulco 744, Mérida 755, Cancún 998) and individual numbers have seven figures. Lada codes are given with all phone

ABOVE: public phone on Isla Mujeres, in the Yucatán.

numbers listed in this guide.

Mexican cell phone numbers have the same area codes, but to call them you may need to use another access code instead of 01, usually **044** or **045**. Numbers beginning **01 800** are toll-free.

International Dialling Codes

To call Mexico from abroad: +52 followed by Lada area code and the number.
To call abroad from Mexico: Australia 00 61; Irish Republic 00 353; New Zealand 00 64; South Africa 00 27; UK 00 44; US and Canada 001.

Telephone Enquiries

Operators for internal services speak Spanish only, but international operators are English-speaking:
• For directory enquiries within Mexico, dial 040.
• For international enquiries and operator-assisted long-distance calls, dial 090.

Time Zones

Most of Mexico is usually in the same time zone as US Central Standard Time (GMT minus 6 hours). Exceptions are the states of Chihuahua, Sonora, Sinaloa and Baja California Sur, which usually follow Mountain Standard Time (GMT minus 7 hours) and Baja California Norte, which is usually in the same zone as US Pacific Time (GMT minus 8 hours). However, Mexico moves onto Daylight Saving Time later than the US, on the first Sunday in April, and ends it earlier, on the last Sunday in October, so for a few days each year the Time Zones of the two countries are not synchronized. In addition, Sonora state does not

observe Daylight Saving at all, so during the summer months it is effectively on Pacific Time, the same as Baja California Norte.

Toilets

Public toilets are quite scarce in Mexico, except in airports, bus stations, museums, malls, and archeological sites. In an emergency, restaurants or cafés are often the best bet; ask for *el servicio* or *el lavabo*. If you're concerned about hygiene, chain restaurants will always be pretty clean.

Tourist Information

Mexican Government Tourist Offices (MGTO)

This is now the common website address for Mexico's tourism authorities worldwide:
www.visitmexico.com
Canada
2 Bloor Street West, Suite 1502, Toronto, Ontario M4W 3E2, tel: 416-925 0704
1 Place Ville Marie, Suite 1931, Montreal, Quebec H3B 2C3, tel: 514-871 1052
999 West Hastings Street, Suite 1110, Vancouver, British Columbia V6C 2W2, tel: 604-669 2845
UK
Wakefield House, 41 Trinity Square, London EC3N 4DJ, tel: 020-7488 9392
US
400 Madison Avenue, Suite 11C, New York, NY 10017, tel: 212-308 2110 ext. 103
2829 16th Street North West, 4th Floor, Washington DC 20009, tel: 202-265 9021
1880 Century Park East, Suite 511, Los Angeles, CA 90067, tel: 310-282 9112
225 North Michigan Avenue, Suite 1850, Chicago, Ill. 60601, tel: 312-228 0194
5975 Sunset Drive, Suite 305, South Miami, Fl 33143, tel: 786-621 2909 ext. 13
4507 San Jacinto, Suite 308, Houston, Texas 77004, tel: 713-772 2581

Local Tourist Offices

Every state in Mexico has its own tourist office, based in the state capital, and many cities also have their own municipal information offices. The quality of local tourist offices varies a great deal. In some the staff are well-informed, up to date on local developments, and very helpful; in others they may be students who have

no specific knowledge and are there only to give out leaflets. Websites, local independent tour companies and, where they exist, local English-language free magazines *(see Media, page 383)* are in general much more useful sources of information than official tourist offices. Tourist offices can be particularly unreliable regarding travel information, so always check bus timings, for example, with the relevant company rather than rely on anything told you by tourist offices. The following are some of the more useful tourist information services around Mexico, but as said there is at least one in each state, and more in coastal resorts.

Acapulco
Av. Costera Miguel Alemán 187, tel: 744-484 4583, www.visitacapulco.com.mx
Baja California Norte
Juan Ruíz de Alarcón 1572, Zona Río, Tijuana, tel: 01-800 028 0888, www.discoverbajacalifornia.com
Cabo San Lucas
Blvd Mauricio Castro, Plaza San José, San José del Cabo, tel: 624-146 9628, from US and Canada 1-866 567 2226, www.loscabosguide.com
Campeche
Main public information office: Casa Seis, Calle 57 (on Parque Principal), Campeche, tel: 01-800 226 7324, from US and Canada 1-800 536 5616, www.campeche.travel
Guadalajara (Jalisco State Tourist Office)
Av. Morelos 102, Plaza Tapatía, tel: 33-3668 1600, http://visitajalisco.gob.mx
Puerto Vallarta
Zona Comercial Continental Plaza, tel: 322-224 1175, www.visitpuertovallarta.com
Mérida and Yucatán
Main city information offices: Teatro Peón Contreras, Calle 60, by Calle 57, and Palacio Municipal, on the Plaza Mayor, tel: 999-928 1966, www.merida.gob.mx/turismo
Yucatán State Tourism Department: www.mayayucatan.com.mx
Mexico City (Distrito Federal)
Nuevo León 56, Colonia Hipódromo, tel: 01-800 008 9090, www.mexicocity.gob.mx
Oaxaca
Independencia 607 (on the Alameda), Oaxaca, tel: 951-516 0123, www.oaxacainfo.gob.mx
Puebla
5 Oriente No 3 (beside the cathedral), Puebla, tel: 01-800 326 8656/222-777 1519, www.puebla.gob.mx
San Cristóbal de las Casas
Palacio Municipal, Av. Miguel Hidalgo 1 (on the Zócalo), tel: 967-678 0665
Veracruz
Palacio Municipal, on the Zócalo,

Veracruz, tel: 229-200 2200, http://portal.veracruz.gob.mx

Websites

See also the state tourist sites listed under Tourist Information Offices www.mexperience.com. Very clear information, interesting background articles, and a booking service. www.mexconnect.com. More of a magazine-style site, Mexico Connect has an inspiring range of features on many aspects of Mexico. www.insidemex.com. Inside Mexico, a guide to living in Mexico produced by expat residents. www.thetruthaboutmexico.com. Informative antidote written by Mexican residents to "Mexico=chaos" media reporting. www.planeta.com/mexico. Eco Travels in Mexico, a useful source for discovering small-scale and ecotourism travel possibilities. http://mexicomike.com. A huge amount of useful information for travelers, and particularly good for drivers. www.zihuatanejo.net. Local guide to Ixtapa-Zihuatanejo and Troncones. http://portalsanmiguel.com. Based in San Miguel de Allende, and a useful guide to activities in the area. www.yucatanliving.com. Imaginative site produced by Mérida-based expats. www.yucatanwildlife.com. Covers every aspect of the peninsula's astonishing wildlife, and tour options.

Tour Operators and Travel Agents

The companies below provide a range of travel services and tours, from the US, the UK and within Mexico.

Andale... Mexico, www.andalemexico.com. Based in Mexico City and Queretaro, this Internet tour agency with international offices offers a much broader than average range of trips and other services around Mexico.

Cathy Matos Mexican Tours, tel (UK): 020 8492 0000, www.mextours. co.uk. The foremost UK Mexico specialist, with expert knowledge and tailor-made and ready-made itineraries. Also the UK agents for Mexicana.

Go... with Jo, tel (US and Canada): 1-800 999 1446, www.gowithjo.com. Texas-based company with range of trips around Mexico, and run with a personal touch.

Haki Cultural Expeditions, tel (Mexico): 55-8421 8064, www.mexico culturaltours.com. Mexican company that specializes in tours to indigenous communities.

Journey Latin America, tel (UK): 020 8747 8315, www.journeylatinamerica. co.uk. One of the best sources in the

UK for flight-only deals and other itineraries in Mexico and around Latin America.

Mexico Adventure, tel (US and Canada): 1-800 390 4639, www.mexico adventure.com. US-based company providing a complete range of tours, packages and other trips in Mexico.

Mexico City Explorer, tel (Mexico): 55-8596 4565, www.mexicocityexplorer. com.mx. Tours of every part of the capital, and an exciting range of trips to other parts of the country.

STS Travel, tel (US and Canada): 1-800 648 4849, www.ststravel.com. US student travel service, with spring break deals a specialty.

Turibus, tel (Mexico): 01-800 280 8887/55-5141 1360, www.turibus.com. mx. Open-topped double-decker buses that provide daily tours of Mexico City, Puebla, Veracruz and Mérida. Passengers can get on and off as many times as they wish during the day.

V isas and Passports

US, Canadian, Australian, New Zealand, British and other EU citizens do not need a visa to enter Mexico as tourists for up to six months, but they are required by nationals of South Africa and certain other countries (for details in English, see the Mexican Immigration Department website, www.inm.gob.mx or consult local Mexican consulates). US citizens need a full passport to travel to and from Mexico by air, and a passport or other WHTI (Western Hemisphere Travel Initiative) compliant document, such as a US Passport Card, to cross the border by land or enter by sea (for details of the WHTI, see the State Department site, http://travel.state.gov). Canadian citizens can officially still enter Mexico with only ID and a birth certificate, but if they transit through the US they must have a WHTI-compliant document, and in practice it's much simpler just to have a full passport. All other travelers must have full passports valid for at least six months from the date of entry.

All air travelers must also fill in a Mexican Tourist Card (FM1), which is handed out on incoming flights, and then stamped at immigration with the length of your permitted stay. Keep it with your passport and then give it up when you leave. Do not lose it, as if you do not have a Tourist Card when you leave you can be fined and delayed.

If you enter Mexico by land from the US, you do not need a Tourist Card for visits to the Zona Fronteriza or "Border Zone" (roughly 20–30km/12–18

Weights and Measures

The metric system is used throughout Mexico.

miles from the border) of up to 72 hours, but if you intend to go further or stay longer you should get one at a border crossing. When traveling by air the charge for a tourist card is absorbed into the ticket, but if you enter Mexico by land from the US, Guatemala or Belize you must pay a fee of around $20. This has to be paid at a government bank office at the border, which can be a little time consuming. There is a special regime for travelers visiting Mexico on cruise ships, so that they do not need a tourist card.

At most airports and US crossing points immigration officers give most visitors stays of 90 or 180 days, but travelers entering from Guatemala or Belize may be given only 30 days or less. If you wish to get an extension, the best thing to do is go to the Immigration Department office in Cancún (Instituto Nacional de Migración, Av. Uxmal by Av. Nader, tel: 998-884 1749), which is open Mon–Fri 9am–1pm, and generally grants tourist extensions very promptly. There are also INM offices in all main cities.

W omen Travelers

Women traveling alone or with another woman in Mexico are likely to attract some attention from Mexican men. To minimize unwanted attention, it's best to dress in a relatively restrained manner, and if such a situation arises to avoid making eye contact; make it clear that you have better things to do and walk purposefully on. In public places and by day this attention is unlikely to be aggressive or persistent, and is often pretty frivolous. However, it is important to avoid empty, dark streets and obviously dubious areas at night, and if you want to take a long walk, try to recruit fellow visitors to come along. Groups of three or more women and women with men are very unlikely to be bothered. In general, men in country areas are often shy and very courteous with all foreigners, including women; you are more likely to find a more aggressive, insistent atmosphere in the biggest cities and biggest resorts.

The most basic traditional cantinas still do not admit women, except at certain times. This is scarcely any loss, as most truly justify the tag "drinking dens." More comfortable cantinas that do admit women are generally very easy to tell apart.

L ANGUAGE

UNDERSTANDING THE LANGUAGE

Pronunciation Tips

Although many Mexicans speak some English, it is always good to have some basic Spanish phrases at your disposal, and outside the main tourist areas it will be essential to get around and to deal with restaurants and hotels. In general, Mexicans are delighted with foreigners who try to speak the language, and they'll be patient – if sometimes amused. Pronunciation is not difficult. The following is a simplified mini-lesson:

Vowels
a as in   *bad*
e as in   *bed*
i as in   *police*
o as in   *holly*
u as in   *rude*

Consonants are approximately like those in English, the main exceptions being:
c is hard before **a**, **o**, or **u** (as in English), and is soft before **e** or **i**, when it sounds like **s**. Thus, *censo* (census) sounds like *senso*.
g is hard before **a**, **o**, or **u** (as in English), but before **e** or **i** Spanish **g** sounds like a guttural **h**. In country areas **g** before **ua** is often slightly suppressed, so that *agua* sounds more like *awa*.
h is silent.
j sounds like a guttural h.
ll sounds like y.
ñ sounds like ny, as in señor.
q is followed by **u** as in English, but the combination always sounds like **k**, not **kw**. ¿Qué quiere Usted? is pronounced: Keh kee-er-eh oosted?
r at the beginning of a work and **rr** within them are heavily rolled.
x between vowels sounds like a

guttural **h**, eg in Mexico or Oaxaca.
y alone, as the word meaning "and", is pronounced **ee**.
Note that **ch** and **ll** are separate letters of the Spanish alphabet; if looking in a phone book or dictionary for a word beginning with **ch**, you will find it after the final **c** entry. A name or word beginning with **ll** will be listed after the final **l** entry (**ñ** and **rr** are also counted as separate letters.)

Useful Words and Phrases

Note that everyone in Mexico understands **OK**, which has become part of everyday Mexican language.
please *por favor*
thank you *gracias*
you're welcome *de nada* (literally, for nothing)
I'm sorry *lo siento*
excuse me *con permiso, disculpe* (if, for example, you would like to pass) *perdón* (if, for example, you have stepped on someone's foot)
yes *sí*
no *no*
Can you speak English? *¿Habla (usted) inglés?*
Do you understand me? *¿Me comprende? / ¿Me entiende?*
I don't understand *No entiendo*
this is good *(esto) está bueno*
this is bad *(esto) está malo*
hello *hola*
good morning *buenos días*
good afternoon *buenas tardes*
good night/evening *buenas noches*
goodbye *adiós*
Where is...? *¿Dónde está?*
exit *la salida*
entrance *la entrada*
money *dinero*
credit card *tarjeta de crédito*
tax *impuesto*

At the Hotel

Where is there an inexpensive hotel? *¿Dónde hay un hotel económico?*
Do you have a double/single room? *¿Tiene una habitación doble/sencilla?*
With a double bed *con cama de matrimonio*
With twin beds *con dos camas*
For one night/two nights *para una noche/dos noches*
Does it have air conditioning? *¿Tiene aire acondicionado* **or** *clima?*
Does it have a bath or a shower? *¿Tiene baño o ducha?*
Can I see the room? *¿Puedo ver la habitación?*
Is there a room with more light? *¿Hay alguna habitación con más luz?*
dining room *el comedor*
key *la llave*
swimming pool *alberca, piscina*
Can you cash a travelers' check? *¿Puede cambiar un cheque de viajero?*

Eating Out

In Spanish, *el menú* is not the main menu, but a fixed menu offered each day (usually for lunch) at a lower price. The main menu is *la carta*.
restaurant *restaurante*
budget restaurant *lonchería, cocina económica*
café, coffee shop *un café*
A coffee please *Un café, por favor*
Please bring me... *Tráigame por favor...*
beer *una cerveza*
cold water *agua fría*
hot water *agua caliente*
soft drink, soda *un refresco*
cheap set menu *la comida corrida*
breakfast *desayuno*
lunch *almuerzo/comida*

dinner *cena*
first course *primer plato*
main course *plato principal*
Another beer, please *Más cerveza, por favor*
The bill/check, please *La cuenta, por favor*
To get the attention of a waiter (waitress) *¡Señor! (¡Señorita! ¡Señora!)*
Can I pay by credit card? *¿Puedo pagar con tarjeta de crédito?*
cambio *change*
tip *propina*

Shopping

market, market place *el mercado*
I want/I would like *Quiero...*
How much is it (this)? *¿Cuánto es (esto)?*
It's very expensive *Es muy caro*
Can you give me a discount? *¿Me puede dar un descuento?*
Do you have...? *¿Tiene usted...?*
I will buy this *Voy a comprar esto*
Please show me another *Muéstreme otro (otra) por favor*
Just a moment, please *Un momento, por favor*

Communications

post office *los correos; la oficina de correos*
public telephone *un teléfono público*
cell/mobile phone *teléfono móvil, celular*
letter *la carta*
postcard *la tarjeta postal*
stamp *una estampilla*
Is there a Net café near here? *¿Hay un centro de internet por aquí?*

Places

police station *la delegación de policía*
embassy *la embajada*
consulate *el consulado*
bank *el banco*
hotel *un hotel*
apartment *un departamento*
restroom *el sanitario/el lavabo/el baño de hombres/mujeres*
ticket office *la oficina de boletos, taquilla*

Transportation

airplane *avión*
airport *el aeropuerto*
ferry boat *el ferry, el transbordador*
small boat *lancha*
subway *el metro*
train *el tren*
first class *primera clase*
second class *segunda clase*

deluxe *de lujo/ejecutivo*
How much is a ticket to...? *¿Cuánto es un boleto a...?*
I want a ticket to... *Quiero un boleto a...*
return ticket *boleto redondo* or *boleto de ida y vuelta*
Please stop here *Pare aquí, por favor*
Straight ahead please *Derecho, por favor*
How many kilometers is it from here to...? *¿Cuántos kilómetros hay de aquí a...?*
How long does it take to go there? *¿Cuánto se tarda en llegar?*
left *a la izquierda*
right *a la derecha*
What is this place called? *¿Cómo se llama este lugar?*
I'm going to... *Voy a...*

On Buses

bus *autobús/camión de pasajeros*
express bus *el camión directo*
bus station *estación de autobuses, central camionera*
first/second class *primera/segunda clase*
bus stop *parada*
reserved seat *asiento reservado*
Where does this bus go? *¿A dónde va este autobus?*
When does the next bus leave for...? *¿Cuándo sale el próximo autobus para...?*
Where does it leave from? *¿De dónde sale?*
I am getting off here! (to call out to a local bus or colectivo driver when you want to get off) *¡Bajan!*

On the Road

car *un carro, un automóvil, un coche*
Where is a gas station? *¿Dónde hay una gasolinera?*
a repair garage *un taller mecánico*
tyre repair shop *una llantera, una vulcanizadora*
auto parts store *una refaccionaria para coches*
fill it up, please *lleno, por favor*
Please check the oil *Cheque el aceite, por favor*
radiator *el radiador*
battery *la batería*
jack *un gato*
towtruck *una grúa*
mechanic *un mecánico*
tire *una llanta*
spare wheel *la llanta de repuesto*

Taxis

taxi *el taxi*
taxi meter *taximetro*
taxi stand *el sitio de taxis*
Please call me a taxi *Pídame un taxi, por favor*

What will be the fare to...? *¿Cuánto sera para llevarme a...?*

Days and Months

Monday *lunes*
Tuesday *martes*
Wednesday *miércoles*
Thursday *jueves*
Friday *viernes*
Saturday *sábado*
Sunday *domingo*
January *enero*
February *febrero*
March *marzo*
April *abril*
May *mayo*
June *junio*
July *julio*
August *agosto*
September *septiembre*
October *octubre*
November *noviembre*
December *diciembre*

Numbers

1 *uno*
2 *dos*
3 *tres*
4 *cuatro*
5 *cinco*
6 *seis*
7 *siete*
8 *ocho*
9 *nueve*
10 *diez*
11 *once*
12 *doce*
13 *trece*
14 *catorce*
15 *quince*
16 *dieciséis*
17 *diecisiete*
18 *dieciocho*
19 *diecinueve*
20 *veinte*
21 *veintiuno*
25 *veinticinco*
30 *treinta*
40 *cuarenta*
50 *cincuenta*
60 *sesenta*
70 *setenta*
80 *ochenta*
90 *noventa*
100 *cien*
101 *ciento uno*
200 *doscientos*
300 *trescientos*
400 *cuatrocientos*
500 *quinientos*
1,000 *mil*
2,000 *dos mil*
10,000 *diez mil*
1,000,000 *un millón*

FURTHER READING

History

The Conquest of New Spain Bernal Díaz del Castillo. A simple soldier's tale, delightful to read, that is one of the world's greatest eyewitness accounts.

Chronicle of the Maya Kings and Queens Simon Martin and Nikolai Grube. Remarkable overview of the huge amount that has been learnt about Classic Maya history in the last 30 years.

The Fall of the Ancient Maya David L. Webster. Explores the great question of what happened to the Maya via a fascinating analysis of the nature of ancient Maya culture.

Five Letters 1519–1526 Hernán Cortés. Long letters in which Cortés recounts his exploits and justifies his actions to his king.

The Gods and Symbols of Ancient Mexico and the Maya Mary Ellen Miller and Karl Taube. Excellent, very helpful illustrated guide to the many spirits of pre-Hispanic Mexico.

Insurgent Mexico John Reed. Exciting account of the 1910 Revolution by the reporter famous for his coverage of the Russian Revolution.

The Lost Chronicles of the Maya Kings David Drew. A very readable overview of Maya history and culture.

Maya Cosmos Linda Schele, David Freidel and Joy Parker. A richly suggestive examination of Maya beliefs, in the past and present. The late Linda Schele played a huge part in expanding knowledge of the Maya and her other books with co-authors (*Blood of Kings, Forest of Kings, The Code of Kings*) are equally fascinating.

Mexico: From the Olmecs to the Aztecs Michael D. Coe and Rex Koontz. An excellent survey of all the ancient Mexican cultures, by one of the most eminent authorities in the field.

The Oxford History of Mexico M.C. Meyer and William Beezley. Scholarly yet engaging one-volume history.

Zapata and the Mexican Revolution John Womack Jr. A vivid account of the life of Mexico's most legendary revolutionary.

Writers on Mexico

First Stop in the New World: Mexico City, the Capital of the 21st Century, David Lida. Up to the minute, very sharp account of the contemporary megalopolis: one to challenge plenty of stereotypes.

Five Families Oscar Lewis. Lewis spent many years studying Mexico's "culture of poverty" and interviewing its victims.

The Forgotten Peninsula: a Naturalist in Baja California Joseph Wood Krutch. One of the best books about Baja.

Incidents of Travel in Central America, Chiapas, and Yucatán and **Incidents of Travel in Yucatán** by John L. Stephens. First published in 1841 and 1843, these books remain among the greatest of all travel books, and have never been out of print. Stephens and illustrator Frederick Catherwood had many adventures, made remarkable discoveries, and were instrumental in revealing the lost Maya civilization to the world.

The Labyrinth of Solitude Octavio Paz. Nobel-Prize winner Paz was the best-known (outside Mexico) of all Mexico's intellectuals, and this book is a must for anyone who wants to go beyond a superficial understanding of the psychology and culture of contemporary Mexicans.

Life in Mexico: The Letters of Fanny Calderón de la Barca, wtih New Material from the Author's Private Journals Fanny Calderón de la Barca. The author was a Scotswoman, whose Spanish husband became Spain's first ambassador to independent Mexico. Madame Calderón de la Barca, intelligent and curious, loved to travel and was a very elegant, observant writer on the emerging country.

The Log from the Sea of Cortés John Steinbeck. Steinbeck tells of an expedition to gather biological specimens from the Sea of Cortés off Baja California, and beautifully evokes its natural riches.

Mayan Tales from Zinacantán Robert M. Laughlin. A fascinating collection of folktales and dream-stories.

Mexican Postcards Carlos Monsiváis. Acute mini-portraits of many aspects of Mexican life, from one of the country's leading contemporary writes.

Mexico: A Biography of Power Enrique Krauze. Krauze is one of Mexico's most respected contemporary historians and political analysts, and his book presents an iconoclastic view of the country's modern history.

Oaxaca Journal Oliver Sacks. Charming book in which the eminent neurologist follows up another of this passions – the search for Oaxaca's rare ferns.

Our Word is our Weapon Subcomandante Marcos. The Zapatista spokesman presents his radical view of the state of modern Mexico.

Sliced Iguana: Travels in Unknown Mexico Isabella Tree. Entertaining reports on the chaos of the capital, the matriarchal communities of Oaxaca and more of the many quirky surprises of modern Mexico.

The Teachings of Don Juan: A Yaqui Way of Knowledge Carlos Castañeda. This and other books by Castañeda provide an imaginative insight into spiritual experience – but don't believe every word. Also *A Separate Reality*; *Journey to Ixtlán*; *Tales of Power*; *The Second Ring of Power*; and *The Eagle's Gift*.

Viva México; a traveller's account of life in Mexico Charles Macomb Flandrau. The charming, unhurried account of British traveler of 1908; some of Flandrau's insights into Mexican character are absolute gems.

Fiction

The Burning Plain/El Llano en Llamas Juan Rulfo. Some of the most powerful Mexican literature: a collection of short stories in which Rulfo's spare, suggestive prose gives the reader a deep understanding of the mestizo culture formed during the colonial era. Rulfo's great masterpiece was the novel **Pedro Páramo**, an intense, allegorical evocation of the memory of violence and its place in rural Mexico in the years after the Revolution.

The Edge of the Storm Agustín Yáñez. A great novel, set in a small town in Jalisco just before the Revolution. The atmosphere is heavy, the characters complex.

Like Water for Chocolate/Como Agua para Chocolate Laura Esquivel. The 1990 bestseller novel about family life, food and the Revolution. Wit, humor, irony and more blend into a very readable book. Also by the same author is **Swift as Desire**, a sad and funny tale about the importance of love.

Mexico City Noir Paco Ignacio Taibo. Taibo is Mexico's most popular modern crime writer, and his thrillers featuring the down-at-heel detective Hector Belascoarán Shayne are vividly entertaining portrayals of the modern country and its often apparently chaotic nature.

The Night of the Iguana Tennessee Williams. Powerful drama made famous by the movie starring Richard Burton.

The Plumed Serpent D.H. Lawrence. Lawrence takes on profound problems – the meaning of life and death, the relations of man to man and woman to man – and argues for a profound change in Mexico. One of the best novels about Mexico, although not one of Lawrence's best.

The Power and the Glory Graham Greene. Mexico was really only a conveniently dramatic backdrop to Greene's meditations on religion, desperation, and commitment, since he knew and understood little about the country, but this novel about a lost priest during the 1930s anti-Catholic campaigns remains powerful.

The Treasure of the Sierra Madre B. Traven. No other foreign author has written so much and so well about Mexico as the mysterious B. Traven (his identity is still a matter of controversy). Most of his books are set in southern Mexico, and his knowledge of that area is astounding. Others to look out for are: *The General from the Jungle*; *The Rebellion of the Hanged*; *March to Caobaland*; *The Bridge in the Jungle*; and *The Carreta*.

Under the Volcano Malcolm Lowry. Lowry's astonishing masterpiece about an alcoholic British consul drinking himself to death in Cuernavaca centers around despair, but in the process it reveals an intense engagement with the Mexican environment.

Where the Air Is Clear Carlos Fuentes. The first, and often considered the best, work by Mexico's most esteemed modern writer. As in all Fuentes' major works, Mexico City, with all its infinite contradictions, is as much a character as any individual: the narrator is a rather mysterious man who spends his life listening to and watching fellow inhabitants of the capital, of every social stratum, as they attempt to cope with the conditions of their lives.

Arts, Crafts, and Traditions

Arts and Crafts of Mexico Chloe Sayer. Excellent photographs, and including step-by-step instructions for making traditional Mexican craft items.

Art and Time in Mexico, photographs Judith Hancock Sandoval, text by Elizabeth Wilder Weismann. Well-illustrated overview of colonial art and architecture.

Days of Death, Days of Life: Ritual in the Popular Culture of Oaxaca, Kristin Norget. In-depth study of the popular culture of one of Mexico's most distinctive cities.

Great Masters of Mexican Folk Art, Cándida Fernández de Calderón. Superb examples of traditional crafts, beautifully illustrated, with an illuminating text on the life of the makers.

The Maya Textile Tradition, Linda Asturias de Barrios and others, with

Send Us Your Thoughts

We do our best to ensure the information in our books is as accurate and up-to-date as possible. The books are updated on a regular basis using local contacts, who painstakingly add, amend and correct as required. However, some details (such as telephone numbers and opening times) are liable to change, and we are ultimately reliant on our readers to put us in the picture.

We welcome your feedback, especially your experience of using the book "on the road". Maybe we recommended a hotel that you liked (or another that you didn't), or you came across a great bar or new attraction we missed.

We will acknowledge all contributions, and we'll offer an Insight Guide to the best letters received.

Please write to us at:
Insight Guides
PO Box 7910
London SE1 1WE
Or email us at:
insight@apaguide.co.uk

photographs by Jeffrey Foxx. Magnificently illustrated examination of the intricate complexity of textile-making in traditional Maya communities.

Mexican Churches Eliot Porter and Ellen Auerbach. A lavish collection of photographs from around the country.

Mexicolor: The Spirit of Mexican Design Melba Levick, Tony Cohan and Masako Takahashi. Fittingly, one of the most colorful books ever published, which beautifully explores Mexico's culture and love of color.

Birds and Wildlife

A Field Guide to the Mammals of Central America and Southeast Mexico Fiona A. Reid. The essential aid for anyone wildlife-spotting in Oaxaca, Chiapas or the Yucatán.

A Guide to the Birds of Mexico and Northern Central America Steve N.G. Howell and Sophie Webb. A well-illustrated handbook, an excellent starter for anyone visiting Mexico who is interested in birds.

Marine Mammals: Baja California-Sea of Cortés-Pacific Coast Uko Gorter. A very thorough, illustrated guide in Rainforest Publications' Mexico Field Guides series.

Southern Mexico Traveller's Wildlife Guide Les Beletsky. Handy one-volume guide covering birds and land and undersea life.

Food and Drink

The Cuisines of Mexico Diana Kennedy. Resident in Mexico for over 50 years, British writer Diana Kennedy is the foremost authority on Mexican food and cooking, in English, and her books are both readable and practical.

The Food and Life of Oaxaca Zarela Martínez. Perceptive, intimate account of the role of food in the life of Oaxaca, also with usable recipes.

Tequila! A Natural and Cultural History Ana Valenzuela-Zapata and Gary Paul Nabhan. The lowdown on the culture surrounding Mexico's most famous lubricant.

Other Insight Guides

Insight Guide *Guatemala, Belize & Yucatán* provides in-depth coverage of this beautiful area, with revealing features and stunning photography.

Smart Guide: *Cancún* will satisfy independent travelers looking for comprehensive listings presented in a snappy, easy-to-find way.

TRANSPORTATION ACCOMMODATIONS EATING OUT ACTIVITIES A – Z LANGUAGE

ART AND PHOTO CREDITS

INDEX

Mexico City Metro